C++ Cookbook™

Other resources from O'Reilly

Related titles

C++ in a Nutshell

C++ Pocket Reference

UML 2.0 in a Nutshell

Learning UML

STL Pocket Reference

Unit Test Frameworks

Practical C++ Programming

oreilly.com

oreilly.com is more than a complete catalog of O'Reilly books. You'll also find links to news, events, articles, weblogs, sample chapters, and code examples.

oreillynet.com is the essential portal for developers interested in open and emerging technologies, including new platforms, programming languages, and operating systems.

Conferences

O'Reilly brings diverse innovators together to nurture the ideas that spark revolutionary industries. We specialize in documenting the latest tools and systems, translating the innovator's knowledge into useful skills for those in the trenches. Visit *conferences.oreilly.com* for our upcoming events.

Safari Bookshelf (*safari.oreilly.com*) is the premier online reference library for programmers and IT professionals. Conduct searches across more than 1,000 books. Subscribers can zero in on answers to time-critical questions in a matter of seconds. Read the books on your Bookshelf from cover to cover or simply flip to the page you need. Try it today with a free trial.

C++ Cookbook™

D. Ryan Stephens, Christopher Diggins,
Jonathan Turkanis, and Jeff Cogswell

O'REILLY®

Beijing · Cambridge · Farnham · Köln · Paris · Sebastopol · Taipei · Tokyo

C++ Cookbook™

by D. Ryan Stephens, Christopher Diggins, Jonathan Turkanis, and Jeff Cogswell

Copyright © 2006 O'Reilly Media, Inc. All rights reserved.
Printed in the United States of America.

Published by O'Reilly Media, Inc., 1005 Gravenstein Highway North, Sebastopol, CA 95472.

O'Reilly books may be purchased for educational, business, or sales promotional use. Online editions are also available for most titles (*safari.oreilly.com*). For more information, contact our corporate/institutional sales department: (800) 998-9938 or *corporate@oreilly.com*.

Editor:	Jonathan Gennick
Production Editor:	Matt Hutchinson
Production Services:	Octal Publishing, Inc.
Cover Designer:	Karen Montgomery
Interior Designer:	David Futato

Printing History:

November 2005:   First Edition.

 This book uses RepKover™, a durable and flexible lay-flat binding.

ISBN: 978-0-596-00761-4

[M]   [1/09]

Table of Contents

Preface

C++ runs on virtually every platform and in an infinite number of applications. If you bought or might buy this book, you are probably an engineer or researcher writing one of these applications. But regardless of what you are writing and what platform you are targeting, odds are that you will be re-solving many of the same problems that other C++ programmers have been solving for years. What we have done in this book is solve many of these common problems and explain each of the solutions.

Whether you have been programming in C++ for years or are relatively new to the language, you are probably familiar with the things you have rewrite on each new project: Date and time parsing/arithmetic, manipulating string and text, working with files, parsing XML, using the standard containers, and so on. These are the kinds of problems this book contains solutions for. In some cases (e.g., date and time arithmetic), the standard library contains very little support. In others (e.g., string manipulation) the standard library contains functionally rich classes, but it can't do everything and some very common tasks are cumbersome.

The format is straightforward. Each recipe has a problem statement and a code solution, and most have a discussion that follows. We have tried to be pragmatic and solve the problems at hand without digressing too far, but in many cases there are related topics that are so useful (or just cool) that we have to provide a page or two of explanation.

This is a book about solving common problems with C++, but not a book about learning C++. We assume that you have at least a basic knowledge of C++ and object-oriented programming. In particular, it will be helpful if you have at least some familiarity with:

- C++ inheritance and virtual functions
- The standard library

- Components of the Standard Template Library (containers, iterators, and algorithms)
- Templates

These are not strict prerequisites for reading this book, but having at least a basic knowledge of them will help.

About the Examples

In crafting our code examples, we strove for simplicity, portability, and performance. The design for each solution followed a similar path: use standard C++ (language or library) if possible; if not, use a de facto standard as the replacement. For example, many of the recipes that deal with strings use the standard string class, and most of the mathematical and scientific recipes use standard numeric types, containers, and templates. The standard library has strong support for these areas, so standard facilities are a perfect fit. By comparison, however, C++ has little or no standardized support for multithreading or XML parsing. Thus, we used the multithreading support provided in the Boost Threads library and the XML parsing functionality provided by the Xerces parser.

Often, there are many ways to do the same thing in C++, which gives developers flexibility, but also invites some controversy. Most of the examples illustrate the best general solution we could come up with, but that doesn't mean that it's the best solution ever. If there are alternative solutions that are better in some ways and not as good in others (maybe the solution that uses the standard library is awkward or unintuitive; in this case, we may provide an alternative that uses Boost), we present the alternative anyway to give you some insight into the various solutions that are available.

Lots of the examples use templates. If you don't have much experience writing templates, you should get some soon. There is very little introductory material on templates in this book, except for two recipes in Chapter 8: 8.11 and 8.12. Most of the interesting developments in C++ are in the areas of template metaprogramming and policy-based design.

At the time of this writing, there is a lot of movement in the C++ community. The first technical report (called TR1) is more or less stable. It is a standardized list of features that will be eventually added to the next version of the C++ standard. It is not required that standard library implementations support it, but many vendors have already begun implementing TR1 and you can expect to see it appearing in shipped compilers soon. Many of the libraries in TR1 first appeared in the Boost project.

We use libraries from Boost a lot. Boost is a set of open source, peer-reviewed, portable libraries that fill in many of the gaps in the standard library. The current version as of this writing is 1.32, and 1.33 should be out any time now. We provide many pointers to specific Boost libraries in the examples. For more information on Boost in general, check out the project web site at *www.boost.org*.

Conventions Used in This Book

The following typographical conventions are used in this book:

Italic

> Indicates new terms, URLs, email addresses, filenames, file extensions, pathnames, directories, Unix utilities, commands, and command-line parameters.

<...>

> Angle-brackets surround elements that you need to specify in commands and command-line parameters when those elements appear inline, in italics.

`Constant width`

> Indicates code or fragments thereof. For example, class names, method names, and the like are rendered in constant width whenever they appear in the text.

`Constant width bold`

> Shows user-input in mixed, input/output examples.

`Constant width italic`

> Indicates user-specified items in syntax examples.

> Indicates a tip, suggestion, or general note.

> Indicates a warning or caution.

Using Code Examples

This book is designed to help you get your job done. In general, you may use the code in this book in your programs and documentation. You do not need to contact us for permission unless you're reproducing a significant portion of the code. For example, writing a program that uses several chunks of code from this book does not require permission. Selling or distributing a CD-ROM of examples from O'Reilly books does require permission. Answering a question by citing this book and quoting example code does not require permission. Incorporating a significant amount of example code from this book into your product's documentation does require permission.

We appreciate, but do not require, attribution. An attribution usually includes the title, author, publisher, and ISBN. For example: "*C++ Cookbook* by D. Ryan

Stephens, Christopher Diggins, Jonathan Turkanis, and Jeff Cogswell. Copyright 2006 O'Reilly Media, Inc., 0-596-00761-2."

If you feel your use of code examples falls outside fair use or the permission given above, feel free to contact us at *permissions@oreilly.com*.

Comments and Questions

Please address comments and questions concerning this book to the publisher:

> O'Reilly Media, Inc.
> 1005 Gravenstein Highway North
> Sebastopol, CA 95472
> (800) 998-9938 (in the United States or Canada)
> (707) 829-0515 (international or local)
> (707) 829-0104 (fax)

We have a web page for this book, where we list errata, examples, and any additional information. You can access this page at:

> *http://www.oreilly.com/catalog/cplusplusckbk*

To comment or ask technical questions about this book, send email to:

> *bookquestions@oreilly.com*

For more information about our books, conferences, Resource Centers, and the O'Reilly Network, see our web site at:

> *http://www.oreilly.com*

Safari Enabled

 When you see a Safari® Enabled icon on the cover of your favorite technology book, that means the book is available online through the O'Reilly Network Safari Bookshelf.

Safari offers a solution that's better than e-books. It's a virtual library that lets you easily search thousands of top tech books, cut and paste code samples, download chapters, and find quick answers when you need the most accurate, current information. Try it for free at *http://safari.oreilly.com*.

Acknowledgments

From D. Ryan Stephens

The most important people I have to thank are my wife, Daphne, and my children, Jesse, Pascal, and Chloe. Writing a book is hard work, but above all it is time-consuming work, and my family has been supportive and has tolerated my late nights in the office in the best possible way.

I also have to thank the technical reviewers, who made this book better than it otherwise would have been. As with so many things, it is always helpful to have a second, third, and fourth set of eyes look over something for clarity and correctness. Many thanks to Dan Saks, Uwe Schnitker, and David Theese.

Finally, I have to thank my editor, Jonathan Gennick, for his advice, which was mostly grammatical, frequently stylistic, occasionally psychologically supportive, and always good.

From Christopher Diggins

I wish to thank Kris Unger, Jonathan Turkanis, Jonathan Gennick, and Ryan Stephens for their helpful suggestions and critiques, and making me a better writer for it. A very special thanks to my wife Mélanie Charbonneau for brightening my life.

From Jonathan Turkanis

Because my chapters touched on so many different commerical products and open source projects—and because I had so many questions about each of them—I have an unusually large number of people to thank.

Let me first thank Ron Liechty, Howard Hinnant, and the engineers at Metrowerks for answering every conceivable question and for providing me with several versions of CodeWarrior.

I'd also like to thank the Boost.Build developers, especially Vladimir Prus, Rene Rivera, and David Abrahams, not just for answering my questions but also for putting together the Boost build system, which was the single most important source of information for Chapter 1.

Thanks also to Walter Bright at Digital Mars; Greg Comeau at Comeau Computing; P. J. Plauger at Dinkumware; Colin Laplace at Bloodshed Software; Ed Mulroy and Pavel Vozenilek at the borland.public.* newsgroups; Arnaud Debaene and Igor Tandetnik at microsoft.public.vc.languages; Earnie Boyd, Greg Chicares, Adib Taraben,

John Vandenberg, and Lennart Borgman at the MinGW/MSYS mailing list; Christopher Faylor, Larry Hall, Igor Pechtchanski, Joshua Daniel Franklin, and Dave Korn at the Cygwin list; Mike Stump and Geoffrey Keating at the GCC developers list; Mark Goodhand at DecisionSoft; and David N. Bertoni at apache.org.

I'm also indebted to Robert Mecklenburg, whose book *Managing Projects with GNU make*, Third Edition (O'Reilly) provided the foundation for my treatment of GNU make.

In addition, Vladimir Prus, Matthew Wilson, Ryan Stephens, and Christopher Diggins provided detailed criticism of early drafts of the manuscript.

Finally, I must thank my editor, Jonathan Gennick, my wife, Jennifer, and my Grandfather, Louis S. Goodman, who taught me how to write.

## CHAPTER 1

Building C++ Applications

1.0 Introduction to Building

This chapter contains recipes for transforming C++ source code into executable programs and libraries. By working through these recipes, you'll learn about the basic tools used to build C++ applications, the various types of binary files involved in the build process, and the systems that have been developed to make building C++ applications manageable.

If you look at the titles of the recipes in this chapter, you might get the impression that I solve the same problems over and over again. You'd be right. That's because there are many ways to build C++ applications, and while I can't cover them all, I try to cover some of the most important methods. In the first dozen or so recipes, I show how to accomplish three fundamental tasks—building static libraries, building dynamic libraries, and building executables—using a variety of methods. The recipes are grouped by method: first, I look at building from the command line, then with the Boost build system (Boost.Build), and then with an Integrated Development Environment (IDE), and finally with GNU *make*.

Before you start reading recipes, be sure to read the following introductory sections. I'll explain some basic terminology, provide an overview of the command-line tools, build systems and IDEs covered in the chapter, and introduce the source code examples.

> Even if you'll be using a build system or IDE, you should start by reading the recipes on building from the command line: these recipes introduce some essential concepts that you'll need to understand later in this chapter.

Basic Terminology

The three basic tools used to build C++ applications are the *compiler*, the *linker*, and the *archiver* (or *librarian*). A collection of these programs and possibly other tools is called a *toolset*.

The compiler takes C++ source files as input and produces *object files*, which contain a mixture of machine-executable code and symbolic references to functions and data. The archiver takes a collection of object files as input and produces a *static library*, or *archive*, which is simply a collection of object files grouped for convenient use. The linker takes a collection of object files and libraries and *resolves* their symbolic references to produce either an *executable* or *dynamic library*. Roughly speaking, the linker operates by matching each use of a symbol to its definition. When an executable or dynamic library is created, it is said to be *linked*; the libraries used to build the executable or dynamic library are said to be *linked against*.

An executable, or *application*, is simply any program that can be executed by the operating system. A dynamic library, also called a *shared library*, is like an executable except that it can't be run on its own; it consists of a body of machine-executable code that is loaded into memory after an application is started and can be shared by one or more applications. On Windows, dynamic libraries are also called *dynamic link libraries* (DLLs).

The object files and static libraries on which an executable depends are needed only when the executable is built. The dynamic libraries on which an executable depends, however, must be present on a user's system when the executable is run.

Table 1-1 shows the file extensions typically associated with these four basic types of files on Microsoft Windows and Unix. When I mention a file that has a different extension on Windows and Unix, I'll sometimes omit the extension if it's clear from the context.

Table 1-1. File extensions on Windows and Unix

File type	Windows	Mac OS X	Other Unix
Object files	.obj	.o	.o
Static libraries	.lib	.a	.a
Dynamic libraries	.dll	.dylib	.so
Executables	.exe	No extension	No extension

 In this chapter, whenever I say Unix, I mean Linux, too.

When you build the examples in this chapter, your tools will generate a number of auxiliary files with extensions that don't appear in Table 1-1. Unless I mention otherwise, you can safely ignore these files. If you really want to know what they do, consult your toolset's documentation.

IDEs and Build Systems

The compiler, linker, and archiver are *command-line tools*, which means they are designed to be run from a shell, such as *bash* on Unix or *cmd.exe* on Microsoft Windows. The names of the input files and output files, together with any other necessary configuration information, are passed to the compiler, linker, and archiver as text on the command line. Invoking these tools by hand is tedious, however. Even for small projects, it can be hard to remember the command-line options for each tool and the order in which the project's source and binary files must be compiled and linked. When a source file is modified, you must determine which object files need to be recompiled, which static libraries need to be updated, and which executables and dynamic libraries need to be relinked. If you rebuild more files than necessary, you've wasted your time; if you don't rebuild enough, you may end up with a failed build or a buggy application. With large C++ projects—which can involve thousands of separate files, including source files, object files, libraries, and executables—building from the command line is simply impossible.

There are two basic approaches to building large C++ applications:

- An IDE provides a graphical interface for organizing a collection of source files and describing the binary files that should be generated from them. Once you specify this information, you can generate the binary files simply by selecting an appropriate command from a menu or toolbar. The IDE is responsible for determining the order in which the binary files should be generated, the tools needed to generate them, and the command-line options that must be passed to the tools. Whenever you modify one or more of your source files, you can instruct the IDE to regenerate only those binary files that are out of date.

  IDEs organize source files into collections called *projects*. An IDE project is usually associated with a single binary file, or with several *variants* of a binary file, such as the debug and release builds of an application. Most IDEs allow users to organize projects into groups called *project groups*, or *solutions*, and to specify the dependencies between projects in a group.

- A *build system* provides a text file format for describing a collection of source files and the binary files that should be generated from them, together with a *build tool* that reads these text files and generates the binary files by invoking the appropriate command-line tools. Typically, these text files are created and edited using a text editor, and the build tool is invoked from the command line. Some build systems, however, provide a graphical interface for editing the text files and invoking the build tool.

While IDEs organize files into *projects*, build systems organize files into *targets*. Most targets correspond to binary files that must be generated; other targets correspond to actions the build tool must perform, such as installing an application.

The most common build tool is the *make* utility; the text files it relies on are called *makefiles*. While there are many versions of *make*, in this chapter I will discuss GNU *make*, the most powerful and portable *make* incarnation. GNU *make* is an extremely flexible tool that can be used for much more than building C++ applications. It also has the advantage of being widely used and well-understood by developers. Unfortunately, getting GNU *make* to do exactly what you want it to do can be a challenge, especially with complex projects involving multiple toolsets. For that reason, I will also discuss *Boost.Build*, a powerful and extensible build system designed from the ground up for building C++ applications.

 For a thorough treatment of GNU *make*, see *Managing Projects with GNU make*, Third Edition, by Robert Mecklenburg (O'Reilly).

Boost.Build was developed by members of the Boost C++ Libraries project. It has been used by a large community of developers for several years, and is currently under active development. Boost.Build uses a build tool called *bjam* and text files called *Jamfiles*. Its greatest strength is the ease with which it allows you to manage complex projects involving multiple platforms and build configurations. Although Boost.Build started out as an extension of Perforce's *Jam* build system, it has since undergone extensive redesign. As this book goes to press, the Boost.Build developers are preparing for the official release of the second major version of the build system, which is the version described in this chapter.

Toolset Overview

In this chapter I'll discuss seven collections of command-line tools: GCC, Visual C++, Intel, Metrowerks, Borland, Comeau, and Digital Mars. Table 1-2 shows the names of the command-line tools from the various toolsets; Table 1-3 shows where they are located on your system, if you have them installed. Tool names for Windows use the *.exe* suffix required for Windows executables; for toolsets that are available for both Windows and Unix, I've put this suffix in brackets.

Table 1-2. Names of command-line tools for various toolsets

Toolset	Compiler	Linker	Archiver
GCC	*g++[.exe]*	*g++*	*ar[.exe]* *ranlib[.exe]*
Visual C++	*cl.exe*	*link.exe*	*lib.exe*

Table 1-2. Names of command-line tools for various toolsets (continued)

Toolset	Compiler	Linker	Archiver
Intel (Windows)	*icl.exe*	*xilink.exe*	*xilib.exe*
Intel (Linux)	*icpc*	*icpc*	*ar* *ranlib*
Metrowerks	*mwcc[.exe]*	*mwld[.exe]*	*mwld[.exe]*
Comeau	*como[.exe]*	*como[.exe]*	Toolset-dependent
Borland	*bcc32.exe*	*bcc32.exe* *ilink32.exe*	*tlib.exe*
Digital Mars	*dmc.exe*	*link.exe*	*lib.exe*

Table 1-3. Location of your command-line tools

Toolset	Location
GCC (Unix)	Typically */usr/bin* or */usr/local/bin*
GCC (Cygwin)	The *bin* subdirectory of your Cygwin installation
GCC (MinGW)	The *bin* subdirectory of your MinGW installation
Visual C++	The *VC/bin* subdirectory of your Visual Studio installation[a]
Intel (Windows)	The *Bin* subdirectory of your Intel compiler installation
Intel (Linux)	The *bin* subdirectory of your Intel compiler installation
Metrowerks	The *Other Metrowerks Tools/Command Line Tools* subdirectory of your CodeWarrior installation
Comeau	The *bin* subdirectory of your Comeau installation
Borland	The *Bin* subdirectory of your C++Builder, C++BuilderX or Borland command-line tools installation

[a] In previous versions of Visual Studio, the *VC* directory was called *VC98* or *Vc7*.

Don't let the number of toolsets scare you—you don't need to learn them all. In most cases you can simply skip the material that doesn't relate to your toolset. If you want to learn a little about other toolsets, however, be sure to read the sections on Visual C++ and GCC, since these are the dominant toolsets on Windows and Unix.

Now let's look at each of the seven toolsets.

The GNU Compiler Collection (GCC)

GCC is a collection of compilers for a wide assortment of languages, including C and C++. It's remarkable for being open source, available on almost every imaginable platform, and highly conformant to the C++ language standard. It's the dominant compiler on many Unix platforms, and is also widely used on Microsoft Windows. Even if GCC is not your primary toolset, you can learn a lot by compiling your code with GCC. Also, if you think you know a way to improve the C++ language, you can test your idea with the GCC code base.

GCC comes with libstdc++, a good open source implementation of the C++ standard library. It can also be used with the open source STLPort C++ standard library and with Dinkumware's standard library.

To obtain GCC, see Recipe 1.1.

The GCC examples in this chapter were tested with GCC 3.4.3 and GCC 4.0.0 on GNU/Linux (Fedora Core 3), with GCC 4.0.0 on Mac OS X (Darwin 8.2.0), and with GCC 3.4.2 (MinGW) and 3.4.4 (Cygwin) on Windows 2000 Professional.

Visual C++

Microsoft's toolset is the dominant toolset on the Windows platform. While several old versions are still in wide use, the most recent version is highly standards conforming. It is also capable of producing highly optimized code. Microsoft's tools are distributed with the Visual C++ and Visual Studio development environments, discussed in the next section. As of this writing, they are also available as part of the Visual C++ Toolkit 2003, which can be downloaded for free from *www.microsoft.com*.

Visual C++ comes with a customized version of the Dinkumware C++ standard library implementation. Dinkumware's C++ standard library is among the most efficient and standards-conforming commercial implementation. It's available for a wide variety of platforms, including many of the other toolsets covered in this chapter.

The Visual C++ examples in this chapter were tested with Microsoft Visual Studio .NET 2003 and Microsoft Visual Studio 2005 (Beta 2). See Table 1-4.

Table 1-4. Versions of Microsoft Visual Studio

Product name	IDE version	Compiler version
Microsoft Visual Studio	6.0	1200
Microsoft Visual Studio .NET	7.0	1300
Microsoft Visual Studio .NET 2003	7.1	1310
Microsoft Visual Studio 2005 (Beta 2)	8.0	1400

Intel

Intel produces several C++ compilers for use with Intel processors. They are notable for generating extremely fast code—perhaps the fastest available for the Intel architecture.

Based on the C++ frontend from the Edison Design Group (EDG), they are also highly standards conforming.

The Intel C++ Compiler for Windows makes use of Microsoft's Visual C++ or Visual Studio development environments, which must be installed for the Intel compiler to function properly. The compiler is designed for compatibility with Visual C++: it can be used as a plug-in to the Visual C++ development environment, it can generate code that is binary-compatible with code generated by the Visual C++ compiler, it offers many of the same command-line options as the Visual C++ compiler, and—unless you tell it not to—it even emulates some Microsoft bugs. The commercial version of the Intel C++ Compiler for Windows is available for purchase at *www.intel.com*. A reasonably priced academic version is also available.

Whereas Intel's compiler for Windows is designed to be compatible with the Visual C++ compiler, Intel's compiler for Linux is designed to be compatible with GCC. It requires GCC to operate, supports a number of GCC options, and by default implements some GCC language extensions. The commercial version of the Intel C++ Compiler for Linux is available for purchase at *www.intel.com*. A noncommercial version is available as a free download.

On Windows, the Intel compiler uses the Dinkumware standard library that ships with Visual C++. On Linux, it uses libstdc++.

> The Intel examples in this chapter were tested with the Intel C++ Compiler 9.0 for Linux on GNU/Linux (Fedora Core 3) and with the Intel C++ Compiler 9.0 for Windows on Windows 2000 Professional.

Metrowerks

Metrowerks's command-line tools, distributed with its CodeWarrior development environment, are among the best available, both in terms of standards conformance and the efficiency of the code they generate. They also come with MSL, Metrowerks's first-rate implementation of the C++ standard library. Until recently, Metrowerks produced tools for Windows, Mac OS, and a variety of embedded platforms. In 2004, however, Metrowerks sold its Intel x86 compiler and debugger technology to Nokia and discontinued its CodeWarrior product line for Windows. In 2005, after Apple Computer announced plans to switch to chips made by Intel, Metrowerks disclosed that the forthcoming CodeWarrior 10 for Mac OS will likely be the final release for that platform. In the future, Metrowerks's focus will be on embedded development targeted at chips made by Freescale Semiconductor.

> By the time you read this, Metrowerks will be a part of Freescale Semiconductor, and the name Metrowerks may no longer be associated with the CodeWarrior product line. I'll still use the name Metrowerks, however, because it's not yet clear what the future names will be.

The Metrowerks examples in this chapter were tested with CodeWarrior 9.6 and 10.0 (Beta) on Mac OS X (Darwin 8.2.0) and with CodeWarrior 9.4 on Windows 2000 Professional.

Borland

Borland's command-line tools were once considered pretty good. As of September 2005, however, the last major update is over three years old and represents only an incremental improvement of over the previous version, which was released in 2000. As a result, Borland's tools are now quite out-of-date. In 2003 Borland announced plans for an ambitious redesign of its C++ compiler, using the EGD frontend; unfortunately, Borland has made no new announcements about this plan for quite some time. Borland's command-line tools remain important, however, because they are still in wide use.

Currently, the most recent versions of Borland's command-line tools can be obtained by purchasing the C++Builder or C++BuilderX development environments, described in the next section, or by downloading the free personal edition of C++BuilderX.

The Borland toolset comes with two C++ standard libraries: STLPort and an outdated version of Rogue Wave's standard library. Borland is also working on producing a version of its tools that will be distributed with the Dinkumware standard library.

 The Borland examples in this chapter were tested with Borland C++ Builder 6.0 (compiler version 5.6.4) on Windows 2000 Professional.

Comeau

The Comeau C++ compiler is widely regarded as the most standards-conforming C++ compiler. In addition to implementing the most recent version of the C++ language, it supports several versions of C and a number of early dialects of C++. It's also among the least expensive, currently priced at $50.

Like the Intel compiler, Comeau uses the EDG frontend and requires a separate C compiler to function correctly. Unlike Intel, Comeau can use a wide variety of C compilers as backends.

Comeau is available for Microsoft Windows and for many Unix platforms. If Comeau is not available on your platform, you can pay Comeau Computing to produce a custom port, but this is substantially more expensive. You can order the Comeau compiler at *www.comeaucomputing.com*.

When I discuss Comeau on Unix, I'll assume the backend compiler is GCC. When I discuss Comeau on Windows, I'll try to indicate how the command-line options depend on the backend compiler. Since Comeau can be used with so many backends, however, it's not always possible to be exhaustive.

Comeau comes with libcomo, an implementation of the C++ standard library based on Silicon Graphics's standard library. It can also be used with Dinkumware's standard library.

The Comeau examples in this chapter assume that you're using libcomo and that you've configured the compiler to find libcomo automatically. The examples have been tested with Comeau 4.3.3 and libcomo 31 using GCC 3.4.3 as backend on GNU/Linux (Fedora Core 3) and using Visual C++ .NET 2003 as backend on Windows 2000 Professional. (See Table 1-4.)

Digital Mars

Digital Mars is a C++ compiler written by Walter Bright. You can download it for free from *www.digitalmars.com*; for a modest fee you can order a CD containing the Digital Mars compiler, an IDE, and some other useful tools. The free version of the compiler can be used to compile all the Digital Mars examples in this chapter except for the ones that require a dynamic version of the runtime library, which is only available on the CD.

Digital Mars is a very fast compiler and produces highly optimized code. Unfortunately, it currently has some problems compiling code that uses advanced template idioms. Fortunately, Walter Bright is very responsive to bug reports and is committed to making Digital Mars standards-conforming.

Digital Mars comes with two standard libraries: a port of the STLPort standard library and an older standard library which is non-conforming and incomplete. For backward compatibility, STLPort must be explicitly enabled by the user. All the Digital Mars examples in this chapter use the STLPort standard library.

The Digital Mars examples in this chapter have been tested using Digital Mars 8.45 on Windows 2000 Professional.

IDE Overview

In this chapter I'll cover four IDEs: Microsoft Visual C++, Metrowerks CodeWarrior, Borland C++Builder, and Bloodshed Software's Dev-C++. There are a number of important IDEs I won't discuss—Apple's Xcode and the Eclipse Project are prominent examples—but the treatment of the four IDEs I do discuss should give you a good start on learning to use other IDEs.

 As with the command-line tools, feel free to skip material that doesn't relate to your IDE.

Visual C++

Microsoft Visual C++ is the dominant C++ development environment for Microsoft Windows. It's available as a standalone application or as part of the Visual Studio suite, and it comes with a wide assortment of tools for Windows development. For portable C++ development, its most notable features are the following:

- A highly conformant C++ compiler
- The Dinkumware C++ standard library
- A good visual debugger
- A project manager that keeps track of dependencies between projects

Several versions of Visual Studio are widely used. Because the names of the various versions can be confusing, I've listed the most widely available versions in Table 1-4.

The first version of Visual C++ to include a first-class C++ compiler and standard library appears in the third row of Table 1-4. All previous versions had serious standards-conformance problems.

CodeWarrior

CodeWarrior is Metrowerks's cross platform development environment. It has many of the same features as Visual C++, including:

- A highly conformant C++ compiler
- An excellent C++ standard library
- A good visual debugger
- A project manager that keeps track of dependencies between projects

One of CodeWarrior's strengths has traditionally been the large number of platform for which it was available; as explained in the last section, however, its Windows product line has been discontinued and its Macintosh product line will likely be discontinued soon. However, it should remain an important platform for embedded development.

 When I discuss the CodeWarrior IDE, I'll assume you're using CodeWarrior 10 for Mac OS X. The CodeWarrior IDE on other platforms is very similar.

C++Builder

C++Builder is Borland's development environment for Microsoft Windows applications. One of its main attractions is its support for Borland's Visual Component Library. For portable C++ development, however, its most notable features are

- An aging C++ compiler
- The STLPort standard library
- A good visual debugger
- A project manager with limited ability to handle dependencies between projects

I cover C++Builder because it is widely used and has a dedicated community of users.

C++Builder should not be confused with C++BuilderX, a cross-platform development environment released by Borland in 2003. Although C++BuilderX is a useful development tool, it has not been a commercial success and it's uncertain whether Borland will release an updated version.

Dev-C++

Bloodshed Software's Dev-C++ is a free C++ development environment for Windows that uses the MinGW port of GCC, described in Recipe 1.1. It features a pretty decent text editor and a visual interface to the GNU debugger.

Dev-C++ offers an incomplete graphical interface to GCC's numerous command-line options: in many cases users must configure their projects by entering command-line options in text boxes. In addition, its project manager can only handle one project at a time and its visual debugger is unreliable. Despite these limitations, Dev-C++ has an active community of users, including many university students. It is a good environment for someone who wants to learn C++ and doesn't own any C++ development tools.

John, Paul, George, and Ringo

Ever since Brian Kernighan and Dennis Ritchie published *The C Programming Language* in 1978, it's been traditional to begin learning a new programming language by writing, compiling and running a toy program that prints "Hello, World!" to the console. Since this chapter covers static and dynamic libraries as well as executables, I'll need a slightly more complex example.

Examples 1-1, 1-2, and 1-3 present the source code for the application *hellobeatles*, which prints:

```
John, Paul, George, and Ringo
```

to the console. This application could have been written as a single source file, but I've split it into three modules: a static library *libjohnpaul*, a dynamic library *libgeorgeringo*, and an executable *hellobeatles*. Furthermore, while each of the libraries could easily have been implemented as a single header file and a single *.cpp* file, I've split the implementation between several source files to illustrate how to compile and link projects containing more than one source file.

 Before you start working through the recipes in this chapter, create four sibling directories *johnpaul*, *geogreringo*, *hellobeatles*, and *binaries*. In the first three directories, place the source files from Examples 1-1, 1-2, and 1-3. The fourth directory will be used for binary files generated by IDEs.

The source code for *libjohnpaul* is presented in Example 1-1. The public interface of *libjohnpaul* consists of a single function, johnpaul( ), declared in the header *johnpaul. hpp*. The function johnpaul( ) is responsible for printing:

```
John, Paul,
```

to the console. The implementation of johnpaul( ) is split between two source files, *john.cpp* and *paul.cpp*, each of which is responsible for printing a single name.

Example 1-1. Source code for libjohnpaul

johnpaul/john.hpp

```
#ifndef JOHN_HPP_INCLUDED
#define JOHN_HPP_INCLUDED

void john(); // Prints "John, "

#endif // JOHN_HPP_INCLUDED
```

johnpaul/john.cpp

```
#include <iostream>
#include "john.hpp"

void john()
{
    std::cout << "John, ";
}
```

johnpaul/paul.hpp

```
#ifndef PAUL_HPP_INCLUDED
#define PAUL_HPP_INCLUDED

void paul(); // Prints " Paul, "

#endif // PAUL_HPP_INCLUDED
```

Example 1-1. Source code for libjohnpaul (continued)

johnpaul/paul.cpp

```
#include <iostream>
#include "paul.hpp"

void paul( )
{
    std::cout << "Paul, ";
}
```

johnpaul/johnpaul.hpp

```
#ifndef JOHNPAUL_HPP_INCLUDED
#define JOHNPAUL_HPP_INCLUDED

void johnpaul( ); // Prints "John, Paul, "

#endif // JOHNPAUL_HPP_INCLUDED
```

johnpaul/johnpaul.cpp

```
#include "john.hpp"
#include "paul.hpp"
#include "johnpaul.hpp"

void johnpaul( )
{
    john( );
    paul( );
}
```

The source code for *libgeorgeringo* is presented in Example 1-2. The public interface of *libgeorgeringo* consists of a single function, georgeringo( ), declared in the header *georgeringo.hpp*. As you might well guess, the function georgeringo( ) is responsible for printing:

```
George, and Ringo
```

to the console. Again, the implementation of georgeringo( ) is split between two source files, *george.cpp* and *ringo.cpp*.

Example 1-2. Source code for libgeorgeringo

georgeringo/george.hpp

```
#ifndef GEORGE_HPP_INCLUDED
#define GEORGE_HPP_INCLUDED

void george( ); // Prints "George, "

#endif // GEORGE_HPP_INCLUDED
```

Example 1-2. Source code for libgeorgeringo (continued)

georgeringo/george.cpp

```
#include <iostream>
#include "george.hpp"

void george()
{
    std::cout << "George, ";
}
```

georgeringo/ringo.hpp

```
#ifndef RINGO_HPP_INCLUDED
#define RINGO_HPP_INCLUDED

void ringo(); // Prints "and Ringo\n"

#endif // RINGO_HPP_INCLUDED
```

georgeringo/ringo.cpp

```
#include <iostream>
#include "ringo.hpp"

void ringo()
{
    std::cout << "and Ringo\n";
}
```

georgeringo/georgeringo.hpp

```
#ifndef GEORGERINGO_HPP_INCLUDED
#define GEORGERINGO_HPP_INCLUDED

// define GEORGERINGO_DLL when building libgeorgreringo.dll
# if defined(_WIN32) && !defined(__GNUC__)
#   ifdef GEORGERINGO_DLL
#     define GEORGERINGO_DECL __declspec(dllexport)
#   else
#     define GEORGERINGO_DECL __declspec(dllimport)
#   endif
# endif // WIN32

#ifndef GEORGERINGO_DECL
# define GEORGERINGO_DECL
#endif

// Prints "George, and Ringo\n"
#ifdef __MWERKS__
# pragma export on
#endif
```

Example 1-2. Source code for libgeorgeringo (continued)

```
GEORGERINGO_DECL void georgeringo( );
#ifdef __MWERKS__
# pragma export off
#endif

#endif // GEORGERINGO_HPP_INCLUDED
```

georgeringo/ georgeringo.cpp

```
#include "george.hpp"
#include "ringo.hpp"
#include "georgeringo.hpp"

void georgeringo( )
{
    george( );
    ringo( );
}
```

The header *georgeringo.hpp* contains some complex preprocessor directives. If you don't understand them, that's okay. I'll explain them in Recipe 1.4.

Finally, the source code for the executable *hellobeatles* is presented in Example 1-3. It consists of a single source file, *hellobeatles.cpp*, which simply includes the headers *johnpaul.hpp* and *georgeringo.hpp* and invokes the function johnpaul( ) followed by the function georgeringo( ).

Example 1-3. Source code for hellobeatles

hellobeatles/ hellobeatles.cpp

```
#include "johnpaul/johnpaul.hpp"
#include " georgeringo/ georgeringo.hpp"

int main( )
{
    // Prints "John, Paul, George, and Ringo\n"
    johnpaul( );
    georgeringo( );
}
```

1.1   Obtaining and Installing GCC

Problem

You wish to obtain GCC, the free GNU C/C++ compiler.

Solution

The solution depends on your operating system.

Windows

Install MinGW, Cygwin, or both.

To install MinGW, go to the MinGW homepage, *www.mingw.org*, and follow the link to the MinGW download page. Download the latest version of the MinGW installation program, which should be named *MinGW-<version>.exe*.

Next, run the installation program. It will ask you to specify where you want to install MinGW. It may also ask you which packages you wish to install; at a minimum, you must install *gcc-core*, *gcc-g++*, *binutils,* and the MinGW runtime, but you may wish to install more. When the installation is complete, you will be able to run *gcc*, *g++*, *ar*, *ranlib*, *dlltool*, and several other GNU tools from the Windows command line. You may wish to add the *bin* subdirectory of your MinGW installation to your PATH environment variable so that you can specify these tools on the command line by their simple names rather than by their full pathnames.

To install Cygwin, go to the Cygwin homepage, *www.cygwin.com*, and follow the link *Install Cygwin Now* to download the Cygwin installation program. Next, run the installation program. It will ask you to make a series of choices, such as where Cygwin should be installed.

 I'm explaining the Cygwin installation process in detail because it can be a bit complicated, depending on what you want to install. The process may have changed by the time you read this, but if it has, it will probably have been made easier.

The most important choice you must make is the selection of packages. If you have enough disk space and a high-speed Internet connection, I recommend that you install all of the packages. To do this, click once on the word Default next to the word All at the top of the hierarchical display of packages. After a possibly long pause, the word Default should change to Install.

If you are short on disk space, or if you have a slow Internet connection, you can choose a smaller selection of packages. To select just the development tools, click once on the word Default next to the word Devel. After a possibly long pause, the word Default should change to Install. For an even smaller collection of packages, expand the list of development packages by clicking on the + icon next to the word Devel. Select the packages *gcc-core*, *gcc-g++*, and *make* by clicking on the word Skip, opposite each package, causing Skip to change to Install.

When you are done selecting packages, press *Finish*. When the installation program completes, the Cygwin installation directory should contain a file named *cygwin.bat*. Running this script will display the Cygwin shell, a command-line environment from which you can run *gcc*, *g++*, *ar*, *ranlib*, *dlltool*, *make*, and any other utilities you chose to install. The installation process adds the *bin* subdirectory of the Cygwin installation to your PATH environment variable, so you can also run these utilities from the Windows shell *cmd.exe*. You will find, however, that the Cygwin shell—a port of the *bash* shell—is a much friendlier environment for running GNU utilities.

Unix

Check whether GCC is installed on your system by entering **g++ -v** from the command line. If GCC is installed, and if C++ language support is available, it should print a message such as the following:

```
Using built-in specs.
Target: powerpc-apple-darwin8
Configured with: /private/var/tmp/gcc/gcc-5026.obj~19/src/configure
--disable-checking --prefix=/usr ...
```

If GCC is not installed, or if it is installed without support for C++, you will have to install it yourself. In general this is a complex process that depends on your platform; among other things, you may have to install GNU *make* and the GNU *binutils* package. Detailed instructions are available at *gcc.gnu.org/install*.

If you use Mac OS X, the easiest way to obtain GCC is to download the Xcode development environment from Apple's web site and follow the simple installation instructions. Xcode is currently available at *developer.apple.com/tools*.

If you use Linux, some version of GCC should already be installed; type **g++ -v** to determine the version. The current version of GCC is 4.0.0; if your version is not relatively recent, use the package management system accompanying your Linux distribution to install the most recent version.

Discussion

Cygwin and MinGW represent very different approaches to porting the GNU tools to Windows. Cygwin is an ambitious project to produce a Unix-like environment hosted by Windows. It provides a Unix-compatibility layer which allows programs written for Unix to be compiled and run on Windows. Consequently, an enormous assortment of Unix utilities are available for Cygwin. Even if you are not a Unix developer, you may soon come to regard the Cygwin tools as indispensable.

MinGW, which stands for "Minimalist GNU for Windows," provides a minimal environment for building Windows executables using GCC. Among other things, MinGW includes a port of GCC, a port of the GNU archiver and linker, and a port of the GNU debugger GDB. It also includes MSYS, a command-line environment capable of executing GNU makefiles and *configure* scripts. MSYS will be discussed in Recipe 1.14.

One important difference between Cygwin and MinGW relates to licensing. With a few exceptions, you can distribute binaries compiled with the MinGW port of GCC under any license you wish. Binaries built with the Cygwin port of GCC, on the other hand, are covered by the GNU General Public License (GPL) by default. If you want to distribute a program compiled under Cygwin without making the source available, you must purchase a license from Red Hat. For complete details, see the Cygwin and MinGW websites.

See Also

Recipe 1.14

1.2 Building a Simple "Hello, World" Application from the Command Line

Problem

You want to build a simple "Hello, World" program, such as that in Example 1-4.

Example 1-4. A simple "Hello, World" program

`hello.cpp`

```
#include <iostream>

int main( )
{
    std::cout << "Hello, World!\n";
}
```

Solution

Follow these steps:

1. Set any environment variables required by your toolset.
2. Enter a command telling your compiler to compile and link your program.

Scripts for setting environment variables are listed in Table 1-5; these scripts are located in the same directory as your command-line tools (Table 1-3). If your toolset does not appear in Table 1-5, you can skip the first step. Otherwise, run the appropriate script from the command line, if you are using Windows, or source the script, if you are using Unix.

Table 1-5. Scripts for setting environment variables required by your command-line tools

Toolset	Script
Visual C++	*vcvars32.bat*
Intel (Windows)	*iclvars.bat*[a]
Intel (Linux)	*iccvars.sh* or *iccvars.csh*
Metrowerks (Mac OS X)	*mwvars.sh* or *mwvars.csh*[b]

Table 1-5. Scripts for setting environment variables required by your command-line tools (continued)

Toolset	Script
Metrowerks (Windows)	cwenv.bat
Comeau	Same as the backend toolset

a With earlier version of the Intel compiler, this script was named *iccvars.bat*.
b In versions of CodeWarrior prior to 10.0, there was a single *csh* script named mwvars.

Commands for compiling and linking *hello.cpp* are given in Table 1-6. To work properly, these commands require that your current directory is the directory containing *hello.cpp* and that the directory containing the command-line compiler appears in your PATH environment variable. If you ran a script in step 1, the latter condition will be satisfied automatically. It's also possible that when you installed your toolset, the setup utility added the directory containing the command-line tools to your PATH. Otherwise, you can either add the directory to your PATH, as shown in Table 1-7, or specify the full file pathname on the command line.

Table 1-6. Commands for compiling and linking hello.cpp in a single step

Toolset	Command Line
GCC	g++ -o hello hello.cpp
Visual C++	cl -nologo -EHsc -GR -Zc:forScope -Zc:wchar_t -Fehello hello.cpp
Intel (Windows)	icl -nologo -EHsc -GR -Zc:forScope -Zc:wchar_t -Fehello hello.cpp
Intel (Linux)	icpc -o hello hello.cpp
Metrowerks	mwcc -wchar_t on -cwd include -o hello hello.cpp
Comeau	como -o hello hello.cpp
Borland	bcc32 -q -ehello hello.cpp
Digital Mars	dmc -Ae -Ar -I<dmcroot>/stlport/stlport -o hello hello.cpp

Table 1-7. Adding a directory to your PATH environment variable for the duration of a command-line session

Shell	Command line
bash, sh, ksh (Unix)	export PATH=<directory>:$PATH
csh, tsch (Unix)	setenv PATH <directory>:$PATH
cmd.exe (Windows)	set PATH=<directory>;%PATH%

For example, if you use Microsoft Visual Studio .NET 2003, and if it is installed in the standard location on the C drive, change to the directory containing *hello.cpp* and enter the commands shown below:

```
> "C:\Program Files\Microsoft Visual Studio .NET 2003\Vc7\bin\
vcvars32.bat"
Setting environment for using Microsoft Visual Studio .NET 2003 tools.
```

```
(If you have another version of Visual Studio or Visual C++ installed
and wish to use its tools from the command line, run vcvars32.bat for
that version.)
> cl -nologo -EHsc -GR -Zc:forScope -Zc:wchar_t -Fehello
hello.cpp
hello
```

You can now run your program:

```
> hello
Hello, World!
```

Similarly, if you are using Intel 9.0 for Linux, and if it is installed in the standard location */opt/intel/cc/9.0*, open a *bash* shell, change to the directory containing *hello. cpp* and enter the commands:

```
$ . /opt/intel/cc/9.0/bin/iccvars.sh
$ icpc -o hello hello.cpp
$ ./hello
Hello, World!
```

Discussion

Environment variables are pairs of strings maintained by your system and accessible to running applications. Command-line tools frequently refer to environment variables to learn details about your system and to obtain configuration information that otherwise would have to be entered on the command line. The environment variable you will encounter most often is PATH, which stores a list of directories that are searched by the operating system when the name of an executable is entered on the command line using its simple name rather than its full pathname. On Windows, the directories in PATH are also searched when a dynamic library is loaded.

Command-line tools make use of environment variables on both Unix and Windows, but on Unix there is typically a dominant C++ compiler and the environment variables it requires are set by default to correct values. On Windows, however, there have traditionally been a number of competing C++ compilers; two different compilers will almost certainly have to look in different locations to find their standard headers and their compiled runtime support libraries, for example. It's, therefore, common for Windows toolsets to provide scripts that set a number of environment variables to record the locations of headers and libraries and other information.

One way to use such a script is to run it from the command line before invoking any of the command-line tools, as I demonstrated for Visual C++ and Intel 9.0 for Linux. It's also possible to make the environment variable settings permanent so that you don't have to run the script each time you start a command-line session; how this is done, depends on your operating system and on your shell. Changing your environment variables permanently is not always a good idea, however, since several toolsets may contain tools with the same name, causing the wrong tool to be invoked during the build process. For example, if you have multiple versions of Visual C++ installed, you must make sure to run the correct version of *vcvars32.bat* before using the command-line tools. As another example, the toolsets Visual C++ and Digital Mars both contain tools named *link.exe* and *lib.exe*.

Now let's look at the command lines in Table 1-7. Remember that you only need to be concerned with the row corresponding to your toolset. In general, the information passed to the compiler falls into four categories:

- The name(s) of the input files
- The name(s) of the output files
- The locations to search for files
- General configuration information

In Table 1-6, there is just a single input file, *hello.cpp*, and it is passed to the compiler simply by writing the name of the file on the command line. It doesn't matter where you place the name of the input file, as long as it doesn't appear in the middle of another command-line option. In Table 1-7, I placed *hello.cpp* at the very end of the command line.

There is also a single output file, *hello.exe* or *hello*, depending on the operating system. In this case, however, the way the file name is passed to the compiler depends on the toolset. Most toolsets use *-o <file>* to specify an output executable, but Visual C++ and Intel for Windows use *-Fe<file>* and Borland uses *-e<file>*. Note that it's not necessary to specify the extension of an executable.

The only information in Table 1-7 that falls into the third category, locations to search for files, appears in the command line for Digital Mars. Since the STLPort library is not Digital Mars's built-in standard library, the compiler must be told, using the *-I* option, where to search for the STLPort headers. The STLPort headers are located in the */stlport/stlport* subdirectory of the Digital Mars installation; I specified this directory in Table 1-7 using the notation *<dmcroot>/stlport/stlport*. For more information on *-I* option, see Recipe 1.5.

Most of the command-line options in Table 1-7 fall into the fourth category: general configuration information. These options don't apply to any particular file; instead they enable or disable particular compiler features.

- The options *-nologo* (Visual C++ and Intel for Windows) and *-q* (Borland) tell the compiler not to print its name and version to the console. This makes the compiler's output easier to read.
- The options *-EHsc* (Visual C++ and Intel for Windows) and *-Ae* (Digital Mars) tell the compiler to enable C++ exception handling.
- The options *-GR* (Visual C++ and Intel for Windows) and *-Ar* (Digital Mars) tell the compiler to enable runtime type information (RTTI).
- The options *-Zc:wchar_t* (Visual C++ and Intel for Windows) and *-wchar_t* on (Metrowerks) tell the compiler to recognize wchar_t as a built-in type.

- The option *-Zc:forScope* (Visual C++ and Intel for Windows) tells the compiler to enforce modern for-scoping rules.
- The option *-cwd* include (Metrowerks) tells the compiler to begin searching for an included header in the directory of the source file that contains the include directive. This is the default behavior for all the toolsets but Metrowerks.

Next, let's consider a second solution to the original problem. Instead of compiling and linking with a single command, you can split the second step into two parts:

2a. Enter a command telling your compiler to compile your program to an object file without linking.

2b. Enter a command telling your linker to create an executable from the object file created in step 2a.

In this simple case, there's no reason to compile and link separately. Separate compilation and linking is frequently necessary, however, so it's important to know how to do it. For example, when creating a static library, you must compile without linking and then pass the resulting object files to the archiver.

The commands for compiling and linking in two steps are presented in Tables 1-8 and 1-9. In several cases I've given an object file the extension *o[bj]* to indicate that a single command line is valid for Windows and Unix except for the extension of the object file.

Table 1-8. Commands for compiling hello.cpp without linking

Toolset	Command line
GCC	*g++ -c -o hello.o hello.cpp*
Visual C++	*cl -c -nologo -EHsc -GR -Zc:forScope -Zc:wchar_t -Fohello hello.cpp*
Intel (Windows)	*icl -c -nologo -EHsc -GR -Zc:forScope -Zc:wchar_t -Fohello hello.cpp*
Intel (Linux)	*icpc -c -o hello.o hello.cpp*
Metrowerks	*mwcc -c -wchar_t on -cwd include -o hello.o[bj]hello.cpp*
Comeau	*como -c -o hello.o[bj] hello.cpp*
Borland	*bcc32 -c -q -o hello.obj hello.cpp*
Digital Mars	*dmc -c -Ae -Ar -I<dmcroot>/stlport/stlport -o hello.obj hello.cpp*

Table 1-9. Commands for linking hello.exe or hello

Toolset	Command line
GCC	*g++ -o hello hello.o*
Visual C++	*link -nologo -out:hello.exe hello.obj*
Intel (Windows)	*xilink -nologo -out:hello.exe hello.obj*
Intel (Linux)	*icpc -o hello hello.o*
Metrowerks	*mwld -o hello hello.o[bj]*

Table 1-9. Commands for linking hello.exe or hello (continued)

Toolset	Command line
Comeau	*como --no_prelink_verbose -o hello hello.o[bj]*
Borland	*bcc32 -q -ehello hello.cpp*
Digital Mars	*link -noi hello.obj, hello.exe,NUL,user32.lib kernel32.lib,,*

For example, to build the executable hello with the GCC toolset, change to the directory containing *hello.cpp* and enter the following commands:

```
$ g++ -c -o hello.o hello.cpp
$ g++ -o hello hello.o
```

You can now run your program as follows:

```
$ ./hello
Hello, World!
```

Table 1-9 is almost identical to Table 1-6. There are just two differences. First, the option -c is used to tell the compiler to compile without linking. Second, the output file is specified to be an object file *hello.obj* or *hello.o* rather than an executable. Most compilers use the option -o *<file>* to specify the output file, but Visual C++ and Intel for Windows use the option -Fo*<file>*. In addition, all the compilers except for Visual C++ and Intel for Windows require that the extension of the object file be specified.

By now, most of the command lines in Table 1-9 should be pretty easy to understand, so I'll just make two observations:

- The Digital Mars linker has an unusual command-line syntax, consisting of six comma-separated fields used for specifying different types of input files. For now you just need to know that the first field is for object files and the second is for the output file. The option *-noi* tells the linker to perform case-sensitive linking, which is necessary for C++ programs.

- The Borland linker, *ilink32.exe*, uses a syntax similar to that of Digital Mars. To simplify the command line, I've used the compiler, *bcc32.exe*, to perform the link step. Behind the scenes, *bcc32.exe* calls *ilink32.exe*.

See Also

Recipes 1.7 and 1.15

1.3   Building a Static Library from the Command Line

Problem

You wish to use your command-line tools to build a static library from a collection of C++ source files, such as those listed in Example 1-1.

Solution

First, use your compiler to compile the source files into object files. If your source files include headers located in other directories, you may need to use the *-I* option to instruct your compiler where to search for headers; for more information, see Recipe 1.5. Second, use your archiver to combine the object files into a static library.

To compile each of the three source files from Example 1-1, use the command lines listed in Table 1-8, modifying the names of the input and output files as needed. To combine the resulting object files into a static library, use the commands listed in Table 1-10.

Table 1-10. Commands for creating the archive libjohnpaul.lib or libjohnpaul.a

Toolset	Command line
GCC (Unix) Intel (Linux) Comeau (Unix)	*ar ru libjohnpaul.a john.o paul.o johnpaul.o* *ranlib libjohnpaul.a*
GCC (Windows)	*ar ru libjohnpaul.a john.o paul.o johnpaul.o*
Visual C++ Comeau (with Visual C++)	*lib -nologo -out:libjohnpaul.lib john.obj paul.obj johnpaul.obj*
Intel (Windows)	*xilib -nologo /out:libjohnpaul.lib john.obj paul.obj johnpaul.obj*
Metrowerks (Windows)	*mwld -library -o libjohnpaul.lib john.obj paul.obj johnpaul.obj*
Metrowerks (Mac OS X)	*mwld -library -o libjohnpaul.a john.o paul.o johnpaul.o*
Borland	*tlib libjohnpaul.lib /u /a /C +john +paul +johnpaul*
Digital Mars	*lib -c -n libjohnpaul.lib john.obj paul.obj johnpaul.obj*

For example, to compile *john.cpp*, *paul.cpp*, and *johnpaul.cpp* into object files using GCC, change to the directory *johnpaul* and enter the following commands to produce the object files *john.o*, *paul.o*, and *johnpaul.o*:

```
$ g++ -c -o john.o john.cpp
$ g++ -c -o paul.o paul.cpp
$ g++ -c -o johnpaul.o johnpaul.cpp
```

Now link the object files into a static library as follows:

```
$ ar ru libjohnpaul.a john.o paul.o johnpaul.o
$ ranlib libjohnpaul.a
```

Discussion

With GCC on Unix you use two separate commands to create a static library: first, you invoke the archiver *ar*, then you invoke a tool named *ranlib*. The *ru* option tells *ar* to add the given object files to the specified archive if there are no existing archive members with the same names, but to update an existing archive member only if the given object file is newer than the existing member. Traditionally, after an archive was created or updated, the tool *ranlib* was used to create or update the archive's symbol table, i.e., the index of the symbols that appear in the various object files it contains. Today, on many systems, the archiver *ar* takes care of building or updating the symbol table by itself, so running *ranlib* is not necessary. In particular, this is true for the GNU version of *ar*. On some systems, however, the GCC compiler may be used in conjunction with a non-GNU version of *ar*; for this reason, it's best to run *ranlib* just to be safe.

As you can see from Table 1-10, the Borland archiver *tlib* uses a slightly unusual syntax: the plus signs before the object files tell *tlib* to add these object files to the library. You should be able to understand all the other command lines fairly easily.

With some toolsets, the linker can be used as an archiver by passing an appropriate command-line option. With other toolsets a separate archiver must be used.

See Also

Recipes 1.8, 1.11, and 1.16

1.4 Building a Dynamic Library from the Command Line

Problem

You wish to use your command-line tools to build a dynamic library from a collection of C++ source files, such as those listed in Example 1-2.

Solution

Follow these steps:

1. Use your compiler to compile the source files into object files. If you're using Windows, use the *-D* option to define any macros necessary to ensure that your dynamic library's symbols will be exported. For example, to build the dynamic library in Example 1-2, you need to define the macro GEORGERINGO_DLL. If you're building a third-party library, the installation instructions should tell you what macros to define.

2. Use your linker to create a dynamic library from the object files created in step 1.

If your dynamic library depends on other libraries, you'll need to tell the compiler where to search for the library headers, and to tell the linker the names of the other libraries and where to find them. This is discussed in detail in Recipe 1.5.

The basic commands for performing the first step are given Table 1-8; you'll need to modify the names of the input and output files appropriately. The commands for performing the second step are given in Table 1-11. If you're using a toolset that comes with static and dynamic variants of its runtime libraries, direct the compiler and linker to use a dynamically linked runtime, as described in Recipe 1.23.

Table 1-11. Commands for creating the dynamic library libgeorgeringo.so, libgeorgeringo.dll, or libgeorgeringo.dylib

Toolset	Command line
GCC	*g++ -shared -fPIC -o libgeorgeringo.so george.o ringo.o georgeringo.o*
GCC (Mac OS X)	*g++ -dynamiclib -fPIC -o libgeorgeringo.dylib george.o ringo.o georgeringo.o*
GCC (Cygwin)	*g++ -shared -o libgeorgeringo.dll* *-Wl,--out-implib,libgeorgeringo.dll.a* *-W1,--export-all-symbols* *-Wl,--enable-auto-image-base george.o ringo.o georgeringo.o*
GCC (MinGW)	*g++ -shared -o libgeorgeringo.dll* *-Wl,--out-implib,libgeorgeringo.a -W1,--export-all-symbols* *-Wl,--enable-auto-image-base george.o ringo.o georgeringo.o*
Visual C++	*link -nologo -dll -out:libgeorgeringo.dll -implib:libgeorgeringo.lib george.obj ringo.obj georgeringo.obj*
Intel (Windows)	*xilink -nologo -dll -out:libgeorgeringo.dll -implib:libgeorgeringo.lib george.obj ringo.obj georgeringo.obj*
Intel (Linux)	*g++ -shared -fPIC -lrt -o libgeorgeringo.so george.o ringo.o georgeringo.o georgeringo.obj*
Metrowerks (Windows)	*mwld -shared -export dllexport -runtime dm -o libgeorgeringo.dll -implib libgeorgeringo.lib george.obj ringo.obj georgeringo.obj*
Metrowerks (Mac OS X)	*mwld -shared -export pragma -o libgeorgeringo.dylib george.o ringo.o georgeringo.o*
CodeWarrior 10.0 (Mac OS X)[a]	Consult the Metrowerks documentation.
Borland	*bcc32 -q -WD -WR -elibgeorgeringo.dll george.obj ringo.obj georgeringo.obj* *implib -c libgeorgeringo.lib libgeorgeringo.dll*
Digital Mars	*dmc -WD -L/implib:libgeorgeringo.lib -o libgeorgeringo.dll george.obj ringo.obj georgeringo.obj user32.lib kernel32.lib*

[a] CodeWarrior 10.0 for Mac OS X will provide dynamic variants of its runtime support libraries; these should be used when building libgeorgeringo.dylib. (See Recipe 1.23.)

 As of September 2005, the Comeau toolset does not support building dynamic libraries on Unix or Windows. Comeau Computing is currently working on dynamic library support, however, and expects it to be implemented for some Unix platforms—including Linux—by the end of 2005.

For example, to compile the source files from Example 1-2 into object files with the Borland compiler, assuming that the directory containing the Borland tools is in your PATH, change to the directory *georgeringo* and enter the following commands:

```
> bcc32 -c -q -WR -o george.obj george.cpp
george.cpp:
> bcc32 -c -q -WR -o ringo.obj ringo.cpp
ringo.cpp:
> bcc32 -c -q -WR -DGEORGERINGO_DLL -o georgeringo.obj georgeringo.cpp
georgeringo.cpp:
```

The compiler option *-WR* is used here to specify a dynamic variant of the runtime library. These three commands will generate the object files *george.obj*, *ringo.obj,* and *georgeringo.obj*. Next, enter the command:

```
> bcc32 -q -WD -WR -elibgeorgeringo.dll george.obj ringo.obj
georgeringo.obj
```

This will generate the dynamic library *libgeorgeringo.dll*. Finally, enter the command:

```
> implib -c libgeorgeringo.lib libgeorgeringo.dll
```

This will generate the import library *libgeorgeringo.lib*.

Discussion

How dynamic libraries are handled varies greatly depending on the operating system and toolset. From the programmer's point of view, the two most important differences are as follows:

Symbol visibility

Dynamic libraries can contain the definitions of classes, functions, and data. On some platforms, all such symbols are automatically accessible to code which uses a dynamic library; other systems offer programmers fine-grained control over which symbols are accessible. Being able to determine which symbols should be visible on a case-by-case basis is generally advantageous; it gives a programmer more explicit control of his library's public interface, and it often provides superior performance. It also makes building and using dynamic libraries more complex, however.

With most Windows toolsets, in order for a symbol defined in a dynamic library to be available to code which uses the dynamically library, it must be explicitly *exported* when the dynamic library is built and *imported* when an executable or dynamic library that uses the dynamic library is built. Some Unix toolsets also offer this flexibility; this is true for recent versions of GCC on several platforms, for Metrowerks on Mac OS X, and for Intel on Linux. In some cases, however, there is no alternative but to make all symbols visible.

Passing libraries to the linker

On Unix, a dynamic library can be specified as input to the linker when code using the dynamic library is linked. On Windows, except when using GCC, dynamic libraries are not specified directly as input to the linker; instead, an import library or module definition file is used.

Import libraries and module definition files

Import libraries, roughly speaking, are static libraries containing the information needed to invoke functions in a DLL at runtime. It's not necessary to know how they work, only how to create and use them. Most linkers create import libraries automatically when you build a DLL, but in some cases it may be necessary to use a separate tool called an *import librarian*. In Table 1-11, I used the Borland import librarian *implib.exe* to avoid the peculiar command-line syntax required by the Borland linker *ilink32.exe*.

A module definition file, or *.def* file, is a text file that describes the functions and data exported by a DLL. A *.def* file can be written by hand or automatically generated by a tool. An example *.def* file for the library *libgeorgeringo.dll* is shown in Example 1-5.

Example 1-5. A module definition file for libgeorgeringo.dll

```
LIBRARY          LIBGEORGERINGO.DLL

EXPORTS
    Georgeringo     @1
```

Exporting symbols from a DLL

There are two standard methods for exporting symbols from a Windows DLL:

- Use the __declspec(dllexport) attribute in the DLL's headers, and build an import library for use when linking code that uses your DLL.

  The __declspec(dllexport) attribute should be inserted at the beginning of the declarations of exported functions and data, following any linkage specifiers, and immediately following the class or struct keyword for exported classes. This is illustrated in Example 1-6. Note that __declspec(dllexport) is not part of the C++ language; it is a language extension implemented by most Windows compilers.

- Create a *.def* file describing the functions and data exported by your dynamic library.

Example 1-6. Using the __declspec(dllexport) attribute

```
__declpec(dllexport) int m = 3;      // Exported data definition
extern __declpec(dllexport) int n;   // Exported data declaration
__declpec(dllexport) void f();       // Exported function declaration
class __declpec(dllexport) c {       // Exported class definition
    /* ... */
};
```

Using a *.def* file has certain advantages; for instance, it can allow functions in a DLL to be accessed by number rather than name, decreasing the size of a DLL. It also eliminates the need for the messy preprocessor directives such as those in the header *georgeringo.hpp* from Example 1-2. It has some serious drawbacks, however. For example, a *.def* file cannot be used to export classes. Furthermore, it can be difficult to remember to update your *.def* file when you add, remove, or modify functions in your DLL. I therefore recommend that you always use __declspec(dllexport). To learn the full syntax of *.def* files as well as how to use them, consult your toolset's documentation.

Importing symbols from a DLL

Just as there are two ways to export symbols from a DLL, there are two ways to import symbols:

- In the headers included by source code that uses your DLL, use the attribute __declspec(dllimport) and pass an import library to the linker when linking code that uses your DLL.
- Specify a *.def* file when linking code which depends on you DLL.

Just as with exporting symbols, I recommend that you use the attribute __declspec(dllimport) in your source code instead of using *.def* files. The attribute __declspec(dllimport) is used exactly like the attribute __declspec(dllexport), discussed earlier. Like __declspec(dllexport), __declspec(dllimport) is not part of the C++ language, but an extension implemented by most Windows compilers.

If you choose to use __declspec(dllexport) and __declspec(dllimport), you must be sure to use __declspec(dllexport) when building your DLL and __declspec(dllimport) when compiling code that uses your DLL. One approach would be to use two sets of headers: one for building your DLL and the other for compiling code that uses your DLL. This is not satisfactory, however, since it is difficult to maintain two separate versions of the same headers.

Instead, the usual approach is to define a macro that expands to __declspec(dllexport) when building your DLL and to __declspec(dllimport) otherwise. In Example 1-2, I used the macro GEORGERINGO_DECL for this purpose. On Windows, GEORGERINGO_DECL expands to __declspec(dllexport) if the macro GEORGERING_SOURCE is defined and to __declspec(dllimport) otherwise. By defining GEORGERING_SOURCE when building the DLL *libgeorgeringo.dll* but not when compiling code that uses *libgeorgeringo.dll*, you obtain the desired result.

Building DLLs with GCC

The Cygwin and MinGW ports of GCC, discussed in Recipe 1.1, handle DLLs differently than other Windows toolsets. When you build a DLL with GCC, all functions, classes, and data are exported by default. This behavior can be modified by passing the option *--no-export-all-symbols* to the linker, by using the attribute __declspec(dllexport) in your source files, or by using a *.def* file. In each of these three cases, unless you use the option *--export-all-symbols* to force the linker to export all symbols, the only exported functions, classes, and data will be those marked __decl-spec(dllexport) or listed in the *.def* file.

It's therefore possible to use the GCC toolset to build DLLs in two ways: like an ordinary Windows toolset, exporting symbols explicitly using __declspec, or like a Unix toolset, exporting all symbols automatically.* I used the latter method in Example 1-2 and Table 1-11. If you choose this method, you should consider using the option *--export-all-symbols* as a safety measure, in case you happen to include headers containing __declspec(dllexport).

GCC differs from other Windows toolsets in a second way: rather than passing the linker an import library associated with a DLL, you can pass the DLL itself. This is usually faster than using an import library. It can also create problems, however, since several versions of a DLL may exist on your system, and you must ensure that the linker selects the correct version. In Table 1-11, to demonstrate how to create import libraries with GCC, I chose not to use this feature.

> With Cygwin, an import library for the DLL *xxx.dll* is typically named *xxx.dll.a*, while with MinGW it is typically named *xxx.a*. This is just a matter of convention.

GCC 4.0's -fvisibility option

Recent versions of GCC on several platforms, including Linux and Mac OS X, give programmers fine-grained control over which symbols in a dynamic library are exported: the command-line option *-fvisibility* can be used to set the default visibility of symbols in a dynamic library, and a special attribute syntax, similar to __declspec(dllexport) on Windows, can be used within source code to modify the visibility of symbols on a case-by-case basis. The *-fvisibility* option has several possible values, but the two interesting cases are *default* and *hidden*. Roughly speaking, *default* visibility means that a symbol is accessible to code in other modules; *hidden* visibility means that it is not. To enable selective exporting of symbols, specify *-fvisibility=hidden* on the command line and use the *visibility attribute* to mark selected symbols as visible, as shown in Example 1-7.

Example 1-7. Using the visibility attribute with the command-line option
-fvisibility=hidden

```
extern __attribute__((visibility("default"))) int m;    // exported
extern int n;                                           // not exported

__attribute__((visibility("default"))) void f();        // exported
void g();                                               // not exported
```

---

* Confusingly, exporting symbols using __declspec(dllexport) is sometimes called *implicit* exporting.

Example 1-7. Using the visibility attribute with the command-line option -fvisibility=hidden (continued)

```
struct __attribute__((visibility("default"))) S { };   // exported
struct T { };                                          // not exported
```

In Example 1-7, the attribute `__attribute__((visibility("default")))` plays the same role as `__declspec(dllexport)` in Windows code.

Using the `visibility` attribute presents some of the same challenges as using `__declspec(dllexport)` and `__declspec(dllimport)`, since you want the attribute to be present when building a shared library, but not when compiling code that uses the shared library, and you want it to be hidden entirely on platforms that don't support it. Just as with `__declspec(dllexport)` and `__declspec(dllimport)`, this problem can be solved with the preprocessor. For example, you can modify the header *georgeringo.hpp* from Example 1-2 to take advantage of the visibility attribute as follows:

```
georgeringo/georgeringo.hpp

#ifndef GEORGERINGO_HPP_INCLUDED
#define GEORGERINGO_HPP_INCLUDED

// define GEORGERINGO_DLL when building libgerogreringo
# if defined(_WIN32) && !defined(__GNUC__)
#   ifdef GEORGERINGO_DLL
#     define GEORGERINGO_DECL __declspec(dllexport)
#   else
#     define GEORGERINGO_DECL __declspec(dllimport)
#   endif
# else // Unix
#   if defined(GEORGERINGO_DLL) && defined(HAS_GCC_VISIBILITY)
#     define GEORGERINGO_DECL __attribute__((visibility("default")))
#   else
#     define GEORGERINGO_DECL
#   endif
# endif

// Prints "George, and Ringo\n"
GEORGERINGO_DECL void georgeringo( );

#endif // GEORGERINGO_HPP_INCLUDED
```

To make this work, you must define the macro `HAS_GCC_VISIBILITY` when building on systems that support the *-fvisibility* option.

 Recent versions of the Intel compiler for Linux also support the *-fvisibility* option.

Symbol Visibility with Metrowerks for Mac OS X

Metrowerks for Mac OS X provides several options for exporting symbols from a dynamic library. When using the CodeWarrior IDE, you can use a *symbol exports file*, which plays a role similar to a *.def* file on Windows. You can also choose to export all symbols, using the option *-export all*, which is the default when building from the command-line. The method I recommend is to use #pragma export in your source code to mark the functions you wish to export, and to specify *-export pragma* on the command-line when building your dynamic library. The use of #export pragma is illustrated in Example 1-2: just invoke #pragma export on in your header files immediately before a group of functions you want to export, and #export pragma off immediately afterwards. If you want your code to work on toolsets other than Metrowerks, you should place the invocations of #pragma export between #ifdef/#endif directives, as illustrated in Example 1-2.

Command-line options

Let's take a quick look at the options used in Table 1-11. Each command line specifies:

- The name of the input files: *george.obj*, *ringo.obj*, and *georgeringo.obj*
- The name of the dynamic library to be created
- On Windows, the name of the import library

In addition, the linker requires an option to tell it to build a dynamic library rather than an executable. Most linkers use the option *-shared*, but Visual C++ and Intel for Windows use *-dll*, Borland and Digital Mars use *-WD*, and GGC for Mac OS X uses *-dynamiclib*.

Several of the options in Table 1-11 help dynamic libraries to be used more effectively at runtime. For example, some Unix linkers should be told to generate *position-independent code* using the option *-fPIC* (GCC and Intel for Linux). This option makes it more likely that multiple processes will be able to share a single copy of the dynamic library's code; on some systems, failing to specify this option can cause a linker error. Similarly, on Windows the GCC linker the option *--enable-auto-image-base* makes it less likely that the operating system will attempt to load two dynamic libraries at the same location; using this option helps to speed DLL loading.

 You can pass options to GCC linker via the compiler by using the compiler option *-Wl,<option>* to g++. (The letter following *W* is a lowercase *l*.)

Most of the remaining options are used to specify runtime library variants, as described in Recipe 1.23.

See Also

Recipes 1.9, 1.12, 1.17, 1.19, and 1.23

1.5   Building a Complex Application from the Command Line

Problem

You wish to use your command-line tools to build an executable that depends on several static and dynamic libraries.

Solution

Start by building the static and dynamic libraries on which your application depends. Follow the instructions distributed with the libraries, if they are from a third party; otherwise, build them as described in Recipes 1.3 and 1.4.

Next, compile your application's *.cpp* files into object files as described in "Building a Simple "Hello, World" Program from the Command Line. You may need to use the *-I* option to tell your compiler where to search for the headers needed by your application, as shown in Table 1-12.

Table 1-12. Specifying directories to search for headers

Toolset	Option
All	-I<directory>

Finally, use your linker to produce an executable from the collection of object files and libraries. For each library, you must either provide a full pathname or tell the linker where to search for it.

At each stage of this process, if you are using a toolset which comes with static and dynamic variants of its runtime libraries, and if your program uses at least one dynamic library, you should direct the compiler or linker to use a dynamically linked runtime library, as described in Recipe 1.23.

Table 1-13 presents commands for linking the application *hellobeatles* from Example 1-3. It assumes that:

- The current directory is *hellobeatles*.
- The static library *libjohnpaul.lib* or *libjohnpaul.a* was created in the directory *johnpaul*.
- The dynamic library *georgeringo.dll*, *georgeringo.so*, or *georgeringo.dylib* and its import library, if any, were created in the directory *georgeringo*.

Since Comeau can't build dynamic libraries, as mentioned in Recipe 1.4, the entry for Comeau in Table 1-13 assumes that *libgeorgeringo* has been built as a static library rather than as a dynamic library. To build *libgeorgeringo* as a static library, remove the modifier `GEORGERINGO_DECL` from the declaration of the function georgeringo( ) in Example 1-2.

Table 1-13. Commands for linking the application hellobeatle.exe

Toolset	Input files	Command line
GCC (Unix)	hellobeatles.o libjohnpaul.a libgeorgeringo.so	*g++ -o hellobeatles hellobeatles.o -L../johnpaul -L../georgeringo -ljohnpaul -lgeorgeringo* or *g++ -o hellobeatles hellobeatles.o ../johnpaul/libjohnpaul.a ../georgeringo/libgeorgeringo.so*
Intel (Linux)		*icpc -o hellobeatles hellobeatles.o -L../johnpaul -L../georgeringo -ljohnpaul -lgeorgeringo* or *icpc -o hellobeatles hellobeatles.o ../johnpaul/libjohnpaul.a ../georgeringo/libgeorgeringo.so*
Comeau (Unix)		*como --no_prelink_verbose -o hellobeatles hellobeatles.o -L../johnpaul -L../georgeringo -ljohnpaul -lgeorgeringo* or *como --no_prelink_verbose -o hellobeatles hellobeatles.o ../johnpaul/libjohnpaul.a ../georgeringo/libgeorgeringo.a*
GCC (Mac OS X)	hellobeatles.o libjohnpaul.a libgeorgeringo.dylib	*g++ -o hellobeatles hellobeatles.o -L../johnpaul -L../georgeringo -ljohnpaul -lgeorgeringo* or *g++ -o hellobeatles hellobeatles.o ../johnpaul/libjohnpaul.a ../georgeringo/libgeorgeringo.dylib*
Metrowerks (Mac OS X)		*mwld -o hellobeatles hellobeatles.o -search -L../johnpaul -search -L../georgeringo -ljohnpaul -lgeorgeringo* or *mwld -o hellobeatles hellobeatles.o ../johnpaul/libjohnpaul.a ../georgeringo/libgeorgering.dylib*
GCC (Cygwin)	hellobeatles.o libjohnpaul.a libgeorgeringo.dll.a	*g++ -o hellobeatles hellobeatles.o -L../johnpaul -L../georgeringo -ljohnpaul -lgeorgeringo* or *g++ -o hellobeatles hellobeatles.o ../johnpaul/libjohnpaul.a ../georgeringo/libgeorgeringo.dll.a*
GCC (MinGW)	hellobeatles.o libjohnpaul.a libgeorgeringo.a	*g++ -o hellobeatles hellobeatles.o -L../johnpaul -L../georgeringo -ljohnpaul -lgeorgeringo* or *g++ --o hellobeatles hellobeatles.o ../johnpaul/libjohnpaul.a ../georgeringo/libgeorgeringo.a*

Table 1-13. Commands for linking the application hellobeatle.exe (continued)

Toolset	Input files	Command line
Visual C++	hellobeatles.obj libjohnpaul.lib libgeorgeringo.lib	link -nologo -out:hellobeatles.exe -libpath:../johnpaul -libpath:../ georgeringo libjohnpaul.lib libgeorgeringo.lib hellobeatles.obj
Intel (Windows)		xilink -nologo -out:hellobeatles-libpath:../johnpaul -libpath:../ georgeringo libjohnpaul.lib libgeorgeringo.lib hellobeatles.obj
Metrowerks (Windows)		mwld -o hellobeatles -search -L../johnpaul libjohnpaul.lib -search -L../georgeringo libgeorgeringo.lib hellobeatles.obj
Metrowerks (Mac OS X)[a]		mwld -o hellobeatles hellobeatles.o -search -L../johnpaul -search -L../ georgeringo libjohnpaul.a libgeorgeringo.dylib
CodeWarrior 10.0 (Mac OS X)[b]		Consult the Metrowerks documentation
Borland		bcc32 -q -WR -WC -ehellobeatles -L../johnpaul -L../georgeringo libjohnpaul.lib libgeorgeringo.lib hellobeatles.obj
Digital Mars		link -noi hellobeatles.obj,hellobeatles.exe,NUL,user32.lib kernel32.lib .. \johnpaul\ ..\georgeringo\ libjohnpaul.lib libgeorgeringo.lib,, or link -noi hellobeatles.obj,hellobeatles.exe,NUL,user32.lib kernel32.lib .. \johnpaul\libjohnpaul.lib ..\georgeringo\libgeorgeringo.lib,,
Comeau (Windows)	hellobeatles.obj libjohnpaul.lib libgeorgeringo.lib	como --no_prelink_verbose -o hellobeatles ../johnpaul/ libjohnpaul.lib . ./georgeringo/libgeorgeringo.lib hellobeatles.obj

[a] *hellobeatles* may not execute properly when built with the indicated command line, since the application will make use of two copies of Metrowerks's static runtime support libraries. (See Recipe 1.23.)
[b] CodeWarrior 10.0 for Mac OS X will provide dynamic variants of its runtime support libraries; these should be used when building *hellobeatles*. (See Recipe 1.23.)

For example, if you use Microsoft Visual Studio .NET 2003, and if it is installed in the standard location on the *C* drive, you can build *hellobeatles.exe* from the command line by changing to the directory *hellobeatles* and entering the following from the commands:

```
> "C:Program Files\Microsoft Visual Studio .NET 2003\VC\bin\
vcvars32.bat"
Setting environment for using Microsoft Visual Studio 2005 tools.
(If you have another version of Visual Studio or Visual C++ installed
and wish to use its tools from the command line, run vsvars32.bat for
that version.)
> cl -c -nologo -EHsc -GR -Zc:forScope -Zc:wchar_t -MD -I..
-Fohellobeatles hellobeatles.cpp
hellobeatles.cpp
> link -nologo -out:hellobeatles.exe -libpath:../johnpaul
-libpath:../georgeringo libjohnpaul.lib libgeorgeringo.lib
hellobeatles.obj
```

Discussion

Searching for included headers

The *-I* option is used to specify an *include path*. When a compiler—actually the pre-processor—encounters an include directive of the form:

```
#include "file"
```

it typically first attempts to find the referenced file by interpreting the given path-name relative to the location of the source file being processed. If this is unsuccessful, it attempts to locate the file in one of the directories specified with the *-I* option, and then in a list of toolset-dependent directories, which can often be configured using environment variables.

The situation is similar when an included header is specified using angle brackets, like so:

```
#include <file>
```

except that compilers generally don't interpret the given pathname relative to the location of the source file being processed.

Passing libraries to the linker

There are several interesting aspects of the command lines in Table 1-13.

On Windows, the input to the linker consists of object files, static libraries, and import libraries; on Unix, it consists of object files, static libraries, and dynamic libraries.

On both Windows and Unix, libraries can be passed to the linker in two ways:

- By specifying a pathname on the command line
- By specifying the simple name of the library together with a location to search for the library

Table 1-13 illustrates both methods.

The locations to search for libraries can usually be specified on the command line. Most linkers use the option *-L<directory>* for this purpose, but Visual C++ and Intel for Windows use *-libpath: <directory>* and Metrowerks uses *-search -L<directory>*. The Digital Mars linker allows library search paths to be listed on the command line alongside library files, with search paths distinguished from library files by a trailing backslash; it also requires that backslashes be used as pathname separators.

Comeau does not provide an option for specifying a library search path on Windows.

In addition to the locations explicitly specified, linkers usually search a list of toolset-dependent directories, which can often be configured using environment variables. On Windows, the list of directories typically includes the *lib* subdirectory of the toolset installation. As a result, if you copy *.lib* files to this directory, you can specify them by name on the command line without specifying a search location. If you combine this method with the technique described in Recipe 1.25, you can avoid passing the linker any information about a library.

The way the name of a library is specified to the linker differs between Unix and Windows. On Windows, the full name of the library is specified, including the file extension. On Unix—and on Windows when using the GCC toolset—libraries are specified using the *-l* option followed by the name of the library, with the file extension and the *lib* prefix removed. This means that the name of a library must begin with *lib* to be automatically found by the linker. More interestingly, it gives the linker the opportunity to choose between several versions of a library. If the linker finds both static and dynamic version of a library, the dynamic library is selected, unless otherwise specified. On some systems, the linker may choose between several versions of a dynamic library based on the portion of the file name following *.so*.

Metrowerks supports both the Windows and the Unix styles for specifying library names.

Finally, be aware that Unix linkers can be very sensitive to the order in which object files and static libraries are specified on the command line: if a static library or object file references a symbol defined in a second static library or object file, the first file must appear before the second file on the command line. To resolve circular dependencies, it is sometimes necessary to specify a given library or object file more than once. Another solution is to pass a sequence of object files and static libraries to linker bracketed by *-(* and *-)*; this causes the file to be searched repeatedly until all references are resolved. This option should be avoided if possible because it can significantly degrade performance.

Running your application

If your application uses a dynamic variant of your toolset's runtime library, the runtime library must be available when your application is run and in a location where it will be found automatically by the operating system's dynamic loader. Typically, this means that the dynamic runtime library must be placed either in the same directory as your application or in one of a list of system-specific directories. This is more of a concern when developing for Windows than when developing for Unix, since on Unix the appropriate runtime libraries are often already installed in the correct locations. The names of the dynamic runtime libraries distributed with the various toolsets are given in Recipe 1.23.

See Also

Recipes 1.10, 1.13, 1.18, and 1.23

1.6 Installing Boost.Build

Problem

You want to obtain and install Boost.Build.

Solution

Consult the Boost.Build documentation at *www.boost.org/boost-build2* or follow these steps:

1. Go to the Boost homepage, *www.boost.org*, and follow the Download link to Boost's SourceForge download area.

2. Download and unpack either the latest release of the package *boost* or the latest release of the package *boost-build*. The former includes the full collection of Boost libraries, while the latter is a standalone release of Boost.Build. Place the unpacked files in a suitable permanent location.

3. Download and unpack the latest version of the package *boost-jam* for your platform; this package includes a prebuilt *bjam* executable. If the package *boost-jam* is not available for your platform, follow the instructions provided with the package you downloaded in step 2 to build the executable from the source.

4. Copy *bjam* to a location in your PATH environment variable.

5. Permanently set the environment variable BOOST_BUILD_PATH to the Boost. Build root directory. If you downloaded the package *boost* in step 1, the root directory is the subdirectory *tools/build/v2* of your Boost installation; otherwise, it is the directory *boost-build*.

6. Configure Boost.Build for your toolsets and libraries by editing the configuration file *user-config.jam*, located in the Boost.Build root directory. The file *user-config.jam* contains comments explaining how to do this.

Discussion

The most difficult part of using Boost.Build is downloading and installing it. Eventually Boost may provide a graphical installation utility, but for the time being, you must follow the above steps.

The purpose of step five is to help the build tool, *bjam*, find the root directory of the build system. This step is not strictly necessary, however, since there is another way to accomplish the same thing: simply create a file called *boost-build.jam*, with the single line:

```
boost-build boost-build-root ;
```

and place it in the root directory of your project or in any of its parent directories. The second method may be preferable if you wish to distribute Boost.Build with your source code, since it makes the installation process easier for end users.

The sixth step is potentially the most complex, but in practice it is usually simple. If you have just a single version of your toolset installed, and if it's installed in a standard location, it's sufficient for *user-config.jam* to consist of a single line of the form:

```
using <toolset> ;
```

For example, if you use Visual C++, the following will usually suffice:

```
using msvc ;
```

And if you use GCC, you can simply write:

```
using gcc ;
```

Things are slightly more complicated if you have more than one version of a toolset installed, or if your toolset is installed in an unusual location. If your toolset is installed in an unusual location, you tell Boost.Build where to find it by passing the command to invoke the toolset's compiler as the third argument to using. For example:

```
using msvc : : "C:/Tools/Compilers/Visual Studio/Vc7/bin/cl" ;
```

If you have several versions of a toolset installed, you can invoke the using rule several times with a single toolset name, passing a version identifier as the second argument and the compiler command as the third argument. For example, you might configure two versions of the Intel toolset as follows:

```
using intel : 7.1 : "C:/Program Files/Intel/Compiler70/IA32/Bin/icl" ;
using intel : 8.0 : "C:/Program Files/Intel/CPP/Compiler80/IA32/Bin/icl" ;
```

The names used by Boost.Build for the seven toolsets covered in this chapter are given in Table 1-14.

Table 1-14. Boost.Build toolset names

Toolset	Name
GCC	gcc
Visual C++	msvc
Intel	intel
Metrowerks	cw
Comeau	como
Borland	borland
Digital Mars	dmc

1.7 Building a Simple "Hello, World" Application Using Boost.Build

Problem

You want to use Boost.Build to build a simple "Hello, World" program, such as the one in Example 1-4.

Solution

Create a text file named *Jamroot* in the directory where you wish the executable and any accompanying intermediate files to be created. In the file *Jamroot*, invoke two *rules*, as follows. First, invoke the exe rule to declare an executable target, specifying your *.cpp* file as a *source*. Next, invoke the install rule, specifying the executable target name and the location where you want the install directory. Finally, run *bjam* to build your program.

For example, to build an executable *hello* or *hello.exe* from the file *hello.cpp* in Example 1-4, create a file named *Jamroot* with the following content in the directory containing *hello.cpp*, as shown in Example 1-8.

Example 1-8. Jamfile for project hello

```
# jamfile for project hello

exe hello : hello.cpp ;

install dist : hello : <location>. ;
```

Next, change to the directory containing *hello.cpp* and *Jamroot* and enter the following command:

```
> bjam hello
```

This command builds the executable *hello* or *hello.exe* in a subdirectory of the current directory. Finally, enter the command:

```
> bjam dist
```

This command copies the executable to the directory specified by the location property, which in this case is the current directory.

> As this book goes to press, the Boost.Build developers are preparing for the official release of Boost.Build version 2. By the time you read this, Version 2 will probably already have been released; if not, you can enable the behavior described in this chapter by passing the command-line option *--v2* to bjam. For example, instead of entering **bjam hello**, enter **bjam --v2 hello**.

Discussion

The file *Jamroot* is an example of a *Jamfile*. While a small collection of C++ source files might be managed using a single Jamfile, a large codebase will typically require many Jamfiles, organized hierarchically. Each Jamfile resides in a separate directory and corresponds to a separate *project*. Most Jamfiles are simply named *Jamfile*, but the highest-level Jamfile—the Jamfile that resides in a directory that is an ancestor of the directories containing all the other Jamfiles—is named *Jamroot*. The project defined by this highest-level Jamfile is known as the *project root*. Each project except the project root has a *parent project*, defined as the project in the nearest ancestor directory containing a Jamfile.

This hierarchical design is quite powerful: for example, it makes it easy to apply a *requirement*, such as thread support, to a project and all its descendants.

Each project is a collection of *targets*. Targets are declared by invoking *rules*, such as the exe rule and the `install` rule. Most targets correspond to binary files, or more precisely, to collections of related binary files, such as the debug and release builds of an application.

The exe rule is used to declare an executable target. An invocation of this rule has the form shown in Example 1-9.

Example 1-9. Invocation of the exe rule

```
exe target-name
    : sources
    : requirements
    : default-build
    : usage-requirements
    ;
```

Here, *target-name* specifies the name of the executable, *sources* specifies a list of source files and libraries; *requirements* specifies properties that will apply to the target regardless of any additional properties requested on the command line or inherited from another project; *default-build* specifies properties that will apply to the target unless a feature with a different value is explicitly requested; *usage-requirements* specifies properties that will be propagated to all other targets that depend on this target.

Properties are specified in the form *<feature>value*. For example, to declare an executable that will always be built with thread support, you could write:

```
exe hello
    : hello.cpp
    : <threading>multi
    ;
```

You don't have to write colons separating trailing arguments to a Boost.Build rule unless you specify values for those arguments.

Several common features, and their possible values, are listed in Table 1-15.

Table 1-15. Common Boost.Build features

Feature	Value	Effect
include	*Path*	Specifies an include path
define	*name*[*=value*]	Defines a macro
threading	multi or single	Enables or disables thread support
runtime-link	static or shared	Specifies runtime library linking[a]
variant	debug or release	Requests a debug or release build

a See Recipe 1.23.

When an executable target—or a target corresponding to a static or dynamic library—is built, the file corresponding to the target is created in a descendent directory of the directory containing the Jamfile. The relative pathname of this directory depends on the toolset and build configuration, but it always begins with *bin*. For example, the executable from Example 1-8 might be created in the directory *bin/ msvc/debug*.

For simplicity I asked you to create the Jamfile from Example 1-8 in the same directory as the source file *hello.cpp*. In a real world project, however, you will often want to keep your source and binary files in separate directories. In Example 1-8 you can place the Jamfile anywhere you like, as long as you adjust the pathname `hello.cpp` so that it points to the file *hello.cpp*.

The `install` rule instructs Boost.Build to copy the one or more files—specified as file names or as main target names—to a specified location. An invocation of this rule has the form shown in Example 1-10.

Example 1-10. Invocation of the install rule

```
install target-name
    : files
    : requirements
    : default-build
    : usage-requirements
    ;
```

Here, `target-name` is the name of the target being declared and `files` is a list of one or more files or targets to be copied. The remaining arguments, `requirements`, `default-build`, and `usage-requirements` have the same meaning as in Example 1-9.

The location where the files are to be copied can be specified either as the target name or as the value of the location property of a target requirement. For example, in Example 1-8 you could have written the install target like so:

```
install . : hello ;
```

You could then install the executable as follows:

```
> bjam .
```

The method used in Example 1-8 is preferable, however, since it's easier to remember a named target than a file pathname.

Finally, let's look briefly at the syntax of the *bjam* command line. To build the target *xxx* with your default toolset, enter the command:

```
> bjam xxx
```

To build the target *xxx* with the toolset *yyy*, enter the command:

```
> bjam xxx toolset=yyy
```

To build the target *xxx* with version *vvv* of toolset *yyy*, enter the command:

```
> bjam xxx toolset=yyy-vvv
```

To build specify a standard library *zzz* from the command line, use the syntax:

```
> bjam xxx stdlib=zzz
```

You can build several targets at once by entering several target names on the command line, and build all targets in the given project by specifying no target. Consequently, you could have built and installed the executable from Example 1-9 by simply entering:

```
> bjam
```

To remove all the files created during the build process, including the executable, enter:

```
> bjam --clean
```

 A property of the form *<feature>value* can be specified on the command line as *feature=value*.

See Also

Recipes 1.2 and 1.15

1.8   Building a Static Library Using Boost.Build

Problem

You want to use Boost.Build to build a static library from a collection of C++ source files, such as those listed in Example 1-1.

Solution

Create a *Jamroot* file in the directory where you wish the static library to be created. In the file *Jamroot*, invoke the lib rule to declare a library target, specifying your *.cpp* files as sources and the property <link>static as a requirement. Add a usage requirement of the form <include>*path* to specify the library's include directory, i.e., the directory with respect to which include directives for library headers should be resolved. You may need to add one or more requirements of the form <include>*path* to tell the compiler where to search for included headers. Finally, run *bjam* from the directory containing *Jamroot*, as described in Recipe 1.7.

For example, to build a static library from the source files listed in Example 1-1, your *Jamroot* might look like Example 1-11.

Example 1-11. A Jamfile to build the static library libjohnpaul.lib or libjohnpaul.a

```
# Jamfile for project libjohnpaul

lib libjohnpaul
    : # sources
      john.cpp paul.cpp johnpaul.cpp
    : # requirements
      <link>static
    : # default-build
    : # usage-requirements
      <include>..
    ;
```

To build the library, enter:

```
> bjam libjohnpaul
```

Discussion

The lib rule is used to declare a target representing a static or dynamic library. It takes the same form as the exe rule, as illustrated in Example 1-9. The usage requirement <include>.. frees projects that depend on your library from having to explicitly specify your library's include directory in their requirements. The requirement <link>static specifies that your target should always be built as a static library. If you want the freedom to build a library target either as static or as dynamic, you can omit the requirement <link>static. Whether the library is built as static or dynamic can then be specified on the command line, or in the requirements of a target that depends on the library target. For example, if the requirement <link>static were omitted in Example 1-11, you could build the target libjohnpaul as a static library by entering the command:

```
> bjam libjohnpaul link=static
```

Writing source code for a library that can be built either as static or dynamic is a bit tricky, however, as discussed in Recipe 1.9.

See Also

Recipes 1.3, 1.11, and 1.16

1.9   Building a Dynamic Library Using Boost.Build

Problem

You wish to use Boost.Build to build a dynamic library from a collection of C++ source files, such as those listed in Example 1-2.

Solution

Create a *Jamroot* file in the directory where you wish the dynamic library—and the import library, if any—to be created. In the file *Jamroot*, invoke the lib rule to declare a library target, specifying your *.cpp* files as sources and the properties <link> shared as a requirement. Add a usage requirement of the form <include>*path* to specify the library's include directory, i.e., the directory with respect to which include directives for library headers should be resolved. If your source files include headers from other libraries, you may need to add several requirements of the form <include>*path* to tell the compiler where to search for included headers. You may also need to add one or more requirements of the form <define>*symbol* to ensure that your dynamic library's symbols will be exported using __declspec(dllexport) on Windows. Finally, run *bjam* from the directory containing *Jamroot*, as described in Recipe 1.7.

For example, to build a dynamic library from the source files listed in Example 1-2, create a file named *Jamroot* in the directory *georgeringo*, as shown in Example 1-12.

Example 1-12. A Jamfile to build the dynamic library georgeringo.so, georgeringo.dll, or georgeringo.dylib

```
# Jamfile for project georgringo

lib libgeorgeringo
    : # sources
      george.cpp ringo.cpp georgeringo.cpp
    : # requirements
      <link>shared
      <define>GEORGERINGO_DLL
```

Example 1-12. A Jamfile to build the dynamic library georgeringo.so, georgeringo.dll, or georgeringo.dylib (continued)

```
: # default-build
: # usage-requirements
  <include>..
;
```

To build the library, enter:

```
> bjam libgeorgeringo
```

Discussion

As discussed in Recipe 1.8, the lib rule is used to declare a target representing a static or dynamic library. The usage requirement `<include>..` frees projects which depend on your library from having to explicitly specify your library's include directory in their requirements. The requirement `<link>shared` specifies that the target should always be built as a dynamic library. If you want the freedom to build a library target either as static or as dynamic, you can omit the requirement `<link>shared` and specify this property on the command line, or in the requirements of a target that depends on the library target. Writing a library which can be built as either static or dynamic requires some care, however, because of the preprocessor directives necessary to ensure that symbols are properly exported on Windows. Rewriting Example 1-2 so that it can be built as either static or dynamic makes a good exercise.

See Also

Recipes 1.4, 1.12, 1.17, and 1.19

1.10   Building a Complex Application Using Boost.Build

Problem

You wish to use Boost.Build to build an executable that depends on several static and dynamic libraries.

Solution

Follow these steps:

1. For each library on which the executable depends—unless it is distributed as a prebuilt binary—create a Jamfile as described in Recipes 1.8 and 1.9.

2. Create a *Jamroot* file in the directory where you want the executable to be created.

---

3. In the file *Jamroot*, invoke the exe rule to declare an executable target. Specify your *.cpp* files and the library targets on which the executable depends as sources. Also, add properties of the form <include>*path* as sources, if necessary, to tell the compiler where to search for library headers.

4. In the file *Jamroot*, invoke the install rule, specifying the properties <install-dependencies>on, <install-type>EXE, and <install-type>SHARED_LIB as requirements.

5. Run *bjam* from the directory containing *Jamroot* as described in Recipe 1.7.

For example, to build an executable from the source files listed in Example 1-3, create a file named *Jamroot* in the directory *hellobeatles* as shown in Example 1-13.

Example 1-13. A Jamfile to build the executable hellobeatles.exe or hellobeatles

```
# Jamfile for project hellobeatles

exe hellobeatles
    : # sources
      ../johnpaul//libjohnpaul
      ../georgeringo//libgeorgeringo
      hellobeatles.cpp
    ;

install dist
    : # sources
      hellobeatles
    : # requirements
      <install-dependencies>on
      <install-type>EXE
      <install-type>SHARED_LIB
      <location>.
    ;
```

Now enter:

> **bjam hellobeatles**

from the directory *hellobeatles*. This first builds the two projects on which the target hellobeatles depends, and then builds the target hellobeatles. Finally, enter:

> **bjam dist**

This copies the executable *hellobeatles* and the dynamic library *georgeringo* to the directory containing *hellobeatles.cpp*.

As discussed in Recipe 1.5, before you can run *hellobeatles*, you may need to place a copy of your toolset's dynamic runtime library in a location where it can be found by the operating system.

Discussion

Library targets

The library targets on which a target depends are specified as sources using the notation *path//target-name*. In Recipes 1.8 and 1.9, I showed how to declare a target for a library to be built from source code by Boost.Build. If a library is available as a prebuilt binary, however, you can declare a target for it as follows:

```
lib target-name
    :
    : <file>file-name
    ;
```

As explained in Recipe 1.7, most main targets correspond not to a single file but to collections of related files, such as the debug and release build of an executable. To declare a target for a prebuilt library that has several variants, you can use the following notation:

```
lib target-name
    :
    : <file>file-name requirements
    ;

lib target-name
    :
    : <file>other-file-name other-requirements
    ;
```

For example, debug and release variants of a prebuilt library might be declared as follows:

```
lib cryptolib
    :
    : <file> ../libraries/cryptolib/cryptolib_debug.lib
      <variant>debug
    ;

lib cryptolib
    :
    : <file> ../libraries/cryptolib/cryptolib.lib
      <variant>release
    ;
```

If a prebuilt library is located in one the directories that is searched automatically by the linker, as described in Recipe 1.5, you can declare a target for it as follows:

```
lib target-name
    :
    : <name>library-name
    ;
```

Here, *library-name* is the name that should be passed to the linker, which may differ from the actual file name, as discussed in Recipe 1.5. To tell the linker to look in a particular directory, you can write

```
lib target-name
    :
    : <name>library-name
      <search>library-path
    ;
```

Installation. A complex application may need to be installed together with a number of additional executables and dynamic libraries on which it depends. Rather than specifying all these files individually, you can use the install-dependencies features, which allows you to specify only the top-level executable target and the type of dependencies that should be installed. In Example 1-13, the requirement <install-dependencies>on turns on the install-dependencies feature, and the requirements <install-type>EXE and <install-type>SHARED_LIB tells Boost.Build to install all dependencies that are executables or shared libraries. Other possible values of the install-type feature include LIB and IMPORT_LIB.

Project organization. All three Jamfiles involved in building the executable *hellobeatles* are named *Jamroot*. This is fine in such a simple example, but in general it's a good idea to organize a collection of Jamfiles hierarchically, with a single top-level Jamfile defining the project root. Arranging projects in this manner allows you to take advantage of some of Boost.Build's more sophisticated features, such as allowing properties to be inherited by child projects. One way to accomplish this in the present case is to change the names of the Jamfiles in the directories *johnpaul*, *georgeringo*, and *hellobeatles* from *Jamroot* to *Jamfile*, and add to a *Jamroot* file in the parent directory with the following content:

```
# jamfile for example application

build-project hellobeatles  ;
```

The rule build-project simply tells *bjam* to build a given project, which can be specified either by pathname or by a symbolic identifier. If you change to the directory containing Jamroot and run *bjam*, the three child projects will be built.

See Also

Recipes 1.5, 1.13, and 1.18

1.11   Building a Static Library with an IDE

Problem

You wish to use your IDE to build a static library from a collection of C++ source files, such as those listed in Example 1-1.

Solution

The basic outline is as follows:

1. Create a new project and specify that you wish to build a static library rather than an executable or a dynamic library.

2. Choose a build configuration (e.g., debug versus release, single-threaded versus multithreaded).

3. Specify the name of your library and the directory in which it should be created.

4. Add your source files to the project.

5. If necessary, specify one or more directories where the compiler should search for included headers. See Recipe 1.13.

6. Build the project.

The steps in this outline vary somewhat depending on the IDE; for example, with some IDEs, several steps are combined into one or the ordering of the steps is different. The second step is covered in detail in Recipes 1.21, 1.22, and 1.23. For now, you should use default settings as much as possible.

For example, here's how to build a static library from the source code in Example 1-1 using the Visual C++ IDE.

Select New → Project from the File menu, select Visual C++* in the left pane, select Win32 Console Application, and enter *libjohnpaul* as your project's name. From the Win32 Application Wizard go to Application Settings, select Static library, uncheck Precompiled header, and press Finish. You should now have an empty project with two build configurations, Debug and Release, the former being the active configuration.

Next, display your project's property pages by right-clicking on the project's name in the Solution Explorer and selecting Properties. Go to Configuration Properties → Librarian → General and enter the pathname of your project's output file in the field labeled Output File. The directory portion of the pathname should point to the directory *binaries* which you created at the beginning of this chapter; the file name portion should be *libjohnpaul.lib*.

---

* In versions of Visual C++ prior to Visual C++ 2005, this option was labeled *Visual C++ Projects*.

Finally, use Add Existing Item... from the Project menu to add the source files listed in Example 1-1 to your project. Your project's property pages should now contain a node labeled "C/C++." Go to Configuration Properties → C/C++ → Code Generation and specify Multi-threaded Debug DLL as the Runtime Library. You can now build your project by selecting Build Solution from the Build menu. Verify that a file named *libjohnpaul.lib* has been created in the directory *binaries*.

 Instead of using Add Existing Item... to add the source files from Example 1-1 to your project, you can use Add New Item... to create blank source files and add them to your project. Then you can type or paste the content from Example 1-1 into the newly created files. Similar remarks hold for other IDEs

Discussion

IDEs differ much more than toolsets. Each IDE provides its own way to create a project, specify its configuration properties, and add files to it. Nonetheless, after you have learned to use several IDEs, learning to use an additional IDE is generally easy.

When learning to use a new a new IDE, the features you should concentrate on are these:

- How to create a new project
- How to specify the type of project (executable, static library, or dynamic library)
- How to add existing files to a project
- How to create new files and add them to a project
- How to specify the name of a project's output file
- How to specify include paths
- How to specify library search paths
- How to specify libraries on which a project depends
- How to build a project
- How to organize collections of projects in to a group and specify their dependencies

This recipe demonstrates many of these features. Most of the other features are covered in Recipes 1.12 and 1.13.

Let's look at how to build a static library using CodeWarrior, C++Builder, and Dev-C++.

CodeWarrior

Select New... from the File menu, and select the Project tab of the New dialog. Enter `libjohnpaul.mcp` as your project's name, select a location where your project's configuration files should be stored, and double-click Mac OS C++ Stationery. From the

New Project dialog, expand the nodes Mac OS X Mach-O and Standard Console, then double-click C++ Console Mach-O. You should now have a project with two targets, Mach-O C++ Console Debug and Mach-O C++ Console Final, the former being the default target.

Since you will need to refer to these targets by name when you create a project which depends on this project, you should give the targets descriptive names. For now, rename just the debug target, as follows. Select the Targets tab on your project's window, and double-click on the name of the debug target to display the Target Settings Window. Then go to Target → Target Settings and enter `libjohnpaul Debug` in the field labeled Target Name.

Next, from the Target Settings Window, go to Target → PPC Mac OS X Target. Specify Library as the Project Type, and enter `libjohnpaul.a` in the field labeled File Name. Go to Target → Target Settings and press Choose... to specify the directory *binaries* as the location where the output file *libjpohnpaul.a* should be created.

Finally, select the Files tab on your project's window and remove the existing source files and libraries files by dragging them to Trash. Then use Add Files... from the Project menu to add the source files listed in Example 1-1 to your project. You can now build your project by selecting Make from the Project menu. Verify that a file named *libjohnpaul.a* has been created in the directory *binaries*.

C++Builder

Select New → Other... from the File menu and then select Library. You should now have an empty project. Select Save Project As... on the File menu, select a directory for storing your project's configuration files and enter *libjohnpaul.bpr* as your project's name.

Next, select Options... from the Project menu to display the Project Options dialog. Then go Directories and Conditionals and use the control next to Final output to specify where your project's output file, *libjohnpaul.lib*, should be created. By default this file will be created in the same directory as *libjohnpaul.bpr*, but you should tell C++Builder to create it in the directory *binaries*. If you wish, you can also use the control next to *Intermediate output* to specify where object files should be created. By default they will be created in the same directory as the source files.

Finally, use Add to Project... from the Project menu to add the source files listed in Example 1-1 to your project. You can now build your project by selecting Make libjohnpaul from the Project menu. Verify that a file named *libjohnpaul.lib* has been created in the directory *binaries*.

Dev-C++

Select New → Project... from the File menu. From the New project dialog, select Static Library and C++ Project and enter *libjohnpaul* as your project's name. After pressing OK, specify the location where your project's configuration file should be located.

Next, select Project Options from the Project menu to display the Project Options dialog. Then go to Build Options and verify that your project's output file is named *libjohnpaul.a*. Enter the pathname of the directory *binaries* under Executable output directory. If you wish, you can enter the directory where object files will be created under Object file output directory.

Finally, use Add to project from the Project menu to add the source files listed in Example 1-1 to your project. You can now build your project by selecting Compile from the Execute menu. Verify that a file named *libjohnpaul.a* has been created in the directory *binaries*.

See Also

Recipes 1.3, 1.8, and 1.16

1.12 Building a Dynamic Library with an IDE

Problem

You wish to use your IDE to build a dynamic library from a collection of C++ source files, such as those listed in Example 1-2.

Solution

The basic outline is as follows:

1. Create a new project and specify that you wish to build a dynamic library rather than static library or an executable.
2. Choose a build configuration (e.g., debug versus release, single-threaded versus multithreaded).
3. Specify the name of your library and the directory where it should be created.
4. Add your source files to the project.
5. On Windows, define any macros necessary to ensure that your dynamic library's symbols will be exported using `__declspec(dllexport)`.
6. If necessary, specify one or more directories where the compiler should search for included headers. See Recipe 1.13.
7. Build the project.

As with Recipe 1.11, the steps in this outline vary somewhat depending on the IDE. The second step is covered in detail in Recipes 1.21, 1.22, and 1.23. For now, you should use default settings wherever possible.

For example, here's how to build a dynamic library from the source code in Example 1-2 using the Visual C++ IDE.

Select New → Project from the File menu, select Visual C++* in the left pane, select Win32 Console Application and enter *libgeorgeringo* as your project's name. From the Win32 Application Wizard go to Application Settings, select DLL and Empty Project, and press Finish. You should now have an empty project with two build configurations, Debug and Release, the former being the active configuration.

Next, display your project's property pages by right-clicking on the project's name in the Solution Explorer and selecting Properties. Go to Configuration Properties → Linker → General and enter the pathname of your project's output file in the field labeled Output File. The directory portion of the pathname should point to the directory binaries which you created at the beginning of this chapter; the file name portion should be *libgeorgeringo.dll*. Similarly, go to Configuration Properties → Linker → Advanced and enter the pathname of your DLL's import library in the field labeled Import Library. The directory portion of the pathname should point to the directory *binaries* which you created at the beginning of this chapter; the file name portion should be *libgeorgeringo.lib*

Next, use Add Existing Item... from the Project menu to add the source files listed in Example 1-2 to your project.

> Instead of using Add Existing Item... to add the source files from Example 1-2 to your project, you can use Add New Item... to create blank source files and add them to your project. Then you can type or paste the content from Example 1-2 into the newly created files. Similar remarks hold for other IDEs.

Your project's property pages should now contain a node labeled C/C++. Go to Configuration Properties → C/C++ → Code Generation and define the macro GEORGERINGO_DLL, as described in Recipe 1.19. Next, go to Configuration Propertiess → C/C++ → Code Generation and specify Multi-threaded Debug DLL as the Run-time Library.

You can now build your project by selecting Build Solution from the Build menu. Verify that two files named *libgeorgeringo.dll* and *libgeorgeringo.lib* have been created in the directory *binaries*.

---

* In versions of Visual C++ prior to Visual C++ 2005, this option was labeled *Visual C++ Projects*.

Discussion

As you saw in Recipe 1.11, each IDE provides its own way to create a project, specify its configuration properties, and add files to it. Let's look at how to build a dynamic library using CodeWarrior, C++Builder, and Dev-C++.

CodeWarrior

Select New... from the File menu, and select the Project tab of the New dialog. Enter **libgeorgeringo.mcp** as your project's name, select a location where your project's configuration files should be stored, and double-click Mac OS C++ Stationery. From the New Project dialog, expand the nodes Mac OS X Mach-O and Standard Console, then double-click C++ Console Mach-O. You should now have a project with two targets, Mach-O C++ Console Debug and Mach-O C++ Console Final, the former being the default target.

Since you will need to refer to these targets by name when you create a project which depends on this project, you should give the targets descriptive names. For now, rename just the debug target, as follows. Select the Targets tab on your project's window, and double-click on the name of the debug target to display the Target Settings Window. Then go to Target → Target Settings and enter **libgeorgeringo Debug** in the field labeled Target Name.

Next, from the Target Settings Window, go to Target → PPC Mac OS X Target. Specify Dynamic Library as the Project Type, and enter **libgeorgeringo.dylib** in the field labeled File Name. Go to Target → Target Settings and press Choose... to specify the directory *binaries* as the location where the output file *libgeorgeringo.dylib* should be created. Then, go to Linker → PPC Mac OS X Linker. Select Use #pragma from the drop-down list labeled Export Symbols, and make sure that the field labeled Main Entry Point is empty.

Finally, select the Files tab on your project's window and remove the existing source files and libraries files by dragging them to Trash. Use Add Files... from the Project menu to add the source files listed in Example 1-2 to your project. Then use Add Files... to add the file *dylib1.o*, in the directory */usr/lib*, and the files *MSL_All_Mach-O_D.dylib* and *MSL_Shared_AppAndDylib_Runtime_D.lib*, in the directory *Metrowerks CodeWarrior/MacOS X Support/Libraries/Runtime/Runtime_PPC/Runtime_MacOSX/Libs*. If you were configuring the release target instead of the debug target, you would add the libraries *MSL_All_Mach-O.dylib* and *MSL_Shared_AppAndDylib_Runtime.lib* instead. You can now build your project by selecting Make from the Project menu. Verify that a file named *libgeorgeringo.dylib* has been created in the directory *binaries*.

C++Builder

Select New → Other... from the File menu and then select DLL Wizard. From the DLL Wizard dialog, select C++ and Multi Threaded. You should now have a project containing a single source file *Unit1.cpp*. Remove *Unit1.cpp* from the project by right-clicking and selecting Remove From Project. Select Save Project As... on the File menu, select a directory for storing your project's configuration files, and enter *libgeorgeringo.bpr* as your project's name.

Next, select Options... from the Project menu to display the Project Options dialog. Then go to Directories and Conditionals and use the control next to Final output to specify that your project's output files should be created in the directory *binaries*. By default, this file will be created in the same directory as *libjohnpaul.bpr*. If you wish, you can also use the control next to Intermediate output to specify where object files should be created. By default they will be created in the same directory as the source files.

Next, define the macro GEORGERINGO_DLL, as described in Recipe 1.19.

Finally, use Add to Project... from the Project menu to add the source files listed in Example 1-2 to your project. You can now build your project by selecting Make libgeorgeringo from the *Project* menu. Verify that two files named *libgeorgeringo.dll* and *libgeorgeringo.lib* have been created in the directory *binaries*.

Dev-C++

Select New → Project... from the File menu. From the New project dialog, select DLL and C++ Project and enter *libgeorgeringo* as your project's name. After pressing *OK*, specify the location where your project's configuration file should be located.

Next, select Project Options from the Project menu to display the Project Option dialog. Then go to Build Options and verify that your project's output file is named *libjohnpaul.dll*. Enter the pathname of the directory *binaries* under Executable output directory. If you wish, you can enter the directory where object files will be created under Object file output directory.

Now, define the macro GEORGERINGO_DLL, as described in Recipe 1.19.

Finally, remove any existing source files from your project by right-clicking and selecting Remove file. Use Save Project as... from the File menu to save your project's configuration file *libgeorgeringo.dev*. Then use Add to project from the Project menu to add the source files listed in Example 1-2 to your project. Build your project by selecting Compile from the Execute menu, and verify that a file named *libjohnpaul.a* has been created in the directory *binaries*.

See Also

Recipes 1.4, 1.9, 1.17, 1.19, and 1.23

1.13   Building a Complex Application with an IDE

Problem

You wish to use your IDE to build an executable that depends on several static and dynamic libraries.

Solution

The basic outline is as follows:

1. If you are building the dependent libraries from the source, and they don't come with their own IDE projects or makefiles, create projects for them, as described in Recipes 1.11 and 1.12.

2. Create a new project and specify that you wish to build an executable rather than a library.

3. Choose a build configuration (e.g., debug versus release, single-threaded versus multithreaded).

4. Specify the name of your executable and the directory in which it should be created.

5. Add your source files to the project.

6. Tell the compiler where to find the headers for the dependent libraries.

7. Tell the linker what libraries to use and where to find them.

8. If your IDE supports project groups, add all the projects mentioned above to a single project group and specify the dependency relationships between them.

9. If your IDE supports project groups, build the project group from step 8. Otherwise, build the projects individually, taking care to build each project before the projects that depend on it.

As with Recipes 1.11 and 1.12, the steps in this outline vary somewhat depending on the IDE. The third step is covered in detail in Recipes 1.21, 1.22, and 1.23. For now, you should use the default settings wherever possible.

For example, here's how to build an executable from the source code in Example 1-3 using the Visual C++ IDE.

Select New → Project from the File menu, select Visual C++* in the left pane, select Win32 Console Application and enter *hellobeatles* as your project's name. From the Win32 Application Wizard go to Application Settings, select Console Application and Empty Project, and press Finish. You should now have an empty project *hellobeatles.vcproj* with two build configurations, Debug and Release, the former

---

* In versions of Visual C++ prior to Visual C++ 2005, this option was labeled *Visual C++ Projects*.

being the active configuration. You should also have a solution *hellobeatles.sln* containing the single project *hellobeatles.vcproj*.

Next, display your project's property pages by right-clicking on the project's name in the Solution Explorer and selecting Properties. Go to Configuration Properties → Linker → General and enter the pathname of your project's output file in the field labeled Output File. The directory portion of the pathname should point to the directory *binaries* which you created at the beginning of this chapter; the file name portion should be *hellobeatles.exe*.

Next, use Add Existing Item... from the Project menu to add the source file *helllobeatles.cpp,* from Example 1-3 to your project. Your project's property pages should now contain a node labeled C/C++. Go to Configuration Properties → C/C++ → Code Generation and specify Multi-threaded Debug DLL as the Runtime Library.

Instead of using Add Existing Item... to add the source file *helllobeatles.cpp* to your project, you can use Add New Item... to create a blank source *.cpp* file and add it to your project. Then you can type or paste the content from Example 1-3 into the newly created files. Similar remarks hold for other IDEs.

Next, go to Configuration Properties → C/C++ → General and enter the directory that contains the directories *johnpaul* and *georgeringo*—the grandparent directory of the source files *john.hpp*, *ringo.hpp*, *etc.*—in the edit control labeled Additional Include Directories. This will allow the `include` directives in the header *hellobeatles.hpp* to be resolved correctly.

Next, using Add → Existing Project... from the File menu, add the project files *libjohnpaul.vcproj* and *libgeorgeringo.vcproj* to the solution *hellobeatles*. Select Project Dependencies... from the Project menu to display the Project Dependencies dialog. Select *hellobeatles* from the drop-down control and click the checkboxes next to *libjohnpaul* and *libgeorgringo*.

If you know that you'll be adding several projects to a single solution, it's not necessary to create a separate solution for each project. You can create an empty solution by selecting New → Blank Solution... from the File menu, and then add new projects to the solution by selecting New → Project... from the File menu.

Finally, build the solution by selecting Build Solution from the Build menu. Verify that files named *libjohnpaul.lib*, *libgeorgeringo.dll*, *libgeorgeringo.lib*, and *hellobeatles.exe* have been created in the directory *binaries*. Now select Start Without Debugging from the Debug menu to run your application.

Discussion

In the preceding example it was easy to specify that *hellobeatles.exe* depends on the libraries *libjohnpaul.lib* and *libgeorgeringo.dll* because both libraries are built from source code using Visual C++ projects. If you are building an application which depends on libraries distributed as pre-built binaries with header files, you can tell Visual C++ how to find them as follows: First, go to Configuration Properties → C/C++ → General and enter the directories that contain the library header files in the edit control labeled Additional Include Directories. Then, go to Configuration Properties → Linker → Input and enter the names of the libraries in the field labeled Additional dependencies. Finally, go to Configuration Properties → Linker → General and enter the pathnames of the directories containing the binary files in the edit control labeled Additional Library Directories. Let's look at how to build an executable from the source code in Example 1-3 using CodeWarrior, C++Builder, and Dev-C++.

CodeWarrior

Select New... from the File menu, and select the Project tab of the New dialog. Enter **hellobeatles.mcp** as your project's name, select a location where your project's configuration files should be stored, and double-click Mac OS C++ Stationery. From the New Project dialog, expand the nodes Mac OS X Mach-O and Standard Console, then double-click C++ Console Mach-O. You should now have a project with two targets, Mach-O C++ Console Debug and Mach-O C++ Console Final, the former being the default target.

Since you will need to refer to these targets by name when you add dependencies to this project, you should give the targets descriptive names. For now, rename just the debug target, as follows. Select the Targets tab on your project's window, and double-click on the name of the debug target to display the Target Settings Window. Then go to Target → Target Settings and enter **hellobeatles Debug** in the field labeled Target Name.

Next, Select the Targets tab on your project's window, and double-click on the name of the debug target to display the Target Settings Window. Go to Target → PPC Mac OS X Target, specify Executable as the Project Type, and enter **hellobeatles** in the field labeled File Name. Go to Target → Target Settings and press Choose... to specify the directory *binaries* as the location where the output file *hellobeatles* should be created.

Select the Files tab on your project's window and remove the existing source files and MSL libraries files by dragging them to Trash. Use Add Files... from the Project menu to add the source file *hellobeatles.cpp* listed in Example 1-3 to your project. Then use Add Files... to add the files *MSL_All_Mach-O_D.dylib* and *MSL_Shared_AppAndDylib_Runtime_D.lib* in the directory *Metrowerks CodeWarrior/MacOS X Support/Libraries/Runtime/Runtime_PPC/Runtime_MacOSX/Libs*. If you were configuring the release target instead of the debug target, you would add the libraries *MSL_All_Mach-O.dylib* and

MSL_Shared_AppAndDylib_Runtime.lib instead. From the Target Settings Window, go to Target → Access Paths and click on the panel labeled User Paths. Use the control labeled Add... to add the directory that contains the directories *johnpaul* and *georgeringo*—the grandparent directory of the source files *john.hpp*, *ringo.hpp*, etc. This will allow the include directives in the header *hellobeatles.hpp* to be resolved correctly.

Using Add Files... from the Project menu, add the project files *libjohnpaul.mcp* and *libgeorgeringo.mcp* to the project *hellobeatles.mcp*. Go to the Targets tab and expand the nodes labeled hellobeatles Debug, libjohnpaul.mcp and libgeorgeringo.mcp. Click on the target icons next to the first child nodes of libjohnpaul.mcp and libgeorgeringo.mcp, labeled libjohgnpaul Debug and libgeorgeringo Debug. Bold arrows should appear on these two icons. Enlarge your project's window, if necessary, to expose a small link icon on the window's far right side. Click twice in this column, opposite the target icons with arrows. Two black dots should appear in this column.

Build the solution by selecting Make from the Project menu. The linker may display a number of warnings about multiply-defined symbols, but these can safely be ignored. You can suppress them by going to Linker → Mac OS X Linker and checking Suppress Warning Messages.

Verify that files named *libjohnpaul.a*, *libgeorgeringo.dylib*, and *hellobeatles* have been created in the directory *binaries*. You can now run *hellobeatles* by placing a copy of the libraries *MSL_All_Mach-O_D.dylib* in the directory *binaries*, changing to the directory *binaries*, and entering `./hellobeatles` from the command line.

C++Builder

Select New from the File menu and then select Console Wizard. From the Console Wizard dialog, select C++, Multi Threaded, and Console Application. You should now have a project containing a single source file *Unit1.cpp*. Remove *Unit1.cpp* from the project by right-clicking and selecting Remove From Project. Select Save Project As... on the File menu, select a directory for storing your project's configuration files and enter your project's name as *hello_beatles*. I've included an underscore in the project name because C++ Builder does not allow a project to have the same name as a source file.

Next, select Options... from the Project menu to display the Project Options dialog. Then go Directories and Conditionals and use the control next to Final output to specify that your project's output file, *hello_beatles.exe*, should be created. By default this file will be created in the same directory as *hello_beatles.bpr*; tell C++Builder to create it in the directory *binaries*. If you wish, you can also use the control next to Intermediate output to specify where object files should be created. By default they will be created in the same directory as the source files.

Next, use Add to Project... from the Project menu to add the source file *helllobeatles.cpp* from Example 1-3 to your project.

Next, from Project Options go to Directories and Conditionals and use the control next to Include path to select directory that contains the directories *johnpaul* and *georgeringo*—the grandparent directory of the source files *john.hpp*, *ringo.hpp*, *etc.* This will allow the `include` directives in the header *hellobeatles.hpp* to be resolved correctly.

Next, right-click on the label ProjectGroup1, select Save Project Group As, select the directory containing the file *hello_beatles.bpr*, and enter your project group's name as *hello_beatles.bpg*.

Next, add the project files *libjohnpaul.bpr* and *libgeorgeringo.bpr* to your project group by right-clicking on the label hello_beatles and selecting Add Existing Project.... Build these two projects, as described in Recipes 1.11 and 1.12, if you have not already done so, then add the output files *libjohnpaul.lib* and *libgeorgeringo.lib* to the project *hello_beatles* using Add to Project... from the Project menu. Use the up-arrow key while holding down the Ctrl key, move the projects *libjohnpaul* and *libgeorgeringo* above the project *hello_beatles* in the Project Manager to ensure that they will be built first.

Finally, build the solution by selecting Make All Projects from the Build menu. Verify that a file named *hellobeatles.exe* has been created in the directory *binaries*. Select Run from the Run menu to run the application.

Dev-C++

Select New → Project... from the File menu. From the New project dialog, select Console Application and C++ Project, and enter *hellobeatles* as your project's name. After pressing OK, specify the location where your project's configuration file should be located.

Next, from Project Options go to Build Options and verify that your project's output file is named *hellobeatles.exe*. Enter the pathname of the directory *binaries* under Executable output directory. If you wish, you can enter the directory where object files will be created under Object file output director.

Next, remove any existing source files from your project by right-clicking and selecting Remove file. Use Save Project as... from the File menu to save your project's configuration file *hellobeatles.dev*. Finally, use Add to project from the Project menu to add the source file *helllobeatles.cpp* from Example 1-3 to your project.

Next, select Project Options from the Project menu to display the Project Options dialog. Then go to Directories → Include Directories, select the directory that contains the directories *johnpaul* and *georgeringo*—the grandparent directory of the source files *john.hpp*, *ringo.hpp*, *etc.*—and press Add. This will allow the `include` directives in the header *hellobeatles.hpp* to be resolved correctly.

Finally, from Project Options go to Directories → Libraries Directories and add the directories that will contain the output files *libjohnpaul.a* and *libgeorgeringo.a* of the projects *libjohnpaul* and *libgeorgeringo*. Then go to Parameters → Linker and enter the options *-ljohnpaul* and *-lgeorgeringo*.

Now build the three projects individually using Compile from the Execute menu, making sure to build *hellobeatles* last. Run *hellobeatles.exe* by selecting Run from the Execute menu.

See Also

Recipes 1.5, 1.10, and 1.18

1.14   Obtaining GNU make

Problem

You want to obtain and install the GNU *make* utility, useful for building libraries and executables from source code.

Solution

The solution depends on your operating system.

Windows

While you can obtain prebuilt binaries for GNU *make* from several locations, to get the most out of GNU *make* it should be installed as part of a Unix-like environment. I recommend using either Cygwin or MSYS, which is a part of the MinGW project.

 Cygwin and MinGW are described in Recipe 1.1.

If you installed Cygwin, as described in Recipe 1.1, you already have GNU *make*. To run it from the Cygwin shell, simply run the command *make*.

To install MSYS, begin by installing MinGW, as described in Recipe 1.1. A future version of the MinGW installer may give you the option of installing MSYS automatically. For now, follow these additional steps.

First, from the MinGW homepage, *http://www.mingw.org*, go to the MinGW download area and download the latest stable version of the MSYS installation program. The name of the installation program should be *MSYS-<version>.exe*.

Next, run the installation program. You will be asked to specify the location of your MinGW installation and the location where MSYS should be installed. When the installation program completes, the MSYS installation directory should contain a file named *msys.bat*. Running this script will display the MSYS shell, a port of the *bash* shell from which you can run GNU *make* and other mingw programs such as *g++*, *ar*, *ranlib*, and *dlltool*.

 To use MSYS it is not necessary for the *bin* subdirectories of either your MinGW installation or your MSYS installation to be in your PATH environment variable.

Unix

First, check whether GNU *make* is installed on your system by running *make -v* from the command line. If GNU *make* is installed, it should print a message like the following:

```
GNU Make 3.80
Copyright (C) 2002  Free Software Foundation, Inc.
This is free software; see the source for copying conditions.
...
```

If your system has a non-GNU version of *make*, it's possible that the GNU version is installed under the name *gmake*. You can check this by entering *gmake -v* from the command line.

If you use Mac OS X, the easiest way to obtain GNU *make* is to download the Xcode development environment from Apple's web site and follow the installation instructions. Xcode is currently available at *developer.apple.com/tools*.

Otherwise, download the latest version of GNU *make* from *ftp://ftp.gnu.org/pub/gnu/make*, unpack it, and follow the installation instructions.

Discussion

The *make* utility comes in many flavors. Most toolsets provide some variant of *make*; for example, Visual C++ comes with a make utility called *nmake.exe*. Usually these toolset-specific versions of *make* have built-in features which make them easy to use with their particular toolset. As a result, a discussion of *make* which covers multiple toolsets will either have to describe several versions of *make* or will have to deal with some cases where there is an imperfect fit between a particular version of *make* and a particular toolset.

Instead of demonstrating more than one *make* utility, I've chosen to focus on GNU *make*, which is easily the most powerful and portable *make* variant. GNU *make* is designed to work first and foremost with GCC; as a result, using GNU *make* with other toolsets, particularly Windows toolsets, can be tricky at times. Still, because GNU *make* is so flexible, it's far easier to use GNU *make* with non-GNU tools than it is to use most of the other makes, such as *nmake.exe*, with a toolset other than the one it was designed for.

Much of GNU *make*'s power comes from its ability to execute complex shell scripts. If you've worked with both Unix and Windows, you know that the Windows shell *cmd.exe* leaves a lot to be desired: it's missing many valuable commands, has a limited ability to execute scripts, and places severe restrictions on the length of command lines. Consequently, forcing GNU *make* to use *cmd.exe* severely limits its usefulness. Fortunately, Cygwin and MSYS provide excellent environments for using GNU *make* on Windows.

MSYS provides the minimal environment necessary to run Unix-style makefiles and *configure* scripts on Windows. Among the useful tools it provides are *awk, cat, cp, grep, ls, mkdir, mv, rm, rmdir,* and *sed*. MSYS was designed to work with GCC, and it does so beautifully; it works somewhat less smoothly with other Windows toolsets, however, particularly those that provide *.bat* files for setting environment variables and those that use slashes (/) instead of a hyphens (-) for command-line options.

Where MSYS is minimalist, Cygwin is maximalist. Cygwin *make* can do everything MSYS *make* can do, and much more. Portable makefiles, however, restrict themselves to a narrow range of GNU utilities, and MSYS supports all of these.

See Also

Recipe 1.1

1.15 Building A Simple "Hello, World" Application with GNU make

Problem

You want to use GNU *make* to build a simple "Hello, World" program, such as that in Example 1-4.

Solution

Before you write your first makefile, you'll need to know a little terminology. A makefile consists of a collection of rules of the form

```
targets: prerequisites
    command-script
```

Here `targets` and `prerequisites` are space-separated strings, and `command-script` consists of zero or more lines of text, each of which begins with a Tab character. Targets and prerequisites are usually files names, but sometimes they are simply formal names for actions for *make* to perform. The command script consists of a sequence of commands to be passed to a shell. Roughly speaking, a rule tells *make* to generate the collection of targets from the collection of prerequisites by executing the command script.

Whitespace in makefiles is significant. Lines containing command scripts must begin with a Tab rather than a Space—this is a source of some of the most common beginner errors. In the following examples, lines which begin with a Tab are indicated by an indentation of four characters.

Now you're ready to begin. Create a text file named *makefile* in the directory containing your source file. In this file, declare four targets. Call the first target all, and specify the name of the executable you wish to build as its sole prerequisite. It should have no command script. Give the second target the same name as your executable. Specify your application's source file as its prerequisite, and specify the command line needed to build the executable from the source file as your target's command script. The third target should be called install. It should have no prerequisites, and should have a command script to copy the executable from the directory containing the makefile to the directory where you want it installed. The last target should be called clean. Like install, it should have no prerequisites. Its command script should remove the executable and the intermediate object file from the current directory. The clean and install targets should both be labeled as *phony targets*, using the PHONY attribute.

For example, to build an executable from the source code in Example 1-4 using GCC, your makefile might look as shown in Example 1-14.

Example 1-14. Makefile to build the executable hello with GCC

```
# This is the default target, which will be built when
# you invoke make
.PHONY: all
all: hello

# This rule tells make how to build hello from hello.cpp
hello: hello.cpp
    g++ -o hello hello.cpp

# This rule tells make to copy hello to the binaries subdirectory,
# creating it if necessary
.PHONY: install
install:
    mkdir -p binaries
    cp -p hello binaries

# This rule tells make to delete hello and hello.o
.PHONY: clean
clean:
    rm -f hello
```

To build an executable from the source code in Example 1-4 using Visual C++, you can use the following makefile shown in Example 1-15.

Example 1-15. Makefile to build the executable hello.exe with Visual C++

```
#default target
.PHONY: all
all: hello.exe

#rule to build hello.exe
hello.exe: hello.cpp
    cl -nologo -EHsc -GR -Zc:forScope -Zc:wchar_t \
        -Fehello hello.cpp

.PHONY: install
install:
    mkdir -p binaries
    cp -p hello.exe binaries

.PHONY: clean
clean:
    rm -f hello.exe
```

Commands and lists of targets or prerequisites can span more than one line of text in a makefile by using the continuation character \, just as in C++ source files.

To build your executable, set any environment variables required by your command-line tools, change to the directory containing *makefile* and enter **make**. To copy your executable to the *binaries* subdirectory, enter **make install**. To delete the executable and the intermediate object file from the makefile directory, enter **make clean**.

If you have installed the Cygwin environment, described in Recipe 1.1, you can execute the makefile in Example 1-15 directly from the Windows shell *cmd.exe*.

You can also execute this makefile from the Cygwin shell, as follows. From *cmd.exe*, run *vcvars32.bat* to set Visual C++'s environment variables. Next, run *cygwin.bat* to start the Cygwin shell. If you place the Cygwin installation directory in your PATH, you can start the Cygwin shell from *cmd.exe* simply by entering **cygwin**. Finally, change to the directory containing the makefile and enter **make**.

Similarly, you can execute the makefile from the MSYS shell: run *vcvars32.bat* from *cmd.exe*, then run *msys.bat* to start the MSYS shell.

If your toolset provides a script to set environment variables, running a makefile from Cygwin or MSYS is slightly more involved than running it from *cmd.exe*. It's necessary for some makefiles, however, since they simply won't work from *cmd.exe*.

Discussion

In the next few recipes, you'll see that GNU *make* is a powerful tool for building complex projects. But what does it actually do? Here's how it works. When *make* is invoked with no arguments, it looks in the current directory for a file named *GNUmakefile*, *makefile* or *Makefile*, and attempts to build the first target it contains, called the *default target*. If the default target is *up to date*—meaning that it exists, that all its prerequisites are up to date, and that none of its prerequisites has been modified more recently than it has—*make*'s job is done. Otherwise, it attempts to generate the default target from its prerequisites by executing its command script. Like the definition of *up to date*, this process is recursive: for each prerequisite which is not up to date, *make* searches for a rule having that prerequisite as a target, and starts the whole process again. This continues until the default target is up to date or until an error occurs.

It follows from the above description that a target having no prerequisites is up to date if and only if it corresponds to a file on the filesystem. Therefore, a target corresponding to a non-existent file is never up to date, and can be used to force a command script to be executed unconditionally. Such targets are called *phony targets*.

 By labeling a target with the .PHONY attribute, as in Examples 1-14 and 1-15, you can tell *make* that the target does not correspond to a file, and so should always be always rebuilt.

Conversely, a prerequisite corresponding to an existing file is always up to date, provided it doesn't appear as the target of a rule.

Now let's look at what happens when we execute the makefile in Example 1-14. The phony target all is always out of date: its only purpose is to tell make to build *hello. exe*. In such a simple makefile, there's no need for an all target; in more complex examples, the all target may have several prerequisites. The rule with target hello tells *make* to build *hello*, if necessary, by invoking *g++*. Assuming that the current directory is empty except for *makefile* and *hello.cpp*, the target hello is not up to date. The prerequisite *is* up to date, however, because the file *hello.cpp* exists, and because hello.cpp does not appear as the target of any rule. Consequently, *make* invokes *g++* to compile and link *hello.cpp*, producing the file *hello*. The prerequisite to the all target is now up to date, so *make* builds the all target—by executing an empty command script—and exits.

When you invoke make with a command-line argument corresponding to a target, make attempts to build that target. Therefore executing **make install** causes the following commands to be executed:

```
mkdir -p binaries
cp -p hello binaries
```

The first command creates the directory *binaries*, if it doesn't already exist; the second command copies *hello* to that directory. Similarly, **make clean** invokes the command

```
rm -f hello
```

which deletes the *hello*.

 If you're using Windows, the `mkdir`, `cp`, and `rm` commands used by the `install` and `clean` targets refer to the GNU tools distributed with Cygwin or MSYS.

Once you understand how *make* analyzes dependencies, Example 1-14 may seem pretty simple. In fact, however, it's considerably more complicated than it needs to be; looking at the various ways it can be simplified is a good way to learn some of the rudiments of makefiles.

Make variables

GNU *make* supports variables whose values are strings. The most common use of variables in makefiles is as symbolic constants; instead of hard-coding the name of a file or a shell command in several locations within a makefile, you can assign the file or command name to a variable and use the variable instead. This leads to simpler and easier to maintain makefiles. For example, you can rewrite the makefile from Example 1-14 using *make* variables, as shown in Example 1-16.

Example 1-16. Makefile to build the executable hello with GCC, modified to use make variables

```
# Specify the target file and the install directory
OUTPUTFILE=hello
INSTALLDIR=binaries

# Default target
.PHONY: all
all: $(OUTPUTFILE)

# Build hello from hello.cpp
$(OUTPUTFILE): hello.cpp
    g++ -o hello hello.cpp

# Copy hello to the binaries subdirectory
.PHONY: install
install:
    mkdir -p $(INSTALLDIR)
    cp -p $(OUTPUTFILE) $(INSTALLDIR)

# Delete hello
.PHONY: clean
clean:
    rm -f $(OUTPUTFILE)
```

Here I've introduced two make variables, OUTPUTFILE and INSTALLDIR. As you can see, make variables can be assigned values using the assignment operator =, and they can be evaluated by enclosing them in parentheses and prefixing a dollar sign.

You can also set the value of a make variable on the command line, using the syntax *make X=Y*. In addition, when make starts up, each environment variable is used to initialize a *make* variable with the same name and value. Values specified on the command line take precedence over values inherited from the environment; values specified in the makefile itself take precedence over values specified on the command line.

GNU make also supports *automatic variables* that take special values when evaluated in a command script. Most importantly, the variable $@ represents the filename of the target, the variable $< represents the filename of the first prerequisite, and the variable $^ represents the sequence of prerequisites, separated by spaces. Using these variables, we can further simplify the makefile from Example 1-16, as shown in Example 1-17.

Example 1-17. Makefile to build the executable hello with GCC, modified to use automatic variables

```
# Specify the target file and the install directory
OUTPUTFILE=hello
INSTALLDIR=binaries

# Default target
.PHONY: all
all: $(OUTPUTFILE)

# Build hello from hello.cpp
$(OUTPUTFILE): hello.cpp
    g++ -o $@ $<

# Install and clean targets as in Example 1-16
```

Within the command script g++ -o $@ $<, the variable $@ expands to hello and the variable $< expands to hello.cpp. Therefore the makefile in Example 1-17 is equivalent to that in Example 1-16, but involves less code duplication.

Implicit Rules

The makefile in Example 1-17 can still be radically simplified. In fact, the command script associated with the target hello is superfluous, as you can demonstrate by executing the makefile in Example 1-18.

Example 1-18. Makefile to build the executable hello with GCC, modified to use implicit rules

```
# Specify the target file and the install directory
OUTPUTFILE=hello
INSTALLDIR=binaries
```

Example 1-18. Makefile to build the executable hello with GCC, modified to use implicit rules (continued)

```
# Default target
.PHONY: all
all: $(OUTPUTFILE)

# Tell make to rebuild hello whenever hello.cpp is modified
$(OUTPUTFILE): hello.cpp

# Install and clean targets as in Example 1-16
```

How does make know how to build the executable *hello* from the source file *hello. cpp*, without being told? The answer is that *make* maintains an internal database of implicit rules representing operations commonly performed when building C and C++ applications. For example, the implicit rule to generate an executable file from a *.cpp* file looks like Example 1-19.

Example 1-19. A pattern rule from make's internal database

```
%: %.cpp
#   commands to execute (built-in):
    $(LINK.cpp) $^ $(LOADLIBES) $(LDLIBS) -o $@
```

Rules with first lines of the form %*xxx*:%*yyy* are known as *pattern rules*; the % character act as a *wildcard*. When no ordinary rule matches an out-of-date prerequisite, *make* searches the available pattern rules. For each pattern rule, make tries to find a string which when substituted for the wildcard character in the target portion of the pattern rule yields the out-of-date prerequisite. If *make* finds such a string, *make* substitutes it for the wildcard character in both the target and prerequisite portions of the pattern rule to produce a new rule. *make* then attempts to build the out-of-date prerequisite using the new rule.

 You can use *make -p* to print GNU *make*'s database of implicit rules.

For example, when the makefile in Example 1-18 is first executed, the prerequisite hello of the default target all is out of date. Although hello does appear as a target in the rule $(OUTPUTFILE): hello.cpp, this rule has no command script, and so is useless for building the file *hello.make* therefore searches its internal database, and finds the rule shown in Example 1-19. By substituting the string hello for the wildcard character in the rule in Example 1-19, *make* generates the following rule, with hello as its target:

```
    hello: hello.cpp
        $(LINK.cpp) $^ $(LOADLIBES) $(LDLIBS) -o $@
```

So far, so good—but clearly there's more to the story. Looking once again through *make*'s internal database reveals that the variable LINK.cpp expands, by default, to $(LINK.cc). LINK.cc, in turn, expands by default to

```
$(CXX) $(CXXFLAGS) $(CPPFLAGS) $(LDFLAGS) $(TARGET_ARCH)
```

Finally, the variable CXX expands by default to g++, and the other four variables—$(CXXFLAGS), $(CPPFLAGS), $(LDFLAGS), and $(TARGET_ARCH)—expand to empty strings. When all these substitutions are carried out, we're left with the following rule, which by now may look familiar.

```
hello: hello.cpp
    g++ $^ -o $@
```

 Confused? I don't blame you. If you study the above explanation and spend some time examining *make*'s internal database, implicit rules will start to make sense.

Customization points

Now that you see how the pattern rule in Example 1-19 causes *make* to build the executable *hello* from the source file *hello.cpp*, you might well wonder why it was necessary to go through so many intermediate steps. Why not simply add the rule

```
%: %.cpp
    g++ $^ -o $@
```

to *make*'s internal database, instead of the complex rule in Example 1-19? The answer is that the intermediate variables such as $(CXX), $(CXXFLAGS), $(CPPFLAGS), and $(LDFLAGS), serve as user *customization points*. For example, you can specify additional flags to be passed to the linker by specifying a value for LDFLAGS on the command line, in a makefile, or by setting an environment variable. The variables CPPFLAGS and CXXFLAGS play a similar role for C++ preprocessor and compiler options, respectively. You can even specify a compiler other than GCC by setting the variable CXX. For example, to build *hello* with Intel for Linux using the makefile in Example 1-18, you can enter **make CXX=icpc** from the command line—assuming you've set the environment variables required by the Intel compiler.

VPATH and the vpath directive

In Example 1-18, *make* is able to apply the correct pattern rule because the *.cpp* file resides in the directory where the output file is to created. If your source files are in a different directory, you can use the VPATH variable to tell make where to search for targets or prerequisites:

```
VPATH = <path-to-cpp-files>
```

You can also use a vpath directive to tell *make* to look in a certain location for particular types of files:

```
# look for .exp files in ../lib
vpath %. exp../lib
```

See Also

Recipes 1.2 and 1.7

1.16 Building a Static Library with GNU Make

Problem

You want to use GNU *make* to build a static library from a collection of C++ source files, such as those listed in Example 1-1.

Solution

First, create a makefile in the directory where you want your static library to be created, and declare a phony target all whose single prerequisite is the static library. Next, declare your static library target. Its prerequisites should be the object files that the library will contain, and its command script should be a command line to build the library from the collection of object files, as demonstrated in Recipe 1.3. If you are using GCC or a compiler with similar command-line syntax, customize the implicit patterns rules, if necessary, by modifying one or more of the variables CXX, CXXFLAGS, *etc.* used in *make's* database of implicit rules, as shown in Recipe 1.15. Otherwise, write a pattern rule telling *make* how to compile *.cpp* files into object files, using the command lines from Table 1-8 and the pattern rule syntax explained in Recipe 1.16. Next, declare targets indicating how each of your library's source files depends on the headers it includes, directly or indirectly. You can write these dependencies by hand or arrange for them to be generated automatically. Finally, add install and clean targets as demonstrated in Recipe 1.15.

For example, to build a static library from the source files listed in Example 1-2 using GCC on Unix, create a makefile in the directory *johnpaul*, as shown in Example 1-20.

Example 1-20. Makefile for libjohnpaul.a using GCC on Unix

```
# Specify extensions of files to delete when cleaning
CLEANEXTS   = o a

# Specify the target file and the install directory
OUTPUTFILE  = libjohnpaul.a
INSTALLDIR  = ../binaries
```

Example 1-20. Makefile for libjohnpaul.a using GCC on Unix (continued)

```
# Default target
.PHONY: all
all: $(OUTPUTFILE)

# Build libjohnpaul.a from john.o, paul.o, and johnpaul.o
$(OUTPUTFILE): john.o paul.o johnpaul.o
    ar ru $@ $^
    ranlib $@

# No rule to build john.o, paul.o, and johnpaul.o from .cpp
# files is required; this is handled by make's database of
# implicit rules

.PHONY: install
install:
    mkdir -p $(INSTALLDIR)
    cp -p $(OUTPUTFILE) $(INSTALLDIR)

.PHONY: clean
clean:
    for file in $(CLEANEXTS); do rm -f *.$$file; done

# Indicate dependencies of .ccp files on .hpp files
john.o: john.hpp
paul.o: paul.hpp
johnpaul.o: john.hpp paul.hpp johnpaul.hpp
```

Similarly, to build a static library using Visual C++, your makefile might look as shown in Example 1-21.

Example 1-21. Makefile for libjohnpaul.lib using Visual C++

```
# Specify extensions of files to delete when cleaning
CLEANEXTS      = obj lib

# Specify the target file and the install directory
OUTPUTFILE     = libjohnpaul.lib
INSTALLDIR     = ../binaries

# Pattern rule to build an object file from a .cpp file
%.obj: %.cpp
    "$(MSVCDIR)/bin/cl" -c -nologo -EHsc -GR -Zc:forScope -Zc:wchar_t \
            $(CXXFLAGS) $(CPPFLAGS) -Fo"$@" $<

# Default target
.PHONY: all
all: $(OUTPUTFILE)

# Build libjohnpaul.lib from john. obj, paul. obj, and johnpaul. obj
$(OUTPUTFILE): john.obj paul.obj johnpaul.obj
    "$(MSVCDIR)/bin/link" -lib -nologo -out:"$@" $^
```

Example 1-21. Makefile for libjohnpaul.lib using Visual C++ (continued)

```
.PHONY: install
install:
    mkdir -p $(INSTALLDIR)
    cp -p $(OUTPUTFILE) $(INSTALLDIR)

.PHONY: clean
clean:
    for file in $(CLEANEXTS); do rm -f *.$$file; done

# Indicate dependency of .cpp files on .hpp files
john.obj: john.hpp
paul.obj: paul.hpp
johnpaul. obj: john.hpp paul.hpp johnpaul.hpp
```

In Example 1-21, I've expressed Visual C++'s *link.exe* command as "$(MSVCDIR)/bin/link", using the environment variable MSVCDIR set by *vcvars32.bat*. This prevents confusion between the Visual C++ linker and the Unix *link* command, supported by Cygwin and MSYS. For consistency, I've also expressed Visual C++'s compile command using MSVCDIR.

Discussion

Let's walk through Example 1-20. I start by defining variables to represent the output file, the install directory, and the extensions of files that should be deleted when the target clean is built. Next, I declare the default target all, as in Example 1-14.

The rule to build the static library looks like this:

```
$(OUTPUTFILE): john.o paul.o johnpaul.o
    ar ru $@ $^
    ranlib $@
```

It's a straightforward adaptation of the entry for GCC in Table 1-10. Here $(OUTPUTFILE) and $@ both expand to libjohnpaul.a, and $^ expands to the list of prerequisites john.o paul.o johnpaul.o.

The next two rules declare install and clean targets, as in Recipe 1.15. The only difference is that in Example 1-20 I use a shell looping construct to remove all files whose extension appears in the list o a — i.e., all object or static library files:

```
    for file in $(CLEANEXTS); do rm -f *.$$file; done
```

I've used a double dollar sign to prevent *make* from expanding the variable $$file rather than passing it on to the shell.

The last three rules specify the dependency relationships between the library's *.cpp* files and the headers they include. There's one rule for each *.cpp* file; its target is the object file to be built from the *.cpp* file, and its prerequisites are the header files included—directly or indirectly—by the *.cpp* file:

```
john.o: john.hpp
paul.o: paul.hpp
johnpaul.o: john.hpp paul.hpp johnpaul.hpp
```

This can be understood as follows. If a *.cpp* file includes a header file—directly or indirectly—it must be rebuilt each time the header is modified. However, since the *.cpp* file exists and does not appear as the target of any rule, it is never out of date, as discussed in Recipe 1.15. Consequently, when the header is modified, no recompilation is triggered. The fix is to declare a rule making these dependencies explicit; whenever one of the headers in question is modified, the object file corresponding to the *.cpp* will become out of date, causing the *.cpp* file to be recompiled.

This solution is only adequate for very small projects, since it's extremely difficult to keep the targets representing source file dependencies synchronized with a changing codebase. Fortunately, there are several methods for generating these dependencies automatically. For example, you can replace the last three rules in Example 1-20 with the following:

```
# Generate dependencies of .cpp files on .hpp files
include john.d paul.d johnpaul.d

%.d: %.cpp
    $(CC) -M $(CPPFLAGS) $< > $@.$$$$; \
    sed 's,\($*\)\.o[ :]*,\1.o $@ : ,g' < $@.$$$$ > $@; \
    rm -f $@.$$$$
```

This bit of code relies on the compiler option *-M* which causes GCC to output dependency information for inclusion in a makefile. For a detailed explanation of how it works—and why it's sometimes inadequate—see *Managing Projects with GNU make*, Third Edition, by Robert Mecklenburg (O'Reilly).

 Put the code to generate dependencies at the end of your makefile.

This method can be adapted to work with most toolsets, since most compilers provide an option similar to GCC's *-M*; in fact, the option is usually either *-M* or *-m*. Visual C++, however, does not provide an option for generating makefile dependencies. If you use Visual C++, you have two choices. You can use the *-Gm* option, together with one of the options *-Zi* or *-ZI*, discussed in Recipe 1.21. The *-Gm* option tells the compiler to build a database, stored in a file with the extension *idb*, containing information about dependencies between source files. The *.idb* file is created when a *.cpp* file, or collection of *.cpp* files, is initially compiled. On subsequent compilations, only those source files which have been modified or which depend on headers which have been modified are recompiled.

Alternatively, you can use the *-showIncludes* option, together with the option *-E*. The *-showIncludes* option causes the compiler to output a message to standard error each time an include directive is encountered. The *-E* option tells the compiler to run the preprocessor and then exit, without building any binary files. Using a bit of shell scripting, you can use the output generated by *-showIncludes* to construct makefile dependencies:

```
include john.d paul.d johnpaul.d

%.d: %.cpp
    "$(MSVCDIR)/bin/cl" -E -showIncludes $< 2> $@.$$$$ > /dev/null; \
    sed -n 's/^Note: including file: *\(.*\)/$*.obj•$*.d:\1/gp' \
        < $@.$$$$ | sed 's:\\:/:g;s: :\\ :gp' > $@;            \
    rm -f $@.$$$$
```

In this example, the character • represents a Tab.

Let's make one last improvement to Example 1-20. Currently, the sequence john paul johnpaul occurs in two places; in the prerequisites of the rule to build the static library, and in the include directive used to generate dependencies. If the list of source files changes, you'll have to update the makefile in two locations. It's better to define a variable SOURCES, and to replace both occurrences of the sequence john paul johnpaul with expressions involving SOURCES:

```
SOURCES = john.cpp paul.cpp johnpaul.cpp
...
# Build libjohnpaul.a from john.o, paul.o, and johnpaul.o
$(OUTPUTFILE): $(subst .cpp,.o,$(SOURCES))
    ar ru $@ $^
    ranlib $@
...

# Generate dependencies of .ccp files on .hpp files
include $(subst .cpp,.d,$(SOURCES))

%.d: %.cpp
    $(CC) -M $(CPPFLAGS) $< > $@.$$$$; \
    sed 's,\($*\)\.o[ :]*,\1.o $@ : ,g' < $@.$$$$ > $@; \
    rm -f $@.$$$$
```

Here I'm using the *make* function $(subst *x,y,str*), which replaces *x* with *y* everywhere in *str*.

 GNU make supports a rich collection of functions for string and filename manipulation and more. It also supports user defined functions. As usual, for a thorough treatment, see *Managing Projects with GNU make*, Third Edition, by Robert Mecklenburg (O'Reilly).

See Also

Recipes 1.2 and 1.7

1.17   Building a Dynamic Library with GNU Make

Problem

You wish to use GNU *make* to build a dynamic library from a collection of C++ source files, such as those listed in Example 1-2.

Solution

First, create a makefile in the directory where you want your dynamic library to be created, and declare a phony target `all` whose single prerequisite is the dynamic library. Next, declare your dynamic library target. Its prerequisites should be the object files from which the library will be built, and its command script should be a command line to build the library from the collection of object files, as demonstrated in Recipe 1.4. If you are using GCC or a compiler with similar command-line syntax, customize the implicit patterns rules, if necessary, by modifying one or more of the variables CXX, CXXFLAGS, *etc.* used in *make's* database of implicit rules, as shown in Recipe 1.15. Otherwise, write a pattern rule telling *make* how to compile *.cpp* files into object files, using the command lines from Table 1-8 and the pattern rule syntax explained in Recipe 1.16. Finally, add `install` and `clean` targets, as demonstrated in Recipe 1.15, and machinery to automatically generate source file dependencies, as demonstrated in Recipe 1.16.

For example, to build a dynamic library from the source files listed Example 1-2 using GCC on Unix, create a makefile in the directory *georgeringo*, as shown in Example 1-22.

Example 1-22. Makefile for libgeorgeringo.so using GCC

```
# Specify extensions of files to delete when cleaning
CLEANEXTS   = o so

# Specify the source files, the target files,
# and the install directory
SOURCES     = george.cpp ringo.cpp georgeringo.cpp
OUTPUTFILE  = libgeorgeringo.so
INSTALLDIR  = ../binaries

.PHONY: all
all: $(OUTPUTFILE)

# Build libgeorgeringo.so from george.o, ringo.o,
# and georgeringo.o; subst is the search-and-replace
# function demonstrated in Recipe 1.16
$(OUTPUTFILE): $(subst .cpp,.o,$(SOURCES))
    $(CXX) -shared -fPIC $(LDFLAGS) -o $@ $^
```

Example 1-22. Makefile for libgeorgeringo.so using GCC (continued)

```
.PHONY: install
install:
    mkdir -p $(INSTALLDIR)
    cp -p $(OUTPUTFILE) $(INSTALLDIR)

.PHONY: clean
clean:
    for file in $(CLEANEXTS); do rm -f *.$$file; done

# Generate dependencies of .ccp files on .hpp files
include $(subst .cpp,.d,$(SOURCES))

%.d: %.cpp
    $(CC) -M $(CPPFLAGS) $< > $@.$$$$; \
    sed 's,\($*\)\.o[ :]*,\1.o $@ : ,g' < $@.$$$$ > $@; \
rm -f $@.$$$$
```

Discussion

The makefile in Example 1-22 is a straightforward application of the ideas from Recipes 1.4, 1.15, and 1.16. The main difference between Example 1-22 and Example 1-20 is the rule for building *lingeorgeringo.so* from the object files *george.o*, *ringo.o*, and *georgeringo.o*:

```
$(OUTPUTFILE): $(subst .cpp,.o,$(SOURCES))
    $(CXX) -shared -fPIC $(LDFLAGS) -o $@ $^
```

Here $(OUTPUTFILE) expands to lingeorgeringo.so and the expression $(subst .cpp,.o,$(SOURCES)) expands to george.o, ringo.o, and georgeringo.o, as illustrated in Recipe 1.16. The command script $(CXX) -shared -fPIC $(LDFLAGS) -o $@ $^ is an adaptation of the GCC command line presented in Table 1-11.

See Also

Recipes 1.4, 1.9, 1.12, 1.19, and 1.23

1.18   Building a Complex Application with GNU make

Problem

You wish to use GNU *make* to build an executable which depends on several static and dynamic libraries.

Solution

Follow these steps:

1. Create makefiles for the libraries used by your application, as described in Recipes 1.16 and 1.17. These makefiles should reside in separate directories.

2. Create a makefile in yet another directory. This makefile can be used to build your application, but only after the makefiles in step 1 have been executed. Give this makefile a phony target all whose prerequisite is your executable. Declare a target for your executable with prerequisites consisting of the libraries which your application uses, together with the object files to be built from your application's *.cpp* files. Write a command script to build the executable from the collection libraries and object files, as described in Recipe 1.5. If necessary, write a pattern rule to generate object files from *.cpp* files, as shown in Recipe 1.16. Add install and clean targets, as shown in Recipe 1.15, and machinery to automatically generate source file dependencies, as shown in Recipe 1.16.

3. Create a makefile in a directory which is an ancestor of the directories containing all the other makefiles—let's call the new makefile the *top-level* makefile and the others the *subordinate* makefiles. Declare a default target all whose prerequisite is the directory containing the makefile created in step 2. Declare a rule whose targets consists of the directories containing the subordinate makefiles, and whose command script invokes *make* in each target directory with a target specified as the value of the variable TARGET. Finally, declare targets specifying the dependencies between the default targets of the subordinate makefiles.

For example, to build an executable from the source files listed in Example 1-3 using GCC on Unix, create a makefile as shown in Example 1-23.

Example 1-23. Makefile for hellobeatles.exe using GCC

```
# Specify the source files, target files, the build directories,
# and the install directory
SOURCES        = hellobeatles.cpp
OUTPUTFILE     = hellobeatles
LIBJOHNPAUL    = libjohnpaul.a
LIBGEORGERINGO = libgeorgeringo.so
JOHNPAULDIR    = ../johnpaul
GEORGERINGODIR   = ../georgeringo
INSTALLDIR     = ../binaries


#
# Add the parent directory as an include path
#
CPPFLAGS      += -I..


#
# Default target
#
```

Example 1-23. Makefile for hellobeatles.exe using GCC (continued)

```
.PHONY: all
all: $(HELLOBEATLES)

#
# Target to build the executable.
#
$(OUTPUTFILE): $(subst .cpp,.o,$(SOURCES))  \
               $(JOHNPAULDIR)/$(LIBJOHNPAUL) \
               $(GEORGERINGODIR)/$(LIBGEORGERINGO)
    $(CXX) $(LDFLAGS) -o $@ $^

.PHONY: install
install:
    mkdir -p $(INSTALLDIR)
    cp -p $(OUTPUTFILE) $(INSTALLDIR)

.PHONY: clean
clean:
    rm -f *.o
    rm -f $(OUTPUTFILE)

# Generate dependencies of .ccp files on .hpp files
include $(subst .cpp,.d,$(SOURCES))

%.d: %.cpp
    $(CC) -M $(CPPFLAGS) $< > $@.$$$$; \
    sed 's,\($*\)\.o[ :]*,\1.o $@ : ,g' < $@.$$$$ > $@; \
    rm -f $@.$$$$
```

Next, create a top-level makefile in the directory containing *johnpaul*, *georgeringo*, *hellobeatles*, and *binaries*, as shown in Example 1-24.

Example 1-24. Top level makefile for the source code from Examples 1-1, 1-2, and 1-3

```
# All the targets in this makefile are phony
.PHONY: all johnpaul georgeringo hellobeatles

# Default target
all: hellobeatles

# The targets johnpaul, georgeringo, and hellobeatles represent
# directories; the command script invokes make in each directory
johnpaul georgeringo hellobeatles:
    $(MAKE) --directory=$@ $(TARGET)

# This rule indicates that the default target of the makefile
# in directory hellobeatles depends on the default targets of
# the makefiles in the directories johnpaul and georgeringo
.PHONY: hellobeatles
hellobeatles: johnpaul georgeringo
```

To build *hellobeatles*, change to the directory containing the top-level makefile, and enter **make**. To copy the files *libjohnpaul.a, libgeorgeringo.so*, and *hellobeatles* to the directory *binaries*, enter **make TARGET=install**. To clean the project, enter **make TARGET=clean**.

Discussion

The approach to managing complex projects demonstrated in this recipe is known as *recursive make*. It allows you to organize a project into a collection of modules, each with its own makefile, and to specify the dependencies between the modules. It's not limited to a single top-level makefile with a collection of child makefiles: the technique can be extended to handle multi-level tree structures. While recursive make was once the standard technique for managing large projects with *make*, there are other methods which are now considered superior. For details, refer once again to *Managing Projects with GNU make*, Third Edition, by Robert Mecklenburg (O'Reilly).

Example 1-23 is a straightforward application of the techniques demonstrated in Recipes 1.15, 1.16, and 1.17. There's really just one interesting point. As illustrated in Recipe 1.15, when compiling *hellobeatles.cpp* from the command line it's necessary to use the option *-I..* so that the compiler can find the headers *johnpaul.hpp* and *georgeringo.hpp*. One solution would be to write an explicit rule for building *hellobeatles.o* with a command script containing the option *-I..*, like so:

```
hellobeatles.o: hello.beatles.cpp
    g++ -c -I.. -o hellobeatles.o hellobeatles.cpp
```

Instead, I've taken advantage of the customization point CPPFLAGS, described in Recipe 1.15, to specify that whenever an object file is compiled from a *.cpp* file, the option *-I..* should be added to the command-line:

```
CPPFLAGS    += -I..
```

I've used the assignment operator +=, instead of =, so that the effect will be cumulative with whatever value of CPPFLAGS may have been specified on the command line or in the environment.

Now let's look at how Example 1-24 works. The most important rule is the one which causes make to be invoked in each of the directories *johnpaul, georgeringo*, and *hellobeatles*:

```
johnpaul georgeringo hellobeatles:
    $(MAKE) --directory=$@ $(TARGET)
```

To understand this rule, you need to know three things. First, the variable MAKE expands to the name of the currently running instance of *make*. Usually this will be make, but on some systems it could be gmake. Second, the command line option *--directory=<path>* causes *make* to be invoked with *<path>* as its current directory.

Third, a rule with several targets is equivalent to a collection of rules, each having one target, and having identical command scripts. So the above rule is equivalent to:

```
johnpaul:
    $(MAKE) --directory=$@ $(TARGET)

georgeringo:
    $(MAKE) --directory=$@ $(TARGET)

hellobeatles:
    $(MAKE) --directory=$@ $(TARGET)
```

This in turn is equivalent to:

```
johnpaul:
    $(MAKE) --directory=johnpaul $(TARGET)

georgeringo:
    $(MAKE) --directory=georgeringo $(TARGET)

hellobeatles:
    $(MAKE) --directory=hellobeatles $(TARGET)
```

The effect of the rule, therefore, is to invoke the makefiles in each of the directories *johnpaul*, *georgeringo*, and *hellobeatles*, with the value of the variable TARGET tacked onto the command line. As a result, you can build target *xxx* of each of the subordinate makefiles by executing the top-level makefile with the option *TARGET=xxx*.

The final rule of the makefile ensures that the subordinate makefiles are executed in the correct order; it simply declares that the target hellobeatles depends on the targets johnpaul and georgeringo:

```
hellobeatles: johnpaul georgeringo
```

In a more complex application, there might be many dependencies between the executable and its component libraries. For each such component, declare a rule indicating the other components on which it directly depends.

See Also

Recipes 1.5, 1.10, and 1.13

1.19 Defining a Macro

Problem

You want to define the preprocessor symbol *name*, assigning it either an unspecified value or the value *value*.

Solution

The compiler options for defining a macro from the command line are shown in Table 1-16. Instructions for defining a macro from your IDE are given in Table 1-17. To define a macro using Boost.Build, simply add a property of the form <define> *name[=value]* to your target's requirements, as shown in Table 1-15 and Example 1-12.

Table 1-16. Defining a macro from the command line

Toolset	Option
All	*-Dname[=value]*

Table 1-17. Defining a macro from your IDE

IDE	Configuration
Visual C++	From your project's property pages, go to Configuration Properties → C/C++ → Preprocessor and enter *name[=value]* under Preprocessor Definitions, using semicolons to separate multiple entries.
CodeWarrior	From the Target Settings Window, go to Language Settings → C/C++ Preprocessor and enter: **#define** *name[=value]* in the area labeled Prefix Text.
C++Builder	From Project Options, go to Directories/Conditionals and enter *name[=value]* under Preprocessor Definitions, using semicolons to separate multiple entries.
Dev-C++	From Project Options, select Parameters and enter: **-D**name[=value] under C++ Compiler.

Discussion

Preprocessor symbols are used frequently in C++ source code to allow a single collection of source files to be used with several build configurations or operating systems. For example, suppose you want to write a function that checks whether a file is a directory. Currently, the C++ standard library does not provide the functionality necessary to perform this task; consequently, your function will need to make use of platform specific features. If you want your code to work both on Windows and on Unix, you'll have to make sure that the code that makes use of Windows-specific features is not visible to the compiler when compiling on Unix, and *vice versa*. The usual way to achieve this is through *conditional compilation*, as illustrated in Example 1-25.

Example 1-25. Conditional compilation using predefined macros

```
#ifdef _WIN32
# include <windows.h>
#else // Not Windows — assume we're on Unix
# include <sys/stat.h>
#endif
```

Example 1-25. Conditional compilation using predefined macros (continued)

```
bool is_directory(const char* path)
{
#ifdef _WIN32
    // Windows implementation
#else
    // Unix implementation
#endif
}
```

On Windows, all the toolsets except the Cygwin port of GCC define the macro _WIN32; macros defined automatically in this way are known as *predefined macros*. Example 1-25 uses the predefined macro WIN32 to determine which operating system it is being compiled under and to enable the appropriate platform-specific code.

Often, however, the configuration information necessary to perform this kind of conditional compilation is not available as predefined macros. In such cases, it's necessary to introduce your own macros and to give them appropriate values using the methods shown in Tables 1-15, 1-16, and 1-17. A good example is Example 1-2. On Windows, you want the function georgeringo( ) to be declared with the attribute __declspec(dllexport) when the DLL *georgeringo.dll* is being built, but with the attribute __declspec(dllimport) otherwise. As described in Recipe 1.4, you can achieve this effect by defining the preprocessor symbol GEORGERINGO_DLL from the command line when building the DLL, but not when compiling code that uses the DLL.

 When you fail to specify a value for a macro, most compilers assign it the value 1, but others assign it an empty value. When macros are used to enable conditional compilation as in Example 1-25, this difference is not important; if you really need a macro to expand to a particular value, however, you should specify that value explicitly using the syntax *-D<name>=<value>*.

See Also

Recipes 1.4, 1.9, 1.12, and 1.17

1.20 Specifying a Command-Line Option from Your IDE

Problem

You want to pass a command-line option to your compiler or linker, but it doesn't correspond to any of the project settings available through your IDE.

Solution

Many IDEs provide a way to pass command-line options directly to the compiler or linker. This is summarized in Tables 1-18 and 1-19.

Table 1-18. Specifying a compiler option from your IDE

IDE	Configuration
Visual C++	From your project's property pages, go to Configuration Properties → C/C++ → Command Line and enter the option under Additional options.
CodeWarrior	n/a
C++Builder	n/a
Dev-C++	From Project Options, select Parameters and enter the option under C++ Compiler.

Table 1-19. Specifying a linker option from your IDE

IDE	Configuration
Visual C++	From your project's property pages, go to Configuration Properties → Linker → Command Line and enter the option under Additional options.
Metrowerks	n/a
C++Builder	n/a
Dev-C++	From Project Options, select Parameters and enter the option under Linker.

Discussion

Visual C++ provides extensive configuration options through its graphical interface, but it also allows you to specify command-line options explicitly. CodeWarrior and C++Builder do not allow you to set command-line options explicitly, but this is generally not a problem, since like Visual C++ they both provide extensive configuration options through their graphical interfaces. Some IDEs, on the other hand, provide little means to configure your command-line tools other than by explicitly typing command-line options into a text field. Dev-C++ occupies a position somewhere in the middle: while Dev-C++ offers more graphical configuration options than some IDEs designed for the GCC toolset, it is still frequently necessary to enter explicit command-line options when using Dev-C++.

1.21   Producing a Debug Build

Problem

You want to build a version of your project that will be easy to debug.

Solution

In general, to produce a debug build, you must;

- Disable optimizations
- Disable expansion of inline function
- Enable generation of debugging information

Table 1-20 presents the compiler and linker options to disable optimization and inlining; Table 1-21 presents the compiler and linker options to enable debugging information.

Table 1-20. Disabling optimization and inlining from the command line

Toolset	Optimization	Inlining
GCC	-O0	-fno-inline[a]
Visual C++ Intel (Windows)	-Od	-Ob0
Intel (Linux)	-O0 -opt off	-Ob0 -inline off
Comeau (Unix)	-O0	--no_inlining
Comeau (Windows)	Same as backend, but using a slash (/) instead of a dash (-)	
Borland	-Od	-vi-
Digital Mars	-o+none -S	-C

[a] It's not necessary to specify this option unless -O3 has also been specified.

Table 1-21. Command-line options for enabling debug information

Toolset	Compiler options	Linker options
Comeau (Unix) GCC Intel (Linux) Metrowerks	*-g*	*-g*
Visual C++ Intel (Windows)	See Table 1-22.	See Table 1-22.
Comeau (Windows)	Same as backend, but using a slash (/) instead of a dash (-).	Same as backend *compiler* option, but using a slash (/) instead of a dash (-).
Borland	*-v*	*-v*
Digital Mars	*-g*	*-co*

Table 1-22. Enabling debugging information with Visual C++ or Intel for Windows

Compiler options	Linker options	IDE options[a]	Description
-Z7	-debug	C7 Compatible	Debug info is stored in .obj and .exe files.
-Zi [-Fd<pdb-file-for-obj>]	-debug[-pdb:<pdb-file-for-exe>]	Program Database	Debug info is stored in .pdb files; use the bracketed options to specify the .pdb files.
-ZI [-Fd<pdb-file-for-obj>]	-debug [-pdb:<pdb-file-for-exe>]	Program Database for Edit & Continue	Debug info is stored in .pdb files; use the bracketed options to specify the .pdb files. Your program can be recompiled during a debugging session.

[a] To access these options, go to Configuration Properties → C/C++ → General → Debug Information Format.

Boost.Build provides a simple mechanism for producing a debug build: simply add <variant>debug to your target's requirements or use the command-line option *variant=debug*, which can be abbreviated simply as *debug*.

Some IDEs also provide a simple way to produce a debug build. For instance, when you create a new project with Visual C++, the IDE generates debug and release build configurations automatically. To request a debug build, simply select Configuration Manager... from the Build menu and select Debug as the active configuration. You can also select Debug from the drop-down list of configurations on the standard toolbar. The next time you build your project, it will produce a debug build.

Similarly, when you create a new project with CodeWarrior using one of Metrowerks's project templates, called *stationery*, the IDE generates debug and release targets automatically. The name of the debug target may vary, but it should always contain the word "debug". To request a debug build, select Set Default Target from the Project menu, and then select the menu item corresponding to the debug target. You can also select the debug target from the drop-down list of targets on your project's window.

C++Builder does not support multiple build configurations for a single project, but it does provide an easy way produce a debug build. To request a debug build, go to Project Options → Compiler and press Full debug. This will disable optimization and inlining and enable debugging information.

If you are using an IDE that doesn't provide preset debug and release configurations, such as Dev-C++, or if you need more control over your project's settings, refer to Tables 1-23 through 1-25.

Table 1-23. Disabling optimization from your IDE

IDE	Configuration
Visual C++	From your project's property pages, go to Configuration Properties → C/C++ → Optimization and set Optimization to Disabled. Use the default settings for the other properties on this page.
CodeWarrior	From the Target Settings Window, go to Code Generation → Global Optimizations and select Off.
C++Builder	From Project Options, go to Compiler and select None under Code optimization.
Dev-C++	From Project Options, go to Compiler → Optimization and set Perform a number of minor optimizations to No; next, go to Compiler → Optimization → Further optimizations and set Optimize, Optimize more, and Best Optimization to No.

Table 1-24. Disabling inlining from your IDE

IDE	Configuration
Visual C++	From your project's property pages, go to Configuration Properties → C/C++ → Optimization and set Inline Function Expansion to Default.
CodeWarrior	From the Target Settings Window, go to Language Settings → C/C++ Language and set Inline Depth to Don't Inline.
C++Builder	From Project Options, go to Compiler and check Disable inline expansions under Debugging.
Dev-C++	See the entry for GCC in Table 1-20 and refer to Recipe 1.20.

Table 1-25. Enabling debug information from your IDE

IDE	Configuration
Visual C++	See Table 1-22.
CodeWarrior	From the Target Settings Window, go to Language Settings → Linker → PPC Mac OS X Linker and check Generate SYM File and Full Path in SYM Files.
C++Builder	From Project Options, go to Compiler and check Debug Information and Line Number Information.
Dev-C++	See the entry for GCC in Table 1-21 and refer to Recipe 1.20.

Discussion

All toolsets provide an option to generate information in object files and executables that allows debuggers to report useful information as a program is executed step by step. This information generally includes the sources file names and line numbers corresponding to particular object or machine code instructions, as well as information about C++ objects occupying particular memory locations, including their names and types.

Most toolsets store debugging information directly in object files and executables, but some, also provide options for generating debugging information in separate database files. For example, with Visual C++, the *-Z7* compiler option specifies that debug information should be placed in object files and executables, while the *-Zi* and *-ZI* options specify that debugging information should be stored in *program database files* with the extension *.pdb*. The *-ZI* option enables a feature called *Edit and Continue*, which allows IDE users to modify and recompile their code without terminating a debugging session. Similarly, CodeWarrior for Mac OS X by default generates debugging information in *.SYM* files.

Most toolsets can generate debugging information even when optimizations and inlining are enabled, although in some cases debugging information may be incompatible with particular optimizations. When optimizations are enabled, however, the compiler has the freedom to improve efficiency by reordering statements or completely reorganizing sections of code, as long as the observable behavior remains the same. This makes debugging difficult, since there may no longer be a close correspondence between locations in the source code and locations in the object or machine code. The same is true for inlining: when the compiler expands a function inline, the object code corresponding to the function body is generated within the body of the calling function. When this code is executed, no stack frame is created for the expanded function; among other things, this means that the debugger will not be able to display the values of the function arguments and local variables. Typically, debuggers do not even attempt to report the source code locations corresponding to the bodies of functions expanded inline.

Because of these considerations, the usual practice is to disable optimizations and inlining when producing a debug build.

See Also

Recipe 1.22

1.22 Producing a Release Build

Problem

You want to produce a small, fast executable or dynamic library for distribution to your customers.

Solution

In general, to produce a release build you must

- Enable optimizations
- Enable the expansion of inline function
- Disable the generation of debugging information

Table 1-26 presents the compiler and linker options to enable optimization and inlining. There are no command-line options for disabling the generation of debugging information: when you build from the command line, debugging information is disabled by default. If you use the GCC toolset, however, you can decrease the size of executables and dynamics libraries by specifying the -s option to the linker.

Table 1-26. *Compiler options to enable optimization and inlining*

Toolset	Optimization	Inlining
GCC	-O3	-finline-functions[a]
Visual C++ Intel	-O2	-Ob1
Metrowerks	-opt full	-inline auto -inline level=8
Comeau (Unix)	-O3	
Comeau (Windows)	Same as backend, but using a slash (/) instead of a dash (-)	--inlining
Borland	-O2	-vi
Digital Mars	-o+time	Enabled by default

[a]This option is enabled automatically when -O3 is specified.

Boost.Build provides a simple mechanism for producing a release build: simply add <variant>release to your target's requirements or use the command-line option *variant=release*, which can be abbreviated simply as *release*.

Some IDEs also provide a simple way to produce a release build. For instance, as I mentioned in Recipe 1.21, when you create a new project with Visual C++, the IDE generates debug and release configurations automatically. To request a release build, simply select Configuration Manager... from the Build menu and select Release as the active configuration. You can also select Release from the drop-down list of configurations on the standard toolbar. The next time you build your project, it will produce a release build.

Similarly, when you create a new project with CodeWarrior using one of Metrowerks's project templates, called *stationery*, the IDE generates debug and release targets automatically. The name of the release target may vary, but it should always contain the word "release" or "final." To request a release build, select Set Default Target from the Project menu, and then select the menu item corresponding to the release target. You can also select the release target from the drop-down list of targets on your project's window.

C++Builder does not support multiple build configurations for a single project, but it does provide an easy way produce a release build. To request a release build, go to Project Options → Compiler and press Release. This will enable optimization and inlining and disable debugging information.

If you are using an IDE which doesn't provide preset debug and release configurations, such as Dev-C++, or if you need more control over your project's settings, refer to Tables 1-27 through 1-29.

Table 1-27. Enabling optimization from your IDE

IDE	Configuration
Visual C++	From your project's property pages, go to Configuration Properties → C/C++ → Optimization and set Optimization to Maximize Speed, Favor Size or Speed to Favor Fast Code, and Global Optimizations, Enable Intrinsic Functions, and Omit Frame Pointers to Yes. Use the default settings for the other properties on this page.
CodeWarrior	From the Target Settings Window, go to Code Generation → Global Optimizations and select Level 4.
C++Builder	From Project Options, go to Compiler and select Speed under Code optimization.
Dev-C++	See the entry for GCC in Table 1-26 and refer to Recipe 1.20.

Table 1-28. Enabling inlining from your IDE

IDE	Configuration
Visual C++	From your project's property pages, go to Configuration Properties → C/C++ → Optimization and set Inline Function Expansion to Any Suitable.
CodeWarrior	From the Target Settings Window, go to Language Settings → C/C++ Language. Set Inline Depth to 8, check Auto-Inline and leave the other inlining options unchecked.
C++Builder	From Project Options, go to Compiler and uncheck Disable inline expansions under Debugging.
Dev-C++	See the entry for GCC in Table 1-26 and refer to Recipe 1.20.

Table 1-29. Disabling debug information from your IDE

IDE	Configuration
Visual C++	From your project's property pages, go to Configuration Properties → C/C++ → General and select Disabled as the Debug Information Format
Metrowerks	From the Target Settings Window, go to Language Settings → Linker → x86 Linker and uncheck Store full paths, Link debug info, and Debug inline functions.
C++Builder	From Project Options, go to Compiler and uncheck Debug Information and Line Number Information.
Dev-C++	Make sure that the command-line option -*g* has not been specified, as described in Recipe 1.20.

Discussion

Most toolsets offer several options for optimization; some offer dozens. Which optimizations you choose depends heavily on the requirements of your project. In an embedded environment, for example, you may want to pick an optimization that produces a smaller executable at the expense of some speed. In other cases, speed may be paramount. Some optimizations will make your program faster on one platform but slower on another. You might even find that certain options make parts of your program faster and other parts slower.

While Tables 1-26 and 1-27 present good general-purpose optimization options, for best results you should carefully consider your requirements, study your toolset's documentation, and conduct extensive tests.

This situation is similar with inlining, although toolsets usually provide fewer options for inlining than for other optimizations.

See Also

Recipe 1.21

1.23 Specifying a Runtime Library Variant

Problem

Your toolset comes with several variants of its runtime support libraries and you want to instruct your compiler and linker which variant to use.

Solution

Runtime libraries supplied with a given toolset can vary depending on whether they are single- or multithreaded, whether they are static or dynamic, and whether or not they were built with debugging information.

If you are using Boost.Build, these three choices can be specified using the `threading`, `runtime-link`, and `variant` features, described in Table 1-15. For example, to specify a statically linked runtime library, add `<runtime-link>static` to your target's requirements, or use the command-line option *runtime-link=static*. To specify a multi-threaded runtime library, add `<threading>multi` to your target's requirements, or use the command-line option *threading=multi*.

If you are building from the command line, use the compiler and linker options presented in Tables 1-30 through 1-36. The command-line options and library names for debug and release configurations as generally quite similar; in the following tables, the letters in brackets should be supplied only for debug configurations. The names of the dynamic variants of the runtime libraries are provided in parentheses; these libraries must be available at runtime if dynamic linking is selected.

Table 1-30. Compiler options for runtime library selection using Visual C++ or Intel (Windows)

	Static linking	Dynamic linking
Single-threaded	*-ML[d]*[a]	n/a
Multithreaded	*-MT[d]*	*-MD[d]* (*msvcrt[d].dll,* *msvcr80[d].dll)*[b]

[a] Beginning with Visual Studio 2005, currently in beta, the options *-ML* and *-MLd* have been deprecated, and single-threaded, statically linked runtime libraries are no longer distributed.

[b] Previous versions of Visual C++ used the DLL's *msvcr71.dll, msvcr71d.dll, msvcr70.dll, msvcr70d.dll*, etc.

Table 1-31. Compiler options for runtime library selection using Metrowerks (Windows)

	Static linking	Dynamic linking
Single-threaded	*-runtime ss[d]*	n/a
Multithreaded	*-runtime sm[d]*	*-runtime dm[d]* *(MSL_All-DLL90_x86[_D].dll)*

Table 1-32. Command-line options for runtime library selection using CodeWarrior 10 for Max OS X

Static linking	Dynamic linking
No options necessary	Consult the Metrowerks documentation for command-line options *(MSL_All_Mach-O[_D].dylib)*.

Table 1-33. Compiler and linker options for runtime library selection using Borland

	Static linking	Dynamic linking
Single-threaded	*-WM*	*-WM- -WR -WC*[a] *(cc3260.dll)*
Multithreaded	*-WM*	*-WM -WR -WC*[a] *(cc3260mt.dll)*

[a] The option *-WC* is required only when building a console application.

Table 1-34. Compiler options for runtime library selection using Digital Mars (all runtime libraries are multithreaded)

Static linking	Dynamic linking
No options necessary	*-ND -D_STLP_USE_DYNAMIC_LIB* *(sccrt70.dll, stlp45dm.dll)*

Table 1-35. Linker options for runtime library selection using GCC

Static linking	Dynamic linking
-static[a]	No options necessary

[a] This option disables all dynamic linking, not just dynamic linking with runtime support libraries.

For example, to specify a dynamically linked release build of the Visual C++ runtime library, use the compiler option *-MD*. To specify a statically linked, single-threaded debug build of the Metrowerks runtime library on Windows, use the compiler option *-runtime ssd*. To specify a single-threaded, dynamically linked build of the Borland runtime library, pass the options *-WM- -WR -WC* to the compiler *and* to the linker.

Instructions for specifying a runtime library variant from your IDE are presented in Table 1-36.

Table 1-36. Specifying a runtime library variant from your IDE

IDE	Configuration
Visual C++	From your project's property pages, go to Configuration Properties → C/C++ → Code Generation and use the drop-down list labeled Runtime Library.
CodeWarrior	For dynamic library projects, add the object file */usr/lib/dylib1.o* and the libraries *MSL_Shared_AppAndDylib_Runtime[_D].lib* and *MSL_All_Mach-O[_D].dylib* to your project, and remove any libraries of the form *MSL_<XXX>_Mach-O[_D].lib*. For executable projects, add the object file */usr/lib/crt1.o* and the libraries *MSL_Shared_AppAndDylib_Runtime[_D].lib* and *MSL_All_Mach-O[_D].dylib* to your project, and remove any libraries of the form *MSL_<XXX>_Mach-O[_D].lib*.
C++Builder	Whether a project will be single- or multithreaded must be specified when you create it. To select a static or dynamic runtime library, go to Linker from Project Options and check or uncheck Use dynamic RTL.
Dev-C++	To select a statically linked runtime library, specify the command-line option *-static*, as described in Recipe 1.20.

Discussion

A runtime library contains implementations of utility functions required by a program while it is running. Runtime libraries generally contain implementations of functions from the C standard library, platform specific functions for accessing operating system services such as threads and file systems, and functions that provide the infrastructure for C++ language features such as runtime type information (RTTI) and exception handling.

In most cases, the more choices you have, the better; the proliferation of runtime library variants, however, presents some problems. The main challenge is ensuring that all the components of an application—static libraries, dynamic libraries, and executables—use a single variant of the runtime library. If not, the application may fail to link, or hard-to-diagnose runtime failures may occur.

 When using third-party libraries, you sometimes have no control over which variants of the runtime libraries are linked against. In such cases, you may be forced to use several runtime library variants in a single application.

So how should you decide which runtime library to use? Two of the choices—single- *versus* multi-threaded and debug *versus* release—are fairly straightforward.

If your project uses multiple threads, or depends on libraries which are multi-threaded, you *must* select a multithreaded variant of the runtime library if your toolset provides one. Calling runtime library functions from multiple threads if the runtime library was not built with thread support can lead to unpredictable runtime behavior. Similarly, if you are producing a debug build, you should use a debug variant of the runtime library, if available.

The last choice—whether to use a static or dynamic runtime library—is more difficult. Using a statically linked runtime has several advantages. First, it can make the overall size of your distribution smaller—if you would otherwise have to distribute a dynamic runtime—since only those functions that your application uses will be linked in. (If you know that the dynamic runtime is already available on your target system, however, linking to the static runtime will probably make your distribution larger.) Second, by linking with the static runtime, you avoid versioning problems that can occur when several different versions of a dynamic library exist on a single system.

Linking with a dynamic runtime library is also attractive, however. This is because a very effective way to organize an application is as a collection of dynamic libraries. For one thing, it allows parts of the application to be updated without requiring the entire application to be reinstalled. Furthermore, applications can sometimes improve their performance significantly by taking advantage of the *delay-loading* feature of DLLs on Windows. But because all components of an application should use a single variant of the runtime library, once an application makes use of a single dynamic library, all the component of that application should use dynamically linked runtimes. As a result, using a dynamically linked runtime makes your application easier to modularize.

I recommend that you choose dynamic linking most of the time. As mentioned earlier, however, sometimes static linking is more appropriate. Sometimes, it's impossible to know in advance what type of linking is appropriate, because you don't know how a library you've written will be used. In that case, a common solution is to provide multiple variants of your library, linked against different variants of the runtime libraries.

See Also

Recipes 1.4, 1.5, 1.21, and 1.25

1.24 Enforcing Strict Conformance to the C++ Standard

Problem

You want your compiler to accept only programs that conform to the C++ language standard.

Solution

Command-line options for specifying strict conformance to the C++ standard are listed in Table 1-37. Instructions for enforcing strict conformance from your IDE are given in Table 1-38.

Some of the compiler options I introduced in Table 1-6 can be considered conformance options. Examples include options to enable basic language features such as wide-character support, exceptions, and runtime type information. I've omitted these in Table 1-37.

Table 1-37. Enforcing strict conformance from the command line

Toolset	Command-line compiler options
GCC	*-ansi -pedantic-errors*
Visual C++	*-Za*
Intel (Windows)	*-Za -Qms0*
Intel (Linux)	*-strict-ansi*[a]
Metrowerks	*-ansi strict -iso_templates on -msext off*
Comeau (Windows)	*--A*
Comeau (Unix)	*--strict or -A*
Borland	*-A*[b]
Digital Mars	*-A*

[a] Versions of the Intel compiler for Linux prior to 9.0 used the option *-strict_ansi*. When using *-strict-ansi* or *-strict_ansi*, it may be necessary to enable Intel's standard library, using the option *-cxxlib-icc*.
[b] With the option *-A*, some of the standard headers from the STLPort library may fail to compile.

Table 1-38. Enforcing strict conformance from your IDE

IDE	Configuration
Visual C++	From your project's property pages, go to Configuration Properties → C/C++ → Language and set Disable Language Extensions, Treat wchar_t as Built-in Type, and Force Conformance in For Loop Scopes to Yes.
Metrowerks	From the Target Settings Window, go to Language Settings → C/C++ Language and check ISO Template Parser, ANSI Strict, and ANSI Keywords Only. Make sure that the options Enable C++ Exceptions, Enable RTTI support, Enable bool Support, and Enable wchar_t Support are checked.
C++Builder	From Project Options, go to Advanced Compiler and check ANSI under Language Compliance.
Dev-C++	See the entry for GCC in Table 1-37 and refer to Recipe 1.20.

Discussion

The C++ language was standardized in 1998 by the International Standards Organization (ISO); in the same year, the ISO standard was adopted by the American National Standards Institute (ANSI). In 2003, a second edition of the standard was approved; the second edition contained corrections and clarifications, but introduced no new language features. Work is currently underway on an updated version of the C++ standard that will contain some important new language features and an expanded standard library.

At the time the standard was approved in 1998, no compiler came close to meeting its requirements—though many were advertised as "ANSI-compliant." Over the years, however, vendors have worked hard to bring their tools into conformance. As of September 2005, the latest versions of the GNU, Microsoft, Intel, Metrowerks, and Comeau compilers are all highly conformant. Comeau and Intel, with their support for exported templates, can now *almost* claim to be 100% conformant.[*]

No compiler is able to enforce perfect conformance to the standard, if that means refusing to compile any invalid program. This is not just because no compiler is 100% conformant: a more fundamental reason is that the C++ standard does not require a compiler to reject all invalid programs. There is a carefully delimited set of circumstances in which a compiler is required to issue a *diagnostic*, indicating an ill-formed program; for many invalid programs, however, no diagnostic is required. These are the programs that invoke what the standard calls *undefined behavior* at runtime. And even when a diagnostic is required, a compiler is permitted to issue the diagnostic and continue with compilation, possibly leading to the successful creation of an executable or library.

The main reason that compilers are not required to reject all nonconforming programs is that in many cases nonconformance is computationally difficult—or even impossible—to detect. Another reason, discussed later, is that nonconforming programs are sometimes useful.

I recommend that you use your compiler's strict conformance option as often as you can. There are some cases where it may not be appropriate, however; to better understand this, let's look at several varieties of nonconforming code.

First, there is code that was legal in an early dialect of C++, before the language was standardized. For example, in the early days of C++, the scope of a variable declared in the initializer of a for loop extended to the end of the block containing the loop:

```
// WARNING: invalid code!
int main( )
{
    for (int i = 0; i < 10; ++i)
    ;
    int j = i; // j == 10
}
```

This is not permitted by the standard, and offers no advantage over the standard scoping rules. The need to compile code like the above should arise only when maintaining legacy applications.

Another category of nonconforming code is code that uses experimental language extensions that might eventually be incorporated into the C++ standard. For example, many compilers provide an integral type long long guaranteed to have a size of

---

[*] Why *almost*? Because even Comeau and Intel have some bugs, and the interpretations of some parts of the standard are disputed.

at least 64 bits. As another example, several compilers provide a built-in operator typeof, with the same syntax as the sizeof operator, which returns the type of an expression. Both of these features are likely to appear in the next version of the C++ standard, although the spelling of typeof is expected to change, probably to decltype.

Be very careful before using an extension like this: before you know it, you may have to port your code to a platform that does not implement the extension, or that implements it with different semantics.

A third category of nonconforming code is code that makes use of platform-specific language extensions necessary to take advantage of operating system features. The attributes __declspec(dllexport) and __declspec(dllimport), for building dynamic libraries on Windows, and the attributes __stdcall, __fastcall and __cdecl, for representing Windows calling conventions, fall into this category. Although these are language extensions, most Windows compilers will accept code containing them even in their strict-conformance mode.

A final category of nonconforming code is code that violates the C++ standard but is perfectly valid according to some other useful standard. A prime example of such a standard is C++/CLI, which is currently in the final stages of standardization by the ECMA. C++/CLI is an extension to C++ that constitutes the C++ interface to the Command Language Infrastructure, the core of Microsoft's .NET Framework. When compiling an application that uses certain C++/CLI extensions, a conforming C++ compiler is required to issue a diagnostic, but it's free to generate a valid C++/CLI application, if it supports the C++/CLI standard.

If you need to compile nonconforming code, first see whether it will compile using the options in Tables 1-37 and 1-38. If not, some compilers offer a range of more fine-grained conformance options that allow some nonconforming constructs to compile but not others. For example, Comeau provides the option *--long_long* to specify that the type long long should be recognized. Finally, some compilers provide options that cause them to report many violations of the standard as warnings rather than errors. For example, GCC provides the option *-pedantic* for this purpose and Comeau provides the options *--a*, for Windows, and *--strict_warnings* or *-a*, for other platforms.

See Also

Recipe 1.2

1.25   Causing a Source File to Be Linked Automatically Against a Specified Library

Problem

You've written a library that you'd like to distribute as a collection of headers and prebuilt static or dynamic libraries, but you don't want users of your library to have to specify the names of the binaries when they link their applications.

Solution

If you are programming for Windows and using the Visual C++, Intel, Metrowerks, Borland, or Digital Mars toolsets, you can use pragma comment in your library's headers to specify the names, and optionally the full file pathnames, of the prebuilt binaries against which any code that includes the headers should be linked.

For example, suppose you want to distribute the library from Example 1-1 as a static library *libjohnpaul.lib* together with the header *johnpaul.hpp*. Modify the header as shown in Example 1-26.

Example 1-26. Using pragma comment

```
#ifndef JOHNPAUL_HPP_INCLUDED
#define JOHNPAUL_HPP_INCLUDED

#pragma comment(lib, "libjohnpaul")

void johnpaul();

#endif // JOHNPAUL_HPP_INCLUDED
```

With this change, the Visual C++, Intel, Metrowerks, Borland, and Digital Mars linkers will automatically search for the library *libjohnpaul.lib* when linking code that includes the header *johnpaul.hpp*.

Discussion

In some ways, linking can be a more difficult phase of the build process than compiling. One of the most common problems during linking occurs when the linker finds the wrong version of a library. This is a particular problem on Windows, where runtime libraries—and the libraries that depend on them—frequently come in many variants. For this reason, libraries for Windows are often distributed with names mangled to reflect the various build configurations. While this helps to reduce version conflict, it also makes linking harder because you have to specify the correct mangled name to the linker.

For this reason, `pragma comment` is a very powerful tool. Among other things, it allows you to specify the correct mangled name of a library in a header file, saving the user the trouble of having to understand your name-mangling convention. If, in addition, you design your installation process to copy the binary files to a location automatically searched by the linker—such as the *lib* subdirectory of the Visual C++, CodeWarrior, or C++Builder root directories—programmers will be able to use your library simply by including your headers.

So far, so good. There's just one problem: `pragma comment` is not recognized by all compilers. If you wish to write portable code, you should invoke a pragma only after verifying that it is supported by the toolset being used. For example, you could modify *johnpaul.cpp* to read:

```
#ifndef JOHNPAUL_HPP_INCLUDED
#define JOHNPAUL_HPP_INCLUDED

#if defined(_MSC_VER) || \
    defined(__ICL) || \
    defined(__MWERKS__) && defined(_WIN32) || \
    defined(__BORLANDC__) \
    defined(__DMC__) \
    /**/
# pragma comment(lib, "libjohnpaul")
#endif

void johnpaul();

#endif // JOHNPAUL_HPP_INCLUDED
```

This example is already pretty complex, and, unfortunately, it's still not exactly right: some compilers that don't support `pragma comment` define the macro `_MSC_VER` for compatibility with Visual C++. Fortunately, Boost provides an easy solution:

```
#ifndef JOHNPAUL_HPP_INCLUDED
#define JOHNPAUL_HPP_INCLUDED

#define BOOST_LIB_NAME libjohnpaul
#define BOOST_AUTO_LINK_NOMANGLE
#include <boost/config/auto_link.hpp>

void johnpaul();

#endif // JOHNPAUL_HPP_INCLUDED
```

Here, the line:

```
#define BOOST_LIB_NAME libjohnpaul
```

specifies your library name, the line:

```
#define BOOST_AUTO_LINK_NOMANGLE
```

indicates that you don't want to use the Boost name-mangling convention, and the line:

```
#include <boost/config/auto_link.hpp>
```

invokes pragma comment for compilers which support it.

See Also

Recipe 1.23

1.26   Using Exported Templates

Problem

You want to build a program that uses exported templates, *meaning that it* declares templates in headers with the export keyword and places template implementations in *.cpp* files.

Solution

First, compile the *.cpp* files containing the template implementations into object files, passing the compiler the command-line options necessary to enable exported templates. Next, compile and link the *.cpp* files that use the exported templates, passing the compiler and linker the command-line options necessary to enable exported templates as well as the options to specify the directories that contain the template implementations.

The options for enabling exported templates are given in Table 1-39. The options for specifying the location of template implementations are given in Table 1-40. If your toolset does not appear in this table, it likely does not support exported templates.

Table 1-39. Options to enable exported templates

Toolset	Script
Comeau (Unix)	*--export, -A* or *--strict*
Comeau (Windows)	*--export* or *--A*
Intel (Linux)	*-export* or *-strict-ansi*[a]

[a] Versions of the Intel compiler for Linux prior to 9.0 used the option *-strict_ansi*.

Table 1-40. Option to specify the location of template implementations

Toolset	Script
Comeau	*--template_directory=<path>*
Intel (Linux)	*-export_dir<path>*

For example, suppose you want to compile the program displayed in Example 1-27. It consists of three files:

- The file *plus.hpp* contains the declaration of an exported function template plus( ).
- The file *plus.cpp* contains the definition of plus( ).
- The file *test.cpp* includes the declaration—but not the definition—of plus( ), and defines a main( ) function that uses plus( ).

Example 1-27. A simple program using exported templates

plus.hpp:

```
#ifndef PLUS_HPP_INCLUDED
#define PLUS_HPP_INCLUDED

export template<typename T>
T plus(const T& lhs, const T& rhs);

#endif // #ifndef PLUS_HPP_INCLUDED
```

plus.cpp:

```
#include "plus.hpp"

template<typename T>
T plus(const T& lhs, const T& rhs)
{
    return rhs + lhs;
}
```

test.cpp:

```
#include <iostream>
#include "plus.hpp"

int main( )
{
    std::cout << "2 + 2 = " << plus(2, 2) << "\n";
}
```

To compile *plus.cpp* to an object file *plus.obj* using Comeau on Unix, change to the directory containing *plus.cpp*, *plus.cpp*, and *test.cpp*, and enter the following command:

```
$ como -c --export plus.cpp
```

This command also generates a file *plus.et* describing the template implementations contained in *plus.cpp*.

 For fun, open the file *plus.et* in a text editor.

Next, compile *test.cpp* to an object file *test.obj*, as follows:

```
$ como -c --export test.cpp
```

Finally, link the executable *test.exe*:

```
$ como --export -o test test.obj
```

The last two commands could also have been combined:

```
$ como --export -o test test.cpp
```

You can now run *test.exe*:

```
$ ./test
  2 + 2 = 4
```

Alternatively, suppose that the files *plus.hpp* and *plus.cpp* are in a directory named *plus*, while *test.cpp* is in a sibling directory *test*. To compile and link *test.cpp*, change to the directory *test* and enter:

```
$ como --export --template_directory=../plus –I../plus -o test
test.cpp
```

Discussion

C++ supports two models for supplying the definitions of function templates and static data members of class templates: the *inclusion model* and the *separation model*. The inclusion model is familiar to all programmers who regularly use C++ templates, but often seems unnatural to programmer accustomed to writing nontemplated code. Under the inclusion model, the *definition* of a function template—or of a static data member of a class template—must be included by each source file that uses it. By contrast, for nontemplated functions and data it is sufficient for a source file simply to include a *declaration*; the definition can be placed in a separate *.cpp* file.

The separation model is closer to the traditional manner of organizing C++ source code. Templates declared with the export keyword do not need to have their definitions included by source files that use them; instead, the definitions can be placed in separate *.cpp* files. The parallel with traditional source code organization is not exact, though, because even though code that uses an exported template does not need to *include* its definition, it still *depends on* the definition in some subtle ways.

The separation model offers several potential benefits:

Reduced compilation times
> Compilation time may improve with the separation model because a template's definition needs to be scanned less frequently and because the separation modules reduce dependencies between modules.

Reduced symbolic "pollution"
> Names of functions, classes, and data used in a template's implementation file can be completely hidden from code that uses the template, reducing the possibility of accidental name clashes. In addition, the author of a template implementation can

worry less about accidental clashes with names from the source files that use the template.

The ability to ship precompiled template implementations
In theory, under the separation mode, a vendor could ship template implementations that have been precompiled into a binary format somewhere between C++ source code and ordinary object files.

All three potential advantages of the separation model are controversial. First, while some users have reported reduced compile times, the separation model can also lead to longer compile times in some cases. At the moment, there is insufficient data to make a definitive judgment. Second, while the separation model does reduce some forms of symbolic pollution, the language rules necessary to support the separation model, particularly the notion of *two-phase lookup*, have complicated the way templated code is written—even when using the inclusion model—and have had some unintended consequences. Third, all existing implementations of the separation model are based on the EDG frontend, and EDG has not yet provided any means to compile source files containing exported template implementations into binary files that can be shipped in lieu of the source.

There was an effort in 2003 to remove exported templates from future versions of the C++ standard, but it failed. Consequently, exported templates are a permanent part of the C++ language, and you should learn to use them.

See Also

Recipe 1.25

## CHAPTER 2

Code Organization

2.0 Introduction

Perhaps one of the reasons C++ has been so popular is its ability to serve small, large, and massive projects well. You can write a few classes for a small prototype or research project, and as the project grows and people are added, C++ will allow you to scale the application into modules that have varying degrees of independence. The trade-off is that you have to make time to do some manual reorganization along the way (adding namespaces, rearranging your header files' physical locations, etc.). Usually this is worth it though, because you can make your application modular and let different people focus only on their logical, functional areas.

The manual labor that you have to invest along the way is inversely proportional to the amount of time you spend designing modularity in the first place. Start with some of the good techniques for modularization, and your code base will scale.

If you don't already use namespaces, you've probably at least heard of them, and very likely you use one already: the std namespace, which is the namespace that contains the standard library. Namespaces are not used as frequently as they ought to be, in my experience, but that's not because they're complicated or using them requires much effort. Recipe 2.3 explains how to modularize code with namespaces.

Many of the recipes in this chapter describe techniques that you apply from within header files. Since there are a number of facilities discussed, each explaining a different part of a header file, I have included Example 2-1 in the introduction, which shows what a typical header file looks like that uses all of the techniques described in this chapter.

Example 2-1. A header file

```
#ifndef MYCLASS_H__  // #include guards, Recipe 2.0
#define MYCLASS_H__

#include <string>
```

Example 2-1. A header file (continued)

```
namespace mylib { // Namespaces, Recipe 2.3

    class AnotherClass; // forward class declarations, Recipe 2.2
    class Logger;

    extern Logger* gpLogger; // External storage declaration, Recipe 2.1

    class MyClass {
    public:
        std::string getVal( ) const;
        // ...
    private:
        static int refCount_;
        std::string val_;
    }

// Inline definitions, Recipe 2.4
inline std::string MyClass::getVal( ) const {
    return(val_);
}

#include "myclass.inl"

} // namespace

#endif // MYCLASS_H__
```

Once you have your header file written and out of the way, most of the time you will need an *implementation* file, too, by which I mean a *.cpp* file that contains definitions and not just declarations. There is less that goes in an implementation file than there is in a header file, but for the sake of completeness, Example 2-2 contains a sample implementation file that goes with the header file presented in Example 2-1.

Example 2-2. An implementation file

```
#include "myclass.h"

namespace mylib {

    MyClass::refCount_ = 0; // Static definition, Recipe 8.4

    MyClass::foo( ) { // Method implementations
        // ...
    }
}
```

Of course, your implementation files will no doubt be full of thoughtful, well-written comments, too, but I left that out for the sake of clarity.

2.1   Making Sure a Header File Gets Included Only Once

Problem

You have a header file that is included by several other files. You want to make sure the preprocessor scans the declarations in the header file no more than once.

Solution

#define a macro in your header file, and include *only* the contents of the header file if the macro hasn't already been defined. You can use this combination of the #ifndef, #define, and #endif preprocessor directives, as I did in Example 2-1:

```
#ifndef MYCLASS_H__ // #include guards
#define MYCLASS_H__

// Put everything here...

#endif // MYCLASS_H__
```

When the preprocessor scans this header file, one of the first things it will encounter is the #ifndef directive and the symbol that follows. #ifndef tells the preprocessor to continue processing on the next line only if the symbol MYCLASS_H__ is not already defined. If it is already defined, then the preprocessor should skip to the closing #endif. The line following #ifndef defines MYCLASS_H__, so if this file is scanned by the preprocessor twice in the same compilation, the second time MYCLASS_H__ is defined. By placing all of your code in between the #ifndef and #endif, you ensure that it is only read once during the compilation process.

Discussion

If you don't use this technique, which is called using *include guards*, you've probably already seen "symbol already defined" compilation errors that result from not taking a protective measure against multiple definitions. C++ does not allow you to define the same symbol more than once, and if you do (on purpose or by accident) you get a compilation error. Include guards prevent such errors, and they are pretty standard practice.

The macros you #define don't have to follow any particular format, but the syntax I used above is common. The idea is to use a symbol that won't conflict with another macro and cause your file to inadvertently be skipped during preprocessing. In practice, you may see other techniques, such as including a header file or module version in the macro, e.g., MYCLASS_H_V301__, or maybe even the author's name. It isn't that important how you name it, so long as you are consistent. These macros should only be referenced by the header file they are protecting, and nowhere else.

In some code you may see *external* include guards, which are the same as the *internal* include guards I described earlier, except that they appear in the file that is including the header file, not the header file itself:

```
#ifndef MYCLASS_H__
#include "myclass.h"
#endif
```

This short-circuits the inclusion process by not even including the file `myclassh.h` if the macro `MYCLASS_H__` is already defined. External include guards were advocated several years ago to improve compile times for large projects, but compilers have improved and they are no longer necessary. Don't use them.

Even if you are working on a small project, it's a good idea to put include guards in your header files. If your header file is included by more than one other file, chances are you're going to get redefinition errors someday. Furthermore, small projects tend to turn into larger projects in a short amount of time, and while a project may have started off with a single executable and a set of header files that are only ever included once, sooner or later the project will grow and compilation errors will start to appear. If you add include guards from the beginning, you won't have to go back and add them to a bunch of files all at once sometime in the future.

2.2   Ensuring You Have Only One Instance of a Variable Across Multiple Source Files

Problem

You need the same variable to be used by different modules in a program, and you can only have one copy of this variable. In other words, a *global* variable.

Solution

Declare and define the variable in a single implementation file in the usual manner, and use the extern keyword in other implementation files where you require access to that variable at runtime. Often, this means including the extern declarations in a header file that is used by all implementation files that need access to the global variable. Example 2-3 contains a few files that show how the extern keyword can be used to access variables defined in another implementation file.

Example 2-3. Using the extern keyword

```
// global.h
#ifndef GLOBAL_H__   // See Recipe 2.0
#define GLOBAL_H__

#include <string>
```

Example 2-3. Using the extern keyword (continued)

```
extern int x;
extern std::string s;

#endif

// global.cpp
#include <string>

int x = 7;
std::string s = "Kangaroo";

// main.cpp
#include <iostream>
#include "global.h"

using namespace std;

int main( ) {

   cout << "x = " << x << endl;
   cout << "s = " << s << endl;
}
```

Discussion

The extern keyword is a way of telling the compiler that the actual storage for a variable is allocated somewhere else. extern tells the linker that the variable it qualifies is somewhere in another object file, and that the linker needs to go find it when creating the final executable or library. If the linker never finds the extern variable you have declared, or it finds more than one of definition for it, you will get a link error.

Example 2-3 isn't terribly exciting, but it illustrates the point well. My two global variables are declared and defined in *global.cpp:*

```
int x = 7;
std::string s = "Kangaroo";
```

I need to be able to access them from other implementation files, so I put an extern declaration for them in the header file *global.h:*

```
extern int x;
extern std::string s;
```

The distinction between declaration and definition is important. In C++, you can declare something many times, so long as the declarations match, but you may only define something once; this is called the *one-definition rule* (you can actually define it more than once, in some cases, but only if the definitions are exactly the same—usually this is not a good idea). The extern keyword is a mechanism for telling the compiler and linker that the definition is somewhere else, to be resolved at link time.

This is not to say that using extern should be a regular practice. You should use it sparingly, and only when you have to, since it permits application-global variables. Sometimes you may need this for truly global objects or data—a logging object; a piece of hardware; a large, shared data object—but most of the time there are more appropriate design alternatives.

2.3 Reducing #includes with Forward Class Declarations

Problem

You have a header file that references classes in other headers, and you need to reduce compilation dependencies (and perhaps time).

Solution

Use forward class declarations where possible to avoid unnecessary compilation dependencies. Example 2-4 gives a short example of a forward class declaration.

Example 2-4. Forward class declaration

```
// myheader.h
#ifndef MYHEADER_H__
#define MYHEADER_H__

class A; // No need to include A's header

class B {
   public:
      void f(const A& a);
   // ...
   private:
      A* a_;
};

#endif
```

Somewhere else there is a header and perhaps an implementation file that declares and defines the class A, but from within *myheader.h* I don't care about the details of A: all I need to know is that A is a class.

Discussion

A forward class declaration is a way to ignore details that you don't need to be concerned with. In Example 2-4, *myheader.h* doesn't need to know anything about the class A except that it exists and that it's a class.

Consider what would happen if you #included the header file for A, or, more realistically, the header files for the half-dozen or so classes you would use in a real header file. Now an implementation file (*myheader.cpp*) includes this header, *myheader.h*, because it contains the declarations for everything. So far, so good. If you change one of the header files included by *myheader.h* (or one of the header files included by one of those files), then all of the implementation files that include *myheader.h* will need to be recompiled.

Forward declare your class and these compilation dependencies go away. Using a forward declaration simply creates a name to which everything else in the header file can refer. The linker has the happy task of matching up definitions in the implementation files that use your header.

Sadly, you can't always use forward declarations. The class B in Example 2-4 only uses pointers or references to A, so I can get away with a forward declaration. However, if I use an A member function or variable, or if I have an object of type A–and not just a pointer or reference to one—in my definition for the class B, suddenly my forward declaration is insufficient. This is because files including *myheader.h* need to know the size of B, and if A is a member variable of B, then the compiler needs to know A's size to figure out B's size. A pointer or a reference to something is always the same size, so in the case where you are using pointers or references, the details of A aren't of interest to the compiler and therefore A's header file isn't necessary.

Not surprisingly, if you include any definition in *myheader.h* that uses members of A, you have to #include A's header. This is because the compiler needs to check the function signature of the A member function or the data type of the A data member you are referencing. To illustrate, this code requires an #include:

```
#include "a.h"

class B {
    public:
        void f(const A& a) {
            foo_ = a.getVal(); // Have to know if a.getVal is valid
        }
    // ...
```

In general, use forward declarations when you can to reduce the amount of #includeing that goes on at compile time.

2.4   Preventing Name Collisions with Namespaces

Problem

You have names from unrelated modules that are clashing, or you want to avoid such clashes by creating logical groups of code in advance.

Solution

Use namespaces to modularize code. With namespaces, you can group large groups of code in separate files into a single namespace. You can nest namespaces as deeply as necessary to partition a large module into submodules, and consumers of your module can selectively expose the elements in your namespace they want to use. Example 2-5 shows a few of the ways you can use a namespace.

Example 2-5. Using namespaces

```
// Devices.h
#ifndef DEVICES_H__
#define DEVICES_H__

#include <string>
#include <list>

namespace hardware {

    class Device {
    public:
        Device() : uptime_(0), status_("unknown") {}
        unsigned long getUptime() const;
        std::string getStatus() const;
        void reset();
    private:
        unsigned long uptime_;
        std::string status_;
    };

    class DeviceMgr {
    public:
        void getDeviceIds(std::list<std::string>& ids) const;
        Device getDevice(const std::string& id) const;
        // Other stuff...
    };
}

#endif // DEVICES_H__

// Devices.cpp
#include "Devices.h"
#include <string>
#include <list>

namespace hardware {

    using std::string;
    using std::list;

    unsigned long Device::getUptime() const {
        return(uptime_);
    }
```

Example 2-5. Using namespaces (continued)

```
    string Device::getStatus() const {
        return(status_);
    }

    void DeviceMgr::getDeviceIds(list<string>& ids) const {
    }

    Device DeviceMgr::getDevice(const string& id) const {
        Device d;
        return(d);
    }
}

// DeviceWidget.h
#ifndef DEVICEWIDGET_H__
#define DEVICEWIDGET_H__

#include "Devices.h"

namespace ui {

    class Widget { /* ... */ };
    class DeviceWidget : public Widget {
    public:
        DeviceWidget(const hardware::Device& dev) : device_(dev) {}
        // Some other stuff
    protected:
        hardware::Device device_;
    };
}
#endif // DEVICEWIDGET_H__

// main.cpp
#include <iostream>
#include "DeviceWidget.h"
#include "Devices.h"

int main() {

    hardware::Device d;
    ui::DeviceWidget myWidget(d);
    // ...
}
```

Discussion

Example 2-5 is a bit complicated, but let's go through it piece by piece, because it illustrates several key points about namespaces. Imagine that you are writing an administrative application that needs to interface with a bunch of hardware devices. You might want to divide your application into two or more namespaces to prevent naming collisions, or just to divide logically the two parts of the application in a way that makes sense.

First, consider the file *Devices.h*. It contains a couple of classes that manage the hardware elements, `Device` and `DeviceMgr`. I don't want them in the global namespace though (meaning their names are visible everywhere else in the program), so I put them in the `hardware` namespace:

```
#ifndef DEVICES_H__  // See Recipe 2.0
#define DEVICES_H__

#include <string>
#include <list>

namespace hardware {

    class Device {
        // ...
    };

    class DeviceMgr {
        // ...
    };
}

#endif // DEVICES_H__
```

The mechanism is simple: wrap everything you want to put in your namespace in a namespace block.

The above excerpt is the declaration of `Device` and `DeviceMgr`, but we still have to think about the implementation, which is in *Devices.cpp*. Once again, wrap everything in a namespace block—it is added to what's already in that namespace:

```
#include "Devices.h"
#include <string>
#include <list>

namespace hardware {

    using std::string;
    using std::list;

    // Implementation for Device and DeviceMgr
}
```

At this point, the `hardware` namespace contains everything we need it to. All that's left is to use it from somewhere. There are a few ways to do this; the way I did it in Example 2-5 is to qualify fully the name to the `Device` class with the namespace name, like this:

```
#ifndef DEVICEWIDGET_H__
#define DEVICEWIDGET_H__
```

```
#include "Devices.h"

namespace ui {

    class Widget { /* ... */ };
    class DeviceWidget : public Widget {
    public:
        DeviceWidget(const hardware::Device& dev) : device_(dev) {}
        // Other stuff...
    protected:
        hardware::Device device_;
    };
}
#endif // DEVICEWIDGET_H__
```

I also did the same thing from main in *main.cpp*:

```
int main( ) {
    hardware::Device d;
    ui::DeviceWidget myWidget(d);
}
```

To add types to one of the namespaces, declare your header and implementation files in the same way as in Example 2-5. Each time you wrap code in a namespace block, it is added to that namespace, so you can have code that's in the same namespace that doesn't have to know anything about the other code in that namespace.

If you use the approach of qualifying class names with their namespace, you will quickly get tired of all the typing. There are a couple of ways to make this problem go away. You can create an alias for a namespace-qualified type with the using keyword:

```
using hardware::Device;

int main( ) {
    Device d;  // No namespace name needed
    ui::DeviceWidget myWidget(d);
}
```

In subsequent code, you can simply refer to the alias instead of the entire namespace name. Or, you can import everything in the namespace by using the namespace instead of one of the types it contains:

```
using namespace hardware;

int main( ) {
    Device d;
    ui::DeviceWidget myWidget(d);
}
```

You have probably already used this, or at least seen it in examples, when using the standard library (many of the examples in this book use this technique). Everything in the standard library is in the std namespace, so quite often, you will see this:

```
using namespace std;
```

Importing an entire namespace is often a bad idea, though, and is generally considered a bad practice. We have imported the std namespace in most of the examples in this book for clarity only, and, in general, recommend against doing so in real programs.

If you are importing an entire namespace, or several of them, the utility of namespaces decreases significantly. One of the reasons namespaces exist is to reduce naming collisions. If you import a bunch of different namespaces, then you increase the probability of naming conflicts. Your code may compile fine and run now, but someone, somewhere else, can add something to the namespace in the future and create a conflict the next time your code is rebuilt.

You can also nest namespaces to divide the contents of a namespace into smaller groups. For example, the hardware namespace I defined in Example 2-5 might actually contain a lot of network classes and more device classes, so I could partition the namespace by nesting some others with more descriptive names:

```
namespace hardware {
    namespace net {
        // network stuff
    }
    namespace devices {
        // device stuff
    }
}
```

Now, I can access elements contained in the namespace with a bit more qualification:

```
// In some other file...
using hardware::devices::Device;
```

Namespaces are handy. There are a few cool things that you can do with namespaces to make your life easier: namespace aliases, automatic name lookup in function parameter namespaces, and name matching for function overloads in using declarations. The last two are wordy, but simple.

A namespace alias is just what it sounds like: a (probably short) name that you can substitute for another (probably long) namespace name. If you don't want to use a using statement, but also don't want to type out a huge fully qualified name every time you use a class, you can create an alias for it:

```
using dev = hardware::devices;
// ...
dev::Device d;
```

You can then use the alias when referring to elements in that namespace.

C++ also provides automatic lookup in function parameter namespaces. So, for example, the following code qualifies its argument with a namespace (dev is the namespace that Device is declared in):

```
void f(dev::Device& d) {
    register(d);  // This is actually dev::register
}
```

When you pass in a function parameter that belongs to a namespace, the compiler includes that namespace when performing name lookup on functions within the body of the function. You may not need this every day, but it saves a lot of typing or an extra using directive when you do. The idea behind this is that functions that operate on some type are often defined in the same namespace as that type. Incidentally, it a good practice, in general, to put functions that operate on certain types in the same namespace as those types, when possible.

The last cool thing about namespaces is name matching for overloads in using declarations. Consider this example:

```
namespace mylib {
    void foo(int);
    void foo(double);
    void foo(std::string);
    // More overloads of foo()...
}

// In some other file...
using mylib::foo; // Which one does this use?
```

The using declaration matches all overloads of foo so you don't have to write one for each overload. The other benefit of this is that if an overload of foo is added, any code with a declaration such as using mylib::foo "sees" it automatically because the using declaration will pick it up (when the code containing the using declaration is compiled, of course).

You have to use namespaces wisely, though, or you may get some unexpected compilation errors or create them for others who use your code. Here are a few popular guidelines when using namespaces:

Use using namespace *xxx sparingly*
> As I explained earlier, importing an entire namespace increases the probability of a name collision, either right now or in the future (someone may add to the namespace you are using, creating a conflict in your code). It also dilutes the modularity provided by namespaces.

Don't use using *statements in header files*
> Header files are included by lots of other files, so if you use a namespace or something in a namespace in a header file, you expose what you are using to the

file that is including your header file. The solution to this problem is to qualify fully everything you need in a header file.

Don't put using *declarations or definitions before* #include *directives*
If you do this, then you expose whatever you're using to the code in the header file, which is probably not what the author of the header file intended.

If you obey these guidelines, using namespaces in a new project or adding them to an existing project should be relatively easy.

2.5   Including an Inline File

Problem

You have a number of member functions or standalone functions that you want to make inline, but you don't want to define them all in the class definition (or even after it) in the header file. This way, you keep declaration and implementation separate.

Solution

Create an *.inl* file and #include it at the end of your header file. This is equivalent to putting the function definition at the end of the header file, but this lets you keep declaration and definition separate. Example 2-6 shows how.

Example 2-6. Using an inline file

```
// Value.h
#ifndef VALUE_H__
#define VALUE_H__

#include <string>

class Value {
public:
   Value (const std::string& val) : val_(val) {}
   std::string getVal() const;
private:
   std::string val_;
};

#include "Value.inl"

#endif VALUE_H__

// Value.inl
inline std::string Value::getVal() const {
   return(val_);
}
```

This solution doesn't require much explanation. #include is replaced with the contents of its argument, so what happens here is that the contents of *Value.inl* are brought into the header file. Any file that includes this header, therefore, has the definition of the inline functions, but you don't have to clutter up your class declaration.

## CHAPTER 3

Numbers

3.0   Introduction

Even if you aren't writing scientific or engineering applications, you will usually have to work with numbers to some degree. This chapter contains solutions to common problems when working with C++'s numeric types.

Several of the recipes contain techniques for converting numbers of various formats (hexadecimal, floating-point, or scientific notation) from numeric types to strings or vice versa. Writing code to make this transformation yourself is cumbersome and tedious, so I present facilities from the standard library or one of the Boost libraries to make the task easier. There are also a few recipes for dealing with only the numeric types: safely converting between them, comparing floating-point numbers within a bounded range, and finding the minimum and maximum values for numeric types.

The recipes in this chapter provide solutions to some general problems you may run into when working with numbers in C++, but it does not attempt to solve problems that are specific to application domains. If you are writing scientific or engineering applications, you should also take a look at Chapter 11, which contains recipes for many common scientific and numerical algorithms.

3.1   Converting a String to a Numeric Type

Problem

You have numbers in string format, but you need to convert them to a numeric type, such as an int or float.

Solution

You can do this in one of two ways, with standard library functions or with the lexical_cast class in Boost (written by Kevlin Henney). The standard library functions are cumbersome and unsafe, but they are standard, and in some cases, you need them, so I present them as the first solution. lexical_cast is safer, easier to use, and just more fun, so I present it in the discussion.

The functions strtol, strtod, and strtoul, defined in <cstdlib>, convert a null-terminated character string to a long int, double, or unsigned long. You can use them to convert numeric strings of any base to a numeric type. The code in Example 3-1 demonstrates a function, hex2int, that you can use for converting a hexadecimal string to a long.

Example 3-1. Converting number strings to numbers

```
#include <iostream>
#include <string>
#include <cstdlib>

using namespace std;

long hex2int(const string& hexStr) {
    char *offset;
    if (hexStr.length() > 2) {
        if (hexStr[0] == '0' && hexStr[1] == 'x') {
            return strtol(hexStr.c_str(), &offset, 0);
        }
    }
    return strtol(hexStr.c_str(), &offset, 16);
}

int main() {
    string str1 = "0x12AB";
    cout << hex2int(str1) << endl;
    string str2 = "12AB";
    cout << hex2int(str2) << endl;
    string str3 = "QAFG";
    cout << hex2int(str3) << endl;
}
```

Here's the output from this program:

```
4779
4779
0
```

The first two strings both contain the hexadecimal number 12AB. The first of the two has the 0x prefix, while the second doesn't. The third string doesn't contain a valid hexadecimal number; the function simply returns 0 in that case.

Discussion

Some people might be inclined to write their own function that converts hexadecimal numbers to integers. But why reinvent the wheel? The standard library already provides this functionality. Example 3-1 provides a wrapper function to simplify the calling of strtol. The strtol function is actually an older function from the C library, and it requires you to pass in a pointer to a null-terminated string, along with the address of another character pointer; this latter pointer receives the address of where the parsing ended. In C++, however, most people prefer to work with the more powerful string class rather than the older-style character pointers. Thus, this hex2int function takes a string parameter.

The strtol function is a bit odd in that it allows you to use two different methods for specifying a base of 16; you can either pass 16 as a third parameter to the function; or, you can pass 0 for the base while preceding your string with the characters 0x (just as you would do for specifying hexadecimal constants in your code; however, remember that with strtol, you're passing a string).

Example 3-1 allows you to use either method. If you pass a string such as 0x12AB, the function will detect the 0x and pass it right on to strtol, with 0 for the third parameter. Otherwise, the function will pass the string with 16 for the third parameter.

strtol and strtoul work the same way; the only difference is the return type. strtod is similar, but does not allow you to specify a base.

These old-school C functions aren't the only way to convert strings to numbers. The Boost project provides a conversion class lexical_cast that does the same thing for numeric strings of base 10. Example 3-2 shows how to use it.

Example 3-2. Using lexical_cast

```
#include <iostream>
#include <string>
#include <boost/lexical_cast.hpp>

using namespace std;

int main( ) {
    string str1 = "750";
    string str2 = "2.71";
    string str3 = "0x7FFF";
    try {
        cout << boost::lexical_cast<int>(str1) << endl;
        cout << boost::lexical_cast<double>(str2) << endl;
        cout << boost::lexical_cast<int>(str3) << endl;
    }
    catch (boost::bad_lexical_cast& e) {
        cerr << "Bad cast: " << e.what( ) << endl;
    }
}
```

The output from Example 3-2 is:

```
750
2.71
Bad cast: bad lexical cast: source type value could not be
interpreted as target
```

You can see that it throws an exception for the last value, which is a hexadecimal number. If you have to convert numbers of a base other than 10, you will have to use the strtol functions.

There are versions of the strtol functions for wide characters, too. The wide character equivalent to strtol is wcstol and it is declared in <cwchar>. The equivalent functions for strtod and strtoul are wcstod and wcstoul. Each of these functions the same way, except that the parameters that are char*'s in the narrow character functions are wchar_t*'s in the wide character functions.

See Also

Recipe 3.2

3.2   Converting Numbers to Strings

Problem

You have numeric types (int, float) and you need to put the results in a string, perhaps formatted a certain way.

Solution

There are a number of different ways to do this, all with benefits and drawbacks. The first technique I will present uses a stringstream class to store the string data, because it is part of the standard library and easy to use. This approach is presented in Example 3-3. See the discussion for alternative techniques.

Example 3-3. Formatting a number as a string

```
#include <iostream>
#include <iomanip>
#include <string>
#include <sstream>

using namespace std;

int main( ) {

   stringstream ss;

   ss << "There are " << 9 << " apples in my cart.";
   cout << ss.str( ) << endl;  // stringstream::str( ) returns a string
                               // with the contents

   ss.str("");                 // Empty the string
   ss << showbase << hex << 16;  // Show the base in hexadecimal
   cout << "ss = " << ss.str( ) << endl;
```

Example 3-3. Formatting a number as a string (continued)

```
    ss.str("");
    ss << 3.14;
    cout << "ss = " << ss.str() << endl;
}
```

The output of Example 3-3 looks like this:

```
    There are 9 apples in my cart.
    ss = 0x10
    ss = 3.14
```

Discussion

A stringstream is a convenient way to put data into a string because it lets you use all of the formatting facilities provided by the standard input and output stream classes. In the simplest case in Example 3-3, I just use the left-shift operator (<<) to write a combination of text and numeric data to my string stream:

```
    ss << "There are " << 9 << " apples in my cart.";
```

The << operator is overloaded for built-in types to format the input accordingly. When you want to get the string that holds your data, use the str member function:

```
    cout << ss.str() << endl;
```

There are lots of stream manipulators in <iomanip>, and you can use them to do all sorts of formatting of your numeric data as you put it in the string. I used showbase and hex to format my number as hexadecimal in Example 3-3, but there are lots more. For example, you can set the precision to display more than the default number of digits:

```
    ss << setprecision(6) << 3.14285;
```

Using manipulators isn't the most intuitive thing though, which is why there is a Recipe on the subject. See Recipe 10.2 for more detailed information about formatting numeric data with stream manipulators.

Of course, as is often the case with C++, there is another way. The Boost Format library (written by Samuel Krempp) contains a format class that makes formatting and conversion extremely easy. Example 3-4 shows you how to do such a conversion.

Example 3-4. Formatting integers as hexadecimal

```
#include <iostream>
#include <boost/format.hpp>

using namespace std;
using boost::format;
using boost::io::str;
using boost::io::format_error;

int main() {
```

Example 3-4. Formatting integers as hexadecimal (continued)

```
try {
    format f("There are %1% ways %2% %3% %4%");

    f % 3;
    f % "to" % "do" % "this.";

    cout << f << endl;

    f.clear(); // Clear buffers to format something else

    f.parse("Those cost $%d.");
    f % 50;

    cout << f << endl;

    int x = 11256099;

    string strx = str(format("%x") % x);
    cout << strx << endl;
}
catch (format_error &e) {
    cout << e.what() << endl;
}
}
```

Here's what you see when you run this program:

```
There are 3 ways to do this.
Those cost $50.
abc123
```

Using a format class involves two steps, creating the format object and then sending it the content. To use the trivial case from Example 3-4, I create the format object using the simplest version of its syntax:

```
format f("There are %1% ways %2% %3% %4%");
```

In the format string, the placeholders are numbers with a % on either side. Then I start sending it the content for the format I provided:

```
f % 3;
f % "to" % "do" % "this.";
```

The % operator has been overridden in the formatting library to add the variables you give it to the format object to its left. You can use it once per line or call it several times in a row. It is analogous to the << operator for streams. Speaking of the << operator, it has also been overridden so you can write format objects directly to an output stream. Alternatively, if you need to put the results in a string, use the str member function:

```
string s = f.str();
```

If you are a `printf` person, you can use `printf` format specifiers:

```
f.parse("Those cost $%d.");
f % 50;
```

If you feed too many or too few content variables to format and try to write it to a stream or extract a formatted string, it will throw a `format_error` (or a subclass thereof) exception.

The `format` class is quite powerful, and it has too many neat formatting capabilities to list here, but it's worth checking out. See Boost's web site at *www.boost.org* to download Boost or to read the documentation.

You can also convert numbers from numeric types to strings using `sprintf` or the related functions. Typically, you should avoid this because it is unsafe and there are better alternatives.

See Also

Chapter 10

3.3   Testing Whether a String Contains a Valid Number

Problem

You have a `string` and you need to find out if it contains a valid number.

Solution

You can use the Boost `lexical_cast` function template to test for a valid number. Using this approach, a valid number can include a preceding minus sign, or a preceding plus sign, but not whitespace. I give a few examples of the kinds of formats that work with `lexical_cast` in Example 3-5.

Example 3-5. Validating a string number

```
#include <iostream>
#include <boost/lexical_cast.hpp>

using namespace std;
using boost::lexical_cast;
using boost::bad_lexical_cast;

template<typename T>
bool isValid(const string& num) {

    bool res = true;
```

Example 3-5. Validating a string number (continued)

```
    try {
        T tmp = lexical_cast<T>(num);
    }
    catch (bad_lexical_cast &e) {
        res = false;
    }

    return(res);
}

void test(const string& s) {

    if (isValid<int>(s))
        cout << s << " is a valid integer." << endl;
    else
        cout << s << " is NOT a valid integer." << endl;

    if (isValid<double>(s))
        cout << s << " is a valid double." << endl;
    else
        cout << s << " is NOT a valid double." << endl;

    if (isValid<float>(s))
        cout << s << " is a valid float." << endl;
    else
        cout << s << " is NOT a valid float." << endl;
}

int main( ) {

    test("12345");
    test("1.23456");
    test("-1.23456");
    test(" - 1.23456");
    test("+1.23456");
    test("  1.23456  ");
    test("asdf");
}
```

Here's the output from this example:

```
    12345 is a valid integer.
    12345 is a valid double.
    12345 is a valid float.
    1.23456 is NOT a valid integer.
    1.23456 is a valid double.
    1.23456 is a valid float.
    -1.23456 is NOT a valid integer.
    -1.23456 is a valid double.
    -1.23456 is a valid float.
     - 1.23456 is NOT a valid integer.
     - 1.23456 is NOT a valid double.
     - 1.23456 is NOT a valid float.
```

```
+1.23456 is NOT a valid integer.
+1.23456 is a valid double.
+1.23456 is a valid float.
   1.23456   is NOT a valid integer.
   1.23456   is NOT a valid double.
   1.23456   is NOT a valid float.
asdf is NOT a valid integer.
asdf is NOT a valid double.
asdf is NOT a valid float.
```

Discussion

The lexical_cast function template converts a value from one type to another. It is declared like this:

```
template<typename Target, typename Source>
Target lexical_cast(Source arg)
```

Source is the type of the original variable, and Target is the type of the variable being converted to. So, for example, if you want to convert from a string to an int, you invoke lexical_cast like this:

```
int i = lexical_cast<int>(str); // str is a string
```

lexical_cast does the parsing and attempts the conversion. If the conversion is not possible, it throws a bad_lexical_cast exception. In Example 3-5, I only want to test for validity and don't need to keep the destination variable around, so I return true if no exception is thrown, false otherwise.

You only have to supply the first template argument to lexical_cast because it's a function template, which means the compiler can deduce the type of the function argument and use that as the second template argument. Explaining this distinction is more confusing than illustrating it, so let me use a code example. Instead of invoking lexical_cast as in the previous code snippet, you could do this:

```
int i = lexical_cast<int, string>(str);
```

This means the same thing, but you don't have to supply the string argument because the compiler can see that str is a string and figure out the rest.

If you are going to write a similar wrapper function to test for validity and return true or false, you would do well to write it as a function template. This way, you only have to write it once with a parameterized type, and a different version will be instantiated each time you use it on a different type.

lexical_cast is also handy for converting from one numeric type to another; I discuss more about that in Recipe 3.6.

See Also

Recipe 3.6

3.4   Comparing Floating-Point Numbers with Bounded Accuracy

Problem

You need to compare floating-point values, but you only want tests for equality, greater-than, or less-than to be concerned with a limited number of digits. For example, you want 3.33333 and 3.33333333 to show as being equal when comparing to a precision of .0001.

Solution

Write your own comparison functions that take a parameter that bounds the accuracy of the comparison. Example 3-6 shows the basic technique for such comparison functions.

Example 3-6. Comparing floating-point numbers

```cpp
#include <iostream>
#include <cmath>     // for fabs()

using namespace std;

bool doubleEquals(double left, double right, double epsilon) {
   return (fabs(left - right) < epsilon);
}

bool doubleLess(double left, double right, double epsilon,
               bool orequal = false) {
   if (fabs(left - right) < epsilon) {
      // Within epsilon, so considered equal
      return (orequal);
   }
   return (left < right);
}

bool doubleGreater(double left, double right, double epsilon,
                  bool orequal = false) {
   if (fabs(left - right) < epsilon) {
      // Within epsilon, so considered equal
      return (orequal);
   }
   return (left > right);
}

int main() {

   double first = 0.33333333;
   double second = 1.0 / 3.0;
```

Example 3-6. Comparing floating-point numbers (continued)

```
    cout << first << endl;
    cout << second << endl;

    // Straight equalify test. Fails when you wouldn't want it to.
    // (boolalpha prints booleans as "true" or "false")
    cout << boolalpha << (first == second) << endl;
    // New equality. Passes as scientific app probably wants.
    cout << doubleEquals(first, second, .0001) << endl;
    // New less-than
    cout << doubleLess(first, second, .0001) << endl;
    // New Greater-than
    cout << doubleGreater(first, second, .0001) << endl;
    // New less-than-or-equal-to
    cout << doubleLess(first, second, .0001, true) << endl;
    // New greater-than-or-equal-to
    cout << doubleGreater(first, second, .0001, true) << endl;
}
```

Following is the output from this example:

```
    0.333333
    0.333333
    false
    true
    false
    false
    true
    true
```

Discussion

The code in Example 3-6 starts with two values, 0.33333333 and whatever the computer figures 1.0 / 3.0 to be. It prints out the two values using the default formatting in cout; these two values appear to be the same at 0.333333. However, when you compare these two values, they are indeed different. The value of 1.0 / 3.0 has more significant digits than 0.33333333, and therefore, as far as your machine is concerned, the two numbers are not equal. In some applications, however, you may want these two numbers to show up as being the same.

The way to handle this is to write three of your own functions for comparing double values: doubleLess, doubleEquals, and doubleGreater, each of which takes two double values as parameters. Additionally, the doubleLess and doubleGreater take an additional parameter, which, when true, causes the functions to behave as *less-than-or-equal* or *greater-than-or-equal*, respectively.

To make these functions handle a precision, first consider the doubleEquals function. Instead of testing for equality, this function tests whether the difference between the two numbers is within a user-specified epsilon. (The example uses .0001 for the epsilon.) If so, then the function returns true, meaning the values are indeed the same.

Thus, the values 0.3333, 0.33333, 0.333333, 0.33333333333, and 0.33333323438 would all show up as being equal.

To handle a *less-than* and *greater-than* operation, first test whether the numbers are equal within the range, as you did in the doubleEquals function. If so, then return true if you want to include equality in the test, and false if you don't. Otherwise, do a straight comparison.

3.5 Parsing a String Containing a Number in Scientific Notation

Problem

You have a string containing a number in scientific notation, and you want to store the number's value in a double variable.

Solution

The most direct way to parse a scientific notation number is by using the C++ library's built-in stringstream class declared in <sstream>, as you can see in Example 3-7.

Example 3-7. Parsing a number in scientific notation

```
#include <iostream>
#include <sstream>
#include <string>

using namespace std;

double sciToDub(const string& str) {

   stringstream ss(str);
   double d = 0;
   ss >> d;

   if (ss.fail()) {
      string s = "Unable to format ";
      s += str;
      s += " as a number!";
      throw (s);
   }

   return (d);
}

int main() {

   try {
      cout << sciToDub("1.234e5") << endl;
      cout << sciToDub("6.02e-2") << endl;
```

Example 3-7. Parsing a number in scientific notation (continued)

```
      cout << sciToDub("asdf") << endl;
   }
   catch (string& e) {
      cerr << "Whoops: " << e << endl;
   }
}
```

Following is the output from this code:

```
123400
0.0602
Whoops: Unable to format asdf as a number!
```

Discussion

The stringstream class is, not surprisingly, a string that behaves like a stream. It is declared in <sstring>. If you need to parse a string that contains a number in scientific notation (see also Recipe 3.2), a stringstream will do the job nicely. The standard stream classes already "know" how to parse numbers, so don't waste your time reimplementing this logic if you don't have to.

In Example 3-7, I wrote the simple function sciToDub that takes a string parameter and returns the double it contains, if it is valid. Within sciToDub, I use the stringstream as follows:

```
   stringstream ss(str); // Construct from a string
   double d = 0;
   ss >> d;

   if (ss.fail()) {
      string s = "Unable to format ";
      s += str;
      s += " as a number!";
      throw (s);
   }
   return (d);
```

The most important part here is that all you have to do is use the right-shift operator (>>) to read from the string stream into a double, just as you would read from cin.

Well, that's not *all* you have to do. If there's a value in the stringstream that can't be written to the variable on the right side of the >> operator, the fail bit is set on the stream. You can check this bit using the fail member function (this is actually a member function of basic_ios, which is a superclass of stringstream). Additionally, the variable on the righthand side of the >> operator is unchanged if the operation fails.

In the interest of being generic, however, you can avoid having to write separate versions of sciToDub for ints, floats, doubles, and whatever else you want to convert to by writing a function template. Consider this new version:

```
template<typename T>
T strToNum(const string& str) {
    stringstream ss(str);
    T tmp;
    ss >> tmp;

    if (ss.fail()) {
        string s = "Unable to format ";
        s += str;
        s += " as a number!";
        throw (s);
    }

    return (tmp);
}
```

Now, if you want to convert a string to a numeric type, you can do it like this:

```
double d = strToNum<double>("7.0");
float f = strToNum<float>("7.0");
int i = strToNum<int>("7.0");
```

You can also make the type of character a template parameter, but that's straightforward to do, so I'll leave it as an exercise for you.

See Also

Recipe 3.2

3.6 Converting Between Numeric Types

Problem

You have number of one type and you need to convert it to another, such as an int to a short or a vice versa, but you want to catch any overflow or underflow errors at runtime.

Solution

Use Boost's numeric_cast class template. It performs runtime checks that throw an exception of type bad_numeric_cast if you will overflow or underflow the variable where you are putting a value. Example 3-8 shows you how to do this.

Example 3-8. Safe numeric conversions

```
#include <iostream>
#include <boost/cast.hpp>
```

Example 3-8. Safe numeric conversions (continued)

```cpp
using namespace std;
using boost::numeric_cast;
using boost::bad_numeric_cast;

int main( ) {

    // Integer sizes
    try {
        int i = 32767;
        short s = numeric_cast<short>(i);

        cout << "s = " << s << endl;

        i++; // Now i is out of range (if sizeof(short) is 2)
        s = numeric_cast<short>(i);
    }
    catch (bad_numeric_cast& e) {
        cerr << e.what( ) << endl;
    }

    try {
        int i = 300;
        unsigned int ui = numeric_cast<unsigned int>(i);

        cout << ui << endl; // Fine

        i *= -1;
        ui = numeric_cast<unsigned int>(i); // i is negative!
    }
    catch (bad_numeric_cast& e) {
        cerr << e.what( ) << endl;
    }

    try {
        double d = 3.14;
        int i = numeric_cast<int>(d);

        i = numeric_cast<int>(d); // This shaves off the 0.14!

        cout << i << endl;   // i = 3

    }
    catch (bad_numeric_cast& e) {
        cerr << e.what( ) << endl;
    }
}
```

Discussion

You are probably aware of the fact that the basic C++ types have different sizes. The C++ standard has strict specifications for the relative size of types—an int is always at least as big as a short int–but it does not specify the absolute size. What this means is that if you take a long int and try to put it in a short, or attempt to put an int in an unsigned int, then you may be losing information about the value in the source variable, such as its sign or even part of its numeric value.

Just knowing that this causes problems isn't enough. You may have tight space requirements and not want to use four bytes for a long when you can get away with two for a short (if your platform, in fact, uses these sizes, which are common but not guaranteed). Because of your space requirements, you want to try to store values in the smallest possible type. If you want to live dangerously but want a safety net, use Boost's numeric_cast to catch loss of data at runtime.

The syntax of numeric_cast is straightforward. It is a function template, declared like this:

```
template<typename Target, typename Source>
inline Target numeric_cast(Source arg)
```

It is just like lexical_cast if you have already read Recipes 3.1 or 3.3. There are two template parameters, Target and Source, which represent the types of the originating and destination values. Because it is a function template, the compiler can deduce the type of the Source template argument, so you only need to supply Target, like this:

```
int i = 32767;
short s = numeric_cast<short>(i);
```

short is the template argument for the Target parameter. The compiler figures out that Source is an int because i is an int.

In this case, I am cramming an int into a short. On my (Windows XP) system, an int is four bytes and a short is two. A short is signed, which means that I have 15 bits to represent a number with and, therefore, 32,767 is the maximum positive value it can hold. The above piece of code goes off without a hitch, but when I increment i by one, it goes beyond the range of a short:

```
i++;
s = numeric_cast<short>(i); // Uh-oh
```

And a bad_numeric_cast exception is thrown—you get the idea. See the rest of Example 3-8: numeric_cast also catches underflow if you try to assign a negative signed value to an unsigned type.

But numeric_cast doesn't solve all of your problems. If you try to put a floating-point value in a nonfloating-point type, you lose everything to the right of the decimal, correct? numeric_cast does not help you with this, so don't think that it can rescue you from all of your risky endeavors. For example, consider this piece of code from Example 3-8:

```
double d = 3.14;
int i = numeric_cast<int>(d);  // Ouch
```

No exception is thrown here. But it is if you try this:

```
double d = -3.14;
unsigned int ui = numeric_cast<unsigned in>(d);
```

Because regardless of you tossing everything to the right of the decimal point out the window, you are losing the negative sign, and that is bad.

See Also

Recipes 3.1 and 3.3

3.7   Getting the Minimum and Maximum Values for a Numeric Type

Problem

You need to know the largest or smallest representable value for your platform for a numeric type, such as an `int` or `double`.

Solution

Use the `numeric_limits` class template in the `<limits>` header to get, among other things, the largest and smallest possible values for a numeric type (see Example 3-9).

Example 3-9. Getting numeric limits

```
#include <iostream>
#include <limits>

using namespace std;

template<typename T>
void showMinMax() {
   cout << "min: " << numeric_limits<T>::min() << endl;
   cout << "max: " << numeric_limits<T>::max() << endl;
   cout << endl;
}

int main() {

   cout << "short:" << endl;
   showMinMax<short>();
   cout << "int:" << endl;
   showMinMax<int>();
   cout << "long:" << endl;
   showMinMax<long>();
   cout << "float:" << endl;
   showMinMax<float>();
   cout << "double:" << endl;
   showMinMax<double>();
```

Example 3-9. Getting numeric limits (continued)

```
    cout << "long double:" << endl;
    showMinMax<long double>( );
    cout << "unsigned short:" << endl;
    showMinMax<unsigned short>( );
    cout << "unsigned int:" << endl;
    showMinMax<unsigned int>( );
    cout << "unsigned long:" << endl;
    showMinMax<unsigned long>( );
}
```

Here's what I get on Windows XP using Visual C++ 7.1:

```
    short:
    min: -32768
    max: 32767

    int:
    min: -2147483648
    max: 2147483647

    long:
    min: -2147483648
    max: 2147483647

    float:
    min: 1.17549e-038
    max: 3.40282e+038

    double:
    min: 2.22507e-308
    max: 1.79769e+308

    long double:
    min: 2.22507e-308
    max: 1.79769e+308

    unsigned short:
    min: 0
    max: 65535

    unsigned int:
    min: 0
    max: 4294967295

    unsigned long:
    min: 0
    max: 4294967295
```

Discussion

Example 3-9 shows a simple example for getting the minimum and maximum values for native numeric types. The `numeric_limits` class template has a specialization for all of the built-in types, including both numeric and nonnumeric. The standard mandates that all of the types I use in Example 3-9 have a specialization of `numeric_limits`, as well as these:

```
bool
char
signed char
unsigned char
wchar_t
```

`min` and `max` are `static` member functions in `numeric_limits` that return the highest and lowest values for the type parameter you pass in.

## CHAPTER 4

Strings and Text

4.0   Introduction

This chapter contains recipes for working with strings and text files. Most C++ programs, regardless of their application, manipulate strings and text files to some degree. Despite the variety of applications, however, the requirements are often the same—for strings: trimming, padding, searching, splitting, and so on; for text files: wrapping, reformatting, reading delimited files, and more. The recipes that follow provide solutions to many of these common needs that do not have ready-made solutions in the C++ standard library.

The standard library is portable, standardized, and, in general, at least as efficient as homemade solutions, so in the following examples I have preferred it over code from scratch. It contains a rich framework for manipulating and managing strings and text, much of which is in the form of the class templates basic_string (for strings), basic_istream, and basic_ostream (for input and output text streams). Almost all of the techniques in this chapter use or extend these class templates. In cases where they didn't have what I wanted, I turned to another area of the standard library that is full of generic, prebuilt solutions: algorithms and containers.

Everybody uses strings, so chances are that if what you need isn't in the standard library, someone has written it. The Boost String Algorithms library, written by Pavol Droba, fills many of the gaps in the standard library by implementing most of the algorithms that you've had to use at one time or another, and it does it in a portable, efficient way. Check out the Boost project at *www.boost.org* for more information and documentation of the String Algorithms library. There is some overlap between the String Algorithms library and the solutions I present in this chapter. In most cases, I provide examples of or at least mention Boost algorithms that are related to the solutions presented.

For most examples, I have provided both a nontemplate and a template version. I did this for two reasons. First, most of the areas of the standard library that use character data are class or function templates that are parameterized on the type of character, narrow (char) or wide (wchar_t). By following this model, you will help maximize the compatibility of your software with the standard library. Second, whether you are working with the standard library or not, class and function templates provide an excellent facility for writing generic software. If you do not need templates, however, you can use the nontemplate versions, though I recommend experimenting with templates if you are new to them.

The standard library makes heavy use of templates and uses typedefs to insulate programmers from some of the verbose syntax that templates use. As a result, I use the terms basic_string, string, and wstring interchangeably, since what applies to one usually applies to them all. string and wstring are just typedefs for basic_string<char> and basic_string<wchar_t>.

Finally, you will probably notice that none of the recipes in this chapter use C-style strings, i.e., null-terminated character arrays. The standard library provides such a wealth of efficient and extensible support for C++ strings that to use C-style string functions (which were provided primarily for backward-compatibility anyway) is to forego the flexibility, safety, and generic nature of what you get for free with your compiler: C++ string classes.

4.1 Padding a String

Problem

You need to "pad," or fill, a string with a number of occurrences of some character to a certain width. For example, you may want to pad the string "Chapter 1" to 20 characters wide with periods, so that it looks like "Chapter 1...........".

Solution

Use string's insert and append member functions to pad a string with characters on the beginning or end. For example, to pad the end of a string to 20 characters with X's:

```
std::string s = "foo";
s.append(20 - s.length(), 'X');
```

To pad the string at the beginning instead:

```
s.insert(s.begin(), 20 - s.length(), 'X');
```

Discussion

The difference in usage between the two functions is insert's first parameter. It is an iterator that points to the character immediately to the right of where the insert should occur. The begin member function returns an iterator pointing to the first element in the string, so in the example, the series of characters is inserted to the left of that. The parameters common to both functions are the number of times to repeat the character and the character itself.

insert and append are actually member functions of the basic_string class template in the <string> header (string is a typedef for basic_string<char> and wstring is a typedef for basic_string<wchar_t>), so they work for strings of narrow or wide characters. Using them as needed, as in the above example, will work fine, but if you are using basic_string member functions from within your own generic utility functions, you should build on the standard library's existing generic design and use a function template. Consider the code in Example 4-1, which defines a generic pad function template that operates on basic_strings.

Example 4-1. A generic pad function template

```
#include <string>
#include <iostream>

using namespace std;

// The generic approach
template<typename T>
void pad(basic_string<T>& s,
         typename basic_string<T>::size_type n, T c) {
    if (n > s.length())
        s.append(n - s.length(), c);
}

int main() {

    string  s  = "Appendix A";
    wstring ws = L"Acknowledgments"; // The "L" indicates that
                                     // this is a wide char
    pad(s, 20, '*');                 // literal
    pad(ws, 20, L'*');

    // cout  << s  << std::endl;  // You shouldn't be able to
    wcout << ws << std::endl;     // run these at the same time
}
```

pad in Example 4-1 pads the given string s up to some width n, with the character c. Since the function template uses a parameterized type for the elements of the string (T), it will work on a basic_string of any kind of character: char, wchar_t, or other custom characters.

4.2   Trimming a String

Problem

You need to trim some number of characters from the end(s) of a string, usually whitespace.

Solution

Use iterators to identify the portion of the string you want to remove, and the erase member function to remove it. Example 4-2 presents the function `rtrim` that trims a character from the end of a string.

Example 4-2. Trimming characters from a string

```
#include <string>
#include <iostream>

// The approach for narrow character strings
void rtrim(std::string& s, char c) {

    if (s.empty())
        return;

    std::string::iterator p;
    for (p = s.end(); p != s.begin() && *--p == c;);

    if (*p != c)
        p++;

    s.erase(p, s.end());
}

int main()
{
    std::string s = "zoo";

    rtrim(s, 'o');

    std::cout << s << '\n';
}
```

Discussion

Example 4-2 will do the trick for strings of chars, but it *only* works for char strings. Just like you saw in Example 4-1, you can take advantage of the generic design of `basic_string` and use a function template instead. Example 4-3 uses a function template to trim characters from the end of any kind of character string.

Example 4-3. A generic version of rtrim

```cpp
#include <string>
#include <iostream>

using namespace std;

// The generic approach for trimming single
// characters from a string
template<typename T>
void rtrim(basic_string<T>& s, T c)
{
   if (s.empty())
      return;

   typename basic_string<T>::iterator p;
   for (p = s.end(); p != s.begin() && *--p == c;);

   if (*p != c)
      p++;

   s.erase(p, s.end());
}

int main() {

   string s = "Great!!!!";
   wstring ws = L"Super!!!!";

   rtrim(s, '!');
   rtrim(ws, L'!');

   cout << s << '\n';
   wcout << ws << L'\n';
}
```

This function works exactly the same way as the previous, nongeneric, version in Example 4-2, but since it is parameterized on the type of character being used, it will work for basic_strings of any kind.

Examples 4-2 and 4-3 remove sequences of a single character from a string. Trimming whitespace is different, however, because whitespace can be one of several characters. Conveniently, the standard library provides a concise way to do this: the isspace function in the <cctype> header (and its wchar_t equivalent, iswspace, in <cwctype>). Example 4-4 defines a generic function that trims trailing whitespace.

Example 4-4. Trim trailing whitespace

```cpp
#include <string>
#include <iostream>
#include <cctype>
#include <cwctype>
```

Example 4-4. Trim trailing whitespace (continued)

```
using namespace std;

template<typename T, typename F>
void rtrimws(basic_string<T>& s, F f) {

    if (s.empty())
        return;

    typename basic_string<T>::iterator p;
    for (p = s.end(); p != s.begin() && f(*--p););

    if (!f(*p))
        p++;

    s.erase(p, s.end());
}

// Overloads to make cleaner calling for client code
void rtrimws(string& s) {
    rtrimws(s, isspace);
}

void rtrimws(wstring& ws) {
    rtrimws(ws, iswspace);
}

int main() {

    string s = "zing          ";
    wstring ws = L"zong         ";

    rtrimws(s);
    rtrimws(ws);

    cout << s << "|\n";
    wcout << ws << L"|\n";
}
```

The function template in Example 4-4, `rtrimws`, is a generic function template, similar to the previous examples, that accepts a `basic_string` and trims whitespace from
the end of it. But unlike the other examples, it takes a function object, and not a
character, that is used to test an element of the string to determine whether it should
be removed.

You don't need to overload `rtrimws` as I did in the example, but it makes the syntax
cleaner when using the function, since the calling code can omit the predicate function argument when using them.

But alas, this solution requires that you write the code yourself. If you would rather
use a library—and a good one at that—Boost's String Algorithms library supplies
lots of functions for trimming strings, and chances are that what you need is already

there. In fact, there are lots of handy trimming functions in the String Algorithms library, so if you can use Boost you should take a look. Table 4-1 lists the function templates in the library that you can use for trimming strings, including some miscellaneous functions. Since these are function templates, they have template parameters that represent the different types used. Here is what each of them mean:

Seq
> This is a type that satisfies the sequence requirements as defined in the C++ standard.

Coll
> This is a type that satisfies a less-restrictive set of requirements than a standard sequence. See the Boost String Algorithms definitions a detailed description of the requirements a collection satisfies.

Pred
> This is a function object or function pointer that takes a single argument and returns a bool—in other words, an unary predicate. You can supply your own unary predicates to some of the trimming functions to trim elements that satisfy certain criteria.

OutIt
> This is a type that satisfies the requirements of an output iterator as defined in the C++ standard, namely that you can increment it and assign to the new location to add an element to the end of the sequence to which it points.

Table 4-1. Boost's string trimming function templates

Declaration	Description

`template<typename Seq>`
`void trim(Seq& s,`
`   const locale& loc =`
`   locale());`
	Trim spaces from both ends of a string in place using the locale's classification function for identifying the space character.

`template<typename Seq,`
`            typename Pred>`
`void trim_if(Seq& s, Pred p);`
	Trim elements from each end of the sequence s for which `p(*it)` is `true`, where `it` is an iterator that refers to an element in the sequence. The trimming ceases when `p(*it) = false`.

`template<typename Seq>`
`Seq trim_copy(const Seq& s,`
`   const locale& loc =`
`   locale());`
	Does the same thing as `trim`, but instead of modifying s it returns a new sequence with the trimmed results.

`template<typename Seq,`
`            typename Pred>`
`Seq trim_copy_if(const Seq& s,`
`   Pred p);`
	Does the same thing as `trim_if`, but instead of modifying s it returns a new sequence with the trimmed results.

`template<typename OutIt,`
`            typename Coll,`
`            typename Pred>`
`OutIt trim_copy_if(OutIt out,`
`   const Coll& c, Pred p);`
	Does the same thing as the previous version of `trim_copy_if`, with a few differences. First, it gives the guarantee of strong exception safety. Second, it takes an output iterator as the first argument and returns an output iterator that refers to one position past the end of the destination sequence. Finally, it takes a collection type instead of a sequence type; see the list before this table for more information.

Table 4-1. Boost's string trimming function templates (continued)

Declaration	Description
trim_left trim_right	Works like trim, but only for the left or right end of a string.
trim_left_if trim_right_if	Works like trim_if, but only for the left or right end of a string.
trim_left_copy trim_right_copy	Works like trim_copy, but only for the left or right end of a string.
trim_left_copy_if trim_right_copy_if	Works like trim_copy_if, but only for the left or right end of a string. Both have two versions, one that operates on a sequence and another that operates on a collection.

The first four function templates described in Table 4-1 are the core functionality of the String Algorithms library's trim functions. The rest are variations on those themes. To see some of them in action, take a look at Example 4-5. It shows some of the advantages of using these functions over string member functions.

Example 4-5. Using Boost's string trim functions

```
#include <iostream>
#include <string>
#include <boost/algorithm/string.hpp>

using namespace std;
using namespace boost;

int main( ) {

    string s1 = "      leading spaces?";

    trim_left(s1); // Trim the original
    string s2 = trim_left_copy(s1); // Trim, but leave original intact

    cout << "s1 = " << s1 << endl;
    cout << "s2 = " << s2 << endl;

    s1 = "YYYYboostXXX";
    s2 = trim_copy_if(s1, is_any_of("XY")); // Use a predicate to

    trim_if(s1, is_any_of("XY"));

    cout << "s1 = " << s1 << endl;
    cout << "s2 = " << s2 << endl;

    s1 = "1234 numbers 9876";
    s2 = trim_copy_if(s1, is_digit( ));

    cout << "s1 = " << s1 << endl;
    cout << "s2 = " << s2 << endl;
```

Example 4-5. Using Boost's string trim functions (continued)

```
   // Nest calls to trim functions if you like
   s1 = "    ****Trim!***    ";
   s2 = trim_copy_if(trim_copy(s1), is_any_of("*"));

   cout << "s1 = " << s1 << endl;
   cout << "s2 = " << s2 << endl;
}
```

Example 4-5 demonstrates how to use the Boost string trim functions. They are generally self-explanatory to use, so I won't go into a detailed explanation beyond what's in Table 4-1. The one function that is in the example that isn't in the table is is_any_of. This is a function template that returns a predicate function object that can be used by the trim_if-style functions. Use it when you want to trim a set of characters. There is a similar classification function named is_from_range that takes two arguments and returns an unary predicate that returns true when a character is within the range. For example, to trim the characters a through d from a string, you could do something like this:

```
   s1 = "abcdXXXabcd";
   trim_if(s1, is_from_range('a', 'd'));
   cout << "s1 = " << s1 << endl;        // Now s1 = XXX
```

Note that this works in a case-sensitive way, since the range a through d does not include the uppercase versions of those letters.

4.3   Storing Strings in a Sequence

Problem

You want to store a set of strings in a sequence that looks and feels like an array.

Solution

Use a vector for array-like storage of your strings. Example 4-6 offers a simple example.

Example 4-6. Store strings in a vector

```
#include <string>
#include <vector>
#include <iostream>

using namespace std;

int main( ) {

   vector<string> v;

   string s = "one";
   v.push_back(s);
```

Example 4-6. Store strings in a vector (continued)

```
    s = "two";
    v.push_back(s);

    s = "three";
    v.push_back(s);

    for (int i = 0; i < v.size(); ++i)
    {
        cout << v[i] << '\n';
    }
}
```

vectors follow array semantics for random access (they also do a lot more), so they are easy and familiar to use. vectors are just one of many sequences in the standard library, however; read on for more of this broad subject.

Discussion

A vector is a dynamically sized sequence of objects that provides array-style operator[] random access. The member function push_back copies its argument via copy constructor, adds that copy as the last item in the vector, and increments its size by one. pop_back does the exact opposite, by removing the last element. Inserting or deleting items from the end of a vector takes amortized constant time, and inserting or deleting from any other location takes linear time. These are the basics of vectors. There is a lot more to them.

In most cases, a vector should be your first choice over a C-style array. First of all, they are dynamically sized, which means they can grow as needed. You don't have to do all sorts of research to figure out an optimal static size, as in the case of C arrays; a vector grows as needed, and it can be resized larger or smaller manually if you need to. Second, vectors offer bounds checking with the at member function (but not with operator[]), so that you can do something if you reference a nonexistent index instead of simply watching your program crash or worse, continuing execution with corrupt data. Look at Example 4-7. It shows how to deal with out-of-bounds indexes.

Example 4-7. Bounds-checking on vectors

```
#include <iostream>
#include <vector>
#include <exception>

using namespace std;

int main() {

    char carr[] = {'a', 'b', 'c', 'd', 'e'};

    cout << carr[100000] << '\n'; // Whoops, who knows what's going
                                  // to happen
```

Example 4-7. Bounds-checking on vectors (continued)

```
vector<char> v;
v.push_back('a');
v.push_back('b');
v.push_back('c');
v.push_back('d');
v.push_back('e');

try {
   cout << v.at(10000) << '\n'; // at checks bounds and throws
} catch(out_of_range& e) {       // out_of_range if it's invalid
   cerr << e.what() << '\n';
}
}
```

If you catch out_of_range, defined in <stdexcept>, you can deal with invalid indexes in a meaningful way. And you can call the what member function to, depending on your implementation, get a useful error message, like this one returned by the code in Example 4-7:

```
invalid vector<T> subscript
```

vectors aren't your only option though. There are lots of ways to store sequences of things in C++. In addition to vectors, there are lists, sets, and double-ended queues (deques). All support many of the same operations, and each supports operations of its own. In addition, each has different algorithmic complexity guarantees, storage requirements, and semantics in general. There is a lot to choose from.

Look at Example 4-6 closely. You will probably notice that I keep changing the value of the string s before I add it to the back of the container with push_back. You could reasonably expect the output to look like this:

```
three
three
three
```

I pushed the same string on the end of the vector three times, so each time I reassign the string, don't all vector elements now just refer to the same thing? No. This is an important point about STL containers.

STL containers store copies of the objects you put into them, not the objects themselves. So after I've put all three of my strings in the container, there are four strings in memory: the three copies that were made and are now "in" the container, and the one copy I've been assigning values to.

Who cares? So a few extra copies have been made: big deal. It is a big deal, because if whatever you are writing uses a lot of strings, you are going to pay for all of that copying with processor time, or memory, or both. Copying elements in and out of containers is the intentional behavior of the STL, and all containers work that way.

A solution to this (certainly not *the* solution) is to store pointers in the container instead. Just remember that the container doesn't delete the pointers when it is destroyed. Your code allocated the memory for the pointer, so your code has to clean it up. This goes for when the container is destroyed entirely, or when the element is removed.

In the interest of providing alternative solutions, let's explore another option. Consider the class template list, defined in <list>, which is a doubly linked list. If you plan on having lots of inserts and deletes in the middle of the sequence, or if you want to ensure that iterators pointing to elements of the sequence are not invalidated when you modify the sequence, you may want to use a list. Example 4-8 uses a list instead of a vector to store a few strings; it also uses for_each to iterate through them and print them out instead of the index operator, as you would have to do with a simple array.

Example 4-8. Storing strings in a list

```
#include <string>
#include <list>
#include <algorithm>
#include <iostream>

using namespace std;

void write(const string& s) {
   cout << s << '\n';
}

int main( ) {
   list<string> lst;

   string s = "knife";
   lst.push_front(s);

   s = "fork";
   lst.push_back(s);

   s = "spoon";
   lst.push_back(s);

   // A list doesn't have random access, so
   // use for_each( ) instead
   for_each(lst.begin( ), lst.end( ), write);
}
```

The point of this digression from the original problem (storing strings in a sequence) is to give a brief introduction to the sequences in the STL. I can't give comprehensive coverage of the topic here. For an overview of the STL, see Chapter 10 of *C++ in a Nutshell*, by Ray Lischner (O'Reilly).

4.4 Getting the Length of a String

Problem

You need the length of a string.

Solution

Use string's length member function:

```
std::string s = "Raising Arizona";
int i = s.length();
```

Discussion

Retrieving the length of a string is a trivial task, but it is a good opportunity to discuss the allocation scheme for strings (both wide and narrow character). strings, unlike C-style null-terminated character arrays, are dynamically sized, and grow as needed. Most standard library implementations start with an arbitrary (low) capacity, and grow by doubling the capacity each time it is reached. Knowing how to analyze this growth, if not the exact algorithm, is helpful in diagnosing string performance problems.

The characters in a basic_string are stored in a buffer that is a contiguous chunk of memory with a static size. The buffer a string uses is an arbitrary size initially, and as characters are added to the string, the buffer fills up until its capacity is reached. When this happens, the buffer grows, sort of. Specifically, a new buffer is allocated with a larger size, the characters are copied from the old buffer to the new buffer, and the old buffer is deleted.

You can find out the size of the buffer (not the number of characters it contains, but its maximum size) with the capacity member function. If you want to manually set the capacity to avoid needless buffer copies, use the reserve member function and pass it a numeric argument that indicates the desired buffer size. There is a maximum size on the possible buffer size though, and you can get that by calling max_size. You can use all of these to observe memory growth in your standard library implementation. Take a look at Example 4-9 to see how.

Example 4-9. String length and capacity

```
#include <string>
#include <iostream>

using namespace std;

int main() {

   string s = "";
   string sr = "";
```

Example 4-9. String length and capacity (continued)

```
sr.reserve(9000);

cout << "s.length    = " << s.length()    << '\n';
cout << "s.capacity  = " << s.capacity()  << '\n';
cout << "s.max_size  = " << s.max_size()  << '\n';

cout << "sr.length   = " << sr.length()   << '\n';
cout << "sr.capacity = " << sr.capacity() << '\n';
cout << "sr.max_size = " << sr.max_size() << '\n';

for (int i = 0; i < 10000; ++i) {

    if (s.length() == s.capacity()) {
        cout << "s reached capacity of " << s.length()
            << ", growing...\n";
    }
    if (sr.length() == sr.capacity()) {
        cout << "sr reached capacity of " << sr.length()
            << ", growing...\n";
    }
    s += 'x';
    sr += 'x';
}
}
```

With Visual C++ 7.1, my output looks like this:

```
s.length    = 0
s.capacity  = 15
s.max_size  = 4294967294
sr.length   = 0
sr.capacity = 9007
sr.max_size = 4294967294
s reached capacity of 15, growing...
s reached capacity of 31, growing...
s reached capacity of 47, growing...
s reached capacity of 70, growing...
s reached capacity of 105, growing...
s reached capacity of 157, growing...
s reached capacity of 235, growing...
s reached capacity of 352, growing...
s reached capacity of 528, growing...
s reached capacity of 792, growing...
s reached capacity of 1188, growing...
s reached capacity of 1782, growing...
s reached capacity of 2673, growing...
s reached capacity of 4009, growing...
s reached capacity of 6013, growing...
sr reached capacity of 9007, growing...
s reached capacity of 9019, growing...
```

What is happening here is that the buffer for the string keeps filling up as I append characters to it. If the buffer is full (i.e., length = capacity), a new, larger buffer is allocated and the original string characters and the newly appended character(s) are copied into the new buffer. s starts with the default capacity of 15 (results vary by compiler), then grows by about half each time.

If you anticipate significant growth in your string, or you have a large number of strings that will need to grow at least modestly, use reserve to minimize the amount of buffer reallocation that goes on. It's also a good idea to experiment with your standard library implementation to see how it handles string growth.

Incidentally, when you want to know if a string is empty, don't check length against zero, just call the empty member function. It is a const member function that returns true if the length of the string is zero.

4.5   Reversing a String

Problem

You want to reverse a string.

Solution

To reverse a string "in place," without using a temporary string, use the reverse function template in the <algorithm> header:

```
std::reverse(s.begin( ), s.end( ));
```

Discussion

reverse works simply enough: it modifies the range you give it such that it is in the opposite order that it was originally. It takes linear time.

In the event that you want to *copy* the string to another string, but backward, use reverse iterators, like this:

```
std::string s = "Los Angeles";
std::string rs;

rs.assign(s.rbegin( ), s.rend( ));
```

rbegin and rend return reverse iterators. Reverse iterators behave as though they are looking at the sequence backward. rbegin returns an iterator that points to the last element, and rend returns an iterator that points to one before the first; this is exactly opposite of what begin and end do.

But do you *need* to reverse the string in the first place? With rbegin and rend, any member functions or algorithms that operate on iterator ranges can be used on the reverse version of the string. And if you want to search through the string, you can use rfind to do what find does but starting from the end of the string and moving backward. For large strings, or large numbers of strings, reversing can be expensive, so avoid it if you can.

4.6   Splitting a String

Problem

You want to split a delimited string into multiple strings. For example, you may want to split the string "Name|Address|Phone" into three separate strings, "Name", "Address", and "Phone", with the delimiter removed.

Solution

Use basic_string's find member function to advance from one occurrence of the delimiter to the next, and substr to copy each substring out of the original string. You can use any standard sequence to hold the results; Example 4-10 uses a vector.

Example 4-10. Split a delimited string

```
#include <string>
#include <vector>
#include <functional>
#include <iostream>

using namespace std;

void split(const string& s, char c,
           vector<string>& v) {
   string::size_type i = 0;
   string::size_type j = s.find(c);

   while (j != string::npos) {
      v.push_back(s.substr(i, j-i));
      i = ++j;
      j = s.find(c, j);

      if (j == string::npos)
         v.push_back(s.substr(i, s.length()));
   }
}

int main( ) {
   vector<string> v;
   string s = "Account Name|Address 1|Address 2|City";

   split(s, '|', v);

   for (int i = 0; i < v.size( ); ++i) {
      cout << v[i] << '\n';
   }
}
```

Discussion

Making the example above a function template that accepts any kind of character is trivial; just parameterize the character type and change references to string to basic_string<T>:

```
template<typename T>
void split(const basic_string<T>& s, T c,
           vector<basic_string<T> >& v) {
    basic_string<T>::size_type i = 0;
    basic_string<T>::size_type j = s.find(c);

    while (j != basic_string<T>::npos) {
        v.push_back(s.substr(i, j-i));
        i = ++j;
        j = s.find(c, j);

        if (j == basic_string<T>::npos)
            v.push_back(s.substr(i, s.length()));
    }
}
```

The logic is identical.

 Notice, though, that I put an extra space between the last two right-angle brackets on the last line of the function header. You have to do this to tell the compiler that it's not reading a right-shift operator.

Example 4-10 splits a string using a simple algorithm. Starting at the beginning, it looks for the first occurrence of the delimiter c, then considers everything before it and after the beginning the next meaningful chunk of text. The example uses the find member function to locate the first occurrence of a character starting at a particular index in the original string, and substr to copy the characters in a range to a new string, which is pushed onto a vector. This is the same behavior as the split function in most scripting languages, and is actually a special case of *tokenizing* a stream of text, which is described in Recipe 4.7.

Splitting strings based on single character delimiters is a common requirement, and it probably won't surprise you that it's in the Boost String Algorithms library. It is easy to use; see Example 4-11 to see how to split a string with Boost's split function.

Example 4-11. Splitting a string with Boost

```
#include <iostream>
#include <string>
#include <list>
#include <boost/algorithm/string.hpp>

using namespace std;
using namespace boost;
```

Example 4-11. Splitting a string with Boost (continued)

```
int main( ) {

    string s = "one,two,three,four";
    list<string> results;

    split(results, s, is_any_of(","));  // Note this is boost::split

    for (list<string>::const_iterator p = results.begin( );
        p != results.end( ); ++p) {
      cout << *p << endl;
    }
}
```

split is a function template that takes three arguments. Its declaration looks like this:

```
    template<typename Seq,
             typename Coll,
             typename Pred>
  Seq& split(Seq& s, Coll& c, Pred p,
             token_compress_mode_type e = token_compress_off);
```

The types Seq, Coll, and Pred, represent the types of the result sequence, the input collection, and the predicate that will be used to determine if something is a delimiter. The sequence argument is a sequence in the C++ standard's definition that contains something that can hold pieces of what is in the input collection. So, for example, in Example 4-11 I used a list<string>, but you could use something else like a vector<string>. The collection argument is the type of the input sequence. A collection is a nonstandard concept that is similar to a sequence, but with fewer requirements (see the Boost documentation at *www.boost.org* for specifics). The predicate argument is an unary function object or function pointer that returns a bool indicating whether its argument is a delimiter or not. It will be invoked against each element in the sequence in the form f(*it), where it is an iterator that refers to an element in the sequence.

is_any_of is a convenient function template that comes with the String Algorithms library that makes your life easier if you are using multiple delimiters. It constructs an unary function object that returns true if the argument you pass in is a member of the set. In other words:

```
    bool b = is_any_of("abc")('a'); // b = true
```

This makes it easy to test for multiple delimiters without having to write the function object yourself.

4.7   Tokenizing a String

Problem

You need to break a string into pieces using a set of delimiters.

Solution

Use the `find_first_of` and `first_first_not_of` member functions on `basic_string` to iterate through the string and alternately locate the next tokens and non-tokens. Example 4-12 presents a simple `StringTokenizer` class that does just that.

Example 4-12. A string tokenizer

```cpp
#include <string>
#include <iostream>

using namespace std;

// String tokenizer class.
class StringTokenizer {

public:

    StringTokenizer(const string& s, const char* delim = NULL) :
        str_(s), count_(-1), begin_(0), end_(0) {

        if (!delim)
            delim_ = " \f\n\r\t\v";   //default to whitespace
        else
            delim_ = delim;

        // Point to the first token
        begin_ = str_.find_first_not_of(delim_);
        end_ = str_.find_first_of(delim_, begin_);
    }

    size_t countTokens() {
        if (count_ >= 0) // return if we've already counted
            return(count_);

        string::size_type n = 0;
        string::size_type i = 0;

        for (;;) {
            // advance to the first token
            if ((i = str_.find_first_not_of(delim_, i)) == string::npos)
                break;
            // advance to the next delimiter
            i = str_.find_first_of(delim_, i+1);
            n++;
            if (i == string::npos)
```

Example 4-12. A string tokenizer (continued)

```
            break;
        }
        return (count_ = n);
    }
    bool hasMoreTokens( ) {return(begin_ != end_);}
    void nextToken(string& s) {
        if (begin_ != string::npos && end_ != string::npos) {
            s = str_.substr(begin_, end_-begin_);
            begin_ = str_.find_first_not_of(delim_, end_);
            end_ = str_.find_first_of(delim_, begin_);
        }
        else if (begin_ != string::npos && end_ == string::npos)
        {
            s = str_.substr(begin_, str_.length( )-begin_);
            begin_ = str_.find_first_not_of(delim_, end_);
        }

    }

private:
    StringTokenizer( ) {};
    string delim_;
    string str_;
    int count_;
    int begin_;
    int end_;
};

int main( ) {
    string s = " razzle dazzle giddyup ";
    string tmp;

    StringTokenizer st(s);

    cout << "there are " << st.countTokens( ) << " tokens.\n";
    while (st.hasMoreTokens( )) {
        st.nextToken(tmp);
        cout << "token = " << tmp << '\n';
    }
}
```

Discussion

Splitting a string with well-defined structure, as in Example 4-10, is nice, but it's not always that easy. Suppose instead that you have to *tokenize* a string instead of simply break it into pieces based on a single delimiter. The most common incarnation of this is tokenizing based on ignoring whitespace. Example 4-12 gives an implementation of a StringTokenizer class (like the standard Java™ class of the same name) for C++ that accepts delimiter characters, but defaults to whitespace.

The most important lines in `StringTokenizer` use `basic_string`'s `find_first_of` and `find_first_not_of` member functions. I describe how they work and when to use them in Recipe 4.9. Example 4-10 produces this output:

```
there are 3 tokens.
token = razzle
token = dazzle
token = giddyup
```

`StringTokenizer` is a more flexible form of the `split` function in Example 4-10. It maintains state, so you can advance from one token to the next instead of parsing the input string all at once. You can also count the number of tokens.

There are a couple of improvements you can make on `StringTokenizer`. First, for simplicity, I wrote `StringTokenizer` to only work with strings, or in other words, narrow character strings. If you want the same class to work for both narrow and wide characters, you can parameterize the character type as I have done in previous recipes. The other thing you may want to do is extend `StringTokenizer` to allow more friendly interaction with sequences and more extensibility. You can always write all of this yourself, or you can use an existing tokenizer class instead. The Boost project has a class named tokenizer that does this. See *www.boost.org* for more details.

See Also

Recipe 4.24

4.8 Joining a Sequence of Strings

Problem

Given a sequence of strings. such as output from Example 4-10, you want to join them together into a single, long string, perhaps with a delimiter.

Solution

Loop through the sequence and append each string to the output string. You can handle any standard sequence as input; Example 4-13 uses a `vector` of strings.

Example 4-13. Join a sequence of strings

```
#include <string>
#include <vector>
#include <iostream>

using namespace std;

void join(const vector<string>& v, char c, string& s) {

    s.clear();
```

Example 4-13. Join a sequence of strings (continued)

```
    for (vector<string>::const_iterator p = v.begin( );
        p != v.end( ); ++p) {
      s += *p;
      if (p != v.end( ) - 1)
        s += c;
    }
}

int main( ) {

    vector<string> v;
    vector<string> v2;
    string s;

    v.push_back(string("fee"));
    v.push_back(string("fi"));
    v.push_back(string("foe"));
    v.push_back(string("fum"));

    join(v, '/', s);

    cout << s << '\n';
}
```

Discussion

Example 4-13 has one technique that is slightly different from previous examples. Look at this line:

```
    for (vector<string>::const_iterator p = v.begin( );
```

The previous string examples simply used iterators, without the "const" part, but you can't get away with that here because v is declared as a reference to a const object. If you have a const container object, you can only use a const_iterator to access its elements. This is because a plain iterator allows writes to the object it refers to, which, of course, you can't do if your container object is const.

I declared v const for two reasons. First, I know I'm not going to be modifying its contents, so I want the compiler to give me an error if I do. The compiler is much better at spotting that kind of thing than I am, especially since a subtle syntactic or semantic error can cause an unwanted assignment. Second, I want to advertise to consumers of this function that I won't do anything to their container, and const is the perfect way to do that. Now, I just have to create a generic version that works on multiple character types.

Just as in Recipe 4.6, making join generic with a function template is easy. All you have to do is change the header to be parameterized on the type of character, like this:

```
template<typename T>
void joing(const std::vector<std::basic_string<T> >& v, T c,
           std::basic_string<T>& s)
```

But vectors may not be your only input. You may be saddled with the task of joining an array of C-style strings. C++ strings are preferable to C-style strings, so if you have to do this, join them into a C++ string. Once you've done that, you can always retrieve a C-style version by calling string's c_str member function, which returns a const pointer to a null-terminated character array.

Example 4-14 offers a generic version of join that joins an array of character arrays into a string. Since the new, generic version is parameterized on the character type, it will work for narrow or wide character arrays.

Example 4-14. Joining C-style strings

```
#include <string>
#include <iostream>

const static int MAGIC_NUMBER = 4;

template<typename T>
void join(T* arr[], size_t n, T c, std::basic_string<T>& s) {
   s.clear();

   for (int i = 0; i < n; ++i) {
      if (arr[i] != NULL)
         s += arr[i];
      if (i < n-1)
         s += c;
   }
}

int main() {
   std::wstring ws;

   wchar_t* arr[MAGIC_NUMBER];

   arr[0] = L"you";
   arr[1] = L"ate";
   arr[2] = L"my";
   arr[3] = L"breakfast";

   join(arr, MAGIC_NUMBER, L'/', ws);
}
```

4.9   Finding Things in Strings

Problem

You want to search a string for something. Maybe it's a single character, another string, or one of (or *not* of) an unordered set of characters. And, for your own reasons, you have to find it in a particular way, such as the first or last occurrence, or the first or last occurrence relative to a particular index.

Solution

Use one of basic_string's "find" member functions. Almost all start with the word "find," and their name gives you a pretty good idea of what they do. Example 4-15 shows how some of the find member functions work.

Example 4-15. Searching strings

```
#include <string>
#include <iostream>

int main( ) {
   std::string s = "Charles Darwin";

   std::cout << s.find("ar") << '\n';             // Search from the
                                                  // beginning
   std::cout << s.rfind("ar") << '\n';            // Search from the end

   std::cout << s.find_first_of("swi")            // Find the first of
             << '\n';                             // any of these chars

   std::cout << s.find_first_not_of("Charles")    // Find the first
             << '\n';                             // that's not in this
                                                  // set

   std::cout << s.find_last_of("abg") << '\n';    // Find the first of
                                                  // any of these chars
                                                  // starting from the
                                                  // end

   std::cout << s.find_last_not_of("aDinrw")      // Find the first
             << '\n';                             // that's not in this
                                                  // set, starting from
                                                  // the end
}
```

Each of the find member functions is discussed in more detail in the "Discussion" section.

Discussion

There are six different find member functions for finding things in strings, each of which provides four overloads. The overloads allow for either basic_string or charT* parameters (charT is the character type). Each has a basic_string::size_type parameter pos that lets you specify the index where the search should begin, and there is one overload with a size_type parameter n that allows you only to search based on the first n characters from the set.

It's hard to keep track of all of these member functions, so Table 4-2 gives a quick reference of each function and its parameters.

Table 4-2. Member functions for searching strings

Member function	Description

`size_type find (const basic_string& str,`
`            size_type pos = 0) const;`
`size_type find (const charT* s,`
`            size_type pos,`
`            size_type n) const;`
`size_type find (const charT* s,`
`            size_type pos = 0) const;`
`size_type find (charT c,`
`            size_type pos = 0) const;`
	Returns the index of the first instance of a character or substring, starting at the beginning or the index indicated by the pos parameter. If n is specified, then match the first n characters in the target string.

`size_type rfind ( ... )`	Find the first instance of a character or substring, from the end to the beginning. In other words, do the same thing as find, but starting from the end of the string.
`size_type find_first_of ( ... )`	Find the first occurrence of any of the characters in the set that is provided as a basic_string or character pointer. If n is specified, then only the first n characters in the set are considered.
`size_type find_last_of ( ... )`	Find the last occurrence of any of the characters in the set that is provided as a basic_string or character pointer. If n is specified, then only the first n characters in the set are considered.
`size_type find_first_not_of ( ... )`	Find the first occurrence of a character that is *not* one of the characters in the set that is provided as a basic_string or character pointer. If n is specified, then only the first n characters in the set are considered.
`size_type find_last_not_of ( ... )`	Find the last occurrence of any of the characters in the set that is provided as a basic_string or character pointer. If n is specified, then only the first n characters in the set are considered.

All of these member functions return the index of the occurrence of what you are looking for as a value of type basic_string<T>::size_type. If the search fails, it returns basic_string<T>::npos, which is a special value (usually -1) that indicates search failure. Even though it is usually -1, you should test for equality with npos to be as portable as possible; this also makes your intent clear, since by comparing to npos you are explicitly checking for search failure and not some magic number.

With this variety of searching algorithms, you should be able to find what you're looking for, and if not, to use them in your own algorithms. If basic_string doesn't provide what you need, however, look in <algorithm> before you roll your own. The standard algorithms operate on sequences by using iterators and, nearly as often, function objects. Conveniently, basic_strings provide iterators for easy traversal, so it is trivial to plug string iterators into standard algorithms. Say you want to find the first occurrence of the same character twice in a row. You can use the adjacent_find function template to find two equal, adjacent elements in a string ("adjacent" means that their positions differ by one iterator, i.e., that *iter == *(iter + 1)).

```
std::string s = "There was a group named Kiss in the 70s";

std::string::iterator p =
    std::adjacent_find(s.begin(), s.end());
```

The result is an iterator that points to the first of the adjacent elements.

If you have to write your own algorithm for operating on strings, don't use a basic_string like you would a C-style string by using operator[] to get at each item. Take advantage of the existing member functions. Each of the find functions takes a size_type parameter that indicates the index where the search should proceed from. Using the find functions repeatedly, you can advance through the string as you see fit. Consider Example 4-16, which counts the number of unique characters in a string.

Example 4-16. Counting unique characters

```
#include <string>
#include <iostream>

template<typename T>
int countUnique(const std::basic_string<T>& s) {
   using std::basic_string;

   basic_string<T> chars;

   for (typename basic_string<T>::const_iterator p = s.begin();
        p != s.end(); ++p) {
     if (chars.find(*p) == basic_string<T>::npos)
        chars += *p;
   }
   return(chars.length());
}

int main() {
   std::string s = "Abracadabra";
```

Example 4-16. Counting unique characters (continued)

```
    std::cout << countUnique(s) << '\n';
}
```

The find functions come in handy quite often. Keep them at the top of the list when you have to find things in strings.

4.10   Finding the nth Instance of a Substring

Problem

Given two strings source and pattern, you want to find the *n*th occurrence of pattern in source.

Solution

Use the find member function to locate successive instances of the substring you are looking for. Example 4-17 contains a simple nthSubstr function.

Example 4-17. Locate the nth version of a substring

```cpp
#include <string>
#include <iostream>

using namespace std;

int nthSubstr(int n, const string& s,
              const string& p) {
   string::size_type i = s.find(p);     // Find the first occurrence

   int j;
   for (j = 1; j < n && i != string::npos; ++j)
     i = s.find(p, i+1); // Find the next occurrence

   if (j == n)
     return(i);
   else
     return(-1);
}

int main( ) {
   string s = "the wind, the sea, the sky, the trees";
   string p = "the";

   cout << nthSubstr(1, s, p) << '\n';
   cout << nthSubstr(2, s, p) << '\n';
   cout << nthSubstr(5, s, p) << '\n';
}
```

Discussion

There are a couple of improvements you can make to nthSubstr as it is presented in Example 4-17. First, you can make it generic by making it a function template instead of an ordinary function. Second, you can add a parameter to account for substrings that may or may not overlap with themselves. By "overlap," I mean that the beginning of the string matches part of the end of the same string, as in the word "abracadabra," where the last four characters are the same as the first four. Example 4-18 demonstrates this.

Example 4-18. An improved version of nthSubstr

```
#include <string>
#include <iostream>

using namespace std;

template<typename T>
int nthSubstrg(int n, const basic_string<T>& s,
               const basic_string<T>& p,
               bool repeats = false) {
   string::size_type i = s.find(p);
   string::size_type adv = (repeats) ? 1 : p.length();

   int j;
   for (j = 1; j < n && i != basic_string<T>::npos; ++j)
      i = s.find(p, i+adv);

   if (j == n)
     return(i);
   else
     return(-1);
}

int main() {
   string s = "AGATGCCATATATATACGATATCCTTA";
   string p = "ATAT";

   cout << p << " as non-repeating occurs at "
        << nthSubstrg(3, s, p) << '\n';
   cout << p << " as repeating occurs at "
        << nthSubstrg(3, s, p, true) << '\n';
}
```

The output for the strings in Example 4-18 is as follows:

```
ATAT as non-repeating occurs at 18
ATAT as repeating occurs at 11
```

See Also

Recipe 4.9

4.11 Removing a Substring from a String

Problem

You want to remove a substring from a string.

Solution

Use the find, erase, and length member functions of basic_string:

```
std::string t = "Banana Republic";
std::string s = "nana";

std::string::size_type i = t.find(s);

if (i != std::string::npos)
   t.erase(i, s.length( ));
```

This will erase s.length( ) elements starting at the index where find found the first occurrence of the substring.

Discussion

There are lots of variations on the theme of finding a substring and removing it. For example, you may want to remove all instances of a substring instead of just one. Or just the last one. Or the seventh one. Each time the steps are the same: find the index of the beginning of the pattern you want to remove, then call erase on that index for the next *n* characters, where *n* is the length of the pattern string. See Recipe 4.9 for the different member functions for finding things in strings.

Chances are you also want to make your substring-removal function generic, so you can use it on strings of any kind of character. Example 4-19 offers a generic version that removes all instances of the pattern from a string.

Example 4-19. Remove all substrings from a string (generic version)

```
#include <string>
#include <iostream>

using namespace std;

template<typename T>
void removeSubstrs(basic_string<T>& s,
                   const basic_string<T>& p) {
   basic_string<T>::size_type n = p.length( );

   for (basic_string<T>::size_type i = s.find(p);
        i != basic_string<T>::npos;
        i = s.find(p))
      s.erase(i, n);
}
```

Example 4-19. Remove all substrings from a string (generic version) (continued)

```
int main( ) {
   string s = "One fish, two fish, red fish, blue fish";
   string p = "fish";

   removeSubstrs(s, p);

   cout << s << '\n';
}
```

The basic_string member function erase is what does the important work here. In <string>, it is overloaded three times. The version I used in Example 4-19 accepts the index to begin erasing at and the number of characters to erase. Another version accepts starting and ending iterator arguments, and there is a version that takes a single iterator and erases the element at that location. To ensure optimal performance, prefer the first two when you plan to delete multiple contiguous elements instead of repeatedly calling s.erase(iter) for each element you want to erase. In other words, use member functions that operate on ranges instead of single elements—especially for those member functions that modify the contents of the string (or sequence). By doing so, you will avoid the extra function calls to erase for each element in the sequence, and you will permit the string implementation to more intelligently manage its data.

4.12   Converting a String to Lower- or Uppercase

Problem

You have a string that you want to convert to lower- or uppercase.

Solution

Use the toupper and tolower functions in the <cctype> header to convert characters to upper- or lowercase. Example 4-20 shows how to do it using these functions. See the discussion for an alternative.

Example 4-20. Converting a string's case

```
#include <iostream>
#include <string>
#include <cctype>
#include <cwctype>
#include <stdexcept>

using namespace std;

void toUpper(basic_string<char>& s) {
   for (basic_string<char>::iterator p = s.begin( );
        p != s.end( ); ++p) {
```

Example 4-20. Converting a string's case (continued)

```
      *p = toupper(*p); // toupper is for char
   }
}

void toUpper(basic_string<wchar_t>& s) {
   for (basic_string<wchar_t>::iterator p = s.begin( );
      p != s.end( ); ++p) {
      *p = towupper(*p); // towupper is for wchar_t
   }
}

void toLower(basic_string<char>& s) {
   for (basic_string<char>::iterator p = s.begin( );
      p != s.end( ); ++p) {
      *p = tolower(*p);
   }
}

void toLower(basic_string<wchar_t>& s) {
   for (basic_string<wchar_t>::iterator p = s.begin( );
      p != s.end( ); ++p) {
      *p = towlower(*p);
   }
}

int main( ) {

   string s = "shazam";
   wstring ws = L"wham";

   toUpper(s);
   toUpper(ws);

   cout << "s =  " << s << endl;
   wcout << "ws = " << ws << endl;

   toLower(s);
   toLower(ws);

   cout << "s =  " << s << endl;
   wcout << "ws = " << ws << endl;
}
```

This produces the following output:

```
s =  SHAZAM
ws = WHAM
s =  shazam
ws = wham
```

Discussion

One would think that the standard string class has a member function that converts the whole thing to upper- or lowercase, but, in fact, it doesn't. If you want to convert a string of characters to upper- or lowercase, you have to do it yourself, sort of.

Not surprisingly, there is more than one way to convert a string's case (and when I say "string," I mean a sequence of characters, either narrow or wide). The simplest way to do it is with using one of the four-character conversion functions toupper, towupper, tolower, and towlower. The first form of each of these is the narrow character version; the second form (with the extra "w") is its wide character equivalent.

Each of these functions converts the case of the character using the current global locale's rules for case conversion. Upper- and lowercase depend on the characters being used in the current locale; some characters don't have an upper- or lowercase version, in which case the functions listed above will return the same character you pass in. See Chapter 13 for more information on locales. The C++ facilities for dealing with different locales are complicated, and I cannot do them justice here.

Doing the actual character conversion is easy. Consider the toUpper function in Example 4-20:

```
void toUpper(basic_string<char>& s) {
    for (basic_string<char>::iterator p = s.begin( );
        p != s.end( ); ++p) {
      *p = toupper(*p);
    }
}
```

The line in bold does the real work. The version for wide characters is nearly identical:

```
void toUpper(basic_string<wchar_t>& s) {
    for (basic_string<wchar_t>::iterator p = s.begin( );
        p != s.end( ); ++p) {
      *p = towupper(*p);
    }
}
```

I overloaded toUpper for the different character types because there is no fully generic toupper function to convert a character's case (unless you are using facets from the <locale> header, which I discuss below). Two simple functions, as above, will get the job done.

There is another way to do this though, and the motivating factor for using this second approach would be your need to use explicit locales. The following versions of toUpper and toLower convert the case of a string, regardless of its character type, as long as the named locale (which defaults to the current locale) supports case conversion for that locale and character type.

```
template<typename C>
void toUpper2(basic_string<C>& s, const locale& loc = locale( )) {
    typename basic_string<C>::iterator p;
```

```
        for (p = s.begin( ); p != s.end( ); ++p) {
            *p = use_facet<ctype<C> >(loc).toupper(*p);
        }
    }


    template<typename C>
    void toLower2(basic_string<C>& s, const locale& loc = locale( )) {
        typename basic_string<C>::iterator p;
        for (p = s.begin( ); p != s.end( ); ++p) {
            *p = use_facet<ctype<C> >(loc).tolower(*p);
        }
    }
```

The lines in bold do the real work. Functionally, they work the same as the upper- and lowercase functions used in Example 4-20, except that they use the internationalization facilities in the <locale> header to do it. See Chapter 13 for a more thorough discussion of locales, facets, and internationalization.

4.13 Doing a Case-Insensitive String Comparison

Problem

You have two strings, and you want to know if they are equal, regardless of the case of the characters. For example, "cat" is not equal to "dog," but "Cat," for your purposes, is equal to "cat," "CAT," or "caT."

Solution

Compare the strings using the equal standard algorithm (defined in <algorithm>), and supply your own comparison function that uses the toupper function in <cctype> (or towupper in <cwctype> for wide characters) to compare the uppercase versions of characters. Example 4-21 offers a generic solution. It also demonstrates the use and flexibility of the STL; see the discussion below for a full explanation.

Example 4-21. Case-insensitive string comparison

```
1    #include <string>
2    #include <iostream>
3    #include <algorithm>
4    #include <cctype>
5    #include <cwctype>
6
7    using namespace std;
8
9    inline bool caseInsCharCompareN(char a, char b) {
10       return(toupper(a) == toupper(b));
11   }
12
13   inline bool caseInsCharCompareW(wchar_t a, wchar_t b) {
14       return(towupper(a) == towupper(b));
```

Example 4-21. Case-insensitive string comparison (continued)

```
15    }
16
17    bool caseInsCompare(const string& s1, const string& s2) {
18        return((s1.size( ) == s2.size( )) &&
19                equal(s1.begin(), s1.end( ), s2.begin( ), caseInsCharCompareN));
20    }
21
22    bool caseInsCompare(const wstring& s1, const wstring& s2) {
23        return((s1.size( ) == s2.size( )) &&
24                equal(s1.begin(), s1.end( ), s2.begin( ), caseInsCharCompareW));
25    }
26
27    int main( ) {
28        string s1 = "In the BEGINNING...";
29        string s2 = "In the beginning...";
30        wstring ws1 = L"The END";
31        wstring ws2 = L"the endd";
32
33        if (caseInsCompare(s1, s2))
34            cout << "Equal!\n";
35
36        if (caseInsCompare(ws1, ws2))
37            cout << "Equal!\n";
38    }
```

Discussion

The critical part of case-insensitive string comparison is the equality test of each corresponding pair of characters, so let's discuss that first. Since I am using the equal standard algorithm in this approach but I want it to use my special comparison criterion, I have to create a standalone function to handle my special comparison.

Lines 9–15 of Example 4-21 define the functions that do the character comparison, caseInsCharCompareN and caseInsCharCompareW. These use toupper and towupper to convert each character to uppercase and then return whether they are equal.

Once I have my comparison functions complete, it's time to use a standard algorithm to handle applying my comparison functions to arbitrary sequences of characters. The caseInsCompare functions defined in lines 17–25 do just that using equal. There are two overloads, one for each character type I care about. They both do the same thing, but each instantiates the appropriate character comparison function for its character type. For this example, I overloaded two ordinary functions, but you can achieve the same effect with templates. See the sidebar "Should I Use a Template?" for a discussion.

equal compares two sequence ranges for equality. There are two versions: one that uses operator==, and another that uses whatever binary predicate (i.e., takes two arguments and returns a bool) function object you supply. In Example 4-21, caseInsCharCompareN and W are the binary predicate functions.

But that's not all you have to do—you need to compare the sizes, too. Consider equal's declaration:

```
template<typename InputIterator1, typename InputIterator2,
         typename BinaryPredicate>
bool equal(InputIterator1 first1, InputIterator1 last1,
           InputIterator2 first2, BinaryPredicate pred);
```

Let n be the distance between first1 and last1, or in other words, the length of the first range. equal returns true if the first n elements of both sequences are equal. That means that if, given two sequences where the first n elements are equal, and the second sequence has more than n elements, equal will return true. Include a size check in your comparison to avoid this false positive.

You don't need to encapsulate this logic in a function. Your code or your client's code can just call the algorithm directly, but it's easier to remember and cleaner to write this:

```
if (caseInsCompare(s1, s2)) {
// they are equal, do something
```

than this:

```
if ((s1.size() == s2.size()) &&
    std::equal(s1.begin(), s1.end(), s2.begin(), caseInsCharCompare<char>)) {
// they are equal, do something
```

whenever you want to do a case-insensitive string comparison.

4.14   Doing a Case-Insensitive String Search

Problem

You want to find a substring in a string without regard for case.

Solution

Use the standard algorithms transform and search, defined in <algorithm>, along with your own special character comparison functions, similar to the approach presented in. Example 4-22 shows how to do this.

Example 4-22. Case-insensitive string search

```
#include <string>
#include <iostream>
#include <algorithm>
#include <iterator>
#include <cctype>

using namespace std;
```

Example 4-22. Case-insensitive string search (continued)

```
inline bool caseInsCharCompSingle(char a, char b) {
    return(toupper(a) == b);
}

string::const_iterator caseInsFind(string& s, const string& p) {
    string tmp;

    transform(p.begin( ), p.end( ),          // Make the pattern
              back_inserter(tmp),            // upper-case
              toupper);

    return(search(s.begin( ), s.end( ),       // Return the iter-
                  tmp.begin( ), tmp.end( ),   // ator returned by
                  caseInsCharCompSingle));    // search
}

int main( ) {
    string s = "row, row, row, your boat";
    string p = "YOUR";
    string::const_iterator it = caseInsFind(s, p);

    if (it != s.end( )) {
        cout << "Found it!\n";
    }
}
```

By returning an iterator that refers to the element in the target string where the pattern string starts, you ensure ease of compatibility with other standard algorithms since most of them accept iterator arguments.

Discussion

Example 4-22 demonstrates the usual mode of operation when working with standard algorithms. Create the functions that do the work, then plug them into the most appropriate algorithms as function objects. The charInsCharCompSingle function does the real work here but, unlike Example 4-21, this character comparison function only uppercases the *first* argument. This is because a little later in caseInsFind, I convert the pattern string to all uppercase before using it to search to avoid having to uppercase each pattern character multiple times.

Once the comparison function is out of the way, use the transform and search standard algorithms to do two things. Use transform to uppercase the entire pattern (but not the target string). After that, use search with the comparison function to find the location of the substring.

Remember that standard algorithms operate on *sequences*, not just strings. They are general algorithms that operate on, primarily but not exclusively, the standard containers, but they make no assumptions about the contents of the containers. All the standard algorithms care about is that you supply a comparison function (or if not, they use the default operators) that somehow compares two elements and returns a bool indicating whether the test is true or false.

There is one thing I should point out that looks odd in Example 4-22. You can see that caseInsCompare returns a const_iterator, as in

```
string::const_iterator caseInsFind(const string& s,
                                   const string& p)
```

What if you want to modify the element that the returned iterator points to? This is a reasonable request. The reason it is const is because the strings being passed into caseInsFind are const, and therefore you can't get a non-const iterator to a const string. If you want an iterator you can use to modify the string, remove the const from the parameters and change the function declaration to return a string::iterator instead.

4.15 Converting Between Tabs and Spaces in a Text File

Problem

You have a text file that contains tabs or spaces, and you want to convert from one to the other. For example, you may want to replace all tabs with three spaces, or you may want to do just the opposite and replace occurrences of some number of spaces with a single tab.

Solution

Regardless of whether you are replacing tabs with spaces or spaces with tabs, use the ifstream and ofstream classes in <fstream>. In the first (simpler) case, read data in with an input stream, one character at a time, examine it, and if it's a tab, write some number of spaces to the output stream. Example 4-23 demonstrates how to do this.

Example 4-23. Replacing tabs with spaces

```
#include <iostream>
#include <fstream>
#include <cstdlib>

using namespace std;

int main(int argc, char** argv) {

   if (argc < 3)
      return(EXIT_FAILURE);

   ifstream in(argv[1]);
   ofstream out(argv[2]);
```

Example 4-23. Replacing tabs with spaces (continued)

```
  if (!in || !out)
    return(EXIT_FAILURE);

  char c;
  while (in.get(c)) {
     if (c == '\t')
        out << "   "; // 3 spaces
     else
        out << c;
  }

  out.close();

  if (out)
     return(EXIT_SUCCESS);
  else
     return(EXIT_FAILURE);
}
```

If, instead, you need to replace spaces with tabs, see Example 4-24. It contains the function spacesToTabs that reads from an input stream, one character at a time, looking for three consecutive spaces. When it finds three in a row, it writes a tab to the output stream. For all other characters, or for fewer than three spaces, whatever is read from the input stream is written to the output stream.

Example 4-24. Replacing spaces with tabs

```
#include <iostream>
#include <istream>
#include <ostream>
#include <fstream>
#include <cstdlib>

using namespace std;

void spacesToTabs(istream& in, ostream& out, int spaceLimit) {

   int consecSpaces = 0;
   char c;

   while (in.get(c)) {
      if (c != ' ') {
         if (consecSpaces > 0) {
            for (int i = 0; i < consecSpaces; i++) {
               out.put(' ');
            }
            consecSpaces = 0;
         }
         out.put(c);
      } else {
         if (++consecSpaces == spaceLimit) {
```

Example 4-24. Replacing spaces with tabs (continued)

```
            out.put('\t');
            consecSpaces = 0;
        }
      }
    }
}

int main(int argc, char** argv) {

    if (argc < 3)
        return(EXIT_FAILURE);

    ifstream in(argv[1]);
    ofstream out(argv[2]);

    if (!in || !out)
        return(EXIT_FAILURE);

    spacesToTabs(in, out, 3);

    out.close();

    if (out)
        return(EXIT_SUCCESS);
    else
        return(EXIT_FAILURE);
}
```

Discussion

The mechanism for both of these solutions is the same; only the algorithms differ. Read characters from an input stream using get, and put them to an output stream with put. Put your logic for doing the translation between calls to these two functions.

You probably noticed in Example 4-24 that in main I declared in and out to be of types ifstream and ofstream, respectively, and that the parameters to spacesToTabs are actually istream and ostream. I did this to allow spacesToTabs to work on any kind of input or output streams (well, not *any* kind of stream—ones that inherit from basic_istream or basic_ostream), and not just file streams. For example, you may have the text you want to reformat in a string stream (istringstream and ostringstream in <sstream>). In that case, do something like this:

```
istringstream istr;
ostringstream ostr;

// fill up istr with text...

spacesToTabs(istr, ostr);
```

As with strings, streams are actually class templates that are parameterized on the type of character the stream operates on. For example, an ifstream is a typedef for basic_ifstream<char>, and a wifstream is a typedef for basic_ifstream<wchar_t>. Thus, if you need spacesToTabs from Examples 4-23 or 4-24 to work on a stream of any kind of character, you can use the class templates instead of the typedefs:

```
template<typename T>
void spacesToTabs(std::basic_istream<T>& in,
                  std::basic_ostream<T>& out,
                  int spaceLimit) { //...
```

4.16 Wrapping Lines in a Text File

Problem

You want to "wrap" text at a specific number of characters in a file. For example, if you want to wrap text at 72 characters, you would insert a new-line character after every 72 characters in the file. If the file contains human-readable text, you probably want to avoid splitting words.

Solution

Write a function that uses input and output streams to read in characters with istream::get(char), do some bookkeeping, and write out characters with ostream::put(char). Example 4-25 shows how to do this for text files that contain human-readable text without splitting words.

Example 4-25. Wrapping text

```
#include <iostream>
#include <fstream>
#include <cstdlib>
#include <string>
#include <cctype>
#include <functional>

using namespace std;

void textWrap(istream& in, ostream& out, size_t width) {

   string tmp;
   char cur = '\0';
   char last = '\0';
   size_t i = 0;

   while (in.get(cur)) {
      if (++i == width) {
         ltrimws(tmp);                    // ltrim as in Recipe
         out << '\n' << tmp;              // 4.1
         i = tmp.length();
         tmp.clear();
      } else if (isspace(cur) &&          // This is the end of
```

Example 4-25. Wrapping text (continued)

```
                  !isspace(last)) { // a word
        out << tmp;
        tmp.clear( );
      }
      tmp += cur;
      last = cur;
    }
}

int main(int argc, char** argv) {
  if (argc < 3)
    return(EXIT_FAILURE);

  int w = 72;
  ifstream in(argv[1]);
  ofstream out(argv[2]);

  if (!in || !out)
    return(EXIT_FAILURE);

  if (argc == 4)
    w = atoi(argv[3]);

  textWrap(in, out, w);

  out.close( );

  if (out)
    return(EXIT_SUCCESS);
  else
    return(EXIT_FAILURE);
}
```

Discussion

textWrap reads characters, one at a time, from the input stream. Each character is appended to a temporary string, tmp, until it reaches the end of a word or the maximum line width. If it reaches the end of a word but is not yet at the maximum line width, the temporary string is written to the output stream. Otherwise, if the maximum line width has been exceeded, a new line is written to the output stream, the whitespace at the beginning of the temporary string is removed, and the string is written to the output stream. In this way, textWrap writes as much as it can to the output stream without exceeding the maximum line width. Instead of splitting a word, it bumps the word to the next line.

Example 4-25 uses streams nearly identically to Recipe 4.15. See that recipe for more information on what streams are and how to use them.

Recipe 4.15

4.17 Counting the Number of Characters, Words, and Lines in a Text File

Problem

You have to count the numbers of characters, words, and lines—or some other type of text element—in a text file.

Solution

Use an input stream to read the characters in, one at a time, and increment local statistics as you encounter characters, words, and line breaks. Example 4-26 contains the function countStuff, which does exactly that.

Example 4-26. Calculating statistics about a text file

```cpp
#include <iostream>
#include <fstream>
#include <cstdlib>
#include <cctype>

using namespace std;

void countStuff(istream& in,
                int& chars,
                int& words,
                int& lines) {

   char cur = '\0';
   char last = '\0';
   chars = words = lines = 0;

   while (in.get(cur)) {
      if (cur == '\n' ||
          (cur == '\f' && last == '\r'))
        lines++;
      else
        chars++;
      if (!std::isalnum(cur) &&    // This is the end of a
          std::isalnum(last))      // word
        words++;
      last = cur;
   }
   if (chars > 0) {                // Adjust word and line
```

Example 4-26. Calculating statistics about a text file (continued)

```
      if (std::isalnum(last))      // counts for special
         words++;                  // case
      lines++;
   }
}

int main(int argc, char** argv) {

   if (argc < 2)
      return(EXIT_FAILURE);

   ifstream in(argv[1]);

   if (!in)
      exit(EXIT_FAILURE);

   int c, w, l;

   countStuff(in, c, w, l);
1
   cout << "chars: " << c << '\n';
   cout << "words: " << w << '\n';
   cout << "lines: " << l << '\n';
}
```

Discussion

The algorithm here is straightforward. Characters are easy: increment the character count each time you call get on the input stream. Lines are only slightly more difficult, since the way a line ends depends on the operating system. Thankfully, it's usually either a new-line character (\n) or a carriage return line feed sequence (\r\l). By keeping track of the current and last characters, you can easily capture occurrences of this sequence. Words are easy or hard, depending on your definition of a word.

For Example 4-26, I consider a word to be a contiguous sequence of alphanumeric characters. As I look at each character in the input stream, when I encounter a nonalphanumeric character, I look at the previous character to see if it was alphanumeric. If it was, then a word has just ended and I can increment the word count. I can tell if a character is alphanumeric by using isalnum from <cctype>. But that's not all—you can test characters for a number of different qualities with similar functions. See Table 4-3 for the functions you can use to test character qualities. For wide characters, use the functions of the same name but with a "w" after the "is," e.g., iswspace. The wide-character versions are declared in the header <cwctype>.

Table 4-3. Character test functions from <cctype> and <cwctype>

Function	Description
isalpha iswalpha	Alpha characters: a–z, A–Z (upper- or lowercase).
isupper iswupper	Alpha characters in uppercase only: A–Z.
islower iswlower	Alpha characters in lowercase only: a–z.
isdigit iswdigit	Numeric characters: 0–9.
isxdigit iswxdigit	Hexadecimal numeric characters: 0–9, a–f, A–F.
isspace iswspace	Whitespace characters: ' ', \n, \t, \v, \r, \l.
iscntrl iswcntrl	Control characters: ASCII 0–31 and 127.
ispunct iswpunct	Punctuation characters that don't belong to the previous groups.
isalnum iswalnum	isalpha or isdigit is true.
isprint iswprint	Printable ASCII characters.
isgraph iswgraph	isalpha or isdigit or ispunct is true.

After all characters have been read in and the end of the stream has been reached, there is a bit of adjustment to do. First, the loop only counts line breaks, and not, strictly speaking, lines. Therefore, it will always be one less than the actual number of lines. To make this problem go away I just increment the line count by one if there are more than zero characters in the file. Second, if the stream ends with an alphanumeric character, the test for the end of the last word will never occur because I can't test the next character. To account for this, I check if the last character in the stream is alphanumeric (also only when there are more than zero characters in the file) and increment the word count by one.

The technique in Example 4-26 of using streams is nearly identical to that described in Recipes 4.14 and 4.15, but simpler since it's just inspecting the file and not making any changes.

See Also

Recipes 4.14 and 4.15

4.18   Counting Instances of Each Word in a Text File

Problem

You want to count the number of occurrences of each word in a text file.

Solution

Use operator>>, defined in <string>, to read contiguous chunks of text from the input file, and use a map, defined in <map>, to store each word and its frequency in the file. Example 4-27 demonstrates how to do this.

Example 4-27. Counting word frequencies

```
1    #include <iostream>
2    #include <fstream>
3    #include <map>
4    #include <string>
5
6    typedef std::map<std::string, int> StrIntMap;
7
8    void countWords(std::istream& in, StrIntMap& words) {
9
10       std::string s;
11
12       while (in >> s) {
13           ++words[s];
14       }
15   }
16
17   int main(int argc, char** argv) {
18
19       if (argc < 2)
20           return(EXIT_FAILURE);
21
22       std::ifstream in(argv[1]);
23
24       if (!in)
25           exit(EXIT_FAILURE);
26
27       StrIntMap w;
28       countWords(in, w);
29
30       for (StrIntMap::iterator p = w.begin();
31           p != w.end(); ++p) {
32           std::cout << p->first << " occurred "
33                   << p->second << " times.\n";
34       }
35   }
```

Discussion

Example 4-27 looks simple enough, but there is more going on than it appears. Most of the subtleties have to do with maps, so let's talk about them first.

If you're not familiar with maps, you should be. A map is a container class template that is part of the STL. It stores key-value pairs in order according to std::less, or your custom comparison function, should you supply one. The kinds of keys and values you can store in it depend only on your imagination; in this example, we are just going to store strings and ints.

I used a typedef on line 6 to make the code cleaner:

```
typedef map<string, int> StrIntMap;
```

Thus, a StrIntMap is a map that stores string/int pairs. Each string is a unique word—which is why I'm using it as the key—that has been read in and its associated int is the number of times it occurs. All that's left is to read in each of the words one-at-a-time, add it to the map if it's not already there, and increment its associated count value if it is.

This is what countWords does. The essential logic is brief:

```
while (in >> s) {
    ++words[s];
}
```

operator>> reads in contiguous chunks of non-whitespace from its lefthand side operand (an istream) and places them in the righthand side operand (a string). Once I've read a "word," all I have to do is update the statistics in the map, and that is done with the following line:

```
++words[s];
```

map defines operator[] for retrieving a value given a key (it actually returns a reference to the value itself), so to increment it, just increment the value indexed at the particular key. But something about this might seem a little weird. What if the key isn't already in the map? Don't we try to increment a nonexistent index, and crash like we would with an array? No, map does operator[] differently than other STL containers or ordinary, C-style arrays.

In a map, operator[] does two things: if the key does not already exist, it creates a value by using that value's type's default constructor and adds that key/value pair to the map, if the key already exists in the map, no modification is made. In both cases, a reference to the value for the specified key is returned, even if that value was just created with its default constructor. This is a handy feature (if you know it's there), because it eliminates the need for client code to check for a key's existence before inserting it.

Now, look at lines 32 and 33. The iterator refers to members called first and second–what are those? maps play a trick on you by using another class template to store your name value pairs: the pair class template defined in <utility> (included by <map> already). If you are iterating through the items stored in a map, you will be pointing to pair objects. Working with pairs is simple, the first item in a pair is stored in the first member, and the second is stored in, well, second.

I used operator>> in Example 4-27 to read in contiguous chunks of text from the input stream, which is different than some of the other examples. I did this to demonstrate that it can be done, but you will almost certainly need to customize the behavior based on your definition of a "word" in a text file. For example, consider an excerpt of the output produced by Example 4-27:

```
with occurred 5 times.
work occurred 3 times.
workers occurred 3 times.
workers. occurred 1 times.
years occurred 2 times.
years. occurred 1 times.
```

Notice that the periods on the end of words are included as part of each word. Most likely, you will want to change the definition of words to mean only alpha or alphanumeric characters, as I did in Recipe 4.17 by using some of the character-testing functions in <cctype> and <cwctype>.

See Also

Recipe 4.17 and Table 4-3

4.19   Add Margins to a Text File

Problem

Given a text file, you want to add margins to it. In other words, you want to pad either side of each line with some character so that each line is the same width.

Solution

Example 4-28 shows how to add margins to a file using streams, strings, and the getline function template.

Example 4-28. Adding margins to a text file

```
#include <iostream>
#include <fstream>
#include <string>
#include <cstdlib>

using namespace std;
const static char PAD_CHAR = '.';
```

Example 4-28. Adding margins to a text file (continued)

```
// addMargins takes two streams and two numbers. The streams are for
// input and output. The first of the two numbers represents the
// left margin width (i.e., the number of spaces to insert at the
// beginning of every line in the file). The second number represents
// the total line width to pad to.
void addMargins(istream& in, ostream& out,
                int left, int right) {

    string tmp;

    while (!in.eof()) {
        getline(in, tmp, '\n');                 // getline is defined
                                                // in <string>

        tmp.insert(tmp.begin(), left, PAD_CHAR);
        rpad(tmp, right, PAD_CHAR);             // rpad from Recipe
                                                // 4.2

        out << tmp << '\n';
    }
}

int main(int argc, char** argv) {

    if (argc < 3)
        return(EXIT_FAILURE);

    ifstream in(argv[1]);
    ofstream out(argv[2]);

    if (!in || !out)
        return(EXIT_FAILURE);

    int left = 8;
    int right = 72;

    if (argc == 5) {
        left = atoi(argv[3]);
        right = atoi(argv[4]);
    }

    addMargins(in, out, left, right);

    out.close();

    if (out)
        return(EXIT_SUCCESS);
    else
        return(EXIT_FAILURE);
}
```

This example makes a few assumptions about the format of the incoming text, so be sure to read the next section for details.

Discussion

addMargins assumes your input looks something like this:

```
The data is still inconclusive. But the weakness
in job creation and the apparent weakness in
high-paying jobs may be opposite sides of a coin.
Companies still seem cautious, relying on
temporary workers and anxious about rising health
care costs associated with full-time workers.
```

This text is wrapped at 50 characters (see Recipe 4.16), and is left justified (see Recipe 4.20). addMargins also assumes you want your output to look something like the following, which uses periods instead of spaces to show where the padding has been done:

```
........The data is still inconclusive. But the weakness................
........in job creation and the apparent weakness in....................
........high-paying jobs may be opposite sides of a coin................
........Companies still seem cautious, relying on.......................
........temporary workers and anxious about rising health...............
........care costs associated with full-time workers....................
```

By default, the left margin is eight characters and the total line length is 72. Of course, if you know your input text will always be left and right justified, you can simply pad each end of each line with as many characters as you see fit. Either way, the logic is straightforward. Many of the techniques used in this recipe have been covered already (streams, padding a string), so I won't discuss them here. The one function that has not yet appeared is getline.

If you want to read in text a line at a time, or to be more precise, you want to read in text up to a particular delimiter, use the getline function template defined in <string>, as I did in Example 4-28:

```
getline(in, tmp, '\n');
```

getline reads characters from the input stream and appends them to tmp until the delimiter '\n' is reached, which is not appended to tmp. basic_istream has a member function by the same name, but it behaves differently. It stores its output in a character buffer, not a string. In this case, I want to take advantage of string member functions, and don't want to have to read a line into a character buffer redundantly and then copy that into a string, so I used the string version of getline.

See Also

Recipes 4.16 and 4.20

4.20   Justify a Text File

Problem

You want to right- or left-justify text.

Solution

Use streams and the standard stream formatting flags `right` and `left` that are part of ios_base, defined in `<ios>`. Example 4-29 shows how they work.

Example 4-29. Justify text

```
#include <iostream>
#include <fstream>
#include <string>
#include <cstdlib>

using namespace std;

int main(int argc, char** argv) {

   if (argc < 3)
      return(EXIT_FAILURE);

   ifstream in(argv[1]);
   ofstream out(argv[2]);

   int w = 72;
   if (argc == 4)
      w = atoi(argv[3]);

   string tmp;
   out.setf(ios_base::right);     // Tell the stream to
                                  // right-justify
   while (!in.eof()) {
      out.width(w);                    // Reset width after
      getline(in, tmp, '\n');          // each write
      out << tmp << '\n';
   }
   out.close();
}
```

This example takes three arguments: an input file, an output file, and the width to right-justify to. You can use an input file like this:

```
With automatic download of Microsoft's (Nasdaq:
MSFT) enormous SP2 security patch to the Windows
XP operating system set to begin, the industry
still waits to understand its ramifications. Home
users that have their preferences set to receive
operating-system updates as they are made
available by Microsoft may be surprised to learn
```

```
    that some of the software they already run on
    their systems could be disabled by SP2 or may run
    very differently.
```

and make it look like this:

```
        With automatic download of Microsoft's (Nasdaq:
       MSFT) enormous SP2 security patch to the Windows
            XP operating system set to begin, the industry
       still waits to understand its ramifications. Home
       users that have their preferences set to receive
             operating-system updates as they are made
       available by Microsoft may be surprised to learn
             that some of the software they already run on
       their systems could be disabled by SP2 or may run
                                      very differently.
```

The second text sample is right-justified to 50 characters.

Discussion

The ios_base class template has lots of flags for formatting numeric and text data that is read from or written to streams. The two that control how text is justified are right and left. They are static const members of ios_base, and are of type fmtflags (which is implementation defined); all of this stuff is defined in <ios>.

To set formatting flags, use ios_base::setf. This ORs the flags you pass in with the existing flags on the stream. For example, this line turns on right-justification:

```
    out.setf(std::ios_base::right);
```

But right-justification doesn't make much sense without a righthand margin to butt up against. To set that margin, use ios_base::width, like this:

```
    out.width(w);
```

This sets the width of the output field to the value passed in, meaning that when you right-justify text, the beginning of the string will be padded with spaces as much as is necessary to align the right end to the margin. Note that I set the width inside the loop while I set the right flag prior to the loop. I had to do this because the width resets to zero after each write to the stream. Format flags are not reset after writes, so I only had to initialize them once and be done with it.

It's always good to be tidy and responsible, though, so there is one more thing you should do when using format flags: clean up after yourself.

Often, the stream you are writing to does not belong to you, especially if you are writing a general-purpose library or API. For example, if you write a fancy logging function that takes an output stream and a string, modifies the string, sets the format flags, and writes it to the stream, you have potentially unwanted side-effects. After client code calls your logging function, its stream has potentially had its format flags rearranged. The solution is to copy the old ones and restore them when you're done.

For example, a responsible error logging function might look like this:

```
using namespace std;

void logError(ostream& out, const string& s) {

    string tmp(s);
    tmp.insert(0, "ERROR: ");

    ios_base::fmtflags flgs =        // setf returns the
        out.setf(ios_base::left);    // flags that were
                                     // already there
    out.width(72);
    out << tmp << '\n';

    out.flags(flgs);                 // reset to original
}
```

The `flags` member function works similarly to `setf`, but it doesn't OR the flags you give it with the stream's current flags, it replaces them. Thus, when you call `flags` and pass in the original formatting flags, you can feel good that you cleaned up after yourself.

4.21 Squeeze Whitespace to Single Spaces in a Text File

Problem

You have a text file with whitespace of varying lengths in it, and you want to reduce every occurrence of a contiguous span of whitespace characters to a single space.

Solution

Use the `operator>>` function template, defined in `<string>`, to read in continuous chunks of non-whitespace from a stream into a string. Then use its counterpart, `operator<<`, to write each of these chunks to an output stream, and append a single character after each one. Example 4-30 gives a short example of this technique.

Example 4-30. Squeezing whitespace to single spaces

```
#include <iostream>
#include <fstream>
#include <string>

using namespace std;

int main(int argc, char** argv) {

    if (argc < 3)
        return(EXIT_FAILURE);
```

Example 4-30. Squeezing whitespace to single spaces (continued)

```
    ifstream in(argv[1]);
    ofstream out(argv[2]);

    if (!in || !out)
        return(EXIT_FAILURE);

    string tmp;

    in >> tmp;          // Grab the first word
    out << tmp;         // Dump it to the output stream

    while (in >> tmp) { // operator>> ignores whitespace, so all I have
        out << ' ';     // to do is add a space and each chunk of non-
        out << tmp;     // whitespace
    }

    out.close();
}
```

Discussion

This is a simple thing to do if you take advantage of streams and strings. Even if you have to implement a variation of this—for example, you may want to preserve new lines—the same facilities do the trick. If you want to add new lines, you can use the solution presented in Recipe 4.16 to insert them in the right place.

See Also

Recipes 4.15 and 4.16

4.22   Autocorrect Text as a Buffer Changes

Problem

You have a class that represents some kind of text field or document, and as text is appended to it, you want to correct automatically misspelled words the way Microsoft Word's Autocorrect feature does.

Solution

Using a map, defined in <map>, strings, and a variety of standard library features, you can implement this with relatively little code. Example 4-31 shows how to do it.

Example 4-31. Autocorrect text

```
#include <iostream>
#include <string>
#include <cctype>
#include <map>
```

Example 4-31. Autocorrect text (continued)

```
using namespace std;

typedef map<string, string> StrStrMap;

// Class for holding text fields
class TextAutoField {

public:
   TextAutoField(StrStrMap* const p) : pDict_(p) {}
   ~TextAutoField( ) {}

   void append(char c);
   void getText(string& s) {s = buf_;}

private:
   TextAutoField( );
   string buf_;
   StrStrMap* const pDict_;
};

// Append with autocorrect
void TextAutoField::append(char c) {

   if ((isspace(c) || ispunct(c)) &&          // Only do the auto-
       buf_.length( ) > 0 &&                  // correct when ws or
       !isspace(buf_[buf_.length( ) - 1])) {  // punct is entered

      string::size_type i = buf_.find_last_of(" \f\n\r\t\v");

      i = (i == string::npos) ? 0 : ++i;

      string tmp = buf_.substr(i, buf_.length( ) - i);
      StrStrMap::const_iterator p = pDict_->find(tmp);

      if (p != pDict_->end( )) {              // Found it, so erase
         buf_.erase(i, buf_.length( ) - i);   // and replace
         buf_ += p->second;
      }
   }
   buf_ += c;
}

int main( ) {

   // Set up the map
   StrStrMap dict;
   TextAutoField txt(&dict);

   dict["taht"] = "that";
   dict["right"] = "wrong";
   dict["bug"] = "feature";
```

Example 4-31. Autocorrect text (continued)

```
    string tmp = "He's right, taht's a bug.";
    cout << "Original: " << tmp << '\n';
    for (string::iterator p = tmp.begin( );
         p != tmp.end( ); ++p) {
      txt.append(*p);
    }

    txt.getText(tmp);

    cout << "Corrected version is: " << tmp << '\n';
}
```

The output of Example 4-31 is:

```
    Original: He's right, taht's a bug.
    Corrected version is: He's wrong, that's a feature.
```

Discussion

strings and maps are handy for situations when you have to keep track of string associations. TextAutoField is a simple text buffer that uses a string to hold its data. What makes TextAutoField interesting is its append method, which "listens" for whitespace or punctuation, and does some processing when either one occurs.

To make this autocorrect behavior a reality, you need two things. First, you need a dictionary of sorts that contains the common misspelling of a word and the associated correct spelling. A map stores key-value pairs, where the key and value can be of any types, so it's an ideal candidate. At the top of Example 4-31, there is a typedef for a map of string pairs:

```
    typedef map<string, string> StrStrMap;
```

See Recipe 4.18 for a more detailed explanation of maps. TextAutoField stores a pointer to the map, because most likely you would want a single dictionary for use by all fields.

Assuming client code puts something meaningful in the map, append just has to periodically do lookups in the map. In Example 4-31, append waits for whitespace or punctuation to do its magic. You can test a character for whitespace with isspace, or for punctuation by using ispunct, both of which are defined in <cctype> for narrow characters (take a look at Table 4-3).

The code that does a lookup requires some explanation if you are not familiar with using iterators and find methods on STL containers. The string tmp contains the last chunk of text that was appended to the TextAutoField. To see if it is a commonly misspelled work, look it up in the dictionary like this:

```
    StrStrMap::iterator p = pDict_->find(tmp);

    if (p != pDict_->end( )) {
```

The important point here is that `map::find` returns an iterator that points to the pair containing the matching key, if it was found. If not, an iterator pointing to one past the end of the map is returned, which is exactly what `map::end` returns (this is how all STL containers that support `find` work). If the word was found in the `map`, erase the old word from the buffer and replace it with the correct version:

```
buf_.erase(i, buf_.length() - i);
buf_ += p->second;
```

Append the character that started the process (either whitespace or punctuation) and you're done.

See Also

Recipes 4.17, 4.18, and Table 4-3

4.23   Reading a Comma-Separated Text File

Problem

You want to read in a text file that is delimited by commas and new lines (or any other pair of delimiters for that matter). Records are delimited by one character, and fields within a record are delimited by another. For example, a comma-separated text file of employee information may look like the following:

```
Smith, Bill, 5/1/2002, Active
Stanford, John, 4/5/1999, Inactive
```

Such files are usually interim storage for data sets exported from spreadsheets, databases, or other file formats.

Solution

See Example 4-32 for how to do this. If you read the text into `strings` one contiguous chunk at a time using `getline` (the function template defined in `<string>`) you can use the `split` function I presented in Recipe 4.6 to parse the text and put it in a data structure, in this case, a `vector`.

Example 4-32. Reading in a delimited file

```cpp
#include <iostream>
#include <fstream>
#include <string>
#include <vector>

using namespace std;

void split(const string& s, char c,
           vector<string>& v) {
   int i = 0;
   int j = s.find(c);
```

Example 4-32. Reading in a delimited file (continued)

```
    while (j >= 0) {
        v.push_back(s.substr(i, j-i));
        i = ++j;
        j = s.find(c, j);

        if (j < 0) {
            v.push_back(s.substr(i, s.length()));
        }
    }
}

void loadCSV(istream& in, vector<vector<string>*>& data) {

    vector<string>* p = NULL;
    string tmp;

    while (!in.eof()) {
        getline(in, tmp, '\n');                  // Grab the next line

        p = new vector<string>();
        split(tmp, ',', *p);                     // Use split from
                                                 // Recipe 4.7
        data.push_back(p);

        cout << tmp << '\n';
        tmp.clear();
    }
}

int main(int argc, char** argv) {

    if (argc < 2)
        return(EXIT_FAILURE);

    ifstream in(argv[1]);

    if (!in)
        return(EXIT_FAILURE);

    vector<vector<string>*> data;

    loadCSV(in, data);

    // Go do something useful with the data...

    for (vector<vector<string>*>::iterator p = data.begin();
         p != data.end(); ++p) {
        delete *p;                               // Be sure to de-
    }                                            // reference p!
}
```

Discussion

There isn't much in Example 4-32 that hasn't been covered already. I discussed `getline` in Recipe 4.19 and vectors in Recipe 4.3. The only piece worth mentioning has to do with memory allocation.

`loadCSV` creates a new vector for each line of data it reads in and stores it in yet another vector of pointers to vectors. Since the memory for each of these vectors is allocated on the heap, somebody has to de-allocate it, and that somebody is you (and not the vector implementation).

The vector has no knowledge of whether it contains a value or a pointer to a value, or anything else. All it knows is that when it's destroyed, it needs to call the destructor for each element it contains. If the vector stores objects, then this is fine; the object is properly destroyed. But if the vector contains pointers, the pointer is destroyed, but not the object it points to.

There are two ways to ensure the memory is freed. First, you can do what I did in Example 4-32 and do it manually yourself, like this:

```
for (vector<vector<string>*>::iterator p = data.begin( );
     p != data.end( ); ++p) {
   delete *p;
}
```

Or you can use a reference-counted pointer, such as the Boost project's `smart_ptr`, which will be part of the forthcoming C++0x standard. But doing so is nontrivial, so I recommend reading up on what a `smart_ptr` is and how it works. For more information on Boost in general, see the homepage at *www.boost.org*.

4.24 Using Regular Expressions to Split a String

Problem

You want to split a string into tokens, but you require more sophisticated searching or flexibility than Recipe 4.7 provides. For example, you may want tokens that are more than one character or can take on many different forms. This often results in code, and causes confusion in consumers of your class or function.

Solution

Use Boost's regex class template. `regex` enables the use of regular expressions on string and text data. Example 4-33 shows how to use regex to split strings.

Example 4-33. Using Boost's regular expressions

```
#include <iostream>
#include <string>
#include <boost/regex.hpp>
```

Example 4-33. Using Boost's regular expressions (continued)

```
int main( ) {

    std::string s = "who,lives:in-a,pineapple     under the sea?";

    boost::regex re(",|:|-|\\s+");       // Create the reg exp
    boost::sregex_token_iterator         // Create an iterator using a
      p(s.begin( ), s.end( ), re, -1);   // sequence and that reg exp
    boost::sregex_token_iterator end;    // Create an end-of-reg-exp
                                         // marker
    while (p != end)
      std::cout << *p++ << '\n';
}
```

Discussion

Example 4-33 shows how to use regex to iterate over matches in a regular expression. The following line sets up the regular expression:

```
boost::regex re(",|:|-|\\s+");
```

What it says, essentially, is that each match of the regular expression is either a comma, or a colon, or a dash, or one or more spaces. The pipe character is the logical operator that ORs each of the delimiters together. The next two lines set up the iterator:

```
boost::sregex_token_iterator
    p(s.begin( ), s.end( ), re, -1);
boost::sregex_token_iterator end;
```

The iterator p is constructed using the regular expression and an input string. Once that has been built, you can treat p like you would an iterator on a standard library sequence. A sregex_token_iterator constructed with no arguments is a special value that represents the end of a regular expression token sequence, and can therefore be used in a comparison to know when you hit the end.

CHAPTER 5

Dates and Times

5.0   Introduction

Dates and times are surprisingly vast and complex topics. As a reflection of this fact, the C++ standard library does not provide a proper date type. C++ inherits the structs and functions for date and time manipulation from C, along with a couple of date/time input and output functions that take into account localization. You can find relief, however, in the Boost date_time Library by Jeff Garland, which is possibly the most comprehensive and extensible date and time library for C++ available. I will be using it in several of the recipes. There is an expectation among the C++ community that future date/time extensions to the standard library will be based on the Boost date_time library.

The Boost date_time library includes two separate systems for manipulating dates and times: one for manipulating times and one for manipulating dates using a Gregorian calendar. The recipes will cover both systems.

For more information on dates and times, specifically reading and writing them, please see Chapter 13.

5.1   Obtaining the Current Date and Time

Problem

You want to retrieve the current date and time from the user's computer, either as a local time or as a Coordinated Universal Time (UTC).

Solution

Call the time function from the <ctime> header, passing a value of 0 as the parameter. The result will be a time_t value. You can use the gmtime function to convert the time_t value to a tm structure representing the current UTC time (a.k.a. Greenwich Mean Time or GMT); or, you can use the localtime function to convert the time_t

---

Gregorian Calendar and Leap Years

The Gregorian calendar is the most widely used calendar in the Western world today. The Gregorian calendar was intended to fix a flaw in the Julian calendar. The slow process of adoption of the Gregorian calendar started in 1582.

The Julian calendar dictates that every fourth year is a leap year, but every hundredth year is a non-leap year. The Gregorian calendar introduced a new exception that every 400 years should be a leap year.

Leap years are designed to compensate for the Earth's rotation around the sun being out of synchronization with the length of the day. In other words, dividing the length of a solar year, by the length of a day is an irrational number. The result is that if the calendar is not adjusted we would have seasonal drift, where the equinoxes and solstices (which determine the seasons) would become further out of synchronization with each new year.

---

value to a `tm` structure representing the local time. The program in Example 5-1 obtains the current date/time, and then converts it to local time and outputs it. Next, the program converts the current date/time to a UTC date/time and outputs that.

Example 5-1. Getting the local and UTC times

```
#include <iostream>
#include <ctime>
#include <cstdlib>

using namespace std;

int main( )
{
  // Current date/time based on current system
  time_t now = time(0);

  // Convert now to tm struct for local timezone
  tm* localtm = localtime(&now);
  cout << "The local date and time is: " << asctime(localtm) << endl;

  // Convert now to tm struct for UTC
  tm* gmtm = gmtime(&now);
  if (gmtm != NULL) {
     cout << "The UTC date and time is: " << asctime(gmtm) << endl;
  }
  else {
    cerr << "Failed to get the UTC date and time" << endl;
    return EXIT_FAILURE;
  }
}
```

Discussion

The `time` function returns a `time_t` type, which is an implementation-defined arithmetic type for representing a time period (a.k.a. a time interval) with at least a resolution of one second. The largest time interval that can be portably represented using a `time_t` is ±2,147,483,648 seconds, or approximately 68 years.

A call to `time(0)` returns a `time_t` representing the time interval from an implementation defined base time (commonly 0:00:00 January 1, 1970) to the current moment.

The Year 2038 Bug

Since a `time_t` is only required to represent time intervals of ±68 years, and many implementations use a base year of 1970 for representing the current time, there is an inability for many popular C++ implementations to represent dates and times after 2038. This means that a lot of software could break in 2038, if programmers don't take adequate precautions.

A more workable representation of the current date and time is achieved by converting to a `tm` struct using the `localtime` or `gmtime` functions. A `tm` struct has the integer fields shown in Example 5-2.

Example 5-2. Layout of a tm struct

```
struct tm {
  int tm_sec;   // seconds of minutes from 0 to 61 (60 and 61 are leap seconds)
  int tm_min;   // minutes of hour from 0 to 59
  int tm_hour;  // hours of day from 0 to 24
  int tm_mday;  // day of month from 0 to 23
  int tm_mon;   // month of year from 0 to 11
  int tm_year;  // year since 1900
  int tm_wday;  // days since sunday
  int tm_yday;  // days since January 1st
  int tm_isdst; // hours of daylight savings time
}
```

When using the `gmtime` function, be sure to check its return value. If the computer running the code doesn't have a local time zone defined, the `gmtime` function will be unable to compute the UTC time, and will return 0. If you pass 0 to the `asctime` function, undefined behavior will result.

The `localtime`, `gmtime`, and `asctime` functions all return pointers to statically allocated objects. This is more efficient for the library, but it means that subsequent calls will change the value of those objects. The code in Example 5-3 shows how this can have surprising effects.

Example 5-3. Pitfalls of using asctime

```
void f( ) {
  char* x = asctime(localtime(time(0)));
  wait_for_15_seconds( ); // do some long processing task
  asctime(localtime(time(0)));
  cout << x << endl; // prints out the current time, not fifteen seconds ago.
}
```

5.2   Formatting a Date/Time as a String

Problem

You want to convert a date and/or time to a formatted string.

Solution

You can use the time_put template class from the <locale> header, as shown in Example 5-4.

Example 5-4. Formatting a datetime string

```
#include <iostream>
#include <cstdlib>
#include <ctime>
#include <cstring>
#include <string>
#include <stdexcept>
#include <iterator>
#include <sstream>

using namespace std;

ostream& formatDateTime(ostream& out, const tm& t, const char* fmt) {
  const time_put<char>& dateWriter = use_facet<time_put<char> >(out.getloc( ));
  int n = strlen(fmt);
  if (dateWriter.put(out, out, ' ', &t, fmt, fmt + n).failed( )) {
    throw runtime_error("failure to format date time");
  }
  return out;
}

string dateTimeToString(const tm& t, const char* format) {
  stringstream s;
  formatDateTime(s, t, format);
  return s.str( );
}

tm now( ) {
  time_t now = time(0);
  return *localtime(&now);
}
```

Example 5-4. Formatting a datetime string (continued)

```
int main( )
{
  try {
    string s = dateTimeToString(now( ), "%A %B, %d %Y %I:%M%p");
    cout << s << endl;
    s = dateTimeToString(now( ), "%Y-%m-%d %H:%M:%S");
    cout << s << endl;
  }
  catch(...) {
    cerr << "failed to format date time" << endl;
    return EXIT_FAILURE;
  }
  return EXIT_SUCCESS;
}
```

Output of the program in Example 5-4 will resemble the following, depending on your local settings:

```
Sunday July, 24 2005 05:48PM
2005-07-24 17:48:11
```

Discussion

The time_put member function put uses a formatting string specifier like the C printf function format string. Characters are output to the buffer as they appear in the format string unless they are preceded by a % sign. A character preceded by a % sign is a format specifier and has the special meaning shown in Table 5-1. Format specifiers may also support modifiers, such as an integer to specify the field width, as in %4B.

Table 5-1. Date/time format specifiers

Specifier	Description
a	Abbreviated weekday name (e.g., Mon)
A	Full weekday name (e.g., Monday)
b	Abbreviated month name (e.g., Dec)
B	Full month name (e.g., May)
c	Complete date and time
d	Day of the month (01–31)
H	Hour (00–23)
I	Hour (01–12)
j	Day of the year (001–366)
m	Month (01–12)
M	Minutes (00–59)
p	AM/PM designation
S	Second, including up to two leap seconds

Table 5-1. Date/time format specifiers (continued)

Specifier	Description
U	Week number (00–53), with week 1 starting on the first Sunday
w	Weekday (0–6), where Sunday is 0
W	Week number (00–53), with week 1 starting on the first Monday
x	Date in form MM/DD/YY
X	Time in form HH/MM/SS with 24-hour clock
y	Year within the current century (00–99)
Y	Year
Z	Time zone abbreviation, or empty if the system doesn't know the time zone

The Boost date_time library discussed in later recipes does not have the formatting capabilities offered by time_put. For convenience Example 5-5 contains several routines to convert from the Boost date/time classes to a tm struct, so that you can use time_put routines.

Example 5-5. Converting from Boost date/time classes to a tm struct

```
using boost::gregorian;
using boost::posix_time;

void dateToTmAux(const date& src, tm& dest) {
  dest.tm_mday = src.day();
  dest.tm_year = src.year() - 1900;
  dest.tm_mon = src.month() - 1;
}

void ptimeToTmAux(const ptime& src, tm& dest) {
  dest.tm_sec = src.seconds();
  dest.tm_min = src.minutes();
  dest.tm_hour = src.hours();
  dateToTmAux(src.date(), dest);
}

tm ptimeToTm(const ptime& t) {
  tm ret = tm();
  ptimeToTmAux(t, ret);
  return ret;
}
```

See Also

Recipe 13.3

5.3 Performing Date and Time Arithmetic

Problem

You want to know the amount of time elapsed between two date/time points.

Solution

If both date/time points falls between the years of 1970 and 2038, you can use a time_t type and the difftime function from the <ctime> header. Example 5-6 shows how to compute the number of days elapsed between two dates.

Example 5-6. Date and time arithmetic with time_t

```
#include <ctime>
#include <iostream>
#include <cstdlib>

using namespace std;

time_t dateToTimeT(int month, int day, int year) {
  // january 5, 2000 is passed as (1, 5, 2000)
  tm tmp = tm( );
  tmp.tm_mday = day;
  tmp.tm_mon = month - 1;
  tmp.tm_year = year - 1900;
  return mktime(&tmp);
}

time_t badTime( ) {
  return time_t(-1);
}

time_t now( ) {
  return time(0);
}

int main( ) {
  time_t date1 = dateToTimeT(1,1,2000);
  time_t date2 = dateToTimeT(1,1,2001);

  if ((date1 == badTime( )) || (date2 == badTime( ))) {
    cerr << "unable to create a time_t struct" << endl;
    return EXIT_FAILURE;
  }
  double sec = difftime(date2, date1);
  long days = static_cast<long>(sec / (60 * 60 * 24));
  cout << "the number of days between Jan 1, 2000, and Jan 1, 2001, is ";
  cout << days << endl;
  return EXIT_SUCCESS;
}
```

The program in Example 5-6 should output :

```
the number of days between Jan 1, 2000, and Jan 1, 2001, is 366
```

Notice that the year 2000 is a leap year because even though it is divisible by 100; it is also divisible by 400, thus it has 366 days.

Discussion

The time_t type is an implementation defined arithmetic type. This means it is either an integer or floating-point type, and thus supports the basic arithmetic operations. You can add, subtract, divide, multiply, and so forth. To compute the distance between two time_t values to seconds, you need to use the difftime function. Do not assume that time_t itself counts seconds, even if it is true. Many C++ implementations may very well quietly change it to count fractions of a second in the near future (this is one reason why difftime returns a double).

If the limitations of time_t are too restricting then you will probably want instead to use the various classes from the Boost date_time library to compute time intervals. Example 5-7 shows how to use the Boost classes to calculate the number of days in the 20th and the 21st centuries.

Example 5-7. Date and time arithmetic with date_duration

```cpp
#include <iostream>
#include <boost/date_time/gregorian/gregorian.hpp>

using namespace std;
using namespace boost::gregorian;

int main()
{
  date_duration dd = date(2000, 1, 1) - date(1900, 1, 1);
  cout << "The twentieth century had " << dd.days() << " days" << endl;
  dd = date(2100, 1, 1) - date(2000, 1, 1);
  cout << "The twenty-first century will have " << dd.days() << " days" << endl;
}
```

The program in Example 5-7 outputs:

```
The twentieth century had 36524 days
The twenty-first century will have 36525 days
```

5.4   Converting Between Time Zones

Problem

You want to convert the current time from one time zone to another.

Solution

To convert between time zones, use the time zone conversion routines from the Boost date_time library. Example 5-8 shows how to finds the time in Tucson, Arizona given a time in New York City.

Example 5-8. Converting between time zones

```
#include <iostream>
#include <boost/date_time/gregorian/gregorian.hpp>
#include <boost/date_time/posix_time/posix_time.hpp>
#include <boost/date_time/local_time_adjustor.hpp>

using namespace std;
using namespace boost::gregorian;
using namespace boost::date_time;
using namespace boost::posix_time;

typedef local_adjustor<ptime, -5, us_dst> EasternTZ;
typedef local_adjustor<ptime, -7, no_dst> ArizonaTZ;

ptime NYtoAZ(ptime nytime) {
  ptime utctime = EasternTZ::local_to_utc(nytime);
  return ArizonaTZ::utc_to_local(utctime);
}

int main()
{
    // May 1st 2004,
    boost::gregorian::date thedate(2004, 6, 1);
    ptime nytime(thedate, hours(19)); // 7 pm
    ptime aztime = NYtoAZ(nytime);
    cout << "On May 1st, 2004, when it was " << nytime.time_of_day().hours();
    cout << ":00 in New York, it was " << aztime.time_of_day().hours();
    cout << ":00 in Arizona " << endl;
}
```

The program in Example 5-8 outputs the following:

```
On May 1st, 2004, when it was 19:00 in New York, it was 16:00 in Arizona
```

Discussion

The time zone conversions in Example 5-8 goes through a two-step process. First, I convert the time to UTC, and then convert the UTC time to the second time zone. Note that the time zones in the Boost date_time library are represented as types using the local_adjustor template class. Each type has conversion functions to convert from the given time zone to UTC (the local_to_utc function), and to convert from UTC to the given time zone (the utc_to_local function).

5.5   Determining a Day's Number Within a Given Year

Problem

You want to determine a day's number within a given year. For example, January 1 is the first day of each year; February 5 is the 36th day of each year, and so on. But since some years have leap days, after February 28, a given day doesn't necessarily have the same numbering each year.

Solution

The solution to this problem requires the solution to several problems simultaneously. First, you have to know how many days are in each month, which, in turn, means you have to know how to determine whether a year is a leap year. Example 5-9 provides routines for performing these computations.

Example 5-9. Routines for determining a day's number within a given year

```cpp
#include <iostream>

using namespace std;

enum MonthEnum  {
  jan = 0, feb = 1, mar = 2, apr = 3, may = 4, jun = 5,
  jul = 6, aug = 7, sep = 8, oct = 9, nov = 10, dec = 11
};

bool isLeapYear(int y) {
  return (y % 4 == 0) && ((y % 100 != 0) || (y % 400 == 0));
}

const int arrayDaysInMonth[] = {
  31, 28, 31, 30, 31, 30, 31, 31, 30, 31, 30, 31
};

int n;
int arrayFirstOfMonth[] = {
  n = 0,
  n += arrayDaysInMonth[jan],
  n += arrayDaysInMonth[feb],
  n += arrayDaysInMonth[mar],
  n += arrayDaysInMonth[apr],
  n += arrayDaysInMonth[may],
  n += arrayDaysInMonth[jun],
  n += arrayDaysInMonth[jul],
  n += arrayDaysInMonth[aug],
  n += arrayDaysInMonth[sep],
  n += arrayDaysInMonth[::oct],
  n += arrayDaysInMonth[nov]
};
```

```
int daysInMonth(MonthEnum month, int year) {
  if (month == feb) {
    return isLeapYear(year) ? 29 : 28;
  }
  else {
    return arrayDaysInMonth[month];
  }
}

int firstOfMonth(MonthEnum month, int year) {
  return arrayFirstOfMonth[month] + isLeapYear(year);
}

int dayOfYear(MonthEnum month, int monthDay, int year) {
  return firstOfMonth(month, year) + monthDay - 1;
}

int main( ) {
  cout << "July 1, 1971, was the " << dayOfYear(jul, 1, 1971);
  cout << " day of the year" << endl;
}
```

The program in Example 5-9 outputs the following:

```
July 1, 1971, was the 181 day of the year
```

Discussion

The code in Example 5-9 is a relatively straightforward but useful set of functions for working with dates and leap years. Notice that I have abandoned what I call the "document and pray" approach used in the previous recipes. What I mean by this is that the months are no longer represented by indexes but rather enumerations. This significantly reduces the chance of programmer error when passing a month to a function as an argument.

The leap year computation shown in Example 5-9 is in accordance to the modern Gregorian calendar. Every fourth year is a leap year, except every hundredth year unless that year is divisible by 400 (e.g., 1896 was a leap year, 1900 wasn't, 2000 was, 2004 was, 2100 will not be).

5.6   Defining Constrained Value Types

Problem

You want self-validating numerical types to represents numbers with a limited range of valid values such as hours of a day or minutes of an hour.

Solution

When working with dates and times, frequently you will want values that are integers with a limited range of valid values (i.e., 0 to 59 for seconds of a minute, 0 to 23 for hours of a day, 0 to 365 for days of a year). Rather than checking these values every time they are passed to a function, you would probably prefer to have them validated automatically by overloading the assignment operator. Since there are so many of these types, it is preferable to implement a single type that can handle this kind of validation for different numerical ranges. Example 5-10 presents a ConstrainedValue template class implementation that makes it easy to define ranged integers and other constrained value types.

Example 5-10. constrained_value.hpp

```
#ifndef CONSTRAINED_VALUE_HPP
#define CONSTRAINED_VALUE_HPP

#include <cstdlib>
#include <iostream>

using namespace std;

template<class Policy_T>
struct ConstrainedValue
{
  public:
    // public typedefs
    typedef typename Policy_T policy_type;
    typedef typename Policy_T::value_type value_type;
    typedef ConstrainedValue self;

    // default constructor
    ConstrainedValue() : m(Policy_T::default_value) { }
    ConstrainedValue(const self& x) : m(x.m) {  }
    ConstrainedValue(const value_type& x) { Policy_T::assign(m, x); }
    operator value_type() const { return m; }

    // uses the policy defined assign function
    void assign(const value_type& x) {
      Policy_T::assign(m, x);
    }

    // assignment operations
    self& operator=(const value_type& x) { assign(x); return *this; }
    self& operator+=(const value_type& x) { assign(m + x); return *this; }
    self& operator-=(const value_type& x) { assign(m - x); return *this; }
    self& operator*=(const value_type& x) { assign(m * x); return *this; }
    self& operator/=(const value_type& x) { assign(m / x); return *this; }
    self& operator%=(const value_type& x) { assign(m % x); return *this; }
    self& operator>>=(int x) { assign(m >> x); return *this; }
    self& operator<<=(int x) { assign(m << x); return *this; }
```

Example 5-10. constrained_value.hpp (continued)

```
    // unary operations
    self operator-() { return self(-m); }
    self operator+() { return self(+m); }
    self operator!() { return self(!m); }
    self operator~() { return self(~m); }

    // binary operations
    friend self operator+(self x, const value_type& y) { return x += y; }
    friend self operator-(self x, const value_type& y) { return x -= y; }
    friend self operator*(self x, const value_type& y) { return x *= y; }
    friend self operator/(self x, const value_type& y) { return x /= y; }
    friend self operator%(self x, const value_type& y) { return x %= y; }
    friend self operator+(const value_type& y, self x) { return x += y; }
    friend self operator-(const value_type& y, self x) { return x -= y; }
    friend self operator*(const value_type& y, self x) { return x *= y; }
    friend self operator/(const value_type& y, self x) { return x /= y; }
    friend self operator%(const value_type& y, self x) { return x %= y; }
    friend self operator>>(self x, int y) { return x >>= y; }
    friend self operator<<(self x, int y) { return x <<= y; }

    // stream operators
    friend ostream& operator<<(ostream& o, self x) { o << x.m; return o; }
    friend istream& operator>>(istream& i, self x) {
      value_type tmp; i >> tmp; x.assign(tmp); return i;
    }

    // comparison operators
    friend bool operator<(const self& x, const self& y) { return x.m < y.m; }
    friend bool operator>(const self& x, const self& y) { return x.m > y.m; }
    friend bool operator<=(const self& x, const self& y) { return x.m <= y.m; }
    friend bool operator>=(const self& x, const self& y) { return x.m >= y.m; }
    friend bool operator==(const self& x, const self& y) { return x.m == y.m; }
    friend bool operator!=(const self& x, const self& y) { return x.m != y.m; }
  private:
    value_type m;
};

template<int Min_N, int Max_N>
struct RangedIntPolicy
{
  typedef int value_type;
  const static value_type default_value = Min_N;
  static void assign(value_type& lvalue, const value_type& rvalue) {
    if ((rvalue < Min_N) || (rvalue > Max_N)) {
      throw range_error("out of valid range");
    }
    lvalue = rvalue;
  }
};

#endif
```

The program in Example 5-11 shows how you can use the `ConstrainedValue` type.

Example 5-11. Using constained_value.hpp

```
#include "constrained_value.hpp"

typedef ConstrainedValue< RangedIntPolicy<1582, 4000> > GregYear;
typedef ConstrainedValue< RangedIntPolicy<1, 12> > GregMonth;
typedef ConstrainedValue< RangedIntPolicy<1, 31> > GregDayOfMonth;

using namespace std;

void gregOutputDate(GregDayOfMonth d, GregMonth m, GregYear y) {
  cout << m << "/" << d << "/" << y << endl;
}

int main( ) {
  try {
    gregOutputDate(14, 7, 2005);
  }
  catch(...) {
    cerr << "whoops, shouldn't be here" << endl;
  }
  try {
    gregOutputDate(1, 5, 1148);
    cerr << "whoops, shouldn't be here" << endl;
  }
  catch(...) {
    cerr << "are you sure you want to be using a Gregorian Calendar?" << endl;
  }
}
```

The output from the program in Example 5-11 is:

```
7/14/2005
are you sure you want to be using a Gregorian Calendar?
```

Discussion

Constrained value types are particularly relevant when working with dates and times, because many values related to date/times are integers that must occur within a specific range of values (e.g., a month must be in the interval [0,11] or a day of the month must be in the interval [0,30]). It is very time consuming and error prone to manually check that every function parameter fits into a certain range. Just imagine if you wanted to make a global change to how a million line program handled date range errors!

The `ConstrainedValue` template class when used with a RangedIntPolicy template can be used to define easily several different types that throw exceptions when assigned values out of range. Example 5-12 shows some different examples of how you can use `ConstrainedValue` to define new self-validating integer types.

Example 5-12. More of usage of ConstrainedValue

```
typedef ConstrainedValue< RangedIntPolicy <0, 59> > Seconds;
typedef ConstrainedValue< RangedIntPolicy <0, 59> > Minutes;
typedef ConstrainedValue< RangedIntPolicy <0, 23> > Hours;
typedef ConstrainedValue< RangedIntPolicy <0, 30> > MonthDays;
typedef ConstrainedValue< RangedIntPolicy <0, 6> > WeekDays;
typedef ConstrainedValue< RangedIntPolicy <0, 365 > > YearDays;
typedef ConstrainedValue< RangedIntPolicy <0, 51> > Weeks;
```

The ConstrainedValue template class is an example of policy-based design. A policy is a class passed as a template parameter that specifies aspects of the implementation or behavior of the parameterized type. The policy passed to a ConstrainedValue is expected to provide the implementation detail of how to assign between the same specializations of the type.

Using policies can improve the flexibility of classes by deferring design decisions to the user of the type. It is common to use policies when a group of types has a common interface but vary in their implementation. Policies are also particularly useful when it is impossible to anticipate and satisfy all possible usage scenarios of a given type.

There are many other policies you can possibly use with a ConstrainedValue type. For instance, rather than throw an exception, you may choose to assign a default value, or assign the nearest legal value. Furthermore, constraints don't even have to be ranges: you might even have a constraint that a value is always even.

## CHAPTER 6

Managing Data with Containers

6.0 Introduction

This chapter describes the data structures in the standard library that you can use to store data. They are generally referred to as containers, since they "contain" objects you add to them. This chapter also describes another sort of container that is not part of the standard library, although it ships with most standard library implementations, namely the *hashed* container.

The part of the library that comprises the containers is often referred to as the Standard Template Library, or STL, because this is what it was called before it was included in the C++ standard. The STL includes not only the containers that are the subject of this chapter, but iterators and algorithms, which are the two other building blocks of the STL that make it a flexible, generic library. Since this chapter is primarily about the standard containers and not the STL in its entirety, I will refer to containers as the "standard containers" and not "STL containers," as is done in much of the C++ literature. Although I discuss iterators and algorithms as much as necessary here, both are discussed in more detail in Chapter 7.

The C++ standard uses precise terminology to describe its collection of containers. A "container" in the C++ standard library is a data structure that has a well-defined interface described in the standard. For example, any C++ standard library class that calls itself a container must support a member function `begin` that has no parameters and that returns an `iterator` referring to the first element in that container. There are a number of required constructors and member functions that define what it is to be a container in C++ terms. There are also optional member functions only some containers implement, usually those that can be implemented efficiently.

The set of all containers is further subdivided into two different kinds of containers: *sequence* containers and *associative* containers. A sequence container (usually just called a sequence) stores objects in an order that is specified by the user, and provides a required interface (in addition to container requirements) for accessing and manipulating the elements. Associative containers store their elements in sorted order, and therefore do not permit you to insert elements at a specific location, although you can provide hints when you insert to improve efficiency. Both sequences and associative containers have a required interface they must support, but only sequences have an additional set of operations that are only supported by sequences for which they can be implemented efficiently. These additional sequence operations provide more flexibility and convenience than the required interface.

This sounds a lot like inheritance. A sequence is a container, an associative container is a container, but a container is not a sequence or an associative container. It's not inheritance, though, in the C++ sense, but it *is* inheritance conceptually. A vector is a sequence, but it is its own, standalone class; it doesn't inherit from a container class or some such thing (standard library implementations are allowed freedom in how they implement vector and other containers, but the standard doesn't mandate that a standard library implementation include a container base class). A great deal of thought went into the design of the containers, and if you would like to read more about it go pick up Matt Austern's *Generic Programming and the STL* (Addison Wesley).

This chapter has two parts. The first few recipes describe how to use vector, which is a standard sequence, since it is one of the more popular data structures. They describe how to use a vector effectively and efficiently. The rest of the recipes discuss most of the other standard containers that are widely applicable, including the two nonstandard hashed containers I mentioned earlier.

6.1   Using vectors Instead of Arrays

Problem

You have to store things (built-in types, objects, pointers, etc.) in a sequence, you require random access to elements, and you can't be confined to a statically sized array.

Solution

Use the standard library's vector class template, which is defined in <vector>; don't use arrays. vector looks and feels like an array, but it has a number of safety and convenience advantages over arrays. Example 6-1 shows a few common vector operations.

Example 6-1. Using common vector member functions

```
#include <iostream>
#include <vector>
#include <string>

using namespace std;

int main( ) {
```

Example 6-1. Using common vector member functions (continued)

```
vector<int>    intVec;
vector<string> strVec;

// Add elements to the "back" of the vector with push_back
intVec.push_back(3);
intVec.push_back(9);
intVec.push_back(6);

string s = "Army";

strVec.push_back(s);
s = "Navy";
strVec.push_back(s);
s = "Air Force";
strVec.push_back(s);

// You can access them with operator[], just like an array
for (vector<string>::size_type i = 0; i < intVec.size(); ++i) {
    cout << "intVec[" << i << "] = " << intVec[i] << '\n';
}

// Or you can use iterators
for (vector<string>::iterator p = strVec.begin();
     p != strVec.end(); ++p) {
    cout << *p << '\n';
}

// If you need to be safe, use at() instead of operator[].  It
// will throw out_of_range if the index you use is > size().
try {
    intVec.at(300) = 2;
}
catch(out_of_range& e) {
    cerr << "out_of_range: " << e.what() << endl;
}
}
```

Discussion

In general, if you need to use an array, you should use a vector instead. vectors offer more safety and flexibility than arrays, and the performance overhead is negligible in most cases—and if you find that it's more than you can tolerate, you can fine-tune vector performance with a few member functions.

If you're not familiar with the containers that come with the standard library, or not acquainted with using class templates (writing them is another matter), the way vectors are declared in Example 6-1 may need some explanation. The declaration for a vector looks like this:

```
vector<typename Value, // The type of element this vector will hold
       typename Allocator = allocator<Value> > // The memory allocator
                                               // to use
```

The standard containers are parameterized by the type of objects you want them to hold. There is also a template parameter for the memory allocator to use, but it defaults to the standard one, and writing one is uncommon, so I don't discuss it here.

If you want a vector that holds ints, declare it as in the example:

```
vector<int>    intVec;
```

And if you need one that holds strings, just change the vector's type argument:

```
vector<string> strVec;
```

vectors can contain any C++ type that supports copy construction and assignment.

The next logical thing to do after you instantiate a vector is to put something in it. Add items to the back of it with push_back:

```
intVec.push_back(3);
intVec.push_back(9);
intVec.push_back(6);
```

This is roughly equivalent to adding elements 0, 1, and 2 to an array. It is "roughly" equivalent because, of course, push_back is a member function that returns void and pushes its argument onto the back of the vector. operator[] returns the memory location referenced by an index in an array. push_back makes sure there is enough room in the vector's internal buffer to add its argument; if there is, it adds the item to the next unused index—if there isn't room, it grows the buffer using an implementation-defined algorithm, *then* adds the argument object.

You can also insert items into the middle of a vector with the insert member function, though you should avoid it because doing so requires linear complexity. See Recipe 6.2 for a more detailed discussion of how to sidestep performance problems when using vectors. To insert an element, get an iterator to the point where you want your insert to begin (for a discussion of iterators, see Recipe 7.1):

```
string s = "Marines";
vector<string>::iterator p = find(strVec.begin(),
                             strVec.end(), s);

if (s != strVec.end())   // Insert s immediately before the element
   strVec.insert(p, s);  // p points to
```

Overloaded versions of insert allow you to insert *n* copies of an object into a vector, as well as insert an entire range from another sequence (that sequence may be another vector, an array, a list, and so on).

Instead of inserting, you might want simply to assign the vector to a preexisting sequence from somewhere else, erasing whatever was there before. The assign member function does this. You can assign an entire range of values, or *n* copies of the same object, to your vector like this:

```
string sarr[3] = {"Ernie", "Bert", "Elmo"};
string s = "Oscar";
```

```
strVec.assign(&sarr[0], &sarr[3]); // Assign this sequence
strVec.assign(50, s);              // Assign 50 copies of s
```

assign will resize the vector's buffer to accommodate the new sequence if it is larger than the previous buffer size.

Once you have put your data in a vector, there are several ways for getting it back out. Probably the most intuitive is operator[], which returns a reference or a const reference to the item at that index, depending on whether the vector you are calling it on is const or not. In this respect, it looks a lot like an array:

```
for (int i = 0; i < intVec.size(); ++i) {
    std::cout << "intVec[" << i << "] = "
              << intVec[i] << '\n'; // rvalue
}
intVec[2] = 32; // lvalue
```

operator[] also behaves like an array in that if you use an index that is higher than the last element in the vector, the results are undefined, which usually means your program will corrupt data or crash. You can avoid this by querying the vector for the number of elements it contains with size(). You should prefer iterators to operator[] though, because using iterators is the conventional way to iterate through any standard container:

```
for (vector<string>::iterator p = strVec.begin();
     p != strVec.end(); ++p) {
    std::cout << *p << '\n';
}
```

Iterators are the more powerful approach because they allow for more generic interaction with containers. For example, if you write an algorithm that operates on a sequence of elements between two iterators, it can run against any standard container. This is a generic approach. If you use random access with operator[], you limit yourself to only those containers that support random access. The former approach is what allows the standard library algorithms in <algorithm> to work seamlessly with the standard containers (and other things that behave like them).

vectors also provide you with safety that you just can't get from a standard array. Unlike arrays, vectors offer range-checking with the at member function. If you give at an invalid index, it will throw an out_of_range exception, which you then have a chance to catch and react accordingly. For example:

```
try {
    intVec.at(300) = 2;
}
catch(std::out_of_range& e) {
    std::cerr << "out_of_range: " << e.what() << std::endl;
}
```

As you know, if you reference an element past the end of an array with operator[], the operator does what you have told it to and fetches whatever is at that memory location. That's not good because either your program crashes from accessing memory it shouldn't, or it silently updates memory that belongs to another heap object, which is usually worse. operator[] works the same way for vector, but at least you can use at when you need to be safe.

So that's the crash course in vectors. But what *is* a vector? If you are writing in C++, you are probably performance-aware, and don't want to be given something and simply told that it works. Fair enough. See Recipe 6.2 for a discussion of how vectors work and tips for using them efficiently.

See Also

Recipe 6.2

6.2   Using vectors Efficiently

Problem

You are using vectors and you have tight space or time requirements and need to reduce or eliminate overhead.

Solution

Understand how a vector is implemented, know the complexity of insertion and deletion member functions, and minimize unnecessary memory churn with the reserve member function. Example 6-2 shows a few of these techniques in action.

Example 6-2. Using a vector efficiently

```
#include <iostream>
#include <vector>
#include <string>

using std::vector;
using std::string;

void f(vector<string>& vec) { // Pass vec by reference (or
                              // pointer, if you have to)
   // ...
}

int main() {

   vector<string> vec(500); // Tell the vector that you plan on
                            // putting a certain number of objects
                            // in it at construction
   vector<string> vec2;

   // Fill up vec...
   f(vec);
```

Example 6-2. Using a vector efficiently (continued)

```
    vec2.reserve(500);        // Or, after the fact, tell the vector
                              // that you want the buffer to be big
                              // enough to hold this many objects

    // Fill up vec2...
}
```

Discussion

The key to using vectors efficiently lies in knowing how they work. Once you have a good idea of how a vector is usually implemented, the performance hot spots become obvious.

How vectors work

A vector is, essentially, a managed array. More specifically, a vector<T> is a chunk of contiguous memory (i.e., an array) that is large enough to hold *n* objects of type T, where *n* is greater than or equal to zero and is less or equal to an implementation-defined maximum size. *n* usually increases during the lifetime of the container as you add or remove elements, but it doesn't decrease. What makes a vector different from an array is the automatic memory management of that array, the member functions for inserting and retrieving elements, and the member functions that provide meta-data about the container, such as the size (number of elements) and capacity (the buffer size), but also the type information: vector<T>::value_type is T's type, vector<T>::pointer is a pointer-to-T type, and so on. These last two, and several others, are part of every standard container, and they allow you to write generic code that works regardless of T's type. Figure 6-1 gives a graphical depiction of what some of vector's member functions provide, given a vector that has a size of 7 and a capacity of 10.

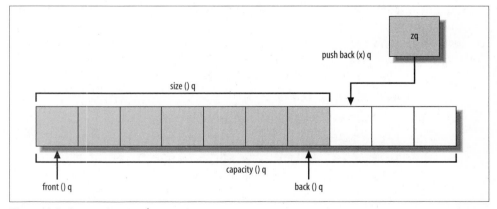

Figure 6-1. A vector's innards

If you are curious how your standard library vendor has implemented vector, compile Example 6-1 and step into every vector member function call, or, open the <vector> header in your standard library implementation and take a look. It may not be the most reader-friendly code you've ever seen, but it should be enlightening. First, if you haven't looked at much library code, it will give you an idea of what implementation techniques are used to write efficient, portable, generic code. Second, it will give you a concrete understanding of whatever container you're using. If you are writing code that may need to run with different standard library implementations, you should do this anyway.

Regardless of the library vendor, however, most implementations of vector are similar. There is a member variable that points to an array of Ts, and the elements you add or assign are copy constructed or assigned into each array element.

Adding a T object to the buffer is usually done by using *placement* new—so called because you give the type of object to be constructed as well as the address where it should be constructed—to copy construct a new object in the next available slot. If, instead, you are assigning a new value to a slot explicitly by using its index (with operator[] or at), T's assignment operator is used. Note that in both cases what happens is that your object is cloned via copy construction or T::operator=. The vector does *not* simply store the address of the object you are adding. It is for this reason that any type stored in a vector must be copy constructible and assignable. These properties mean that an equivalent object of T can be created by calling T's copy constructor or assignment operator. This is important, because of the copy-in, copy-out semantics of vectors—if copy constructing or assigning one of your objects does not work properly, then what you get out of a vector might be different than what you put in. This is bad.

Once you have added a bunch of objects to a vector, its buffer becomes full and it must grow to accommodate any new objects. The algorithm for growth is implementation defined, but what usually happens is that the buffer size of n is increased to $2n + 1$. The important concept here is how vector grows the buffer. You can't just tell the operating system to extend your hunk of heap memory indefinitely; you have to request a new chunk of memory that is bigger than the one you just had. As a result, the process of increasing the buffer size is as follows:

1. Allocate memory for a new buffer.
2. Copy the old data into the new buffer.
3. Delete the old buffer.

This allows the vector to keep all of its objects in one contiguous chunk of memory.

Optimizing vector performance

The previous section should give you a good idea of how objects are stored in a vector. And from that overview, the major performance points should have jumped out at you, but in case they didn't, I'll discuss them.

To begin with, a vector (or any other standard library container) doesn't store your object, it stores a *copy* of your object. This means that each time you put something in a vector, you aren't really "putting" it anywhere; you're copying it somewhere else with its copy constructor or assignment operator. Similarly, when you retrieve a value from a vector, you are copying what is in the vector at that location to your local variable. Consider a simple assignment to a local variable from an element in a vector:

```
vector<MyObj> myVec;
// Put some MyObj objects in myVec
MyObj obj = myVec[10];  // Copy the object at index 10
```

This assignment calls obj's assignment operator with the object returned by myVec[10] as its righthand side. The performance overhead from lots of object copies will add up quickly, so it's best if you avoid it.

Put pointers in the vector instead of the objects themselves to reduce copy overhead. Storing pointers will require fewer CPU cycles to add or retrieve data, because pointers are quicker to copy than objects, and it will reduce the memory required by the vector's buffer. Just remember that if you add pointers to a standard library container, the container doesn't delete them when it's destroyed. Containers destroy only the objects they contain, i.e., the variable holding the addresses of the objects pointed to, but a container doesn't know that what it's storing is a pointer or an object, all it knows is that it's some object of type T.

Resizing the memory buffer is also not cheap. Copying every element in the buffer is a lot of work, and such a thing is best avoided. To protect against this, specify the buffer size explicitly. There are a couple of ways to do this. The simplest way to do it is during construction:

```
vector<string> vec(1000);
```

This reserves enough space for 1,000 strings and it initializes each slot in the buffer with string's default constructor. With this approach, you pay for constructing each of these objects, but you add some measure of safety by initializing every element in the buffer with an empty string. This means that if you reference an element that hasn't been assigned, you simply get an empty object.

If you want to initialize the buffer to something special, you can pass in the object that you want to copy into each slot in the buffer:

```
string defString = "uninitialized";
vector<string> vec(100, defString);
string s = vec[50]; // s = "uninitialized"
```

With this form, vec will copy construct 100 elements from defString.

The other way to reserve buffer space is to call the reserve member function some-time after the vector has been constructed:

```
vector<string> vec;
vec.reserve(1000);
```

The biggest difference between calling reserve and specifying the size at construction is that reserve doesn't initialize the slots in the buffer with anything. Specifically, this means that you shouldn't reference indexes where you haven't already put something:

```
vector<string> vec(100);
string s = vec[50];      // No problem: s is now an empty string
vector<string> vec2;
vec2.reserve(100);
s = vec2[50];            // Undefined
```

Using reserve or specifying a number of default objects at construction will help you avoid nasty buffer reallocation. That helps with performance, but also avoids another problem: anytime a buffer is reallocated, any iterators you may have that refer to its elements become invalid.

Finally, inserting anywhere but the end of a vector is not a good idea. Look again at Figure 6-1. Since a vector is just an array with some other bells and whistles, it should be easy to see why you should insert only at the end. The objects in the vector are stored contiguously, so when you insert anywhere but at the end, say, at index n, the objects from $n+1$ to the end must be shifted down by one (toward the end) to make room for the new item. This operation is linear, which means it is expensive for vectors of even modest size. Deleting an element in a vector has a similar effect: it means that all indexes larger than n must be shifted up one slot. If you need to be able to insert and delete anywhere but the end of a container, you should use a list instead.

6.3   Copying a vector

Problem

You need to copy the contents of one vector into another.

Solution

There are a couple of ways to do this. You can use a copy constructor when you create a vector, or you can use the assign member function. Example 6-3 shows how to do both.

Example 6-3. Copying vector contents

```cpp
#include <iostream>
#include <vector>
#include <string>
#include <algorithm>

using namespace std;

// Util function for printing vector contents
template<typename T>
void vecPrint (const vector<T>& vec) {
   cout << "{";
   for (typename vector<T>::const_iterator p = vec.begin( );
        p != vec.end( ); ++p) {
      cout << "{" << *p << "} ";
   }
   cout << "}" << endl;
}

int main( ) {

   vector<string> vec(5);
   string foo[] = {"My", "way", "or", "the", "highway"};

   vec[0] = "Today";
   vec[1] = "is";
   vec[2] = "a";
   vec[3] = "new";
   vec[4] = "day";

   vector<string> vec2(vec);
   vecPrint(vec2);

   vec.at(0) = "Tomorrow";

   vec2.assign(vec.begin( ), vec.end( )); // Copy each element over
   vecPrint(vec2);                        // with assign

   vec2.assign(&foo[0], &foo[5]); // Assign works for anything that
   vecPrint(vec2);                // behaves like an iterator

   vector<string>::iterator p;

   p = find(vec.begin( ), vec.end( ), "new");

   vec2.assign(vec.begin( ), p); // Copy a subset of the full range
   vecPrint(vec2);               // of vec
}
```

Discussion

Copying a vector is easy; there are two ways to do it. You can copy construct one vector from another, just like any other object, or you can use the assign member function. There is little to say about the copy constructor; just pass in the vector you want it to clone, and you're done.

```
vector<string> vec2(vec);
```

In this case, vec2 will contain the same number of elements that are in vec, and each one of those elements will be a copy of its corresponding index in vec. Each element is copied with string's copy constructor. Since this is construction, vec2's buffer is sized at least large enough to hold everything in vec.

assign works similarly, except that there is some additional work that goes on behind the scenes, since now you are dealing with a target vector that may already have data in it. First, the objects that are in the way, so to speak, must be destroyed. assign first calls the destructor for each of the objects that vec2 already contains. Once they are gone, it checks vec2's buffer size to ensure it is big enough to hold what it is about to receive from vec. If not, assign resizes the buffer to accommodate the new data. Finally, it copies each element over.

Additionally, you can use assign for copying a subset of a sequence. For example, if you just want to assign a subset of the elements in vec, just specify the range you want to pull when calling assign:

```
vector<string>::iterator p;
p = std::find(vec.begin( ), vec.end( ), "new");
vec2.assign(vec.begin( ), p);
vecPrint(vec2);
```

In this case, assign will copy everything up to, but not including, p. This is because, as is the convention in all standard library containers and algorithms, assign(first, last) copies the element pointed to by first up to, but not including, the element pointed to by last. Such a range, that includes the first element but not the last element, is often denoted as *[first, last)*.

Use assign or the copy constructor instead of looping yourself. That is, don't copy each element by looping through vec and pushing each element on the back of vec2. This requires more (redundant) code on your part, and disallows any optimizations the implementer of your standard library may have used when writing assign or the copy constructor.

6.4   Storing Pointers in a vector

Problem

For efficiency or other reasons, you can't store copies of your objects in a vector, but you need to keep track of them somehow.

Solution

Store pointers to your objects in a vector instead of copies of the objects themselves. But if you do, don't forget to delete the objects that are pointed to, because the vector won't do it for you. Example 6-4 shows how to declare and work with vectors of pointers.

Example 6-4. Using vectors of pointers

```
#include <iostream>
#include <vector>

using namespace std;

static const int NUM_OBJECTS = 10;

class MyClass { /*...*/ };

int main( ) {

   vector<MyClass*> vec;

   MyClass* p = NULL;

   // Load up the vector with MyClass objects
   for (int i = 0; i < NUM_OBJECTS; i++) {
      p = new MyClass( );
      vec.push_back(p);
   }

   // Do something useful with this data, then delete the objects when
   // you're done
   for (vector<MyClass*>::iterator pObj = vec.begin( );
        pObj != vec.end( ); ++pObj) {
      delete *pObj; // Note that this is deleting what pObj points to,
                    // which is a pointer
   }

   vec.clear( ); // Purge the contents so no one tries to delete them
              // again
}
```

Discussion

You can store pointers in a vector just like you would anything else. Declare a vector of pointers like this:

```
vector<MyClass*> vec;
```

The important thing to remember is that a vector stores *values* without regard for what those values represent. It, therefore, doesn't know that it's supposed to delete pointer values when it's destroyed. If you allocate memory, then put pointers to that memory in a vector, you have to delete the memory yourself when you are done with it. Don't be fooled by the term "container" into thinking that somehow when you store a pointer in a vector that it assumes ownership.

You should also explicitly empty the vector after you have deleted the pointers for the same reason that you should set pointer variables to NULL when you're done with them. This will prevent them from erroneously being deleted again.

6.5   Storing Objects in a list

Problem

You need to store items in a sequence, but your requirements don't match up well with a vector. Specifically, you need to be able to efficiently add and remove items in the middle of the sequence, not just at the end.

Solution

Use a list, declared in <list>, to hold your data. lists offer better performance and more flexibility when modifying the sequence at someplace other than the beginning or the end. Example 6-5 shows you how to use a list, and shows off some of its unique operations.

Example 6-5. Using a list

```
#include <iostream>
#include <list>
#include <string>
#include <algorithm>

using namespace std;

// A simple functor for printing
template<typename T>
struct printer {
   void operator()(const T& s) {
      cout << s << '\n';
   }
};

bool inline even(int n) {
   return(n % 2 == 0);
}

printer<string> strPrinter;
printer<int>    intPrinter;

int main() {
```

Example 6-5. Using a list (continued)

```
    list<string> lstOne;
    list<string> lstTwo;

    lstOne.push_back("Red");
    lstOne.push_back("Green");
    lstOne.push_back("Blue");

    lstTwo.push_front("Orange");
    lstTwo.push_front("Yellow");
    lstTwo.push_front("Fuschia");

    for_each(lstOne.begin( ), // Print each element in the list
             lstOne.end( ),   // with a custom functor, print
             strPrinter);

    lstOne.sort( );          // list has a member for sorting
    lstTwo.sort( );

    lstOne.merge(lstTwo);    // Merge the two lists and print
    for_each(lstOne.begin( ), // the results (the lists must be
             lstOne.end( ),   // sorted before merging)
             strPrinter);

    list<int> intLst;

    intLst.push_back(0);
    intLst.push_back(1);
    intLst.push_back(2);
    intLst.push_back(3);
    intLst.push_back(4);

    // Remove all values greater than 2
    intLst.remove_if(bind2nd(greater<int>( ), 2));

    for_each(intLst.begin( ),
             intLst.end( ),
             intPrinter);

    // Or, remove all even values
    intLst.remove_if(even);
}
```

Discussion

A `list` is a sequence provides constant complexity for inserting or deleting elements at any position, but it requires linear complexity to find elements. `lists` are usually implemented as a doubly linked `list`, which means that each element is stored in a node that has a pointer to its previous and next elements in the sequence. It meets all the requirements of a standard sequence container, plus provides a few unique member functions.

Declaring a list is straightforward, just give it the type of the elements you're going to store in it, and, optionally, specify a memory allocation class:

```
list<typename Value, // The type of element stored in the list
     typename Allocator = allocator<Value> > // The memory allocator
                                             // to use
```

The Value template parameter is the type of the elements that will be stored in the list. It must be a type that supports copy construction and assignment. Allocator is the memory allocation class to use; the standard allocator is the default (and will be sufficient for most of your needs).

Following is a typical list declaration (from Example 6-5):

```
list<string> lstOne;
```

After you've declared your list, put some things in it with push_front or push_back, like this:

```
lstOne.push_back("Red");     // Add these to the end of the list
lstOne.push_back("Green");
lstOne.push_back("Blue");

lstTwo.push_front("Orange");  // Add these to the beginning
lstTwo.push_front("Yellow");
lstTwo.push_front("Fuschia");
```

Pushing elements on a list takes constant time, but not *amortized* constant time as with a vector. A list implementation does not need to occasionally resize its buffer, so you won't have the intermittent performance penalty you would with a vector. The list will just have to update a handful of pointers, and not much else.

Use pop_front or pop_back (no arguments) to remove elements from the beginning or end of the list. Despite their name, the "pop" member functions don't return the popped element, as you might expect à la typical stack semantics; to get a reference to the element at the beginning or end of a sequence, use back or front.

Typically, a list looks like what is displayed in Figure 6-2. Each node has (at least) three parts: the object it contains, a pointer to the previous node, and a pointer to the next node. For the rest of this recipe, I will refer to the next and previous pointers as next_ and prev_.

Once you see how a list is implemented, it's probably obvious why some of the operations have different complexity than a vector. Adding an element anywhere in the list requires only that the preceding and following items have their next_ and prev_ pointers adjusted. One nice thing about lists is that only iterators pointing to the affected object(s) are invalidated when you insert or erase elements. Iterators to other elements are unaffected.

The insertion and deletion methods are insert and erase. insert takes an iterator as its first argument, and either an object of type T, a number and then an object of type T, or an ending iterator as its second argument. The iterator points to the item that is

---

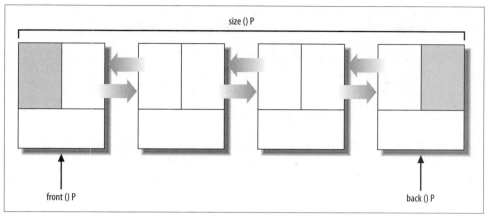

Figure 6-2. A doubly linked list

to have the insert performed immediately preceding it. Each of the insert overloads is used like this:

```
list<string> strLst;
list<string>::iterator p;
// ...
string s = "Scion";

p = find(strLst.begin( ), strLst.end( ),  // std::find from <algorithm>
         "Toyota");

strLst.insert(p, s);       // Insert s right before p
strLst.insert(p, 16, s);   // Insert 16 copies of s right before p
strLst.insert(p, myOtherStrLst.begin( ),  // Insert everything in
              myOtherStrLst.end( ));       // myOtherStrLst before p
```

Erasing elements is similar:

```
p = find(strLst.begin( ), strLst.end( ),  // std::find from <algorithm>
         "Toyota");

strLst1.erase(p);    // Erase this element
strLst2.erase(p, strLst.end( )); // Erase p to the end
strLst3.clear( ); // Erase all elements
```

In addition to the standard container member functions, list provides a few interesting ones. The first is splice.

splice does what it sounds like: it splices two lists together. Here's how I could have spliced lstTwo into lstOne in Example 6-5:

```
list<string>::iterator p =  // Find somewhere to insert the other
  std::find(lstOne.begin( ), // list
            lstOne.end( ), "Green");
lstOne.splice(p, lstTwo);    // Insert lstTwo right before "Green"
```

p is an iterator that refers to an element in lstOne. lstTwo is inserted into lstOne immediately preceding p. As with an insertion, all that really needs to be done here is to change the next_ and prev_ pointers on the affected nodes, so this operation takes constant time. lstTwo is empty after you splice it into lstOne, which is why it is not a const parameter. You can also insert a single element from lstTwo into lstOne, or a range of items from lstTwo. In both cases, the items that are spliced in are removed from the originating list.

If your lists are sorted (list has its own sort member function; std::sort won't work with a list), and you want to merge them together and preserve their sorted order, use merge instead of splice. merge will combine the two lists into one, and if two elements are equivalent, the one from lstOne comes first in the final list. As with splice, the argument list is empty afterward.

list also has some cool aggregate operations for removing things. Imagine that you want to erase all occurrences of an element. All you have to do is call remove with an argument that, when compared to each item in the list, will give (*p == item) != false, where p is a list iterator. Call remove like this:

```
strLst.remove("Harry");
```

This will remove all elements from strLst where el == "Harry". If you want to remove elements that satisfy some other predicate, such as being larger than some value, use remove_if instead:

```
bool inline even(int n) {
    return(n % 2 == 0);
}

list<int> intLst;
// Fill up intLst...
intLst.remove_if(even);  // Removes all elements where even(*p)
                         // is != false
```

If your predicates are more complicated, consider using some of the functors in <functional>. For example, if you want to remove elements that are greater than some value, you can use greater (from <algorithm>) and bind2nd combined with remove_if:

```
intLst.remove_if(std::bind2nd(std::greater<int>( ), 2));
```

This will remove all values greater than 2 from intLst. The syntax is a little esoteric, but what's happening is straightforward. bind2nd takes two arguments, a function object (call it f) and a value (v), and returns a function object that takes a single argument (arg) and invokes f(arg, v). bind2nd is a slick way to do just this sort of thing without having to write a bunch of little functions.

A list is a good alternative to vector when you need a standard sequence container. list's different internal representation permits it to provide different complexities for many of the standard sequence operations and a few interesting operations of its own.

See Also

Recipe 6.1

6.6 Mapping strings to Other Things

Problem

You have objects that you need to store in memory, and you want to store them by their string keys. You need to be able to add, delete, and retrieve items quickly (with, at most, logarithmic complexity).

Solution

Use the standard container map, declared in <map>, to map keys (strings) to values (any type that obeys value semantics). Example 6-6 shows how.

Example 6-6. Creating a string map

```
#include <iostream>
#include <map>
#include <string>

using namespace std;

int main( ) {

   map<string, string> strMap;

   strMap["Monday"]    = "Montag";
   strMap["Tuesday"]   = "Dienstag";
   strMap["Wednesday"] = "Mittwoch";
   strMap["Thursday"]  = "Donnerstag";
   strMap["Friday"]    = "Freitag";
   strMap["Saturday"]  = "Samstag";
   // strMap.insert(make_pair("Sunday", "Sonntag"));
   strMap.insert(pair<string, string>("Sunday", "Sonntag"));

   for (map<string, string>::iterator p = strMap.begin( );
     p != strMap.end( ); ++p ) {
        cout << "English: " << p->first
             << ", German: " << p->second << endl;
   }

   cout << endl;

   strMap.erase(strMap.find("Tuesday"));
```

Example 6-6. Creating a string map (continued)

```
    for (map<string, string>::iterator p = strMap.begin( );
       p != strMap.end( ); ++p ) {
          cout << "English: " << p->first
               << ", German: " << p->second << endl;
    }
}
```

Discussion

A map is an associative container that maps keys to values, provides logarithmic complexity for inserting and finding, and constant time for erasing single elements. It is common for developers to use a map to keep track of objects by using a string key. This is what Example 6-6 does; in this case, the mapped type happens to be a string, but it could be nearly anything.

A map is declared like this:

```
    map<typename Key,                              // The type of the key
        typename Value,                            // The type of the value
        typename LessThanFun = std::less<Key>,     // The function/functor
                                                   // used for sorting
        typename Alloc = std::allocator<Key> > // Memory allocator
```

Key and Value are the types of the key and associated value that will be stored in the map. LessThanFun is a function or functor that takes two arguments and returns true if the first is less than the second; the standard functor less is used by default. Alloc is the memory allocator, which defaults to the standard allocator.

Using a map is easy enough. Declare the type of the key and value like this:

```
    map<string, string> strMap;
```

This creates a map where both the key and the value are strings. Put objects in your map with operator[], which is intuitive and easy to read:

```
    strMap["Monday"]    = "Montag";
    strMap["Tuesday"]   = "Dienstag";
    strMap["Wednesday"] = "Mittwoch"; // ...
```

This inserts elements into the map with the index (e.g., "Monday") as the key and the righthand side as the value. They are stored in order according to the LessThanFun template parameter, if you supplied one; if not, map uses std::less<Key>.

To get values out of a map, use operator[] on the righthand side of assignment, like this:

```
    wedInGerman = strMap["Wednesday"];
```

In the manner of all standard containers, the value associated with the key "Wednesday" is copied into the object wedInGerman using operator=.

operator[] is a convenient way to insert or update items in, or retrieve values from a map, but it has subtle behavior that might not be what you expect. Strictly speaking, operator[k] returns a reference to the value associated with k—whether k exists in the map or not. If the k is in the map already, its associated value object is returned. If it doesn't, k is inserted and the value type's default constructor is used to create a value object for that key. To make this concrete, consider what the following code does:

```
map<string, string> mapZipCodes;  // There are zero elements now

string myZip = mapZipCodes["Tempe"];  // Nothing is in the map yet,
                                      // but what is count( ) now?
```

What's in myZip, and how many elements are in mapZipCodes now? Since operator[] inserts the key you give it if it doesn't already exist, myZip is an empty string and there is now one element in mapZipCodes. This might not be the behavior you expect, but whether it is or not, be aware that operator[] is not a const member function: there is always the possibility that it will change the state of the map by adding a node.

The insert member function provides an alternative for adding pairs to the map. insert performs a strict insert, not an insert/update as operator[] does. If you are using a map (and not a multimap, which can have duplicate keys), insert does nothing if the key already exists. By comparison, operator[] replaces the value object for the key you supply if it already exists.

But the syntax of insert requires a little more work than operator[], and this has to do with how a map stores your data. Consider this line from Example 6-6:

```
strMap.insert(std::make_pair("Sunday", "Sonntag"));
```

A map stores your key/value pairs in a pair object. A pair is a simple utility class template (declared in <utility> and included by <map>) that holds two values of two types. To declare a pair of strings, do this:

```
pair<string, string> myPair;
```

The first and second elements in the pair are accessible by the public members first and second. If you use operator[] to access elements in a map, then you don't usually have to deal with pairs directly, but with many of the other member functions you do, so it's good to know how to create and reference pair objects. Iterators, for example, simply dereference to a pair object, so when you use them, as I did in Example 6-6, you ought to know how to get at the key and its value.

```
for (map<string, string>::iterator p = strMap.begin( );
    p != strMap.end( ); ++p )
        cout << "English: " << p->first
             << ", German: " << p->second << endl;
```

The key is stored in first and the value is stored in second.

This doesn't explain why I used make_pair, though. make_pair is a helper function template that creates a pair object out of the arguments you give it. Some prefer this to calling the pair constructor because a class template can't use argument deduction to figure out its template parameters, whereas a function template can. Thus, these two lines of code are functionally equivalent:

```
strMap.insert(std::make_pair("Sunday", "Sonntag"));
strMap.insert(std::pair<string, string>("Sunday", "Sonntag"));
```

maps prohibit duplicate keys. If you want to allow duplicate keys, you have to use a multimap, which is a map that permits multiple equivalent keys. Its interface is identical to map, but the behavior of the member functions is necessarily different. Table 6-1 lists the member functions that are in one but not the other, and explains any behavioral differences in the common member functions. maps and multimaps have some typedefs that describe the different values that are stored in them. In Table 6-1, I use them as follows:

key_type
> This is the type of the key. In a string map declared as map<string, MyClass*>, key_type would be string.

mapped_type
> This is the type of the value that the key maps to. In a string map declared as map<string, MyClass*>, mapped_type would be MyClass*.

value_type
> This is the type of the object that contains a key and a value, which, in a map or mutimap, is a pair<const key_type, mapped_type>.

Table 6-1. map versus multimap

Member function	map, multimap, or both	Behavior
T& operator[] (const key_type& k)	map	Returns a reference to the value object stored with key k. If k is not already in the map, it is added and a value object is created with its default constructor.

iterator
  insert(const value_type& v)
pair<iterator, bool>
  insert(const value_type& v)
	Both	The first version inserts v into the mutimap and returns an iterator that points to the inserted pair. The second version inserts v into a map if there is not already a key in the map equivalent to the key of v. The pair returned contains an iterator that points to the pair that was inserted, if any, and a bool indicating whether the insert was successful or not.

iterator find(const key_type& k)	Both	Returns an iterator or a const_iterator that points to the mapped_type that corresponds to k. In a multimap, the iterator returned is not guaranteed to point to the first value equivalent to k. If there is no key equivalent to k, the returned iterator is equivalent to end( ).

Table 6-1 also shows the behavioral differences between map and multimap.

If operator[] doesn't work for you, there are other ways to find things in a map. You can use the find member function:

```
map<string, string>::const_iterator p
    = strMap.find("Thursday");

if (p != strMap.end())
    cout << "Thursday = " << p->second << endl;
```

Just be aware that when you are using a multimap, the item returned isn't guaranteed to be the *first* element that is equivalent to the search key. If you want the first element that is not less than some value or not more than some value, use lower_bound or upper_bound. lower_bound returns an iterator to the first key/value pair equal to or greater than its key_type argument. In other words, if your map is filled with days of the week as in Example 6-6, the following will return an iterator that points to the pair containing "Friday" and "Freitag":

```
p = strMap.lower_bound("Foo");

if (p != strMap.end())
    cout << p->first << " = " << p->second << endl;
```

This is because "Friday" is the first key greater than or equal to "Foo". upper_bound works the same way, but in the opposite manner.

I mentioned at the beginning of this discussion that the elements in a map are stored in sorted order according to their keys, so if you iterate from begin to end, each element is "greater" than the previous element (in a multimap it is greater than or equal to). But if you aren't using something as trivial as strings or numbers as your keys, you may have to specify how keys are compared when the map has to determine what should be inserted where.

By default, keys are sorted using the standard functor less (declared in <functional>). less is a binary function (takes two arguments of the same type) that returns a bool indicating whether the first argument is less than the second. In other words, less(a, b) returns a < b. If this is not what you want, create your own functor and declare the map using it instead. For example, if you have a Person object as your key, and each Person has a last name and a first name, you may want to compare last names and first names. Example 6-7 presents one way to do this.

Example 6-7. Using your own sorting functor

```
#include <iostream>
#include <map>
#include <string>

using namespace std;

class Person {
    friend class PersonLessThan;
public:
```

Example 6-7. Using your own sorting functor (continued)

```
    Person(const string& first, const string& last) :
        lastName_(last), firstName_(first) {}
    // ...
    string getFirstName() const {return(firstName_);}
    string getLastName() const {return(lastName_);}
private:
    string lastName_;
    string firstName_;
};

class PersonLessThan {
public:
    bool operator()(const Person& per1,
                    const Person& per2) const {
        if (per1.lastName_ < per2.lastName_)          // Compare last
            return(true);                             // names, then
        else if (per1.lastName_ == per2.lastName_)    // first
            return(per1.firstName_ < per2.firstName_);
        else
            return(false);
    }
};

int main() {

    map<Person, string, PersonLessThan> personMap;

    Person per1("Billy", "Silly"),
        per2("Johnny", "Goofball"),
        per3("Frank", "Stank"),
        per4("Albert", "Goofball");

    personMap[per1] = "cool";
    personMap[per2] = "not cool";
    personMap[per3] = "not cool";
    personMap[per4] = "cool";

    for (map<Person, string, PersonLessThan>::const_iterator p =
            personMap.begin(); p != personMap.end(); ++p) {
        cout << p->first.getFirstName() << " " << p->first.getLastName()
            << " is " << p->second << endl;
    }
}
```

maps are a great way to store key/value pairs. Once you understand the subtle behavior, such as how operator[] works and how the pairs are actually stored (as pair<Key, Value> objects), maps provide great ease of use and good performance.

See Also

Recipe 6.7

6.7   Using Hashed Containers

Problem

You are storing keys and values, you need constant-time access to elements, and you don't need the elements to be stored in sorted order.

Solution

Use one of the hashed associated containers, hash_map or hash_set. Be aware, however, that these are not standard containers specified by the C++ Standard, rather they are extensions that most standard library implementations include. Example 6-8 shows how to use a hash_set.

Example 6-8. Storing strings in a hash_set

```
#include <iostream>
#include <string>
#include <hash_set>

int main( ) {

    hash_set<std::string> hsString;
    string s = "bravo";

    hsString.insert(s);
    s = "alpha";
    hsString.insert(s);
    s = "charlie";
    hsString.insert(s);

    for (hash_set<string>::const_iterator p = hsString.begin( );
         p != hsString.end( ); ++p)
      cout << *p << endl; // Note that these aren't guaranteed
                          // to be in sorted order
}
```

Discussion

Hashed containers are popular data structures in any language, and it is unfortunate that C++ Standard does not require an implementation to supply them. All is not lost, however, if you want to use a hashed container: chances are that the standard library implementation you are using includes hash_map and hash_set, but the fact that they are not standardized means their interfaces may differ from one standard library implementation to the next. I will describe the hashed containers that are provided in the STLPort standard library implementation.

STLPort is a free, portable standard library implementation that has been around for a long time and provides hashed containers. If you are using a different library, the interface may be different, but the general idea is the same.

The main characteristics of hashed containers (called hashed associative containers by much of the C++ literature) are that they provide, in the average case, constant-time location, insertion, and deletion of elements; in the worst case, operations require linear complexity. The trade-off for all of these constant-time operations is that the elements in a hashed container are not stored in order, as they are in a map.

Look at Example 6-8. Using a hashed container (in this case, a hash_set) is simple enough—declare it like most other containers and start inserting things into it:

```
hash_set<string> hsString;  // A hash_set of strings
string s = "bravo";
hsString.insert(s);   // Insert a copy of s
```

Using a hash_map is similar, except that (minimally) you have to specify both the key and the data types that will be used. This is identical to a map:

```
hash_map<string, string>
    hmStrings;  // Map strings to strings
string key = "key";
string val = "val";
hmStrings[key] = val;
```

These are just the basics of using hashed containers; there are a handful of additional template parameters that let you specify the hash function to use, the function to use to test for key equivalency, and an object to use for memory allocation. I discuss these a little later.

There are four hashed containers in most libraries, and they resemble the other associative containers in the standard library (i.e., map and set), they are hash_map, hash_multimap, hash_set, and hash_multiset. Hashed containers are all implemented using a hash *table*. A hash table is a data structure that allows constant-time access to elements by, basically, using a hash function to "jump" to a location close to where the desired object is stored instead of traversing through a tree-like structure. The difference between hash_map and hash_set is how the data are stored in the hash table.

The declarations for the hash table–based containers in STLPort are as follows:

```
hash_map<Key,              // The type of the key
        Value,             // The type of the value
                           // associated with the key
        HashFun = hash<Key>,    // The hash function to use
        EqualKey = equal_to<Key>, // Function to use for key
                           // equivalence test
        Alloc = alloc>     // The allocator to use
```

```
hash_set<Key,                        // The type of the key
        HashFun = hash<Key>,         // The hash function to use
        EqualKey = equal_to<Key>,    // Function to use for key
                                     // equivalence test
        Alloc = alloc>               // The allocator to use
```

A hash_map is a hash table that stores values as pair<const Key, Data> objects. What this means is that when I describe hash tables below, the "elements" in the table are key/value pairs; hash_maps don't store the key and value separately (neither do maps). A hash_set simply stores the key as the value type.

The HashFun template parameter is a function that turns objects of type Key into a value that can be stored as a size_t. This is discussed more below. The EqualKey template parameter is a function that takes two arguments and returns true if they are equivalent. In hash_map and hash_set containers, no two keys can be equivalent; hash_multimap and hash_multiset can have multiple equivalent keys. As with all containers, Alloc is the memory allocator that will be used.

A hash table has two parts. There is one relatively large vector where each index in the vector is a "bucket." Each bucket is actually a pointer to the first node in a relatively short singly or doubly linked list (singly in STLPort). These lists are where the actual data are stored. You can get the number of buckets in a hashed container with the bucket_count member function. Figure 6-3 should give you an idea of what a hash map looks like in memory.

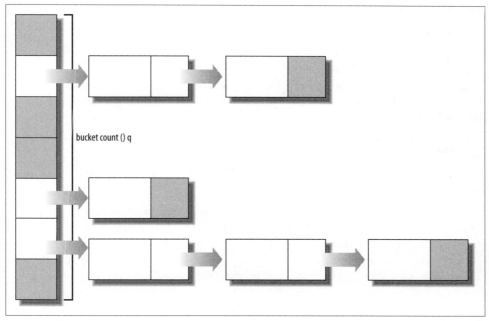

bucket count () q

Figure 6-3. A hash table

Consider the use of the hash_set in Example 6-8. When you insert an element, the container first has to figure out what bucket the element belongs to. It does that by calling the hash function for the container on the key you passed in (hash functions are discussed shortly) and calculates its modulus with the number of buckets. This gives an index in the bucket vector.

If you aren't familiar with what "hashing" is, it's a straightforward concept. Given some value (say, a char array), a hash function is a function that takes a single argument and returns a hash value of type size_t (i.e., a number). Ideally, you will want a hash function that generates hash values that are usually unique, but they don't have to be. This function is not one-to-one in the mathematical sense: more than one string can map to the same hash value. I'll discuss why that's okay in a moment.

STLPort includes such a hash function as a function template in <hash_map> and <hash_set>. The function doesn't work for just any object though, because it's not possible to make a fully generic hash function that works on any kind of input. Instead, there are a number of specializations for the built-in types that are most commonly used as the keys in a hash table. For example, if you want to see what a hash value looks like, hash a character string:

```
std::hash<const char*> hashFun;

std::cout << "\"Hashomatic\" hashes to "
          << hashFun("Hashomatic") << '\n';
```

What you will see is something like this:

```
"Hashomatic" hashes to 189555649
```

STLPort provides specializations for the following types: char*, const char*, char, unsigned char, signed char, short, unsigned short, int, unsigned int, long, and unsigned long. That sounds like a lot, but what it means, ultimately, is that the library has built-in hash function support for character strings or numbers. If you want to hash something else, you have to supply your own hash function.

When you put something in a hash table, it figures out which bucket the item belongs in with the modulo operator and the number of buckets, e.g., hashFun(key) % bucket_count( ). This is a fast operation that points right to the index in the main vector where the bucket begins.

You can use a hashed container like any ordinary associative container, such as by using operator[] to add elements to a hash_map. The difference is that you know you'll be getting constant time instead of logarithmic time with inserts and searches. Consider Example 6-9, which contains a simple class for mapping login names to Session objects. It uses a few of the capabilities of a hashed container that I have discussed in this recipe.

Example 6-9. A simple session manager

```cpp
#include <iostream>
#include <string>
#include <hash_map>

using namespace std;

class Session { /* ... */ };

// Make reading easier with a typedef
typedef hash_map<string, Session*> SessionHashMap;

class SessionManager {

public:
   SessionManager () : sessionMap_(500) {}  // Initialize hash table
                                            // with 500 buckets
  ~SessionManager () {
      for (SessionHashMap::iterator p = sessionMap_.begin();
           p != sessionMap_.end(); ++p)
         delete (*p).second; // Destroy the Session object
   }

   Session* addSession(const string& login) {
      Session* p = NULL;
      if (!(p = getSession(login))) {
         p = new Session();
         sessionMap_[login] = p; // Assign the new session with
      }                          // operator[]
      return(p);
   }
   Session* getSession(const string& login) {
      return(sessionMap_[login]);
   }
   // ...

private:
   SessionHashMap sessionMap_;
};
```

Each key maps to a single bucket, and more than one key may be in the bucket. A bucket is usually a singly or doubly linked list.

There is a great deal of literature on hash functions and tables. If you are interested in this sort of thing, do a Google search for "C++ hash function."

See Also

Recipe 6.6

6.8   Storing Objects in Sorted Order

Problem

You have to store a set of objects in order, perhaps because you frequently need to access ordered ranges of these objects and you don't want to pay for resorting them each time you do this.

Solution

Use the associative container set, declared in <set>, which stores items in sorted order. It uses the standard less class template, (which invokes operator< on its arguments) by default, or you can supply your own sorting predicate. Example 6-10 shows how to store strings in a set.

Example 6-10. Storing strings in a set

```
#include <iostream>
#include <set>
#include <string>

using namespace std;

int main( ) {

    set<string> setStr;
    string s = "Bill";

    setStr.insert(s);
    s = "Steve";
    setStr.insert(s);
    s = "Randy";
    setStr.insert(s);
    s = "Howard";
    setStr.insert(s);

    for (set<string>::const_iterator p = setStr.begin( );
        p != setStr.end( ); ++p)
      cout << *p << endl;
}
```

Since the values are stored in sorted order, the output will look like this:

```
Bill
Howard
Randy
Steve
```

Discussion

A set is an associative container that provides logarithmic complexity insertion and find, and constant-time deletion of elements (once you have found the element you want to delete). sets are unique associative containers, which means that no two elements can be equivalent, though you can use a multiset if you need to store multiple instances of equivalent elements. You can think of a set as a set in the mathematical sense, that is, a collection of items, with the added bonus that order is maintained among the elements.

You can insert and find elements, but, like a list, a set does not allow random access to elements. If you want something in a set, you have to look for it with the find member function, or iterate through the elements using set<T>::iterator or set<T>::const_iterator.

The declaration of a set should look familiar:

```
set<typename Key,                         // The type of the element
    typename LessThanFun = std::less<Key>, // The function/functor
                                          // used for sorting
    typename Alloc = std::allocator<Key> > // Memory allocator
```

You always have to specify the Key, you sometimes should supply your own LessThanFun, and you should rarely need to supply your own allocator (so I won't discuss how to write an allocator here).

The Key template parameter is, as is usually the case with the other standard containers, the type of the element that will be stored. It is typedef'd on the set as set<Key>::key_type, so you have access to the type at runtime. The Key class has to support copy construction and assignment, and you're all set.

Example 6-10 shows how to use a set with strings. Using a set to store objects of any other class works the same way; declare the set with the class name as the template parameter:

```
std::set<MyClass> setMyObjs;
```

This is all you have to do to use a set in the simplest way possible. But most of the time, life won't be so simple. For example, if you are storing pointers in the set, you can't rely on the default sorting predicate because it's just going to sort the objects by their address. To make sure elements are sorted properly, you will have to supply your own predicate for making less-than comparisons. Example 6-11 shows how.

Example 6-11. Storing pointers in a set

```
#include <iostream>
#include <set>
#include <string>
#include <functional>
#include <cassert>
```

Example 6-11. Storing pointers in a set (continued)

```
using namespace std;

// Class for comparing strings given two string pointers
struct strPtrLess {
   bool operator( )(const string* p1,
                    const string* p2) {
   assert(p1 && p2);
   return(*p1 < *p2);
   }
};

int main( ) {
   set<string*, strPtrLess> setStrPtr;   // Give it my special
                                         // less-than functor
   string s1 = "Tom";
   string s2 = "Dick";
   string s3 = "Harry";

   setStrPtr.insert(&s1);
   setStrPtr.insert(&s2);
   setStrPtr.insert(&s3);

   for (set<string*, strPtrLess>::const_iterator p =
       setStrPtr.begin( ); p != setStrPtr.end( ); ++p)
     cout << **p << endl;   // Dereference the iterator and what
                            // it points to
}
```

strPtrLess returns true if the string pointed to by p1 is less than the one pointed to by p2. This makes it a binary predicate, because it takes two arguments and returns a bool. Since operator< is defined for strings, I can just use that to make the comparison. In fact, if you want to take a more generic approach, use a class template for your comparison predicate:

```
template<typename T>
class ptrLess {
public:
   bool operator( )(const T* p1,
                    const T* p2) {
   assert(p1 && p2);
   return(*p1 < *p2);
   }
};
```

This will work for pointers to anything that has operator< defined. You can declare a set with it like this:

```
set<string*, ptrLess<string> > setStrPtr;
```

sets support many of the same functions as the standard sequence containers (e.g., begin, end, size, max_size), and other associative containers (e.g., insert, erase, clear, find).

When you are using a set, remember that you pay for the sorting every time you modify the state of the set. When the number of elements is large, the logarithmic complexity of adding or deleting elements can add up—do you really need the objects to be sorted all the time? If not, you may get better performance by storing items in a vector or a list and sorting them only when you have to, which can usually be done in n*log(n) complexity.

6.9   Storing Containers in Containers

Problem

You have a number of instances of a standard container (lists, sets, etc.), and you want to keep track of them by storing them in yet another container.

Solution

Store pointers to your containers in a single, master container. For example, you can use a map to store a string key and a pointer to a set as its value. Example 6-12 presents a simple transaction log class that stores its data as a map of string-set pointer pairs.

Example 6-12. Storing set pointers in a map

```
#include <iostream>
#include <set>
#include <map>
#include <string>

using namespace std;

typedef set<string> SetStr;
typedef map<string, SetStr*> MapStrSetStr;

// Dummy database class
class DBConn {
public:
   void beginTxn() {}
   void endTxn() {}
   void execSql(string& sql) {}
};

class SimpleTxnLog {

public:
   SimpleTxnLog() {}
  ~SimpleTxnLog() {purge();}

   // Add an SQL statement to the list
   void addTxn(const string& id,
               const string& sql) {
```

Example 6-12. Storing set pointers in a map (continued)

```
        SetStr* pSet = log_[id];      // This creates the entry for
        if (pSet == NULL) {           // this id if it isn't there
            pSet = new SetStr();
            log_[id] = pSet;
        }
        pSet->insert(sql);
    }

    // Apply the SQL statements to the database, one transaction
    // at a time
    void apply() {
        for (MapStrSetStr::iterator p = log_.begin();
             p != log_.end(); ++p) {
            conn_->beginTxn();

            // Remember that a map iterator actually refers to an object
            // of pair<Key,Val>.  The set pointer is stored in p->second.
            for (SetStr::iterator pSql = p->second->begin();
                 pSql != p->second->end(); ++pSql) {
                string s = *pSql;
                conn_->execSql(s);
                cout << "Executing SQL: " << s << endl;
            }

            conn_->endTxn();
            delete p->second;
        }
        log_.clear();
    }

    void purge() {
        for (MapStrSetStr::iterator p = log_.begin();
             p != log_.end(); ++p)
          delete p->second;

        log_.clear();
    }
    // ...

private:
  MapStrSetStr log_;
  DBConn* conn_;
};
```

Discussion

Example 6-12 offers one situation where you might need to store containers within a container. Imagine that you need to store a series of SQL statements in batches, to be executed against a relational database all at once sometime in the future. That's what SimpleTxnLog does. It could stand to have a few more member functions to make it useful, and some exception handling to make it safe, but the purpose of the example is to show how to store one kind of container in another.

To begin with, I created some typedefs to make the code easier to read:

```
typedef std::set<std::string> SetStr;
typedef std::map<std::string, SetStr*> MapStrSetStr;
```

When you are using templates of templates (of templates…ad nauseam), the declarations will get very long, which makes them hard to read, so make your life easier by employing typedef. Furthermore, using typedef makes it easier to change something about the template declaration without having to search and replace through multiple source files.

The DBConn class is a dummy class that is supposed to represent a connection to a relational database. The interesting part comes when we get into the definition of SimpleTxnLog, in the addTxn member function. At the beginning of the function, I do this to see if there is already a set object for the id that was passed in:

```
SetStr* pSet = log_[id];
```

log_ is a map (see Recipe 6.6), so operator[] does a lookup of id to see if there is a data object associated with it. If there is, the data object is returned and pSet is non-NULL; if there isn't, it creates it and returns the associated pointer, which will be NULL. Then, I can check to see if pSet points to anything to determine if I need to create another set:

```
if (pSet == NULL) {
   pSet = new SetStr();  // SetStr = std::set<std::string>
   log_[id] = pSet;
}
```

Once I create the set, I have to assign it back to the associated key in the map, since pSet is a copy of the data object stored in the map (a set pointer), not the value itself. Once I do that, all that's left is to add an element to the set and return:

```
pSet->insert(sql);
```

With the above steps, I added a pointer to an address of one container (a set) to another (a map). What I didn't do was add a set *object* to a map. The difference is important. Since containers have copy-in, copy-out semantics, doing the following would copy the entire set s into the map:

```
set<string> s;
// Load up s with data...
log_[id] = s; // Copy s and add the copy to log_
```

This will cause a lot of extra copying that you probably don't want. Therefore, the general rule to follow when using containers of containers is to use containers of *pointers* to containers.

CHAPTER 7

Algorithms

7.0 Introduction

This chapter describes how to work with the standard algorithms and how to use them on the standard containers. These algorithms were originally part of what is often referred to as the Standard Template Library (STL), which is the set of algorithms, iterators, and containers that now belong to the standard library (Chapter 6 contains recipes for working with the standard containers). I will refer to these simply as the standard algorithms, iterators, and containers, but keep in mind that they are the same ones that other authors' refer to as part of the STL. One of the pillars of the standard library is iterators, so the first recipe explains what they are and how to use them. After that, there are a number of recipes that explain how to use and extend the standard algorithms. Finally, if what you need isn't in the standard library, Recipe 7.10 explains how to write your own algorithm.

The recipes presented here are largely biased toward working with the standard containers for two reasons. First, the standard containers are ubiquitous, and it's better to learn the standard than to reinvent the wheel. Second, the algorithms in the standard library implementations provide a good model to follow for interoperability and performance. If you watch how the pros do it in the standard library code, you are likely to learn a few valuable lessons along the way.

All standard algorithms use iterators. Even if you are already familiar with the concept of iterators, which is the subject of the first recipe, take a look at Table 7-1, which contains a list of the conventions I use in the rest of the chapter when listing function declarations for the standard algorithms.

Table 7-1. Iterator category abbreviations

Abbreviation	Meaning
In	Input iterator
Out	Output iterator

Table 7-1. Iterator category abbreviations (continued)

Abbreviation	Meaning
Fwd	Forward iterator
Bid	Bidirectional iterator
Rand	Random-access iterator

The standard algorithms also make use of function objects, or *functors*. A function object is a class that has overridden operator( ) so that it can be called like a function. A functor that returns a bool (and does not maintain state, and is therefore called *pure*) is called a *predicate*, and they are another regular feature in the standard algorithms. Generally, a predicate takes one or two arguments: if it takes one argument, it is an *unary* predicate; and if it takes two, it is called a *binary* predicate. For the sake of brevity, I use the abbreviations listed in Table 7-2 when listing function declarations.

Table 7-2. Functor types

Type Name	Description
UnPred	An unary predicate. Takes one argument and returns a bool.
BinPred	A binary predicate. Takes two arguments and returns a bool.
UnFunc	An unary function. Takes one argument and returns anything.
BinFunc	A binary function. Takes two arguments and returns anything.

In most cases, a function pointer can be used when a functor argument is required. When I use the term functor, I also mean function pointer unless otherwise noted.

7.1   Iterating Through a Container

Problem

You have a range of iterators—most likely from a standard container—and the standard algorithms don't fit your needs, so you need to iterate through them.

Solution

Use an iterator or a const_iterator to access and advance through each of the elements in your container. In the standard library, algorithms and containers communicate using iterators, and one of the very ideas of the standard algorithms is that they insulate you from having to use iterators directly unless you are writing your own algorithm. Even so, you should understand the different kinds of iterators so you can use the standard algorithms and containers effectively. Example 7-1 presents some straightforward uses of iterators.

Example 7-1. Using iterators with containers

```
#include <iostream>
#include <list>
#include <algorithm>
#include <string>

using namespace std;

static const int ARRAY_SIZE = 5;

template<typename T,
         typename FwdIter>
FwdIter fixOutliersUBound(FwdIter p1,
                          FwdIter p2,
                          const T& oldVal,
                          const T& newVal) {
    for ( ;p1 != p2; ++p1) {
        if (greater<T>(*p1, oldVal)) {
            *p1 = newVal;
        }
    }
}

int main( ) {

    list<string> lstStr;

    lstStr.push_back("Please");
    lstStr.push_back("leave");
    lstStr.push_back("a");
    lstStr.push_back("message");

    // Create an iterator for stepping through the list
    for (list<string>::iterator p = lstStr.begin( );
         p != lstStr.end( ); ++p) {
        cout << *p << endl;
    }

    // Or I can use a reverse_iterator to go from the end
    // to the beginning.  rbegin returns a reverse_iterator
    // to the last element and rend returns a reverse_iterator
    // to one-before-the-first.
    for (list<string>::reverse_iterator p = lstStr.rbegin( );
         p != lstStr.rend( ); ++p) {
        cout << *p << endl;
    }

    // Iterating through a range
    string arrStr[ARRAY_SIZE] = {"My", "cup", "cup", "runneth", "over"};

    for (string* p = &arrStr[0];
         p != &arrStr[ARRAY_SIZE]; ++p) {
        cout << *p << endl;
    }
```

Example 7-1. Using iterators with containers (continued)

```
    // Using standard algorithms with a standard sequence
    list<string> lstStrDest;
    unique_copy(&arrStr[0], &arrStr[ARRAY_SIZE],
                  back_inserter(lstStrDest));
}
```

Discussion

An iterator is a type that is used to refer to a single object in a container. The standard containers use iterators as the primary means for accessing the elements they contain. An iterator behaves like a pointer: you dereference an iterator (using the * or -> operators) to access what it refers to, and you can move an iterator forward and backward with syntax that looks like pointer arithmetic. An iterator is not exactly like a pointer, however, for a few reasons. Before I get into that though, let's cover the essentials of how to use iterators.

Using iterators

You declare an iterator using the type that you plan on iterating through. For example, in Example 7-1 I am using a list<string>, so I declare an iterator like this:

```
    list<string>::iterator p = lstStr.begin();
```

The ::iterator part of this declaration may look a little unusual if you are not used to working with the standard containers. It is a nested typedef on the list class template created for just this reason—so that users of the container can create iterators for this particular instantiation of a template. This is a standardized convention that all of the standard containers obey; for example, you can declare an iterator to a list<int> or to a set<MyClass> like this:

```
    list<int>::iterator p1;
    set<MyClass>::iterator p2;
```

To get back to the example, the iterator p is initialized with the first element in the sequence, which is returned by begin. To advance forward to the next element, use operator++. You can use preincrement (++p) or postincrement (p++), just as you would with a pointer to an array element, but preincrement doesn't create a temporary value to return each time, so it's more efficient and is the preferred approach. Postincrement (p++) has to create a temporary variable because it returns the value of p before the increment. However, it can't increment the value after it has returned, so it has to make a copy of the current value, increment the current value, then return the temporary value. Creating these temporary variables adds up after a while, so if you don't require postincrement behavior, use preincrement.

You will know when to stop advancing to the next element when you hit the end. Or, strictly speaking, when you hit one past the end. The convention with the standard containers is that there is a mystical value that represents one past the end of the sequence, and that value is returned by end. This works conveniently in a for loop, as in the example:

```
for (list<string>::iterator p = lstStr.begin();
     p != lstStr.end(); ++p) {
   cout << *p << endl;
}
```

As soon as p equals end, you know that p can advance no further. If the container is empty, begin == end is true, so the body of the loop is never executed. (However, use the empty member function to test a container for emptiness, don't compare begin to end or check that size == 0).

That's the simple functional explanation of iterators, but that's not all. First, an iterator as declared a moment ago works as an rvalue or an lvalue, which means you can assign from its dereferenced value or assign *to* it. To overwrite every element in the string list, I could write something like this:

```
for (list<string>::iterator p = lstStr.begin();
     p != lstStr.end(); ++p) {
   *p = "mustard";
}
```

Since *p refers to an object of type string, string::operator=(const char*) is used to assign the new string to the element in the container. But what if lstStr is a const object? In that case, an iterator won't work because dereferencing it returns a non-const object. You will need to use a const_iterator, which is an iterator that returns an rvalue only. Imagine that you decide to write a simple function for printing the contents of a container. Naturally, you will want to pass the container as a const reference:

```
template<typename T>
void printElements(const T& cont) {
   for(T::const_iterator p = cont.begin();
       p != cont.end(); ++p) {
      cout << *p << endl;
   }
}
```

Using const in this situation is the right thing to do, and a const_iterator will make the compiler keep you honest if your code tries to modify *p.

The other thing you will need to do sooner or later is iterate through the container backward. You can do this with a normal iterator, but there is a reverse_iterator that was created for just this purpose. A reverse_iterator looks and feels like an ordinary iterator, except that increment and decrement work exactly opposite to an ordinary iterator, and instead of using a container's begin and end methods, you use rbegin and rend, which return reverse_iterators. A reverse_iterator views the sequence in the opposite direction. For example, instead of initializing a reverse_iterator with begin, you use rbegin, which returns a reverse_iterator that refers to the last element in the sequence. operator++ advances backward, or toward the beginning, in the sequence.

rend returns a `reverse_iterator` that points to one-before-the-first element. Here's what it looks like:

```
for (list<string>::reverse_iterator p = lstStr.rbegin();
        p != lstStr.rend(); ++p) {
    cout << *p << endl;
}
```

But you may not be able to use a `reverse_iterator`, in which case, you can use an ordinary `iterator`, as in:

```
for (list<string>::iterator p = --lstStr.end();
        p != --lstStr.begin(); --p) {
    cout << *p << endl;
}
```

Finally, if you happen to know how far forward or backward you need to advance, you can use arithmetic with integral values to move more than one position forward or backward. Perhaps you want to get right to the middle of the list; you might do this:

```
size_t i = lstStr.size();

list<string>::iterator p = begin();
p += i/2;  // Move to the middle of the sequence
```

But beware: depending on the type of container you are using, this operation may be constant or linear complexity. If you are using a container that stores elements contiguously, such as a `vector` or `deque`, the `iterator` can calculate where it needs to jump to and do it in constant time. But if you are using a node-based container, such as a `list`, you can't use these random-access operations. Instead, you have to advance until you find the element you're after. This is expensive. This is why your requirements for how you iterate through a container or how you plan to find elements in it will dictate the best container to use for your situation. (See Chapter 6 for more information on how the standard containers work.)

When using containers that allow random access, you should prefer `iterators` to using `operator[]` with an index variable to access each element. This is especially important if you are writing a generic algorithm as a function template because not all containers support random-access `iterators`.

There are other things you can do with an iterator, but not just any `iterator`. `iterators` belong to one of five categories that have varying degrees of functionality. It's not as simple as a class hierarchy though, so that's what I describe next.

Iterator categories

Iterators supplied by different types of containers do not necessarily do all of the same things. For example, a `vector<T>::iterator` lets you use `operator+=` to jump forward some number of elements, while a `list<T>::iterator` does not. The difference between these two kinds of iterators is their *category*.

An iterator category is an interface conceptually (not technically; there is no use of abstract base classes to implement iterator categories). There are five categories, and each offers an increasing number of capabilities. They are, from least functional to most, as follows:

Input iterator

> An input iterator supports advancing forward with p++ or ++p, and dereferencing with *p. You get back an rvalue when you dereference though. Input iterators are used for things like streams, where dereferencing an input iterator means pulling the next element off the stream, so you can only read a particular element once.

Output iterator

> An output iterator supports advancing forward with p++ or ++p, and dereferencing with *p. It's different from an input iterator though, in that you can't read from one, you can only write to it—and only write to an element once. Also unlike an input iterator, you get back an lvalue and not an rvalue, so you can assign to it but not read from it.

Forward iterator

> A forward iterator merges the functionality of an input iterator and an output iterator: it supports ++p and p++, and you can treat *p as an rvalue or an lvalue. You can use a forward iterator anywhere you need an input or an output iterator, with the added benefit that you can read from or write to a dereferenced forward iterator as many times as you see fit.

Bidirectional iterator

> As the name implies, a bidirectional iterator goes forward and backward. It is a forward iterator that adds the ability to go backward using --p or p--.

Random-access iterator

> A random-access iterator does everything a bidirectional iterator does, but it also supports pointer-like operations. You can use p[n] to access the element that is n positions after p in the sequence, or you can add to or subtract from p with +, +=, -, or -= to move the iterator forward some number of elements in constant time. You can also compare two iterators p1 and p2 with <, >, <=, or >= to determine their relative order (as long as they both point to the same sequence).

Or maybe you like to see things in Venn diagrams. In that case, see Figure 7-1.

Most of the standard containers support at least bidirectional iterators, some (vector and deque) provide random-access iterators. The iterator category a container supports is specified in the standard.

Most of the time, you will use iterators for the simpler tasks: finding an element and erasing it, or otherwise doing something to it. For this you need only a forward iterator, which is available from all containers. But when you need to write

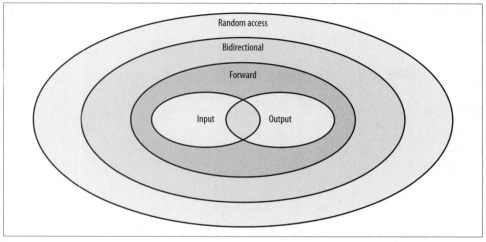

Figure 7-1. Iterator categories

a nontrivial algorithm, or use one from the standard library, you will often require more than a simple forward iterator. But how do you specify what you need? That's where iterator categories come in.

The different categories of iterators allow standard (or nonstandard) algorithms to specify the range of functionality they require. Generally, standard algorithms operate on ranges specified with iterators, and not entire containers. The declaration of a standard algorithm tells you what category of iterator it expects. For example, std::sort requires random-access iterators, since it needs to be able to reference nonadjacent elements in constant time. Thus, the declaration for sort looks like this:

```
template<typename RandomAccessIterator>
void sort(RandomAccessIterator first, RandomAccessIterator last);
```

By the name of the iterator type, you can see that it expects it to be a random-access iterator. If you try to compile sort on an iterator category other than random access, it will fail, because lesser iterator categories do not implement the pointer-arithmetic-like operations.

The iterator category provided by a particular container and that required by a particular standard algorithm is what determines which algorithms work with which containers. Many of the standard algorithms are the subject of the rest of this chapter. Table 7-1 shows the abbreviations I use in the rest of this chapter for the kinds of iterators each algorithm accepts as arguments.

This recipe discussed iterators as they are used with containers. The iterator pattern is not specific to containers, and thus there are other kinds of iterators. There are stream iterators, stream buffer iterators, and raw storage iterators, but those are not covered here.

See Also

Chapter 6

7.2   Removing Objects from a Container

Problem

You want to remove objects from a container.

Solution

Use the container's erase member function to erase a single element or a range of elements, and possibly use one of the standard algorithms to make the job easier. Example 7-2 shows a couple of different ways to remove elements from a sequence.

Example 7-2. Removing elements from a container

```
#include <iostream>
#include <string>
#include <list>
#include <algorithm>
#include <functional>
#include "utils.h" // For printContainer(): see 7.10

using namespace std;

int main( ) {

    list<string> lstStr;

    lstStr.push_back("On");
    lstStr.push_back("a");
    lstStr.push_back("cloudy");
    lstStr.push_back("cloudy");
    lstStr.push_back("day");

    list<string>::iterator p;

    // Find what you want with find
    p = find(lstStr.begin( ), lstStr.end( ), "day");

    p = lstStr.erase(p); // Now p points to the last element

    // Or, to erase all occurrences of something, use remove
    lstStr.erase(remove(lstStr.begin( ), lstStr.end( ), "cloudy"),
                 lstStr.end( ));
    printContainer(lstStr); // See 7.10
}
```

Discussion

Use a container's erase member function to remove one or more elements from it. All containers have two overloads of erase: one that takes a single iterator argument that points to the element you want to delete, and another that takes two iterators that represent a range of elements you want deleted. To erase a single element, obtain an iterator referring to that element and pass the iterator to erase, as in Example 7-2:

```
p = find(lstStr.begin( ), lstStr.end( ), "day");
p = lstStr.erase(p);
```

This will delete the object that p refers to by calling its destructor, and then do any necessary reorganization of the remaining elements in the range. The reorganization that happens depends on the type of container, and therefore the complexity of the operation will vary from one kind of container to another. The signature and behavior also differs slightly when you are using a sequence container versus an associative container.

In sequences, erase returns an iterator that refers to the first element immediately following the last element that was deleted, which may be end if the last element in the sequence was the last one deleted. The complexity of the operation is different for each container because sequences are implemented in different ways. For example, since all elements in a vector are stored in a contiguous chunk of memory, removing an element from anywhere except the end requires shifting all the elements following it toward the beginning to fill the gap. This is a hefty performance penalty (linear), which is why you shouldn't use a vector if you have to delete (or insert, for that matter) elements anywhere except at the end. I discuss this very matter in more detail in Recipe 6.2.

In associative containers, erase returns void. The complexity is amortized constant if you are deleting a single element, and logarithmic plus the number of elements deleted if you are deleting a range of elements. This is because associative containers are often implemented as balanced trees (e.g., red-black tree).

erase is handy, but not very interesting. If you want more flexibility in how you express what should be deleted, you will have to turn to the standard algorithms (in <algorithm>). Consider this line from Example 7-2:

```
lstStr.erase(std::remove(lstStr.begin( ), lstStr.end( ), "cloudy"),
        lstStr.end( ));
```

Notice that I am still using erase, but this time, for my own reasons, I want to delete all occurrences of the word "cloudy" from my list<string>. remove returns an iterator, which I pass to erase as the beginning of the doomed range, and I pass end to erase as the end point for the range. This deletes each object obj (by calling its delete method) in the range for which obj == "cloudy" is true. But it may not behave exactly as you expect. Here is where I need to clarify some terminology.

remove doesn't actually *remove* anything. It moves everything that isn't equal to the value you specify to the beginning of the sequence, and returns an iterator that refers to the first element following them. Then, it is up to you to actually call erase on the container to delete the objects between [p, end), where p is the iterator returned by remove.

remove has some variants, too. What if you want to remove elements that satisfy some predicate, and not simply those equal to some value? Use remove_if. For example, imagine you have a class named Conn that represents some sort of connection. If the connection has an idle time greater than some value, you want to remove it. First, create a functor as follows:

```
struct IdleConnFn :
    public std::unary_function<const Conn, bool> {   // Include this line
    bool operator( ) (const Conn& c) const {         // so it works with
        if (c.getIdleTime( ) > TIMEOUT) {            // other stuff in
            return(true);                            // <functional>
        }
        else
            return(false);
    }
} idle;
```

Then you can call remove_if with erase and pass in your functor, like this:

```
vec.erase(std::remove_if(vec.begin(), vec.end( ), idle), vec.end( ));
```

You want to derive such functors from unary_function for a good reason. unary_function defines some typedefs that are used by other functors in <functional>, and if they aren't there, the other functors won't compile. For example, if you are particularly malicious, and you want to remove connections that aren't idle, you can employ the not1 functor with your idle-checking functor:

```
vec.erase(std::remove_if(vec.begin( ), vec.end( ), std::not1(idle)),
          vec.end( ));
```

Finally, you may want to leave the original sequence alone (maybe it's const) and copy the results minus some elements into a new sequence. You can do that with remove_copy and remove_copy_if, which work the same way as remove and remove_if, except that there is also an output iterator you pass in where the resulting data is supposed to go. For example, to copy strings from one list to another, do this:

```
std::remove_copy(lstStr.begin( ), lstStr.end( ), lstStr2, "cloudy");
```

The thing you have to remember when using remove_copy, or any standard algorithm that writes to an output range, is that the output range must already be large enough to accommodate the elements that are about to be written to it.

erase and remove (and its family of related algorithms) offer a convenient way to erase certain elements from a sequence. They provide a clean, ready-made alternative to looping yourself to find all the elements you want, then erasing them one by one.

See Also

Recipes 6.2 and 7.1

7.3   Randomly Shuffling Data

Problem

You have a sequence of data, and you need to jumble it into some random order.

Solution

Use the `random_shuffle` standard algorithm, defined in `<algorithm>`. `random_shuffle` takes two random-access `iterators`, and (optionally) a random-number generation functor, and rearranges the elements in the range at random. Example 7-3 shows how to do this.

Example 7-3. Shuffling a sequence at random

```
#include <iostream>
#include <vector>
#include <algorithm>
#include <iterator>
#include "utils.h" // For printContainer(): see 7.11

using namespace std;

int main( ) {

   vector<int> v;
   back_insert_iterator<std::vector<int> > p =
      back_inserter(v);

   for (int i = 0; i < 10; ++i)
     *p = i;

   printContainer(v, true);

   random_shuffle(v.begin( ), v.end( ));

   printContainer(v, true);
}
```

Your output might look like this:

```
   -----
   0 1 2 3 4 5 6 7 8 9
   -----
   8 1 9 2 0 5 7 3 4 6
```

Discussion

random_shuffle is intuitive to use. Give it a range, and it will shuffle the range at random. There are two versions, and their prototypes look like this:

```
void random_shuffle(RndIter first, RndIter last);
void random_shuffle(RndIter first, RndIter last, RandFunc& rand);
```

In the first version, the "random" is using an implementation-specific random-number generation function, which should be sufficient for most of your needs. If it isn't—perhaps you want a nonuniform distribution, e.g., Gaussian—you can write your own and supply that instead using the second version.

Your random-number generator must be a functor that a single argument and returns a single value, both of which are convertible to iterator_traits<RndIter>::difference_type. In most cases, an integer will do. For example, here's my knock-off random-number generator:

```
struct RanNumGenFtor {
    size_t operator( )(size_t n) const {
        return(rand( ) % n);
    }
} rnd;

random_shuffle(v.begin( ), v.end( ), rnd);
```

The applications to random_shuffle are limited to sequences that provide random-access iterators (strings, vectors, and deques), arrays, or your custom containers that do the same. You can't randomly shuffle an associative container because its contents are stored in sorted order. In fact, you can't use any algorithm that modifies its range (often referred to as a *mutating* algorithm) on an associative container.

7.4   Comparing Ranges

Problem

You have two ranges, and you need to compare them for equality or you need to see which one comes first based on some ordering on the elements.

Solution

Depending on what kind of comparison you want to do, use one of the standard algorithms equal, lexicographical_compare, or mismatch, defined in <algorithm>. Example 7-4 shows several of them in action.

Example 7-4. Different kinds of comparisons

```
#include <iostream>
#include <vector>
#include <string>
```

Example 7-4. Different kinds of comparisons (continued)

```
#include <algorithm>
#include "utils.h"

using namespace std;
using namespace utils;

int main( ) {

    vector<string> vec1, vec2;

    vec1.push_back("Charles");
    vec1.push_back("in");
    vec1.push_back("Charge");

    vec2.push_back("Charles");
    vec2.push_back("in");
    vec2.push_back("charge");   // Note the small "c"

    if (equal(vec1.begin(), vec1.end( ), vec2.begin( ))) {
        cout << "The two ranges are equal!" << endl;
    } else {
        cout << "The two ranges are NOT equal!" << endl;
    }

    string s1 = "abcde";
    string s2 = "abcdf";
    string s3 = "abc";

    cout << boolalpha  // Show bools as "true" or "false"
         << lexicographical_compare(s1.begin( ), s1.end( ),
                                    s1.begin( ), s1.end( )) << endl;
    cout << lexicographical_compare(s1.begin( ), s1.end( ),
                                    s2.begin( ), s2.end( )) << endl;
    cout << lexicographical_compare(s2.begin( ), s2.end( ),
                                    s1.begin( ), s1.end( )) << endl;
    cout << lexicographical_compare(s1.begin( ), s1.end( ),
                                    s3.begin( ), s3.end( )) << endl;
    cout << lexicographical_compare(s3.begin( ), s3.end( ),
                                    s1.begin( ), s1.end( )) << endl;

    pair<string::iterator, string::iterator> iters =
        mismatch(s1.begin(), s1.end(), s2.begin());

    cout << "first mismatch  = " << *(iters.first) << endl;
    cout << "second mismatch = " << *(iters.second) << endl;
}
```

The output of Example 7-4 looks like this:

```
The two sequences are NOT equal!
false
true
false
```

```
false
true
first mismatch  = e
second mismatch = f
```

Discussion

Use equal to compare two sequences for equality. It takes three or four arguments, depending on the version you use. Here's how equal is declared:

```
bool equal(In1 first1, In1 last1, In2 first2);
bool equal(In1 first1, In1 last1, In2 first2, BinPred pred);
```

equal compares each element between first1 and last1 with each element starting at first2 using operator==. If you supply pred, equal uses that to test equality instead. Ensure that the sequences each have the same length before calling equal; it assumes the second range is at least as long as the first, and if it isn't, the behavior is undefined.

If you want to know more about how or where two sequences differ, you can use lexicographical_compare or mismatch. lexicographical_compare compares two sequences and returns true if the first is lexicographically less than the second, which means that each pair of elements in the two sequences is compared using the < operator. The declaration of lexicographical_compare looks like this:

```
bool lexicographical_compare(In1 first1, In1 last1,
                             In2 first2, In2 last2);
bool lexicographical_compare(In1 first1, In1 last1,
                             In2 first2, In2 last2,
                             Compare comp);
```

As soon as operator< returns true, or the first sequence ends before the second, true is returned. Otherwise, false is returned. Consider the character sequences in Example 7-4:

```
string s1 = "abcde";
string s2 = "abcdf";
string s3 = "abc";

lexicographical_compare(s1.begin( ), s1.end( ),  // abcde < abcde
                        s1.begin( ), s1.end( )); // = false
lexicographical_compare(s1.begin( ), s1.end( ),  // abcde < abcdf
                        s2.begin( ), s2.end( )); // = true
lexicographical_compare(s2.begin( ), s2.end( ),  // abcdf < abcde
                        s1.begin( ), s1.end( )); // = false
lexicographical_compare(s1.begin( ), s1.end( ),  // abcde < abc
                        s3.begin( ), s3.end( )); // = false
lexicographical_compare(s3.begin( ), s3.end( ),  // abc < abcde
                        s1.begin( ), s1.end( )); // = true
```

The complexity of lexicographical_compare is linear and will do a number of comparisons equal to the minimum of the two sequence lengths, or until the first time an element in one of the sequences is less than the corresponding element in the other. The comparisons are implemented entirely using operator<, so if iter1 and iter2 are iterators into the two sequences, the comparison stops as soon as *iter1 < *iter2 or *iter2 < *iter1.

mismatch will tell you where two sequences differ. Its declaration is a little different than equal and lexicographical_compare, though, because it returns a pair<> of iterators instead of a bool. Here it is:

```
pair<In1, In2> mismatch(In1 first1, In1 last1, In2 first2);
pair<In1, In2> mismatch(In1 first1, In1 last1, In2 first2, BinPred);
```

The two iterators returned point to the differing elements in each of the sequences. Consider Example 7-4:

```
string s1 = "abcde";
string s2 = "abcdf";
pair<string::iterator, string::iterator> iters =
    mismatch(s1.begin(), s1.end(), s2.begin());

cout << "first mismatch  = " << *(iters.first) << '\n'; // 'e'
cout << "second mismatch = " << *(iters.second) << '\n';// 'f'
```

You have to ensure that the second range is at least as long as the first. If the second sequence is shorter than the first, mismatch has no way to know it and will continue making comparisons to elements past the end of the second sequence, which has undefined behavior if it extends past the end of the second sequence. Additionally, if there is no mismatch, the first iterator will be pointing to last1, which may not be valid (e.g., if you passed in end( ) as last1).

You may have noticed from the declarations of each of these algorithms that the types of the iterators for each of the two sequences are different. This means that the two sequences can be containers of different types, so long as the type of the element those iterators refer to have operator< defined for them. For example, you may want to compare a string to a vector<char>:

```
string s = "Coke";
vector<char> v;

v.push_back('c');
v.push_back('o');
v.push_back('k');
v.push_back('e');

std::cout << std::lexicographical_compare(s.begin( ), s.end( ),
                                          v.begin( ), v.end( )) << '\n';
```

This compares each of the characters in the two sequences without regard for the type of container that holds them.

The C++ standard library provides several different ways to compare sequences. If none of these suits your needs, look at the source code for them; it will provide a good example of how you can write your own efficient, generic algorithm.

See Also

Recipe 7.1

7.5   Merging Data

Problem

You have two sorted sequences and you need to merge them.

Solution

Use either the merge or inplace_merge function template. merge merges two sequences and puts the results in a third, and inplace_merge merges two contiguous sequences. Example 7-5 shows how.

Example 7-5. Merging two sequences

```
#include <iostream>
#include <string>
#include <list>
#include <vector>
#include <algorithm>
#include <iterator>
#include "utils.h" // For printContainer(): see 7.10

using namespace std;

int main( ) {

   vector<string> v1, v2, v3;

   v1.push_back("a");
   v1.push_back("c");
   v1.push_back("e");

   v2.push_back("b");
   v2.push_back("d");
   v2.push_back("f");

   v3.reserve(v1.size( ) + v2.size( ) + 1);

   // Use a back_inserter from iterator to avoid having to put
   // a bunch of default objects in the container.  But this doesn't
   // mean you don't have to use reserve!
   merge(v1.begin( ), v1.end( ),
         v2.begin( ), v2.end( ),
         back_inserter<vector<string> >(v3));

   printContainer(v3);
```

Example 7-5. Merging two sequences (continued)

```
    // Now make a mess
    random_shuffle(v3.begin( ), v3.end( ));
    sort(v3.begin(), v3.begin( ) + v3.size( ) / 2);
    sort(v3.begin() + v3.size( ) / 2, v3.end( ));

    printContainer(v3);

    inplace_merge(v3.begin(), v3.begin( ) + 3, v3.end( ));

    printContainer(v3);

    // If you are using two lists, though, use list::merge instead.
    // As a general rule, blah blah...
    list<string> lstStr1, lstStr2;

    lstStr1.push_back("Frank");
    lstStr1.push_back("Rizzo");
    lstStr1.push_back("Bill");
    lstStr1.push_back("Cheetoh");

    lstStr2.push_back("Allie");
    lstStr2.push_back("McBeal");
    lstStr2.push_back("Slick");
    lstStr2.push_back("Willie");

    lstStr1.sort( );  // Sort these or merge makes garbage!
    lstStr2.sort( );

    lstStr1.merge(lstStr2); // Note that this only works with other
                            // lists of the same type

    printContainer(lstStr1);
}
```

The output of Example 7-5 looks like this:

```
    -----
    a
    b
    c
    d
    e
    f
    -----
    b
    d
    e
    a
    c
    f
    -----
    a
    b
```

```
c
d
e
f
-----
Allie
Bill
Cheetoh
Frank
McBeal
Rizzo
Slick
Willie
```

Discussion

merge merges two sorted sequences and places the result into a third, optionally using a caller-supplied comparison functor to determine when one element is less than another—it uses operator< by default. The complexity is linear: the number of comparisons performed during the merge is the sum of the two sequence lengths minus one. The types of the elements in each sequence must be comparable with operator< (or the comparison functor you supply), and they must be convertible to the type of element in the output sequence via copy constructor or assignment; or there must be conversion operators defined such that the type of the element in the output sequence has assignment and copy construction defined for both types.

The declarations for merge look like this:

```
void merge(In1 first1, In1 last1, In2 first2, In2 last2, Out result)
void merge(In1 first1, In1 last1, In2 first2, In2 last2, Out result,
        BinPred comp)
```

Using merge is simple enough. Both sequences must be sorted (or the output will be garbage), and neither is modified by merge. The output iterator where the results are going to go must have enough room to accommodate the sum of the lengths of each input sequence. You can do this by explicitly reserving enough storage, or, as I did in Example 7-5, by using a back_inserter:

```
merge(v1.begin( ), v1.end( ),
      v2.begin( ), v2.end( ),
      back_inserter(v3));
```

A back_inserter is a class defined in <iterator> that provides a convenient way to create an output iterator that calls push_back on a sequence every time you assign a value to it. This way, you don't have to explicitly size the output sequence. The following call creates a back_inserter for a vector<string> named v3.

```
back_inserter(v3);
```

You don't have to specify the template arguments because a `back_inserter` is a function template, not a class template, so the type of the call arguments can be deduced. An equivalent call with explicit template arguments would look like this:

```
back_inserter<vector<string> >(v3);
```

Note, however, that sometimes you ought to explicitly size the output sequence, especially when the output sequence is a `vector`. A `vector` may need to keep resizing itself if you simply add items to it with `push_back`, and resizing is an expensive operation. See Recipe 6.2 for more details.

If there are two equivalent elements in the sequences, the one from the first sequence will precede the one from the second. Therefore, if you call `merge` twice with the input sequences switched, the resulting output sequences may be different (predictable and correct, but different).

Merging `list`s is a good example of a situation where you can use a sequence's member function or a similar standard algorithm. You should prefer a member function over a standard algorithm that does the same thing, but this doesn't always work, and here's an example of why.

Consider your list of strings from Example 7-5:

```
lstStr1.sort( );  // Sort these or merge makes garbage!
lstStr2.sort( );
lstStr1.merge(lstStr2); // This is list::merge
```

There are two reasons why this is different than calling `std::merge`. To begin with, both `list`s must have the same type of elements. This is because `list::merge` is declared like this:

```
void merge(list<T, Alloc>& lst)
template <typename Compare>
void merge(list<T, Alloc>& lst, Compare comp)
```

Where `T` is the same type as in the list class template itself. So you can't, for example, merge a list of null-terminated character arrays into a list of `string`s.

The other thing that's different is that `list::merge` erases the input sequence, while `std::merge` leaves the two input sequences untouched. Most likely, `list::merge` will have better performance, since in most cases the elements in the list are relinked instead of copied; but relinking is not guaranteed, so step into the source or experiment to be sure.

You can also merge two contiguous sequences with `inplace_merge`. `inplace_merge` is different from `merge` because it merges its two sequence arguments, well, in place. In other words, if you have two sequences that are contiguous (i.e., they are parts of the same sequence), and they are sorted, and you want the entire sequence sorted, you can use `inplace_merge` instead of a sort algorithm. The advantage is that `inplace_merge` can run in linear time if there is enough additional memory available. If there isn't, it runs in $n \log n$, which is the average complexity of sort anyway.

The declaration for inplace_merge is a little different from merge:

```
void inplace_merge(Bid first, Bid mid, Bid last)
void inplace_merge(Bid first, Bid mid, Bid last, BinPred comp)
```

inplace_merge requires bidirectional iterators, so you can't use it interchangeably with merge, but in most cases either should work. Like merge, it uses operator< by default to determine elements' relative order, and comp if you supply it.

7.6   Sorting a Range

Problem

You have a range of elements that you need to sort.

Solution

There are a handful of algorithms you can use for sorting a range. You can do a conventional sort (ascending or descending order) with sort, defined in <algorithm>, or you can use one of the other sorting functions, such as partial_sort. Have a look at Example 7-6 to see how.

Example 7-6. Sorting

```
#include <iostream>
#include <istream>
#include <string>
#include <list>
#include <vector>
#include <algorithm>
#include <iterator>
#include "utils.h" // For printContainer(): see 7.10

using namespace std;

int main() {

    cout << "Enter a series of strings: ";
    istream_iterator<string> start(cin);
    istream_iterator<string> end; // This creates a "marker"
    vector<string> v(start, end);

    // The sort standard algorithm will sort elements in a range.  It
    // requires a random-access iterator, so it works for a vector.
    sort(v.begin(), v.end());
    printContainer(v);

    random_shuffle(v.begin(), v.end()); // See 7.2

    string* arr = new string[v.size()];
```

Example 7-6. Sorting (continued)

```
    // Copy the elements into the array
    copy(v.begin(), v.end(), &arr[0]);

    // Sort works on any kind of range, so long as its arguments
    // behave like random-access iterators.
    sort(&arr[0], &arr[v.size()]);
    printRange(&arr[0], &arr[v.size()]);

    // Create a list with the same elements
    list<string> lst(v.begin(), v.end());

    lst.sort(); // The standalone version of sort won't work; you have
                // to use list::sort.  Note, consequently, that you
                // can't sort only parts of a list.

    printContainer(lst);
}
```

A run of Example 7-6 might look like this:

```
    Enter a series of strings: a z b y c x d w
    ^Z
    -----
    a b c d w x y z
    -----
    w b y c a x z d
    -----
    a b c d w x y z
    -----
    a b c d w x y z
```

Discussion

Sorting is a common thing, and there are two ways you can sort a sequence. You can keep elements in sorted order by using an associative container, but then you pay logarithmic time for insertions. Or, you can sort them only as needed, for which you have several options.

The sort standard algorithm does just what you'd expect: it sorts the elements in a range in ascending order using operator<. Its declaration looks like this:

```
    void sort(Rnd first, Rnd last);
    void sort(Rnd first, Rnd last, BinPred comp);
```

As with most other algorithms, you can supply your own comparison operator for sorting if operator< isn't what you want. Complexity is, in the average case, $n \log n$. It can be quadratic in the worst case.

If you require that equivalent elements retain their relative order, use stable_sort. It has the same signature, but guarantees that equivalent elements will not have their relative order changed. Its complexity is also a little different in that it is $n \log n$ in the worst case, as long as there is memory available. If there isn't enough extra memory available, it can be at most $n (\log n)^2$.

sort doesn't work for any container, though. It requires random-access iterators, so if you are using a container that doesn't provide them, it won't work. The standard sequence containers deque, vector, and string/wstring (which are not containers, but satisfy almost all of the sequence container requirements), all provide random access iterators. list is the only one that doesn't. If you need to sort a list, you can use list::sort. For example, in Example 7-6 you will probably notice that list::sort takes no arguments:

```
lst.sort( );
```

This makes it distinct from std::sort, in that you can't sort only parts of a list. If you need to sort parts of a sequence, you may be better off using a sequence other than a list.

The concept of sorting is pretty straightforward, but there are a few variations on the theme that are implemented in the standard library. The following list describes each of them:

partial_sort
: Takes three random-access iterators: first, middle, and last, and optionally a comparison functor. It has two postconditions: the elements in the range (first, middle) are all less than those in the range (middle, last), and the range (first, middle) is sorted according to operator< or your comparison functor. In other words, it sorts until the first n elements are sorted.

partial_sort_copy
: Does the same thing as partial_sort, but places the results in an output range. It takes the first n elements from the source range and copies them into the destination range in sorted order. If the destination range (n) is shorter than the source range (m), only n items are copied into the destination range.

nth_element
: Takes three random-access iterator arguments: first, nth, and last, and an optional comparison functor It puts the element referred to by nth at the index where it would be if the entire range were sorted. Consequently, all elements in the range (first, nth) are less than the element at the nth position (those in (nth, last) are not sorted, but are all greater than the ones preceding nth). You would use this if you only want one or a few elements sorted in a range, but you don't want to pay for sorting the entire range if you don't have to.

You can also partition the elements in a range according to your own criterion (functor), and that is the subject of Recipe 7.7.

See Also

Recipe 7.7

7.7   Partitioning a Range

Problem

You have a range of elements that you need to partition in some well-defined way. For example, you may want all elements less than a particular value moved to the front of the range.

Solution

Use the partition standard algorithm with a predicate functor to move the elements around however you like. See Example 7-7.

Example 7-7. Partitioning a range

```
#include <iostream>
#include <istream>
#include <string>
#include <vector>
#include <algorithm>
#include <functional>
#include <iterator>
#include "utils.h" // For printContainer(): see Recipe 7.10

using namespace std;

int main() {

    cout << "Enter a series of strings: ";
    istream_iterator<string> start(cin);
    istream_iterator<string> end; // This creates a "marker"
    vector<string> v(start, end);

    // Rearrange the elements in v so that those that are less
    // than "foo" occur before the rest.
    vector<string>::iterator p =
       partition(v.begin(), v.end(),
               bind2nd(less<string>(), "foo"));
    printContainer(v);

    cout << "*p = " << *p << endl;
}
```

The output for Example 7-7 would look like the following:

```
Enter a series of strings: a d f j k l
^Z
-----
a d f j k l
*p = j
```

After the partition, the iterator p refers to the first element for which less(*p, "foo") is not true.

Discussion

partition takes the beginning and end of a range and a predicate, and moves all elements for which the predicate is true to the beginning of the range. It returns an iterator to the first element where the predicate is not true, or the end of the range if all elements satisfy the predicate. Its declaration looks like this:

```
Bi partition(Bi first, Bi last, Pred pred);
```

pred is a functor that takes one argument and returns true or false. There is no default predicate; you have to supply one that makes sense for what you are trying to partition. You can write your own predicate, or use one from the standard library. For example, from Example 7-7, you can see that I used less and bind2nd to create a functor for me:

```
vector<string>::iterator p =
    partition(v.begin( ), v.end( ),
            bind2nd(less<string>( ), "foo"));
```

What this does is move all elements less than "foo" before everything that is not. bind2nd is not required here, but it is a convenient way to create automatically a functor that takes one argument and returns the result of less<string>(*i, "foo") for each element i in the sequence. You can also use stable_partition if you want equivalent elements to retain their relative order.

> partition, and other algorithms that change the order of the elements in a range, do not work with the standard associative containers set, multiset, map, and multimap. This is because associative containers keep their elements in a well-defined order and only the containers themselves are allowed to move or remove elements. You can use partition with any range for which you can obtain at least bidirectional iterators, which includes all of the standard sequence containers deque, vector, and list.

See Also

Recipe 7.9

7.8   Performing Set Operations on Sequences

Problem

You have sequences that you want to rearrange using set operations like union, difference, or intersection.

Solution

Use the standard library functions built for exactly this purpose: set_union, set_dif-
ference, and set_intersection. Each of these performs its respective set operation
and places the results in an output range. See how to do this in Example 7-8.

Example 7-8. Using set operations

```cpp
#include <iostream>
#include <algorithm>
#include <string>
#include <set>
#include <iterator>
#include "utils.h" // For printContainer(): see 7.10

using namespace std;

int main() {

   cout << "Enter some strings: ";
   istream_iterator<string> start(cin);
   istream_iterator<string> end;
   set<string> s1(start, end);

   cin.clear();

   cout << "Enter some more strings: ";
   set<string> s2(++start, end);

   set<string> setUnion;
   set<string> setInter;
   set<string> setDiff;

   set_union(s1.begin(), s1.end(),
             s2.begin(), s2.end(),
             inserter(setUnion, setUnion.begin()));

   set_difference(s1.begin(), s1.end(),
                  s2.begin(), s2.end(),
                  inserter(setDiff, setDiff.begin()));

   set_intersection(s1.begin(), s1.end(),
                    s2.begin(), s2.end(),
                    inserter(setInter, setInter.begin()));

   cout << "Union:\n";
   printContainer(setUnion);
   cout << "Difference:\n";
   printContainer(setDiff);
   cout << "Intersection:\n";
   printContainer(setInter);
}
```

The output to this program looks like this (printContainer just prints the contents of a container):

```
Enter some strings: a b c d
^Z
Enter some more strings: d e f g
^Z
Union: a b c d e f g
Difference: a b c
Intersection: d
```

Discussion

The set operations in the standard library all look and work pretty much the same. Each takes two ranges, performs its respective operation on them, and places the results in an output iterator. You have to make sure there is enough room in the output sequence, or use an inserter or a back_inserter (see the discussion in Recipe 7.5 to see how to use a back_inserter).

The declaration for set_union looks like this:

```
Out set_union(In first1, In last1, In first2, In last2, Out result)
```

The declarations for set_difference, set_intersection, and set_symmetric_difference all look the same.

To use these functions, do as I did in Example 7-8. To find the intersection of two sets, for example, you might call set_intersection like this:

```
set_intersection(s1.begin( ), s1.end( ),
                 s2.begin( ), s2.end( ),
                 inserter(setInter, setInter.begin( )));
```

The last argument to set_intersection needs further explanation. inserter is a function template defined in <iterator> that takes a container and an iterator and returns an output iterator that calls insert on its first argument when values are assigned to it. If you use it on a sequence container, it inserts values before the iterator you pass in as its last argument. If you use it on an associative container as I did in the previous code snippet, this iterator is ignored and elements are inserted where they belong according to the container's sort criteria.

sets are a convenient example for my purposes, but you can call the set operations on any sequence, not just sets. For example, you may have lists that you want to do some set operations on:

```
list<string> lst1, lst2, lst3;

// Fill them with data

lst1.sort( );// Elements must be sorted
lst2.sort( );
```

```
set_symmetric_difference(lst1.begin( ), lst1.end( ),
                         lst2.begin( ), lst2.end( ),
                         back_inserter(lst3));
```

However, since lists are not stored in sorted order, you have to sort them first or the results of the set operations are invalid. Notice also that I used a back_inserter in this example instead of an inserter. back_inserter works similarly to inserter, except that it uses push_back to add elements to the container you give it. You don't need to do it this way; for example, you could resize the output container so that it's always big enough:

```
lst3.resize(lst1.size( ) + lst2.size( ));
```

```
set_symmetric_difference(lst1.begin( ), lst1.end( ),
                         lst2.begin( ), lst2.end( ),
                         lst3.begin( ));
```

If the output sequence is large enough, you can just pass in an iterator pointing to the first element in the sequence with begin.

In case you don't know what set_symmetric_difference is, I'll tell you. It's the union of the differences of two sets in opposite order. That is, if a and b are sets, the symmetric difference is a − b ∪ b − a. Another way to put it is to say that the symmetric difference is the set of all elements that appear in one set but not the other.

There's one more thing you should know about the set operations. Since sequences don't have to be unique, you can have a "set" with duplicate values. Strictly speaking, of course, mathematical sets can't contain duplicates, so this may not be intuitive. Consider what the output of Example 7-8 might look like if I used lists instead of sets (you can enter duplicate values when running Example 7-8, but they aren't added to the sets because set::insert fails when the element being inserted already exists in the set):

```
Enter some strings: a a a b c c
^Z
Enter some more strings: a a b b c
^Z
Union: a a a b b c c
Difference: a c
Intersection: a a b c
```

What's happening here is that the set operations iterate through both sequences and compare corresponding values to determine what to put in the output sequence.

Finally, the set operations in their default form (using operator< to compare elements) probably don't work like you want them to if your sets contain pointers. To get around this, write a functor that compares pointers' objects, as in Recipe 7.4.

See Also

Recipe 7.4

7.9   Transforming Elements in a Sequence

Problem

You have a sequence of elements and you have to do something to each one, either in place or as it is copied to another sequence.

Solution

Use the transform or for_each standard algorithms. Both are simple, but allow you to do almost anything you want to the elements in your sequence. See Example 7-9 for an illustration.

Example 7-9. Transforming data

```
#include <iostream>
#include <istream>
#include <string>
#include <list>
#include <algorithm>
#include <iterator>
#include <cctype>
#include "utils.h" // For printContainer(): see 7.10

using namespace std;

// Convert a string to upper case
string strToUpper(const string& s) {
    string tmp;
    for (string::const_iterator p = s.begin(); p != s.end(); ++p)
        tmp += toupper(*p);
    return(tmp);
}

string strAppend(const string& s1, const string& s2) {
    return(s1 + s2);
}

int main() {

    cout << "Enter a series of strings: ";
    istream_iterator<string> start(cin);
    istream_iterator<string> end;
    list<string> lst(start, end), out;

    // Use transform with an unary function...
    transform(lst.begin(), lst.end(),
              back_inserter(out),
              strToUpper);

    printContainer(out);
```

Example 7-9. Transforming data (continued)

```
    cin.clear( );

    cout << "Enter another series of strings: ";
    list<string> lst2(++start, end);
    out.clear( );

    // ...or a binary function and another input sequence.
    transform(lst.begin(), lst.end( ), lst2.begin( ),
              back_inserter(out),
              strAppend);

    printContainer(out);
}
```

Discussion

The obvious function for transforming data is transform. It has two forms. The first form takes a sequence, an output iterator, and an unary functor. It applies the functor to each element in the sequence and assigns the return value to the next element pointed to by the output iterator. The output iterator can be another sequence or the beginning of the originating sequence. In this respect, transform handles both copy-style or in-place transformations.

Here's what the declarations for transform look like:

```
    Out transform(In first, In last, Out result, UnFunc f);
    Out transform(In first1, In last1, In first2, In last2,
                  Out result, BinFunc f);
```

Both versions return an iterator that refers to one past the end of the result sequence.

Using either version is straightforward. To copy strings from one sequence to another, but in uppercase, do as I did in Example 7-9:

```
    std::transform(lst.begin( ), lst.end( ),
                   std::back_inserter(out), strToUpper);
```

If you want to modify the originating sequence, just pass in the beginning of the sequence as the result iterator:

```
    std::transform(lst.begin( ), lst.end( ),
                   lst.begin( ), strToUpper);
```

Using two sequences and a binary operation works the same way, and you can use either one of the input sequences as the output sequence.

If you want to transform elements in place, you might want to avoid the overhead of assigning each element to the return value of some function. Or if the functor you want to use modifies its source object, you can use for_each instead:

```
    void strToUpperInPlace(string& s) {
        for (string::iterator p = s.begin( ); p != s.end( ); ++p)
            *p = std::toupper(*p);
```

```
    }
    // ...
    std::for_each(lst.begin( ), lst.end( ), strToUpperInPlace);
```

If what you want to do is change the sequence itself and not necessarily change each of its elements, see Recipe 7.6, where I describe many of the standard algorithms for rearranging the elements in a sequence.

See Also

Recipes 7.1 and 7.6

Discussion

7.10 Writing Your Own Algorithm

Problem

You need to execute an algorithm on a range and none of the standard algorithms meets your requirements.

Solution

Write your algorithm as a function template and advertise your iterator requirements with the names of your template parameters. See Example 7-10 for a variation on the copy standard algorithm.

Example 7-10. Writing your own algorithm

```
#include <iostream>
#include <istream>
#include <iterator>
#include <string>
#include <functional>
#include <vector>
#include <list>
#include "utils.h" // For printContainer( ): see 7.11

using namespace std;

template<typename In, typename Out, typename UnPred>
Out copyIf(In first, In last, Out result, UnPred pred) {
   for ( ;first != last; ++first)
      if (pred(*first))
         *result++ = *first;
   return(result);
}

int main( ) {
```

Example 7-10. Writing your own algorithm (continued)

```
    cout << "Enter a series of strings: ";
    istream_iterator<string> start(cin);
    istream_iterator<string> end; // This creates a "marker"
    vector<string> v(start, end);

    list<string> lst;

    copyIf(v.begin( ), v.end( ), back_inserter<list<string> >(lst),
        bind2nd(less<string>( ), "cookie"));

    printContainer(lst);
}
```

A sample run of Example 7-10 will look something like this:

```
Enter a series of strings: apple banana danish eclaire
^Z
-----
apple banana
```

You can see that it only copies values less than "cookie" into the destination range.

Discussion

The standard library contains the copy function template, which copies elements from one range to another, but there is no standard version that takes a predicate and conditionally copies each element (i.e., a copy_if algorithm), so that's what I have implemented in Example 7-10. The behavior is simple enough: given a source range and the beginning of the destination range, copy elements to the destination range for which my unary predicate functor returns true.

The algorithm is simple, but there's more going on with the implementation than meets the eye. Starting with the declaration, you can see that there are three template parameters:

```
template<typename In, typename Out, typename UnPred>
Out copyIf(In first, In last, Out result, UnPred pred) {
```

The first template parameter, In, is the type of the input iterator. Since this is the input range, all copyIf needs to be able to do is extract the dereferenced value from the iterator and increment the iterator to the next element. This describes the input iterator category (iterator categories are described in Recipe 7.1), so that's the kind of iterator we will advertise we need by naming the template parameter In. There is no standard convention (In and Out are my conventions, which I described in the first recipe of this chapter), but it's easy enough to get your point across with similar naming conventions: InIter, Input_T, or even InputIterator. The second template parameter, Out, is the type of the iterator that refers to the range where elements will be copied to. copyIf needs to be able to write to the dereferenced value of the output iterator and increment the iterator, which is the description of an output iterator.

By advertising your iterator requirements with the template parameter names, you make the calling conventions of the algorithm self-documenting. But why use two different iterator categories?

There are at least a couple of reasons why I used two different iterator categories in copyIf. First, the operations on each range are slightly different, and since I will never need to go backward in the input range, or assign to it, all I need is an input iterator. Similarly, I will never need to read from the output range, so all I need there is an output iterator. There are requirements for each of the iterators that do not apply to the other, so it would make no sense to (for example) have one bidirectional iterator type and use that for both ranges. Second, using two different iterator types lets the caller read from one kind of range and write to another. In Example 7-10, I read from a vector and wrote to a list:

```
vector<string> v(start, end);
list<string> lst;

copyIf(v.begin( ), v.end( ), back_inserter<list<string> >(lst),
    bind2nd(less<string>( ), "cookie"));
```

If you try doing this using a single iterator type on your algorithm, it won't compile.

In Example 7-10, I passed a back_inserter as the beginning of the output range instead of, say, the iterator returned from lst.begin. I did this because lst has no elements in it, and in this algorithm (as in the copy standard algorithm), the destination range has to be big enough to hold all of the elements that will be copied to it. Otherwise, incrementing the output iterator result inside copyIf will have undefined behavior. A back inserter returns an output iterator that calls push_back on its container whenever you increment the iterator. This increases the size of lst by one each time the output iterator result is incremented. I describe the back_inserter class template in more detail in Recipe 7.5.

When writing your own algorithm for working with ranges (i.e., the standard containers), you should work with iterator arguments and not container arguments. You may be tempted, for example, to declare copyIf to take two container arguments instead of a source range and destination output iterator, but this is a less general solution than using ranges. You can't work with only a subset of elements in a container if you take container arguments, for one. Furthermore, in the body of copyIf, you would depend on the containers' begin and end member functions to get the range you were after, and the return type would depend on the type of container used as the output range. This means that using nonstandard ranges will not work with copyIf, such as built-in arrays or your own custom containers. These, and other reasons, are why the standard algorithms all operate on ranges.

Finally, if you do write your own algorithm, double-check the standard algorithms for what you need. They may seem like very simple algorithms at first glance, but their apparent simplicity is because of their generality, and nine times out of ten they can be extended in some fashion to meet your needs. Reusing the standard algorithms is something you should strive for, since it goes along way in ensuring portability and efficiency.

See Also

Recipe 7.5

7.11   Printing a Range to a Stream

Problem

You have a range of elements that you want to print to a stream, most likely cout for debugging.

Solution

Write a function template that takes a range or a container, iterates through each element, and uses the copy algorithm and an ostream_iterator to write each element to a stream. If you want more control over formatting, write your own simple algorithm that iterates through a range and prints each element to the stream. (See Example 7-11.)

Example 7-11. Printing a range to a stream

```
#include <iostream>
#include <string>
#include <algorithm>
#include <iterator>
#include <vector>

using namespace std;

int main( ) {

    // An input iterator is the opposite of an output iterator: it
    // reads elements from a stream as if it were a container.
    cout << "Enter a series of strings: ";
    istream_iterator<string> start(cin);
    istream_iterator<string> end;
    vector<string> v(start, end);

    // Treat the output stream as a container by using an
    // output_iterator.  It constructs an output iterator where writing
    // to each element is equivalent to writing it to the stream.
    copy(v.begin( ), v.end( ), ostream_iterator<string>(cout, ", "));
}
```

The output for Example 7-11 might look like this:

```
Enter a series of strings: z x y a b c
^Z
z, x, y, a, b, c,
```

Discussion

A stream `iterator` is an `iterator` that is based on a stream instead of a range of elements in some container, and stream `iterators` allow you to treat stream input as an input `iterator` (read from the dereferenced value and increment the `iterator`) or an output `iterator` (just like an input `iterator`, but you write to its dereferenced value instead of read from it). This makes for concise reading of values (especially strings) from a stream, which is what I have done in a number of other examples in this chapter, and writing values to a stream, which is what I have done in Example 7-11. I know this recipe is about printing a range *to* a stream, but allow me to stray from the path for a moment to explain input stream `iterators` since I use them in so many examples in this chapter.

There are three key parts to the `istream_iterator` in Example 7-11. The first part is creating the `istream_iterator` that refers to the start of the stream input. I do it like this:

```
istream_iterator<string> start(cin);
```

This creates an `iterator` named `start` that refers to the first element in the input sequence, just as `vec.begin` (`vec` is a `vector`) returns an `iterator` that refers to the first element in a vector. The template argument string tells the `istream_iterator` that the elements in this sequence are `strings`. The constructor argument `cin` is the input stream to read from. This is an abstraction, though, because there is no first element at this point because nothing has come in from `cin`. That will happen in a moment.

The second part to the input stream `iterator` is the end marker, which I created like this:

```
istream_iterator<string> end;
```

The standard containers use the special value of one past the end to indicate the point at which any algorithm using the range should stop. Since an input stream iterator has no actual last element in memory, it uses a constructor with no arguments to create a logical endpoint value that represents the point at which any algorithm should stop iterating.

The last part of the `istream_iterator` technique is how I use it to extract values. A convenient way to pull all values entered on a stream into a container is to use the container's range constructor. For example, if you construct a `vector` with two iterators, the constructor will copy each element out of the range the `iterators` refer to into itself. If I pass in the `start` and `end` `iterators` I just created, it looks like this:

```
vector<string> v(start, end);
```

This is where the values are actually read from the stream. When v is constructed, it starts at start and iterates forward until it reaches end. Each time v reads from *start, it is equivalent to invoking something like this on cin:

```
cin >> v[i]; // v is a vector<string>
```

In other words, the next value is pulled from cin, is converted to a string, and is inserted into the vector.

 When you are using cin as the input stream, it is up to your platform to decide what constitutes an end-of-file marker where the stream should end. On Windows, I have to press Enter, Ctrl-Z, Enter to end the stream input. Experiment on your platform to see what you have to do, but chances are it's a combination of these same key combinations.

Output stream iterators behave similarly to input stream iterators. In Example 7-11, I copy from my vector of values to cout by creating an ostream_iterator that refers to cout, like this:

```
copy(v.begin( ), v.end( ), ostream_iterator<string>(cout, ", "));
```

The template argument to ostream_iterator tells it that the elements I will be assigning to it are strings. The first constructor argument to ostream_iterator is the stream I will write to (which can be any output stream, including ofstreams and ostringstreams) and the second is the delimiter I want to use. This provides a handy way to dump a range of values to the standard output, which I do often when debugging.

If you want more control over the appearance of the output—such as wrapping the sequence with brackets or curly braces, or avoiding the last delimiter on the end of the sequence—doing so requires only a few more lines of code. Example 7-12 shows the body of printContainer and printRange, the first of which I have been using throughout examples in this chapter.

Example 7-12. Writing your own printing function

```
#include <iostream>
#include <string>
#include <algorithm>
#include <iterator>
#include <vector>

using namespace std;

template<typename C>
void printContainer(const C& c, char delim = ',', ostream& out = cout) {
    printRange(c.begin( ), c.end( ), delim, out);
}

template<typename Fwd>
void printRange(Fwd first, Fwd last, char delim = ',', ostream& out = cout) {
    out << "{";
```

Example 7-12. Writing your own printing function (continued)

```
    while (first != last) {
        out << *first;
        if (++first != last)
            out << delim << ' ';
    }
    out << "}" << endl;
}

int main( ) {

    cout << "Enter a series of strings: ";
    istream_iterator<string> start(cin);
    istream_iterator<string> end;
    vector<string> v(start, end);

    printContainer(v);
    printRange(v.begin( ), v.end( ), ';', cout);
}
```

The function printRange is the more general approach, since it operates on a range (this is explained in more detail in Recipe 7.10), but printContainer is more convenient for printing an entire container. There are many more ways to do this. A couple that come to mind are defining a version of operator<< that operates on an output stream and a container and using the for_each standard algorithm with a custom functor to write out each element in a stream.

## CHAPTER 8

Classes

8.0   Introduction

This chapter contains solutions to common problems related to working with C++ classes. The recipes are mostly independent, but they are organized into two parts, which each make up about half the chapter. The first half of the chapter contains solutions to common problems you may experience when constructing objects of a class, such as using a function to create objects (which is often called a Factory pattern) or using constructors and destructors to manage resources. The second half contains solutions to problems post-construction, such as determining an object's type at runtime, and miscellaneous implementation techniques, such as how to create an interface with an abstract base class.

Classes are, of course, the central feature of C++ that supports object-oriented programming, and there are lots of different things you can do with classes. This chapter does not contain recipes that explain the basics of classes: virtual functions (polymorphism), inheritance, and encapsulation. I assume you are already familiar with these general object-oriented design principles, whether it's with C++ or another language such as Java or Smalltalk. Rather, the purpose of this chapter is to provide recipes for some of the mechanical difficulties you may run into when implementing object-oriented designs with C++.

Object-oriented design and the related design patterns is a huge subject, and the literature on the subject is vast and comprehensive. I mention only a few design patterns by name in this chapter, and they are the ones for which C++ facilities provide an elegant or perhaps not-so-obvious solution. If you are unfamiliar with the concept of design patterns, I recommend you read *Design Patterns* by Gamma, et al (Addison Wesley), because it is a useful thing to know in software engineering; however, it is not a prerequisite for this chapter.

8.1   Initializing Class Member Variables

Problem

You need to initialize member variables that are native types, pointers, or references.

Solution

Use an initializer list to set the initial values for member variables. Example 8-1 shows how you can do this for native types, pointers, and references.

Example 8-1. Initializing class members

```
#include <string>

using namespace std;

class Foo {
public:
    Foo() : counter_(0), str_(NULL) {}
    Foo(int c, string* p) :
        counter_(c), str_(p) {}
private:
    int counter_;
    string* str_;
};

int main() {

    string s = "bar";
    Foo(2, &s);
}
```

Discussion

You should always initialize native variables, especially if they are class member variables. Class variables, on the other hand, should have a constructor defined that will initialize its state properly, so you do not always have to initialize them. Leaving a native variable in an uninitialized state, where it contains garbage, is asking for trouble. But there are a few different ways to do this in C++, which is what this recipe discusses.

The simplest things to initialize are native types. ints, chars, pointers, and so on are easy to deal with. Consider a simple class and its default constructor:

```
class Foo {
public:
    Foo() : counter_(0), str_(NULL) {}
    Foo(int c, string* p) :
        counter_(c), str_(p) {}
private:
```

```
    int counter_;
    string* str_;
};
```

Use an initializer list in the constructor to initialize member variables, and avoid doing so in the body of the constructor. This leaves the body of the constructor for any logic that must occur at construction, and makes the member variables' initialization easy to locate. A minor benefit over just assigning member variables in the constructor body, to be sure, but the benefits of using an initializer list becomes more apparent when you have class or reference member variables, or when you are trying to deal with exceptions effectively.

 Members are initialized in the order they are declared in the class declaration, *not* in the order they are declared in the initializer list.

Consider a class member variable using the same Foo class from Example 8-1:

```
class Foo {
public:
    Foo() : counter_(0), str_(NULL), cls_(0) {}
    Foo(int c, string* p) :
        counter_(c), str_(p), cls_(0) {}
private:
    int counter_;
    string* str_;
    SomeClass cls_;
};
```

In Foo's default constructor, you don't need to initialize cls_ because its default constructor will be called. But if you need to construct Foo with an argument, you should add the argument to the initializer list as I did earlier instead of assigning it in the body of the constructor. By taking the initializer list route, you avoid an extra step in the construction of cls_ (because if you assign cls_ a value in the constructor body, cls_ is constructed by its default constructor first, then assigned using the assignment operator, versus being constructed once), but you also gain automatic exception handling. If an object is constructed in the initializer list, and that object throws an exception during construction, the runtime environment destroys all other previously constructed objects in the list, and the exception continues to the caller of the constructor. On the other hand, if you assign the argument in the body of the constructor, then you have to handle the exception with a try/catch block.

References are more complicated: initialization of reference variables (and const members) actually *requires* use of the initializer list. According to the standard, a reference must always refer to a single variable, and can never be changed to refer to another variable. At no time can a reference variable not refer to an object. Therefore, for it to be assigned anything meaningful when a class member variable is a reference, it must happen at *initialization*, i.e., in the initializer list.

The following is not allowed in C++:

```
int& x;
```

That is, you cannot declare a reference variable without initializing it. Instead, you must initialize it to refer to some object. For nonmember variables, initialization looks like this:

```
int a;
int& x = a;
```

Well, that's all fine, but this creates a problem for classes. Suppose you want to have a member variable in a class that is a reference, like so:

```
class HasARef {
public:
    int& ref;
};
```

Most compilers will accept this until you try to create an instance of the class, like this:

```
HasARef me;
```

At this point, you'll get an error. Here's the error you get from gcc:

```
error: structure `me' with uninitialized reference members
```

Instead, use the initializer list:

```
class HasARef {
public:
    int &ref;
    HasARef(int &aref) : ref(aref) {}
};
```

Then, when you're ready to create an instance of the class, you provide a variable that the ref variable will refer to, like so:

```
int var;
HasARef me(var);
```

That's how you initialize member variables safely and effectively. In general, use the initializer list when possible and avoid initializing member variables in the body of the constructor unless you have to. Even if you do have to do something to the variable in the body of the constructor, you can at least use the initializer list to set it to a valid initial value, and then update it in the body of the constructor.

See Also

Recipe 9.2

8.2 Using a Function to Create Objects (a.k.a. Factory Pattern)

Problem

Instead of creating a heap object with new, you need a function (member or standalone) to do the creation for you so that the type of the object being created is decided dynamically. This sort of behavior is what the Abstract Factory design pattern achieves.

Solution

You have a couple of choices here. You can:

- Have the function create an instance of the object on the heap, and return a pointer to the object (or update a pointer that was passed in with the new object's address)
- Have the function create and return a temporary object

Example 8-2 shows how to do both of these. The Session class in the example could be any class that you don't want application code to create directly (i.e., with new), but rather you want creation managed by some other class; in this example, the managing class is SessionFactory.

Example 8-2. Functions that create objects

```
#include <iostream>

class Session {};

class SessionFactory {

public:
   Session Create();
   Session* CreatePtr();
   void Create(Session*& p);
   // ...
};

// Return a copy of a stack object
Session SessionFactory::Create() {
   Session s;
   return(s);
}

// Return a pointer to a heap object
Session* SessionFactory::CreatePtr() {
   return(new Session());
}
```

Example 8-2. Functions that create objects (continued)

```
// Update the caller's pointer with the address
// of a new object
void SessionFactory::Create(Session*& p) {
   p = new Session();
}

static SessionFactory f; // The one factory object

int main() {
   Session* p1;
   Session* p2 = new Session();

   *p2 = f.Create();    // Just assign the object returned from Create
   p1 = f.CreatePtr(); // or return a pointer to a heap object
   f.Create(p1);       // or update the pointer with the new address
}
```

Discussion

Example 8-2 shows a few different ways to write a function that returns an object. You may want to do this instead of using new if the object being allocated is coming from a pool, is tied to hardware, or you want destruction of the objects to be managed by something other than the caller. There are many reasons to use this approach (which is why, incidentally, there is a design pattern for it); I have given only a few. Thankfully, implementation of the Factory pattern in C++ is straightforward.

Returning the address of a new heap object or updating a reference to a pointer argument are the most common ways to do this. Their implementation is shown in Example 8-2, and it is trivial, so there is no more to explain here. Less common, however, is returning an entire object from a function, most likely because it brings some caveats.

Returning a temporary object works by creating the object on the stack within the body of the function. When the function returns, the compiler copies the data from the temporary object to another temporary object that is actually returned by the function. Finally, the object in the calling function is assigned the value of the temporary object with its assignment operator. What this means is that two objects are actually created: the object in the factory function, and a temporary object that is returned from the function, and *then* its contents are copied to the target object. This is a lot of extra copying (although the compiler may optimize the temporary object away), so be aware of what's going on especially if you're working with large objects or frequent calls to this factory member function.

Also, this technique of copying a temporary object only works for objects that can behave as *value objects*, meaning that when one is copied the new version is equivalent to the original. For most objects this makes sense, but for others it doesn't. For example, consider creating an object of a class that listens on a network port. When you instantiate the object, it may begin listening on the target port, so you don't want to copy it to a new object because then you will have two objects attempting to listen on the same port. In this case, you would want to return the address of a heap object.

You should also take a look at Recipe 8.12 if you are writing a function or member function to create objects. With function templates, you can write a single function that returns a new object of any type. For example:

```
template<typename T>
T* createObject( ) {
    return(new T( ));
}

MyClass* p1 = createObject( );
MyOtherClass* p2 = createObject( );
// ...
```

This approach is handy if you want a single factory function to be able to create objects of any number of classes (or a group of related classes) in the same way, without having to write a redundant factory function multiple times.

See Also

Recipe 8.12

8.3   Using Constructors and Destructors to Manage Resources (or RAII)

Problem

For a class that represents some resource, you want to use its constructor to acquire it and the destructor to release it. This technique is often referred to as *resource acquisition is initialization* (RAII).

Solution

Allocate or acquire the resource in the constructor, and free or release the resource in the destructor. This reduces the amount of code a user of the class must write to deal with exceptions. See Example 8-3 for a simple illustration of this technique.

Example 8-3. Using constructors and destructors

```
#include <iostream>
#include <string>

using namespace std;
```

Example 8-3. Using constructors and destructors (continued)

```cpp
class Socket {
public:
    Socket(const string& hostname) {}
};

class HttpRequest {
public:
    HttpRequest (const string& hostname) :
        sock_(new Socket(hostname)) {}
    void send(string soapMsg) {sock_ << soapMsg;}
  ~HttpRequest () {delete sock_;}
private:
    Socket* sock_;
};

void sendMyData(string soapMsg, string host) {
    HttpRequest req(host);
    req.send(soapMsg);
    // Nothing to do here, because when req goes out of scope
    // everything is cleaned up.
}

int main() {
    string s = "xml";
    sendMyData(s, "www.oreilly.com");
}
```

Discussion

The guarantees made by constructors and destructors offer a nice way to let the compiler clean up after you. Typically, you initialize an object and allocate any resources it uses in the constructor, and clean them up in the destructor. This is normal. But programmers have a tendency to use the create-open-use-close sequence of events, where the user of the class is required to do explicit "opening" and "closing" of resources. A file class is a good example.

The usual argument for RAII goes something like this. I could easily have designed my HttpRequest class in Example 8-3 to make the user do a little more work. For example:

```cpp
class HttpRequest {
public:
    HttpRequest ();
    void open(const std::string& hostname);
    void send(std::string soapMsg);
    void close();
  ~HttpRequest ();
private:
    Socket* sock_;
};
```

With this approach, a responsible version of sendMyData might look like this:

```
void sendMyData(std::string soapMsg, std::string host) {
    HttpRequest req;

    try {
        req.open();
        req.send(soapMsg);
        req.close();
    }
    catch (std::exception& e) {
        req.close();
        // Do something useful...
    }
}
```

This is more work without any benefit. This sort of design forces the user to write more code and to deal with exceptions by cleaning up your class (assuming you don't call close in your destructor).

The RAII approach has wide applicability, especially when you want a guarantee that something will be undone if an exception is thrown without having to put try/catch code all over the place. Consider a desktop application that wants to display a message on the status bar or title bar while some work is being done:

```
void MyWindow::thisTakesALongTime() {
    StatusBarMessage("Copying files...");
    // ...
}
```

All the StatusBarMessage class has to do is update the appropriate window with status information when it is constructed, and reset it back to the empty string (or

message was there previously) when it is destroyed. Here's the key point: if

n returns or an exception is thrown StatusBarMessage still gets its work

compiler *guarantees* that the destructor will be called for a stack variable

e has exited. Without this approach, the author of thisTakesALongTime

arefully account for every control path so the wrong message doesn't

he window if the operation fails, the user cancels it, etc. Once again, this

ss code and fewer errors for the author of the calling function.

panacea, but if you have not used it before, chances are you can find a

number of places where it is useful. Another good example is locking. If you are using RAII to manage locks on resources such as threads, pooled objects, network connections, etc., you will find that this approach allows for stronger exception-safety and less code. In fact, this is how the Boost multithreading library implements locks to make for clean programming on the part of the user. See Chapter 12 for a discussion of the Boost Threads library.

8.4   Automatically Adding New Class Instances to a Container

Problem

You need to store all instances of a class in a single container without requiring the users of the class to do anything special.

Solution

Include in the class a static member that is a container, such as a list, defined in `<list>`. Add an object's address to the container at construction and remove it upon destruction. Example 8-4 shows how.

Example 8-4. Keeping track of objects

```
#include <iostream>
#include <list>
#include <algorithm>

using namespace std;

class MyClass {
protected:
   int value_;
public:
   static list<MyClass*> instances_;
   MyClass(int val);
  ~MyClass();
   static void showList();
};

list<MyClass*> MyClass::instances_;

MyClass::MyClass(int val) {
   instances_.push_back(this);
   value_ = val;
}

MyClass::~MyClass() {
   list<MyClass*>::iterator p =
       find(instances_.begin(), instances_.end(), this);
   if (p != instances_.end())
      instances_.erase(p);
}

void MyClass::showList() {
   for (list<MyClass*>::iterator p = instances_.begin();
```

Example 8-4. Keeping track of objects (continued)

```
        p != instances_.end( ); ++p)
      cout << (*p)->value_ << endl;
}

int main( ) {
   MyClass a(1);
   MyClass b(10);
   MyClass c(100);
   MyClass::showList( );
}
```

Example 8-4 will create output like this:

```
   1
   10
   100
```

Discussion

The approach in Example 8-4 is straightforward: use a static list to hold pointers to objects. When an object is created, add its address to the list; when it's destroyed, remove it. There are a couple of things to remember.

As with any static data member, you have to declare it in the class header and define it in an implementation file. Example 8-4 is all in one file, so it doesn't apply here, but remember that you should define the static variable in an implementation file, not a header. See Recipe 8.5 for an explanation of why.

You don't have to use a static member. You can, of course, use a global object, but then the design is not self-contained. Furthermore, you have to allocate the global object somewhere else, pass it in to MyClass at construction, and, in general, do a bit more bookkeeping.

Be aware that the shared use of a global container like Example 8-4 will not work if multiple threads are instantiating objects of MyClass. You need to serialize access to the shared object through mutexes; see Chapter 12 for recipes relating to this and other multithreading techniques.

If you want to keep track of all instances of a class, you may also want to use a Factory pattern. Essentially, this approach would mean that clients call a function to get a new object instead of using the new operator. See Recipe 8.2 for more details on how to do this.

See Also

Recipe 8.2

8.5 Ensuring a Single Copy of a Member Variable

Problem

You have a member variable that you want only one instance of, no matter how many instances of the class are created. This kind of member variable is generally called a static member or a *class* variable, as opposed to an *instance* variable, which is one that is instantiated with every object of a class.

Solution

Declare the member variable with the static keyword, then initialize it in a separate source file (not the header file where you declared it) as in Example 8-5.

Example 8-5. Using a static member variable

```
// Static.h
class OneStatic {
public:
    int getCount() {return count;}
    OneStatic();
protected:
    static int count;
};

// Static.cpp
#include "Static.h"

int OneStatic::count = 0;

OneStatic::OneStatic() {
    count++;
}

// StaticMain.cpp
#include <iostream>
#include "static.h"

using namespace std;

int main() {
    OneStatic a;
    OneStatic b;
    OneStatic c;

    cout << a.getCount() << endl;
    cout << b.getCount() << endl;
    cout << c.getCount() << endl;
}
```

Discussion

`static` is C++'s way of allowing only one copy of something. If you declare a member variable `static`, only one of it will ever be constructed, regardless of the number of objects of that class that are instantiated. Similarly, if you declare a variable `static` in a function, it is constructed at most once and retains its value from one function call to another. With member variables, you have to do a little extra work to make sure member variables are allocated properly, though. This is why there are three files in Example 8-5.

First, you have to use the `static` keyword when you declare the variable. This is easy enough: add this keyword in the class header in the header file *Static.h*:

```
protected:
    static int count;
```

Once you have done that, you have to define the variable in a source file somewhere. This is what allocates storage for it. Do this by fully qualifying the name of the variable and assigning it a value, like this:

```
int OneStatic::count = 0;
```

In Example 8-5, I put this definition in the file *Static.cpp*. This is what you have to do; you should not put the definition in the header file. If you do, storage will be allocated in each implementation file that includes the header file, and either you will get a linker error or, worse, there will be several instances of this member variable in memory. This is not what you want if you need a `static` member variable.

In the main file, *StaticMain.cpp*, you can see what happens. Several instances of the class `OneStatic` are created, and the default constructor of `OneStatic` increments the static member variable by one each time. As a result, the output from `main` in *StaticMain.cpp* is:

```
3
3
3
```

Each call to `getCount` returns the same integer value, even though each is invoked on a different instance of the class.

8.6   Determining an Object's Type at Runtime

Problem

At runtime, you need to interrogate dynamically the type of particular class.

Solution

Use runtime type identification (commonly referred to as RTTI) to query the address of the object for the type of object it points to. Example 8-6 shows how.

Example 8-6. Using runtime type identification

```
#include <iostream>
#include <typeinfo>

using namespace std;

class Base {};
class Derived : public Base {};

int main( ) {

    Base b, bb;
    Derived d;

    // Use typeid to test type equality
    if (typeid(b) == typeid(d)) { // No
        cout << "b and d are of the same type.\n";
    }
    if (typeid(b) == typeid(bb)) { // Yes
        cout << "b and bb are of the same type.\n";
    }
    if (typeid(d) == typeid(Derived)) { // Yes
        cout << "d is of type Derived.\n";
    }
}
```

Discussion

Example 8-6 shows you how to use the operator typeid to determine and compare the type of an object. typeid takes an expression or a type and returns a reference to an object of type_info or a subclass of it (which is implementation defined). You can use what is returned to test for equality or retrieve a string representation of the type's name. For example, you can compare the types of two objects like this:

```
    if (typeid(b) == typeid(d)) {
```

This will return true if the type_info objects returned by both of these are equal. This is because typeid returns a reference to a static object, so if you call it on two objects that are the same type, you will get two references to the same thing, which is why the equality test returns true.

You can also use typeid with the type itself, as in:

```
    if (typeid(d) == typeid(Derived)) {
```

This allows you to explicitly test for a particular type.

Probably the most common use of typeid is for debugging. To write out the name of the type, use type_info::name, like this:

```
    std::cout << typeid(d).name( ) << std::endl;
```

When you are passing objects around of varying types, this can be a useful debugging aid. The null-terminated string returned by name is implementation defined, but you can expect (but not depend on) the name of the type most of the time. This works for native types, too.

Do not abuse this technique by basing program logic on type information unless you absolutely have to. In general, it is considered bad design to have logic that does something along the lines of:

If obj has a type of X, do something else, if obj has a type of Y, do something else.

This approach is a bad design because the client code now contains superfluous dependencies on the type of the object being used. It also results in a lot of messy if/then code that is duplicated everywhere you want particular behavior for an object of type X or Y. Object-oriented programming and polymorphic behavior exist in large part so you don't have to write this kind of logic. If you want type-specific, dynamic behavior for some family of related classes, then they should all subclass the same base class and use virtual functions to dynamically invoke potentially different behavior based on the type.

RTTI adds overhead, so compilers don't usually enable it by default. Chances are your compiler has a command-line parameter to turn on RTTI. Also, this isn't the only way you can query type information, see Recipe 8.7 for another technique.

See Also

Recipe 8.7

8.7   Determining if One Object's Class Is a Subclass of Another

Problem

You have two objects, and you need to know if their respective classes have a base class/derived class relationship or if they are unrelated.

Solution

Use the dynamic_cast operator to attempt to downcast from one type to another. The result tells you about the class's relationships. Example 8-7 presents some code for doing this.

Example 8-7. Determining class relationships

```
#include <iostream>
#include <typeinfo>
```

Example 8-7. Determining class relationships (continued)

```
using namespace std;

class Base {
public:
   virtual ~Base( ) {} // Make this a polymorphic class
};
class Derived : public Base {
public:
   virtual ~Derived( ) {}
};

int main( ) {

   Derived d;

   // Query the type relationship
   if (dynamic_cast<Base*>(&d)) {
      cout << "Derived is a subclass of Base" << endl;
   }
   else {
      cout << "Derived is NOT a subclass of Base" << endl;
   }
}
```

Discussion

Use the `dynamic_cast` operator to query the relationship between two types. `dynamic_cast` takes a pointer or reference to a given type and tries to convert it to a pointer or reference of a derived type, i.e., casting down a class hierarchy. If you have a `Base*` that points to a `Derived` object, `dynamic_cast<Base*>(&d)` returns a pointer of type `Derived` *only if* d is an object of a type that's derived from `Base`. If this is not possible (because `Derived` is not a subclass, directly or indirectly, of `Base`), the cast fails and `NULL` is returned if you passed `dynamic_cast` a pointer to a derived object. If it is a reference, then the standard exception `bad_cast` is thrown. Also, the base class must be publicly inherited and it must be unambiguous. The result tells you if one class is a descendant of another. Here's what I did in Example 8-7:

```
   if (dynamic_cast<Base*>(&d)) {
```

This returns a non-NULL pointer because d is an object of a class that is a descendant of `Base`. Use this on any pair of classes to determine their relationship. The only requirement is that the object argument is a *polymorphic* type, which means that it has at least one virtual function. If it does not, it won't compile. This doesn't usually cause much of a headache though, because a class hierarchy without virtual functions is uncommon.

If the syntax is too messy for you, you can use a macro to hide some of the details:

```
   #define IS_DERIVED_FROM(baseClass, x) (dynamic_cast<baseClass*>(&(x)))
   //...
   if (IS_DERIVED_FROM(Base, l)) { // ...
```

This type information is not free, though, because dynamic_cast must traverse the class hierarchy at runtime to determine if one class is a descendant of another, so be smart about where you use it. Additionally, compilers don't include this information by default since there is overhead required for RTTI, and not everyone uses this feature, so you may have to enable it with a compiler switch.

See Also

Recipe 8.6

8.8 Giving Each Instance of a Class a Unique Identifier

Problem

You want each object of a class to have a unique identifier.

Solution

Use a static member variable to keep track of the next available identifier to use. In the constructor, assign the next available value to the current object and increment the static member. See Example 8-8 to get an idea of how this works.

Example 8-8. Assigning unique identifiers

```
#include <iostream>

class UniqueID {
protected:
   static int nextID;
public:
   int id;
   UniqueID( );
   UniqueID(const UniqueID& orig);
   UniqueID& operator=(const UniqueID& orig);
};

int UniqueID::nextID = 0;

UniqueID::UniqueID( ) {
   id = ++nextID;
}

UniqueID::UniqueID(const UniqueID& orig) {
   id = orig.id;
}

UniqueID& UniqueID::operator=(const UniqueID& orig) {
   id = orig.id;
```

Example 8-8. Assigning unique identifiers (continued)
```
    return(*this);
}

int main( ) {
    UniqueID a;
    std::cout << a.id << std::endl;
    UniqueID b;
    std::cout << b.id << std::endl;
    UniqueID c;
    std::cout << c.id << std::endl;
}
```

Discussion

Use a `static` variable to keep track of the next identifier to use. In Example 8-8, I used a `static int`, but you can use anything as the unique identifier, so long as you have a function that can generate the unique values.

In this case, the identifiers are not reused until you reach the maximum size of an int. Once you delete an object, that object's unique value is gone until the program restarts or the identifier value maxes out and flips over. This uniqueness throughout the program can have some interesting advantages. For example, if you're working with a memory management library that shuffles memory around and invalidates pointers, you can be assured that the unique value will remain the same per object. If you use the unique values in conjunction with Recipe 8.4, but use a `map` instead of a `list`, you can easily locate your objects given the unique identifier. To do this, you would simply `map` unique IDs to object instances, like so:

```
    static map<int, MyClass*> instmap;
```

This way, any code that keeps track of an object's identifier can find it later without having to maintain a reference to it.

But that's not the whole story. Consider the case where you need to add one of these objects to a standard container (`vector`, `list`, `set`, etc.). The standard containers store copies of the objects you add to them, not references or pointers to the objects themselves (unless, of course, it is a container of pointers). Thus, the standard containers expect objects they contain to behave as *value* objects, which means objects that, when assigned with the assignment operator, or copied with a copy constructor, create new versions that are equal to the old versions.

This means that you have to make a decision on how you want your unique objects to behave. When you create an object with a unique identifier and add it to a container you then have two objects with the same identifier unless you've done something different in your assignment operator. You need to deal with the unique value in your assignment operator and copy constructor in a way that makes sense. Does it make sense for the object in the container to be equal to the original object? If so, the standard copy constructor and assignment operators will get the job done, but you should be explicit so users of your class know you did it that way on purpose and didn't just forget how containers work and get lucky. For example, to use the same identifier values your copy constructor and assignment operator would look like this:

```
UniqueID::UniqueID(const UniqueID& orig) {
    id = orig.id;
}

UniqueID& UniqueID::operator=(const UniqueID& orig) {
    id = orig.id;
    return(*this);
}
```

But maybe it makes more sense to create another unique value for the object in the container in the context of your application. In that case, just use the static variable again as you did in the ordinary constructor, like this:

```
UniqueID::UniqueID(const UniqueID& orig) {
    id = ++nextID;
}

UniqueID& UniqueID::operator=(const UniqueID& orig) {
    id = ++nextID;
    return(*this);
}
```

You may still not be in the clear though. If `UniqueID` will be used by multiple threads, you are going to run into trouble because access to the static variable is not synchronized. See Chapter 12 for more information on making resources usable by multiple threads.

See Also

Recipe 8.3

8.9   Creating a Singleton Class

Problem

You have a class that must only ever be instantiated once, and you need to provide a way for clients to access that class in such a way that the same, single object is returned each time. This is commonly referred to as a *singleton* pattern, or a singleton class.

Solution

Create a static member that is a pointer to the current class, restrict the use of constructors to create the class by making them private, and provide a public static member function that clients can use to access the single, static instance. Example 8-9 demonstrates how to do this.

Example 8-9. Creating a singleton class

```cpp
#include <iostream>

using namespace std;

class Singleton {
public:
    // This is how clients can access the single instance
    static Singleton* getInstance();

    void setValue(int val) {value_ = val;}
    int  getValue()             {return(value_);}

protected:
    int value_;

private:
    static Singleton* inst_;   // The one, single instance
    Singleton() : value_(0) {} // private constructor
    Singleton(const Singleton&);
    Singleton& operator=(const Singleton&);
};

// Define the static Singleton pointer
Singleton* Singleton::inst_ = NULL;

Singleton* Singleton::getInstance() {
    if (inst_ == NULL) {
        inst_ = new Singleton();
    }
    return(inst_);
}

int main() {

    Singleton* p1 = Singleton::getInstance();

    p1->setValue(10);

    Singleton* p2 = Singleton::getInstance();

    cout << "Value = " << p2->getValue() << '\n';
}
```

Discussion

There are many situations where you want at most one instance of a class—this is why Singleton is a design pattern. With a few simple steps, it's easy to implement a singleton class in C++.

When you decide that you only want one instance of something, the static keyword should come to mind. As I described in Recipe 8.5, a static member variable is one such that there is at most one instance of it in memory. Use a `static` member variable to keep track of the one object of your singleton class, as I did in Example 8-9:

```
private:
    static Singleton* inst_;
```

Keep it `private` to keep client code from knowing about it. Be sure to initialize it to `NULL` with a static variable definition in an implementation file:

```
Singleton* Singleton::inst_ = NULL;
```

To keep clients from instantiating this class, make the constructors private, especially the default constructor.

```
private:
    Singleton( ) {}
```

This way, if anyone tries to create a new singleton class on the heap or the stack, they'll get a friendly compiler error.

Now that you've created a static variable to keep track of the one `Singleton` object, and you've prohibited creation of `Singleton` objects by restricting their constructors, all that's left is to provide a way for clients to access the one instance of the `Singleton` object. Do this with a `static` member function:

```
Singleton* Singleton::getInstance( ) {
    if (inst_ == NULL) {
        inst_ = new Singleton( );
    }
    return(inst_);
}
```

You can see how this works. If the `static Singleton` pointer is `NULL`, create the object. If it has already been created, just return its address. Clients can access the one instance of `Singleton` by calling this `static` member:

```
Singleton* p1 = Singleton::getInstance( );
```

And if you don't want clients to deal with pointers, you can return a reference, too:

```
Singleton& Singleton::getInstance( ) {
    if (inst_ == NULL) {
        inst_ = new Singleton( );
    }
    return(*inst_);
}
```

The point here is that in both cases you have prevented clients from creating instances of a `Singleton` object and provided a single interface through which they can gain access.

See Also

Recipe 8.3

8.10   Creating an Interface with an Abstract Base Class

Problem

You need to define an interface that subclasses will implement, but the concept that the interface defines is just an abstraction, and is not something that should be instantiated itself.

Solution

Create an abstract class that defines the interface by declaring at least one of its functions as pure `virtual`. Subclass this abstract class by clients who will use different implementations to fulfill the same interface guarantees. Example 8-10 shows how you might define an abstract class for reading a configuration file.

Example 8-10. Using an abstract base class

```
#include <iostream>
#include <string>
#include <fstream>

using namespace std;

class AbstractConfigFile {

public:
   virtual ~AbstractConfigFile( ) {}

   virtual void getKey(const string& header,
                       const string& key,
                             string& val) const = 0;
   virtual void exists(const string& header,
                       const string& key,
                             string& val) const = 0;
};

class TXTConfigFile : public AbstractConfigFile {

public:
           TXTConfigFile( ) : in_(NULL) {}
           TXTConfigFile(istream& in) : in_(&in) {}
   virtual ~TXTConfigFile( ) {}

   virtual void getKey(const string& header,
                       const string& key,
                             string& val) const {}
   virtual void exists(const string& header,
                       const string& key,
                             string& val) const {}
```

Example 8-10. Using an abstract base class (continued)

```
protected:
    istream* in_;
};

class MyAppClass {
public:
    MyAppClass() : config_(NULL) {}
    ~MyAppClass() {}
    void setConfigObj(const AbstractConfigFile* p) {config_ = p;}
    void myMethod();

private:
    const AbstractConfigFile* config_;
};

void MyAppClass::myMethod() {

    string val;
    config_->getKey("Foo", "Bar", val);
    // ...
}

int main() {

    ifstream in("foo.txt");
    TXTConfigFile cfg(in);

    MyAppClass m;

    m.setConfigObj(&cfg);

    m.myMethod();
}
```

Discussion

An abstract base class (often referred to as an ABC) is a class that can't be instantiated and, therefore, serves only as an interface. A class is abstract if it declares at least one pure virtual function or inherits one without implementing it. Thus, if a subclass of an ABC needs to be instantiated, it has to implement each of the virtual functions, which means that it supports the interface declared by the ABC.

A subclass that inherits an ABC (and implements all of its pure virtuals) upholds the contract defined by the interface. Consider the classes MyAppClass and TXTConfigFile in Example 8-10. MyAppClass has a pointer member that points to an object of type AbstractConfigFile:

```
const AbstractConfigFile* config_;
```

(I made it const because `MyAppClass` should not be changing the config file, only reading from it.) Users can set the config file for `MyAppClass` with a setter member function, `setConfigObj`.

When it is time to use the config file for `MyAppClass`, as `MyAppClass::myMethod` does, it can call any of the functions declared on `AbstractConfigFile` without regard for the actual kind of config file that was used. It could be a `TXTConfigFile`, `XMLConfigFile`, or anything else that inherits from `AbstractConfigFile`.

This polymorphic behavior is the benefit of inheritance in general: if your code refers to a base class object, invoking virtual functions on it will dynamically use the correct versions of subclasses of that class, so long as the actual object you're referring to is an object of that subclass. But this is the case whether the base class is an ABC or not, so what's the difference?

There are two differences. A pure interface class (an ABC that provides no implementation) serves only as a contract that subclasses must obey if they want to be instantiated. Often, this means that the is-a test for a subclass of a pure interface class may fail (meaning you can't say that an object of the subclass is an object of the base class), but that the behaves-like-a test succeeds. This permits you to have some separation of what something is versus what it can do. Think of Superman. He is a person, but he is also a superhero. Superheroes can fly like a bird, but it is not correct to say that a superhero is a bird. You might design a class hierarchy for Superman like I did in Example 8-11.

Example 8-11. Using a pure interface

```
class Person {
public:
    virtual void eat()   = 0;
    virtual void sleep() = 0;
    virtual void walk()  = 0;
    virtual void jump()  = 0;
};

class IAirborne {
public:
    virtual void fly()  = 0;
    virtual void up()   = 0;
    virtual void down() = 0;
};

class Superhero : public Person,      // A superhero *is* a person
                  public IAirborne {  // and flies
public:
    virtual void eat();
    virtual void sleep();
    virtual void walk();
    virtual void jump();
    virtual void fly();
```

Example 8-11. Using a pure interface (continued)

```
    virtual void up( );
    virtual void down( );
    virtual ~Superhero( );
};

void Superhero::fly( ) {
    // ...
}

// Implement all of the pure virtuals in Superhero's superclasses...

int main( ) {

    Superhero superman;
    superman.walk( ); // Superman can walk like a person
    superman.fly( );  // or fly like a bird
}
```

Lots of different kinds of things fly, though, so you don't want an interface called, for example, IBird. IAirborne indicates that anything that supports this interface can fly. All it does is allow client code to rest assured that if it is working with an object derived from IAirborne, the client code can call fly, up, and down.

The second difference is that an ABC can define an abstract entity that makes no sense as an object because it is inherently general. In this case, the is-a test holds for the inheritance, but the ABC is abstract because, by itself, it has no implementation that can be instantiated as an object. Consider the AbstractConfigFile class in Example 8-10: Does it make any sense to instantiate an AbstractConfigFile? No, it only makes sense to instantiate different *kinds* of config files that have concrete representation.

Here is a quick list of rules regarding abstract classes and pure virtual functions. A class is abstract if:

- It declares at least one pure virtual function
- It inherits, but does not implement, at least one pure virtual function

An abstract class cannot be instantiated. However, with an abstract class you can:

- Have data members
- Have nonvirtual member functions
- Provide implementations for pure virtual functions
- Do most of the things you can in an ordinary class

In other words, you can do just about everything you can do with an ordinary class except instantiate it.

Using ABCs in C++ requires discretion when it comes to implementation. Whether you use an ABC as a pure interface or not is up to you. For example, assume for a moment that in the superhero example I decided that the Person class should be abstract, but since every kind of person has a first and last name, I want to add those members to the class and the associated getter and setter member functions so that authors of subclasses don't have to.

```
class Person {
public:
   virtual void    eat()   = 0;
   virtual void    sleep() = 0;
   virtual void    walk()  = 0;
   virtual void    jump()  = 0;
   virtual void    setFirstName(const string& s) {firstName_ = s;}
   virtual void    setLastName(const string& s) {lastName_ = s;}
   virtual string getFirstName() {return(firstName_);}
   virtual string getLastName() {return(lastName_);}
protected:
   string firstName_;
   string lastName_;
};
```

Now, if the Superhero subclass wants to override one of these functions, it can. All it has to do is use the base class name to qualify which version it is invoking. For example:

```
string Superhero::getLastName() {
   return(Person::getLastName() + " (Superhero)");
}
```

Incidentally, you can still make these functions pure and provide a default implementation. You just have to use the = 0 syntax following the declaration and put the actual definition somewhere else, like this:

```
class Person {
// ...
virtual void    setFirstName(const string& s) = 0;
// ...
Person::setFirstName(const string& s) {
   firstName_ = s;
}
```

By doing this, you force subclasses to override it, but they can still call the default version if they want to by using the fully qualified class name.

Finally, if you provide a virtual destructor in your base class (pure or not), you have to provide a body for it. This is because the subclass destructor will call the base class destructor automatically.

8.11 Writing a Class Template

Problem

You have a class whose members need to be different types in different situations, and using conventional polymorphic behavior is cumbersome or redundant. In other words, as the class designer, you want a class user to be able to choose the types of various parts of your class when he instantiates it, rather than setting them all in the original definition of the class.

Solution

Use a class template to parameterize types that can be used to declare class members (and much more). That is, write your class with placeholders for types; thus, leaving it to the user of the class template to choose which types to use. See Example 8-12 for an example of a tree node that can point to any type.

Example 8-12. Writing a class template

```cpp
#include <iostream>
#include <string>

using namespace std;

template<typename T>
class TreeNode {
public:
   TreeNode(const T& val) : val_(val), left_(NULL), right_(NULL) {}
  ~TreeNode() {
      delete left_;
      delete right_;
   }

   const T& getVal() const {return(val_);}
   void setVal(const T& val) {val_ = val;}
   void addChild(TreeNode<T>* p) {
      const T& other = p->getVal();
      if (other > val_)
         if (right_)
            right_->addChild(p);
         else
            right_ = p;
      else
         if (left_)
            left_->addChild(p);
         else
            left_ = p;
   }
   const TreeNode<T>* getLeft() {return(left_);}
   const TreeNode<T>* getRight() {return(right_);}

private:
   T val_;
   TreeNode<T>* left_;
   TreeNode<T>* right_;
};

int main() {
```

Example 8-12. Writing a class template (continued)

```
    TreeNode<string> node1("frank");
    TreeNode<string> node2("larry");
    TreeNode<string> node3("bill");

    node1.addChild(&node2);
    node1.addChild(&node3);
}
```

Discussion

Class templates provide a way for a class designer to parameterize types, so that they can be supplied by a user of the class at the point the class is instantiated. Templates might be a bit confusing though, so let me go through the example before coming back to how it works.

Consider the declaration of the TreeNode class template in Example 8-12:

```
    template<typename T>
    class TreeNode { //...
```

The template<typename T> part is what makes this a class template and not an ordinary class. What this line says is that T is the name of a type that will be given when the class is used, but not right now where it is declared. The parameter T can then be used throughout the declaration and definition of TreeNode as if it were any other type, native or user defined. For example, I have a private member named val_ that I want to be of type T, so I declare it like this:

```
    T val_;
```

This simply declares a class member named val_ of some type that will be determined later in the same way I would declare an int, float, MyClass, or string named val_. In this respect, you can think of it as something like a macro (i.e., using #define), although the similarity with macros is little more than that.

Your type parameter can be used in any way you would use an ordinary parameter: return values, pointers, member function parameters, and so on. Consider my getter and setter methods for val_:

```
    const T& getVal() const {return(val_);}
    void setVal(const T& val) {val_ = val;}
```

getVal returns a const reference to val_, which is of type T, and setVal takes a reference to a T and sets val_ equal to it. Things get a little messier when it comes to the getLeft and getRight member functions, so I'll come back to those in a minute. Bear with me.

Now that TreeNode has been declared with a type placeholder, some client code somewhere has to use it. Here's how.

TreeNode is a simple implementation of a binary tree. To create a tree that stores string values, create your nodes like this:

```
TreeNode<string> node1("frank");
TreeNode<string> node2("larry");
TreeNode<string> node3("bill");
```

The type between the angle brackets is what gets used for T when this class template is *instantiated*. Template instantiation is the process the compiler goes through when it builds a version of TreeNode where T is string. A binary, physical representation of TreeNode<string> is created when it is instantiated (and only when it is instantiated). What you get is a memory layout that is equivalent to if you had just written TreeNode without the template keyword and type parameter, and used a string everywhere you used a T.

Instantiation of a template for a given type parameter is analogous to instantiation of an object of a class. The key difference is that template instantiation occurs at *compile* time, while object instantiation occurs at runtime. This means that if, instead of a string, you wanted your binary tree to store ints, you would declare nodes like this:

```
TreeNode<int> intNode1(7);
TreeNode<int> intNode2(11);
TreeNode<int> intNode3(13);
```

As with the string version, a binary entity is created for the TreeNode class template using int as the internal type.

A minute ago, I said I would revisit the getLeft and getRight member functions. Now that you are familiar with template instantiations (if you weren't already), the declaration and definition of getLeft and getRight may make more sense:

```
const TreeNode<T>* getLeft() {return(left_);}
const TreeNode<T>* getRight() {return(right_);}
```

What this says is that each of these member functions returns a pointer to an instantiation of TreeNode for T. Therefore, when TreeNode is instantiated for, say, a string, getLeft and getRight are instantiated like this:

```
const TreeNode<string>* getLeft() {return(left_);}
const TreeNode<string>* getRight() {return(right_);}
```

You aren't limited to one template parameter though. You can use a bunch of them, if you like. Imagine that you want to keep track of the number of children below a given node, but users of your class may be pressed for space and not want to use an int if they can get away with a short. Similarly, they may want to supply something other than a simple, built-in type to tally the node usage, like their own number class. In any case, you can allow them to do so with another template parameter:

```
template<typename T, typename N = short>
class TreeNode {
```

```
// ...
   N getNumChildren( );

private:
   TreeNode( ) {}
   T val_;
   N numChildren_;
// ...
```

This way, the person using your class can supply an int, short, or anything else he wants to keep track of subtree size on each node.

You can also supply default arguments for template parameters, as I just did in the example, with the same syntax you would use to declare default function parameters:

```
template<typename T, typename N = short>
```

As with default function arguments, you can only supply them for a given parameter if it is either the last parameter or each parameter to the right of it has a default argument.

In Example 8-12, the definition for the template is given in the same place as the declaration. Usually, I do this to conserve space in example code, but, in this case, there is another reason. Templates (classes or functions—see Recipe 8.12) are only compiled into binary form when they are instantiated. Thus, you cannot have the template declaration in a header file and its implementation in a source file (i.e., *.cpp*). The reason is that there is nothing to compile! There are exceptions to this, but, generally speaking, if you are writing a class template, you should put its implementation in the header file or in an inline file that is included by the header.

If you do this, you will need to use a syntax that is a little unfamiliar. Declare the member functions and the rest of the class template as you would an ordinary class, but when you are defining the member functions, you have to include some extra tokens to tell the compiler that this is for a class template. For example, you would define getVal like this (compare this to Example 8-12):

```
template<typename T>
const T& TreeNode<T>::getVal( ) const {
   return(val_);
}
```

The body of the function looks the same.

Be careful with templates though, because if you write one that is used everywhere, you can get *code bloat*, which is what happens when the same template with the same parameters (e.g., TreeNode<int, short>) is compiled into separate object files. Essentially, the same binary representation of an instantiated template is in multiple files, and this can make your library or executable much larger than it needs to be.

One way to avoid this is to use explicit instantiation, which is a way to tell the compiler that it needs to instantiate a version of the class template for a particular set of template arguments. If you do this in a place that is a common location that will be linked to by multiple clients, you can avoid code bloat. For example, if I know that throughout my application I will be using TreeNode<string>, I would put a line like this in a common source file:

```
// common.cpp
template class TreeNode<string>;
```

Build a shared library with that file and then code that uses TreeNode<string> can use the library dynamically without having to contain its own compiled version. Other code can include the header for the class template, then link to this library and therefore avoid needing its own copy. This requires some experimentation though, because not all compilers have the same problems with code bloat to the same degree, but this is the general approach you can use to minimize it.

C++ templates (both class and function) are a vast subject, and there is a long list of mind-bending techniques for powerful, efficient designs that use templates. A great example of applications of class templates is the standard library containers, e.g., vector, list, set, etc., which is the subject of Chapter 15. Most of the interesting developments that are happening in the C++ literature have to do with templates. If you are interested in the subject, you should check out the newsgroups *comp.lang.std.c++* and *comp.lang.c++*. There are always interesting questions and answers there.

See Also

Recipe 8.12

8.12   Writing a Member Function Template

Problem

You have a single member function that needs to take a parameter that can be of any type, and you can't or don't want to be constrained to a particular type or category of types (by using a base class pointer parameter).

Solution

Use a member function template and declare a template parameter for the type of object the function parameter is supposed to have. See Example 8-13 for a short example.

Example 8-13. Using a member function template

```
class ObjectManager {
public:
   template<typename T>
   T* gimmeAnObject();
```

Example 8-13. Using a member function template (continued)

```
      template<typename T>
      void gimmeAnObject(T*& p);
};

template<typename T>
T* ObjectManager::gimmeAnObject() {
   return(new T);
}

template<typename T>
void ObjectManager::gimmeAnObject(T*& p) {
   p = new T;
}

class X { /* ... */ };
class Y { /* ... */ };

int main() {
   ObjectManager om;

   X* p1 = om.gimmeAnObject<X>(); // You have to specify the template
   Y* p2 = om.gimmeAnObject<Y>(); // parameter

   om.gimmeAnObject(p1);  // Not here, though, since the compiler can
   om.gimmeAnObject(p2);  // deduce T from the arguments
}
```

Discussion

When talking about function or class templates, the words parameter and argument have some ambiguity. There are two kinds of each: template and function. Template parameters are the parameters in the angle brackets, e.g., T in Example 8-13, and function parameters are parameters in the conventional sense.

Consider the ObjectManager class in Example 8-13. It is a simplistic version of the Factory pattern discussed in Recipe 8.2, so I have defined the member function gimmeAnObject as something that creates new objects that client code would use instead of calling new directly. I can do this by either returning a pointer to a new object or by modifying a pointer passed in by the client code. Let's take a look at each approach.

Declaration of a template member function requires that you provide the template keyword and the template parameters.

```
      template<typename T>
      T* gimmeAnObject();

      template<typename T>
      void gimmeAnObject(T*& p);
```

Both of these member functions happen to use T as the template parameter, but they don't need to; they each represent the template parameter for that member function only, so the names are unrelated. You have to do the same thing for your template member function definition, i.e., use the template keyword and list all the template parameters. Here's what my definitions look like:

```
template<typename T>
T* ObjectManager::gimmeAnObject() {
    return(new T);
}

template<typename T>
void ObjectManager::gimmeAnObject(T*& p) {
    p = new T;
}
```

There are a couple of ways to call template member functions. First, you can invoke them with explicit use of the template parameter, like this:

```
X* p1 = om.gimmeAnObject<X>();
```

X is just some class name. Or, you can let the compiler deduce the arguments for the template parameters by passing in arguments of the type(s) of the template parameters. For example, you can invoke the second form of gimmeAnObject without passing in anything in angle brackets:

```
om.gimmeAnObject(p1);
```

This is because the compiler can deduce T by looking at p1 and recognizing that it's an X*. Template deduction only works for function templates (member or not) and only works when the template parameters are deduced from the *function* arguments.

Member function templates aren't the most popular feature in C++, but they come in handy from time to time, so it's good to know how to write one. I often see the need crop up when I want a member function to work for types that are not related by inheritance. For example, if I have a member function foo that I want to take a single argument that is always going to be a class that inherits from some base class, I don't need a template: I can just make the parameter type a base class pointer or reference. Then, any objects of subclasses of the parameter class will work just fine—such is the way of C++.

But you may want a function that operates on parameters that don't all inherit from the same base class(es). In this case, you can either write the same member function several times—once for each type—or make it a template member function. Using templates also permits specialization, which is a way of providing implementations of templates for particular template arguments. But that's beyond the scope of a single recipe, so I won't discuss it further here, but it's a powerful technique, so if template programming appeals to you, I encourage you check it out.

See Also

Recipe 8.11

8.13 Overloading the Increment and Decrement Operators

Problem

You have a class where the familiar increment and decrement operators make sense, and you want to overload operator++ and operator-- to make incrementing and decrementing objects of your class easy and intuitive to users.

Solution

Overload the prefix and postfix forms of ++ and -- to do what you want. Example 8-14 shows the conventional technique for overloading the increment and decrement operators.

Example 8-14. Overloading increment and decrement

```
#include <iostream>

using namespace std;

class Score {
public:
    Score( ) : score_(0) {}
    Score(int i) : score_(i) {}

    Score& operator++( ) { // prefix
        ++score_;
        return(*this);
    }
    const Score operator++(int) { // postfix
        Score tmp(*this);
        ++(*this); // Take advantage of the prefix operator
        return(tmp);
    }
    Score& operator--( ) {
        --score_;
        return(*this);
    }
    const Score operator--(int x) {
        Score tmp(*this);
        --(*this);
        return(tmp);
```

Example 8-14. Overloading increment and decrement (continued)

```
    }
    int getScore() const {return(score_);}

private:
    int score_;
};

int main() {
    Score player1(50);

    player1++;
    ++player1; // score_ = 52
    cout << "Score = " << player1.getScore() << '\n';
    (--player1)--; // score_ = 50
    cout << "Score = " << player1.getScore() << '\n';
}
```

Discussion

The increment and decrement operators often make sense for classes that represent some sort of integer value. They are easy to use, as long as you understand the difference between prefix and postfix and you follow the conventions for return values.

Think about incrementing an integer. For some integer i, there are two ways to do it with the ++ operator:

```
i++; // postfix
++i; // prefix
```

Both increment i: the first version creates a temporary copy of i increments i, then returns the temporary value, the second increments i then returns it. C++ allows operator overloading, which means you can make your favorite user-defined type (a class or an enum) behave like an int in this regard.

Overload operator++ and operator-- to get what you want. Example 8-14 illustrates how to overload both the prefix and postfix versions:

```
Score& operator++() { // prefix
    ++score_;
    return(*this);
}
const Score operator++(int) { // postfix
    Score tmp(*this);
    ++(*this);
    return(tmp);
}
```

Prefix appears as you would expect, but for the compiler to distinguish between the two, an int parameter is included as part of the postfix operator declaration. It has no semantic use; at runtime, it is always passed as zero so you can ignore it.

Once you do this, you can use the Score class as you would an int:

```
Score player1(50);

player1++;
++player1; // score_ = 52
```

You probably noticed that the signatures for the prefix version of operator++ return a reference to the current class. You should do this (instead of, say, returning void) so that the object that is being incremented or decremented can be used in other expressions. Consider this line from the example:

```
(--player1)--;
```

Strange, yes, but it illustrates a point. If prefix operator-- didn't return anything meaningful, then this expression would not compile. Another example would be a function call:

```
foo(--player1);
```

The function foo expects an argument of type Score, and that's exactly what you have to return from prefix operator-- for this to compile.

Operator overloading is a powerful feature that lets you use the same operators on user-defined types that you would on built-in types. Proponents of other languages that do not allow operator overloading bemoan the potential for confusion and complexity, and admittedly, lots of operators can be overloaded for any kind of custom behavior. But when it comes to simple increment and decrement, it's nice to be able to customize your classes' behavior to your liking.

See Also

Recipe 8.14

8.14 Overloading Arithmetic and Assignment Operators for Intuitive Class Behavior

Problem

You have a class for which some of C++'s unary or binary operators make sense, and you want users of your class to be able to use them when working with objects of your class. For example, if you have a class named Balance that contains, essentially, a floating-point value (i.e., an account balance), it would be convenient if you could use Balance objects with some standard C++ operators, like this:

```
Balance checking(50.0), savings(100.0);

checking += 12.0;
Balance total = checking + savings;
```

Solution

Overload the operators you want to use as member functions and standalone functions to allow arguments of various types for which the given operator makes sense, as in Example 8-15.

Example 8-15. Overloading unary and binary operators

```
#include <iostream>

using namespace std;

class Balance {
    // These have to see private data
    friend const Balance operator+(const Balance& lhs, const Balance& rhs);
    friend const Balance operator+(double lhs, const Balance& rhs);
    friend const Balance operator+(const Balance& lhs, double rhs);

public:
    Balance() : val_(0.0) {}
    Balance(double val) : val_(val) {}
    ~Balance() {}

    // Unary operators
    Balance& operator+=(const Balance& other) {
        val_ += other.val_;
        return(*this);
    }
    Balance& operator+=(double other) {
        val_ += other;
        return(*this);
    }

    double getVal() const {return(val_);}

private:
    double val_;
};

// Binary operators
const Balance operator+(const Balance& lhs, const Balance& rhs) {
    Balance tmp(lhs.val_ + rhs.val_);
    return(tmp);
}

const Balance operator+(double lhs, const Balance& rhs) {
    Balance tmp(lhs + rhs.val_);
    return(tmp);
}

const Balance operator+(const Balance& lhs, double rhs) {
    Balance tmp(lhs.val_ + rhs);
```

Example 8-15. Overloading unary and binary operators (continued)

```
    return(tmp);
}

int main( ) {

    Balance checking(500.00), savings(23.91);

    checking += 50;
    Balance total = checking + savings;

    cout << "Checking balance: " << checking.getVal() << '\n';
    cout << "Total balance: "    << total.getVal() << '\n';
}
```

Discussion

The most common case for operator overloading is assignment and arithmetic. There are all sorts of classes for which arithmetic and assignment operators (addition, multiplication, modulo, left/right bit shift) make sense, whether you are using them for math or something else. Example 8-15 shows the fundamental techniques for overloading these operators.

Let's start with what is probably the most common operator to be overloaded, the assignment operator. The assignment operator is what's used when you assign one object to another, as in the following statement:

```
    Balance x(0), y(32);
    x = y;
```

The second line is a shorthand way of calling Balance::operator=(y). The assignment operator is different than most other operators because a default version is created for you by the compiler if you don't supply one. The default version simply copies each member from the target object to the current object, which, of course, is not always what you want, so you can override it to provide your own behavior, or overload it to allow assignment of types other than the current type.

For the Balance class in Example 8-15, you might define the assignment operator like this:

```
    Balance& operator=(const Balance& other) {
        val_ = other.val_;
        return(*this);
    }
```

The first thing that may jump out at you, if you're not familiar with operator overloading, is the operator= syntax. This is the way all operators are declared; you can think of each operator as a function named operator[*symbol*], where the symbol is the operator you are overloading. The only difference between operators and ordinary functions is the calling syntax. In fact, you can call operators using this syntax if you feel like doing a lot of extra typing and having ugly code:

```
x.operator=(y);  // Same thing as x = y, but uglier
```

The operation of my assignment operator implementation is simple. It updates the val_ member on the current object with the value from the other argument, and then returns a reference to the current object. Assignment operators return the current object as a reference so that callers can use assignment in expressions:

```
Balance x, y, z;
// ...
x = (y = z);
```

This way, the return value from (y = z) is the modified object y, which is then passed to the assignment operator for the object x. This is not as common with assignment as it is with arithmetic, but you should return a reference to the current object just to stick with convention (I discuss the issue as it relates to arithmetic operators shortly).

Simple assignment is only the beginning though; most likely you will want to use the other arithmetic operators to define more interesting behavior. Table 8-1 lists all of the arithmetic and assignment operators.

Table 8-1. Arithmetic and assignment operators

Operator	Behavior
=	Assignment (must be member function)
+ +=	Addition
- -=	Subtraction
* *=	Multiplication or dereferencing
/ /=	Division
% %=	Modulo
++	Increment
--	Decrement
^ ^=	Bitwise exclusive or
~	Bitwise complement
& &=	Bitwise and
| |=	Bitwise or

Table 8-1. Arithmetic and assignment operators (continued)

Operator	Behavior
`<<` `<<=`	Left shift
`>>` `>>=`	Right shift

For most of the operators in Table 8-1 there are two tokens: the first is the version of the operator that is used in the conventional manner, e.g., 1 + 2, and the second is the version that also assigns the result of an operation to a variable, e.g., x += 5. Note that the increment and decrement operators ++ and -- are covered in Recipe 8.13.

Implementing each of the arithmetic or assignment operators is pretty much the same, with the exception of the assignment operator, which can't be a standalone function (i.e., it has to be a member function).

The addition operator is a popular choice for overloading, especially since it can be used in contexts other than math, such as appending one string to another, so let's consider the addition assignment operator first. It adds the righthand argument to the lefthand argument and assigns the resulting value to the lefthand argument, as in the statements:

```
int i = 0;
i += 5;
```

After the second line has executed, the int i is modified by having 5 added to it. Similarly, if you look at Example 8-15, you would expect the same behavior from these lines:

```
Balance checking(500.00), savings(23.91);
checking += 50;
```

That is, you would expect that after the += operator is used, the value of checking has increased by 50. Using the implementation in Example 8-15, this is exactly what happens. Look at the function definition for the += operator:

```
Balance& operator+=(double other) {
    val_ += other;
    return(*this);
}
```

For an assignment operator, the parameter list is what will be supplied to the operator as its righthand side; in this case, an integer. The body of the function is trivial: all we are doing here is adding the argument to the private member variable. When all the work is done, return *this. You should return *this from assignment and arithmetic member operators so they can be used as expressions whose results can be the input to something else. For example, imagine if I had declared operator+= this way:

```
void operator+=(double other) { // Don't do this
    val_ += other;
}
```

Then someone wants to use this operator on an instance of my class somewhere and pass the results to other function:

```
Balance moneyMarket(1000.00);
// ...
updateGeneralLedger(moneyMarket += deposit); // Won't compile
```

This creates a problem because `Balance::operator+=` returns `void`, and a function like `updateGeneralLedger` expects to get a `Balance` object. If you return the current object from arithmetic and assignment member operators, then you won't have this problem. This doesn't apply to all operators though. Other operators like the array subscript operator `[]` or the relational operator `&&`, return an object other than `*this`, so this guideline holds for just arithmetic and assignment member operators.

That takes care of assignment operators that also do some arithmetic, but what about arithmetic that doesn't do assignment? The other way to use an arithmetic operator is like this:

```
int i = 0, j = 2;
i = j + 5;
```

In this case, `j` is added to 5 and the result is assigned to `i` (which, if `i` were an object and not a native type, would use `i`'s class's assignment operator), but `j` is unchanged. If you want the same behavior from your class, you can overload the addition operator as a standalone function. For example, you might want statements like this to make sense:

```
Balance checking(500.00), savings(100.00), total(0);
total = checking + savings;
```

You can do this in two steps. The first step is to create the function that overloads the + operator:

```
Balance operator+(const Balance& lhs, const Balance& rhs) {
    Balance tmp(lhs.val_ + rhs.val_);
    return(tmp);
}
```

This takes two `const Balance` objects, adds their private members, creates a temporary object, and returns it. Notice that, unlike the assignment operators, this returns an object, not an object reference. This is because the object returned is a temporary, and returning a reference would mean that the caller has a reference to a variable that is no longer there. This won't work by itself though, because it needs access to the private members of its arguments (assuming you've made the data members nonpublic). To allow this, the Balance class has to declare this function as a friend:

```
class Balance {
    // These have to see private data
    friend Balance operator+(const Balance& lhs, const Balance& rhs);
    // ...
```

Anything declared as a friend has access to all members of a class, so this does the trick. Just remember to declare the parameters const, since you probably don't want the objects modified.

This gets you most of the way, but you're not quite all the way there yet. Users of your class may put together expressions like this:

```
total = savings + 500.00;
```

This will work with the code in Example 8-15 because the compiler can see that the Balance class has a constructor that takes a float, so it creates a temporary Balance object out of 500.00 using that constructor. There are two problems with this though: the overhead with creating temporary objects and Balance doesn't have a constructor for each possible argument that can be used with the addition operator. Let's say you have a class named Transaction that represents a credit or debit amount. A user of Balance may do something like this:

```
Transaction tx(-20.00);
total = savings + tx;
```

This won't compile because there is no operator that adds a Balance object and a Transaction object. So create one:

```
Balance operator+(const Balance& lhs, const Transaction& rhs) {
    Balance tmp(lhs.val_ + Transaction.amount_);
    return(tmp);
}
```

There is some extra legwork though. You have to declare this operator a friend of the Transaction class, too, and you have to create an identical version of this that takes the arguments in the opposite order if you want to be able to use the arguments to + in any order, or if you want the operation to be commutative, i.e., x + y = y + x:

```
Balance operator+(const Transaction& lhs, const Balance& rhs) {
    Balance tmp(lhs.amount_ + rhs.val_);
    return(tmp);
}
```

By the same token, if you want to avoid the extra temporary object that is created when a constructor is invoked automatically, you can create your own operators to deal with any other kind of variable:

```
Balance operator+(double lhs, const Balance& rhs) {
    Balance tmp(lhs + rhs.val_);
    return(tmp);
```

```
    }
    Balance operator+(const Balance& lhs, double rhs) {
        Balance tmp(lhs.val_ + rhs);
        return(tmp);
    }
```

Again, you need to create two of them to allow expressions like this to work:

```
    total = 500.00 + checking;
```

In this case, the construction of a temporary object is small and, relatively speaking, inexpensive. But a temporary object is still a temporary object, and in simple, single statements, it won't create noticeable overhead, but you should always consider such minor optimizations in a broader context—what if a million of these temporary objects are created because a user wants to increment every element in a vector<Balance>? Your best bet is to know how the class will generally be used and measure the performance overhead if you aren't sure.

It is reasonable to ask, at this point, why we need to create standalone functions for these nonassignment arithmetic operators, and not just use member functions as we did with assignment. In fact, you *can* declare these kinds of operators as member functions on the class you are interested in, but it doesn't make for commutative operators. To make an operator commutative on a user-defined type, you would have to declare it as a member function on both classes that could be involved in the operation, and that will work (albeit with each of the classes knowing about each other classes internal members), but it won't work for operators that you want to use with native types unless there are constructors that can be used, and even in that case, you have to pay for the temporary objects.

Operator overloading is a powerful feature of C++, and like multiple inheritance, it has proponents and critics. In fact, most other popular languages don't support it at all. If you use it with care, however, it can make for powerful, concise code that uses your class.

Most of the standard operators have some conventional meaning, and in general, you should follow the conventional meanings. For example, the << operator means left-bit shift, or it means "put to" if you are dealing with streams, as in:

```
    cout << "This is written to the standard output stream.\n";
```

If you decide to override << for one or more of your classes, you should make it do one of these two things, or at least something that is analogous to them. Overloading an operator is one thing, but giving an operator an entirely new semantic meaning is another. Unless you are introducing a new convention that is ubiquitous throughout your application or library (which still doesn't mean it's a good idea), and it makes good intuitive sense to someone other than you, you should stick with the standard meanings.

To overload operators effectively, there is a lot of legwork. But you only have to do it once, and it pays off every time you use your class in a simple expression. If you use operator overloading conservatively and judiciously, it can make code easy to write and read.

See Also

Recipe 8.13

8.15 Calling a Superclass Virtual Function

Problem

You need to invoke a function on a superclass of a particular class, but it is overridden in subclasses, so the usual syntax of p->method( ) won't give you the results you are after.

Solution

Qualify the name of the member function you want to call with the target base class; for example, if you have two classes. (See Example 8-16.)

Example 8-16. Calling a specific version of a virtual function

```
#include <iostream>

using namespace std;

class Base {
public:
   virtual void foo() {cout << "Base::foo()" << endl;}
};

class Derived : public Base {
public:
   virtual void foo() {cout << "Derived::foo()" << endl;}
};

int main() {
   Derived* p = new Derived();

   p->foo();       // Calls the derived version
   p->Base::foo(); // Calls the base version
}
```

Discussion

Making a regular practice of overriding C++'s polymorphic facilities is not a good idea, but there are times when you have to do it. As with so many techniques in C++, it is largely a matter of syntax. When you want to call a specific base class's version of a virtual function, just qualify it with the name of the class you are after, as I did in Example 8-16:

```
p->Base::foo( );
```

This will call the version of foo defined for Base, and not the one defined for whatever subclass of Base p points to.

## CHAPTER 9

Exceptions and Safety

9.0 Introduction

This chapter contains recipes for using C++'s exception-handling features. C++ has strong support for exception handling, and by employing a few techniques you can write code that handles exceptional circumstances effectively and is easy to debug.

The first recipe describes C++'s semantics for throwing and catching exceptions, then it explains how to write a class to represent exceptions. This is a good starting point if you have little or no experience with exceptions. It also describes the standard exception classes that are defined in <stdexcept> and <exception>.

The rest of the recipes illustrate techniques for using exceptions optimally, and they define several key terms along the way. Just throwing an exception when something unexpected happens, or catching an exception only to print an error message and abort does not make for good software. To use C++'s exception-handling facilities effectively, you have to write code that doesn't leak resources if an exception is thrown, and that otherwise has well-defined behavior when an exception is thrown. These are known as the *basic* and *strong* exception-safety guarantees. I describe techniques you can use that allow you to make these guarantees for constructors and various member functions.

9.1 Creating an Exception Class

Problem

You want to create your own exception class for throwing and catching.

Solution

You can throw or catch any C++ type that lives up to some simple requirements, namely that it has a valid copy constructor and destructor. Exceptions are a complicated subject though, so there are a number of things to consider when designing a class to represent exceptional circumstances. Example 9-1 shows what a simple exception class might look like.

Example 9-1. A simple exception class

```cpp
#include <iostream>
#include <string>

using namespace std;

class Exception {

public:
  Exception(const string& msg) : msg_(msg) {}
  ~Exception() {}

  string getMessage() const {return(msg_);}
private:
  string msg_;
};

void f() {
  throw(Exception("Mr. Sulu"));
}

int main() {

  try {
    f();
  }
  catch(Exception& e) {
    cout << "You threw an exception: " << e.getMessage() << endl;
  }
}
```

Discussion

C++ supports exceptions with three keywords: try, catch, and throw. The syntax looks like this:

```cpp
try {
  // Something that may call "throw", e.g.
  throw(Exception("Uh-oh"));
}
catch(Exception& e) {
  // Do something useful with e
}
```

An exception in C++ (Java and C# are similar) is a way to put a message in a bottle at some point in a program, abandon ship, and hope that someone is looking for your message somewhere down the call stack. It is an alternative to other, simpler techniques, such as returning an error code or message. The semantics of using exceptions (e.g., "trying" something, "throwing" an exception, and subsequently "catching" it) are distinct from other kinds of C++ operations, so before I describe how to create an exception class I will give a short overview of what an exception *is* and what it means to throw or catch one.

When an exceptional situation arises, and you think the calling code should be made aware of it, you can stuff your message in the bottle with the throw statement, as in:

```
throw(Exception("Something went wrong"));
```

When you do this, the runtime environment constructs an Exception object, then it begins unwinding the call stack until it finds a try block that has been entered but not yet exited. If the runtime environment never finds one, meaning it gets all the way to main (or the top-level scope in the current thread) and can't unwind the stack any further, a special global function named terminate is called. But if it does find a try block, it then looks at each of the catch statements for that try block for one that is catching something with the same type as what was just thrown. Something like this would suffice:

```
catch(Exception& e) { //...
```

At this point, a new Exception is created with Exception's copy constructor from the one that was thrown. (The one in scope at the throw is a temporary, so the compiler may optimize it away.) The original exception is destroyed since it has gone out of scope, and the body of the catch statement is executed.

If, within the body of the catch statement, you want to propagate the exception that you just caught, you can call throw with no arguments:

```
throw;
```

This will continue the exception handling process down the call stack until another matching handler is found. This permits each scope to catch the exception and do something useful with it, then re-throw it when it is done (or not).

That's a crash course in how exceptions are thrown and caught. Now that you're equipped with that knowledge, consider Example 9-1. You can construct an Exception with a character pointer or a string, and then throw it. But this class is not terribly useful, because it is little more than a wrapper to a text message. As a matter of fact, you could get nearly the same results by just using a string as your exception object instead:

```
try {
    throw(string("Something went wrong!"));
}
catch (string& s) {
    cout << "The exception was: " << s << endl;
}
```

Not that this is necessarily a good approach; my goal is to demonstrate the nature of an exception: that it can be any C++ type. You can throw an int, char, class, struct, or any other C++ type if you really want to. But you're better off using a hierarchy of exception classes, either those in the standard library or your own hierarchy.

One of the biggest advantages to using an exception class hierarchy is that it allows you to express the nature of the exceptional circumstance with the *type* of exception class itself, rather than an error code, text string, severity level, or something else. This is what the standard library has done with the standard exceptions defined in `<stdexcept>`. The base class for the exceptions in `<stdexcept>` is exception, which is actually defined in `<exception>`. Figure 9-1 shows the class hierarchy for the standard exception classes.

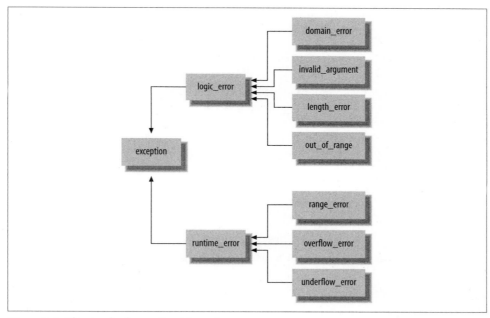

Figure 9-1. The standard exception hierarchy

Each standard exception class, by its name, indicates what category of condition it is meant to identify. For example, the class `logic_error` represents circumstances that should have been caught during code writing or review, and its subclasses represent subcategories of that: situations such as violating a precondition, supplying an out-of-range index, offering an invalid argument, etc. The complementary case to a logical error is a runtime error, which is represented by `runtime_error`. This indicates situations that, more than likely, could not have been caught at code time such as range, overflow, or underflow.

This is a limited set of exceptional situations, and the standard exception classes probably don't have everything you want. Chances are you want something more application-specific like `database_error`, `network_error`, `painting_error` and so on. I will discuss this more later. Before that, though, let's talk about how the standard exceptions work.

Since the standard library uses the standard exception classes (imagine that), you can expect classes in the standard library to throw one when there is a problem, as in trying to reference an index beyond the end of a vector:

```
std::vector<int> v;
int i = -1;

// fill up v...

try {
    i = v.at(v.size());  // One past the end
}
catch (std::out_of_range& e) {
    std::cerr << "Whoa, exception thrown: " << e.what() << '\n';
}
```

vector<>::at will throw an out_of_range exception if you give it an index that is less than zero or greater than size() − 1. Since you know this, you can write a handler to deal with this kind of exceptional situation specifically. If you're not expecting a specific exception, but instead would rather handle all exceptions the same way, you can catch the base class for all exceptions:

```
catch(std::exception& e) {
    std::cerr << "Nonspecific exception: " << e.what() << '\n';
}
```

Doing so will catch any derived class of exception. what is a virtual member function that provides an implementation-defined message string.

I am about to come full circle. The point of Example 9-1 followed by so much discussion is to illustrate the good parts of an exception class. There are two things that make an exception class useful: a hierarchy where the class communicates the nature of the exception and a message for the catcher to display for human consumers. The exception class hierarchy will permit developers who are using your library to write safe code and debug it easily, and the message text will allow those same developers to present a meaningful error message to end-users of the application.

Exceptions are a complicated topic, and handling exceptional circumstances safely and effectively is one of the most difficult parts of software engineering, in general, and C++, in particular. How do you write a constructor that won't leak memory if an exception is thrown in its body, or its initializer list? What does exception-safety mean? I will answer these and other questions in the recipes that follow.

9.2 Making a Constructor Exception-Safe

Problem

Your constructor needs to uphold basic and strong exception-safety guarantees. See the discussion that follows for the definitions of "basic" and "strong" guarantees.

Solution

Use try and catch in the constructor to clean up properly if an exception is thrown during construction. Example 9-2 presents examples of the simple Device and Broker classes. Broker constructs two Device objects on the heap, but needs to be able to properly clean them up if an exception is thrown during construction.

Example 9-2. An exception-safe constructor

```
#include <iostream>
#include <stdexcept>

using namespace std;

class Device {
public:
   Device(int devno) {
      if (devno == 2)
         throw runtime_error("Big problem");
   }
   ~Device() {}
};

class Broker {

public:
   Broker (int devno1, int devno2) :
      dev1_(NULL), dev2_(NULL) {
      try {
         dev1_ = new Device(devno1);   // Enclose the creation of heap
         dev2_ = new Device(devno2);   // objects in a try block...
      }
      catch (...) {
         delete dev1_;                 // ...clean up and rethrow if
         throw;                        // something goes wrong.
      }
   }
   ~Broker() {
      delete dev1_;
      delete dev2_;
   }

private:
   Broker();
   Device* dev1_;
```

Example 9-2. An exception-safe constructor (continued)

```
    Device* dev2_;
};

int main( ) {

    try {
        Broker b(1, 2);
    }
    catch(exception& e) {
        cerr << "Exception: " << e.what( ) << endl;
    }
}
```

Discussion

To say that a constructor, member function, destructor, or anything else is "exception-safe" is to guarantee that it won't leak resources and possibly that it won't leave its object in an inconsistent state. In C++, these two kinds of guarantees have been given the names *basic* and *strong*.

The *basic* exception-safety guarantee, which is quite intuitive, says that if an exception is thrown, the current operation won't leak resources and the objects involved in the operation will still be usable (meaning you can call other member functions and destroy the object, i.e., it won't be in a corrupt state). It also means the program will be left in a consistent state, although it might not be a predictable state. The rules are straightforward: if an exception is thrown anywhere in the body of (for example) a member function, heap objects are not orphaned and the objects involved in the operation can be destroyed or reset by the caller. The other guarantee, called the *strong* exception-safety guarantee, ensures that the object state remains unchanged if the operation fails. The latter applies to postconstruction operations on an object, since, by definition, an object that throws an exception during construction is never fully constructed and therefore never in a valid state. I will return to the subject of member functions in Recipe 9.4. For now, let's focus on construction.

Example 9-2 defines two classes, Device and Broker, that don't do much, but could easily represent any sort of device/broker scenario where you have some class that opens a connection to each of two devices and manages communication between them. A broker is useless if only one of the devices is available, so you want transactional semantics when you instantiate a broker, such that if one of the two throws an exception when it is being acquired, the other is released. This will ensure memory and other resources are not leaked.

try and catch will do the job. In the constructor, wrap the allocation of heap objects in a try block and catch anything that is thrown during their construction like this:

```
    try {
        dev1_ = new Device(devno1);
        dev2_ = new Device(devno2);
```

```
   }
catch (...) {
   delete dev1_;
   throw;
}
```

The ellipsis in the catch handler means that anything that is thrown will be caught. This is what you need here, because all you're doing is cleaning up after yourself if something goes wrong, then rethrowing regardless of what sort of exception was thrown. You need to rethrow so the client code that is trying to instantiate the Broker object can do something useful with the exception, like write its error message somewhere.

I only delete dev1_ in the catch handler because the last chance for an exception to be thrown is in the call to new for dev2_. If this throws an exception, than dev2_ will not be assigned a value and, therefore, I don't need to delete it. However, if you do something after dev2_'s initialization, you will need to be sure to clean it up. For example:

```
try {
   dev1_ = new Device(devno1);
   dev2_ = new Device(devno2);
   foo_ = new MyClass();       // Might throw
}
catch (...) {
   delete dev1_;
   delete dev2_;
   throw;
}
```

In this case, you don't need to worry about deleting pointers that were never assigned real values (as long as you properly initialized them in the first place), since deleting a NULL pointer has no effect. In other words, if the assignment to dev1_ throws an exception, your catch handler still calls delete dev2_, but that's okay as long as you initialized it to NULL in the initializer list.

As I said in Recipe 9.1, designing a sound, flexible exception strategy can be tricky, and exception-safety is no different. For a detailed look at designing exception-safe code, see *Exceptional C++* by Herb Sutter (Addison Wesley).

See Also

Recipe 9.3

9.3   Making an Initializer List Exception-Safe

Problem

You have to initialize your data members in the constructor's initializer list, and, therefore, cannot use the approach described in Recipe 9.2.

Solution

Use a special syntax for try and catch that catches exceptions thrown in the initializer list. Example 9-3 shows how.

Example 9-3. Handling exceptions in an initializer

```
#include <iostream>
#include <stdexcept>

using namespace std;

// Some device
class Device {
public:
   Device(int devno) {
      if (devno == 2)
         throw runtime_error("Big problem");
   }
   ~Device() {}
private:
   Device();
};

class Broker {

public:
   Broker (int devno1, int devno2)
      try : dev1_(Device(devno1)),    // Create these in the initializer
            dev2_(Device(devno2)) {} // list.
      catch (...) {
         throw; // Log the message or translate the error here (see
                // the discussion)
      }
   ~Broker() {}

private:
   Broker();
   Device dev1_;
   Device dev2_;
};

int main() {
```

Example 9-3. Handling exceptions in an initializer (continued)

```
    try {
        Broker b(1, 2);
    }
    catch(exception& e) {
        cerr << "Exception: " << e.what() << endl;
    }
}
```

Discussion

The syntax for handling exceptions in initializers looks a little different from the traditional C++ syntax because it uses the try block as the constructor body. The critical part of Example 9-3 is the Broker constructor:

```
Broker (int devno1, int devno2)    // Constructor header is the same
    try :                          // Same idea as a try {...} block
        dev1_(Device(devno1)),     // The initializers follow
        dev2_(Device(devno2)) {
      // This is the constructor body.
    }
    catch (...) {                  // The catch handler is *after*
        throw;                     // the constructor body
    }
```

try and catch behave as you would expect; the only difference from the usual syntax of a try block is that when you want to catch exceptions thrown in an initializer list, try is followed by a colon, then the initializer list, and *then* the try block, which is also the body of the constructor. If anything is thrown in either the initializer list or the constructor body, the catch handler that follows the constructor body will get it. You can still embed additional try/catch pairs in the body of the constructor if you have to, but nested try/catch blocks usually get ugly.

In addition to moving the member initialization to the initializer list, Example 9-3 is different from Example 9-2 for another reason. The Device object members aren't created on the heap this time with new. I did this to illustrate a couple of points regarding safety and member objects.

First, using stack instead of heap objects lets the compiler provide its built-in safety. If any of the objects in the initializer list throws an exception during construction, its memory is deallocated automatically as the stack unwinds in the exception-handling process. Second, and even better, any other objects that have already been successfully constructed are destroyed without you having to catch the exception and delete them explicitly.

But maybe you require or prefer heap members. Consider an approach like the original Broker class in Example 9-2. You can just initialize your pointers in the initializer list, right?

```
class BrokerBad {

public:
    BrokerBad (int devno1, int devno2)
        try : dev1_(new Device(devno1)),    // Create heap objects with
              dev2_(new Device(devno2)) {} // initializers
        catch (...) {
            if (dev1_) {
                delete dev1_;                // Shouldn't compile, and
                delete dev2_;                // is a bad approach if it
            }                                // does
            throw; // Rethrow the same exception
        }
    ~BrokerBad() {
        delete dev1_;
        delete dev2_;
    }

private:
    BrokerBad();
    Device* dev1_;
    Device* dev2_;
};
```

No. There are two problems here. To begin with, this should not be allowed by your compiler because the catch block of a constructor should not allow program code to access member variables—at that point, they don't exist. Second, even if your compiler permits it, it is a bad idea. Consider the case where the construction of dev1_'s object throws an exception. This is the code that will be executed in the catch handler:

```
catch (...) {
    if (dev1_) {      // What value does this contain?
        delete dev1_; // Now you are deleting an undefined value
        delete dev2_;
    }
    throw; // Rethrow the same exception
}
```

If an exception is thrown during the construction of dev1_, then new doesn't get a chance to return the address to the newly allocated memory and dev1_ is unchanged. Then what does it contain? It's undefined, because it was never initialized with a value. As a result, when you call delete dev1_, you will probably be deleting a garbage pointer address, which means your program will crash, you will get fired, and you will have to live with that shame for the rest of your life.

To avoid such a life-altering fiasco, initialize your pointers to NULL in the initializer list, and then create the heap objects in the constructor. This way it's easy to catch anything that goes wrong and clean up the mess, since calling delete on NULL pointers is okay.

```
BrokerBetter (int devno1, int devno2) :
dev1_(NULL), dev2_(NULL) {
```

```
        try {
            dev1_ = new Device(devno1);
            dev2_ = new Device(devno2);
        }
        catch (...) {
            delete dev1_; // This will always be valid
            throw;
        }
    }
```

So, to summarize, if you must use pointer members, initialize them to NULL in the initializer list, then allocate their objects in the constructor using a try/catch block. You can deallocate any memory in the catch handler. However, if you can work with automatic members, construct them in the initializer list and use the special try/catch syntax to deal with any exceptions.

See Also

Recipe 9.2

9.4   Making Member Functions Exception-Safe

Problem

You are writing a member function and you need it to uphold the basic and strong exception-safety guarantees, namely that it won't leak resources and it won't leave the object in an invalid state if an exception is thrown.

Solution

Be aware of what operations can throw exceptions and do them first, usually in a try/catch block. Once the code that can throw exceptions is done executing, then you can update the object state. Example 9-4 offers one way to make a member function exception-safe.

Example 9-4. An exception-safe member function

```
class Message {

public:
    Message(int bufSize = DEFAULT_BUF_SIZE) :
        bufSize_(bufSize),
        initBufSize_(bufSize),
        msgSize_(0),
        buf_(NULL) {
        buf_ = new char[bufSize];
    }

    ~Message() {
        delete[] buf_;
    }
```

Example 9-4. An exception-safe member function (continued)

```
    // Append character data
    void appendData(int len, const char* data) {
        if (msgSize_+len > MAX_SIZE) {
            throw out_of_range("Data size exceeds maximum size.");
        }
        if (msgSize_+len > bufSize_) {

            int newBufSize = bufSize_;
            while ((newBufSize *= 2) < msgSize_+len);

            char* p = new char[newBufSize];    // Allocate memory
                                               // for new buffer

            copy(buf_, buf_+msgSize_, p);      // Copy old data
            copy(data, data+len, p+msgSize_);  // Copy new data

            msgSize_ += len;
            bufSize_ = newBufSize;

            delete[] buf_;  // Get rid of old buffer and point to new
            buf_ = p;
        }
        else {
            copy(data, data+len, buf_+msgSize_);
            msgSize_ += len;
        }
    }

    // Copy the data out to the caller's buffer
    int getData(int maxLen, char* data) {
        if (maxLen < msgSize_) {
            throw out_of_range("This data is too big for your buffer.");
        }
        copy(buf_, buf_+msgSize_, data);
        return(msgSize_);
    }

private:
    Message(const Message& orig) {}          // We will come to these
    Message& operator=(const Message& rhs) {} // in Recipe 9.5
    int bufSize_;
    int initBufSize_;
    int msgSize_;
    char* buf_;
};
```

Discussion

The class Message in Example 9-4 is a class for holding character data; you might use
such a thing to wrap text or binary data as it is passed from one system to another.
The member function of interest here is appendData, which appends the caller's data

to the data already in the buffer, growing the buffer if necessary. It upholds the strong exception-safety guarantee, though it may not be clear at first glance why this is the case.

Look at this part of appendData:

```
if (msgSize_+len > bufSize_) {

    int newBufSize = bufSize_;
    while ((newBufSize *= 2) < msgSize_+len);

    char* p = new char[newBufSize];
```

The point of this block of code is to grow the buffer. I grow the size of the buffer by doubling it until it's big enough. This piece of code is safe because the only part that can throw an exception is the call to new, and I don't update the object state or allocate any other resources before that happens. It will throw bad_alloc if the operating system is unable to allocate the requested piece of memory.

If the memory is allocated successfully, then I can start updating the state of the object by copying the data and updating the member variables:

```
    copy(buf_, buf_+msgSize_, p);
    copy(data, data+len, p+msgSize_);

    msgSize_ += len;
    bufSize_ = newBufSize;

    delete[] buf_;
    buf_ = p;
```

None of these operations can throw exceptions, so we are in the clear. (This is only because the data in the buffer is a sequence of chars; see the discussion that follows Example 9-5 for further explanation.)

This solution is simple, and it is the general strategy for making member functions strongly exception-safe: Do everything that might throw an exception first, then, when all of the dangerous work is over with, take a deep breath and update the object state. appendData just uses a temporary variable to hold the new buffer size. This solves the problem with the buffer size, but does it truly uphold the basic guarantee of not leaking resources? Yes, but barely.

copy calls operator= on each element in the sequence that it is copying. In Example 9-4, each element is a char, so we are safe because a single assignment of one character to another can't throw anything. But I said, barely, because you shouldn't let the safety of this special case make you think an exception will never come out of copy.

Imagine for a moment that instead of a narrow character buffer, you have to write a Message class that can contain an array of anything. You might write it as a class template to look like Example 9-5.

Example 9-5. A generic message class

```
template<typename T>
class MessageGeneric {

public:
   MessageGeneric(int bufSize = DEFAULT_BUF_SIZE) :
      bufSize_(bufSize),
      initBufSize_(bufSize),
      msgSize_(0),
      buf_(new T[bufSize]) {}

  ~MessageGeneric() {
      delete[] buf_;
   }

   void appendData(int len, const T* data) {
      if (msgSize_ +len > MAX_SIZE) {
         throw out_of_range("Data size exceeds maximum size.");
      }
      if (msgSize_ +len > bufSize_) {

         int newBufSize = bufSize_;
         while ((newBufSize *= 2) < msgSize_+len);

         T* p = new T[newBufSize];

         copy(buf_, buf_+msgSize_, p);      // Can these throw?
         copy(data, data+len, p+msgSize_);

         msgSize_ += len;
         bufSize_ = newBufSize;

         delete[] buf_;  // Get rid of old buffer and point to new
         buf_ = p;
      }
      else {
         copy(data, data+len, buf_+msgSize_);
         msgSize_ += len;
      }
   }

   // Copy the data out to the caller's buffer
   int getData(int maxLen, T* data) {
      if (maxLen < msgSize_) {
         throw out_of_range("This data is too big for your buffer.");
      }
      copy(buf_, buf_+msgSize_, data);
      return(msgSize_);
   }

private:
   MessageGeneric(const MessageGeneric& orig) {}
   MessageGeneric& operator=(const MessageGeneric& rhs) {}
```

Example 9-5. A generic message class (continued)

```
    int bufSize_;
    int initBufSize_;
    int msgSize_;
    T* buf_;
};
```

Now you have to be more careful, because you can't make assumptions about the target type. For example, how do you know that T::operator= won't throw? You don't, so you have to be prepared for that possibility.

Wrap the calls to copy in a try block:

```
    try {
        copy(buf_, buf_+msgSize_, p);
        copy(data, data+len, p+msgSize_);
    }
    catch(...) {   // I don't care what was thrown; all I know
        delete[] p; // is that I have to clean up after myself,
        throw;      // then rethrow.
    }
```

Since you are catching any type that is thrown with the ellipsis operator, you can rest assured that if T::operator= throws, you will catch it and be able to clean up the heap memory you just allocated.

Strictly speaking, copy doesn't actually throw anything, T::operator= does. This is because copy (and the rest of the algorithms in the standard library) are generally *exception-neutral*, which means that if whatever it is invoking throws an exception, it will propagate it to the caller and not eat it (catch it and not rethrow). It reserves the right to catch exceptions, do some clean-up, then rethrow them, but ultimately anything that is thrown by a class or function the standard library is using will find its way to the caller.

Making your member functions exception-safe is tedious work. It requires that you consider all possible points where an exception can be thrown and that you deal with them the right way. When can an exception be thrown? Anywhere a function call is made. Operators for native data types can't throw, and destructors should *never* throw, but anything else, be it a standalone function, member function, operator, constructor, and so on, is a potential source of an exception. Examples 9-5 and 9-6 provide examples that use a narrow scope of exceptions. The classes contain very few member variables, and the behavior of the class is discrete. As the number of member functions and variables increase, and you introduce inheritance and virtual functions, remaining strongly exception-safe becomes more challenging.

Finally, as with most application requirements, you only need to be as exception-safe as you need to be. In other words, if you are writing a dialog-based wizard for generating web pages, your development schedule will probably preclude the necessary research and testing for making it strongly exception-safe. Thus, it may be acceptable to your client for users to encounter the occasional, ambiguous error message, "Unknown error, aborting." On the other hand, if you are writing software that controls the angle of a helicopter rotor, your client will probably push for more safety assurances than the occasional "Unknown error, aborting" message.

9.5   Safely Copying an Object

Problem

You need the basic class copy operations—copy construction and assignment—to be exception-safe.

Solution

Employ the tactics discussed in Recipe 9.4 by doing everything that might throw first, then changing the object state with operations that can't throw only after the hazardous work is complete. Example 9-6 presents the Message class again, this time with the assignment operator and copy constructor defined.

Example 9-6. Exception-safe assignment and copy construction

```
#include <iostream>
#include <string>

const static int DEFAULT_BUF_SIZE = 3;
const static int MAX_SIZE        = 4096;

class Message {

public:
   Message(int bufSize = DEFAULT_BUF_SIZE) :
      bufSize_(bufSize),
      initBufSize_(bufSize),
      msgSize_(0),
      key_("") {
      buf_ = new char[bufSize]; // Note: now this is in the body
   }

   ~Message() {
      delete[] buf_;
   }

   // Exception-safe copy ctor
   Message(const Message& orig) :
      bufSize_(orig.bufSize_),
      initBufSize_(orig.initBufSize_),
      msgSize_(orig.msgSize_),
      key_(orig.key_) { // This can throw...
```

Example 9-6. Exception-safe assignment and copy construction (continued)

```
        buf_ = new char[orig.bufSize_];  // ...so can this
        copy(orig.buf_, orig.buf_+msgSize_, buf_); // This can't
    }

    // Exception-safe assignment, using the copy ctor
    Message& operator=(const Message& rhs) {

        Message tmp(rhs);     // Copy construct a temporary
        swapInternals(tmp);   // Swap members with it
        return(*this);        // When we leave, tmp is destroyed, taking
                              // the original data with it
    }

    const char* data() {
        return(buf_);
    }

private:
    void swapInternals(Message& msg) {
        // Since key_ is not a built-in data type it can throw,
        // so do it first.
        swap(key_, msg.key_);

        // If it hasn't thrown, then do all the primitives
        swap(bufSize_,     msg.bufSize_);
        swap(initBufSize_, msg.initBufSize_);
        swap(msgSize_,     msg.msgSize_);
        swap(buf_,         msg.buf_);
    }
    int bufSize_;
    int initBufSize_;
    int msgSize_;
    char* buf_;
    string key_;
};
```

Discussion

The copy constructor and the private member swapInternals do all the work here. The copy constructor initializes the primitive members and one of the nonprimitive members in the initializer list. Then it allocates a new buffer and copies the data into it. Simple enough, but why do it in this order? You could argue that all the initialization goes in the initializer list, but doing so can open the door for subtle bugs.

For example, you may want to put the buffer allocation in the initializer list, like this:

```
    Message(const Message& orig) :
        bufSize_(orig.bufSize_),
        initBufSize_(orig.initBufSize_),
        msgSize_(orig.msgSize_),
        key_(orig.key_),
```

```
    buf_(new char[orig.bufSize_]) {
    copy(orig.buf_, orig.buf_+msgSize_, buf_);
}
```

You might expect that everything will be fine, because if the new in the buffer allocation fails, all the other fully constructed objects will be destroyed. But this behavior is
not guaranteed, because the members are initialized in the order in which they are
declared in the class header, *not* the order in which you list them in the initializer list.
The order of the member declaration looks like this:

```
int bufSize_;
int initBufSize_;
int msgSize_;
char* buf_;
string key_;
```

As a result, buf_ will be initialized before key_. If the initialization of key_ throws
something, buf_ will not be destroyed and you will have created a hunk of unrefer-
enced memory. You can guard against this by using a try/catch block in the constructor (see Recipe 9.2), but it is easier just to put buf_'s initialization in the body of
the constructor where it is guaranteed to be called after the initializer list.

The call to copy won't throw because it's copying primitive values. But this is where
the subtleties of exception-safety come in: it can throw if it is copying objects (e.g., if
this is a generic container of T elements), in which case, you will need to catch it and
delete the associated memory.

The other way you may want to copy an object is by using the assignment operator,
operator=. Since it and the copy constructor have similar needs (e.g., make my members equal to my argument's members), reuse what you have already done and make
your life easier. The only twist is that you can make things slick by using a private
member to swap member data. I wish I had invented this technique, but I have to
credit Herb Sutter and Stephen Dewhurst since their writing is where I first saw it.

It may make sense to you at first glance, but I will explain just in case it doesn't.
Consider the first line, which copy constructs a temporary object, tmp:

```
Message tmp(rhs);
```

Now we have just created a clone of the object we are assigning from. Essentially, tmp
is now equivalent to rhs. Now, swap its members with *this's members:

```
swapInternals(tmp);
```

I will come back to swapInternals in a moment. For now, all we care about is that
now the *this's members are the same as tmp's were a second ago. And tmp was a
copy of rhs, so now *this is equivalent to rhs. But wait: we still have this temporary
object hanging around. No problem, when you return *this, tmp is automatically
destroyed when it goes out of scope, taking the old members with it.

```
return(*this);
```

That's it. But is it exception-safe? Constructing tmp is, since our constructor is exception-safe. The call to swapInternals is what does the majority of the work, so let's have a look at what it does to see if it's safe.

swapInternals exchanges each data member in the current object with those in the object that is passed in. It does this by using swap, which takes two arguments *a* and *b*, creates a temporary copy of *a*, assigns *b* to *a*, and then assigns the temporary to *b*. As such, it is exception-safe and exception-neutral because the only exceptions that come out of it are those that may be thrown by the objects it is operating on. It uses no dynamic memory, so it upholds the basic guarantee of not leaking resources.

Since key_ isn't a primitive, which means that operations on it may throw an exception, I swap it first. That way, if it throws an exception, none of the other member variables are corrupted. This doesn't guarantee that key_ won't be corrupted though. When working with object members, you are at the mercy of their exception-safety guarantees. If that doesn't throw, I'm home free because I know that swapping native variables won't throw. Therefore, swapInternals is both basically and strongly exception-safe.

This brings up an interesting point though. What if you have more than one object member? If you had two string members, the beginning of swapInternals may look like this:

```
void swapInternals(Message& msg) {
    swap(key_, msg.key_);
    swap(myObj_, msg.myObj_);
    // ...
```

There is a problem: If the second swap throws an exception, how can we safely undo the first swap? In other words, now key_ has been updated with the new value, but the swap of myObj_ failed, so key_ is now corrupt. If the caller catches the exception and wants to proceed as though nothing happened, he is now working with something different than what he started with. Copying key_ to a temporary string first is one approach, but it can't guarantee safety because doing that copy may throw an exception.

One way to get around this is to use heap objects:

```
void swapInternals(Message& msg) {
    // key_ is a string* and myObj_ is a MyClass*
    swap(key_, msg.key_);
    swap(myObj_, msg.myObj_);
```

Of course, this means that now you have more dynamic memory to manage, but making exception-safety guarantees will often affect your design, so it is a good idea to start thinking about it early in the design process.

The theme for this recipe is unchanged from the previous recipes about exception-safety. Do the work that might cause problems first, wait with a try/catch block just in case something goes wrong, and, if something does go wrong, then clean up after yourself. If nothing goes wrong, pat yourself on the back and update the object state.

See Also

Recipes 9.2 and 9.3

## CHAPTER 10

Streams and Files

10.0 Introduction

Streams are one of the most powerful (and complicated) components of the C++ standard library. Using them for plain, unformatted input and output is generally straightforward, but changing the format to suit your needs with standard manipulators, or writing your own manipulators, is not. Therefore, the first few recipes describe different ways to format stream output. The two after that describe how to write objects of a class to a stream or read them from one.

Then the recipes shift from reading and writing file content to operating on the files themselves (and directories). If your program uses files, especially if it's a daemon or server-side process, you will probably create files and directories, clean them up, rename them, and so on. There are a number of recipes that explain how to do these unglamorous, but necessary, tasks in C++.

The last third of the recipes demonstrate how to manipulate file and pathnames themselves using many of the standard string member functions. Standard strings contain an abundance of functions for inspecting and manipulating their contents, and if you have to parse path and filenames they come in handy. If what you need is not discussed in these recipes, take a look at Chapter 7, too—what you're after might be described there.

File manipulation requires direct interaction with the operating system (OS), and there are often subtle differences (and occasionally glaring incompatibilities) between OSs. Many of the typical file and directory manipulation needs are part of the standard C system calls, and work the same or similarly on different systems. Where there are differences between OSs' versions of libraries, I note it in the recipes.

As I have discussed in previous chapters, Boost is an open source project that has generated a number of high-quality, portable libraries. But since this is a book about C++ and not the Boost project, I have preferred standard C++ solutions whenever possible. In many cases, however, (most notably Recipe 10.12) there isn't a Standard

C++ solution, so I have used the Boost Filesystem library written by Beman Dawes, which provides a portable filesystem interface, to give a portable solution. Take a look at the Boost Filesystem library if you have to do portable filesystem interaction—you will save yourself lots of time and effort. For more information on the Boost project, see *www.boost.org*.

10.1 Lining Up Text Output

Problem

You need to line up your text output vertically. For example, if you are exporting tabular data, you may want it to look like this:

```
Jim           Willcox         Mesa           AZ
Bill          Johnson         San Mateo      CA
Robert        Robertson       Fort Collins   CO
```

You will probably also want to be able to right- or left-justify the text.

Solution

Use ostream or wostream, for narrow or wide characters, defined in <ostream>, and the standard stream manipulators to set the field width and justify the text. Example 10-1 shows how.

Example 10-1. Lining up text output

```cpp
#include <iostream>
#include <iomanip>
#include <string>

using namespace std;

int main( ) {

    ios_base::fmtflags flags = cout.flags( );
    string first, last, citystate;
    int width = 20;

    first = "Richard";
    last  = "Stevens";
    citystate = "Tucson, AZ";

    cout << left                          // Left-justify in each field
         << setw(width) << first          // Then, repeatedly set the width
         << setw(width) << last           // and write some data
         << setw(width) << citystate << endl;

    cout.flags(flags);
}
```

The output looks like this:

```
Richard            Stevens            Tucson, AZ
```

Discussion

A manipulator is a function that operates on a stream. Manipulators are applied to a stream with operator<<. The stream's format (input or output) is controlled by a set of flags and settings on the ultimate base stream class, ios_base. Manipulators exist to provide convenient shorthand for adjusting these flags and settings without having to explicitly set them via setf or flags, which is cumbersome to write and ugly to read. The best way to format stream output is to use manipulators.

Example 10-1 uses two manipulators to line up text output into columns. The manipulator setw sets the field width, and left left-justifies the value within that field (the counterpart to left is, not surprisingly, right). A "field" is just another way of saying that you want the output to be padded on one side or the other to make sure that the value you write is the only thing printed in that field. If, as in Example 10-1, you left-justify a value, then set the field width, the next thing you write to the stream will begin with the first character in the field. If the data you send to the stream is not wide enough to span the entire field width, the right side of it will be padded with the stream's fill character, which is, by default, a single space. You can change the fill character with the setfill manipulator, like this:

```
myostr << setfill('.') << "foo";
```

If the value you put in the field is larger than the field width, the entire value is printed and no padding is added.

Table 10-1 contains a summary of manipulators that operate on any kind of value (text, float, integer, etc.). There is a set of manipulators that apply only to floating-point output, and they are described in Recipe 10.2.

Table 10-1. Text manipulators

Manipulator	Description	Sample output

left
right
	Justify values within the current field width to either the left or right side, and pad the remaining space with the fill character.	Left-justified:
		  apple
		  bananna
		  cherry
		
		Right-justified (with a field width of 10):
		     apple
		   bananna
		    cherry

setw(int n)	Set the width of the field to n characters wide.	See earlier example.

Table 10-1. Text manipulators (continued)

Manipulator	Description	Sample output
setfill(int c)	Use the character c to pad fields that have remaining space.	cout << setfill('.') << setw(10) << right << "foo" produces: ....foo
boolalpha noboolalpha	Display Boolean values as the current locale's representation of the words true and false, instead of 1 and 0.	cout << boolalpha << true produces: true
endl	Write a newline to the stream and flush the output buffer.	n/a
ends	Write a null character ('\0') to the stream.	n/a
flush	Flush the output buffer.	n/a

Some of the manipulators in Table 10-1 (and Table 10-2 in the next recipe) toggle binary stream flags, and are actually implemented as two manipulators that turn a flag on or off. Take boolalpha, for example. If you want Boolean values to be displayed as their written equivalents in the current locale (e.g., "true" and "false"), use the boolalpha manipulator. To turn this behavior off, so that 0 and 1 are printed instead, use noboolalpha, which is the default.

All manipulators have the behavior that they stay in effect until they are explicitly changed, except for setw. In Example 10-1, you can see that it is called before each write, but left is used only once. This is because the width is reset to zero after each value is written to the stream with operator<<; to keep the same width for each field, I had to call setw each time.

The standard manipulators provide a lot of functionality, but they don't do everything. If you want to write your own manipulators, see Recipe 10.2.

As with all other character-based classes in the standard library, manipulators work on streams that use narrow or wide characters. Therefore, you can use them with templates to write formatting utilities that operate on streams of any kind of character. Example 10-2 presents the class template TableFormatter, which formats data into equal-width columns and writes it to a stream.

Example 10-2. A generic class for tabular data

```
#include <iostream>
#include <iomanip>
#include <string>
#include <vector>

using namespace std;
```

Example 10-2. A generic class for tabular data (continued)

```cpp
// TableFormatter formats data for output to a stream of characters
// of type T.
template<typename T>
class TableFormatter {

public:
   TableFormatter(basic_ostream<T>& os) : out_(os) {}
  ~TableFormatter() {out_ << flush;}

   template<typename valT>
   void writeTableRow(const vector<valT>& v, int width);
   //...

private:
  basic_ostream<T>& out_;
};

template<typename T>     // refers to class template param list
template<typename valT> // refers to mem fn template param list
void TableFormatter<T>::writeTableRow(const std::vector<valT>& v,
                                     int width) {

   ios_base::fmtflags flags = out_.flags();

   out_.flush();
   out_ << setprecision(2) << fixed;  // Set the precision, in case
                                      // this is floating-point data
   for (vector<valT>::const_iterator p = v.begin();
        p != v.end(); ++p)
     out_ << setw(width) << left << *p;  // Set the width, justify,
                                         // and write the element
   out_ << endl;     // Flush
   out_.setf(flags); // Set the flags back to normal
}

int main() {

   TableFormatter<char> fmt(cout);

   vector<string> vs;

   vs.push_back( "Sunday" );
   vs.push_back( "Monday" );
   vs.push_back( "Tuesday" );

   fmt.writeTableRow(vs, 12);
   fmt.writeTableRow(vs, 12);
   fmt.writeTableRow(vs, 12);

   vector<double> vd;
```

Example 10-2. A generic class for tabular data (continued)

```
    vd.push_back(4.0);
    vd.push_back(3.0);
    vd.push_back(2.0);
    vd.push_back(1.0);

    fmt.writeTableRow(vd, 5);
}
```

The output from Example 10-2 looks like this:

```
    Sunday      Monday      Tuesday
    4.00 3.00 2.00 1.00
```

See Also

Table 10-1, Recipe 10.2

10.2   Formatting Floating-Point Output

Problem

You need to present floating-point output in a well-defined format, either for the sake of precision (scientific versus fixed-point notation) or simply to line up decimal points vertically for easier reading.

Solution

Use the standard manipulators provided in `<iomanip>` and `<ios>` to control the format of floating-point values that are written to the stream. There are too many combinations of ways to cover here, but Example 10-3 offers a few different ways to display the value of pi.

Example 10-3. Formatting pi

```
#include <iostream>
#include <iomanip>
#include <string>

using namespace std;

int main( ) {

    ios_base::fmtflags flags =  // Save old flags
        cout.flags( );

    double pi = 3.14159265;

    cout << "pi = " << setprecision(5)  // Normal (default) mode; only
        << pi << '\n';                  // show 5 digits, including both
                                        // sides of decimal point.
```

Example 10-3. Formatting pi (continued)

```
cout << "pi = " << fixed          // Fixed-point mode;
     << showpos                   // show a "+" for positive nums,
     << setprecision(3)           // show 3 digits to the *right*
     << pi << '\n';               // of the decimal.

cout << "pi = " << scientific     // Scientific mode;
     << noshowpos                 // don't show plus sign anymore
     << pi * 1000 << '\n';

cout.flags(flags);   // Set the flags to the way they were
}
```

This will produce the following output:

```
pi = 3.1416
pi = +3.142
pi = 3.142e+003
```

Discussion

Manipulators that specifically manipulate floating-point output divide into two categories. There are those that set the format, which, for the purposes of this recipe, set the general appearance of floating-point and integer values, and there are those that fine-tune the display of each format. The formats are as follows:

Normal (the default)

In this format, the number of digits displayed is fixed (with a default of six) and the decimal is displayed such that only a set number of digits are displayed at one time. So, by default, pi would be displayed as 3.14159, and pi times 100 would display 314.159.

Fixed

In this format, the number of digits displayed to the *right* of the decimal point is fixed, while the number of those displayed to the left is not. In this case, again with a default precision of six, pi would be displayed as 3.141593, and pi times 100 would be 314.159265. In both cases, the number of digits displayed to the right of the decimal point is six while the total number of digits can grow indefinitely.

Scientific

The value is shown as a single digit, followed by a decimal point, followed by a number of digits determined by the precision setting, followed by the letter "e" and the power of ten to raise the preceding value to. In this case, pi times 1,000 would display as 3.141593e+003.

Table 10-2 shows all manipulators that affect floating-point output (and sometimes numeric output in general). See Table 10-1 for general manipulators you can use together with the floating-point manipulators.

Table 10-2. Floating-point and numeric manipulators

Manipulator	Description	Sample output
Fixed	Show floating-point values with a fixed number of digits to the right of the decimal point.	With a default precision of six digits: `pi = 3.141593`
scientific	Show floating-point values using scientific notation, which means a decimal number and an exponent multiplier.	pi * 1000, with a default precision of six digits: `pi = 3.141593e+003`

setprecision	Control the number of digits displayed in the output. (See further explanation later.)	Pi in the default format, with a precision of 3:
		`pi = 3.14`
		In fixed format:
		`pi = 3.142`
		In scientific format:
		`pi = 3.142e+000`

showpos noshowpos	Show a plus sign in front of positive numbers. This works for any kind of number, decimal or integer.	+3.14

showpoint
noshowpoint
	Show the decimal, even if there are only zeros after it. This works only for floating-point values, and not for integers.	The following line, with a precision of 2:
		`    cout << showpoint << 2.0`
		will display like this:
		`2.00`

showbase noshowbase	Show the base for the number: decimal (none), octal (leading zero), or hexadecimal (leading 0x). See the next entry.	Decimal: 32 Octal: 040 Hexadecimal: 0x20
dec oct hex	Set the base for the numbers to be displayed to decimal, octal, or hexadecimal. The base is not shown by default; use showbase to display the base.	See previous entry.
Uppercase nouppercase	Display values in uppercase.	This sets the case for numeric output, such as 0X for hexadecimal numbers and E for numbers in scientific notation.

In all three formats, all manipulators have the same effects except setprecision. In the default mode, "precision" refers to the number of digits on both sides of the decimal point. For example, to display pi in the default format with a precision of 2, do this:

```
cout << "pi = " << setprecision(2)
    << pi << '\n';
```

Your output will look like this:

```
pi = 3.1
```

By comparison, consider if you want to display pi in fixed-point format instead:

```
cout << "pi = " << fixed
    << setprecision(2)
    << pi << '\n';
```

Now the output will look like this:

```
pi = 3.14
```

This is because, in fixed-point format, the precision refers to the number of digits to the *right* of the decimal point. If we multiply pi by 1,000 in the same format, the number of digits to the right of the decimal remains unchanged:

```
cout << "pi = " << fixed
     << setprecision(2)
     << pi * 1000 << '\n';
```

produces:

```
pi = 3141.59
```

This is nice, because you can set your precision, set your field width with setw, right-justify your output with right (see Recipe 10.1), and your decimal points will all be lined up vertically.

Since a manipulator is just a convenient way of setting a format flag on the stream, remember that the settings stick around until you undo them or until the stream is destroyed. Save the format flags (see Example 10-3) before you start making changes, and restore them when you are done

See Also

Recipe 10.3

10.3 Writing Your Own Stream Manipulators

Problem

You need a stream manipulator that does something the standard ones can't. Or, you want to have a single manipulator set several flags on the stream instead of calling a set of manipulators each time you want a particular format.

Solution

To write a manipulator that doesn't take an argument (à la left), write a function that takes an ios_base parameter and sets stream flags on it. If you need a manipulator that takes an argument, see the discussion a little later. Example 10-4 shows how to write a manipulator that doesn't take an argument.

Example 10-4. A simple stream manipulator

```
#include <iostream>
#include <iomanip>
#include <string>

using namespace std;
```

Example 10-4. A simple stream manipulator (continued)

```
// make floating-point output look normal
inline ios_base& floatnormal(ios_base& io) {
   io.setf(0, ios_base::floatfield);
   return(io);
}
int main( ) {

   ios_base::fmtflags flags =  // Save old flags
      cout.flags( );

   double pi = 3.14159265;

   cout << "pi = " << scientific    // Scientific mode
        << pi * 1000 << '\n';

   cout << "pi = " << floatnormal
        << pi << '\n';

   cout.flags(flags);
}
```

Discussion

There are two kinds of manipulators: those that accept arguments and those that don't. Manipulators that take no arguments are easy to write. All you have to do is write a function that accepts a stream parameter, does something to it (sets a flag or changes a setting), and returns it. Writing a manipulator that takes one or more arguments is more complicated because you need to create additional classes and functions that operate behind the scenes. Since argument-less manipulators are simple, let's start with those.

After reading Recipe 10.1, you may have realized that there are three floating-point formats and only two manipulators for choosing the format. The default format doesn't have a manipulator; you have to set a flag on the stream to get back to the default format, like this:

```
myiostr.setf(0, ios_base::floatfield);
```

But for consistency and convenience, you may want to add your own manipulator that does the same thing. That's what Example 10-4 does. The floatnormal manipulator sets the appropriate stream flag to output floating-point data in the default format.

The compiler knows what to do with your new function because the standard library already defines an operator for basic_ostream (basic_ostream is the name of the class template that ostream and wostream are instantiations of) like this:

```
basic_ostream<charT,traits>& operator<<
(basic_ostream<charT,traits>& (* pf)(basic_ostream<charT,traits>&))
```

In this example, `pf` is a pointer to a function that takes a `basic_ostream` reference argument and returns a `basic_ostream` reference. This operator just calls your function with the current stream as an argument.

Writing manipulators that take arguments is more complicated. To understand why, consider how a manipulator without arguments works. When you use a manipulator like this:

```
myostream << myManip << "foo";
```

You use it without parenthesis, so that it actually resolves to the address of your manipulator function. `operator<<` is what actually calls the manipulator function, and it passes in the stream so the manipulator can do its work.

For the sake of comparison, say you have a manipulator that takes a numeric argument, so that, ideally, you would use it like this:

```
myostream << myFancyManip(17) << "apple";
```

How is this going to work? If you assume `myFancyManip` is a function that takes an integer argument, then there is a problem: How do you pass the stream to the function without including in the parameters and using it explicitly? Here's what you might do:

```
myostream << myFancyManip(17, myostream) << "apple";
```

But this is ugly and redundant. One of the conveniences of a manipulator is the ability to just add it in line with a bunch of `operator<<`s and to read and use it easily.

The solution is to send the compiler on a detour. Instead of `operator<<` just invoking your manipulator function on the stream, you need to introduce an ephemeral object that returns something `operator<<` can use. Here's how.

First, you need to define a temporary class to do the work. For the sake of simplicity, say you want to write a manipulator called `setWidth` that does the same thing as `setw`. The temporary structure you need to build should look something like this:

```
class WidthSetter {

public:
    WidthSetter (int n) : width_(n) {}
    void operator()(ostream& os) const {os.width(width_);}
private:
    int width_;
};
```

The function of this class is simple. Construct it with an integer argument, and when `operator()` is invoked with a stream argument, set the width on the stream to the value that the object was initialized with. The point of this behavior is that `WidthSetter` will be constructed by one function and used by another. Your manipulator function is what will construct it, and it should look like this:

```
WidthSetter setWidth(int n) {
    return(WidthSetter(n));    // Return the initialized object
}
```

All this does is return a `WidthSetter` object that was initialized with the integer value. This is the manipulator that you will use in line with operator<<s, like this:

```
myostream << setWidth(20) << "banana";
```

But this alone is not enough, because if `setWidth` just returns a `WidthSetter` object, operator<< won't know what to do with it. You have to overload operator<< so it knows how to handle a `WidthSetter`:

```
ostream& operator<<(ostream& os, const WidthSetter& ws) {
    ws(os);        // Pass the stream to the ws object
    return(os); // to do the real work
}
```

That solves the problem, but in a nongeneric way. You don't want to have to write a `WidthSetter`-style class for every argument-accepting manipulator you write (maybe you do, but never mind that), so a better approach is to use templates and function pointers to make a nice, generic infrastructure on which you can base any number of manipulators. Example 10-5 provides the `ManipInfra` class and a version of operator<< that uses template arguments to deal with the different kinds of characters a stream may handle and the different kinds of arguments a stream manipulator might use.

Example 10-5. Manipulator infrastructure

```
#include <iostream>
#include <string>

using namespace std;

// ManipInfra is a small, intermediary class that serves as a utility
// for custom manipulators with arguments. Call its constructor with a
// function pointer and a value from your main manipulator function.
// The function pointer should be a helper function that does the
// actual work. See examples below.
template<typename T, typename C>
class ManipInfra {

public:
    ManipInfra (basic_ostream<C>& (*pFun)
                (basic_ostream<C>&, T), T val)
        : manipFun_(pFun), val_(val) {}
    void operator()(basic_ostream<C>& os) const
        {manipFun_(os, val_);}  // Invoke the function pointer with the
private:                        // stream and value
    T val_;
```

Example 10-5. Manipulator infrastructure (continued)

```cpp
    basic_ostream<C>& (*manipFun_)
        (basic_ostream<C>&, T);
};

template<typename T, typename C>
basic_ostream<C>& operator<<(basic_ostream<C>& os,
                             const ManipInfra<T, C>& manip) {
    manip(os);
    return(os);
}

// Helper function that is ultimately called by the ManipInfra class
ostream& setTheWidth(ostream& os, int n) {
    os.width(n);
    return(os);
}

// Manipulator function itself.  This is what is used by client
// code
ManipInfra<int, char> setWidth(int n) {
    return(ManipInfra<int, char>(setTheWidth, n));
}

// Another helper that takes a char argument
ostream& setTheFillChar(ostream& os, char c) {
    os.fill(c);
    return(os);
}

ManipInfra<char, char> setFill(char c) {
    return(ManipInfra<char, char>(setTheFillChar, c));
}

int main() {

  cout << setFill('-')
       << setWidth(10) << right << "Proust\n";
}
```

If the sequence of events is still hazy, I suggest running Example 10-5 in the debugger. Once you see it in action, it will make perfect sense.

10.4   Making a Class Writable to a Stream

Problem

You have to write a class to an output stream, either for human readability or persistent storage, i.e., serialization.

Solution

Overload operator<< to write the appropriate data members to the stream.
Example 10-6 shows how.

Example 10-6. Writing objects to a stream

```cpp
#include <iostream>
#include <string>

using namespace std;

class Employer {
    friend ostream& operator<<              // This has to be a friend
        (ostream& out, const Employer& empr); // so it can access non-
public:                                      // public members
    Employer() {}
    ~Employer() {}

    void setName(const string& name) {name_ = name;}
private:
    string name_;
};

class Employee {
    friend ostream& operator<<
        (ostream& out, const Employee& obj);
public:
    Employee() : empr_(NULL) {}
    ~Employee() {if (empr_) delete empr_;}

    void setFirstName(const string& name) {firstName_ = name;}
    void setLastName(const string& name) {lastName_ = name;}
    void setEmployer(Employer& empr) {empr_ = &empr;}
    const Employer* getEmployer() const {return(empr_);}

private:
    string firstName_;
    string lastName_;
    Employer* empr_;
};

// Allow us to send Employer objects to an ostream...
ostream& operator<<(ostream& out, const Employer& empr) {

    out << empr.name_ << endl;

    return(out);
}

// Allow us to send Employee objects to an ostream...
ostream& operator<<(ostream& out, const Employee& emp) {
```

Example 10-6. Writing objects to a stream (continued)

```
      out << emp.firstName_ << endl;
      out << emp.lastName_ << endl;
      if (emp.empr_)
        out << *emp.empr_ << endl;

      return(out);
}

int main( ) {

      Employee emp;
      string first = "William";
      string last = "Shatner";
      Employer empr;
      string name = "Enterprise";
      empr.setName(name);

      emp.setFirstName(first);
      emp.setLastName(last);
      emp.setEmployer(empr);

      cout << emp;   // Write to the stream
}
```

Discussion

The first thing you need to do is declare operator<< as a friend of the class you want to write to a stream. You should use operator<< instead of a member function like writeToStream(ostream& os) because the left-shift operator is the convention for writing everything else in the standard library to a stream. You need to declare it as a friend because, in most cases, you want to write private members to the stream, and non-friend functions can't access them.

After that, define the version of operator<< that operates on an ostream or wostream (defined in <ostream>) and your class that you have already declared as a friend. This is where you have to decide which data members should be written to the stream. Typically, you will want to write all data members to the stream, as I did in Example 10-6:

```
      out << emp.firstName_ << endl;
      out << emp.lastName_ << endl;
```

In Example 10-6, I wrote the object pointed to by empr_ by invoking operator<< on it:

```
      if (emp.empr_)
          out << *emp.empr_ << endl;
```

I can do this because empr_ points to an object of the Employer class, and, like Employee, I have defined operator<< for it.

When you are done writing your class's members to the stream, your operator<<
must return the stream it was passed. You need to do this whenever you overload
operator<<, so it can be used in succession, like this:

```
cout << "Here's my object: " << myObj << '\n';
```

The approach I give is simple, and when you want to be able to write a class to an output stream for human consumption, it will work just fine, but that's only part of the
story. If you are writing an object to a stream, it's usually for one of two reasons. Either
that stream goes somewhere that will be read by a person (cout, console window, a log
file, etc.), or the stream is a temporary or persistent storage medium (a stringstream, a
network connection, a file, etc.), and you plan on reassembling the object from that
stream in the future. If you need to recreate the object from a stream (the subject of
Recipe 10.5), you need to think carefully about your class relationships.

Implementing serialization for anything other than trivial classes is hard work. If
your class references (via pointer or reference) other classes—as most nontrivial
classes do—you have to accommodate the potential for circular references in a
meaningful way when writing out objects, and you have to reconstruct references
correctly when reading them in. If you have to build something from scratch, then
you'll have to handle these design considerations, but if you can use an external
library, you should try the Boost Serialization library, which provides a framework
for serializing objects in a portable way.

See Also

Recipe 10.5

10.5   Making a Class Readable from a Stream

Problem

You have written an object of some class to a stream, and now you need to read that
data from the stream and use it to initialize an object of the same class.

Solution

Use operator>> to read data from the stream into your class to populate its data
members, which is simply the reverse of what Example 10-6 does. See Example 10-7
for an implementation.

Example 10-7. Reading data into an object from a stream

```
#include <iostream>
#include <istream>
#include <fstream>
#include <string>
```

Example 10-7. Reading data into an object from a stream (continued)

```
using namespace std;

class Employee {
    friend ostream& operator<<           // These have to be friends
        (ostream& out, const Employee& emp); // so they can access
    friend istream& operator>>           // nonpublic members
        (istream& in, Employee& emp);

public:
    Employee( ) {}
   ~Employee( ) {}

    void setFirstName(const string& name) {firstName_ = name;}
    void setLastName(const string& name) {lastName_ = name;}

private:
    string firstName_;
    string lastName_;
};

// Send an Employee object to an ostream...
ostream& operator<<(ostream& out, const Employee& emp) {

    out << emp.firstName_ << endl;
    out << emp.lastName_ << endl;

    return(out);
}

// Read an Employee object from a stream
istream& operator>>(istream& in, Employee& emp) {

    in >> emp.firstName_;
    in >> emp.lastName_;

    return(in);
}

int main( ) {

    Employee emp;
    string first = "William";
    string last = "Shatner";

    emp.setFirstName(first);
    emp.setLastName(last);

    ofstream out("tmp\\emp.txt");

    if (!out) {
        cerr << "Unable to open output file.\n";
        exit(EXIT_FAILURE);
    }
```

Example 10-7. Reading data into an object from a stream (continued)

```
    out << emp;  // Write the Emp to the file
    out.close();

    ifstream in("tmp\\emp.txt");

    if (!in) {
        cerr << "Unable to open input file.\n";
        exit(EXIT_FAILURE);
    }

    Employee emp2;

    in >> emp2;  // Read the file into an empty object
    in.close();

    cout << emp2;
}
```

Discussion

The steps for making a class readable from a stream are nearly identical to, but the opposite of, those for writing an object to a stream. If you have not already read Recipe 10.4, you should do so for Example 10-7 to make sense.

First, you have to declare an operator>> as a friend of your target class, but, in this case, you want it to use an istream instead of an ostream. Then define operator>> (instead of operator<<) to read values from the stream directly into each of your class's member variables. When you are done reading in data, return the input stream.

See Also

Recipe 10.4

10.6 Getting Information About a File

Problem

You want information about a file, such as its size, device, last modification time, etc.

Solution

Use the C system call stat in <sys/stat.h>. See Example 10-8 for a typical use of stat that prints out a few file attributes.

Example 10-8. Obtaining file information

```
#include <iostream>
#include <ctime>
```

Example 10-8. Obtaining file information (continued)

```cpp
#include <sys/types.h>
#include <sys/stat.h>
#include <cerrno>
#include <cstring>

int main(int argc, char** argv )
{
   struct stat fileInfo;

   if (argc < 2) {
      std::cout << "Usage: fileinfo <file name>\n";
      return(EXIT_FAILURE);
   }

   if (stat(argv[1], &fileInfo) != 0) {  // Use stat() to get the info
      std::cerr << "Error: " << strerror(errno) << '\n';
      return(EXIT_FAILURE);
   }

   std::cout << "Type:         : ";
   if ((fileInfo.st_mode & S_IFMT) == S_IFDIR) { // From sys/types.h
      std::cout << "Directory\n";
   } else {
      std::cout << "File\n";
   }

   std::cout << "Size          : " <<
      fileInfo.st_size << '\n';                  // Size in bytes
   std::cout << "Device        : " <<
      (char)(fileInfo.st_dev + 'A') << '\n';  // Device number
   std::cout << "Created       : " <<
      std::ctime(&fileInfo.st_ctime);          // Creation time
   std::cout << "Modified      : " <<
      std::ctime(&fileInfo.st_mtime);          // Last mod time
}
```

Discussion

The C++ standard library supports manipulation of file *content* with streams, but it has no built-in support for reading or altering the metadata the OS maintains about a file, such as its size, ownership, permissions, various timestamps, and other information. However, standard C contains a number of standard system call libraries that you can use to get this kind of information about a file, and that's what Example 10-8 uses.

There are two parts to obtaining file information. First, there is a struct named stat that contains members that hold data about a file, and second there is a system call (function) of the same name, which gets information about whatever file you specify and populates a stat struct with it. A *system call* is a function that provides some service from the OS. A number of system calls are part of Standard C, and many of them are standardized across the different versions of Unix. The stat struct looks like this (from Kernigan and Richie's *The C Programming Language* [Prentice Hall]):

```
struct stat {
    dev_t   st_dev;    /* device of inode */
    ino_t   st_ino;    /* inode number */
    short   st_mode;   /* mode bits */
    short   st_nlink;  /* number of links to file */
    short   st_uid;    /* owner's user id */
    short   st_gid;    /* owner's group id */
    dev_t   st_rdev;   /* for special files */
    off_t   st_size;   /* file size in characters */
    time_t  st_atime;  /* time last accessed */
    time_t  st_mtime;  /* time last modified */
    time_t  st_ctime;  /* time inode last changed */
};
```

The meaning of each of stat's members depends on the OS. For example, st_uid and st_gid mean nothing on Windows systems; whereas on Unix systems, they actually contain the user and group ids of the file's owner. Take a look at your OS documentation to see which values are supported and how to interpret them.

Example 10-8 shows how to display some of the portable members of stat. st_mode contains a bit mask describing the type of file. You can use it to determine if the file is a directory or not. st_size is the file size in bytes. The three time_t members are timestamps of the access, modification, and creation times of the files.

The remaining members contain operating-system specific information. Consider st_dev: on Windows systems, it contains the device number (drive) as an offset from ASCII letter A (which is why I add an 'A' to it in the example—this gives you the drive letter). But that won't give you the same results on Unix; pass the value returned to the ustat system call to obtain the filesystem name.

If you need more information about a file, the best thing to do is to do some investigating in your OS's documentation. The standard C system calls are Unix-centric, so they are usually more useful on Unix systems (and have a number of other system calls that can be used in conjunction with them). If you are not using Unix, chances are there are proprietary libraries that ship with your OS's development environment that provide more detailed information.

10.7 Copying a File

Problem

You need to copy one file to another in a portable manner, i.e., without using OS-specific APIs.

Solution

Use C++ file streams in `<fstream>` to copy data from one stream to another. Example 10-9 gives an example of a buffered stream copy.

Example 10-9. Copying a file

```
#include <iostream>
#include <fstream>

const static int BUF_SIZE = 4096;

using std::ios_base;

int main(int argc, char** argv) {

    std::ifstream in(argv[1],
        ios_base::in | ios_base::binary);  // Use binary mode so we can
    std::ofstream out(argv[2],             // handle all kinds of file
        ios_base::out | ios_base::binary); // content.

    // Make sure the streams opened okay...

    char buf[BUF_SIZE];

    do {
        in.read(&buf[0], BUF_SIZE);       // Read at most n bytes into
        out.write(&buf[0], in.gcount());  // buf, then write the buf to
    } while (in.gcount() > 0);            // the output.

    // Check streams for problems...

    in.close();
    out.close();
}
```

Discussion

Copying a file may appear to be a simple matter of reading from one stream and writing to another. But the C++ streams library is large, and there are a number of different ways to do the reading and the writing, so you should know a little about the library to avoid costly performance mistakes.

Example 10-9 runs fast because it buffers input and output. The read and write functions operate on entire buffers at a time—instead of a character-at-a-time copy loop—by reading from the input stream to the buffer and writing from the buffer to the output stream in chunks. They also do not do any kind of formatting on the data like the left- and right-shift operators, which keeps things fast. Additionally, since the streams are in binary mode, EOF characters can be read and written without incident. Depending on your hardware, OS, and so on, you will get different results for different buffer sizes. Experiment to find the best parameters for your system.

But there's more to it than this. All C++ streams already buffer data when reading or writing, so Example 10-9 is actually doing *double* buffering. The input stream has its own internal stream buffer that holds characters that have been read from the source but not extracted with read, operator<<, getc, or any other member functions, and the output stream has a buffer that holds output that has been written to the stream but not the destination (in the case of an ofstream, it's a file but it could be a string, a network connection, or who-knows-what). Therefore, the best thing to do is to let the buffers exchange data directly. You can do this with operator<<, which behaves differently than usual when used with stream buffers. For example, instead of the do/while loop in Example 10-9, use this:

```
out << in.rdbuf();
```

Don't place this statement in the body of the loop, replace the loop with this single line. It looks a little odd, since, typically, operator<< says, "take the righthand side and send it to the lefthand stream," but bear with me and it will make sense. rdbuf returns the buffer from the input stream, and the implementation of operator<< that takes a stream buffer as a righthand argument reads a character at a time from the input buffer and writes it to the output buffer. When the input buffer is emptied, it knows it has to refill itself with data from the real source, and operator<< is none the wiser.

Example 10-9 shows how to copy the *contents* of a file yourself, but your OS is responsible for managing the filesystem, which encompasses copying them, so why not let the OS do the work? In most cases, the answer to this question is that a direct call to the OS API is, of course, not portable. Boost's Filesystem library masks a lot of the OS-specific APIs for you by providing the function copy_file, which makes different OS calls based on the platform it was compiled for. Example 10-10 contains a short program that copies a file from one location to another.

Example 10-10. Copying a file with Boost

```
#include <iostream>
#include <string>
#include <boost/filesystem/operations.hpp>
#include <boost/filesystem/fstream.hpp>

using namespace std;
using namespace boost::filesystem;

int main(int argc, char** argv) {

    // Parameter checking...

    try {
        // Turn the args into absolute paths using native formatting
        path src = complete(path(argv[1], native));
        path dst = complete(path(argv[2], native));
```

Example 10-10. Copying a file with Boost (continued)

```
      copy_file(src, dst);
   }
   catch (exception& e) {
      cerr << e.what() << endl;
   }

   return(EXIT_SUCCESS);
}
```

This a small program, but there are a few key parts that need explaining because other recipes in this chapter use the Boost Filesystem library. To begin with, the central component of the Boost Filesystem library is the path class, which represents, in an OS-independent way, a path to a file or directory. You can create a path using either a portable or OS-native string. In Example 10-10, I create a path out of the program arguments (that I then pass to complete, which I discuss in a moment):

```
      path src = complete(path(argv[1], native));
```

The first argument is the text of the path, e.g., "tmp\\foo.txt" and the second argument is the name of a function that accepts a string argument and returns a boolean that validates that a path is valid according to certain rules. The native function means to use the OS's native format for validation. I used it in Example 10-10 because the arguments are passed in from the command line where they are presumably typed in by a human user, who will probably use the native OS format when specifying files. There are a number of functions that you can use to validate file and directory names, all of which are self-explanatory: portable_posix_name, windows_name, portable_name, portable_directory_name, portable_file_name, and no_check. See the documentation for specifics.

complete composes an absolute path using the current working directory and the relative path you pass it. Thus, I can do this to create an absolute path to the source file:

```
      path src = complete(path("tmp\\foo.txt", native));
```

complete handles the case where the first argument is already an absolute filename by using the value given rather than trying to merge it with the current working directory. In other words, the following code invoked from a current directory of "c:\myprograms" ignores the current working directory since the path given is already complete:

```
      path src = complete(path("c:\\windows\\garbage.txt", native));
```

Many of the Boost Filesystem functions will throw an exception if a precondition is not met. The documentation has all the details, but a good example is with the copy_file function itself. A file must exist before it can be copied, so if the source file does not exist, the operation cannot succeed; therefore, copy_file will throw an exception.

Catch the exception as I did in Example 10-10 and you will get an error message that explains the problem.

10.8   Deleting or Renaming a File

Problem

You have to remove or rename a file, and you want to do it portably, i.e., without using OS-specific APIs.

Solution

The Standard C functions remove and rename, in <cstdio>, will do this. See Example 10-11 for a brief demonstration of them.

Example 10-11. Removing a file

```
#include <iostream>
#include <cstdio>
#include <cerrno>

using namespace std;

int main(int argc, char** argv) {

   if (argc != 2) {
      cerr << "You must supply a file name to remove." << endl;
      return(EXIT_FAILURE);
   }

   if (remove(argv[1]) == -1) {  // remove() returns -1 on error
      cerr << "Error: " << strerror(errno) << endl;
      return(EXIT_FAILURE);
   }
   else {
      cout << "File '" << argv[1] << "' removed." << endl;
   }
}
```

Discussion

These system calls are easy to use: just call one or the other with the filename you want to delete or rename. If something goes wrong, the return value is non-zero and errno is set to the appropriate error number. You can use strerror or perror (both declared in <cstdio>) to print out the implementation-defined error message.

To rename a file, you can replace the remove call in Example 10-11 with the following code:

```
if (rename(argv[1], argv[2])) {
    cerr << "Error: " << strerror(errno) << endl;
    return(EXIT_FAILURE);
}
```

The Boost Filesystem library also provides the ability to remove or rename a file. Example 10-12 shows a short program for removing a file (or directory, but see the discussion after the example).

Example 10-12. Removing a file with Boost

```
#include <iostream>
#include <string>
#include <boost/filesystem/operations.hpp>
#include <boost/filesystem/fstream.hpp>

using namespace std;
using namespace boost::filesystem;

int main(int argc, char** argv) {

    // Do parameter checking...

    try {
        path p = complete(path(argv[1], native));
        remove(p);
    }
    catch (exception& e) {
        cerr << e.what() << endl;
    }
    return(EXIT_SUCCESS);
}
```

The important part of Example 10-12 is the remove function. Call it with a valid path argument that refers to a file or an empty directory, and it will be removed. For an explanation of the path class and complete function, both of which are part of the Boost Filesystem library, take a look at the discussion in Recipe 10.7. See Recipe 10.11 for an example of how to remove a directory and all the files it contains.

Renaming a file or directory is similar. Replace the code in the try block in Example 10-12 with this code:

```
path src = complete(path(argv[1], native));
path dst = complete(path(argv[2], native));
rename(src, dst);
```

This will rename src to dst, so long as each is a valid path. src and dst don't have to have a common base directory, and in that respect, the rename function logically moves a file or directory to a new base directory, so long as dst exists.

See Also

Recipe 10.7

10.9   Creating a Temporary Filename and File

Problem

You have to store some stuff on disk temporarily, and you don't want to have to write a routine that generates a unique name yourself.

Solution

Use either the tmpfile or tmpnam functions, declared in <cstdio>. tmpfile returns a FILE* that is already opened for writing, and tmpnam generates a unique filename that you can open yourself. Example 10-13 shows how to use tmpfile.

Example 10-13. Creating a temporary file

```
#include <iostream>
#include <cstdio>

using namespace std;

int main( ) {

   FILE* pf = NULL;
   char buf[256];

   pf = tmpfile( );  // Create and open a temp file

   if (pf) {
      fputs("This is a temp file", pf);  // Write some data to it
   }

   fseek(pf, 5, SEEK_SET);  // Reset the file position
   fgets(buf, 255, pf);     // Read a string from it
   fclose(pf);

   cout << buf << '\n';
}
```

Discussion

There are two ways to create a temporary file; Example 10-13 shows the first way. The function tmpfile is declared in <cstdio>, takes no parameters, and returns a FILE* if successful, NULL if not. The FILE* is the same type you can use with the C input/output functions fread, fwrite, fgets, fputs, etc. tmpfile opens the temporary file in "wb+" mode, which means you can write to it or read from it in binary mode (i.e., the characters are not interpreted as they are read). When your program terminates normally, the temporary file created by tmpfile is automatically deleted.

This may or may not work for you depending on your requirements. You will notice that tmpfile does not give you a filename—how do you pass the file to another program? You can't; you'll have to use a similar function instead: tmpnam.

tmpnam doesn't actually create a temporary file, it just creates a unique file *name* that you can use to go open a file using that name yourself. tmpnam takes a single char* parameter and returns a char*. You can pass in a pointer to a char buffer (that has to be at least as big as the macro L_tmpnam, also defined in <cstdio>), where tmpnam will copy the temporary name, and it will return a pointer to the same buffer. If you pass in NULL, tmpfile will return a pointer to a static buffer that contains the filename, which means that subsequent calls to tmpnam will overwrite it. (See Example 10-14.)

Example 10-14. Creating a temporary filename

```
#include <iostream>
#include <fstream>
#include <cstdio>
#include <string>

using namespace std;

int main( ) {

    char* pFileName = NULL;

    pFileName = tmpnam(NULL);
    // Right here is where another program may get the same temp
    // filename.

    if (!pFileName) {
        cerr << "Couldn't create temp file name.\n";
        return(EXIT_FAILURE);
    }

    cout << "The temp file name is: " << pFileName << '\n';

    ofstream of(pFileName);

    if (of) {
        of << "Here is some temp data.";
        of.close( );
    }

    ifstream ifs(pFileName);
    string s;

    if (ifs) {
        ifs >> s;
```

Example 10-14. Creating a temporary filename (continued)

```
    cout << "Just read in \"" << s << "\"\n";
    ifs.close();
  }
}
```

But there is something important you should know about tmpnam. It has a race condition whereby more than one process may generate the same filename if one calls tmpname and the other calls tmpname before the first process opens the file. This is bad for two reasons. First, a malicious program can do this to intercept the data in a temporary file, and second, an unsuspecting program can get the same filename and simply corrupt or delete data.

10.10 Creating a Directory

Problem

You have to create a directory, and you want to do it portably, i.e., without using OS-specific APIs.

Solution

On most platforms, you will be able to use the mkdir system call that is shipped with most compilers as part of the C headers. It takes on different forms in different OSs, but regardless, you can use it to create a new directory. There is no standard C++, portable way to create a directory. Check out Example 10-15 to see how.

Example 10-15. Creating a directory

```
#include <iostream>
#include <direct.h>
#include <cstring>
#include <errno.h>
#include <cstdlib>

using namespace std;

int main(int argc, char** argv) {

   if (argc < 2) {
      cerr << "Usage: " << argv[0] << " [new dir name]\n";
      return(EXIT_FAILURE);
   }

   if (mkdir(argv[1]) == -1) {  // Create the directory
      cerr << "Error: " << strerror(errno);
      return(EXIT_FAILURE);
   }
}
```

Discussion

The system call for creating directories differs somewhat from one OS to another, but don't let that stop you from using it anyway. Variations of mkdir are supported on most systems, so creating a directory is just a matter of knowing which header to include and what the function's signature looks like.

Example 10-15 works on Windows, but not Unix. On Windows, mkdir is declared in <direct.h>. It takes one parameter (the directory name), returns -1 if there is an error, and sets errno to the corresponding error number. You can get the implementation-defined error text by calling strerror or perror.

On Unix, mkdir is declared in <sys/stat.h>, and its signature is slightly different. The error semantics are just like Windows, but there is a second parameter that specifies the permissions to apply to the new directory. Instead, you must specify the permissions using the traditional chmod format (see the chmod man page for specifics), e.g., 0777 means owner, group, and others all have read, write, and execute permissions. Thus, you might call it like this on Unix:

```
#include <iostream>
#include <sys/types.h>
#include <sys/stat.h>
#include <cstring>
#include <errno.h>
#include <cstdlib>

using namespace std;

int main(int argc, char** argv) {

    if (argc < 2) {
        cerr << "Usage: " << argv[0] << " [new dir name]\n";
        return(EXIT_FAILURE);
    }

    if (mkdir(argv[1], 0777) == -1) {  // Create the directory
        cerr << "Error: " << strerror(errno);
        return(EXIT_FAILURE);
    }
}
```

If you want portability, and don't want to write all the #ifdefs yourself, you should consider using the Boost Filesystem library. You can create a directory using the create_directory function, as shown in Example 10-16, which contains a short program that creates a directory.

Example 10-16. Creating a directory with Boost

```
#include <iostream>
#include <string>
#include <cstdlib>
```

Example 10-16. Creating a directory with Boost (continued)

```
#include <boost/filesystem/operations.hpp>
#include <boost/filesystem/fstream.hpp>

using namespace std;
using namespace boost::filesystem;

int main(int argc, char** argv) {

   // Parameter checking...

   try {
      path p = complete(path(argv[1], native));
      create_directory(p);
   }
   catch (exception& e) {
      cerr << e.what() << endl;
   }

   return(EXIT_SUCCESS);
}
```

The create_directory function creates a directory identified by the path argument you give it. If that directory already exists, a filesystem_error exception is thrown (derived from the standard exception class). For an explanation of the path class and complete function, both of which are part of the Boost Filesystem library, take a look at the discussion in Recipe 10.7. See Recipe 10.11 for an example of how to remove a directory and all the files it contains. If, on the other hand, portability is not a concern, consult your OS's proprietary filesystem API, which will most likely offer more flexibility.

See Also

Recipe 10.12

10.11 Removing a Directory

Problem

You need to remove a directory, and you want to do it portably, i.e., without using OS-specific APIs.

Solution

On most platforms, you will be able to use the rmdir system call that is shipped with most compilers as part of the C headers. There is no standard C++, portable way to remove a directory. rmdir takes on different forms in different OSs, but regardless, you can use it to remove a directory. See Example 10-17 for a short program that removes a directory.

Example 10-17. Removing a directory

```
#include <iostream>
#include <direct.h>

using namespace std;

int main(int argc, char** argv) {

   if (argc < 2) {
      cerr << "Usage: " << argv[0] << " [dir name]" << endl;
      return(EXIT_FAILURE);
   }

   if (rmdir(argv[1]) == -1) {  // Remove the directory
      cerr << "Error: " << strerror(errno) << endl;;
      return(EXIT_FAILURE);
   }
}
```

Discussion

The signature of `rmdir` is the same on most OSs, but the header file where it is declared is not. On Windows, it is declared in `<direct.h>`, and on Unix, it is declared in `<unistd.h>`. It takes one parameter (the directory name), returns -1 if there is an error, and sets errno to the corresponding error number. You can get the implementation-defined error text by calling `strerror` or `perror`.

If the target directory is not empty `rmdir` will return an error. To list the contents of a directory, to enumerate them for deletion, etc., see Recipe 10.12.

If you want portability, and don't want to write a bunch of `#ifdefs` around the various OS-specific directory functions, you should consider using the Boost Filesystem library. The Boost Filesystem library uses the concept of a path to refer to a directory or file, and paths can be removed with a single function, `remove`.

The function `removeRecurse` in Example 10-18 recursively removes a directory and all of its contents. The most important part is the `remove` function (which is `boost::filesystem::remove`, not a standard library function). It takes a `path` argument, and removes it if it is a file or an *empty* directory, but it doesn't remove a directory that contains files.

Example 10-18. Removing a directory with Boost

```
#include <iostream>
#include <string>
#include <cstdlib>
#include <boost/filesystem/operations.hpp>
#include <boost/filesystem/fstream.hpp>

using namespace std;
using namespace boost::filesystem;

void removeRecurse(const path& p) {
```

Example 10-18. Removing a directory with Boost (continued)

```
    // First, remove the contents of the directory
    directory_iterator end;
    for (directory_iterator it(p);
         it != end; ++it) {

        if (is_directory(*it)) {
            removeRecurse(*it);
        }
        else {
            remove(*it);
        }
    }
    // Then, remove the directory itself
    remove(p);
}

int main(int argc, char** argv) {

    if (argc != 2) {
        cerr << "Usage: " << argv[0] << " [dir name]\n";
        return(EXIT_FAILURE);
    }

    path thePath = system_complete(path(argv[1], native));

    if (!exists(thePath)) {
        cerr << "Error: the directory " << thePath.string()
             << " does not exist.\n";
        return(EXIT_FAILURE);
    }

    try {
        removeRecurse(thePath);
    }
    catch (exception& e) {
        cerr << e.what() << endl;
        return(EXIT_FAILURE);
    }
    return(EXIT_SUCCESS);
}
```

The code that iterates through the directory contents requires some explanation, and that is the subject of Recipe 10.12.

The Boost Filesystem library is handy, but remember that Boost is not a formal standard and therefore is not guaranteed to run everywhere. If you examine the source code for the Boost Filesystem library, you will notice that essentially, it compiles native OS calls based on the target platform. If portability is not a concern, consult your OS's proprietary filesystem API, which will most likely offer more flexibility.

See Also

Recipe 10.12

10.12 Reading the Contents of a Directory

Problem

You need to read the contents of a directory, most likely to do something to each file or subdirectory that's in it.

Solution

To write something portable, use the Boost Filesystem library's classes and functions. It provides a number of handy utilities for manipulating files, such as a portable path representation, directory iterators, and numerous functions for renaming, deleting, and copying files, and so on. Example 10-19 demonstrates how to use a few of these facilities.

Example 10-19. Reading a directory

```
#include <iostream>
#include <boost/filesystem/operations.hpp>
#include <boost/filesystem/fstream.hpp>

using namespace boost::filesystem;

int main(int argc, char** argv) {

   if (argc < 2) {
      std::cerr << "Usage: " << argv[0] << " [dir name]\n";
      return(EXIT_FAILURE);
   }

   path fullPath =     // Create the full, absolute path name
      system_complete(path(argv[1], native));

   if (!exists(fullPath)) {
      std::cerr << "Error: the directory " << fullPath.string()
                << " does not exist.\n";
      return(EXIT_FAILURE);
   }

   if (!is_directory(fullPath)) {
      std::cout << fullPath.string() << " is not a directory!\n";
      return(EXIT_SUCCESS);
   }

   directory_iterator end;
   for (directory_iterator it(fullPath);
        it != end; ++it) {             // Iterate through each
                                       // element in the dir,
      std::cout << it->leaf();         // almost as you would
      if (is_directory(*it))           // an STL container
         std::cout << " (dir)";
```

Example 10-19. Reading a directory (continued)

```
        std::cout << '\n';
    }

    return(EXIT_SUCCESS);
}
```

Discussion

Like creating or deleting directories (see Recipes 10.10 and 10.11), there is no standard, portable way to read the contents of a directory. To make your C++ life easier, the Filesystem library in the Boost project provides a set of portable routines for operating on files and directories. It also provides many more—see the other recipes in this chapter or the Boost Filesystem web page at *www.boost.com* for more information.

Example 10-19 is a simple directory listing program (like ls on Unix or dir on MS-DOS). First, it builds an absolute pathname out of the argument passed to the program, like this:

```
    path fullPath = complete(path(argv[1], native));
```

The data type of a path is called, appropriately, path. This is the type that the filesystem routines operate on, and is easily convertible to a string by calling path::string. Once the path has been assembled, the program checks its existence (with exists), then checks to see if it is a directory with another utility function, is_directory. If it is, then everything is in good shape and it can proceed to the real work of listing the directory contents.

There is a class called directory_iterator in filesystem that uses standard iterator semantics, like the standard containers, to allow you to use an iterator like you would a pointer to a directory element. Unlike standard containers, however, there is no end member function you can call on a directory that represents one-past-the-last-element (i.e., vector<T>::end). Instead, if you create a directory_iterator with the default constructor, it represents an end marker that you can use for comparison to determine when you are done. So do this:

```
    directory_iterator end;
```

and then you can create an iterator from your path, and compare it to end, like this:

```
    for (directory_iterator it(fullPath);
         it != end; ++it) {
        // do whatever you want to *it
        std::cout << it->leaf();
    }
```

The leaf member function returns a string representing the element referred to by a path, and not the full path itself, which is what you get if you call the string member function.

If you have to write something that is portable, but for some reason you cannot use Boost, take a look at the Boost code itself. It contains #ifdefs that deal with (for the most part) Windows versus Posix OS interface environments and path particulars, such as drive letters versus device names.

See Also

Recipes 10.10 and 10.11

10.13 Extracting a File Extension from a String

Problem

Given a filename or a complete path, you need to retrieve the file extension, which is the part of a filename that follows the last period. For example, in the filenames *src.cpp*, *Window.class*, and *Resume.doc*, the file extensions are *.cpp*, *.class*, and *.doc*.

Solution

Convert the file and/or pathname to a string, use the rfind member function to locate the last period, and return everything after that. Example 10-20 shows how to do this.

Example 10-20. Getting a file extension from a filename

```
#include <iostream>
#include <string>

using std::string;

string getFileExt(const string& s) {

   size_t i = s.rfind('.', s.length());
   if (i != string::npos) {
      return(s.substr(i+1, s.length() - i));
   }

   return("");
}

int main(int argc, char** argv) {

   string path = argv[1];

   std::cout << "The extension is \"" << getFileExt(path) << "\"\n";
}
```

Discussion

To get an extension from a filename, you just need to find out where the last dot "." is and take everything to the right of that. The standard string class, defined in <string> contains functions for doing both of these things: rfind and substr.

rfind will search *backward* for whatever you sent it (a char in this case) as the first argument, starting at the index specified by the second argument, and return the index where it was found. If the pattern wasn't found, rfind will return string::npos. substr also takes two arguments. The first is the index of the first element to copy, and the second is the number of characters to copy.

The standard string class contains a number of member functions for finding things. See Recipe 4.9 for a longer discussion of string searching.

See Also

Recipes 4.9 and 10.12

10.14 Extracting a Filename from a Full Path

Problem

You have the full path of a filename, e.g., *d:\apps\src\foo.c*, and you need to get the filename, *foo.c*.

Solution

Employ the same technique as the previous recipe and use rfind and substr to find and get what you want from the full pathname. Example 10-21 shows how.

Example 10-21. Extracting a filename from a path

```
#include <iostream>
#include <string>

using std::string;

string getFileName(const string& s) {

   char sep = '/';

#ifdef _WIN32
   sep = '\\';
#endif

   size_t i = s.rfind(sep, s.length());
   if (i != string::npos) {
      return(s.substr(i+1, s.length() - i));
   }
```

Example 10-21. Extracting a filename from a path (continued)

```
    return("");
}

int main(int argc, char** argv) {

    string path = argv[1];

    std::cout << "The file name is \"" << getFileName(path) << "\"\n";
}
```

Discussion

See the previous recipe for details on how `rfind` and `substr` work. The only thing noteworthy about Example 10-21 is that, as you probably are already aware, Windows has a path separator that is a backslash instead of a forward-slash, so I added an `#ifdef` to conditionally set the path separator.

The `path` class in the Boost Filesystem library makes getting the last part of a full pathname—which may be a file or directory name—easy with the `path::leaf` member function. Example 10-22 shows a simple program that uses it to print out whether a path refers to a file or directory.

Example 10-22. Getting a filename from a path

```
#include <iostream>
#include <cstdlib>
#include <boost/filesystem/operations.hpp>

using namespace std;
using namespace boost::filesystem;

int main(int argc, char** argv) {

    // Parameter checking...

    try {
        path p = complete(path(argv[1], native));
        cout << p.leaf() << " is a "
            << (is_directory(p) ? "directory" : "file") << endl;
    }
    catch (exception& e) {
        cerr << e.what() << endl;
    }

    return(EXIT_SUCCESS);
}
```

See the discussion in Recipe 10.7 for more information about the path class.

See Also

Recipe 10.15

10.15 Extracting a Path from a Full Path and Filename

Problem

You have the full path of a filename, e.g., `d:\apps\src\foo.c`, and you need to get the pathname, `d:\apps\src`.

Solution

Use the same technique as the previous two recipes by invoking `rfind` and `substr` to find and get what you want from the full pathname. See Example 10-23 for a short sample program.

Example 10-23. Get the path from a full path and filename

```
#include <iostream>
#include <string>

using std::string;

string getPathName(const string& s) {

   char sep = '/';

#ifdef _WIN32
   sep = '\\';
#endif

   size_t i = s.rfind(sep, s.length());
   if (i != string::npos) {
      return(s.substr(0, i));
   }

   return("");
}

int main(int argc, char** argv) {

   string path = argv[1];

   std::cout << "The path name is \"" << getPathName(path) << "\"\n";
}
```

Discussion

Example 10-23 is trivial, especially if you've already looked at the previous few recipes, so there is no more to explain. However, as with many of the other recipes, the Boost Filesystem library provides a way to extract everything but the last part of the filename with its branch_path function. Example 10-24 shows how to use it.

Example 10-24. Getting the base path

```cpp
#include <iostream>
#include <cstdlib>
#include <boost/filesystem/operations.hpp>

using namespace std;
using namespace boost::filesystem;

int main(int argc, char** argv) {

   // Parameter checking...

   try {
      path p = complete(path(argv[1], native));
      cout << p.branch_path().string() << endl;
   }
   catch (exception& e) {
      cerr << e.what() << endl;
   }
   return(EXIT_SUCCESS);
}
```

Sample output from Example 10-24 looks like this:

```
D:\src\ccb\c10>bin\GetPathBoost.exe c:\windows\system32\1033
c:/windows/system32
```

See Also

Recipes 10.13 and 10.14

10.16 Replacing a File Extension

Problem

Given a filename, or a path and filename, you want to replace the file's extension. For example, if you are given thesis.tex, you want to convert it to thesis.txt.

Solution

Use string's rfind and replace member functions to find the extension and replace it. Example 10-25 shows you how to do this.

Example 10-25. Replacing a file extension

```
#include <iostream>
#include <string>

using std::string;

void replaceExt(string& s, const string& newExt) {

   string::size_type i = s.rfind('.', s.length( ));

   if (i != string::npos) {
      s.replace(i+1, newExt.length( ), newExt);
   }
}

int main(int argc, char** argv) {

   string path = argv[1];

   replaceExt(path, "foobar");
   std::cout << "The new name is \"" << path << "\"\n";
}
```

Discussion

This solution is similar to the ones in the preceding recipes, but in this case I used replace to replace a portion of the string with a new string. replace has three parameters. The first parameter is the index where the replace should begin, and the second is the number of characters to delete from the destination string. The third parameter is the value that will be used to replace the deleted portion of the string.

See Also

Recipe 4.9

10.17 Combining Two Paths into a Single Path

Problem

You have two paths and you have to combine them into a single path. You may have something like /usr/home/ryan as a first path, and utils/compilers as the second, and wish to get /usr/home/ryan/utils/compilers, without having to worry whether or not the first path ends with a path separator.

Solution

Treat the paths as strings and use the append operator, operator+=, to compose a full path out of partial paths. See Example 10-26.

Example 10-26. Combining paths

```
#include <iostream>
#include <string>

using std::string;

string pathAppend(const string& p1, const string& p2) {

    char sep = '/';
    string tmp = p1;

#ifdef _WIN32
    sep = '\\';
#endif

    if (p1[p1.length()] != sep) { // Need to add a
        tmp += sep;                // path separator
        return(tmp + p2);
    }
    else
        return(p1 + p2);
}

int main(int argc, char** argv) {

    string path = argv[1];

    std::cout << "Appending somedir\\anotherdir is \""
              << pathAppend(path, "somedir\\anotherdir") << "\"\n";
}
```

Discussion

The code in Example 10-26 uses strings that represent paths, but there's no additional checking on the path class for validity and the paths used are only as portable as the values they contain. If, for example, these paths are retrieved from the user, you don't know if they're using the right OS-specific format, or if they contain illegal characters.

For many other recipes in this chapter I have included examples that use the Boost Filesystem library, and when working with paths, this approach has lots of benefits. As I discussed in Recipe 10.7, the Boost Filesystem library contains a path class that is a portable representation of a path to a file or directory. The operations in the Filesystem library mostly work with path objects, and as such, the path class can handle path composition from an absolute base and a relative path. (See Example 10-27.)

Example 10-27. Combining paths with Boost

```
#include <iostream>
#include <string>
#include <cstdlib>
```

Example 10-27. Combining paths with Boost (continued)

```
#include <boost/filesystem/operations.hpp>
#include <boost/filesystem/fstream.hpp>

using namespace std;
using namespace boost::filesystem;

int main(int argc, char** argv) {

    // Parameter checking...

    try {
        // Compose a path from the two args
        path p1 = complete(path(argv[2], native),
                           path(argv[1], native));
        cout << p1.string() << endl;

        // Create a path with a base of the current dir
        path p2 = system_complete(path(argv[2], native));
        cout << p2.string() << endl;
    }
    catch (exception& e) {
        cerr << e.what() << endl;
    }

    return(EXIT_SUCCESS);
}
```

The output of the program in Example 10-27 might look like this:

```
D:\src\ccb\c10>bin\MakePathBoost.exe d:\temp some\other\dir
d:/temp/some/other/dir
D:/src/ccb/c10/some/other/dir
```

or:

```
D:\src\ccb\c10>bin\MakePathBoost.exe d:\temp c:\WINDOWS\system32
c:/WINDOWS/system32
c:/WINDOWS/system32
```

What you can see here is that `complete` and `system_complete` merge paths when possible, or return the absolute path when merging paths makes no sense. For example, in the first output, the first argument given to the program is an absolute directory and the second is a relative directory. `complete` merges them together and produces a single, absolute path. The first argument to `complete` is the relative path, and the second is the absolute path, and if the first argument is already an absolute path, the second argument is ignored. That's why in the second output you can see that the argument "d:\temp" is ignored since the second argument I give is already an absolute path.

`system_complete` only takes a single argument (the relative path in this case) and appends it to the current working directory to produce another absolute path. Again, if you give it a path that is already absolute, it ignores the current working directory and simply returns the absolute path you gave it.

These paths are not reconciled with the filesystem though. You have to explicitly test to see if a path object represents a valid filesystem path. For example, to check if one of these paths exists, you can use the exists function on a path:

```
path p1 = complete(path(argv[2], native),
                    path(argv[1], native));
if (exists(p1)) {
    // ...
```

There are many more functions you can use to get information about a path: is_directory, is_empty, file_size, last_write_time, and so on. See the Boost Filesystem library documentation at *www.boost.org* for more information.

See Also

Recipe 10.7

CHAPTER 11

Science and Mathematics

11.0   Introduction

C++ is a language well suited for scientific and mathematical programming, due to its flexibility, expressivity, and efficiency. One of the biggest advantages of C++ for numerical processing code is that it can help you avoid redundancy.

Historically, numerical code in many programming languages would repeat algorithms over and over for different kinds of numerical types (e.g., short, long, single, double, custom numerical types, etc.). C++ provides a solution to this problem of redundancy through templates. Templates enable you to write algorithms independantly of the data representation, a technique known commonly as generic programming.

C++ is not without its shortcomings with regards to numerical processing code. The biggest drawback with C++—in contrast to specialized mathematical and scientific programming languages—is that the standard library is limited in terms of support of algorithms and data-types relevant to numerical programming. The biggest oversights in the standard library are arguably the lack of matrix types and arbitrary precision integers.

In this chapter, I will provide you with solutions to common numerical programming problems and demonstrate how to use generic programming techniques to write numerical code effectively. Where appropriate, I will recommend widely used open-source libraries with commercially friendly licenses and a proven track record. This chapter introduces the basic techniques of generic programming gradually from recipe to recipe.

Many programmers using C++ still distrust templates and generic programming due to their apparent complexity. When templates were first introduced into the language they were neither well implemented nor well understood by programmers and compiler implementers alike. As a result, many programmers, including yours truly, avoided generic programming in C++ for several years while the technology matured.

Today, generic programming is widely accepted as a powerful and useful programming paradigm, and is supported by the most popular programming languages. Furthermore, C++ compiler technology has improved by leaps and bounds, and modern compilers deal with templates in a much more standardized and efficient manner. As a result, modern C++ is a particularly powerful language for scientific and numerical applications.

11.1 Computing the Number of Elements in a Container

Problem

You want to find the number of elements in a container.

Solution

You can compute the number of elements in a container by using the size member function or the distance function from the <algorithm> header as in Example 11-1.

Example 11-1. Computing the Number of Elements in a Container

```
#include <algorithm>
#include <iostream>
#include <vector>

using namespace std;

int main( ) {
  vector<int> v;
  v.push_back(0);
  v.push_back(1);
  v.push_back(2);
  cout << v.size( ) << endl;
  cout << distance(v.begin( ), v.end( )) << endl;
}
```

The program in Example 11-1 produces the following output:

```
3
3
```

Discussion

The size member function, which returns the number of elements in a standard container, is the best solution in cases where the container object is accessible. I also demonstrated distance in Example 11-1, because when writing generic code it is common to work with only a pair of iterators. When working with iterators, you often don't have access to the type of the container or to its member functions.

The distance function, like most STL algorithms, is actually a template function. Since the type of the template argument can be deduced automatically by the compiler from the function arguments, you don't have to explicitly pass it as a template parameter. You can, of course, write out the template parameter explicitly if you want to, as follows:

```
cout << distance<vector<int>::iterator>(v.begin( ), v.end( )) << endl;
```

The distance function performance depends on the kind of iterator used. It takes constant time if the input iterator is a random-access iterator; otherwise, it operates in linear time. (Iterator concepts are explained in Recipe 7.1.)

See Also

Recipe 15.1

11.2   Finding the Greatest or Least Value in a Container

Problem

You want to find the maximum or minimum value in a container.

Solution

Example 11-2 shows how to find the minimum and maximum elements in a container by using the functions max_element and min_element found in the <algorithm> header. These functions return iterators that point to the first occurence of an element with the largest or smallest value, respectively.

Example 11-2. Finding the minimum or maximum element from a container

```
#include <algorithm>
#include <vector>
#include <iostream>

using namespace std;

int getMaxInt(vector<int>& v) {
  return *max_element(v.begin( ), v.end( ));
}

int getMinInt(vector<int>& v) {
  return *min_element(v.begin( ), v.end( ));
}

int main( ) {
  vector<int> v;
  for (int i=10; i < 20; ++i) v.push_back(i);
```

```
    cout << "min integer = " << getMinInt(v) << endl;
    cout << "max integer = " << getMaxInt(v) << endl;
}
```

The program in Example 11-2 produces the following output:

```
    min integer = 10
    max integer = 19
```

Discussion

You may have noticed the dereferencing of the return value from the calls to min_
element and max_element. This is because these functions return iterators and not
actual values, so the results have to be dereferenced. You may find it a minor incon-
venience to have to dereference the return type, but it avoids unnecssarily copying
the return value. This can be especially significant when the return value has expensive copy semantics (e.g., large strings).

The generic algorithms provided by the standard library are obviously quite useful,
but it is more important for you to be able to write your own generic functions for
getting the minimum and maximum value from a container. For instance, let's say
that you want a single function which returns the minimum and maximum values by
modifying reference parameters instead of returning them in a pair or some other
structure. This is demonstrated in Example 11-3.

Example 11-3. Generic function for returning the minimum and maximum value

```
#include <algorithm>
#include <vector>
#include <iostream>

using namespace std;

template<class Iter_T, class Value_T>
void computeMinAndMax(Iter_T first, Iter_T last, Value_T& min, Value_T& max) {
  min = *min_element(first, last);
  max = *max_element(first, last);
}

int main() {
  vector<int> v;
  for (int i=10; i < 20; ++i) v.push_back(i);
  int min = -1;
  int max = -1;
  computeMinAndMax(v.begin(), v.end(), min, max);
  cout << "min integer = " << min << endl;
  cout << "max integer = " << max << endl;
}
```

In Example 11-3, I have written a `computeMinAndMax` function template which takes two template parameters, one is the type of the iterator and the other is the type of the minimum and maximum values. Because both template parameters are also function parameters, the C++ compiler is able to deduce the two separate types, `Iter_T` and `Value_T`, just as I demonstrated in Recipe 11.1. This saves me from having to specify the template parameters explicitly like:

```
compute_min_max<vector<int>::iterator, int>(...)
```

The `min_element` and `max_element` functions work by using `operator<` to compare the values referenced by the iterators. This means that if an iterator does not reference a type that supports comparison through the less-than operator, a compiler error will result. The `min_element` and `max_element` functions, however, can be used with a user-defined comparison functor, i.e., a function pointer or a function object.

Functors

Many STL algorithms accept user-defined function objects or pointers. Collectively, these are known as *functors*. Sometimes in the literature, the term "function object" is used interchangeably with the term functor, but I've reserved the use of function object for refering specifically to instances of classes or structs that overload `operator()`.

Of the two options, which one should you use? In the majority of cases, a function object is more efficient because most compilers can more easily inline a function object.

Another reason for using a function object is that it can have a state. You can pass values to its constructor, which it stores in its fields for use later on. This gives function objects an expressive equivalency as with the concept of closures found in other programming languages.

Finally, function objects can be defined within another function or class. Function pointers have to be declared in a namespace scope.

The specific kind of functor needed by `min_element` and `max_element` is one that takes two values of the type referenced by the iterator and returns a `boolean` value if one is less than the other. A functor which returns a `boolean` value is known as a predicate. Consider for instance the case of finding the greatest element of a set of user defined type in Example 11-4.

Example 11-4. Finding the maximum element for user-defined types

```
#include <algorithm>
#include <vector>
#include <iostream>

using namespace std;
```

Example 11-4. Finding the maximum element for user-defined types (continued)

```cpp
struct ChessPlayer {
  ChessPlayer(const char* name, int rating)
    : name_(name), rating_(rating)
  { }
  const char* name_;
  int rating_;
};

struct IsWeakerPlayer {
  bool operator( )(const ChessPlayer& x, const ChessPlayer& y) {
    return x.rating_ < y.rating_;
  }
};

int main( )
{
  ChessPlayer kasparov("Garry Kasparov", 2805);
  ChessPlayer anand("Viswanathan Anand ", 2788);
  ChessPlayer topalov("Veselin Topalov", 2788);
  vector<ChessPlayer> v;
  v.push_back(kasparov);
  v.push_back(anand);
  v.push_back(topalov);
  cout << "the best player is ";
  cout << max_element(v.begin(), v.end( ), IsWeakerPlayer( ))->name_;
  cout << endl;
}
```

The program in Example 11-4 produces the following output:

```
the best player is Garry Kasparov
```

In Example 11-4 I have shown how to provide max_element with a custom predicate. The predicate is the function object IsWeakerPlayer.

Another alternative to pasing a user-defined predicate in Example 11-4 is to override operator< for the ChessPlayer struct. This works fine for the specific case of the example, but it presumes that the most important way to sort players is by rating. It may be that sorting by name is more prevalent. Since choosing one method of sorting over another in this case is an arbitrary choice, I prefer to leave operator< undefined.

11.3   Computing the Sum and Mean of Elements in a Container

Problem

You want to compute the sum and mean of elements in a container of numbers.

Solution

You can use the accumulate function from the <numeric> header to compute the sum, and then divide by the size to get the mean. Example 11-5 demonstrates this using a vector.

Example 11-5. Computing the sum and mean of a container

```
#include <numeric>
#include <iostream>
#include <vector>

using namespace std;

int main( ) {
  vector<int> v;
  v.push_back(1);
  v.push_back(2);
  v.push_back(3);
  v.push_back(4);
  int sum = accumulate(v.begin( ), v.end( ), 0);
  double mean = double(sum) / v.size( );
  cout << "sum = " << sum << endl;
  cout << "count = " << v.size( ) << endl;
  cout << "mean = " << mean << endl;
}
```

The program in Example 11-5 produces the following output:

```
sum = 10
count = 4
mean = 2.5
```

Discussion

The accumulate function generally provides the most efficient and simplest method to find the sum of all the elements in a container.

Even though this recipe has a relatively simple solution, writing your own generic function to compute a mean is not so easy. Example 11-6 shows one way to write such a generic function:

Example 11-6. A generic function to compute the mean

```
template<class Iter_T>
double computeMean(Iter_T first, Iter_T last) {
  return static_cast<double>(accumulate(first, last, 0.0))
    / distance(first, last);
}
```

The computeMean function in Example 11-6 is sufficient for most purposes but it has one restriction: it doesn't work with input iterators such as istream_iterator.

An istream_iterator allows only a single pass over the data, so you can call either
accumulate or distance but once you call either function, the data is invalidated and
any further attempts to iterate over the data will likely fail. Example 11-7 demonstrates how to write instead a more generic algorithm for computing the mean of a
sequence of numbers in a single pass.

Example 11-7. A more generic function to compute the mean

```
#include <stdexcept>
#include <iostream>
#include <iterator>

using namespace std;

template<class Value_T, class Iter_T>
Value_T computeMean(Iter_T first, Iter_T last) {
  if (first == last) throw domain_error("mean is undefined");
  Value_T sum;
  int cnt = 0;
  while (first != last) {
    sum += *first++;
    ++cnt;
  }
  return sum / cnt;
}

int main( ) {
  cout << "please type in several integers separated by newlines" << endl;
  cout << "and terminated by an EOF character (i.e., Ctrl-Z)" << endl;
  double mean = computeMean<double>(
    istream_iterator<int>(cin),
    istream_iterator<int>( ));
  cout << "the mean is " << mean << endl;
}
```

When writing generic code, you should always try to write for the most basic kind of iterator possible. This implies that whenever you can you should try to write generic algorithms that operate in a single pass over the input. By taking this approach, your generic code is not restricted only to containers, but can also be used with input iterators such as istream_iterator. As further motivation, single pass algorithms are often more efficient.

It may be surprising that I decided to write the computeMean function in Example 11-7 to require that the return type is passed as a template parameter as opposed to deducing it from the iterator type. This is because it is common for statistics to be computed and represented with a higher level of precision than the numbers in the container. For example, the code in Example 11-7 returns the mean of a set of integers as a double value.

11.4   Filtering Values Outside a Given Range

Problem

You want to ignore values from a sequence that fall above or below a given range.

Solution

Use the remove_copy_if function found in the <algorithm>, as shown in Example 11-8.

Example 11-8. Removing elements from a sequence below a value

```
#include <algorithm>
#include <vector>
#include <iostream>
#include <iterator>

using namespace std;

struct OutOfRange
{
  OutOfRange(int min, int max)
    : min_(min), max_(max)
  { }
  bool operator( )(int x) {
    return (x < min_) || (x > max_);
  }
  int min_;
  int max_;
};

int main( )
{
  vector<int> v;
  v.push_back(6);
  v.push_back(12);
```

Example 11-8. Removing elements from a sequence below a value (continued)

```
    v.push_back(18);
    v.push_back(24);
    v.push_back(30);
    remove_copy_if(v.begin( ), v.end( ),
        ostream_iterator<int>(cout, "\n"), OutOfRange(10,25));
}
```

The program in Example 11-8 produces the following output:

```
    12
    18
    24
```

Discussion

The `remove_copy_if` function copies the elements from one container to another container (or output iterator), ignoring any elements that satisfy a predicate that you provide (it probably would have been more accurate if the function was named `copy_ignore_if`). The function, however, does not change the size of the target container. If, as is often the case, the number of elements copied by `remove_copy_if` is fewer than the size of the target container, you will have to shrink the target container by calling the erase member function.

The function `remove_copy_if` requires a unary predicate (a functor that takes one argument and returns a `boolean` value) that returns true when an element should not be copied. In Example 11-8 the predicate is the function object `OutOfRange`. The `OutOfRange` constructor takes a lower and upper range, and overloads `operator( )`. The `operator( )` function takes an integer parameter, and returns true if the passed argument is less than the lower limit, or greater than the upper limit.

11.5   Computing Variance, Standard Deviation, and Other Statistical Functions

Problem

You want to compute one or more of the common statistics such as variance, standard deviation, skew, and kurtosis of a sequence of numbers.

Solution

You can use the `accumulate` function from the `<numeric>` header to compute many meaningful statistical functions beyond simply the sum by passing custom function objects. Example 11-9 shows how to compute several important statistical functions, using `accumulate`.

Example 11-9. Statistical functions

```cpp
#include <numeric>
#include <cmath>
#include <algorithm>
#include <functional>
#include <vector>
#include <iostream>

using namespace std;

template<int N, class T>
T nthPower(T x) {
  T ret = x;
  for (int i=1; i < N; ++i) {
    ret *= x;
  }
  return ret;
}

template<class T, int N>
struct SumDiffNthPower {
  SumDiffNthPower(T x) : mean_(x) { };
  T operator()(T sum, T current) {
    return sum + nthPower<N>(current - mean_);
  }
  T mean_;
};

template<class T, int N, class Iter_T>
T nthMoment(Iter_T first, Iter_T last, T mean)  {
  size_t cnt = distance(first, last);
  return accumulate(first, last, T(), SumDiffNthPower<T, N>(mean)) / cnt;
}

template<class T, class Iter_T>
T computeVariance(Iter_T first, Iter_T last, T mean) {
  return nthMoment<T, 2>(first, last, mean);
}

template<class T, class Iter_T>
T computeStdDev(Iter_T first, Iter_T last, T mean) {
  return sqrt(computeVariance(first, last, mean));
}

template<class T, class Iter_T>
T computeSkew(Iter_T begin, Iter_T end, T mean) {
  T m3 = nthMoment<T, 3>(begin, end, mean);
  T m2 = nthMoment<T, 2>(begin, end, mean);
  return m3 / (m2 * sqrt(m2));
}

template<class T, class Iter_T>
T computeKurtosisExcess(Iter_T begin, Iter_T end, T mean) {
```

Example 11-9. Statistical functions (continued)

```
  T m4 = nthMoment<T, 4>(begin, end, mean);
  T m2 = nthMoment<T, 2>(begin, end, mean);
  return m4 / (m2 * m2) - 3;
}

template<class T, class Iter_T>
void computeStats(Iter_T first, Iter_T last, T& sum, T& mean,
  T& var, T& std_dev, T& skew, T& kurt)
{
  size_t cnt = distance(first, last);
  sum = accumulate(first, last, T());
  mean = sum / cnt;
  var = computeVariance(first, last, mean);
  std_dev = sqrt(var);
  skew = computeSkew(first, last, mean);
  kurt = computeKurtosisExcess(first, last, mean);
}

int main()
{
  vector<int> v;
  v.push_back(2);
  v.push_back(4);
  v.push_back(8);
  v.push_back(10);
  v.push_back(99);
  v.push_back(1);
  double sum, mean, var, dev, skew, kurt;
  computeStats(v.begin(), v.end(), sum, mean, var, dev, skew, kurt);
  cout << "count = " << v.size() << "\n";
  cout << "sum = " << sum << "\n";
  cout << "mean = " << mean << "\n";
  cout << "variance = " << var << "\n";
  cout << "standard deviation = " << dev << "\n";
  cout << "skew = " << skew << "\n";
  cout << "kurtosis excess = " << kurt << "\n";
  cout << endl;
}
```

The program in Example 11-9 produces the following output:

```
count = 6
sum = 124
mean = 20.6667
variance = 1237.22
standard deviation = 35.1742
skew = 1.75664
kurtosis excess = 1.14171
```

Discussion

Some of the most important statistical functions (e.g., variance, standard deviation, skew, and kurtosis) are defined in terms of standardized sample moments about the mean. The precise definitions of statistical functions vary somewhat from text to text. This text uses the unbiased definitions of the statistical functions shown in Table 11-1.

Table 11-1. Definitions of statistical functions

Statistical function	Equation
*n*th central moment (μ_n)	$\Sigma\,(x_i - mean)^n\,P(x_i)$
Variance	μ_2
Standard deviation	$\sqrt{\mu_2}$
Skew	$\mu_3/\mu_2^{3/2}$
Kurtosis excess	$(\mu_4/\mu_2^2) - 3$

A *moment* is a characterization of a sequence of numbers. In other words, it is a way to describe a set of number mathematically. Moments form the basis of several important statistical functions, such as the variance, standard deviation, skew, and kurtosis. A *central moment* is a moment that is computed about the mean as opposed to about the origin. A *sample moment* is a moment that is computed from a discrete set of numbers instead of a function. A *standardized moment* is a moment divided by a power of the standard deviation (the standard deviation is the square root of the second moment).

The simplest way to code the statistical functions is to define them all in terms of moments. Since there are several different moments used, each one accepting a constant integer value, I pass the constant as a template parameter. This allows the compiler to potentially generate more efficient code because the integer is known at compile time.

The moment function is defined using the mathematical summation operator Σ. Whenever you think of the summation operation you should think of the `accumulate` function from the `<numeric>` header. The accumulate function has two forms: one accumulates using `operator+` and the other uses an accumulator functor that you need to provide. Your accumulator functor will accept two values: the accumulated value so far, and the value at a specific position in the sequence.

Example 11-10 illustrates how `accumulate` works by showing how the user supplied functor is called repeatedly for each element in a series.

Example 11-10. Sample implementation of accumulate

```
template<class Iter_T, class Value_T, class BinOp_T>
Iter_T accumulate(Iter_T begin, Iter_T end, Value_T value, BinOp_T op) {
  while (begin != end) {
    value = op(value, *begin++)
  }
  return value;
}
```

11.6   Generating Random Numbers

Problem

You want to generate some random floating-point numbers in the interval of [0.0, 1.0] with a uniform distribution.

Solution

The C++ standard provides the C runtime function rand in the <cstdlib> header that returns a random number in the range of 0 to RAND_MAX inclusive. The RAND_MAX macro represents the highest value returnable by the rand function. A demonstration of using rand to generate random floating-point numbers is shown in Example 11-11.

Example 11-11. Generating random numbers using rand

```
#include <cstdlib>
#include <ctime>
#include <iostream>

using namespace std;

double doubleRand() {
  return double(rand()) / (double(RAND_MAX) + 1.0);
}

int main() {
  srand(static_cast<unsigned int>(clock()));
  cout << "expect 5 numbers within the interval [0.0, 1.0)" << endl;
  for (int i=0; i < 5; i++) {
    cout << doubleRand() << "\n";
  }
  cout << endl;
}
```

The program in Example 11-11 should produce output similar to:

```
expect 5 numbers within the interval [0.0, 1.0)
0.010437
0.740997
0.34906
0.369293
0.544373
```

Discussion

To be precise, random number generation functions, including `rand`, return pseudo-random numbers as opposed to truly random numbers, so whenever I say random, I actually mean pseudo-random.

Before using the `rand` function you need to seed (i.e., initialize) the random number generator with a call to `srand`. This assures that subsequent calls to `rand` won't produce the same sequence of numbers each time the program is run. The simplest way to seed the random number generator is to pass the result from a call to `clock` from the `<ctime>` header as an `unsigned int`. Reseeding a random number generator causes number generation to be less random.

The `rand` function is limited in many ways. To begin with, it only generates integers, and only does so using a uniform distribution. Furthermore, the specific random number generation algorithm used is implementation specific and, thus, random number sequences are not reproducible from system to system given the same seed. This is a problem for certain kinds of applications, as well as when testing and debugging.

A much more sophisticated alternative to `rand` is the Boost Random library by Jens Maurer that has inspired the random number facilities proposed for TR1.

 TR1 stands for Technical Report One, and is an official proposed extension to the C++ 98 standard library.

The Boost Random library provides several high-quality random number generation functions for both integer and floating-point types, and support for numerous kinds of distributions. Example 11-12 demonstrates how you can produce random floating-point numbers in the interval [0,1).

Example 11-12. Using the Boost Random library

```
#include <boost/random.hpp>
#include <iostream>
#include <cstdlib>

using namespace std;
using namespace boost;

typedef boost::mt19937 BaseGenerator;
typedef boost::uniform_real<double> Distribution;
typedef boost::variate_generator<BaseGenerator, Distribution> Generator;

double boostDoubleRand() {
  static BaseGenerator base;
  static Distribution dist;
  static Generator rng(base, dist);
  return rng();
}
```

Example 11-12. Using the Boost Random library (continued)

```
int main( ) {
  cout << "expect 5 numbers within the interval [0,1)" << endl;
  for (int i=0; i < 5; i++) {
    cout << boostDoubleRand( ) << "\n";
  }
  cout << endl;
}
```

The main advantage of the Boost Random library, is that the pseudo-random number generation algorithm has guaranteed and reproducible randomness properties based on the precise algorithm chosen. In Example 11-12 I use the Mersenne Twister generator (mt19937) because it offers a good blend of performance and randomness.

11.7   Initializing a Container with Random Numbers

Problem

You want to fill an arbitrary container with random numbers.

Solution

You can use either the generate or generate_n functions from the <algorithm> header with a functor that returns random numbers. See Example 11-13 for an example of how to do this.

Example 11-13. Initializing containers with random numbers

```
#include <algorithm>
#include <vector>
#include <iterator>
#include <iostream>
#include <cstdlib>

using namespace std;

struct RndIntGen
{
  RndIntGen(int l, int h)
    : low(l), high(h)
  { }
  int operator( )( ) const {
    return low + (rand( ) % ((high - low) + 1));
  }
private:
  int low;
  int high;
};
```

Example 11-13. Initializing containers with random numbers (continued)

```
int main( ) {
  srand(static_cast<unsigned int>(clock( )));
  vector<int> v(5);
  generate(v.begin( ), v.end( ), RndIntGen(1, 6));
  copy(v.begin( ), v.end( ), ostream_iterator<int>(cout, "\n"));
}
```

The program in Example 11-13 should produce output similar to:

```
3
1
2
6
4
```

Discussion

The standard C++ library provides the functions generate and generate_n specifically for filling containers with the result of a generator function. These functions
accept a nullary functor (a function pointer or function object with no arguments)
whose result is assigned to contiguous values in the container. Sample implementations of the generate and generate_n functions are shown in Example 11-14.

Example 11-14. Sample implementations of generate and generate_n

```
template<class Iter_T, class Fxn_T>
void generate(Iter_T first, Iter_T last, Fxn_T f) {
  while (first != last) *first++ = f( );
}

template<class Iter_T, class Fxn_T>
void generate_n(Iter_T first, int n, Fxn_T f) {
  for (int i=0; i < n; ++i) *first++ = f( );
}
```

11.8 Representing a Dynamically Sized Numerical Vector

Problem

You want a type for manipulating numerical vectors with dynamic size.

Solution

You can use the valarray template from the <valarray> header. Example 11-15
shows how you can use the valarray template.

Example 11-15. Using valarray

```
#include <valarray>
#include <iostream>

using namespace std;

int main( ) {
  valarray<int> v(3);
  v[0] = 1; v[1] = 2; v[2] = 3;
  cout << v[0] << ", " << v[1] << ", " << v[2] << endl;
  v = v + v;
  cout << v[0] << ", " << v[1] << ", " << v[2] << endl;
  v /= 2;
  cout << v[0] << ", " << v[1] << ", " << v[2] << endl;
}
```

The program in Example 11-15 will output the following:

```
1, 2, 3
2, 4, 6
1, 2, 3
```

Discussion

Despite its name, vector is not intended to be used as a numerical vector; rather, the valarray template is. The valarray is designed so that C++ implementations, especially those on high-performance machines, can apply specialized vector optimizations to it. The other big advantage of valarray is that it provides numerous overloaded operators specifically for working with numerical vectors. These operators provide such functionality as vector addition and scalar multiplication.

The valarray template can also be used with the standard algorithms like a C-style array. See Example 11-16 to see how you can create iterators to the beginning of, and one past the end of, a valarray.

Example 11-16. Getting iterators to valarray

```
template<class T>
T* valarray_begin(valarray<T>& x) {
  return &x[0];
}

template<class T>
T* valarray_end(valarray<T>& x) {
  return valarray_begin(x) + x.size( );
}
```

Even though it appears somewhat academic, you should not try to create an end iterator for a valarray by writing &x[x.size( )]. If this works, it is only by accident since indexing a valarray past the last valid index results in undefined behaviour.

The lack of begin and end member functions in valarray is decidedly non-STL-like. This lack emphasizes that valarray does not model an STL container concept. Despite that, you can use valarray with any of the generic algorithms where a random-access iterator is required.

11.9   Representing a Fixed-Size Numerical Vector

Problem

You want an efficient representation for manipulating constant-sized numerical vectors

Solution

On many common software architectures, it is more efficient to use a custom vector implementation than a valarray when the size is known at compile time. Example 11-17 provides a sample implementation of a fixed-size vector template called a kvector.

Example 11-17. kvector.hpp

```
#include <algorithm>
#include <cassert>

template<class Value_T, unsigned int N>
class kvector
{
public:
  // public fields
  Value_T m[N];

  // public typedefs
  typedef Value_T value_type;
  typedef Value_T* iterator;
  typedef const Value_T* const_iterator;
  typedef Value_T& reference;
  typedef const Value_T& const_reference;
  typedef size_t size_type;

  // shorthand for referring to kvector
  typedef kvector self;

  // member functions
  template<typename Iter_T>
  void copy(Iter_T first, Iter_T last) { copy(first, last, begin()); }
  iterator begin() { return m; }
  iterator end() { return m + N; }
  const_iterator begin() const { return m; }
  const_iterator end() const { return m + N; }
  reference operator[](size_type n) { return m[n]; }
  const_reference operator[](size_type n) const { return m[n]; }
  static size_type size() { return N; }
```

Example 11-17. kvector.hpp (continued)

```
// vector operations
self& operator+=(const self& x) {
    for (int i=0; i<N; ++i) m[i] += x.m[i]; return *this;
}
self& operator-=(const self& x) {
    for (int i=0; i<N; ++i) m[i] -= x.m[i]; return *this;
}

// scalar operations
self& operator=(value_type x) {
  std::fill(begin(), end(), x); return *this;
}
self& operator+=(value_type x) {
  for (int i=0; i<N; ++i) m[i] += x; return *this;
}
self& operator-=(value_type x) {
  for (int i=0; i<N; ++i) m[i] -= x; return *this;
}
self& operator*=(value_type x) {
    for (int i=0; i<N;  ++i) m[i] *= x; return *this;
}
self& operator/=(value_type x) {
    for (int i=0; i<N; ++i) m[i] /= x; return *this;
}
self& operator%=(value_type x) {
    for (int i=0; i<N; ++i) m[i] %= x; return *this;
 }
self operator-() {
  self x;
  for (int i=0; i<N; ++i) x.m[i] = -m[i];
  return x;
}

// friend operators
friend self operator+(self x, const self& y) { return x += y; }
friend self operator-(self x, const self& y) { return x -= y; }
friend self operator+(self x, value_type y) { return x += y; }
friend self operator-(self x, value_type y) { return x -= y; }
friend self operator*(self x, value_type y) { return x *= y; }
friend self operator/(self x, value_type y) { return x /= y; }
friend self operator%(self x, value_type y) { return x %= y; }
};
```

Usage of the kvector class template is demonstrated in Example 11-18.

Example 11-18. Using kvector

```
#include "kvector.hpp"

#include <algorithm>
#include <numeric>
#include <iostream>
```

Example 11-18. Using kvector (continued)

```
using namespace std;

int main( ) {
  kvector<int, 4> v = { 1, 2, 3, 4 };
  cout << "sum = " << accumulate(v.begin( ), v.end( ), 0) << endl;
  v *= 3;
  cout << "sum = " << accumulate(v.begin( ), v.end( ), 0) << endl;
  v += 1;
  cout << "sum = " << accumulate(v.begin( ), v.end( ), 0) << endl;
}
```

The program in Example 11-18 will produce the following output:

```
sum = 10
sum = 30
sum = 34
```

Discussion

The kvector template in Example 11-17 is a cross between a valarray and the array template proposed for TR1. Like valarray, kvector represents a sequence of values of a given numerical type, but like tr1::array, the size is known at compile time.

Salient features of kvector are that it supports array initialization syntax and it provides begin and end member functions. In effect, a kvector is considered a pseudo-container, which means that it satisfies some but not all of the requirements of a standard container concept. The result of this is that it is much easier to use kvector with standard algorithms than a valarray.

Another advantage of the kvector template class is that it supports array initialization syntax as follows:

```
int x;
kvector<int, 3> k = { x = 1, x + 2, 5 };
```

This initializing syntax is only possible because kvector is an aggregate. An *aggregate* is an array or a class with no user declared constructors, no private or protected non-static data members, no base classes, and no virtual functions. Note that you can still declare a kvector filled with default values as follows:

```
kvector<int, 3> k = {};
```

This fills the vector with zeros.

As you can see, I had to made a design trade-off between fully satisfying the standard container requirements or allowing the array initialization syntax. A similar design trade-off was made in the design of the TR1 array template.

Perhaps the biggest advantage of the kvector over dynamic vector implementations is performance. The kvector template is much more efficient than most dynamic vector implementations for two main reasons: compilers are very good at optimizing fixed-size loops, and there are no dynamic allocations. The performance difference is particularly noticeable for small matricies (e.g., 2×2 or 3×3), which are common in many kinds of applications.

What Is the "self" typedef?

The self typedef I use in Example 11-17 and in later examples is a convenient shorthand that I use to refer to the type of the current class. It makes code much easier to write and understand when the self typedef is used rather than writing out the name of the class.

11.10 Computing a Dot Product

Problem

You have two containers of numbers that are the same length and you want to compute their dot product.

Solution

Example 11-19 shows how you can compute a dot product using the inner_product function from the <numeric> header.

Example 11-19. Computing the dot product

```
#include <numeric>
#include <iostream>
#include <vector>

using namespace std;

int main( ) {
  int v1[] = { 1, 2, 3 };
  int v2[] = { 4, 6, 8 };
  cout << "the dot product of (1,2,3) and (4,6,8) is ";
  cout << inner_product(v1, v1 + 3, v2, 0) << endl;
}
```

The program in Example 11-19 produces the following output:

```
    the dot product of (1,2,3) and (4,6,8) is 40
```

Discussion

The dot product is a form of inner product known as the Euclidean Inner Product. The inner_product function is declared as follows:

```
template<class In, class In2, class T>
T inner_product(In first, In last, In2 first2, T init);

template<class In, class In2, class T, class BinOp, class BinOp2>
T inner_product(In first, In last, In2 first2, T init, BinOp op, Binop2 op2);
```

The first form of inner_product sums the result of multiplying corresponding elements from two containers. The second form of the inner_product function allows you to supply your own pairwise operation and accumulation function. See Example 11-20 to see a sample implementation demonstrating how inner_product works.

Example 11-20. Sample implementation of inner_product()

```
template<class In, class In2, class T, class BinOp, class BinOp2>
T inner_product(In first, In last, In2 first2, T init, BinOp op, Binop2 op2) {
  while (first != last) {
    BinOp(init, BinOp2(*first++, *first2++));
  }
  return init;
}
```

Because of its flexible implementation, you can use inner_product for many more purposes than just computing a dot product (e.g., you can use it to compute the distance between two vectors or compute the norm of a vector).

See Also

Recipes 11.11 and 11.12

11.11 Computing the Norm of a Vector

Problem

You want to find the norm (i.e., the length) of a numerical vector.

Solution

You can use the inner_product function from the <numeric> header to multiply a vector with itself as shown in Example 11-21.

Example 11-21. Computing the norm of a vector

```
#include <numeric>
#include <vector>
```

Example 11-21. Computing the norm of a vector (continued)

```cpp
#include <cmath>
#include <iostream>

using namespace std;

template<typename Iter_T>
long double vectorNorm(Iter_T first, Iter_T last) {
  return sqrt(inner_product(first, last, first, 0.0L));
}

int main( ) {
  int v[] = { 3, 4 };
  cout << "The length of the vector (3,4) is ";
  cout << vectorNorm(v, v + 2) << endl;
}
```

The program in Example 11-21 produces the following output:

```
The length of the vector (3,4) is 5
```

Discussion

Example 11-21 uses the `inner_product` function from the `<numeric>` header to find the dot product of the numerical vector with itself. The square root of this is known as the vector norm or the length of a vector.

Rather than deduce the result type in the `vectorNorm` function, I chose to return a `long double` to lose as little data as possible. If a vector is a series of integers, it is unlikely that in a real example, that the distance can be meaningfully represented as an integer as well.

11.12 Computing the Distance Between Two Vectors

Problem

You want to find the Euclidean distance between two vectors.

Solution

The Euclidean distance between two vectors is defined as the square root of the sum of squares of differences between corresponding elements. This can be computed as shown in Example 11-22.

Example 11-22. Finding the distance between two vectors

```cpp
#include <cmath>
#include <iostream>

using namespace std;
```

Example 11-22. Finding the distance between two vectors (continued)

```
template<class Iter_T, class Iter2_T>
double vectorDistance(Iter_T first, Iter_T last, Iter2_T first2) {
  double ret = 0.0;
  while (first != last) {
    double dist = (*first++) - (*first2++);
    ret += dist * dist;
  }
  return ret > 0.0 ? sqrt(ret) : 0.0;
}

int main() {
  int v1[] = { 1, 5 };
  int v2[] = { 4, 9 };
  cout << "distance between vectors (1,5) and (4,9) is ";
  cout << vectorDistance(v1, v1 + 2, v2) << endl;
}
```

The program in Example 11-22 produces the following output:

```
distance between vectors (1,5) and (4,9) is 5
```

Discussion

Example 11-22 is a straightforward recipe that shows how to write a simple generic function in the style of the STL. To compute the vector distances, I could have instead used the inner_product function I chose not to use a functor, because it was more complex than was strictly needed. Example 11-23 shows how you can compute vector distance using a functor and the inner_product function from the <numeric> header.

Example 11-23. Computing the distance between vectors using inner_product

```
#include <numeric>
#include <cmath>
#include <iostream>
#include <functional>

using namespace std;

template<class Value_T>
struct DiffSquared {
  Value_T operator()(Value_T x, Value_T y) const {
    return (x - y) * (x - y);
  }
};

template<class Iter_T, class Iter2_T>
double vectorDistance(Iter_T first, Iter_T last, Iter2_T first2)  {
  double ret = inner_product(first, last, first2, 0.0L,
    plus<double>(), DiffSquared<double>());
  return ret > 0.0 ? sqrt(ret) : 0.0;
}
```

Example 11-23. Computing the distance between vectors using inner_product (continued)

```
int main( ) {
  int v1[] = { 1, 5 };
  int v2[] = { 4, 9 };
  cout << "distance between vectors (1,5) and (4,9) is ";
  cout << vectorDistance(v1, v1 + 2, v2) << endl;
}
```

Because an implementation of `inner_product( )` may contain special optimizations for your platform and compiler, I prefer to use it where possible.

11.13 Implementing a Stride Iterator

Problem

You have a contiguous series of numbers and you want to iterate through the elements *n* at a time.

Solution

Example 11-24 presents a stride iterator class as a separate header file.

Example 11-24. stride_iter.hpp

```
#ifndef STRIDE_ITER_HPP
#define STRIDE_ITER_HPP

#include <iterator>
#include <cassert>

template<class Iter_T>
class stride_iter
{
public:
  // public typedefs
  typedef typename std::iterator_traits<Iter_T>::value_type value_type;
  typedef typename std::iterator_traits<Iter_T>::reference reference;
  typedef typename std::iterator_traits<Iter_T>::difference_type
    difference_type;
  typedef typename std::iterator_traits<Iter_T>::pointer pointer;
  typedef std::random_access_iterator_tag iterator_category;
  typedef stride_iter self;

  // constructors
  stride_iter( ) : m(NULL), step(0) { };
  stride_iter(const self& x) : m(x.m), step(x.step) { }
  stride_iter(Iter_T x, difference_type n) : m(x), step(n) { }

  // operators
  self& operator++( ) { m += step; return *this; }
  self operator++(int) { self tmp = *this; m += step; return tmp; }
```

Example 11-24. stride_iter.hpp (continued)

```
    self& operator+=(difference_type x) { m += x * step; return *this; }
    self& operator--() { m -= step; return *this; }
    self operator--(int) { self tmp = *this; m -= step; return tmp; }
    self& operator-=(difference_type x) { m -= x * step; return *this; }
    reference operator[](difference_type n) { return m[n * step]; }
    reference operator*() { return *m; }

    // friend operators
    friend bool operator==(const self& x, const self& y) {
      assert(x.step == y.step);
      return x.m == y.m;
    }
    friend bool operator!=(const self& x, const self& y) {
      assert(x.step == y.step);
      return x.m != y.m;
    }
    friend bool operator<(const self& x, const self& y) {
      assert(x.step == y.step);
      return x.m < y.m;
    }
    friend difference_type operator-(const self& x, const self& y) {
      assert(x.step == y.step);
      return (x.m - y.m) / x.step;
    }
    friend self operator+(const self& x, difference_type y) {
      assert(x.step == y.step);
      return x += y * x.step;
    }
    friend self operator+(difference_type x, const self& y) {
      assert(x.step == y.step);
      return y += x * x.step;
    }
private:
  Iter_T m;
  difference_type step;
};

#endif
```

Example 11-25 shows how to use the stride_iter from Example 11-24 to iterate over a sequence of elements two at a time.

Example 11-25. Using stride_iter

```
#include "stride_iter.hpp"

#include <algorithm>
#include <iterator>
#include <iostream>

using namespace std;
```

Example 11-25. Using stride_iter (continued)

```
int main( ) {
  int a[] = { 0, 1, 2, 3, 4, 5, 6, 7 };
  stride_iter<int*> first(a, 2);
  stride_iter<int*> last(a + 8, 2);
  copy(first, last, ostream_iterator<int>(cout, "\n"));
}
```

The program in Example 11-25 produces the following output:

```
0
2
4
6
```

Discussion

Stride iterators are commonplace in matrix implementations. They provide a simple and efficient way to implement matricies as a sequential series of numbers. The stride iterator implementation presented in Example 11-24 acts as a wrapper around another iterator that is passed as a template parameter.

I wanted the stride iterator to be compatible with the STL so I had to choose one of the standard iterator concepts and satisfy the requirements. The stride iterator in Example 11-24 models a random-access iterator.

In Example 11-26, I have provided a separate implementation for stride iterators when the step size is known at compile time, called a `kstride_iter`. Since the step size is passed as a template parameter, the compiler can much more effectively optimize the code for the iterator, and the size of the iterator is reduced.

Example 11-26. kstride_iter.hpp

```
#ifndef KSTRIDE_ITER_HPP
#define KSTRIDE_ITER_HPP

#include <iterator>

template<class Iter_T, int Step_N>
class kstride_iter
{
public:
  // public typedefs
  typedef typename std::iterator_traits<Iter_T>::value_type value_type;
  typedef typename std::iterator_traits<Iter_T>::reference reference;
  typedef typename std::iterator_traits<Iter_T>::difference_type difference_type;
  typedef typename std::iterator_traits<Iter_T>::pointer pointer;
  typedef std::random_access_iterator_tag iterator_category;
  typedef kstride_iter self;

  // constructors
  kstride_iter( ) : m(NULL) { }
```

Example 11-26. kstride_iter.hpp (continued)

```
  kstride_iter(const self& x) : m(x.m) { }
  explicit kstride_iter(Iter_T x) : m(x) { }

  // operators
  self& operator++() { m += Step_N; return *this; }
  self operator++(int) { self tmp = *this; m += Step_N; return tmp; }
  self& operator+=(difference_type x) { m += x * Step_N; return *this; }
  self& operator--() { m -= Step_N; return *this; }
  self operator--(int) { self tmp = *this; m -= Step_N; return tmp; }
  self& operator-=(difference_type x) { m -= x * Step_N; return *this; }
  reference operator[](difference_type n) { return m[n * Step_N]; }
  reference operator*() { return *m; }

  // friend operators
  friend bool operator==(self x, self y) { return x.m == y.m; }
  friend bool operator!=(self x, self y) { return x.m != y.m; }
  friend bool operator<(self x, self y) { return x.m < y.m; }
  friend difference_type operator-(self x, self y) {
    return (x.m - y.m) / Step_N;
  }
  friend self operator+(self x, difference_type y) { return x += y * Step_N; }
  friend self operator+(difference_type x, self y) { return y += x * Step_N; }
private:
  Iter_T m;
};

#endif
```

Example 11-27 shows how to use the kstride_iter.

Example 11-27. Using kstride_iter

```
#include "kstride_iter.hpp"

#include <algorithm>
#include <iterator>
#include <iostream>

using namespace std;

int main( ) {
  int a[] = { 0, 1, 2, 3, 4, 5, 6, 7 };
  kstride_iter<int*, 2> first(a);
  kstride_iter<int*, 2> last(a + 8);
  copy(first, last, ostream_iterator<int>(cout, "\n"));
}
```

11.14 Implementing a Dynamically Sized Matrix

Problem

You need to store and represent Matricies of numbers where the dimensions (number of rows and columns) are not known at compile time.

Solution

Example 11-28 provides a general purpose and efficient implementation of a dynamically sized matrix class using the stride iterator from Recipe 11.12 and a valarray.

Example 11-28. matrix.hpp

```
#ifndef MATRIX_HPP
#define MATRIX_HPP

#include "stride_iter.hpp" // see Recipe 11.12

#include <valarray>
#include <numeric>
#include <algorithm>

template<class Value_T>
class matrix
{
public:
  // public typedefs
  typedef Value_T value_type;
  typedef matrix self;
  typedef value_type* iterator;
  typedef const value_type* const_iterator;
  typedef Value_T* row_type;
  typedef stride_iter<value_type*> col_type;
  typedef const value_type* const_row_type;
  typedef stride_iter<const value_type*> const_col_type;

  // constructors
  matrix() : nrows(0), ncols(0), m() { }
  matrix(int r, int c) : nrows(r), ncols(c), m(r * c) { }
  matrix(const self& x) : m(x.m), nrows(x.nrows), ncols(x.ncols) { }

  template<typename T>
  explicit matrix(const valarray<T>& x)
  : m(x.size() + 1), nrows(x.size()), ncols(1)
  {
    for (int i=0; i<x.size(); ++i) m[i] = x[i];
  }
```

Example 11-28. matrix.hpp (continued)

```cpp
// allow construction from matricies of other types
template<typename T>
explicit matrix(const matrix<T>& x)
: m(x.size() + 1), nrows(x.nrows), ncols(x.ncols)
{
  copy(x.begin(), x.end(), m.begin());
}

// public functions
int rows() const { return nrows; }
int cols() const { return ncols; }
int size() const { return nrows * ncols; }

// element access
row_type row_begin(int n) { return &m[n * cols()]; }
row_type row_end(int n) { return row_begin() + cols(); }
col_type col_begin(int n) { return col_type(&m[n], cols()); }
col_type col_end(int n) { return col_begin(n) + cols(); }
const_row_type row_begin(int n) const { return &m[n * cols()]; }
const_row_type row_end(int n) const { return row_begin() + cols(); }
const_col_type col_begin(int n) const { return col_type(&m[n], cols()); }
const_col_type col_end(int n) const { return col_begin() + cols(); }
iterator begin() { return &m[0]; }
iterator end() { return begin() + size(); }
const_iterator begin() const { return &m[0]; }
const_iterator end() const { return begin() + size(); }

// operators
self& operator=(const self& x) {
  m = x.m; nrows = x.nrows; ncols = x.ncols; return *this;
}
self& operator=(value_type x) { m = x; return *this; }
row_type operator[](int n) { return row_begin(n); }
const_row_type operator[](int n) const { return row_begin(n); }
self& operator+=(const self& x) { m += x.m; return *this; }
self& operator-=(const self& x) { m -= x.m; return *this; }
self& operator+=(value_type x) { m += x; return *this; }
self& operator-=(value_type x) { m -= x; return *this; }
self& operator*=(value_type x) { m *= x; return *this; }
self& operator/=(value_type x) { m /= x; return *this; }
self& operator%=(value_type x) { m %= x; return *this; }
self operator-() { return -m; }
self operator+() { return +m; }
self operator!() { return !m; }
self operator~() { return ~m; }

// friend operators
friend self operator+(const self& x, const self& y) { return self(x) += y; }
friend self operator-(const self& x, const self& y) { return self(x) -= y; }
friend self operator+(const self& x, value_type y) { return self(x) += y; }
friend self operator-(const self& x, value_type y) { return self(x) -= y; }
friend self operator*(const self& x, value_type y) { return self(x) *= y; }
```

Example 11-28. matrix.hpp (continued)

```
  friend self operator/(const self& x, value_type y) { return self(x) /= y; }
  friend self operator%(const self& x, value_type y) { return self(x) %= y; }
private:
  mutable valarray<Value_T> m;
  int nrows;
  int ncols;
};
```

```
#endif
```

Example 11-29 shows how you might use the `matrix` template class.

Example 11-29. Using the matrix template

```
#include "matrix.hpp"

#include <iostream>

using namespace std;

int main( ) {
  matrix<int> m(2,2);
  m = 0;
  m[0][0] = 1;
  m[1][1] = 1;
  m *= 2;
  cout << "(" << m[0][0] << "," << m[0][1] << ")" << endl;
  cout << "(" << m[1][0] << "," << m[1][1] << ")" << endl;
}
```

The program in Example 11-29 produces the following output:

```
(2,0)
(0,2)
```

Discussion

The design of the matrix template in Example 11-28 is heavily inspired by Bjarne Stroustrup's matrix template from *The C++ Programming Language*, Third Edition (Addison Wesley). Stroustrup's implementation differs in that its iterator uses `slice` and a pointer to the valarray for indexing. The matrix implementation in Example 11-27 uses instead the stride iterator from Recipe 11.12, making the iterators more compact and, on some implementations, more efficient.

The `matrix` template class allows indexing of the element *i*th row and *j*th column using a double subscripting operation. For example:

```
matrix<int> m(100,100);
cout << "the element at row 24 and column 42 is " << m[24][42] << endl;
```

The `matrix` template class also provides `begin` and `end` member functions, which means that it can be used easily with the various STL algorithms.

There is a line of code in Example 11-28 that might have caused you to raise your eyebrows. That is the declaration:

```
mutable valarray<Value_T> m;
```

The declaration of the member field m as being mutable was a necessary evil. If it wasn't for this line I would not have been able to provide const iterators, because you can't create an iterator to a const valarray.

See Also

Recipes 11.15 and 11.16

11.15 Implementing a Constant-Sized Matrix

Problem

You want an efficient matrix implementation where the dimensions (i.e., number of rows and columns) are constants known at compile time.

Solution

When the dimensions of a matrix are known at compile time, the compiler can more easily optimize an implementation that accepts the row and columns as template parameters as shown in Example 11-30.

Example 11-30. kmatrix.hpp

```
#ifndef KMATRIX_HPP
#define KMATRIX_HPP

#include "kvector.hpp"
#include "kstride_iter.hpp"

template<class Value_T, int Rows_N, int Cols_N>
class kmatrix
{
public:
  // public typedefs
  typedef Value_T value_type;
  typedef kmatrix self;
  typedef Value_T* iterator;
  typedef const Value_T* const_iterator;
  typedef kstride_iter<Value_T*, 1> row_type;
  typedef kstride_iter<Value_T*, Cols_N> col_type;
  typedef kstride_iter<const Value_T*, 1> const_row_type;
  typedef kstride_iter<const Value_T*, Cols_N> const_col_type;

  // public constants
  static const int nRows = Rows_N;
  static const int nCols = Cols_N;
```

Example 11-30. kmatrix.hpp (continued)

```cpp
// constructors
kmatrix() { m = Value_T(); }
kmatrix(const self& x) { m = x.m; }
explicit kmatrix(Value_T& x) { m = x.m; }

// public functions
static int rows() { return Rows_N; }
static int cols() { return Cols_N; }
row_type row(int n) { return row_type(begin() + (n * Cols_N)); }
col_type col(int n) { return col_type(begin() + n); }
const_row_type row(int n) const {
  return const_row_type(begin() + (n * Cols_N));
}
const_col_type col(int n) const {
  return const_col_type(begin() + n);
}
iterator begin() { return m.begin(); }
iterator end() { return m.begin() + size(); }
const_iterator begin() const { return m; }
const_iterator end() const { return m + size(); }
static int size() { return Rows_N * Cols_N; }

// operators
row_type operator[](int n) { return row(n); }
const_row_type operator[](int n) const { return row(n); }

// assignment operations
self& operator=(const self& x) { m = x.m; return *this; }
self& operator=(value_type x) { m = x; return *this; }
self& operator+=(const self& x) { m += x.m; return *this; }
self& operator-=(const self& x) { m -= x.m; return *this; }
self& operator+=(value_type x) { m += x; return *this; }
self& operator-=(value_type x) { m -= x; return *this; }
self& operator*=(value_type x) { m *= x; return *this; }
self& operator/=(value_type x) { m /= x; return *this; }
self operator-() { return self(-m); }

// friends
friend self operator+(self x, const self& y) { return x += y; }
friend self operator-(self x, const self& y) { return x -= y; }
friend self operator+(self x, value_type y) { return x += y; }
friend self operator-(self x, value_type y) { return x -= y; }
friend self operator*(self x, value_type y) { return x *= y; }
friend self operator/(self x, value_type y) { return x /= y; }
friend bool operator==(const self& x, const self& y) { return x != y; }
friend bool operator!=(const self& x, const self& y) { return x.m != y.m; }
private:
  kvector<Value_T, (Rows_N + 1) * Cols_N> m;
};

#endif
```

Example 11-31 shows a program that demonstrates how to use the kmatrix template class.

Example 11-31. Using kmatrix

```cpp
#include "kmatrix.hpp"

#include <iostream>

using namespace std;

template<class Iter_T>
void outputRowOrColumn(Iter_T iter, int n) {
  for (int i=0; i < n; ++i) {
    cout << iter[i] << " ";
  }
  cout << endl;
}

template<class Matrix_T>
void initializeMatrix(Matrix_T& m) {
  int k = 0;
  for (int i=0; i < m.rows(); ++i) {
    for (int j=0; j < m.cols(); ++j) {
      m[i][j] = k++;
    }
  }
}

template<class Matrix_T>
void outputMatrix(Matrix_T& m) {
  for (int i=0; i < m.rows(); ++i) {
    cout << "Row " << i << " = ";
    outputRowOrColumn(m.row(i), m.cols());
  }
  for (int i=0; i < m.cols(); ++i) {
    cout << "Column " << i << " = ";
    outputRowOrColumn(m.col(i), m.rows());
  }
}

int main()
{
  kmatrix<int, 2, 4> m;
  initializeMatrix(m);
  m *= 2;
  outputMatrix(m);
}
```

The program in Example 11-31 produces the following output:

```
Row 0 = 0 2 4 6
Row 1 = 8 10 12 14
Column 0 = 0 8
```

```
Column 1 = 2 10
Column 2 = 4 12
Column 3 = 6 14
```

Discussion

This design and usage for the kmatrix class template in Example 11-30 and Example 11-31 is very similar to the matrix class template presented in Recipe 11.14. The only significant difference is that to declare an instance of a kmatrix you pass the dimensions as template parameters, as follows:

```
kmatrix<int, 5, 6> m; // declares a matrix with five rows and six columns
```

It is common for many kinds of applications requiring matricies that the dimensions are known at compile-time. Passing the row and column size as template parameters enables the compiler to more easily apply common optimizations such as loop-unrolling, function inlining, and faster indexing.

 Like the constant-sized vector template presented earlier (kvector), the kmatrix template is particularly effective when using small matrix sizes.

See Also

Recipes 11.14 and 11.16

11.16 Multiplying Matricies

Problem

You want to perform efficient multiplication of two matricies.

Solution

Example 11-32 shows an implementation of matrix multiplication that can be used with both the dynamic- or fixed-size matrix implementations. This algorithm technically produces the result of the equation A=A+B*C, which is, perhaps surprisingly, an equation more efficiently computed than A=B*C.

Example 11-32. Matrix multiplication

```
#include "matrix.hpp" // recipe 11.13
#include "kmatrix.hpp" // recipe 11.14
#include <iostream>
#include <cassert>

using namespace std;
```

Example 11-32. Matrix multiplication (continued)

```
template<class M1, class M2, class M3>
void matrixMultiply(const M1& m1, const M2& m2, M3& m3)
{
  assert(m1.cols() == m2.rows());
  assert(m1.rows() == m3.rows());
  assert(m2.cols() == m3.cols());
  for (int i=m1.rows()-1; i >= 0; --i) {
    for (int j=m2.cols()-1; j >= 0; --j) {
      for (int k = m1.cols()-1; k >= 0; --k) {
        m3[i][j] += m1[i][k] * m2[k][j];
      }
    }
  }
}

int main()
{
  matrix<int> m1(2, 1);
  matrix<int> m2(1, 2);
  kmatrix<int, 2, 2> m3;
  m3 = 0;
  m1[0][0] = 1; m1[1][0] = 2;
  m2[0][0] = 3; m2[0][1] = 4;
  matrixMultiply(m1, m2, m3);
  cout << "(" << m3[0][0] << ", " << m3[0][1] << ")" << endl;
  cout << "(" << m3[1][0] << ", " << m3[1][1] << ")" << endl;
}
```

Example 11-32 produces the following output:

```
(3, 4)
(6, 8)
```

Discussion

When multiplying two matricies, the number of columns in the first matrix must be equal to the number of rows in the second matrix. The resulting matrix has the number of rows of the first matrix and the number of columns of the second matrix. I assure that these conditions are true during debug builds by using the assert macro found in the <cassert> header.

The key to efficient matrix multiplication is to avoid any superfluous creation and copying of temporaries. Thus, the matrix multiplication function in Example 11-32 was written to pass the result by reference. If I had written a straightforward multiplication algorithm by overriding operator* it would result in the overhead of an unneccessary allocation, copy, and deallocation of a temporary matrix. This can be potentially very expensive when dealing with large matricies.

The reason the matrix multiplication equation in Example 11-32 computes A=A+B*C instead of A=B*C is that it avoids unneccessarily initializing the values of A.

See Also

Recipe 11.17

11.17 Computing the Fast Fourier Transform

Problem

You want to compute the Discrete Fourier Transform (DFT) efficiently using the Fast Fourier Transform (FFT) algorithm.

Solution

The code in Example 11-33 provides a basic implementation of the FFT.

Example 11-33. FFT implementation

```
#include <iostream>
#include <complex>
#include <cmath>
#include <iterator>

using namespace std;

unsigned int bitReverse(unsigned int x, int log2n) {
  int n = 0;
  int mask = 0x1;
  for (int i=0; i < log2n; i++) {
    n <<= 1;
    n |= (x & 1);
    x >>= 1;
  }
  return n;
}

const double PI = 3.1415926536;

template<class Iter_T>
void fft(Iter_T a, Iter_T b, int log2n)
{
  typedef typename iterator_traits<Iter_T>::value_type complex;
  const complex J(0, 1);
  int n = 1 << log2n;
  for (unsigned int i=0; i < n; ++i) {
    b[bitReverse(i, log2n)] = a[i];
  }
```

Example 11-33. FFT implementation (continued)

```
  for (int s = 1; s <= log2n; ++s) {
    int m = 1 << s;
    int m2 = m >> 1;
    complex w(1, 0);
    complex wm = exp(-J * (PI / m2));
    for (int j=0; j < m2; ++j) {
      for (int k=j; k < n; k += m) {
        complex t = w * b[k + m2];
        complex u = b[k];
        b[k] = u + t;
        b[k + m2] = u - t;
      }
      w *= wm;
    }
  }
}

int main( ) {
  typedef complex<double> cx;
  cx a[] = { cx(0,0), cx(1,1), cx(3,3), cx(4,4),
    cx(4, 4), cx(3, 3), cx(1,1), cx(0,0) };
  cx b[8];
  fft(a, b, 3);
  for (int i=0; i<8; ++i)
    cout << b[i] << "\n";
}
```

The program in Example 11-33 produces the following output:

```
(16,16)
(-4.82843,-11.6569)
(0,0)
(-0.343146,0.828427)
(0,0)
(0.828427,-0.343146)
(0,0)
(-11.6569,-4.82843)
```

Discussion

The Fourier transform is an important equation for spectral analysis, and is required frequently in engineering and scientific applications. The FFT is an algorithm for computing a DFT that operates in N log2(N) complexity versus the expected N² complexity of a naive implementation of a DFT. The FFT achieves such an impressive speed-up by removing redundant computations.

Finding a good FFT implementation written in idiomatic C++ (i.e., C++ that isn't mechanically ported from old Fortran or C algorithms) and that isn't severely restricted by a license is very hard. The code in Example 11-33 is based on public domain code that can be found on the digital signal processing newswgoup on usenet (*comp.dsp*). A big advantage of an idiomatic C++ solution over the more common C-style FFT implementations is that the standard library provides the complex template that significantly reduces the amount of code needed. The fft( ) function in Example 11-33, was written to be as simple as possible rather than focusing on efficiency.

11.18 Working with Polar Coordinates

Problem

You want to represent and manipulate polar coordinates.

Solution

The complex template from the <complex> header provides functions for conversion to and from polar coordinates. Example 11-34 shows how you can use the complex template class to represent and manipulate polar coordinates.

Example 11-34. Using complex template class to represent polar coordinates

```
#include <complex>
#include <iostream>

using namespace std;

int main( ) {
  double rho = 3.0; // magnitude
  double theta = 3.141592 / 2; // angle
  complex<double> coord = polar(rho, theta);
  cout << "rho = " << abs(coord) << ", theta = " << arg(coord) << endl;
  coord += polar(4.0, 0.0);
  cout << "rho = " << abs(coord) << ", theta = " << arg(coord) << endl;
}
```

Example 11-34 produces the following output:

```
rho = 3, theta = 1.5708
rho = 5, theta = 0.643501
```

Discussion

There is a natural relationship between polar coordinates and complex numbers. Even though the two are somewhat interchangeable, it is generally not a good idea to use the same type to represent different concepts. Since using the complex template to represent polar coordinates is inelegant, I have provided a polar coordinate class that is more natural to use in Example 11-35.

Example 11-35. A polar coordinate class

```
#include <complex>
#include <iostream>
```

Example 11-35. A polar coordinate class (continued)

```cpp
using namespace std;

template<class T>
struct BasicPolar
{
  public:
    typedef BasicPolar self;

    // constructors
    BasicPolar() : m() {  }
    BasicPolar(const self& x) : m(x.m) {  }
    BasicPolar(const T& rho, const T& theta) : m(polar(rho, theta)) { }

    // assignment operations
    self operator-() { return Polar(-m); }
    self& operator+=(const self& x) { m += x.m; return *this; }
    self& operator-=(const self& x) { m -= x.m; return *this; }
    self& operator*=(const self& x) { m *= x.m; return *this; }
    self& operator/=(const self& x) { m /= x.m; return *this; }
    operator complex<T>() const { return m; }

    // public member functions
    T rho() const { return abs(m); }
    T theta() const { return arg(m); }

    // binary operations
    friend self operator+(self x, const self& y) { return x += y; }
    friend self operator-(self x, const self& y) { return x -= y; }
    friend self operator*(self x, const self& y) { return x *= y; }
    friend self operator/(self x, const self& y) { return x /= y; }

    // comparison operators
    friend bool operator==(const self& x, const self& y) { return x.m == y.m; }
    friend bool operator!=(const self& x, const self& y) { return x.m != y.m; }
  private:
    complex<T> m;
};

typedef BasicPolar<double> Polar;

int main() {
  double rho = 3.0; // magnitude
  double theta = 3.141592 / 2; // angle
  Polar coord(rho, theta);
  cout << "rho = " << coord.rho() << ", theta = " << coord.theta() << endl;
  coord += Polar(4.0, 0.0);
  cout << "rho = " << coord.rho() << ", theta = " << coord.theta() << endl;
  system("pause");
}
```

In Example 11-35, I have defined the Polar type as a typedef'd specialization of the BasicPolar template. This way you can have a convenient default but you can still specialize the BasicPolar template using another numerical type if you prefer. This technique is used in the standard library with the string class being a specialization of the basic_string template.

11.19 Performing Arithmetic on Bitsets

Problem

You want to perform basic arithmetic and comparison operations on a set of bits as if it were a binary representation of an unsigned integer number.

Solution

The functions in Example 11-36 provide functions that allow arithmetic and comparison of bitset class template from the <bitset> header as if it represents an unsigned integer.

Example 11-36. bitset_arithmetic.hpp

```
#include <stdexcept>
#include <bitset>

bool fullAdder(bool b1, bool b2, bool& carry) {
  bool sum = (b1 ^ b2) ^ carry;
  carry = (b1 && b2) || (b1 && carry) || (b2 && carry);
  return sum;
}

bool fullSubtractor(bool b1, bool b2, bool& borrow) {
  bool diff;
  if (borrow) {
    diff = !(b1 ^ b2);
    borrow = !b1 || (b1 && b2);
  }
  else {
    diff = b1 ^ b2;
    borrow = !b1 && b2;
  }
  return diff;
}

template<unsigned int N>
bool bitsetLtEq(const std::bitset<N>& x, const std::bitset<N>& y)
{
  for (int i=N-1; i >= 0; i--) {
    if (x[i] && !y[i]) return false;
    if (!x[i] && y[i]) return true;
  }
  return true;
}
```

Example 11-36. bitset_arithmetic.hpp (continued)

```
template<unsigned int N>
bool bitsetLt(const std::bitset<N>& x, const std::bitset<N>& y)
{
  for (int i=N-1; i >= 0; i--) {
    if (x[i] && !y[i]) return false;
    if (!x[i] && y[i]) return true;
  }
  return false;
}

template<unsigned int N>
bool bitsetGtEq(const std::bitset<N>& x, const std::bitset<N>& y)
{
  for (int i=N-1; i >= 0; i--) {
    if (x[i] && !y[i]) return true;
    if (!x[i] && y[i]) return false;
  }
  return true;
}

template<unsigned int N>
bool bitsetGt(const std::bitset<N>& x, const std::bitset<N>& y)
{
  for (int i=N-1; i >= 0; i--) {
    if (x[i] && !y[i]) return true;
    if (!x[i] && y[i]) return false;
  }
  return false;
}

template<unsigned int N>
void bitsetAdd(std::bitset<N>& x, const std::bitset<N>& y)
{
  bool carry = false;
  for (int i = 0; i < N; i++) {
    x[i] = fullAdder(x[i], y[i], carry);
  }
}

template<unsigned int N>
void bitsetSubtract(std::bitset<N>& x, const std::bitset<N>& y) {
  bool borrow = false;
  for (int i = 0; i < N; i++) {
    if (borrow) {
      if (x[i]) {
        x[i] = y[i];
        borrow = y[i];
      }
      else {
        x[i] = !y[i];
        borrow = true;
      }
```

Example 11-36. bitset_arithmetic.hpp (continued)

```
    }
    else {
      if (x[i]) {
        x[i] = !y[i];
        borrow = false;
      }
      else {
        x[i] = y[i];
        borrow = y[i];
      }
    }
  }
}

template<unsigned int N>
void bitsetMultiply(std::bitset<N>& x, const std::bitset<N>& y)
{
  std::bitset<N> tmp = x;
  x.reset();

  // we want to minimize the number of times we shift and add
  if (tmp.count() < y.count()) {
    for (int i=0; i < N; i++)
      if (tmp[i]) bitsetAdd(x, y << i);
  }
  else {
    for (int i=0; i < N; i++)
      if (y[i]) bitsetAdd(x, tmp << i);
  }
}

template<unsigned int N>
void bitsetDivide(std::bitset<N> x, std::bitset<N> y,
  std::bitset<N>& q, std::bitset<N>& r)
{
  if (y.none()) {
    throw std::domain_error("division by zero undefined");
  }
  q.reset();
  r.reset();
  if (x.none()) {
    return;
  }
  if (x == y) {
    q[0] = 1;
    return;
  }
  r = x;
  if (bitsetLt(x, y)) {
    return;
  }
```

Example 11-36. bitset_arithmetic.hpp (continued)

```cpp
  // count significant digits in divisor and dividend
  unsigned int sig_x;
  for (int i=N-1; i>=0; i--) {
    sig_x = i;
    if (x[i]) break;
  }
  unsigned int sig_y;
  for (int i=N-1; i>=0; i--) {
    sig_y = i;
    if (y[i]) break;
  }

  // align the divisor with the dividend
  unsigned int n = (sig_x - sig_y);
  y <<= n;

  // make sure the loop executes the right number of times
  n += 1;

  // long division algorithm, shift, and subtract
  while (n--)
  {
    // shift the quotient to the left
    if (bitsetLtEq(y, r))
    {
      // add a new digit to quotient
      q[n] = true;
      bitsetSubtract(r, y);
    }
    // shift the divisor to the right
    y >>= 1;
  }
}
```

Example 11-37 shows how you might use the *bitset_arithmetic.hpp* header file.

Example 11-37. Using the bitset_arithmetic.hpp functions

```cpp
#include "bitset_arithmetic.hpp"

#include <bitset>
#include <iostream>
#include <string>

using namespace std;

int main( ) {
  bitset<10> bits1(string("100010001"));
  bitset<10> bits2(string("000000011"));
  bitsetAdd(bits1, bits2);
  cout << bits1.to_string<char, char_traits<char>, allocator<char> >() << endl;
}
```

The program in Example 11-37 produces the following output:

```
0100010100
```

Discussion

The bitset class template comes with basic operations for manipulating sets of bits but doesn't provide any arithmetic or comparion operations. This is because the library can't safely assume what kind of numerical type a programmer might expect an arbitrary set of bits to represent.

The functions in Example 11-36 treat a bitset as a representation of an unsigned integer type, and provide you with functions for adding, subtracting, multiplying, dividing, and comparing them. These functions can provide a basis for writing custom-sized integer types, and are used for such a purpose in Recipe 11.20.

I did not use the most efficient algorithms I could for Example 11-36. Instead I chose the simplest possible algorithms because they are more easily understood. A much more efficient implementation would use similar algorithms, but would operate on words rather than single bits.

See Also

Recipe 11.20

11.20 Representing Large Fixed-Width Integers

Problem

You need to perform arithmetic of numbers larger than can be represented by a long int.

Solution

The BigInt template in Example 11-38 uses the bitset from the <bitset> header to allow you to represent unsigned integers using a fixed number of bits specified as a template parameter.

Example 11-38. big_int.hpp

```
#ifndef BIG_INT_HPP
#define BIG_INT_HPP

#include <bitset>

#include "bitset_arithmetic.hpp" // Recipe 11.20

template<unsigned int N>
class BigInt
```

Example 11-38. big_int.hpp (continued)

```cpp
{
  typedef BigInt self;
public:
  BigInt() : bits() { }
  BigInt(const self& x) : bits(x.bits) { }
  BigInt(unsigned long x) {
    int n = 0;
    while (x) {
      bits[n++] = x & 0x1;
      x >>= 1;
    }
  }
  explicit BigInt(const std::bitset<N>& x) : bits(x) { }

  // public functions
  bool operator[](int n) const { return bits[n]; }
  unsigned long toUlong() const { return bits.to_ulong(); }

  // operators
  self& operator<<=(unsigned int n) {
    bits <<= n;
    return *this;
  }
  self& operator>>=(unsigned int n) {
    bits >>= n;
    return *this;
  }
  self operator++(int) {
    self i = *this;
    operator++();
    return i;
  }
  self operator--(int) {
    self i = *this;
    operator--();
    return i;
  }
  self& operator++() {
    bool carry = false;
    bits[0] = fullAdder(bits[0], 1, carry);
    for (int i = 1; i < N; i++) {
      bits[i] = fullAdder(bits[i], 0, carry);
    }
    return *this;
  }
  self& operator--() {
    bool borrow = false;
    bits[0] = fullSubtractor(bits[0], 1, borrow);
    for (int i = 1; i < N; i++) {
      bits[i] = fullSubtractor(bits[i], 0, borrow);
    }
    return *this;
```

Example 11-38. big_int.hpp (continued)

```cpp
  }
  self& operator+=(const self& x) {
    bitsetAdd(bits, x.bits);
    return *this;
  }
  self& operator-=(const self& x) {
    bitsetSubtract(bits, x.bits);
    return *this;
  }
  self& operator*=(const self& x) {
    bitsetMultiply(bits, x.bits);
    return *this;
  }
  self& operator/=(const self& x) {
    std::bitset<N> tmp;
    bitsetDivide(bits, x.bits, bits, tmp);
    return *this;
  }
  self& operator%=(const self& x) {
    std::bitset<N> tmp;
    bitsetDivide(bits, x.bits, tmp, bits);
    return *this;
  }
  self operator~() const { return ~bits; }
  self& operator&=(self x) { bits &= x.bits; return *this; }
  self& operator|=(self x) { bits |= x.bits; return *this; }
  self& operator^=(self x) { bits ^= x.bits; return *this; }

  // friend functions
  friend self operator<<(self x, unsigned int n) { return x <<= n; }
  friend self operator>>(self x, unsigned int n) { return x >>= n; }
  friend self operator+(self x, const self& y) { return x += y; }
  friend self operator-(self x, const self& y) { return x -= y; }
  friend self operator*(self x, const self& y) { return x *= y; }
  friend self operator/(self x, const self& y) { return x /= y; }
  friend self operator%(self x, const self& y) { return x %= y; }
  friend self operator^(self x, const self& y) { return x ^= y; }
  friend self operator&(self x, const self& y) { return x &= y; }
  friend self operator|(self x, const self& y) { return x |= y; }

  // comparison operators
  friend bool operator==(const self& x, const self& y) {
    return x.bits == y.bits;
  }
  friend bool operator!=(const self& x, const self& y) {
    return x.bits != y.bits;
  }
  friend bool operator>(const self& x, const self& y) {
    return bitsetGt(x.bits, y.bits);
  }
  friend bool operator<(const self& x, const self& y) {
    return bitsetLt(x.bits, y.bits);
```

Example 11-38. big_int.hpp (continued)

```
  }
  friend bool operator>=(const self& x, const self& y) {
    return bitsetGtEq(x.bits, y.bits);
  }
  friend bool operator<=(const self& x, const self& y) {
    return bitsetLtEq(x.bits, y.bits);
  }
private:
  std::bitset<N> bits;
};

#endif
```

The BigInt template class could be used to represent factorials, as shown in Example 11-39.

Example 11-39. Using the big_int class

```
#include "big_int.hpp"

#include <iostream>
#include <vector>
#include <iterator>
#include <algorithm>

using namespace std;

void outputBigInt(BigInt<1024> x) {
  vector<int> v;
  if (x == 0) {
    cout << 0;
    return;
  }
  while (x > 0) {
    v.push_back((x % 10).to_ulong());
    x /= 10;
  }
  copy(v.rbegin(), v.rend(), ostream_iterator<int>(cout, ""));
  cout << endl;
}

int main() {
  BigInt<1024> n(1);
  // compute 32 factorial
  for (int i=1; i <= 32; ++i) {
    n *= i;
  }
  outputBigInt(n);
}
```

The program in Example 11-39 outputs:

```
263130836933693530167218012160000000
```

Discussion

Large integers are common in many applications. In cryptography, for example, integers of 1,000 bits and larger are not uncommon. However, the current C++ standard provides integers only as large as a `long int`.

 The number of bits in a `long int` is implementation specific, but is guaranteed to be at least 32. And t probably won't ever be as large as 1,000. Remember that one of those bits is reserved for the sign.

The next version of the standard (C++ 0x) is expected to follow the C99 standard and provide a `long long` type that will be defined as being at least as large as a `long int`, and possibly bigger. Despite this there will always be occasions where an integer type larger than the largest primitive is needed.

The implementation I presented here is based on a binary representation of numbers using a `bitset`, at a cost of some performance. What I lost in performance I more than made up for in simplicity. A more efficient implementation of arbitrary precision numbers could easily fill the book.

See Also

Recipe 11.19

11.21 Implementing Fixed-Point Numbers

Problem

You want to perform computations on real numbers using a fixed-point representation of a real number rather than using a floating-point type.

Solution

Example 11-40 provides the implementation of a fixed-point real number, where the number of places to the right of the binary point is a template parameter. For instance `basic_fixed_real<10>` has 10 binary digits to the right of the binary point, allowing it to represent numbers up to a precision of 1/1,024.

Example 11-40. Representing real numbers using a fixed-point implementation

```
#include <iostream>

using namespace std;
```

Example 11-40. Representing real numbers using a fixed-point implementation (continued)

```
template<int E>
struct BasicFixedReal
{
  typedef BasicFixedReal self;
  static const int factor = 1 << (E - 1);
  BasicFixedReal() : m(0) { }
  BasicFixedReal(double d) : m(static_cast<int>(d * factor)) { }
  self& operator+=(const self& x) { m += x.m; return *this; }
  self& operator-=(const self& x) { m -= x.m; return *this; }
  self& operator*=(const self& x) { m *= x.m; m >>= E; return *this; }
  self& operator/=(const self& x) { m /= x.m; m *= factor; return *this; }
  self& operator*=(int x) { m *= x; return *this; }
  self& operator/=(int x) { m /= x; return *this; }
  self operator-() { return self(-m); }
  double toDouble() const { return double(m) / factor;  }

  // friend functions
  friend self operator+(self x, const self& y) { return x += y; }
  friend self operator-(self x, const self& y) { return x -= y; }
  friend self operator*(self x, const self& y) { return x *= y; }
  friend self operator/(self x, const self& y) { return x /= y; }

  // comparison operators
  friend bool operator==(const self& x, const self& y) { return x.m == y.m; }
  friend bool operator!=(const self& x, const self& y) { return x.m != y.m; }
  friend bool operator>(const self& x, const self& y) { return x.m > y.m; }
  friend bool operator<(const self& x, const self& y) { return x.m < y.m; }
  friend bool operator>=(const self& x, const self& y) { return x.m >= y.m; }
  friend bool operator<=(const self& x, const self& y) { return x.m <= y.m; }
private:
  int m;
};

typedef BasicFixedReal<10> FixedReal;

int main() {
  FixedReal x(0);
  for (int i=0; i < 100; ++i) {
    x += FixedReal(0.0625);
  }
  cout << x.toDouble() << endl;
}
```

The program in Example 11-40 outputs:

```
6.25
```

Discussion

A fixed-point number, like a floating-point number, is an approximate representation of a real number. A floating-point number is stored as a mantissa (m), and an exponent (e), to form the equation $m * b^e$, where b is some constant.

A fixed-point number is almost the same but the exponent is also a constant. This constant is passed to the basic_fixed_real in Example 11-40 as a template parameter.

By representing *e* as a constant, it allows fixed-point numbers to be represented internally as integers and for the arithmetic operations on them to be performed using integer artithmetic. This can often improve the speed of basic arithmetic operations especially addition and subtraction.

Fixed-point representations are less flexible than floating-point numbers, as they can only represent a narrow range of values. The fixed_real type in Example 11-40 has a range that can only represent values from −2,097,151 to +2,097,151 with a precision of 1/1,024.

Implementing addition and subtraction of fixed-point numbers is straightforward enough: I simply add or subtract the underlying representation. To perform division and multiplication, I need an extra step of shifting the mantissa left or right to adjust for the binary point.

CHAPTER 12
Multithreading

12.0 Introduction

This chapter describes how to write multithreaded programs in C++ using the Boost Threads library written by William Kempf. Boost is a set of open source, peer-reviewed, portable, high-performance libraries ranging from simple data structures to a complex parsing framework. The Boost Threads library is a framework for multithreading. For more information on Boost, see *www.boost.org*.

Standard C++ contains no native support for multithreading, so it is not possible to write portable multithreaded code the same way you would write portable code that uses other standard library classes like string, vector, list, and so on. The Boost Threads library goes a long way toward making a standard, portable multithreading library though, and it is designed to minimize many common multithreading headaches.

Unlike the standard library or third-party libraries, however, using a multithreading library is not as easy as unzipping it into a directory, adding your #includes, and coding away. For all but trivial multithreaded applications, you must design carefully using proven patterns and known tactics to avoid bugs that are otherwise virtually guaranteed to happen. In a typical, single-threaded application, it is easy to find common programming errors: off-by-one loops, dereferencing a null or deleted pointer, loss of precision on floating-point conversions, and so on. Multithreaded programs are different. Not only is it tedious to keep track of what several threads are doing in your debugger, but multithreaded programs are nondeterministic, meaning that bugs may only show up under rare or complicated circumstances.

It is for this reason that this chapter should not be your introduction to multithreaded programming. If you have already done some programming with threads, but not with C++ or the Boost Threads library, this chapter will get you on your way. But describing the fundamentals of multithreaded programming is beyond the scope of this book. If you have never done any multithreaded programming before, then you may want to read an introductory book on multithreading, though such titles are scant because most programmers don't use threads (though they probably ought to).

Much of the Boost documentation and some of the following recipes discuss the classes using the *concept/model* idea. A *concept* is an abstract description of something, usually a class, and its behavior, without any assumptions about its implementation. Typically, this description includes construction and destruction behavior, and each of the methods, including their preconditions, parameters, and postconditions. For example, the concept of a Mutex is something that can be locked and unlocked by one thread at a time. A *model* is a concrete manifestation of a concept, such as the mutex class in the Boost Threads library. A *refinement* on a concept is a specialization of it, such as a ReadWriteMutex, which is a Mutex with some additional behavior.

Finally, threads are doing one of three things: working, waiting for something, or ready to go but not waiting for anything or doing any work. These states are called *run*, *wait*, and *ready*. These are the terms I will use in the following recipes.

12.1   Creating a Thread

Problem

You want to create a thread to perform some task while the main thread continues its work.

Solution

Create an object of the class thread, and pass it a functor that does the work. The creation of the thread object will instantiate an operating system thread that begins executing at operator( ) on your functor (or the beginning of the function if you passed in a function pointer instead). Example 12-1 shows you how.

Example 12-1. Creating a thread

```
#include <iostream>
#include <boost/thread/thread.hpp>
#include <boost/thread/xtime.hpp>

struct MyThreadFunc {
   void operator()() {
      // Do something long-running...
   }
} threadFun;

int main() {

   boost::thread myThread(threadFun); // Create a thread that starts
                                      // running threadFun
```

Example 12-1. Creating a thread (continued)

```
    boost::thread::yield( ); // Give up the main thread's timeslice
                             // so the child thread can get some work
                             // done.

    // Go do some other work...

    myThread.join( ); // The current (i.e., main) thread will wait
                      // for myThread to finish before it returns

}
```

Discussion

Creating a thread is deceptively simple. All you have to do is create a thread object on the stack or the heap, and pass it a functor that tells it where it can begin working. For this discussion, a "thread" is actually two things. First, it's an object of the class thread, which is a C++ object in the conventional sense. When I am referring to this object, I will say "thread object." Then there is the thread of execution, which is an operating system thread that is represented by the thread object. When I say "thread" (not in fixed-width font), I mean the operating system thread.

Let's get right to the code in the example. The thread constructor takes a functor (or function pointer) that takes no arguments and returns void. Look at this line from Example 12-1:

```
    boost::thread myThread(threadFun);
```

This creates the myThread object on the stack, which represents a new operating system thread that begins executing threadFun. At that point, the code in threadFun and the code in main are, at least in theory, running in parallel. They may not exactly be running in parallel, of course, because your machine may have only one processor, in which case this is impossible (recent processor architectures have made this not quite true, but I'll ignore dual-core processors and the like for now). If you have only one processor, then the operating system will give each thread you create a slice of time in the run state before it is suspended. Because these slices of time can be of varying sizes, you can never be guaranteed which thread will reach a particular point first. This is the aspect of multithreaded programming that makes it difficult: *multithreaded program state is nondeterministic*. The same multithreaded program, run multiple times, with the same inputs, can produce different output. Coordinating resources used by multiple threads is the subject of Recipe 12.2.

After creating myThread, the main thread continues, at least for a moment, until it reaches the next line:

```
    boost::thread::yield( );
```

This puts the current thread (in this case the main thread) in a sleep state, which means the operating system will switch to another thread or another process using

---

some operating-system-specific policy. yield is a way of telling the operating system that the current thread wants to give up the rest of its slice of time. Meanwhile, the new thread is executing threadFun. When threadFun is done, the child thread goes away. Note that the thread object doesn't go away, because it's still a C++ object that's in scope. This is an important distinction.

The thread object is something that exists on the heap or the stack, and works just like any other C++ object. When the calling code exits scope, any stack thread objects are destroyed and, alternatively, when the caller calls delete on a thread*, the corresponding heap thread object disappears. But thread objects are just proxies for the actual operating system threads, and when they are destroyed the operating system threads aren't guaranteed to go away. They merely become detached, meaning that they cannot later be rejoined. This is not a bad thing.

Threads use resources, and in any (well-designed) multithreaded application, access to such resources (objects, sockets, files, raw memory, and so on) is controlled with mutexes, which are objects used for serializing access to something among multiple threads (see Recipe 12.2). If an operating system thread is killed, it will not release its locks or deallocate its resources, similarly to how killing a process does not give it a chance to flush its buffers or release operating system resources properly. Simply ending a thread when you think it ought to be finished is like pulling a ladder out from under a painter when his time is up.

Thus, we have the join member function. As in Example 12-1, you can call join to wait for a child thread to finish. join is a polite way of telling the thread that you are going to wait until it's done working:

```
myThread.join();
```

The thread that calls join goes into a wait state until the thread represented by myThread is finished. If it never finishes, join never returns. join is the best way to wait for a child thread to finish.

You may notice that if you put something meaningful in threadFun, but comment out the use of join, the thread doesn't finish its work. Try this out by putting a loop or some long operation in threadFun. This is because when the operating system destroys a process, all of its child threads go with it, whether they're done or not. Without the call to join, main doesn't wait for its child thread: it exits, and the operating system thread is destroyed.

If you need to create several threads, consider grouping them with a thread_group object. A thread_group object can manage threads in a couple of ways. First, you can call add_thread with a pointer to a thread object, and that object will be added to the group. Here's a sample:

```
boost::thread_group grp;
boost::thread* p = new boost::thread(threadFun);
grp.add_thread(p);
// do something...
grp.remove_thread(p);
```

When grp's destructor is called, it will delete each of the thread pointers that were added with add_thread. For this reason, you can only add pointers to heap thread objects to a thread_group. Remove a thread by calling remove_thread and passing in the thread object's address (remove_thread finds the corresponding thread object in the group by comparing the pointer values, not by comparing the objects they point to). remove_thread will remove the pointer to that thread from the group, but you are still responsible for delete-ing it.

You can also add a thread to a group without having to create it yourself by calling create_thread, which (like a thread object) takes a functor as an argument and begins executing it in a new operating system thread. For example, to spawn two threads in a group, do this:

```
boost::thread_group grp;

grp.create_thread(threadFun);
grp.create_thread(threadFun); // Now there are two threads in grp

grp.join_all(); // Wait for all threads to finish
```

Whether you add threads to the group with create_thread or add_thread, you can call join_all to wait for all of the threads in the group to complete. Calling join_all is the same as calling join on each of the threads in the group: when all of the threads in the group have completed their work join_all returns.

Creating a thread object allows a separate thread of execution to begin. Doing it with the Boost Threads library is deceptively easy, though, so design carefully. Read the rest of the recipes in this chapter for more cautionary information about threads.

See Also

Recipe 12.2

12.2   Making a Resource Thread-Safe

Problem

You are using multiple threads in a program and you need to ensure a resource is not modified by more than one thread at a time. In general, this process is called making the resource *thread-safe*, or *serializing* access to it.

Solution

Use the class mutex, defined in *boost/thread/mutex.hpp*, to synchronize access among threads. Example 12-2 shows a simple use of a mutex object to control concurrent access to a queue.

Example 12-2. Making a class thread-safe

```cpp
#include <iostream>
#include <boost/thread/thread.hpp>
#include <string>

// A simple queue class; don't do this, use std::queue
template<typename T>
class Queue {
public:
   Queue( ) {}
  ~Queue( ) {}

   void enqueue(const T& x) {
      // Lock the mutex for this queue
      boost::mutex::scoped_lock lock(mutex_);
      list_.push_back(x);
      // A scoped_lock is automatically destroyed (and thus unlocked)
      // when it goes out of scope
   }

   T dequeue( ) {
      boost::mutex::scoped_lock lock(mutex_);

      if (list_.empty( ))
         throw "empty!";      // This leaves the current scope, so the
      T tmp = list_.front( ); // lock is released
      list_.pop_front( );
      return(tmp);
   } // Again: when scope ends, mutex_ is unlocked

private:
   std::list<T> list_;
   boost::mutex mutex_;
};

Queue<std::string> queueOfStrings;

void sendSomething( ) {
   std::string s;
   for (int i = 0; i < 10; ++i) {
      queueOfStrings.enqueue("Cyrus");
   }
}

void recvSomething( ) {
   std::string s;

   for (int i = 0; i < 10; ++i) {
      try {s = queueOfStrings.dequeue( );}
      catch(...) {}
   }
}
```

Example 12-2. Making a class thread-safe (continued)

```
int main( ) {
   boost::thread thr1(sendSomething);
   boost::thread thr2(recvSomething);

   thr1.join( );
   thr2.join( );
}
```

Discussion

Making classes, functions, blocks of code, or other objects thread-safe is at the heart of multithreaded programming. If you are designing a piece of software to be multi-threaded, chances are that each thread will have its own set of resources, such as stack and heap objects, operating system resources, and so on. But sooner or later you will need to share something among threads. It may be a shared queue of incoming work requests (as in a multithreaded web server) or something as simple as an output stream (as in a log file, or even cout). The standard way of coordinating the safe sharing of resources is with a *mutex*, which provides mutually exclusive access to something.

The rest of this discussion describes what a mutex is in general and how to use boost::mutex in particular to serialize access to resources. I use the concept/model approach terminology that I mentioned briefly in the introduction to this chapter. A *concept* is an abstract (language-independent) description of something, and a *model* of a concept is its concrete representation in C++ class form. A *refinement* of a concept is a given concept with some additional or augmented behavior.

Concurrent programming is a complicated subject though and there are many more techniques than can fit in a single recipe. There are lots of different patterns that can be used, and different strategies that should be used for different applications. If you plan to do a significant amount of multithreaded programming, or if you are designing performance-critical applications, you ought to pick up a good book on multi-threaded patterns. Many of the problems that make debugging multithreaded programs so difficult can be successfully averted with careful, tedious design.

Using mutexes

The mutex concept is simple: a mutex is something that represents a resource and can be locked or unlocked by only one thread at a time. It is a flag used to coordinate access to a resource by multiple consumers. In the Boost Threads library, the mutex concept is modeled by the boost::mutex class. In Example 12-2, write access to the Queue class is maintained with a mutex member variable:

```
    boost::mutex mutex_;
```

mutex_ must be locked by any member function that must change the state of the queue of items that is maintained. The mutex object itself has no knowledge of what it's representing. It's just a locked/unlocked flag that is shared by all consumers of some resource.

In Example 12-2, when a Queue member function needs to change the state of the object, it must first lock mutex_. Only one thread at a time can lock it, which is what prevents multiple objects from modifying the state of a Queue object. Thus, a mutex is a simple signaling mechanism, but it is more than just a bool or int, because a mutex *requires* serialized access, which can only be guaranteed by the operating system kernel. If you try doing the same thing with a bool, it won't work because there's nothing that prevents multiple threads from modifying the state of a bool at the same time. (Different operating systems have different ways of doing this, which is why it is not easy to implement a portable threading library.)

mutex objects are locked and unlocked using several different locking strategies, the simplest of which is the scoped_lock. A scoped_lock is a class that, when constructed using a mutex argument, locks it until the lock is destroyed. Look at the enqueue member function in Example 12-2 to see how scoped_lock works with a mutex:

```
void enqueue(const T& x) {
    boost::mutex::scoped_lock lock(mutex_);
    list_.push_back(x);
} // unlocked!
```

When lock is destroyed, mutex_ is unlocked. If the lock is constructed on a mutex that is already locked by another thread, the current thread goes into a wait state until the lock becomes available.

This design may seem a little odd at first—why not have lock and unlock methods on mutex? The approach of using a scoped_lock class that locks on construction and unlocks on destruction is actually much more convenient and less error-prone. When you create a lock using the scoped_lock approach, it locks the object for its lifetime, which means that you don't have to unlock explicitly anything on every control path. On the other hand, if you have to unlock a locked mutex explicitly, you have to ensure that any exceptions that are thrown in your function (or anywhere above your function on the call stack) are caught and the mutex is unlocked. With a scoped_lock, if an exception is thrown or the function returns, the scoped_lock object is automatically destroyed and the mutex is unlocked.

Using a mutex will get the job done, but it leaves a little to be desired. It makes no distinction between reading and writing, which is significant, because it is inefficient to force threads to wait in line to use a resource when many or all of them are doing a read-only operation, which should not require exclusive access. For this, the Boost Threads library provides read_write_mutex. Example 12-3 shows how you might implement Example 12-2 using a read_write_mutex with a front member function that allows the caller to retrieve a copy of the first item on the queue without popping it.

Example 12-3. Using a read/write mutex

```cpp
#include <iostream>
#include <boost/thread/thread.hpp>
#include <boost/thread/read_write_mutex.hpp>
#include <string>

template<typename T>
class Queue {
public:
   Queue() :   // Use a read/write mutex and give writers priority
      rwMutex_(boost::read_write_scheduling_policy::writer_priority) {}
  ~Queue() {}

   void enqueue(const T& x) {
      // Use a r/w lock since enqueue updates the state
      boost::read_write_mutex::scoped_write_lock writeLock(rwMutex_);
      list_.push_back(x);
   }

   T dequeue() {
      // Again, use a write lock
      boost::read_write_mutex::scoped_write_lock writeLock(rwMutex_);

      if (list_.empty())
         throw "empty!";
      T tmp = list_.front();
      list_.pop_front();
      return(tmp);
   }

   T getFront() {
      // This is a read-only operation, so you only need a read lock
      boost::read_write_mutex::scoped_read_lock readLock(rwMutex_);
      if (list_.empty())
         throw "empty!";
      return(list_.front());
   }

private:
   std::list<T> list_;
   boost::read_write_mutex rwMutex_;
};

Queue<std::string> queueOfStrings;

void sendSomething() {
   std::string s;
```

Example 12-3. Using a read/write mutex (continued)

```
    for (int i = 0; i < 10; ++i) {
        queueOfStrings.enqueue("Cyrus");
    }
}

void checkTheFront( ) {
    std::string s;

    for (int i = 0; i < 10; ++i) {
        try {s = queueOfStrings.getFront( );}
        catch(...) {}
    }
}

int main( ) {

    boost::thread thr1(sendSomething);
    boost::thread_group grp;

    grp.create_thread(checkTheFront);
    grp.create_thread(checkTheFront);
    grp.create_thread(checkTheFront);
    grp.create_thread(checkTheFront);

    thr1.join( );
    grp.join_all( );
}
```

There are a few things I should point out here. Notice that now I am using a read_ write_mutex, like this:

```
    boost::read_write_mutex rwMutex_;
```

The locks are also different when you're using read/write mutexes. In Example 12-3, when I want to lock the Queue for writing, I create a scoped_write_lock:

```
    boost::read_write_mutex::scoped_write_lock writeLock(rwMutex_);
```

And when I just need to read the Queue, I use a scoped_read_lock:

```
    boost::read_write_mutex::scoped_read_lock readLock(rwMutex_);
```

Read/write locks are handy, but they don't prevent you from shooting yourself in the foot. There is no compile-time check on the resource represented by rwMutex_ to make sure you're not changing it when you only have a read lock. Take extra care to ensure a thread only modifies the state of an object when it has a write lock because the compiler won't.

Exactly how these locks are scheduled is determined by the scheduling policy you chose when you constructed the mutex. There are four that are provided by the Boost Threads library:

reader_priority
> Threads waiting for a read lock will be granted the lock before those waiting for a write lock.

writer_priority
> Threads waiting for a write lock will be granted the lock before those waiting for a read lock.

alternating_single_read
> Alternate between read and write locks. Grant a single reader a read lock when it is the readers' "turn." This policy gives writers priority in general. For example, if the mutex is write-locked, and there are several pending read locks and one pending write lock, one read lock will be granted, then the waiting write lock will be granted, then all remaining read locks will be granted. This assumes no new locks are requested during this period.

alternating_many_reads
> Alternate between read and write locks. Grant all readers' locks when it is the readers' "turn." In other words, this policy empties the queue of all waiting read locks in between write locks.

Each of these policies has different pros and cons, and they will perform differently depending on your application. Deciding which policy to use takes careful consideration, because simply going with reader or writer priority can result in starvation, which I describe in more detail below.

Dangers

There are three basic problems that occur when you are programming with multiple threads: deadlock, starvation, and race conditions. There are techniques for avoiding each of them, with varying degrees of sophistication that are beyond the scope of this recipe. I will describe what each of the problems is so you know how what to watch out for, but if you plan on doing multithreaded application development, you should do some homework on multithreaded patterns first.

Deadlock is a situation that involves at least two threads and two resources. Consider two threads, A and B, and two resources, X and Y, where A has a lock on X and B has a lock on Y. A deadlock occurs when A tries to lock Y and B tries to lock X. If threads are not designed to break the deadlock somehow, then they will wait forever.

The Boost Threads library lets you avoid deadlocks with refinements to the mutex and locking concepts. A *try* mutex is one that supports attempts at locking, using a *try* lock that either succeeds or fails, but does not block and wait for the lock to become available. Using models of these concepts in the form of try_mutex and scoped_try_lock, your code can go and do something else if the resource you need to access is locked. There is also yet another refinement to the concept of a try lock, and that is a timed lock. With a timed lock, a thread can give up after blocking for a specific amount of time. I do not discuss timed locks in detail here; have a look at the Boost Threads documentation for details.

For example, in the Queue class in Example 12-2, you wanted to use a try mutex so dequeue returns a bool indicating whether or not it was able to dequeue the first item. This way, consumers of dequeue don't have to wait around if the queue is locked. Here's how you could rewrite dequeue:

```
bool dequeue(T& x) {
    boost::try_mutex::scoped_try_lock lock(tryMutex_);

    if (!lock.locked())
        return(false);
    else {
        if (list_.empty())
            throw "empty!";
        x = list_.front();
        list_.pop_front();
        return(true);
    }
}
private:
boost::try_mutex tryMutex_;
// ...
```

The mutex being used and the lock are different than those used in Example 12-2. Be sure to correctly qualify the names of the mutex and lock classes you are using, otherwise, you won't get the behavior you expect.

When you serialize access to something, you tell consumers of it to line up and wait their turn. If each of them stays in the same position in line, everybody gets a chance to use the resource. But if you let some consumers cut in line, it is possible that those at the back of the line never get their turn. This is starvation.

When using a mutex, consumers wait in a group and not a line. There is no guaranteed order among threads that are waiting for the lock. For read/write mutexes, the Boost Threads library uses the four scheduling policies described earlier. Therefore, when using read/write mutexes, be aware of what the different scheduling policies mean, and what your threads are doing. If you are using writer_priority, and you have lots of threads creating write locks, your readers will starve; the same goes for reader_priority, since these scheduling policies always prefer one type of lock over another. Through testing, if you recognize that one kind of thread isn't making as much progress as it should, consider switching to an alternating_many_reads or alternating_single_read policy. You specify the policy when constructing a read/write mutex.

Finally, a race condition is a situation where your code has made an assumption about the order or atomicity of locks that has proven false. For example, consider a

consumer of the Queue class that interrogates the element on the front and conditionally dequeues it:

```
if (q.getFront() == "Cyrus") {
    str = q.dequeue();
    // ...
```

This code works fine in a single-threaded environment, because q won't be modified
between the first and second lines. However, when using multiple threads, you have
to account for the situation where another thread modifies q at any moment—in fact,
you should *assume* that shared objects are modified when a thread doesn't have
them locked. After line 1, another thread can come along and dequeue the next item
from q, which means that line 2 gets something unexpected or nothing at all. Both
getFront and dequeue lock the single mutex used to modify q, but in between it is
unlocked, and if another thread is waiting on the lock, it may snatch it up before line
2 has a chance.

A solution, for this particular race condition, is to ensure that a lock is held for the
duration of the operation. Create a member function called dequeueIfEquals that
only dequeues the next object if it equals the argument. dequeueIfEquals can use a
lock like anything else:

```
T dequeueIfEquals(const T& t) {
    boost::mutex::scoped_lock lock(mutex_);
    if (list_.front() == t)
        // ...
```

There are other kinds of race conditions, but this example should give you a general
idea of what to watch out for. As the number of threads and shared resources you are
using increases, the race conditions become more subtle and difficult to catch.
Therefore, you should take special care to design to prevent them.

Ensuring serialized access to resources is the most difficult thing about multithreading, because when you don't do it right, debugging it can be a nightmare. Since a
multithreaded program is inherently nondeterministic (because threads can execute
in different order and for different lengths of time each time the program is run), it is
painful to try and pinpoint exactly where or how a thread modifies something it
shouldn't. More so than with single-threaded programming, a sound design will
minimize debugging and rework.

12.3   Notifying One Thread from Another

Problem

You are using a pattern where one thread (or group of threads) does something and
it needs to let another thread (or group of threads) know about it. You may have a
master thread that is handing out work to slave threads, or you may use one group of

threads to populate a queue and another to remove the data from it and do something useful.

Solution

Use mutex and condition objects, declared in *boost/thread/mutex.hpp* and *boost/thread/condition.hpp*. You can create a condition for each situation you want threads to wait for, and notify any waiting threads on the condition. Example 12-4 shows how to use signaling in a master/slave threading model.

Example 12-4. Signaling between threads

```
#include <iostream>
#include <boost/thread/thread.hpp>
#include <boost/thread/condition.hpp>
#include <boost/thread/mutex.hpp>
#include <list>
#include <string>

class Request { /*...*/ };

// A simple job queue class; don't do this, use std::queue
template<typename T>
class JobQueue {
public:
   JobQueue( ) {}
  ~JobQueue( ) {}

   void submitJob(const T& x) {
      boost::mutex::scoped_lock lock(mutex_);
      list_.push_back(x);
      workToBeDone_.notify_one( );
   }

   T getJob( ) {
      boost::mutex::scoped_lock lock(mutex_);

      workToBeDone_.wait(lock); // Wait until this condition is
                                // satisfied, then lock the mutex
      T tmp = list_.front( );
      list_.pop_front( );
      return(tmp);
   }

private:
   std::list<T> list_;
   boost::mutex mutex_;
   boost::condition workToBeDone_;
};

JobQueue<Request> myJobQueue;
```

Example 12-4. Signaling between threads (continued)

```
void boss( ) {
    for (;;) {
        // Get the request from somewhere
        Request req;
        myJobQueue.submitJob(req);
    }
}

void worker( ) {
    for (;;) {
        Request r(myJobQueue.getJob( ));
        // Do something with the job...
    }
}

int main( ) {
    boost::thread thr1(boss);
    boost::thread thr2(worker);
    boost::thread thr3(worker);

    thr1.join( );
    thr2.join( );
    thr3.join( );
}
```

Discussion

A condition object uses a `mutex`, and lets you wait for a situation other than its becoming unlocked. Consider Example 12-4, which is a modified version of the Queue class presented in Example 12-2. I have modified `Queue` to be a specific kind of queue, namely a `JobQueue`, where objects representing jobs are submitted by a master thread and are retrieved by slave threads.

The most important change for the `JobQueue` class is the `condition` member variable `workToBeDone_`. This is a condition that indicates whether or not there is work in the queue. When a thread wants to retrieve an element from the job queue, it calls `getJob`, which tries to acquire a lock on the mutex and then waits for the new condition with the following lines:

```
boost::mutex::scoped_lock lock(mutex_);
workToBeDone_.wait(lock);
```

The first line locks the mutex in the usual manner. The second line then *unlocks* the mutex and waits, or goes to sleep, until the condition is met. The unlocking of the mutex allows other threads to use that mutex—one of them might need it to set up the condition we are waiting for—otherwise, other threads would be unable to lock the mutex while one thread was waiting on the condition.

In `submitJob`, after the job has been added to the internal list, I added the following line:

```
workToBeDone_.notify_one( );
```

This "satisfies" the condition that `getJob` is waiting for. Technically, this means that if there are any threads who have called `wait` on this condition, that one of them is put in a run state. In `getJob`, that means that execution continues at the following line:

```
workToBeDone_.wait(lock);
```

But not just yet. `wait` does two things: it waits until someone calls `notify_one` or `notify_all` on the condition that it's waiting on, then it tries to lock the mutex it's associated with. So what actually happens when `submitJob` calls `notify_all` is that the waiting thread is put in a run state and the next thing it does is try to lock the mutex that `submitJob` still has locked, so it goes back into a wait state until `submitJob` is complete. Thus, `condition::wait` requires that the mutex be locked when you call it, at which point it is unlocked, then locked again when the condition is met.

Notify all threads that are waiting for some condition to be true by calling `notify_all`. This works the same way as `notify_one`, except that all threads that are waiting on the condition are changed to a run state. They all try and acquire the next lock though, so what happens after that depends on the kind of mutex and the type of locks used.

A condition gives you something subtle that you don't get when you are using mutexes and locks alone. Consider the case of the `Queue` class presented earlier. Threads waiting to `dequeue` something wait until they can acquire a write lock, then pop the next item off the queue. This may appear to work fine without any sort of signaling mechanism, but does it really? What about when the queue is empty? You have a few choices for how you implement `dequeue` if you are waiting for a condition to become true: acquire the lock; check to see if there are items in the queue or not, if not, return; use another mutex that is locked when the queue is empty and unlocked when it has data (not a good idea); or return a special value when the queue is empty. These are either problematic or inefficient. If you simply return when the queue is empty by throwing an exception or returning a special value, then your clients have to keep checking to see when something arrives. This is a needless drain on resources.

A `condition` lets consumer threads sleep so the processor can do something else while a condition is not met. Imagine a web server that uses a pool of worker threads to handle incoming requests. It is far better to have child threads in a wait state when there is no activity then to have them looping, or sleeping and waking up occasionally to check the queue.

12.4 Initializing Shared Resources Once

Problem

You have a number of threads that are using a resource that must only be initialized once.

Solution

Either initialize the resource before the threads are started, or if you can't, use the call_once function defined in <boost/thread/once.hpp> and the type once_flag. Example 12-5 shows how to use call_once.

Example 12-5. Initializing something once

```
#include <iostream>
#include <boost/thread/thread.hpp>
#include <boost/thread/once.hpp>

// Some sort of connection class that should only be initialized once
struct Conn {
   static void init() {++i_;}
   static boost::once_flag init_;
   static int i_;
   // ...
};

int Conn::i_ = 0;
boost::once_flag Conn::init_ = BOOST_ONCE_INIT;

void worker() {
   boost::call_once(Conn::init, Conn::init_);
   // Do the real work...
}

Conn c;  // You probably don't want to use a global, so see the
         // next Recipe

int main() {

   boost::thread_group grp;

   for (int i = 0; i < 100; ++i)
      grp.create_thread(worker);

   grp.join_all();

   std::cout << c.i_ << '\n'; // c.i_ = 1
}
```

Discussion

A shared resource has to be initialized somewhere, and you may want the first thread to use it to do the initializing. A variable of type once_flag (whose exact type is platform-dependent) and the call_once function can keep multiple threads from re-initializing the same object. You have to do two things.

First, initialize your once_flag variable to the macro BOOST_ONCE_INIT. This is a platform-dependent value. In Example 12-5, the class Conn represents some sort of connection (database, socket, hardware, etc.) that I only want initialized once even though multiple threads may try to initialize it. This sort of thing comes up often when you want to load a library dynamically, perhaps one specified in an application config file. The once_flag is a static class variable because I only want one initialization, no matter how many instances of the class there may be. So, I give the flag a starting value of BOOST_ONCE_INIT like this:

```
boost::once_flag Conn::initFlag_ = BOOST_ONCE_INIT;
```

Then, in my worker function, I invoke call_once, which synchronizes access to my init flag and, therefore, forbids concurrent initialization. I pass two arguments to call_once:

```
boost::call_once(Conn::init, Conn::initFlag_);
```

The first argument is the address of the function that will be doing the initialization. The second is the flag. This way, multiple threads can try to initialize the Conn class, but only the first will succeed.

12.5 Passing an Argument to a Thread Function

Problem

You have to pass an argument to your thread function, but the thread creation facilities in the Boost Threads library only accept functors that take no arguments.

Solution

Create a functor adapter that takes your parameters and returns a functor that takes no parameters. You can use the functor adapter where you would have otherwise put the thread functor. Take a look at Example 12-6 to see how this is done.

Example 12-6. Passing an argument to a thread function

```
#include <iostream>
#include <string>
#include <functional>
#include <boost/thread/thread.hpp>
```

Example 12-6. Passing an argument to a thread function (continued)

```cpp
// A typedef to make the declarations below easier to read
typedef void (*WorkerFunPtr)(const std::string&);

template<typename FunT,    // The type of the function being called
         typename ParamT> // The type of its parameter
struct Adapter {
    Adapter(FunT f, ParamT& p) : // Construct this adapter and set the
        f_(f), p_(&p) {}         // members to the function and its arg

    void operator()() { // This just calls the function with its arg
        f_(*p_);
    }
private:
    FunT    f_;
    ParamT* p_;  // Use the parameter's address to avoid extra copying
};

void worker(const std::string& s) {
    std::cout << s << '\n';
}

int main() {

    std::string s1 = "This is the first thread!";
    std::string s2 = "This is the second thread!";

    boost::thread thr1(Adapter<WorkerFunPtr, std::string>(worker, s1));
    boost::thread thr2(Adapter<WorkerFunPtr, std::string>(worker, s2));

    thr1.join();
    thr2.join();
}
```

Discussion

The fundamental problem you need to solve here is not specific to threading or Boost, but a general problem when you have to pass a functor with one signature to something that requires a different signature. The solution is to create an adapter.

The syntax can get a little messy, but essentially what Example 12-6 does is create a temporary functor that the thread constructor can call as a function with no arguments like it expects. First things first; use a typedef to make function pointer syntax easier to read:

```cpp
typedef void (*WorkerFunPtr)(const std::string&);
```

This creates a type `WorkerFunPtr` that is a pointer to a function that takes a `string` reference as an argument and returns `void`. After that, I created the `Adapter` class template. It provides a way to instantiate a dynamic functor. Take a look at the constructor:

```
template<typename FunT,
         typename ParamT>
struct Adapter {
    Adapter(FunT f, ParamT& p) :
        f_(f), p_(&p) {}
// ...
```

All the constructor does is initialize the two members, which can be any types, but we expect them to be a function pointer and some parameter p of any type. I store the address of the parameter instead of copying it by value to be efficient.

Now consider this line from the main thread:

```
boost::thread thr1(Adapter<WorkerFunPtr, std::string>(worker, s1));
```

The argument to `thr1`'s constructor is an instantiation of the `Adapter` class template, using the two types `WorkerFunPtr` and `std::string` as its arguments. That instance uses those two types for Adapter's `f_` and `p_` members. Finally, `Adapter` overrides `operator( )`, so it can be called like a function. When it is called, it simply does this:

```
f_(*p_);
```

Using the `Adapter` class template, you can pass arguments to thread functions, albeit with a little extra syntax. If you want to pass more than one argument, just add another type and member variable to `Adapter`. The nice thing about this approach is that you can create a set of generic adapter class templates and use them in various other contexts.

CHAPTER 13

Internationalization

13.0 Introduction

This chapter describes solutions to some common requirements when internationalizing C++ programs. Making software work in different locales (usually referred to as *localization*) usually requires solving two problems: formatting user-visible strings such that they obey local conventions (such as those for date, time, money, and numbers), and reconciling data in different character sets. This chapter deals mostly with the first issue, and only briefly with the second, because there is little standardized support for different character sets since most aspects of it are largely implementation dependent.

Most software will also run in countries other than the one where it was written. To support this practical reality, the C++ standard library has several facilities for writing code that will run in different countries. The design of these facilities, however, is different than many other standard library facilities such as strings, file input and output, containers, algorithms, and so forth. For example, the class that is used to represent a locale is locale, and is provided in the <locale> header. locale provides facilities for writing to and reading from streams using locale-specific formatting, and for getting information about a locale, such as the currency symbol or the date format. The standard only requires that a single locale be provided though, and that is the "C" or *classic* locale. The classic locale uses ANSI C conventions: American English conventions and 7-bit ASCII character encoding. It is up to the implementation whether it will provide locale instances for the various languages and regions.

There are three fundamental parts to the <locale> header. First, there is the locale class. It encapsulates all aspects of behavior for a locale that C++ supports, and it is your entry point to the different kinds of locale information you need to do locale-aware formatting. Second, the most granular part of a locale, and the concrete classes you will be working with, are called *facets*. An example of a facet is a class such as time_put for writing a date to a stream. Third, each facet belongs to a *category*, which is a way of grouping related facets together. Examples of categories are numeric, time, and monetary (the `time_put` facet I mentioned a moment ago belongs to the time category). I mention categories briefly in this chapter, but they only really come in handy when you are doing some more sophisticated stuff with locales, so I don't cover their use in depth here.

Every C++ program has at least one locale, referred to as the global locale (it is often implemented as a global static object). By default, it is the classic "C" locale unless you change it to something else. One of the `locale` constructors allows you to instantiate the user's preferred locale, although an implementation is free to define exactly what a user's "preferred" locale is.

In most cases, you will only use locales when writing to or reading from streams. This is the main focus of this chapter.

13.1   Hardcoding a Unicode String

Problem

You have to hardcode a Unicode, i.e., wide-character, string in a source file.

Solution

Do this by hardcoding the string with a prefix of `L` and typing the character into your source editor as you would any other string, or use the hexadecimal number that represents the Unicode character you're after. Example 13-1 shows how to do it both ways.

Example 13-1. Hardcoding a Unicode string

```
#include <iostream>
#include <fstream>
#include <string>

using namespace std;

int main( ) {

    // Create some strings with Unicode characters
    wstring ws1 = L"Infinity: \u221E";
    wstring ws2 = L"Euro: _";

    wchar_t w[] = L"Infinity: \u221E";

    wofstream out("tmp\\unicode.txt");
    out << ws2 << endl;
    wcout << ws2 << endl;
}
```

Discussion

Hardcoding a Unicode string is mostly a matter of deciding how you want to enter the string in your source editor. C++ provides a wide-character type, wchar_t, which can store Unicode strings. The exact implementation of wchar_t is implementation defined, but it is often UTF-32. The class wstring, defined in <string>, is a sequence of wchar_ts, just like the string class is a sequence of chars. (Strictly speaking, of course, wstring is a typedef for basic_string<wchar_t>).

The easiest way to enter Unicode characters is to use the L prefix to a string literal, as in Example 13-1:

```
wstring ws1 = L"Infinity: \u2210";  // Use the code itself
wstring ws2 = L"Euro: €";           // Or just type it in
```

Now, you can write these wide-character strings to a wide-character stream, like this:

```
wcout << ws1 << endl; // wcout is the wide char version of cout
```

This goes for files, too:

```
wofstream out("tmp\\unicode.txt");
out << ws2 << endl;
```

The trickiest part of dealing with different character encodings isn't embedding the right characters in your source files, it's knowing what kind of character data you are getting back from a database, HTTP request, user input, and so on, and this is beyond the realm of the C++ standard. The C++ standard does not require a particular encoding, rather that the character encoding used by your operating system to store source files can be anything, as long as it supports at least the 96 characters used by the C++ language. For characters that are not part of this character set, called the *basic source character set*, the standard indicates that they must be available by using the \u*XXXX* or \U*XXXXXXXX* escape sequences, where each *X* is a hexadecimal digit.

13.2   Writing and Reading Numbers

Problem

You need to write a number to a stream in a formatted way that obeys local conventions, which are different depending on where you are.

Solution

Imbue the stream you are writing to with the current locale and then write the numbers to it, as in Example 13-2, or you can set the global locale and then create a stream. The latter approach is explained in the discussion.

Example 13-2. Writing numbers using localized formatting

```
#include <iostream>
#include <locale>
#include <string>

using namespace std;

// There is a global locale in the background that is set up by the
// runtime environment. It is the "C" locale by default. You can
// replace it with locale::global(const locale&).
int main() {
    locale loc(""); // Create a copy of the user's locale
    cout << "Locale name = " << loc.name() << endl;

    cout.imbue(loc); // Tell cout to use the formatting of
                     // the user's locale

    cout << "pi in locale " << cout.getloc().name() << " is "
        << 3.14 << endl;
}
```

Discussion

Example 13-2 shows how to use the user's locale to format a floating-point number. Doing so requires two steps, creating an instance of the `locale` class and then associating, or *imbuing*, the stream with it.

To begin with, Example 13-2 creates `loc`, which is a copy of the user's locale. You have to do this using `locale`'s constructor with an empty string (and not the default constructor), like this:

```
locale loc("");
```

The difference is subtle but important, and I'll come back to it in a moment. Creating a locale object in this way creates a copy of the "user's locale," which is something that is implementation defined. This means that if the machine has been configured to use American English, `locale::name()` will return a locale string such as `"en_US"`, `"English_United States.1252"`, `"english-american"`, and so on. The actual string is implementation defined, and the only one required to work by the C++ standard is `"C"`.

By comparison, `locale`'s default constructor returns a copy of the current *global* locale. There is a single, global `locale` object for every C++ program that is run (probably implemented as a `static` variable somewhere in the runtime library— exactly how this is done is implementation defined). By default, it is the C locale, and you can replace it with `locale::global(locale& loc)`. When streams are created, they use the global locale at the time of creation, which means that `cin`, `cout`, `cerr`, `wcin`, `wcout`, and `wcerr` use the C locale, so you have to change them explicitly if you want the formatting to obey a certain locale's conventions.

Locale names are not standardized. Usually, however, they look something like this:

```
<language>_<country>.<codepage>
```

Where language is either a full language name, such as "Spanish", or a two-letter code, such as "sp"; country is a country, such as "Colombia", or a two-letter country code such as "CO", and code page is the code page, e.g., 1252. The language is the only required part. Experiment using explicit locales on various systems to get a feel for what the different names will look like using different compilers. If the locale name you use is invalid, it will throw a runtime_error. Example 13-3 gives a few examples of explicit locale names.

Example 13-3. Naming locales explicitly

```cpp
#include <iostream>
#include <fstream>
#include <locale>
#include <string>

using namespace std;

int main() {
   try {
      locale loc("");
      cout << "Locale name = " << loc.name() << endl;

      locale locFr("french");
      locale locEn("english-american");
      locale locBr("portuguese-brazilian");

      cout.imbue(locFr); // Tell cout to use French formatting

      cout << "3.14 (French) = " << 3.14 << endl;
      cout << "Name = " << locFr.name() << endl;

      cout.imbue(locEn); // Now change to English (American)

      cout << "3.14 (English) = " << 3.14 << endl;
      cout << "Name = " << locEn.name() << endl;

      cout.imbue(locFr); // Tell cout to use Brazilian formatting

      cout << "3.14 (Brazil) = " << 3.14 << endl;
      cout << "Name = " << locBr.name() << endl;
   }
   catch (runtime_error& e) {
      // If you use an invalid locale name, a runtime_error exception
      // is thrown.
      cerr << "Error: " << e.what() << endl;
   }
}
```

The output of this program on Windows with Visual C++ 7.1 looks like this:

```
Locale name = English_United States.1252
3.14 (French) = 3,14
Name = French_France.1252
3.14 (English) = 3.14
Name = English_United States.1252
3.14 (Brazil) = 3,14
Name = Portuguese_Brazil.1252
```

You can see that my machine's locale is U.S. English using codepage 1252. The example also shows pi using a couple of other locales. Note that France and Brazil use a comma instead of a decimal point. The thousands separator is different, too: French and Portuguese use a space instead of a comma, so that 1,000,000.25 in America would be written as 1 000 000,25 in French and Portuguese.

Creating locales with explicit names is something you shouldn't have to do in most cases anyway. For using locales to print numbers, dates, currency, or anything else, you should simply instantiate a locale using an empty string, and imbue your streams with it.

Locale behavior can be a bit confusing, so I will summarize important points:

- The default global locale is the "C" locale, because it is the only one guaranteed to exist in every implementation, per the standard.
- The standard streams are all created using the global locale at program start-up, which is the "C" locale.
- You can create a copy of the user's current runtime locale by passing an empty string to the locale constructor, e.g., locale("").
- You can create a locale object for a named locale by passing in a string that identifies the locale, e.g., locale("portuguese-brazilian"). The strings are not standardized, though.
- Once you have a locale object that represents the user's default locale or a named locale, you can set the global locale with locale::global. All streams that are created subsequently will use the global locale.
- You can set the locale for a stream explicitly with the imbue member function.

When writing software to use locales, only use localized formatting for user-visible data. That is, if you need to display a number in a format the user is familiar with, instantiate a locale and imbue the stream with it to display the number correctly to the user. But if you are writing data to a file or some other intermediate serialized storage, use the C locale for portability. If your code explicitly changes the global locale, then you will need to explicitly imbue your file streams with the C locale. You can do this two ways, by creating a locale using the name "C," or by calling locale::classic( ), like this:

```
ofstream out("data.dat");
out.imbue(locale::classic( ));
out << pi << endl; // Write using C locale
```

Reading numbers is similar. For example, to read in a number in French and write it in the C locale, do this:

```
double d;
cin.imbue(locale("french"));
cin >> d;
cout << "In English: " << d;
```

If you run this program and enter **300,00**, it will print out 300.

To make a stream obey a locale's numeric conventions, explicitly imbue the stream with the target locale object. Or, if you want all streams created to use a particular locale, install it as the global locale. Currency is handled somewhat differently; see Recipe 13.4 for examples of how to write and read currency.

See Also

Recipe 13.4

13.3   Writing and Reading Dates and Times

Problem

You need to display or read dates and times using local formatting conventions.

Solution

Use the time_t type and tm struct from <ctime>, and the date and time facets provided in <locale>, to write and read dates and times (facets are described in the discussion in a moment). See Example 13-4 for a sample.

Example 13-4. Writing and reading dates

```
#include <iostream>
#include <ctime>
#include <locale>
#include <sstream>
#include <iterator>

using namespace std;

void translateDate(istream& in, ostream& out) {

   // Create a date reader
   const time_get<char>& dateReader =
     use_facet<time_get<char> >(in.getloc());

   // Create a state object, which the facets will use to tell
   // us if there was a problem.
   ios_base::iostate state = 0;
```

Example 13-4. Writing and reading dates (continued)

```
    // End marker
    istreambuf_iterator<char> end;

    tm t; // Time struct (from <ctime>)

    // Now that all that's out of the way, read in the date from
    // the input stream and put it in a time struct.
    dateReader.get_date(in, end, in, state, &t);

    // Now the date is in a tm struct. Print it to the out stream
    // using its locale. Make sure you only print out what you
    // know is valid in t.
    if (state == 0 || state == ios_base::eofbit) {
        // The read succeeded.
        const time_put<char>& dateWriter =
            use_facet<time_put<char> >(out.getloc());

        char fmt[] = "%x";

        if (dateWriter.put(out, out, out.fill(),
                           &t, &fmt[0], &fmt[2]).failed())
            cerr << "Unable to write to output stream.\n";
    } else {
        cerr << "Unable to read cin!\n";
    }
}

int main() {

    cin.imbue(locale("english"));
    cout.imbue(locale("german"));
    translateDate(cin, cout);
}
```

This program produces the following output:

```
3/28/2005
28.03.2005
```

Discussion

Writing and reading date and time data requires some knowledge of locale's design details. Read the introduction to this chapter if you aren't already familiar with the concepts of locales and facets.

C++ does not have a standard class for representing dates and times; the closest it gets is the time_t type and struct tm from <ctime>. If you want to write and read dates using standard library facilities, you will have to be able to convert whatever nonstandard date representation you are using to a struct tm. It is worthwhile to do so, since the implementation(s) you are using has probably already built in support for formatting locale-sensitive dates.

Earlier, I stated that a facet was an aspect of a locale that requires locale-specific behavior. More concretely, a facet is a `const` instantiation of a class template for a character type that looks up how it behaves based on the locale class you give it at construction. In Example 13-4, I create an instance of the `time_get` facet like this:

```
const time_get<char>& dateReader =
  use_facet<time_get<char> >(in.getloc());
```

The function template `use_facet` looks up a given facet for a given locale. All of the standard facets are class templates that accept a character type parameter, and since I am reading and writing chars, I instantiate my `time_get` class for chars. The standard requires that an implementation provide template specializations for char and `wchar_t`, so they are guaranteed to exist (although it is not guaranteed to support a given locale other than the C locale). The `time_get` object I created is `const` because the locale functionality provided by an implementation is a set of rules for formatting various kinds of data in different locales, and the rules are not user-editable, thus, the state of a given facet should not be changed by consumer code.

The locale I pass to `use_facet` is the one associated with the stream I am about to write to. `getloc()` is declared in `ios_base` and returns the locale associated with an input or output stream. Using the locale that is already associated with the stream you want to read from or write to is the best approach; passing in the locale name as a parameter or being specified in some other manner is error prone.

Once I've created the object that's going to do the actual reading, I need to create something to capture stream state:

```
ios_base::iostate state = 0;
```

Facets don't modify the state of the stream itself, e.g., set `stream::failbit = 1`; instead, they will set the state in your state object to indicate that a date couldn't be read. This is because failure to read a formatted value isn't a problem with the stream necessarily—the input stream of characters may still be perfectly valid—but reading it in the format you expect may not be possible.

The actual date information is stored in a `struct tm`. All I have to do is create a local tm variable and pass its address to the `time_get` or `time_put` facets.

Once I have read in the date, I can check the state variable I used to see if all went as expected. If it is equal to zero or `ios_base::eofbit`, then that indicates that the stream state is okay and that my date was read in with no problem. Since in Example 13-4 I want to write the date out to another stream, I have to create an object for just that purpose. I do it like this:

```
const time_put<char>& dateWriter =
  use_facet<time_put<char> >(out.getloc());
```

This works the same way as the previous instantiation of a `time_get` class, but in the other direction. After that, I created a formatting string (with `printf`-like formatting syntax) that will print the date. "%x" prints the date and "%X" prints the time. Be careful though: this example only read in the date, so the members of the struct tm that have to do with time are undefined at this point.

Now, I can write to the output stream. Here's how:

```
if (dateWriter.put(out,        // Output stream iterator
                   out,        // Output stream
                   out.fill(), // Fill char to use
                   &t,         // Addr of tm struct
                   &fmt[0],    // Begin and end of format string
                   &fmt[2]
                  ).failed()) // iter_type.failed( ) tells us if
                              // there was a problem writing
```

time_put::put writes the date to the output stream you pass it using the locale it (the time_put object) was created with. time_put::put returns an ostreambuf_iterator, which has a member function failed that you can call to see if the iterator is in a corrupt state.

get_date isn't the only member function you can use to get components of a date from a stream. There are a few of them:

get_date
    Gets the date from a stream using a locale's formatting rules

get_time
    Gets the time from a stream using a locale's formatting rules

get_weekday
    Gets the weekday name, e.g., Monday, lundi, понедельник

get_year
    Gets the year from a stream using a locale's formatting rules

Something else that you may find handy is the date_order member function. It returns an enumeration (time_base::dateorder in <locale>) that indicates the order of month, day, and year in the date. This can be useful if you have to parse the date output by time_get::put. Example 13-5 shows how to check the date order.

Example 13-5. Looking at date order

```
#include <iostream>
#include <locale>
#include <string>

using namespace std;

int main( ) {

   cin.imbue(locale("german"));

   const time_get<char>& dateReader =
     use_facet<time_get<char> >(cin.getloc( ));
```

Example 13-5. Looking at date order (continued)

```
  time_base::dateorder d = dateReader.date_order();

  string s;

  switch (d) {
  case time_base::no_order:
    s = "No order";
    break;
  case time_base::dmy:
    s = "day/month/year";
    break;
  case time_base::mdy:
    s = "month/day/year";
    break;
  case time_base::ymd:
    s = "year/month/day";
    break;
  case time_base::ydm:
    s = "year/day/month";
    break;
  }

  cout << "Date order for locale " << cin.getloc().name()
       << " is " << s << endl;
}
```

There is also another handy feature you can use when it comes to instantiating facets: has_facet. This is a function template that returns a bool indicating whether the facet you want is defined for a given locale. So to be safe, take advantage of has_facet whenever you are instantiating a facet. If it returns false, you can always default to the classic C locale, since it's guaranteed to be there by a standard-conforming implementation. has_facet looks like this:

```
  if (has_facet<time_put<char> >(loc)) {
    const time_put<char>& dateWriter =
      use_facet<time_put<char> >(loc);
```

Once you get over the syntax of the time_get and time_put classes, you will find them straightforward to use. As always, you can use typedef to minimize the number of unsightly angle brackets:

```
  typedef time_put<char> TimePutNarrow;
  typedef time_get<char> TimeGetNarrow;
  // ...
  const TimeGetNarrow& dateReader = use_facet<TimeGetNarrow>(loc);
```

Writing and reading dates in locale-specific formats is a bit tedious, but once you have an understanding of locale's expectations of you, it is effective and powerful. Chapter 5 is entirely dedicated to the subject of dates and times, so for more detailed formatting information when writing dates and times, see Recipe 5.2.

See Also

Chapter 5 and Recipe 5.2

13.4 Writing and Reading Currency

Problem

You need to write or read a formatted currency value to or from a stream.

Solution

Use the money_put and money_get facets to write and read currency, as shown in Example 13-6.

Example 13-6. Writing and reading currency

```
#include <iostream>
#include <locale>
#include <string>
#include <sstream>

using namespace std;

long double readMoney(istream& in, bool intl = false) {

    long double val;

    // Create a reader facet
    const money_get<char>& moneyReader =
      use_facet<money_get<char> >(in.getloc());

    // End marker
    istreambuf_iterator<char> end;

    // State variable for detecting errors
    ios_base::iostate state = 0;

    moneyReader.get(in, end, intl, in, state, val);

    // failbit will be set if something went wrong
    if (state != 0 && !(state & ios_base::eofbit))
        throw "Couldn't read money!\n";

    return(val);
}

void writeMoney(ostream& out, long double val, bool intl = false) {

    // Create a writer facet
    const money_put<char>& moneyWriter =
      use_facet<money_put<char> >(out.getloc());
```

Example 13-6. Writing and reading currency (continued)

```
    // Write to the stream. Call failed() (the return value is an
    // ostreambuf_iterator) to see if anything went wrong.
    if (moneyWriter.put(out, intl, out, out.fill(), val).failed())
        throw "Couldn't write money!\n";
}

int main() {

    long double val = 0;
    float exchangeRate = 0.775434f;   // Dollars to Euros
    locale locEn("english");
    locale locFr("french");

    cout << "Dollars: ";
    cin.imbue(locEn);
    val = readMoney(cin, false);

    cout.imbue(locFr);
    // Set the showbase flag so the currency char is printed
    cout.setf(ios_base::showbase);
    cout << "Euros: ";
    writeMoney(cout, val * exchangeRate, true);
}
```

If you run Example 13-6, your output might look like this:

```
    Dollars: $100
    Euros: EUR77,54
```

Discussion

The money_put and money_get facets write and read formatted currency values to and from a stream. They work almost identically to the date/time and numeric facets described in previous recipes. The standard requires instantiations of these for narrow and wide characters, e.g., money_put<char> and money_put<wchar_t>. As with the other facets, the get and put functions are verbose, but once you use them a few times, the parameters are easy to remember. money_get and money_put use a moneypunct class that stores formatting information.

First, let's discuss writing money to a stream. The display of currency involves several pieces: the currency sign, the positive or negative sign, the thousands separator, and the decimal point. Most of these are optional, except the decimal point.

You create a money_put object with a character type and a locale, like this:

```
    const money_put<char>& moneyWriter =
      use_facet<money_put<char> >(out.getloc());
```

Both the char and wchar_t versions of money_put are required by the C++ standard. It is a good idea to use the locale of the stream you are writing to to avoid mismatches that result from trying to keep the stream and the money_put object in sync. Next, call the put method to write the currency value to an output stream:

```
if (moneyWriter.put(out,        // Output iterator
                    intl,       // bool: use intl format?
                    out,        // ostream&
                    out.fill(), // fill char to use
                    val)        // currency value as long double
               .failed())
        throw "Couldn't write money!\n";
```

money_put::put writes the date to the output stream you pass it using the locale it (the money_put object) was created with. money_put::put returns an ostreambuf_iterator that points to one past the last character output, which has a member function failed you can call to see if the iterator is in a corrupt state.

The parameters to money_put::put are all self-explanatory, except maybe the second one (the intl argument in the example). It is a bool that determines whether the currency symbol is used (e.g., $, €), or the international three-letter code is used (e.g., USD, EUR). Set it to false to use the symbol, true to use the international code.

Writing currency to an output stream obeys some of the formatting flags on the stream. Here is each flag and the effect it has on currency:

ios_base::internal
> Wherever there is a space or nothing in the formatting of the currency, the fill character will be used (and not a space). See the discussion of moneypunct below for more information about the patterns used for formatting.

ios_base::left *and* ios_base::right
> Causes the currency value to be left or right justified, and the remaining space up to the width value is padded with the fill character (see the description of width next). This is handy because it makes for easy tabular formatting of currency.

ios_base::width
> money_put values will follow the standard rules for stream field width. By default, values are left justified. If the field is larger than the value, the fill character given to money_put is used.

ios_base::showbase
> When this is true, the currency symbol is printed; otherwise, it is not.

As I said earlier, money_get and money_put use a moneypunct class, which is what actually stores the formatting information. You don't need to worry about the moneypunct class unless you are implementing a standard library, but you can use it to explore the formatting used for a particular locale. moneypunct contains information such as the currency symbol used, the character used for the decimal point, the format of positive and negative values, and so on. Example 13-7 presents a short program for printing out currency format information for a given locale.

Example 13-7. Printing currency format info

```
#include <iostream>
#include <locale>
#include <string>

using namespace std;

string printPattern(moneypunct<char>::pattern& pat) {

    string s(pat.field);  // pat.field is a char[4]
    string r;

    for (int i = 0; i < 4; ++i) {
        switch (s[i]) {
        case moneypunct<char>::sign:
          r += "sign ";
          break;
        case moneypunct<char>::none:
          r += "none ";
          break;
        case moneypunct<char>::space:
          r += "space ";
          break;
        case moneypunct<char>::value:
          r += "value ";
          break;
        case moneypunct<char>::symbol:
          r += "symbol ";
          break;
        }
    }
    return(r);
}

int main() {

    locale loc("danish");

    const moneypunct<char>& punct =
      use_facet<moneypunct<char> >(loc);

    cout << "Decimal point:        " << punct.decimal_point() << '\n'
         << "Thousands separator: " << punct.thousands_sep() << '\n'
         << "Currency symbol:      " << punct.curr_symbol() << '\n'
         << "Positive sign:        " << punct.positive_sign() << '\n'
         << "Negative sign:        " << punct.negative_sign() << '\n'
         << "Fractional digits:    " << punct.frac_digits() << '\n'
         << "Positive format:      "
         << printPattern(punct.pos_format()) << '\n'
         << "Negative format:      "
         << printPattern(punct.neg_format()) << '\n';
```

Example 13-7. Printing currency format info (continued)

```
    // Grouping is represented by a string of chars, but the meaning
    // of each char is its integer value, not the char it represents.
    string s = punct.grouping( );
    for (string::iterator p = s.begin( ); p != s.end( ); ++p)
        cout << "Groups of: " << (int)*p << '\n';
}
```

Most of these methods are self-explanatory, but a few require further explanation. First, the grouping method returns a string of characters that is interpreted as a string of integers. Each character represents the grouping at that particular index in the number, starting at the right side of the number. And if there is no value for an index, the value for the next previous index is used. In other words, for standard American formatting, there will be a value of 3 at index 0 in the string, which means at index 0, the numbers should be grouped in triplets. Since there are no more values, all indexes greater than zero should also use grouping in triplets.

pos_format and neg_format return an object of type moneypunct<T>::pattern, which has a member field that is a T[4], where T is the character type. Each element in field is one of the enumerations moneypunct<T>::part, which has five possible values: none, space, symbol, sign, and value. A string representation of currency has four parts (thus the array of length four). Typically, the sequence of parts will be something like symbol space sign value, which would mean to print a value as $ -32.00. Often, the positive sign is the empty string since a value with no sign is generally assumed to be positive. The negative sign can be more than one character, such as "()," in which case the first character is printed where the symbol part occurs in neg_format, and the remainder is printed at the end, so you can have negative values represented as $(32.00).

Most of the time you will not need to worry about the formatting information stored in moneypunct. But if you have to do a lot of formatting of money in different locales, it's worthwhile to experiment and see how different locales are formatted.

See Also

Recipes 13.2 and 13.3

13.5   Sorting Localized Strings

Problem

You have a sequence of strings that contain non-ASCII characters, and you need to sort according to local convention.

Solution

The locale class has built-in support for comparing characters in a given locale by overriding operator. You can use an instance of the locale class as your comparison functor when you call any standard function that takes a functor for comparison. (See Example 13-8.)

Example 13-8. Locale-specific sorting

```cpp
#include <iostream>
#include <locale>
#include <string>
#include <vector>
#include <algorithm>

using namespace std;

bool localeLessThan (const string& s1, const string& s2) {

    const collate<char>& col =
      use_facet<collate<char> >(locale()); // Use the global locale

    const char* pb1 = s1.data();
    const char* pb2 = s2.data();

    return (col.compare(pb1, pb1 + s1.size(),
                        pb2, pb2 + s2.size()) < 0);
}

int main() {

    // Create two strings, one with a German character
    string s1 = "diät";
    string s2 = "dich";

    vector<string> v;
    v.push_back(s1);
    v.push_back(s2);

    // Sort without giving a locale, which will sort according to the
    // current global locale's rules.
    sort(v.begin(), v.end());
    for (vector<string>::const_iterator p = v.begin();
        p != v.end(); ++p)
      cout << *p << endl;

    // Set the global locale to German, and then sort
    locale::global(locale("german"));
    sort(v.begin(), v.end(), localeLessThan);
    for (vector<string>::const_iterator p = v.begin();
        p != v.end(); ++p)
      cout << *p << endl;
}
```

The first sort follows ASCII sorting convention, and therefore the output looks like this:

```
dich
diät
```

The second sort uses the proper ordering according to German semantics, and it is just the opposite:

```
diät
dich
```

Discussion

Sorting becomes more complicated when you're working in different locales, and the standard library solves this problem. The facet `collate` provides a member function `compare` that works like `strcmp`: it returns -1 if the first string is less than the second, 0 if they are equal, and 1 if the first string is greater than the second. Unlike `strcmp`, `collate::compare` uses the character semantics of the target locale.

Example 13-8 presents the function `localeLessThan`, which returns `true` if the first argument is less than the second according to the global locale. The most important part of the function is the call to compare:

```
col.compare(pb1,            // Pointer to the first char
            pb1 + s1.size(), // Pointer to one past the last char
            pb2,
            pb2 + s2.size())
```

Depending on the execution character set of your implementation, Example 13-8 may return the results I showed earlier or not. But if you want to ensure string comparison works in a locale-specific manner, you should use `collate::compare`. Of course, the standard does not require an implementation to support any locales other than "C," so be sure to test for all the locales you support.

CHAPTER 14

XML

14.0 Introduction

XML is important in many areas, including information storage and retrieval, publishing, and network communication; in this chapter, you'll learn to work with XML in C++. Because this book is about C++ rather than XML, I'll assume you already have some experience with the various XML-related technologies I discuss, including SAX, DOM, XML Schema, XPath, and XSLT. Don't worry if you're not an expert in all of these areas; the recipes in this chapter are more or less independent of each other, so you should be able to skip some of the recipes and still understand the rest. In any case, each recipe provides a quick explanation of the XML concepts and tools it uses.

If you come from another programming language, such as Java, you may expect to find the tools for XML processing in C++ to be included in the C++ standard library. Unfortunately, XML was in its infancy when the C++ standard was approved, and while there's strong interest in adding XML processing to a future version of the C++ standard library, for now you will have to rely on the collection of excellent third-party XML libraries available in C++.

Before you start reading recipes, you may want to download and install the libraries I'll be covering in this chapter. Table 14-1 shows the homepage of each library; Table 14-2 shows the features of each library and the recipes that use the library. The table doesn't show each library's exact level of conformance to the various XML specifications and recommendations because this information is likely to change in the near future.

Table 14-1. C++ libraries for XML

Library name	Homepage
TinyXml	*www.grinninglizard.com/tinyxml*
Xerxes	*xml.apache.org/xerces-c*

Table 14-1. C++ libraries for XML (continued)

Library name	Homepage
Xalan	*xml.apache.org/xalan-c*
Pathan 1	*software.decisionsoft.com/pathanIntro.html*
Boost.Serialization	*www.boost.org/libs/serialization*

Table 14-2. How each library is used

Library name	Features	Recipes
TinyXml	DOM (nonstandard)	14.1
Xerxes	SAX2, DOM, XML Schema	14.2–14.8
Xalan	XSLT, XPath	14.7–14.8
Pathan	XPath	14.8
Boost.Serialization	XML Serialization	14.9

14.1   Parsing a Simple XML Document

Problem

You have a collection of data stored in an XML document. You want to parse the document and turn the data it contains into a collection of C++ objects. Your XML document is small enough to fit into memory and doesn't use an internal Document Type Definition (DTD) or XML Namespaces.

Solution

Use the TinyXml library. First, define an object of type TiXmlDocument and call its LoadFile( ) method, passing the pathname of your XML document as its argument. If LoadFile( ) returns true, your document has been successfully parsed. If parsing was successful, call the RootElement( ) method to obtain a pointer to an object of type TiXmlElement representing the document root. This object has a hierarchical structure that reflects the structure of your XML document; by traversing this structure, you can extract information about the document and use this information to create a collection of C++ objects.

For example, suppose you have an XML document *animals.xml* representing a collection of circus animals, as shown in Example 14-1. The document root is named animalList and has a number of child animal elements each representing an animal owned by the Feldman Family Circus. Suppose you also have a C++ class named Animal, and you want to construct a std::vector of Animals corresponding to the animals listed in the document.

Example 14-1. An XML document representing a list of circus animals

```xml
<?xml version="1.0" encoding="UTF-8"?>

<!-- Feldman Family Circus Animals -->

<animalList>
    <animal>
        <name>Herby</name>
        <species>elephant</species>
        <dateOfBirth>1992-04-23</dateOfBirth>
        <veterinarian name="Dr. Hal Brown" phone="(801)595-9627"/>
        <trainer name="Bob Fisk" phone="(801)881-2260"/>
    </animal>
    <animal>
        <name>Sheldon</name>
        <species>parrot</species>
        <dateOfBirth>1998-09-30</dateOfBirth>
        <veterinarian name="Dr. Kevin Wilson" phone="(801)466-6498"/>
        <trainer name="Eli Wendel" phone="(801)929-2506"/>
    </animal>
    <animal>
        <name>Dippy</name>
        <species>penguin</species>
        <dateOfBirth>2001-06-08</dateOfBirth>
        <veterinarian name="Dr. Barbara Swayne" phone="(801)459-7746"/>
        <trainer name="Ben Waxman" phone="(801)882-3549"/>
    </animal>
</animalList>
```

Example 14-2 shows how the definition of the class `Animal` might look. `Animal` has five data members corresponding to an animal's name, species, date of birth, veterinarian, and trainer. An animal's name and species are represented as `std::string`s, its date of birth is represented as a `boost::gregorian::date` from Boost.Date_Time, and its veterinarian and trainer are represented as instances of the class `Contact`, also defined in Example 14-2. Example 14-3 shows how to use TinyXml to parse the document *animals.xml*, traverse the parsed document, and populate a `std::vector` of Animals using data extracted from the document.

Example 14-2. The header animal.hpp

```cpp
#ifndef ANIMALS_HPP_INCLUDED
#define ANIMALS_HPP_INCLUDED

#include <ostream>
#include <string>
#include <stdexcept> // runtime_error
#include <boost/date_time/gregorian/gregorian.hpp>
#include <boost/regex.hpp>

// Represents a veterinarian or trainer
class Contact {
public:
```

Example 14-2. The header animal.hpp (continued)

```
    Contact() { }
    Contact(const std::string& name, const std::string& phone)
        : name_(name)
    {
        setPhone(phone);
    }
    std::string name() const { return name_; }
    std::string phone() const { return phone_; }
    void setName(const std::string& name) { name_ = name; }
    void setPhone(const std::string& phone)
    {
        using namespace std;
        using namespace boost;
        // Use Boost.Regex to verify that phone
        // has the form (ddd)ddd-dddd
        static regex pattern("\\([0-9]{3}\\)[0-9]{3}-[0-9]{4}");
        if (!regex_match(phone, pattern)) {
            throw runtime_error(string("bad phone number:") + phone);
        }
        phone_ = phone;
    }
private:
    std::string name_;
    std::string phone_;
};

// Compare two Contacts for equality; used in Recipe 14.9
// (for completeness, you should also define operator!=)
bool operator==(const Contact& lhs, const Contact& rhs)
{
    return lhs.name() == rhs.name() && lhs.phone() == rhs.phone();
}

// Writes a Contact to an ostream
std::ostream& operator<<(std::ostream& out, const Contact& contact)
{
    out << contact.name() << " " << contact.phone();
    return out;
}

// Represents an animal
class Animal {
public:
    // Default constructs an Animal; this is
    // the constructor you'll use most
    Animal() { }

    // Constructs an Animal with the given properties;
    // you'll use this constructor in Recipe 14.9
    Animal( const std::string& name,
            const std::string& species,
            const std::string& dob,
```

Example 14-2. The header animal.hpp (continued)

```
                 const Contact& vet,
                 const Contact& trainer )
        : name_(name),
          species_(species),
          vet_(vet),
          trainer_(trainer)
    {
        setDateOfBirth(dob);
    }

    // Getters
    std::string            name() const { return name_; }
    std::string            species() const { return species_; }
    boost::gregorian::date dateOfBirth() const { return dob_; }
    Contact                veterinarian() const { return vet_; }
    Contact                trainer() const { return trainer_; }

    // Setters
    void setName(const std::string& name) { name_ = name; }
    void setSpecies(const std::string& species) { species_ = species; }
    void setDateOfBirth(const std::string& dob)
    {
        dob_ = boost::gregorian::from_string(dob);
    }
    void setVeterinarian(const Contact& vet) { vet_ = vet; }
    void setTrainer(const Contact& trainer) { trainer_ = trainer; }
private:
    std::string            name_;
    std::string            species_;
    boost::gregorian::date dob_;
    Contact                vet_;
    Contact                trainer_;
};

// Compare two Animals for equality; used in Recipe 14.9
// (for completeness, you should also define operator!=)
bool operator==(const Animal& lhs, const Animal& rhs)
{
    return lhs.name() == rhs.name() &&
           lhs.species() == rhs.species() &&
           lhs.dateOfBirth() == rhs.dateOfBirth() &&
           lhs.veterinarian() == rhs.veterinarian() &&
           lhs.trainer() == rhs.trainer();
}

// Writes an Animal to an ostream
std::ostream& operator<<(std::ostream& out, const Animal& animal)
{
    out << "Animal {\n"
        << "  name=" << animal.name() << ";\n"
        << "  species=" << animal.species() << ";\n"
        << "  date-of-birth=" << animal.dateOfBirth() << ";\n"
```

Example 14-2. The header animal.hpp (continued)

```
            << "  veterinarian=" << animal.veterinarian() << ";\n"
            << "  trainer=" << animal.trainer() << ";\n"
            << "}";
    return out;
}


#endif // #ifndef ANIMALS_HPP_INCLUDED
```

Example 14-3. Parsing animals.xml with TinyXml

```cpp
#include <exception>
#include <iostream>      // cout
#include <stdexcept>     // runtime_error
#include <cstdlib>       // EXIT_FAILURE
#include <cstring>       // strcmp
#include <vector>
#include <tinyxml.h>
#include "animal.hpp"

using namespace std;

// Extracts the content of an XML element that contains only text
const char* textValue(TiXmlElement* e)
{
    TiXmlNode* first = e->FirstChild();
    if ( first != 0 &&
         first == e->LastChild() &&
         first->Type() == TiXmlNode::TEXT )
    {
        // the element e has a single child, of type TEXT;
        // return the child's
        return first->Value();
    } else {
        throw runtime_error(string("bad ") + e->Value() + " element");
    }
}

// Constructs a Contact from a "veterinarian" or "trainer" element
Contact nodeToContact(TiXmlElement* contact)
{
    using namespace std;
    const char *name, *phone;
    if ( contact->FirstChild() == 0 &&
         (name = contact->Attribute("name")) &&
         (phone = contact->Attribute("phone")) )
    {
        // The element contact is childless and has "name"
        // and "phone" attributes; use these values to
        // construct a Contact
        return Contact(name, phone);
    } else {
        throw runtime_error(string("bad ") + contact->Value() + " element");
```

Example 14-3. Parsing animals.xml with TinyXml (continued)

```
    }
}

// Constructs an Animal from an "animal" element
Animal nodeToAnimal(TiXmlElement* animal)
{
    using namespace std;

    // Verify that animal corresponds to an "animal" element
    if (strcmp(animal->Value( ), "animal") != 0) {
        throw runtime_error(string("bad animal: ") + animal ->Value( ));
    }

    Animal result; // Return value
    TiXmlElement* element = animal->FirstChildElement( );

    // Read name
    if (element && strcmp(element->Value( ), "name") == 0) {
        // The first child element of animal is a "name"
        // element; use its text value to set the name of result
        result.setName(textValue(element));
    } else {
        throw runtime_error("no name attribute");
    }

    // Read species
    element = element->NextSiblingElement( );
    if (element && strcmp(element->Value( ), "species") == 0) {
        // The second child element of animal is a "species"
        // element; use its text value to set the species of result
        result.setSpecies(textValue(element));
    } else {
        throw runtime_error("no species attribute");
    }

    // Read date of birth
    element = element->NextSiblingElement( );
    if (element && strcmp(element->Value( ), "dateOfBirth") == 0) {
        // The third child element of animal is a "dateOfBirth"
        // element; use its text value to set the date of birth
        // of result
        result.setDateOfBirth(textValue(element));
    } else {
        throw runtime_error("no dateOfBirth attribute");
    }

    // Read veterinarian
    element = element->NextSiblingElement( );
    if (strcmp(element->Value( ), "veterinarian") == 0) {
        // The fourth child element of animal is a "veterinarian"
        // element; use it to construct a Contact object and
        // set result's veterinarian
```

Example 14-3. Parsing animals.xml with TinyXml (continued)

```
        result.setVeterinarian(nodeToContact(element));
    } else {
        throw runtime_error("no veterinarian attribute");
    }

    // Read trainer
    element = element->NextSiblingElement();
    if (strcmp(element->Value(), "trainer") == 0) {
        // The fifth child element of animal is a "trainer"
        // element; use it to construct a Contact object and
        // set result's trainer
        result.setTrainer(nodeToContact(element));
    } else {
        throw runtime_error("no trainer attribute");
    }

    // Check that there are no more children
    element = element->NextSiblingElement();
    if (element != 0) {
        throw runtime_error(
                string("unexpected element:") +
                element->Value()
            );

    }

    return result;
}

int main()
{
    using namespace std;

    try {
        vector<Animal> animalList;

        // Parse "animals.xml"
        TiXmlDocument doc("animals.xml");
        if (!doc.LoadFile())
            throw runtime_error("bad parse");

        // Verify that root is an animal-list
        TiXmlElement* root = doc.RootElement();
        if (strcmp(root->Value(), "animalList") != 0) {
            throw runtime_error(string("bad root: ") + root->Value());
        }

        // Traverse children of root, populating the list
        // of animals
        for ( TiXmlElement* animal = root->FirstChildElement();
                animal;
                animal = animal->NextSiblingElement() )
```

Example 14-3. Parsing animals.xml with TinyXml (continued)

```
        {
            animalList.push_back(nodeToAnimal(animal));
        }

        // Print the animals' names
        for ( vector<Animal>::size_type i = 0,
                                    n = animalList.size( );
              i < n;
              ++i )
        {
            cout << animalList[i] << "\n";
        }
    } catch (const exception& e) {
        cout << e.what( ) << "\n";
        return EXIT_FAILURE;
    }
}
```

Discussion

TinyXml is an excellent choice for applications that need to do just a bit of XML processing. Its source distribution is small, it's easy to build and integrate with projects, and it has a very simple interface. It also has a very permissive license. Its main limitations are that it doesn't understand XML Namespaces, can't validate against a DTD or schema, and can't parse XML documents containing an internal DTD. If you need to use any of these features, or any of the XML-related technologies such as XPath or XSLT, you should use the other libraries covered in this chapter.

The TinyXml parser produces a representation of an XML document as a tree whose nodes represent the elements, text, comments and other components of an XML document. The root of the tree represents the XML document itself. This type of representation of a hierarchical document as a tree is known as a Document Object Model (DOM). The TinyXml DOM is similar to the one designed by the World Wide Web Consortium (W3C), although it does not conform to the W3C specification. In keeping with the minimalist spirit of TinyXml, the TinyXml DOM is simpler than the W3C DOM, but also less powerful.

The nodes in the tree representing an XML document can be accessed through the interface TiXmlNode, which provides methods to access a node's parent, to enumerate its child nodes, and to remove child nodes or insert additional child nodes. Each node is actually an instance of a more derived type; for example, the root of the tree is an instance of TiXmlDocument, nodes representing elements are instances TiXmlElement, and nodes representing text are instances of TiXmlText. The type of a TiXmlNode can be determined by calling its Type( ) method; once you know the type of a node, you can obtain a representation of the node as a more derived type by calling one of the convenience methods such as toDocument( ), toElement( ) and toText( ).

These derived types contain additional methods appropriate to the type of node they represent.

It's now easy to understand Example 14-3. First, the function textValue( ) extracts the text content from an element that contains only text, such as name, species, or dateOfBirth. It does this by first checking that an element has only one child, and that the child is a text node. It then obtains the child's text by calling the Value( ) method, which returns the textual content of a text node or comment node, the tag name of an element node, and the filename of a root node.

Next, the function nodeToContact( ) takes a node corresponding to a veterinarian or trainer element and constructs a Contact object from the values of its name and phone attributes, which it retrieves using the Attribute( ) method.

Similarly, the function nodeToAnimal( ) takes a node corresponding to an animal element and constructs an Animal object. It does this by iterating over the node's children using the NextSiblingElement( ) method, extracting the data contained in each element, and setting the corresponding property of the Animal object. The data is extracted using the function textValue( ) for the elements name, species, and dateOfBirth and the function nodeToContact( ) for the elements veterinarian and trainer.

In the main function, I first construct a TiXmlDocument object corresponding to the file *animals.xml* and parse it using the LoadFile( ) method. I then obtain a TiXmlElement corresponding to the document root by calling the RootElement( ) method. Next, I iterate over the children of the root element, constructing an Animal object from each animal element using the function nodeToAnimal( ). Finally, I iterate over the collection of Animal objects, writing them to standard output.

One feature of TinyXml that is not illustrated in Example 14-3 is the SaveFile( ) method of TiXmlDocument, which writes the document represented by a TiXmlDocument to a file. This allows you to parse an XML document, modify it using the DOM interface, and save the modified document. You can even create a TiXmlDocument from scratch and save it to disk:

```
// Create a document hello.xml, consisting
// of a single "hello" element
TiXmlDocument doc;
TiXmlElement root("hello");
doc.InsertEndChild(root);
doc.SaveFile("hello.xml");
```

See Also

Recipes 14.3 and 14.4

14.2   Working with Xerces Strings

Problem

You want to be able to handle the wide-character strings used by the Xerces library safely and easily. In particular, you want to be able to store strings returned by Xerces functions as well as to convert between Xerces strings and C++ standard library strings.

Solution

You can store wide-character strings returned by Xerces library functions using the template std::basic_string specialized for the Xerces wide-character type XMLCh:

```
typedef std::basic_string<XMLCh> XercesString;
```

To translate between Xerces strings and narrow-character strings, use the overloaded static method transcode( ) from the class xercesc::XMLString, defined in the header *xercesc/util/XMLString.hpp*. Example 14-4 defines two overloaded utility functions, toNative and fromNative, that use transcode to translate from narrow-character strings to Xerces strings and *vice versa*. Each function has two variants, one that takes a C-style string and one that takes a C++ standard library string. These utility functions are all you'll need to convert between Xerces string and narrow-character strings; once you define them, you'll never need to call transcode directly.

Example 14-4. The header xerces_strings.hpp, for converting between Xerces strings and narrow-character strings

```
#ifndef XERCES_STRINGS_HPP_INCLUDED
#define XERCES_STRINGS_HPP_INCLUDED

#include <string>
#include <boost/scoped_array.hpp>
#include <xercesc/util/XMLString.hpp>

typedef std::basic_string<XMLCh> XercesString;

// Converts from a narrow-character string to a wide-character string.
inline XercesString fromNative(const char* str)
{
    boost::scoped_array<XMLCh> ptr(xercesc::XMLString::transcode(str));
    return XercesString(ptr.get( ));
}

// Converts from a narrow-character string to a wide-charactr string.
inline XercesString fromNative(const std::string& str)
{
    return fromNative(str.c_str( ));
}
```

Example 14-4. The header xerces_strings.hpp, for converting between Xerces strings and narrow-character strings (continued)

```
// Converts from a wide-character string to a narrow-character string.
inline std::string toNative(const XMLCh* str)
{
    boost::scoped_array<char> ptr(xercesc::XMLString::transcode(str));
    return std::string(ptr.get());
}

// Converts from a wide-character string to a narrow-character string.
inline std::string toNative(const XercesString& str)
{
    return toNative(str.c_str());
}

#endif // #ifndef XERCES_STRINGS_HPP_INCLUDED
```

To convert between Xerces strings and std::wstrings, simply use the std::basic_string constructor taking a pair of iterators. For example, you can define the following two functions:

```
// Converts from a Xerces String to a std::wstring
std::wstring xercesToWstring(const XercesString& str)
{
    return std::wstring(str.begin(), str.end());
}

// Converts from a std::wstring to a XercesString
XercesString wstringToXerces(const std::wstring& str)
{
    return XercesString(str.begin(), str.end());
}
```

These functions rely on the fact that wchar_t and XMLCh are integral types each of which can be implicitly converted to the other; it should work regardless of the size of wchar_t, as long as no values outside the range of XMLCh are used. You can define similar functions taking C-style strings as arguments, using the std::basic_string constructor that takes a character array and a length as arguments.

Discussion

Xerces uses the null-terminated sequences of characters of type XMLCh to represent Unicode strings. XMLCh is a typedef for an implementation-defined integral type having a size of at least 16 bits—wide enough to represent almost all known characters in any language using a single character. Xerces uses the UTF-16 character encoding, which means that theoretically some Unicode characters must be represented by a sequence of more than one XMLCh; in practice, however, you can think of an XMLCh as directly representing a Unicode code point, i.e., the numerical value of a Unicode character.

At one time, XMLCh was defined as a typedef for wchar_t, which meant you could easily store a copy of a Xerces string as a std::wstring. Currently, however, Xerces defines XMLCh as a typedef for unsigned short on all platforms. Among other things, this means that on some platforms XMLCh and wchar_t don't even have the same width. Since Xerces may change the definition of XMLCh in the future, you can't count on XMLCh to be identical to any particular type. So if you want to store a copy of a Xerces string, you should use a std::basic_string<XMLCh>.

When using Xerces you will frequently need to convert between narrow-character strings and Xerces strings; Xerces provides the overloaded function transcode( ) for this purpose. transcode( ) can convert a Unicode string to a narrow-character string in the "native" character encoding or a narrow-character string in the "native" encoding to a Unicode string. What constitutes the native encoding is not precisely defined, however, so if you are programming in an environment where there are several commonly used character encodings, you may need to take matters into your own hands and perform your own conversion, either by using a std::codecvt facet, or by using Xerces's *pluggable transcoding services*, described in the Xerces documentation. In many cases, however, transcode( ) is all you need.

The null-terminate string returned by transcode( ) is dynamically allocated using the array form of operator new; it's up to you to delete it using delete []. This presents a slight memory-management problem, since typically you will want to make a copy of the string or write it to a stream before you delete it, and these operations can throw exceptions. I've addressed this problem in Example 14-4 by using the template boost::scoped_array, which takes ownership of a dynamically allocated array and deletes it automatically when it goes out of scope, even if an exception is thrown. For example, look at the implementation of fromNative:

```
inline XercesString fromNative(const char* str)
{
    boost::scoped_array<XMLCh> ptr(xercesc::XMLString::transcode(str));
    return XercesString(ptr.get());
}
```

Here, ptr takes ownership of the null-terminated string returned by transcode( ) and frees it even if the XercesString constructor throws a std::bad_alloc exception.

14.3 Parsing a Complex XML Document

Problem

You have a collection of data stored in an XML document that uses an internal DTD or XML Namespaces. You want to parse the document and turn the data it contains into a collection of C++ objects.

Solution

Use Xerces's implementation of the SAX2 API (the Simple API for XML, Version 2.0). First, derive a class from `xercesc::ContentHandler`; this class will receive notifications about the structure and content of your XML document as it is being parsed. Next, if you like, derive a class from `xercesc::ErrorHandler` to receive warnings and error notifications. Construct a parser of type `xercesc::SAX2XMLReader`, register instances of your handler classes using the parser's `setContentHandler( )` and `setErrorHandler( )` methods. Finally, invoke the parser's `parse( )` method, passing the file pathname of your document as its argument.

For example, suppose you want to parse the XML document *animals.xml* from Example 14-1 and construct a `std::vector` of Animals representing the animals listed in the document. (See Example 14-2 for the C++ definition of the class Animal.) In Example 14-3, I showed how to do this using TinyXml. To make the problem more challenging, let's add namespaces to the document, as shown in Example 14-5.

Example 14-5. List of circus animals, using XML Namespaces

```
<?xml version="1.0" encoding="UTF-8"?>

<!-- Feldman Family Circus Animals with Namespaces -->

<ffc:animalList xmlns:ffc="http://www.feldman-family-circus.com">
    <ffc:animal>
        <ffc:name>Herby</ffc:name>
        <ffc:species>elephant</ffc:species>
        <ffc:dateOfBirth>1992-04-23</ffc:dateOfBirth>
        <ffc:veterinarian name="Dr. Hal Brown" phone="(801)595-9627"/>
        <ffc:trainer name="Bob Fisk" phone="(801)881-2260"/>
    </ffc:animal>

    <!-- etc. -->

</ffc:animalList>
```

To parse this document with SAX2, define a `ContentHandler`, as shown in Example 14-6, and an `ErrorHandler`, as shown in Example 14-7. Then construct a `SAX2XMLReader`, register your handlers, and run the parser. This is illustrated in Example 14-8.

Example 14-6. A SAX2 ContentHandler for parsing the document animals.xml

```
#include <stdexcept>                      // runtime_error
#include <vector>
#include <xercesc/sax2/Attributes.hpp>
#include <xercesc/sax2/DefaultHandler.hpp> // Contains no-op
                                           // implementations of
                                           // the various handlers
#include "xerces_strings.hpp"             // Example 14-4
#include "animal.hpp"
```

Example 14-6. A SAX2 ContentHandler for parsing the document animals.xml (continued)

```cpp
using namespace std;
using namespace xercesc;

// Returns an instance of Contact based
// on the given collection of attributes
Contact contactFromAttributes(const Attributes &attrs)
{
    // For efficiency, store frequently used string
    // in static variables
    static XercesString name = fromNative("name");
    static XercesString phone = fromNative("phone");

    Contact result;    // Contact to be returned.
    const XMLCh* val;  // Value of name or phone attribute.

    // Set Contact's name.
    if ((val = attrs.getValue(name.c_str())) != 0) {
        result.setName(toNative(val));
    } else {
        throw runtime_error("contact missing name attribute");
    }

    // Set Contact's phone number.
    if ((val = attrs.getValue(phone.c_str())) != 0) {
        result.setPhone(toNative(val));
    } else {
        throw runtime_error("contact missing phone attribute");
    }

    return result;
}

// Implements callbacks that receive character data and
// notifications about the beginnings and ends of elements
class CircusContentHandler : public DefaultHandler {
public:
    CircusContentHandler(vector<Animal>& animalList)
        : animalList_(animalList)
        { }

    // If the current element represents a veterinarian or trainer,
    // use attrs to construct a Contact object for the current
    // Animal; otherwise, clear currentText_ in preparation for the
    // characters() callback
    void startElement(
            const XMLCh *const uri,        // namespace URI
            const XMLCh *const localname,  // tagname w/ out NS prefix
            const XMLCh *const qname,      // tagname + NS pefix
            const Attributes &attrs )      // elements's attributes
    {
        static XercesString animalList = fromNative("animalList");
        static XercesString animal = fromNative("animal");
```

```
        static XercesString vet = fromNative("veterinarian");
        static XercesString trainer = fromNative("trainer");
        static XercesString xmlns =
            fromNative("http://www.feldman-family-circus.com");

        // Check namespace URI
        if (uri != xmlns)
            throw runtime_error(
                    string("wrong namespace uri: ") + toNative(uri)
                );
        if (localname == animal) {
            // Add an Animal to the list; this is the new
            // "current Animal"
            animalList_.push_back(Animal( ));
        } else if (localname!= animalList) {
            Animal& animal = animalList_.back( );
            if (localname == vet) {
                // We've encountered a "veterinarian" element.
                animal.setVeterinarian(contactFromAttributes(attrs));
            } else if (localname == trainer) {
                // We 've encountered a "trainer" element.
                animal.setTrainer(contactFromAttributes(attrs));
            } else {
                // We've encountered a "name" , "species", or
                // "dateOfBirth" element. Its content will be supplied
                // by the callback function characters( ).
                currentText_.clear( );
            }
        }
    }

    // If the current element represents a name, species, or date
    // of birth, use the text stored in currentText_ to set the
    // appropriate property of the current Animal.
    void endElement(
            const XMLCh *const uri,         // namespace URI
            const XMLCh *const localname,   // tagname w/ out NS prefix
            const XMLCh *const qname )      // tagname + NS pefix
    {
        static XercesString animalList = fromNative("animal-list");
        static XercesString animal = fromNative("animal");
        static XercesString name = fromNative("name");
        static XercesString species = fromNative("species");
        static XercesString dob = fromNative("dateOfBirth");

        if (localname!= animal && localname!= animalList) {
            // currentText_ contains the content of the element
            // which has ended. Use it to set the current Animal's
            // properties.
            Animal& animal = animalList_.back( );
            if (localname == name) {
                animal.setName(toNative(currentText_));
```

```
            } else if (localname == species) {
                animal.setSpecies(toNative(currentText_));
            } else if (localname == dob) {
                animal.setDateOfBirth(toNative(currentText_));
            }
        }
    }
    // Receives notifications when character data is encountered
    void characters( const XMLCh* const chars,
                     const unsigned int length )
    {
        // Append characters to currentText_ for processing by
        // the method endElement()
        currentText_.append(chars, length);
    }
private:
    vector<Animal>&  animalList_;
    XercesString     currentText_;
};
```

Example 14-7. A SAX2 ErrorHandler

```
#include <stdexcept> // runtime_error
#include <xercesc/sax2/DefaultHandler.hpp>

// Receives Error notifications.
class CircusErrorHandler : public DefaultHandler {
public:
    void warning(const SAXParseException& e)
    {
        /* do nothing */
    }
    void error(const SAXParseException& e)
    {
        throw runtime_error(toNative(e.getMessage()));
    }
    void fatalError(const SAXParseException& e) { error(e); }
};
```

Example 14-8. Parsing the document animals.xml with the SAX2 API

```
#include <exception>
#include <iostream>       // cout
#include <memory>         // auto_ptr
#include <vector>
#include <xercesc/sax2/SAX2XMLReader.hpp>
#include <xercesc/sax2/XMLReaderFactory.hpp>
#include <xercesc/util/PlatformUtils.hpp>
#include "animal.hpp"
#include "xerces_strings.hpp"  // Example 14-4

using namespace std;
using namespace xercesc;
```

Example 14-8. Parsing the document animals.xml with the SAX2 API (continued)

```
// RAII utility that initializes the parser and frees resources
// when it goes out of scope
class XercesInitializer {
public:
    XercesInitializer( ) { XMLPlatformUtils::Initialize( ); }
    ~XercesInitializer( ) { XMLPlatformUtils::Terminate( ); }
private:
    // Prohibit copying and assignment
    XercesInitializer(const XercesInitializer&);
    XercesInitializer& operator=(const XercesInitializer&);
};

int main( )
{
    try {
        vector<Animal> animalList;

        // Initialze Xerces and obtain parser
        XercesInitializer        init;
        auto_ptr<SAX2XMLReader>  ]
            parser(XMLReaderFactory::createXMLReader( ));

        // Register handlers
        CircusContentHandler     content(animalList);
        CircusErrorHandler       error;
        parser->setContentHandler(&content);
        parser->setErrorHandler(&error);

        // Parse the XML document
        parser->parse("animals.xml");

        // Print animals' names
        for ( vector<Animal>::size_type i = 0,
                                  n = animalList.size( );
             i < n;
             ++i )
        {
            cout << animalList[i] << "\n";
        }
    } catch (const SAXException& e) {
        cout << "xml error: " << toNative(e.getMessage( )) << "\n";
        return EXIT_FAILURE;
    } catch (const XMLException& e) {
        cout << "xml error: " << toNative(e.getMessage( )) << "\n";
        return EXIT_FAILURE;
    } catch (const exception& e) {
        cout << e.what( ) << "\n";
        return EXIT_FAILURE;
    }
}
```

Discussion

Some XML parsers parse an XML document and return it to the user as a complex C++ object. The TinyXml parser and the W3C DOM parser that you'll see in the next recipe both work this way. The SAX2 parser, by contrast, uses a collection of callback function to deliver information about an XML document to the user as the document is being parsed. The callback functions are grouped into several handler interfaces: a ContentHandler receives notifications about an XML document's elements, attributes, and text, an ErrorHandler receives warnings and error notifications, and a DTDHandler receives notifications about an XML document's DTD.

Designing a parser around a collection of callback function has several important advantages. For example, it makes it possible to parse documents that are too large to fit into memory. In addition, it can save processing time by avoiding the numerous dynamic allocations needed to construct nodes in an internal representation of an XML document, and by allowing the user to construct her own representation of a document's data directly, instead of having to traverse the document tree as I did in Example 14-3.

Example 14-8 is pretty straightforward: I obtain a SAX2 parser, register a ContentHandler and ErrorHandler, parse the document animals.xml, and print the list of Animals populated by the ContentHandler. There are two interesting points: First, the function XMLReaderFactory::createXMLReader( ) returns a dynamically allocated instance of SAX2XMLReader that must be freed explicitly by the user; I use a std::auto_ptr for this purpose to make sure that the parser is deleted even in the event of an exception. Second, the Xerces framework must be initialized using xercesc::XMLPlatformUtils::Initialize( ) and be cleaned up using xercesc:: XMLPlatformUtils::Terminate( ). I encapsulate this initialization and cleanup in a class called XercesInitializer, which calls XMLPlatformUtils::Initialize( ) in its constructor and XMLPlatformUtils::Terminate( ) in its destructor. This ensures that Terminate( ) is called even if an exception is thrown. This is an example of the *Resource Acquisition Is Initialization* (RAII) technique demonstrated in Example 8-3.

Let's look at how the class CircusContentHandler from Example 14-6 implements the SAX2 ContentHandler interface. The SAX 2 parser calls the method startElement( ) each time it encounters the opening tag of an element. If the element has an associated namespace, the first argument, uri, contains the element's namespace URI, and the second argument, localname, contains the portion of the element's tag name following its namespace prefix. If the element has no associated namespace, these two arguments are empty strings. The third argument contains the element's tag name, if the element has no associated namespace; if the element does have an associated namespace, this argument may contain the element's tag name as it appears in the document being parsed, but it may also be an empty string. The fourth argument is an instance of the class Attributes, which represents the element's collection of attributes.

In the implementation of startElement( ) in Example 14-6, I ignore the animalList element. When I encounter an animal element, I add a new Animal to its list of animals—let's call this Animal the *current* Animal—and delegate the job of setting the Animal's properties to the handlers for other elements. When I encounter a veterinarian or trainer element, I call the function contactFromAttributes to construct an instance of Contact from the element's collection of attributes, and then use this Contact to set the current Animal's veterinarian or trainer property. When I encounter a name, species, or dateOfBirth element, I clear the member variable currentText_, which will be used to store the element's textual content.

The SAX2 parser calls the method characters( ) to deliver the character data contained by an element. The parser is allowed to deliver an element's character in a series of calls to characters( ); until an element's closing tag is encountered, there's no guarantee that all its character data has been delivered. Consequently, in the implementation of characters( ), I simply append the provided characters to the member variable currentText_, which I use to set the current Animal's name, species, or date of birth as soon as a closing name, species, or dateOfBirth tag is encountered.

The SAX2 parser calls the method endElement( ) each time it leaves an element. Its arguments have the same interpretation as the first three arguments to startElement( ). In the implementation of endElement( ) in Example 14-6, I ignore all elements other than name, species, and dateOBirth. When a callback corresponding to one of these elements occurs—signaling that the parser is just leaving the element—I use the character data stored in currentText_ to set the current Animal's name, species, or date of birth.

Several important features of SAX2 are not illustrated in Examples 14-6, 14-7, and 14-8. For example, the class SAX2XMLReader provides an overload of the method parse( ) taking an instance of xercesc::InputSource as an argument instead of a C-style string. InputSource is an abstract class encapsulating a source of character data; its concrete subclasses, including xercesc::MemBufInputSource and xercesc::URLInputSource, allow the SAX2 parser to parse XML documents stored in locations other than the local file-system.

Furthermore, the ContentHandler interface contains many additional methods, such as startDocument( ) and endDocmuent( ), which signal the start and end of the XML document, and setLocator( ), which allows you to specify a Locator object which keeps track of the current position in the file being parsed. There are also other handler interfaces, including DTDHandler and EntityResolver–from the core SAX 2.0 specification—and DeclarationHandler and LexicalHandler–from the standardized extensions to SAX 2.0.

It's also possible for a single class to implement several handler interfaces. The class xercesc::DefaultHandler makes this easy, because it derives from all the handler interfaces and provides no-op implementations of their virtual functions. Consequently, I could have added the methods from `CircusErrorHandler` to `CircusContentHandler`, and modified Example 14-8 as follows:

```
// Register handlers
CircusContentHandler handler(animalList);
parser->setContentHandler(&handler);
parser->setErrorHandler(&handler);
```

There's one last feature of Example 14-8 you should notice: `CircusContentHandler` makes no attempt to verify that the document being parsed has the correct structure—for instance, that its root is an `animalList` element or that all the children of the root are animal elements. This is in sharp contrast with Example 14-3. For example, the main( ) function in Example 14-3 verifies that the top-level element is an `animalList`, and the function `nodeToAnimal( )` verifies that its argument represents an animal element with exactly five child elements of type `name`, `species`, `dateOfBirth`, `veterinarian`, and `trainer`.

It's possible to modify Example 14-6 so that it performs this type of error checking. The `ContentHandler` in Example 14-9, for instance, verifies that the document's root element is an `animalList`, that its children are of type `animal`, and the children of an animal element don't contain other elements. It works by maintaining three boolean flags, `parsingAnimalList_`, `parsingAnimal_`, and `parsingAnimalChild_`, which record the region of the document that is being parsed at any given time. The methods `startElement( )` and `endElement( )` simply update these flags and check them for consistency, delegating the task of updating the current `Animal` to the helper methods `startAnimalChild( )` and `endElementChild( )`, whose implementations are very similar to the implementations of `startElement( )` and `endElement( )` in Example 14-6.

Example 14-9. A SAX2 ContentHandler for animals.xml that checks the document's structure

```
// Implements callbacks which receive character data and
// notifications about the beginnings and ends of elements
class CircusContentHandler : public DefaultHandler {
public:
    CircusContentHandler(vector<Animal>& animalList)
        : animalList_(animalList),    // list to be populated
          parsingAnimalList_(false), // parsing state
          parsingAnimal_(false),     // parsing state
          parsingAnimalChild_(false) // parsing state
        { }

    // Receives notifications from the parser each time
    // beginning of an element is encountered
    void startElement(
            const XMLCh *const uri,       // Namespace uri
            const XMLCh *const localname, // simple tag name
            const XMLCh *const qname,     // qualified tag name
            const Attributes &attrs )     // Collection of attributes
    {
```

```
        static XercesString animalList = fromNative("animalList");
        static XercesString animal = fromNative("animal");
        static XercesString xmlns =
            fromNative("http://www.feldman-family-circus.com");

        // Validate the namespace uri
        if (uri != xmlns)
            throw runtime_error(
                    string("wrong namespace uri: ") + toNative(uri)
                );

        // (i) Update the flags parsingAnimalList_, parsingAnimal_,
        //      and parsingAnimalChild_, which indicate where we are
        //      within the document
        // (ii) verify that the elements are correctly
        //       nested;
        // (iii) Delegate most of the work to the method
        //        startAnimalChild( )
        if (!parsingAnimalList_) {
            // We've just encountered the document root
            if (localname == animalList) {
                parsingAnimalList_ = true; // Update parsing state.
            } else {
                // Incorrect nesting
                throw runtime_error(
                        string("expected 'animalList', got ") +
                        toNative(localname )
                    );
            }
        } else if (!parsingAnimal_) {
            // We've just encountered a new animal
            if (localname == animal) {
                parsingAnimal_ = true;            // Update parsing state.
                animalList_.push_back(Animal( )); // Add an Animal to the list.
            } else {
                // Incorrect nesting
                throw runtime_error(
                        string("expected 'animal', got ") +
                        toNative(localname )
                    );
            }
        } else {
            // We're in the middle of parsing an animal element.
            if (parsingAnimalChild_) {
                // Incorrect nesting
                throw runtime_error("bad animal element");
            }
            // Update parsing state.
            parsingAnimalChild_ = true;
```

```
                // Let startAnimalChild( ) do the real work
                startAnimalChild(uri, localname, qname, attrs);
        }
    }


    void endElement(
            const XMLCh *const uri,        // Namespace uri
            const XMLCh *const localname,  // simple tag name
            const XMLCh *const qname )     // qualified tag name
    {
        static XercesString animalList = fromNative("animal-list");
        static XercesString animal = fromNative("animal");

        // Update the flags parsingAnimalList, parsingAnimal_,
        // and parsingAnimalChild_; delegate most of the work
        // to endAnimalChild( )
        if (localname == animal) {
            parsingAnimal_ = false;
        } else if (localname == animalList) {
            parsingAnimalList_ = false;
        } else {
            endAnimalChild(uri, localname, qname);
            parsingAnimalChild_ = false;
        }
    }

    // Receives notifications when character data is encountered
    void characters(const XMLCh* const chars, const unsigned int length)
    {
        // Append characters to currentText_ for processing by
        // the method endAnimalChild( )
        currentText_.append(chars, length);
    }
private:
    // If the current element represents a veterinarian or trainer,
    // use attrs to construct a Contact object for the current
    // Animal; otherwise, clear currentText_ in preparation for the
    // characters( ) callback
    void startAnimalChild(
            const XMLCh *const uri,        // Namespace uri
            const XMLCh *const localname,  // simple tag name
            const XMLCh *const qname,      // qualified tag name
            const Attributes &attrs )      // Collection of attributes
    {
        static XercesString vet = fromNative("veterinarian");
        static XercesString trainer = fromNative("trainer");

        Animal& animal = animalList_.back( );
        if (localname == vet) {
            // We've encountered a "veterinarian" element.
```

```
                    animal.setVeterinarian(contactFromAttributes(attrs));
            } else if (localname == trainer) {
                // We've encountered a "trainer" element.
                animal.setTrainer(contactFromAttributes(attrs));
            } else {
                // We've encountered a "name" , "species", or
                // "dateOfBirth" element. Its content will be supplied
                // by the callback function characters( ).
                currentText_.clear( );
            }
        }
    }

    // If the current element represents a name, species, or date
    // of birth, use the text stored in currentText_ to set the
    // appropriate property of the current Animal.
    void endAnimalChild(
            const XMLCh *const uri,        // Namespace uri
            const XMLCh *const localname, // simple tag name
            const XMLCh *const qname )     // qualified tag name
    {
        static XercesString name = fromNative("name");
        static XercesString species = fromNative("species");
        static XercesString dob = fromNative("dateOfBirth");

        // currentText_ contains the content of the element which has
        // just ended. Use it to set the current Animal's properties.
        Animal& animal = animalList_.back( );
        if (localname == name) {
            animal.setName(toNative(currentText_));
        } else if (localname == species) {
            animal.setSpecies(toNative(currentText_));
        } else if (localname == dob) {
            animal.setDateOfBirth(toNative(currentText_));
        }
    }

    vector<Animal>&  animalList_;         // list to be populated
    bool             parsingAnimalList_;  // parsing state
    bool             parsingAnimal_;      // parsing state
    bool             parsingAnimalChild_; // parsing state
    XercesString     currentText_;        // character data of the
                                          // current text node
};
```

Comparing Example 14-9 with Example 14-6, you can see how complex it can be to verify a document's structure using callbacks. What's more, Example 14-6 still doesn't perform as much checking as Example 14-3: it doesn't verify that the children of an animal element appear in the correct order, for instance. Fortunately, there are much easier ways to verify a document's structure using SAX2, as you'll see in the Recipes 14.5 and 14.6.

See Also

Recipes 14.1, 14.4, 14.5, and 14.6

14.4   Manipulating an XML Document

Problem

You want to represent an XML document as a C++ object so that you can manipulate its elements, attributes, text, DTD, processing instructions, and comments.

Solution

Use Xerces's implementation of the W3C DOM. First, use the class xercesc::DOMImplementationRegistry to obtain an instance of xercesc::DOMImplementation, then use the DOMImplementation to create an instance of the parser xercesc::DOMBuilder. Next, register an instance of xercesc::DOMErrorHandler to receive notifications of parsing errors, and invoke the parser's parseURI() method with your XML document's URI or file pathname as its argument. If the parse is successful, parseURI will return a pointer to a DOMDocument representing the XML document. You can then use the functions defined by the W3C DOM specification to inspect and manipulate the document.

When you are done manipulating the document, you can save it to a file by obtaining a DOMWriter from the DOMImplementation and calling its writeNode() method with a pointer to the DOMDocument as its argument.

Example 14-10 shows how to use DOM to parse the document *animals.xml* from Example 14-1, locate and remove the node corresponding to Herby the elephant, and save the modified document.

Example 14-10. Using DOM to load, modify, and then save an XML document

```
#include <exception>
#include <iostream>      // cout
#include <xercesc/dom/DOM.hpp>
#include <xercesc/framework/LocalFileFormatTarget.hpp>
#include <xercesc/sax/SAXException.hpp>
#include <xercesc/util/PlatformUtils.hpp>
#include "animal.hpp"
#include "xerces_strings.hpp"

using namespace std;
using namespace xercesc;

/*
 * Define XercesInitializer as in Example 14-8
 */
```

Example 14-10. Using DOM to load, modify, and then save an XML document (continued)

```
// RAII utility that releases a resource when it goes out of scope.
template<typename T>
class DOMPtr {
public:
    DOMPtr(T* t) : t_(t) { }
    ~DOMPtr() { t_->release(); }
    T* operator->() const { return t_; }
private:
    // prohibit copying and assigning
    DOMPtr(const DOMPtr&);
    DOMPtr& operator=(const DOMPtr&);
    T* t_;
};

// Reports errors encountered while parsing using a DOMBuilder.
class CircusErrorHandler : public DOMErrorHandler {
public:
    bool handleError(const DOMError& e)
    {
        std::cout << toNative(e.getMessage()) << "\n";
        return false;
    }
};

// Returns the value of the "name" child of an "animal" element.
const XMLCh* getAnimalName(const DOMElement* animal)
{
    static XercesString name = fromNative("name");

    // Iterate though animal's children
    DOMNodeList* children = animal->getChildNodes();
    for ( size_t i = 0,
                  len = children->getLength();
          i < len;
          ++i )
    {
        DOMNode* child = children->item(i);
        if ( child->getNodeType() == DOMNode::ELEMENT_NODE &&
             static_cast<DOMElement*>(child)->getTagName() == name )
        {
            // We've found the "name" element.
            return child->getTextContent();
        }
    }
    return 0;
}

int main()
{
    try {
        // Initialize Xerces and retrieve a DOMImplementation;
        // specify that you want to  use the Load and Save (LS)
```

Example 14-10. Using DOM to load, modify, and then save an XML document (continued)

```
    // feature
    XercesInitializer   init;
    DOMImplementation*  impl =
        DOMImplementationRegistry::getDOMImplementation(
            fromNative("LS").c_str()
        );
    if (impl == 0) {
        cout << "couldn't create DOM implementation\n";
        return EXIT_FAILURE;
    }

    // Construct a DOMBuilder to parse animals.xml.
    DOMPtr<DOMBuilder>  parser =
        static_cast<DOMImplementationLS*>(impl)->
            createDOMBuilder(DOMImplementationLS::MODE_SYNCHRONOUS, 0);

    // Enable namespaces (not needed in this example)
    parser->setFeature(XMLUni::fgDOMNamespaces, true);

    // Register an error handler
    CircusErrorHandler  err;
    parser->setErrorHandler(&err);

    // Parse animals.xml; you can use a URL here
    // instead of a file name
    DOMDocument* doc =
        parser->parseURI("animals.xml");

    // Search for Herby the elephant: first, obtain a pointer
    // to the "animalList" element.
    DOMElement*  animalList = doc->getDocumentElement();
    if (animalList->getTagName() != fromNative("animalList")) {
        cout << "bad document root: "
            << toNative(animalList->getTagName())
            << "\n";
        return EXIT_FAILURE;
    }

    // Next, iterate through the "animal" elements, searching
    // for Herby the elephant.
    DOMNodeList* animals =
        animalList->getElementsByTagName(fromNative("animal").c_str());
    for ( size_t i = 0,
                 len = animals->getLength();
          i < len;
          ++i )
    {
        DOMElement* animal =
          static_cast<DOMElement*>(animals->item(i));
        const XMLCh* name = getAnimalName(animal);
        if (name != 0 && name == fromNative("Herby")) {
            // Found Herby -- remove him from document.
```

```
                animalList->removeChild(animal);
                animal->release( ); // optional.
                break;
            }
        }

        // Construct a DOMWriter to save animals.xml.
        DOMPtr<DOMWriter> writer =
            static_cast<DOMImplementationLS*>(impl)->createDOMWriter( );
        writer->setErrorHandler(&err);

        // Save animals.xml.
        LocalFileFormatTarget file("animals.xml");
        writer->writeNode(&file, *animalList);
    } catch (const SAXException& e) {
        cout << "xml error: " << toNative(e.getMessage( )) << "\n";
        return EXIT_FAILURE;
    } catch (const DOMException& e) {
        cout << "xml error: " << toNative(e.getMessage( )) << "\n";
        return EXIT_FAILURE;
    } catch (const exception& e) {
        cout << e.what( ) << "\n";
        return EXIT_FAILURE;
    }
}
```

Discussion

Like the TinyXml parser, the Xerces DOM parser produces a representation of an XML document as a tree-structured C++ object with nodes representing the document's components. Xerces is a much more sophisticated parser, however: for instance, unlike TinyXml, it understands XML Namespaces and can parse complex DTDs. It also constructs a much more detailed representation of an XML document, including its processing instructions and the namespace URIs associated with elements and attributes. Most importantly, it provides access to this information through the interface described in the W3C DOM specification.

The W3C specification, which is still a work in progress, is divided into several "levels"; currently, there are three levels. The classes DOMImplementation, DOMDocument, DOMElement, and DOMNodeList, used in Example 14-10, are specified in DOM Level 1. The classes DOMBuilder and DOMWrite are specified in DOM Level 3, as part of the Load and Save recommendation.

 The names of Xerces classes aren't always the same as the names of the W3C DOM interfaces they implement; this is because Xerces implements several specifications in a single namespace, and attaches prefixes to some class names to avoid name clashes.

Example 14-10 should now be pretty easy to understand. I start by initializing Xerces as shown in Example 14-8. Then I obtain a DOMImplementation from the DOMImplementationRegistry, requesting the Load and Save feature by passing the string "LS" to the static method DOMImplementationRegistry::getDOMImplementation(). I next obtain a DOMBuilder from the DOMIMplementation. I have to cast the DOMIMplementation to type DOMIMplementationLS, because Load and Save features are not accessible from the DOMIMplementation interface specified by W3C DOM level 1. The first argument to createDOMBuilder() indicates that the returned parser will operate in *synchronous mode*. The other possible mode, *asynchronous mode*, is not currently supported by Xerces.

After obtaining a DOMBuilder, I enable XML Namespace support, register an ErrorHandler, and parse the document. The parser returns a representation of the document as a DOMDocument; using the DOMDocument's getElementsByTagName() method, I obtain a DOMElement object corresponding to the document's animalList element and iterate over its children using an object of type DOMNodeList. When I find an element that has a child element of type name containing the text "Herby", I remove it from the document by calling the root element's removeChild() method.

Just as SAX2XMLReader has a parse() method taking an instance of InputSource, DOMBuilder has a parse() method taking an instance of xercesc::DOMInputSource, an abstract class encapsulating a source of character data. DOMInputSource has a concrete subclass Wrapper4DOMInputSource that can be used to transform an arbitrary InputSource into a xercesc::DOMInputSource. See Recipe 14.3.

Finally, I obtain a DOMWriter object from the DOMImplementation, in much the same way that I obtained a DOMBuilder, and save the modified XML document to disk by calling its writeNode() method with the document's root element as argument.

You must free pointers returned by methods of the form DOMImplementation::createXXX() by calling the method release(). Use the DOMPtr utility from Example 14-10 to make sure such pointers are released even if an exception is thrown. Pointers returned by methods of the form DOMDocument::createXXX() need not be explicitly released, although they can be if they are no longer needed. See the Xerces documentation for details.

14.5   Validating an XML Document with a DTD

Problem

You want to verify that an XML document is valid according to a DTD.

Solution

Use the Xerces library with either the SAX2 (Simple API for XML) or the DOM parser.

To validate an XML document using SAX2, obtain a SAX2XMLReader, as in Example 14-8. Next, enable DTD validation by calling the parser's setFeature( ) method with the arguments xercesc::XMLUni::fgSAX2CoreValidation and true. Finally, register an ErrorHandler to receive notifications of DTD violations and call the parser's parse( ) method with your XML document's name as its argument.

To validate an XML document using DOM, first construct an instance of XercesDOMParser. Next, enable DTD validation by calling the parser's setValidationScheme( ) method with the argument xercesc:: XercesDOMParser::Val_Always. Finally, register an ErrorHandler to receive notifications of DTD violations and call the parser's parse( ) method with your XML document's name as its argument.

> Here I'm using the class XercesDOMParser, an XML parser that has been part of Xerces since before the DOM Level 3 DOMBuilder interface was introduced. Using a XercesDOMParser makes the example a bit simpler, but you can use a DOMBuilder instead if you like. See Discussion and Recipe 14.4.

For example, suppose you modify the XML document *animals.xml* from Example 14-1 to contain a reference to an external DTD, as illustrated in Examples 14-11 and 14-12. The code to validate this document using the SAX2 API is presented in Example 14-13; the code to validate it using the DOM parser is presented in Example 14-14.

Example 14-11. DTD animals.dtd for the file animals.xml

```
<!-- DTD for Feldman Family Circus Animals -->

<!ELEMENT animalList (animal+)>
<!ELEMENT animal ( name, species, dateOfBirth,
                   veterinarian, trainer ) >
<!ELEMENT name (#PCDATA)>
<!ELEMENT species (#PCDATA)>
<!ELEMENT dateOfBirth (#PCDATA)>
<!ELEMENT veterinarian EMPTY>
<!ELEMENT trainer EMPTY>
<!ATTLIST veterinarian
    name  CDATA #REQUIRED
    phone CDATA #REQUIRED
>
<!ATTLIST trainer
    name  CDATA #REQUIRED
    phone CDATA #REQUIRED
>
```

Example 14-12. The file animals.xml, modified to contain a DTD

```
<?xml version="1.0" encoding="UTF-8"?>

<!-- Feldman Family Circus Animals with DTD -->

<!DOCTYPE animalList SYSTEM "animals.dtd">

    <!-- same as Example 14-1 -->

</animalList>
```

Example 14-13. Validating the document animals.xml against a DTD using the SAX2 API

```
/*
 * Same includes as Example 14-8, except <vector> is not needed
 */

#include <stdexcept> // runtime_error
#include <xercesc/sax2/DefaultHandler.hpp>

using namespace std;
using namespace xercesc;

/*
 * Define XercesInitializer as in Example 14-8
 * and CircusErrorHandler as in Example 14-7
 */

int main( )
{
    try {
        // Initialize Xerces and obtain a SAX2 parser
        XercesInitializer init;
        auto_ptr<SAX2XMLReader>
            parser(XMLReaderFactory::createXMLReader( ));

        // Enable validation
        parser->setFeature(XMLUni::fgSAX2CoreValidation, true);

        // Register error handler to receive notifications
        // of DTD violations
        CircusErrorHandler error;
        parser->setErrorHandler(&error);
        parser->parse("animals.xml");
    } catch (const SAXException& e) {
        cout << "xml error: " << toNative(e.getMessage( )) << "\n";
        return EXIT_FAILURE;
    } catch (const XMLException& e) {
        cout << "xml error: " << toNative(e.getMessage( )) << "\n";
        return EXIT_FAILURE;
    } catch (const exception& e) {
        cout << e.what( ) << "\n";
        return EXIT_FAILURE;
    }
}
```

Example 14-14. Validating the document animals.xml against the DTD animals.dtd using XercesDOMParser

```cpp
#include <exception>
#include <iostream>        // cout
#include <stdexcept>       // runtime_error
#include <xercesc/dom/DOM.hpp>
#include <xercesc/parsers/XercesDOMParser.hpp>
#include <xercesc/sax/HandlerBase.hpp>
#include <xercesc/util/PlatformUtils.hpp>
#include "xerces_strings.hpp"  // Example 14-4

using namespace std;
using namespace xercesc;

/*
 * Define XercesInitializer as in Example 14-8
 * and CircusErrorHandler as in Example 14-7
 */

int main( )
{
    try {
        // Initialize Xerces and construct a DOM parser.
        XercesInitializer        init;
        XercesDOMParser          parser;

        // Enable DTD validation
        parser.setValidationScheme(XercesDOMParser::Val_Always);

        // Register an error handler to receive notifications
        // of schema violations
        CircusErrorHandler       handler;
        parser.setErrorHandler(&handler);

        // Parse and validate.
        parser.parse("animals.xml");
    } catch (const SAXException& e) {
        cout << "xml error: " << toNative(e.getMessage( )) << "\n";
        return EXIT_FAILURE;
    } catch (const XMLException& e) {
        cout << "xml error: " << toNative(e.getMessage( )) << "\n";
        return EXIT_FAILURE;
    } catch (const exception& e) {
        cout << e.what( ) << "\n";
        return EXIT_FAILURE;
    }
}
```

Discussion

DTDs provide a simple way to constrain an XML document. For example, using a DTD, you can specify what elements may appear in a document; what attributes an element may have; and whether a particular element can contain child elements, text, or both. It's also possible to impose constraints on the type, order, and number of an element's children and on the values an attribute may take.

The purpose of DTDs is to identify the subset of well-formed XML documents that are interesting in a certain application domain. In Example 14-1, for instance, it's important that each animal element has child elements name, species, dateofBirth, veterinarian, and trainer, that the name, species, and dateOfBirth elements contain only text, and that the veterinarian and trainer elements have both a name and a phone attribute. Furthermore, an animal element should have no phone attribute, and a veterinarian element should have no species children.

These are the types of restrictions enforced by the DTD in Example 14-11. For example, the following *element declaration* states that an animal element must have child elements name, species, dateOfBirth, veterinarian, and trainer, in that order.

```
<!ELEMENT animal ( name, species, dateOfBirth,
                   veterinarian, trainer ) >
```

Similarly, the following *attribute declaration* indicates that a trainer element must have name and phone attributes; the fact that no other attribute declarations for trainer appears in the DTD indicates that these are the only two attributes a trainer element may have:

```
<!ATTLIST trainer
    name  CDATA #REQUIRED
    phone CDATA #REQUIRED
>
```

An XML document that contains a DTD and conforms to its constraints is said to be *valid*. An XML parser that checks for validity in addition to checking for syntax errors is called a *validating parser*. Although SAX2XMLReader parser and XercesDOMParser are not validating parsers by default, they both provide a validation feature that can be enabled as shown in Examples 14-13 and 14-14. Similarly, a DOMBuilder, described in Recipe 14.4, can be made to validate by calling its setFeature( ) method with the arguments fgXMLUni::fgDOMValidation and true.

 The classes SAX2XMLReader, DOMBuilder, DOMWriter, and XercesDOMParser support a number of optional features. With SAX2XMLReader and DOMBuilder, you can enable and disable these features using the methods setFeature( ) and setProperty( ). The first method takes a string and a boolean value; the second takes a string and a void*. You can also query the enabled features using getFeature( ) and getProperty( ). For convenience, Xerces provides constants representing the names of features and properties. The class DOMWriter supports setFeature( ) but not setProperty( ). The class XercesDOMParser supports neither method; it provides separate setter and getter methods for each feature. See the Xerces documentation for a complete list of supported features.

See Also

Recipe 14.6

14.6   Validating an XML Document with a Schema

Problem

You want to verify that an XML document is valid according to a schema, as specified in the XML Schema 1.0 recommendation.

Solution

Use the Xerces library with either the SAX2 or the DOM parser.

Validating an XML document against a schema using the SAX2 API is exactly the same as validating a document that contains a DTD, assuming the schema is contained in or referenced from the target document. If you want to validate an XML document against an external schema, you must call the parser's setProperty( ) method to enable external schema validation. The first argument to setProperty( ) should be XMLUni::fgXercesSchemaExternalSchemaLocation or XMLUni::fgXercesSchemaExternalNoNameSpaceSchemaLocation, depending on whether the schema has a target namespace. The second argument should be the location of the schema, expressed as a const XMLCh*. Make sure to cast the second argument to void*, as explained in Recipe 14.5.

Validating an XML document against a schema using the XercesDOMParser is similar to validating a document against a DTD, assuming the schema is contained in or referenced from the target document. The only difference is that schema and namespace support must be explicitly enabled, as shown in Example 14-15.

Example 14-15. Enabling schema validation with a XercesDOMParser

```
XercesDOMParser parser;
parser.setValidationScheme(XercesDOMParser::Val_Always);
parser.setDoSchema(true);
parser.setDoNamespaces(true);
```

If you want to validate an XML document against an external schema with a target namespace, call the parser's setExternalSchemaLocation( ) method with your schema's location as its argument. If you want to validate an XML document against an external schema that has no target namespace, call the parser's setExternalNoNamespaceSchemaLocation( ) instead.

Similarly, to validate an XML document against a schema using a DOMBuilder, enable its validation feature as follows:

```
DOMBuilder* parser = ...;
parser->setFeature(XMLUni::fgDOMNamespaces, true);
```

```
parser->setFeature(XMLUni::fgDOMValidation, true);
parser->setFeature(XMLUni::fgXercesSchema, true);
```

To validate against an external schema using DOMBuilder, set the property XMLUni::fgXercesSchemaExternalSchemaLocation or XMLUni::fgXercesSchemaExternalNoNameSpaceSchemaLocation to the location of the schema.

For example, suppose you want to validate the document *animals.xml* from Example 14-1 using the schema in Example 14-16. One way to do this is to add a reference to the schema to *animals.xml*, as shown in Example 14-17. You can then validate the document with the SAX2 API, as shown in Example 14-13, or using DOM, as shown in Example 14-14, with the modification indicated in Example 14-15.

Example 14-16. Schema animals.xsd for the file animals.xml

```xml
<?xml version="1.0" encoding="UTF-8"?>

<!-- Schema for Feldman Family Circus Animals -->

<xsd:schema xmlns:xsd="http://www.w3.org/2001/XMLSchema" elementFormDefault="qualified">
<xsd:element name="animalList">
    <xsd:complexType>
        <xsd:sequence>
            <xsd:element name="animal" minOccurs="0" maxOccurs="unbounded">
                <xsd:complexType>
                    <xsd:sequence>
                        <xsd:element name="name" type="xsd:string"/>
                        <xsd:element name="species" type="xsd:string"/>
                        <xsd:element name="dateOfBirth" type="xsd:date"/>
                        <xsd:element name="veterinarian" type="contact"/>
                        <xsd:element name="trainer" type="contact"/>
                    </xsd:sequence>
                </xsd:complexType>
            </xsd:element>
        </xsd:sequence>
    </xsd:complexType>
</xsd:element>

<xsd:complexType name="contact">
    <xsd:attribute name="name" type="xsd:string"/>
    <xsd:attribute name="phone" type="phone"/>
</xsd:complexType>

<xsd:simpleType name="phone">
    <xsd:restriction base="xsd:string">
        <xsd:pattern value="\(\d{3}\)\d{3}-\d{4}"/>
    </xsd:restriction>
</xsd:simpleType>

</xsd:schema>
```

Example 14-17. The file animals.xml, modified to contain a reference to a schema

```xml
<?xml version="1.0" encoding="UTF-8"?>

<!-- Feldman Family Circus Animals with Schema -->

<animalList xmlns:xsi="http://www.w3.org/2001/XMLSchema-instance"
            xsi:noNamespaceSchemaLocation="animals.xsd">

    <!-- same as Example 14-1 -->

</animalList>
```

Another way is to omit the reference to the schema and enable external schema validation. Example 14-18 shows how to do this with the DOM parser.

Example 14-18. Validating an XML document against an external schema, using DOM

```cpp
/*
 * Same includes as in Example 14-14
 */

using namespace std;
using namespace xercesc;

/*
 * Define XercesInitializer as in Example 14-8
 * and CircusErrorHandler as in Example 14-7
 */

int main( )
{
    try {
        // Initialize Xerces and construct a DOM parser.
        XercesInitializer      init;
        XercesDOMParser        parser;

        // Enable validation
        parser.setValidationScheme(XercesDOMParser::Val_Always);
        parser.setDoSchema(true);
        parser.setDoNamespaces(true);
        parser.setExternalNoNamespaceSchemaLocation(
            fromNative("animals.xsd").c_str( )
        );

        // Register an error handler to receive notifications
        // of schema violations
        CircusErrorHandler       handler;
        parser.setErrorHandler(&handler);

        // Parse and validate.
        parser.parse("animals.xml");
    } catch (const SAXException& e) {
        cout << "xml error: " << toNative(e.getMessage( )) << "\n";
```

```
        return EXIT_FAILURE;
    } catch (const XMLException& e) {
        cout << "xml error: " << toNative(e.getMessage()) << "\n";
        return EXIT_FAILURE;
    } catch (const exception& e) {
        cout << e.what() << "\n";
        return EXIT_FAILURE;
    }
}
```

Discussion

Like DTDs, discussed in the previous recipe, schemas constrain XML documents. The purpose of a schema is to identify the subset of well-formed XML documents that are interesting in a certain application domain. Schemas differ from DTDs in three respects, however. First, the DTD concept and the associated notion of *validity* are defined in the XML specification itself, while schemas are described in a separate specification, the XML Schema recommendation. Second, while DTDs use the specialized syntax illustrated in Example 14-11, schemas are expressed as well-formed XML documents. Third, schemas are far more expressive than DTDs. Because of these last two points, schemas are widely regarded as superior to DTDs.

For example, the DTD in Example 14-11 was only able to require that veterinarian elements have exactly two attributes, name and phone, with values consisting of characters. By contrast, the schema in Example 14-16 requires that the value of the phone attribute also match the regular expression \(\d{3}\)\d{3}-\d{4}, i.e., that it have the form (ddd)xxx-dddd, where d represents an arbitrary digit. Similarly, while the DTD was only able to require that the dateOfBirth element has textual content, the schema requires that the text be of the form yyyy-mm-dd, where yyyy ranges from 0001 to 9999, mm ranges from 01 to 12, and dd ranges from 01 to 31. The ability to impose these additional requirements is a great benefit, since it shifts work from the programmer to the parser.

See Also

Recipe 14.5

14.7 Transforming an XML Document with XSLT

Problem

You want to transform an XML document using an XSLT stylesheet.

Solution

Use the Xalan library. First, construct an instance of the XSTL engine `xalanc::XalanTransformer`. Next, construct two instances of `xalanc::XSLTInputSource`—one to represent the document to be transformed and the other to represent your stylesheet—and an instance of `xalanc::XSLTResultTarget` to represent the document to be generated by the transformation. Finally, call the XSLT engine's `transform( )` method, passing the two `XSLTInputSource`s and the `XSLTResultTarget` as arguments.

For example, suppose you want to be able to view the list of circus animals from Example 14-1 with your web browser. An easy way to do this is with XSLT. Example 14-19 shows an XSLT stylesheet that takes an XML document like *animals.xml* as input and generates an HTML document containing a table with one data row per animal listing the animal's name, species, date of birth, veterinarian, and trainer. Example 14-20 shows how to use the Xalan library to apply this stylesheet to the document *animals.xml*. The HTML generated by the program in Example 14-20 is shown in Example 14-21, reformatted for readability.

Example 14-19. Stylesheet for animals.xml

```xml
<?xml version="1.0" encoding="utf-8"?>

<!-- Stylesheet for Feldman Family Circus Animals -->

<xsl:stylesheet version="1.1"
                xmlns:xsl="http://www.w3.org/1999/XSL/Transform">
    <xsl:output method="html"/>
    <xsl:template match="/">
        <html>
        <head>
            <title>Feldman Family Circus Animals</title>
        </head>
        <body>
            <h1>Feldman Family Circus Animals</h1>
            <table cellpadding="3" border="1">
                <tr>
                    <th>Name</th>
                    <th>Species</th>
                    <th>Date of Birth</th>
                    <th>Veterinarian</th>
                    <th>Trainer</th>
                </tr>
                <xsl:apply-templates match="animal">
                </xsl:apply-templates>
            </table>
        </body>
        </html>
    </xsl:template>
    <xsl:template match="animal">
        <tr>
            <td><xsl:value-of select="name"/></td>
```

Example 14-19. Stylesheet for animals.xml (continued)

```
            <td><xsl:value-of select="species"/></td>
            <td><xsl:value-of select="dateOfBirth"/></td>
            <xsl:apply-templates select="veterinarian"/>
            <xsl:apply-templates select="trainer"/>
        </tr>
    </xsl:template>
    <xsl:template match="veterinarian|trainer">
        <td>
            <table>
                <tr>
                    <th>name:</th>
                    <td><xsl:value-of select="attribute::name"/></td>
                </tr>
                <tr>
                    <th>phone:</th>
                    <td><xsl:value-of select="attribute::phone"/></td>
                </tr>
            </table>
        </td>
    </xsl:template>
</xsl:stylesheet>
```

Example 14-20. Applying the stylesheet animals.xsl to the file animals.xml using Xalan

```cpp
#include <exception>
#include <iostream>      // cout
#include <xalanc/Include/PlatformDefinitions.hpp>
#include <xalanc/XalanTransformer/XalanTransformer.hpp>
#include <xalanc/XSLT/XSLTInputSource.hpp>
#include <xalanc/XSLT/XSLTResultTarget.hpp>
#include <xercesc/util/PlatformUtils.hpp>
#include "xerces_strings.hpp"  // Example 14-4

using namespace std;
using namespace xercesc;
using namespace xalanc;

// RAII utility that initializes the parser and frees resources
// when it goes out of scope
struct XalanInitializer {
    XalanInitializer()
    {
        XMLPlatformUtils::Initialize();
        XalanTransformer::initialize();
    }
    ~XalanInitializer()
    {
        XalanTransformer::terminate();
        XMLPlatformUtils::Terminate();
    }
};
```

Example 14-20. Applying the stylesheet animals.xsl to the file animals.xml using Xalan (continued)

```
int main( )
{
    try {
        XalanInitializer  init;                // Initialize Xalan.
        XalanTransformer  xslt;                // XSLT engine.
        XSLTInputSource   xml("animals.xml");  // XML document from
                                               // Example 14-1.
        XSLTInputSource   xsl("animals.xsl");  // Stylesheet from
                                               // Example 14-19.
        XSLTResultTarget  html("animals.html"); // xslt's output.

        // Perform transformation.
        if (xslt.transform(xml, xsl, html) != 0) {
            cout << "xml error: " << xslt.getLastError() << "\n";
        }
    } catch (const XMLException& e) {
        cout << "xml error: " << toNative(e.getMessage()) << "\n";
        return EXIT_FAILURE;
    } catch (const exception& e) {
        cout << e.what() << "\n";
        return EXIT_FAILURE;
    }
}
```

Example 14-21. HTML document generated by the program in Example 14-20

```
<html>
<head>
    <META http-equiv="Content-Type" content="text/html; charset=UTF-8">
    <title>Feldman Family Circus Animals</title>
</head>
<body>
    <h1>Feldman Family Circus Animals</h1>
    <table cellpadding="3" border="1">
    <tr>
        <th>Name</th>
        <th>Species</th>
        <th>Date of Birth</th>
        <th>Veterinarian</th>
        <th>Trainer</th>
    </tr>
    <tr>
        <td>Herby</td>
        <td>elephant</td>
        <td>1992-04-23</td>
        <td>
            <table>
                <tr><th>name:</th><td>Dr. Hal Brown</td></tr>
                <tr><th>phone:</th><td>(801)595-9627</td></tr>
            </table>
        </td>
        <td>
```

```
            <table>
                <tr><th>name:</th><td>Bob Fisk</td></tr>
                <tr><th>phone:</th><td>(801)881-2260</td></tr>
            </table>
        </td>
    </tr>
    <tr>
        <td>Sheldon</td>
        <td>parrot</td>
        <td>1998-09-30</td>
        <td>
            <table>
                <tr><th>name:</th><td>Dr. Kevin Wilson</td></tr>
                <tr><th>phone:</th><td>(801)466-6498</td></tr>
            </table>
        </td>
        <td>
            <table>
                <tr><th>name:</th><td>Eli Wendel</td></tr>
                <tr><th>phone:</th><td>(801)929-2506</td></tr>
            </table>
        </td>
    </tr>
    <tr>
        <td>Dippy</td>
        <td>penguin</td>
        <td>2001-06-08</td>
        <td>
            <table>
                <tr><th>name:</th><td>Dr. Barbara Swayne</td></tr>
                <tr><th>phone:</th><td>(801)459-7746</td></tr>
            </table>
        </td>
        <td>
            <table>
                <tr><th>name:</th><td>Ben Waxman</td></tr>
                <tr><th>phone:</th><td>(801)882-3549</td></tr>
            </table>
        </td>
    </tr>
</table>
</body>
</html>
```

Discussion

XSL Transformations (XSLT) is a language for transforming XML documents into other XML documents. XSLT is a component of the Extensible Stylesheet Language (XSL) family of specifications, which provides a framework for specifying visual representations of XML documents. XSLT is useful for more than formatting, however;

for example, it is used by web servers to generate HTML documents on-the-fly and by documentation generation systems such as DocBook.

XSLT transformations are expressed as XML documents called *stylesheets*. A stylesheet acts on a *source document* to produce a *result document*. A stylesheet consists of a collection of *templates*, which *match* nodes in the source document and are *applied* to produce fragments of the result document. Templates are applied recursively to the source document, generating fragments of the result document incrementally until no more matches remain. Pattern matching is governed by the XPath language, a language designed to extract information—strings, numbers, boolean values, and sets of nodes—from XML documents.

The stylesheet in Example 14-19 contains three templates. The primary template has a match attribute equal to /, indicating that it matches the root of the source document, meaning the node that is the parent of the source document's root element 'and any top-level processing instructions and comments. When this template is applied, it generates a fragment of an HTML document containing the heading "Feldman Family Circus Animals" and a table with a single row consisting of five th elements containing the labels Name, Species, Date of Birth, Veterinarian, and Trainer. This template contains an apply-templates element with match attribute equal to animal. This causes the stylesheet's second template—with match attribute animal–to be applied once for each of the animal children of the document root, generating a table row for each child. The row generated for an animal element consists of five td elements. The first three td elements contain the text value of the animal element's name, species, and dateOfBirth children, extracted using XSLT's value-of instruction. The last two td elements contains table elements created by applying the stylesheet's third template—with match attribute veterinarian|trainer–to the animal element's veterinarian and trainer children.

Although I chose to specify local files for the stylesheet, source document, and result document in Example 14-20, XSLTInputSources and XSLTResultTargets can be constructed from C++ standard library streams, allowing a XalanTransformer to accept input and generate output at arbitrary locations. Furthermore, instead of accepting input as instances of XSLTInputSource, a XalanTransformer can operate on a precompiled stylesheet, represented as an instance of xalanc::XalanCompiledStylesheet, and a preparsed source document, represented as an instance of xalanc::XalanParsedSource. This is illustrated in Example 14-22. If you need to apply a single stylesheet to multiple source documents, using a XalanCompiledStylesheet can be much more efficient than using an XSLTInputSource.

Example 14-22. Performing an XSLT transformation with a precompiled stylesheet

```
/*
 * Same includes as Example 14-20
 */
```

Example 14-22. Performing an XSLT transformation with a precompiled stylesheet (continued)

```cpp
using namespace std;
using namespace xercesc;
using namespace xalanc;

/*
 * Define XalanInitializer as in Example 14-20
 */

int main( )
{
    try {
        XalanInitializer    init;      // Initialize Xalan.
        XalanTransformer    xslt;      // XSLT engine.
        XSLTResultTarget    html("animals.html"); // xslt's output.

        // Parse source
        XSLTInputSource     xml("animals.xml");
        XalanParsedSource*  parsedXml = 0;
        if (xslt.parseSource(xml, parsedXml) != 0) {
            cout << "xml error: " << xslt.getLastError( ) << "\n";
        }

        // Compile stylesheet.
        XSLTInputSource          xsl("animals.xsl");
        XalanCompiledStylesheet* compiledXsl = 0;
        if (xslt.compileStylesheet(xsl, compiledXsl) != 0) {
            cout << "xml error: " << xslt.getLastError( ) << "\n";
        }

        // Perform transformation.
        if (xslt.transform(xml, xsl, html)) {
            cout << "xml error: " << xslt.getLastError( ) << "\n";
        }
    } catch (const XMLException& e) {
        cout << "xml error: " << toNative(e.getMessage( )) << "\n";
        return EXIT_FAILURE;
    } catch (const exception& e) {
        cout << e.what( ) << "\n";
        return EXIT_FAILURE;
    }
}
```

See Also

Recipe 14.8

14.8   Evaluating an XPath Expression

Problem

You want to extract information from a parsed XML document by evaluating an XPath expression.

Solution

Use the Xalan library. First, parse the XML document to obtain a pointer to a xalanc::XalanDocument. This can be done by using instances of XalanSourceTreeInit, XalanSourceTreeDOMSupport, and XalanSourceTreeParserLiaison—each defined in the namespace xalanc—like so:

```
#include <xercesc/framework/LocalFileInputSource.hpp>
#include <xalanc/XalanSourceTree/XalanSourceTreeDOMSupport.hpp>
#include <xalanc/XalanSourceTree/XalanSourceTreeInit.hpp>
#include <xalanc/XalanSourceTree/XalanSourceTreeParserLiaison.hpp>
...
int main( )
{
    ...
    // Initialize the XalanSourceTree subsystem
    XalanSourceTreeInit        init;
    XalanSourceTreeDOMSupport  support;

    // Interface to the parser
    XalanSourceTreeParserLiaison  liaison(support);

    // Hook DOMSupport to ParserLiaison
    support.setParserLiaison(&liaison);
    LocalFileInputSource       src(document-location);
    XalanDocument*             doc = liason.ParseXMLStream(doc);
    ...
}
```

Alternatively, you can use the Xerces DOM parser to obtain a pointer to a DOMDocument, as in Example 14-14, and then use instances of XercesDOMSupport, XercesParserLiaison, and XercesDOMWrapperParsedSource—each defined in namespace xalanc—to obtain a pointer to a XalanDocument corresponding to the DOMDocument:

```
#include <xercesc/dom/DOM.hpp>
#include <xalanc/XalanTransformer/XercesDOMWrapperParsedSource.hpp>
#include <xalanc/XercesParserLiaison/XercesParserLiaison.hpp>
#include <xalanc/XercesParserLiaison/XercesDOMSupport.hpp>
...
int main( ) {
    ...
    DOMDocument*               doc = ... ;
    XercesDOMSupport           support;
    XercesParserLiaison        liaison(support);
    XercesDOMWrapperParsedSource src(doc, liaison, support);
```

```
XalanDocument*                    xalanDoc = src.getDocument( );
    ...
}
```

Next, obtain a pointer to the node that serves as the context node when evaluating the XPath expression. You can do this by using XalanDocument's DOM interface. Construct an XPathEvaluator to evaluate the XPath expression and a XalanDocumentPrefixResolver to resolve namespace prefixes in the XML document. Finally, call the XPathEvaluator's evaluate( ) method, passing the DOMSupport, the context node, the XPath expression, and the PrefixResolver as arguments. The result of evaluating the expression is returned as an object of type XObjectPtr; the operations you can perform on this object depend on its XPath data type, which you can query using the getType( ) method.

For example, suppose you want to extract a list of animals' names from the document *animals.xml* from Example 14-1. You can do this by parsing the document and evaluating the XPath expression animalList/animal/name/child::text( ) with the document root as context node. This is illustrated in Example 14-23.

Example 14-23. Evaluating an XPath expression using Xalan

```
#include <cstddef>        // size_t
#include <exception>
#include <iostream>       // cout
#include <xercesc/dom/DOM.hpp>
#include <xercesc/parsers/XercesDOMParser.hpp>
#include <xercesc/sax2/DefaultHandler.hpp>
#include <xercesc/util/PlatformUtils.hpp>
#include <xalanc/DOMSupport/XalanDocumentPrefixResolver.hpp>
#include <xalanc/XalanTransformer/XercesDOMWrapperParsedSource.hpp>
#include <xalanc/XercesParserLiaison/XercesParserLiaison.hpp>
#include <xalanc/XercesParserLiaison/XercesDOMSupport.hpp>
#include <xalanc/XPath/XObject.hpp>
#include <xalanc/XPath/XPathEvaluator.hpp>
#include "animal.hpp"
#include "xerces_strings.hpp"

using namespace std;
using namespace xercesc;
using namespace xalanc;

// RAII utility that initializes the parser and the XPath engine
// and frees resources when it goes out of scope
class XPathInitializer {
public:
    XPathInitializer( )
    {
        XMLPlatformUtils::Initialize( );
        XPathEvaluator::initialize( );
    }
    ~XPathInitializer( )
    {
        XPathEvaluator::terminate( );
```

Example 14-23. Evaluating an XPath expression using Xalan (continued)

```
        XMLPlatformUtils::Terminate( );
    }
private:
    // Prohibit copying and assignment
    XPathInitializer(const XPathInitializer&);
    XPathInitializer& operator=(const XPathInitializer&);
};

// Receives Error notifications
class CircusErrorHandler : public DefaultHandler {
public:
    void error(const SAXParseException& e)
    {
        throw runtime_error(toNative(e.getMessage( )));
    }
    void fatalError(const SAXParseException& e) { error(e); }
};

int main( )
{
    try {
        // Initialize Xerces and XPath and construct a DOM parser.
        XPathInitializer    init;
        XercesDOMParser     parser;

        // Register error handler
        CircusErrorHandler error;
        parser.setErrorHandler(&error);

        // Parse animals.xml.
        parser.parse(fromNative("animals.xml").c_str( ));
        DOMDocument* doc = parser.getDocument( );
        DOMElement*  animalList = doc->getDocumentElement( );

        // Create a XalanDocument based on doc.
        XercesDOMSupport              support;
        XercesParserLiaison           liaison(support);
        XercesDOMWrapperParsedSource  src(doc, liaison, support);
        XalanDocument*                xalanDoc = src.getDocument( );

        // Evaluate an XPath expression to obtain a list
        // of text nodes containing animals' names
        XPathEvaluator                evaluator;
        XalanDocumentPrefixResolver   resolver(xalanDoc);
        XercesString                  xpath =
            fromNative("animalList/animal/name/child::text( )");
        XObjectPtr                    result =
            evaluator.evaluate(
                support,        // DOMSupport
                xalanDoc,       // context node
                xpath.c_str( ), // XPath expr
                resolver );     // Namespace resolver
        const NodeRefListBase&        nodeset = result->nodeset( );
```

Example 14-23. Evaluating an XPath expression using Xalan (continued)

```
            // Iterate through the node list, printing the animals' names
            for ( size_t i = 0,
                        len = nodeset.getLength( );
                  i < len;
                  ++i )
            {
                const XMLCh* name =
                  nodeset.item(i)->getNodeValue( ).c_str( );
                std::cout << toNative(name) << "\n";
            }
        } catch (const DOMException& e) {
            cout << "xml error: " << toNative(e.getMessage( )) << "\n";
            return EXIT_FAILURE;
        } catch (const exception& e) {
            cout << e.what( ) << "\n";
            return EXIT_FAILURE;
        }
    }
```

Discussion

XPath is a pattern matching language designed to extract information from XML documents. XPath's main construct—the *path expression*—provides a hierarchical syntax for referring to elements, attributes, and text nodes based on their names, attributes, textual content, inheritance relations, and other properties. In addition to operating on sets of nodes, or *node sets*, the XPath language can handle strings, numbers, and boolean values. XPath Version 2.0, which is not currently supported by the Xalan library, provides an even richer data model, based on the XML Schema recommendation. (See Recipe 14.5.)

XPath expressions are evaluated in the context of a node in an XML document, called the context node, which is used to interpret relative constructs such as parent, child, and descendent. In Example 14-23, I specified the *root* of the XML document as the context node; this is the node that is the parent of the XML document's root element and of any top-level processing instructions and comments. When evaluated with the root node as the context node, the path expression animalList/animal/name/child::text( ) matches all text node children of name elements whose parent element is an animal element and whose grandparent is an animalList element.

The evaluate( ) method of XPathEvaluator returns an XObjectPtr representing the result of evaluating the XPath expression. The data type of an XObjectPtr can be queried by dereferncing it to obtain an XObject and calling the method getType( ); the underlying data can then be accessed by calling num( ), boolean( ), str( ), or nodeset( ). Since the XPath expression in Example 14-23 represents a node set, I used the nodeset( ) method to obtain a reference to a NodeRefListBase, which provides access to the nodes in a node set through its getLength( ) and item( ) methods. The method item( ) returns a pointer to a XalanNode, whose getNodeValue( ) method returns a string with an interface similar to std::basic_string.

Since XPath provides an easy way to locate nodes in an XML document, it's natural to wonder whether you can use Xalan XPath expressions to obtain instances of xercesc::DOMNode from a xercesc::DOMDocument. Indeed it is possible, but it is slightly awkward; what's more, by default, the xercesc::DOMNodes obtained in this way are part of a *read-only* view of the XML document tree, which limits the usefulness of XPath as a tool for DOM manipulation. There are ways to work around this restriction, but they are complex and potentially dangerous.

Fortunately, the Pathan library provides an implementation of XPath that is compatible with Xerces and which allows easy manipulation of the Xerces DOM. Example 14-24 shows how to use Pathan to locate and remove the node corresponding to Herby the elephant in the XML document from Example 14-1, by evaluating the XPath expression animalList/animal[child::name='Herby']. Comparing this example with Example 14-10 makes it clear how powerful the XPath language is.

Example 14-24. Locating a node and removing it using Pathan

```
#include <exception>
#include <iostream>      // cout
#include <xercesc/dom/DOM.hpp>
#include <xercesc/framework/LocalFileFormatTarget.hpp>
#include <xercesc/util/PlatformUtils.hpp>
#include <pathan/XPathNamespace.hpp>
#include <pathan/XPathResult.hpp>
#include <pathan/XPathEvaluator.hpp>
#include <pathan/XPathExpression.hpp>
#include "xerces_strings.hpp"  // Example 14-4

using namespace std;
using namespace xercesc;

/*
 * Define XercesInitializer as in Example 14-8, and
 * CircusErrorHandler and DOMPtr as in Example 14-10
 */

int main( )
{
    try {
        // Initialize Xerces and retrieve a DOMImplementation.
        XercesInitializer    init;
        DOMImplementation*  impl =
            DOMImplementationRegistry::getDOMImplementation(
                fromNative("LS").c_str( )
            );
        if (impl == 0) {
            cout << "couldn't create DOM implementation\n";
            return EXIT_FAILURE;
        }
```

Example 14-24. Locating a node and removing it using Pathan (continued)

```
            // Construct a DOMBuilder to parse animals.xml.
            DOMPtr<DOMBuilder>  parser =
                static_cast<DOMImplementationLS*>(impl)->
                    createDOMBuilder(
                        DOMImplementationLS::MODE_SYNCHRONOUS, 0
                    );
            CircusErrorHandler  err;
            parser->setErrorHandler(&err);

            // Parse animals.xml.
            DOMDocument*  doc =
                parser->parseURI("animals.xml");
            DOMElement*   animalList = doc->getDocumentElement( );

            // Create XPath expression.
            auto_ptr<XPathEvaluator>
                evaluator(XPathEvaluator::createEvaluator());
            auto_ptr<XPathNSResolver>
                resolver(evaluator->createNSResolver(animalList));
            auto_ptr<XPathExpression>
                xpath(
                    evaluator->createExpression(
                        fromNative(
                            "animalList/animal[child::name='Herby']"
                        ).c_str(),
                        resolver.get()
                    )
                );
auto_ptr<XPathEvaluator>    evaluator(XPathEvaluator::createEvaluator());
auto_ptr<XPathNSResolver>   resolver(evaluator->createNSResolver(animalList));
auto_ptr<XPathExpression>   xpath(
        evaluator->createExpression(
            fromNative("animalList/animal[child::name='Herby']").c_str(),
            resolver.get()
    ));

            // Evaluate the expression.
            XPathResult* result =
                xpath->evaluate(
                    doc,
                    XPathResult::ORDERED_NODE_ITERATOR_TYPE,
                    0
                );

            DOMNode* herby;
            if (herby = result->iterateNext( )) {
                animalList->removeChild(herby);
                herby->release( ); // optional.
            }

            // Construct a DOMWriter to save animals.xml.
            DOMPtr<DOMWriter> writer =
```

Example 14-24. Locating a node and removing it using Pathan (continued)

```
            static_cast<DOMImplementationLS*>(impl)->createDOMWriter( );
        writer->setErrorHandler(&err);

        // Save animals.xml.
        LocalFileFormatTarget file("circus.xml");
        writer->writeNode(&file, *animalList);
    } catch (const DOMException& e) {
        cout << toNative(e.getMessage( )) << "\n";
        return EXIT_FAILURE;
    } catch (const XPathException &e) {
        cout << e.getString( ) << "\n";
        return EXIT_FAILURE;
    } catch (const exception& e) {
        cout << e.what( ) << "\n";
        return EXIT_FAILURE;
    }
}
```

Example 14-24 uses Pathan 1, which implements the XPath 1.0 recommendation, the same version currently supported by Xalan. Pathan 2, currently available in a beta version, provides a preliminary implementation of the XPath 2.0 recommendation. Pathan 2 represents a more faithful implementation of the XPath standard; I recommend using Pathan 2 instead of Pathan 1 as soon as a non-beta version becomes available.

See Also

Recipe 14.7

14.9   Using XML to Save and Restore a Collection of Objects

Problem

You want to be able to save a collection of C++ objects to an XML document and read it back into memory later.

Solution

Use the Boost Serialization library. This library allows you to save and restore objects using classes called *archives*. To make use of this library, you must first make each of your classes *serializable*, which just means that instances of the class can be written to an archive, or *serialized*, and read back into memory, or *deserialized*. Then, at runtime, you can save your objects to an XML archive using the << operator and restore them using the >> operator.

To make a class serializable, add a member function template `serialize` with the following signature:

```
template<typename Archive>
void serialize(Archive& ar, const unsigned int version);
```

The implementation of `serialize` should write each data member of the class to the specified archive as a name-value pair, using the & operator. For example, if you want to serialize and deserialize instances of the class Contact from Example 14-2, add a member function `serialize`, as shown in Example 14-25.

Example 14-25. Adding support for serialization to the class Contact from Example 14-2

```
#include <boost/serialization/nvp.hpp> // "name-value pair"

class Contact {
...
private:
    friend class boost::serialization::access;
    template<typename Archive>
    void serialize(Archive& ar, const unsigned int version)
    {
        // Write (or read) each data-member as a name-value pair
        using boost::serialization::make_nvp;
        ar & make_nvp("name", name_);
        ar & make_nvp("phone", phone_);
    }
    ...
};
```

Similarly, you can make the class Animal from Example 14-2 serializable, as shown in Example 14-26.

Example 14-26. Adding support for serialization to the class Animal from Example 14-2

```
...
// Include serialization support for boost::gregorian::date
#include <boost/date_time/gregorian/greg_serialize.hpp>
...
class Contact {
...
private:
    friend class boost::serialization::access;
    template<typename Archive>
    void serialize(Archive& ar, const unsigned int version)
    {
        // Write (or read) each data-member as a name-value pair
        using boost::serialization::make_nvp;
        ar & make_nvp("name", name_);
        ar & make_nvp("species", species_);
        ar & make_nvp("dateOfBirth", dob_);
        ar & make_nvp("veterinarian", vet_);
        ar & make_nvp("trainer", trainer_);
```

Example 14-26. Adding support for serialization to the class Animal from Example 14-2 (continued)

```
    }
...
};
```

You can now serialize an `Animal` by creating an XML archive of type `boost::archive::xml_oarchive` and writing the animal to the archive using the `<<` operator. The `xml_oarchive` constructor takes a `std::ostream` as an argument; often this will be an output stream for writing to a file, but in general it can be a stream for writing to any type of resource. After an `Animal` is serialized, it can be read back into memory by constructing an XML archive of type `boost::archive::xml_iarchive`, connecting it to the same resource as the original archive, and invoking the `>>` operator.

Example 14-27 shows how to use Boost.Serialization to save a `std::vector` of `Animals` to the file *animals.xml* and then load it back into memory. The contents of the file *animals.xml* after running the program in Example 14-27 are shown in Example 14-28.

Example 14-27. Serializing a std::vector of Animals

```cpp
#include <fstream>
#include <boost/archive/xml_oarchive.hpp> // Archive for writing XML
#include <boost/archive/xml_iarchive.hpp> // Archive for reading XML
#include <boost/serialization/vector.hpp> // machinery for serializing
#include "animal.hpp"                      // std::vector

int main( )
{
    using namespace std;
    using namespace boost::archive;        // namespace for archives
    using namespace boost::serialization;  // namespace for make_nvp

    try {
        // Populate list of animals
        vector<Animal> animalList;
        animalList.push_back(
            Animal( "Herby", "elephant", "1992-04-23",
                    Contact("Dr. Hal Brown", "(801)595-9627"),
                    Contact("Bob Fisk", "(801)881-2260") ));
        animalList.push_back(
            Animal( "Sheldon", "parrot", "1998-09-30",
                    Contact("Dr. Kevin Wilson", "(801)466-6498"),
                    Contact("Eli Wendel", "(801)929-2506") ));
        animalList.push_back(
            Animal( "Dippy", "penguin", "2001-06-08",
                    Contact("Dr. Barbara Swayne", "(801)459-7746"),
                    Contact("Ben Waxman", "(801)882-3549") ));

        // Construct XML output archive and serialize list
        ofstream       fout("animals.xml");
        xml_oarchive   oa(fout);
```

Example 14-27. Serializing a std::vector of Animals (continued)

```
        oa << make_nvp("animalList", animalList);
        fout.close();

        // Construct XML intput archive and deserialize list
        ifstream        fin("animals.xml");
        xml_iarchive    ia(fin);
        vector<Animal>  animalListCopy;
        ia >> make_nvp("animalList", animalListCopy);
        fin.close();

        if (animalListCopy != animalList) {
            cout << "XML serialization failed\n";
            return EXIT_FAILURE;
        }

    } catch (const exception& e) {
        cout << e.what() << "\n";
        return EXIT_FAILURE;
    }
}
```

Example 14-28. The file animals.xml after running the program from Example 14-27

```
<?xml version="1.0" encoding="UTF-8" standalone="yes" ?>
<!DOCTYPE boost_serialization>
<boost_serialization signature="serialization::archive" version="3">
<animalList class_id="0" tracking_level="0" version="0">
    <count>3</count>
    <item class_id="1" tracking_level="0" version="0">
        <name>Herby</name>
        <species>elephant</species>
        <dateOfBirth class_id="2" tracking_level="0" version="0">
            <date>19920423</date>
        </dateOfBirth>
        <veterinarian class_id="3" tracking_level="0" version="0">
            <name>Dr. Hal Brown</name>
            <phone>(801)595-9627</phone>
        </veterinarian>
        <trainer>
            <name>Bob Fisk</name>
            <phone>(801)881-2260</phone>
        </trainer>
    </item>
    <item>
        <name>Sheldon</name>
        <species>parrot</species>
        <dateOfBirth>
            <date>19980930</date>
        </dateOfBirth>
        <veterinarian>
            <name>Dr. Kevin Wilson</name>
            <phone>(801)466-6498</phone>
```

```
        </veterinarian>
        <trainer>
            <name>Eli Wendel</name>
            <phone>(801)929-2506</phone>
        </trainer>
    </item>
    <item>
        <name>Dippy</name>
        <species>penguin</species>
        <dateOfBirth>
            <date>20010608</date>
        </dateOfBirth>
        <veterinarian>
            <name>Dr. Barbara Swayne</name>
            <phone>(801)459-7746</phone>
        </veterinarian>
        <trainer>
            <name>Ben Waxman</name>
            <phone>(801)882-3549</phone>
        </trainer>
    </item>
</animalList>
```

Discussion

The Boost Serialization library provides the most comprehensive and flexible way to save and restore C++ objects. It's an extremely sophisticated framework; for example, it's able to serialize complex data structures containing cyclic references and pointers to polymorphic objects. Furthermore, the library is useful for much more than XML serialization: in addition to XML archives, it provides several types of text and binary archives. The XML and text archives are portable, meaning that data can be serialized on one system and deserialized on another; the binaries archives are nonportable but compact.

The XML documents produced by Boost.Serialization do not conform to any preexisting specification, and the format may change in future versions of Boost. As a result, you cannot use these documents in conjunction with other C++ serialization frameworks. Nonetheless, XML serialization is useful because the serialized output is easy for humans to read and can be processed by XML processing tools.

Examples 14-25 and 14-26 demonstrate *intrusive serialization*: the classes Animal and Contact were modified to make them serializable. Boost.Serialization also supports *nonintrusive serialization*, allowing classes to be made serializable without modifying their definitions, provided that all of an object's state is accessible through its public interface. You've already seen an example of nonintrusive serialization in Example 14-27: the template std::vector is serializable, despite the fact that its definition is unmodifiable by end-users. In fact, all standard library containers are serializable; to make serialization available for a container defined in the standard header *xxx*, simply include the header *boost/serialization/xxx.hpp*. To learn more about non-intrusive serialization, consult the Boost.Serialization documentation.

Examples 14-25 and 14-26 also illustrate the dual role of the & operator: it acts like the << operator when an object is being serialized and like the >> operator when an object is being deserialized. This is convenient, because it allows serialization and deserialization to be implemented as a single function. In some cases, however, it's not appropriate to use a single function for serialization and deserialization; for those cases, Boost.Serialization provides a mechanism for splitting the serialize() method into separate load() and save() methods. If you need to take advantage of this feature, consult the Boost.Serialization documentation.

In Examples 14-25, 14-26, and 14-27, I use the function boost::serialization::make_nvp to construct name-value pairs. Boost.Serialization also provides a macro BOOST_SERIALIZATION_NVP that allows you to serialize a variable by specifying only its name. The first component of the pair will be constructed automatically by the preprocessor using the "stringizing" operator # to convert the macro parameters to string constants:

```
// Same as ar & make_nvp("name_", name_);
ar & BOOST_SERIALIZATION_NVP(name_);
```

In the examples, I use make_nvp instead of BOOST_SERIALIZATION_NVP to give me more control over the tag names, making the contents of XML archives easier to read.

The Boost.Serialization documentation recommends that the serialize() method be declared private to reduce user errors when adding serialization support to classes derived from other serializable classes. To allow Boost.Serialization to call your class's serialize() method, you must declare the class boost::serialization::access to be a friend.

Finally, the second parameter of the serialize() method in Examples 14-25 and 14-26 is part of Boost.Serialization's support for *class versioning*. The first time an object of a certain class is saved to an archive, the class's version is also saved; when an instance of the class is deserialized, Boost.Serialization passes the stored version as the second argument to serialize. This information can be used to customize deserialization; for example, serialize might load the value of a member variable only if the class version recorded in the archive is as least as high as the first version of the class to declare that variable. By default, a class's version is 0. To specify a class's version, invoke the macro BOOST_CLASS_VERSION–defined in the header *boost/serialization/version.hpp*—passing the name of the class and class's version as arguments.

## CHAPTER 15

Miscellaneous

15.0 Introduction

This chapter describes a few facets of C++ that don't neatly fit into any of the other chapters: function and member pointers, const variables and member functions, and standalone (i.e., nonmember) operators and a few other topics.

15.1 Using Function Pointers for Callbacks

Problem

You plan to call some function func1, and at runtime you need it to invoke another function func2. For one reason or another, however, you cannot simply hardcode the name of func2 within func1. func2 may not be known definitively at compile time, or perhaps func1 belongs to a third-party API that you can't change and recompile. In either case, you need a *callback* function.

Solution

In the case of the functions above, declare func1 to take a pointer to a function, and pass it the address of func2 at runtime. Use a typedef to make the messy syntax easier to read and debug. Example 15-1 shows how to implement a callback function with a function pointer.

Example 15-1. A callback function

```
#include <iostream>

// An example of a callback function
bool updateProgress(int pct) {

    std::cout << pct << "% complete...\n";
    return(true);
}
```

Example 15-1. A callback function (continued)

```
// A typedef to make for easier reading
typedef bool (*FuncPtrBoolInt)(int);

// A function that runs for a while
void longOperation(FuncPtrBoolInt f) {

    for (long l = 0; l < 100000000; l++)
        if (l % 10000000 == 0)
            f(l / 1000000);
}

int main( ) {

    longOperation(updateProgress); // ok
}
```

Discussion

In a situation such as that shown in Example 15-1, a function pointer is a good idea if updateProgress and longOperation shouldn't know anything about each other. For example, a function that updates the progress by displaying it to the user—either in a user interface (UI) dialog box, in a console window, or somewhere else—does not care about the context in which it is invoked. Similarly, the longOperation function may be part of some data loading API that doesn't care whether it's invoked from a graphical UI, a console window, or by a background process.

The first thing you will want to do is determine what the signature of the function is you plan to call and create a typedef for it. typedef is your friend when it comes to function pointers, because their syntax is ugly. Consider how you would declare a function pointer variable f that contains the address of a function that takes a single integer argument and returns a boolean. It would look like this:

```
bool (*f)(int);  // f is the variable name
```

One could argue, convincingly, that this is no big deal and that I'm just a whiner. But what if you want a vector of such function pointers?

```
vector<bool (*)(int)> vf;
```

Or an array of them?

```
bool (*af[10])(int);
```

Function pointers do not look like ordinary C++ variable declarations whose format is often a (qualified) type name followed by a variable name. This is why they can make for messy reading.

Thus, in Example 15-1, I used a typedef like this:

```
typedef bool (*FuncPtrBoolInt)(int);
```

Once that was out of the way, I was free to declare function pointers that have the signature of returning bool and accepting a single integer argument as I would any other sort of parameter, like so:

```
void longOperation(FuncPtrBoolInt f) {
   // ...
```

Now, all longOperation needs to do is call f like it would any function:

```
f (1/1000000);
```

In this way, f can be any function that accepts an integer argument and returns bool. Consider a caller of longOperation that doesn't care about the progress. It can pass in a function pointer of a no-op function:

```
bool whoCares(int i) {return(true);}
//...
longOperation(whoCares);
```

More importantly, which function to pass to longOperation can be determined dynamically at runtime.

15.2   Using Pointers to Class Members

Problem

You need to refer to a data member or a member function with its address.

Solution

Use the class name and the scope operator (::) with an asterisk to correctly qualify the name. Example 15-2 shows how.

Example 15-2. Obtaining a pointer to a member

```
#include <iostream>
#include <string>

class MyClass {

public:
   MyClass() : ival_(0), sval_("foo") {}
   ~MyClass() {}

   void incr() {++ival_;}
   void decr() {ival_--;}

private:
   std::string sval_;
   int ival_;
};

int main() {
```

Example 15-2. Obtaining a pointer to a member (continued)

```
    MyClass obj;

    int         MyClass::* mpi = &MyClass::ival_;  // Data member
    std::string MyClass::* mps = &MyClass::sval_;  // pointers

    void (MyClass::*mpf)();  // A pointer to a member function that
                            // takes no params and returns void
    void (*pf)();            // A normal function pointer

    int* pi = &obj.ival_;   // int pointer referring to int member--no
                            // problem.

    mpf = &MyClass::incr;   // A pointer to a member function. You can't
                            // write this value to a stream. Look at it
                            // in your debugger to see what its
                            // representation looks like.

    pf = &MyClass::incr;    // Error: &MyClass::incr is not an instance
                            // of a function

    std::cout << "mpi = " << mpi << '\n';
    std::cout << "mps = " << mps << '\n';
    std::cout << "pi =  " << pi << '\n';
    std::cout << "*pi = " << *pi << '\n';

    obj.*mpi = 5;
    obj.*mps = "bar";

    (obj.*mpf)(); // now obj.ival_ is 6

    std::cout << "obj.ival_ = " << obj.ival_ << '\n';
    std::cout << "obj.sval_ = " << obj.sval_ << '\n';
}
```

Discussion

Pointers to members look and act differently than ordinary pointers. First of all, they have funny syntax (not funny ha-ha, funny strange). Consider the following line, from Example 15-2:

```
    int MyClass::* mpi = &MyClass::ival_;
```

This declares and assigns a pointer to an integer that happens to be a member of the class MyClass. Two things make this different than an ordinary int*. First, you have to include the class name and the scope operator in between the data type and the asterisk. Second, when you assign this pointer, you aren't actually assigning it the address of something in memory. The value &MyClass::ival_ is not a concrete value in memory—it can't be; it refers to the *class* name, not an *object* name—but what is it? Think of it as an offset of the data member from the object's start address.

The variable mpi has to be used with an instance of the class to which it applies. A little further down in Example 15-2, this line uses mpi to assign an integer to the value pointed to by mpi:

```
obj.*mpi = 5;
```

obj is an instance of the class MyClass. By referring to the member using the dot notation (or -> if you have a pointer to obj) and dereferencing mpi, you get a reference to obj.ival_.

Pointers to member functions are essentially the same. Example 15-2 declares a pointer to a member function of MyClass that returns void and takes no arguments:

```
void (MyClass::*mpf)();
```

Assign it to a value with the address-of operator:

```
mpf = &MyClass::incr;
```

To invoke it, place parenthesis around the main expression to ensure the compiler knows what you're doing, like this:

```
(obj.*mpf)();
```

There is one difference in data member pointers and function pointers though. If you want to point an ordinary, nonmember pointer at a data member, just do it as you would expect:

```
int* pi = &obj.ival_;
```

Of course, you use an object name and not a class name, because you are getting the address of the concrete data member of a specific object somewhere in memory. (Typically, though, you don't want to give out addresses to your class's data members, lest they be inadvertently changed by reckless client code.)

By contrast, you can't do the same thing with a member function because it makes no sense. Consider a function pointer that assumes the same function signature as MyClass::incr (i.e., returns void and takes no arguments):

```
void (*pf)();
```

Now, try to assign the address of a member function to it:

```
pf = &MyClass::incr; // Nope
pf = &obj.incr;      // No dice
```

Neither of these will compile, and for good reason. A member function requires an object context to make any sense, since it most likely refers to member variables. Invoking a member function without an object would require that the member function not use any of the object's members, which is presumably why it's a member function and not a standalone function.

See Also

Recipe 15.1

15.3 Ensuring That a Function Doesn't Modify an Argument

Problem

You are writing a function, and you need to guarantee that its arguments will not be modified when it is invoked.

Solution

Declare your arguments with the keyword const to prevent your function from changing the arguments. See Example 15-3 for a short sample.

Example 15-3. Guaranteeing unmodified arguments

```
#include <iostream>
#include <string>

void concat(const std::string& s1, // These are declared const, so they
            const std::string& s2, // cannot be changed
            std::string& out) {
   out = s1 + s2;
}

int main( ) {

   std::string s1 = "Cabo ";
   std::string s2 = "Wabo";
   std::string s3;

   concat(s1, s2, s3);

   std::cout << "s1 = " << s1 << '\n';
   std::cout << "s2 = " << s2 << '\n';
   std::cout << "s3 = " << s3 << '\n';
}
```

Discussion

Example 15-3 demonstrates a straightforward use of const. There are a couple of good reasons for declaring your function parameters const when you don't plan on changing them. First, you communicate your intent to human readers of your code. By declaring a parameter as const, what you are saying, essentially, is that the const parameters are for *input*. This lets consumers of your function, code with the assumption that the values will not change. Second, it tells the compiler to disallow any modifying operations, in the event you do so by accident. Consider an unsafe version of concat from Example 15-3:

```
void concatUnsafe(std::string& s1,
                  std::string& s2,
```

```
                std::string& out) {
        out = s1 += s2; // Whoops, wrote to s1
    }
```

Despite my fastidious coding habits, I have made a silly mistake and typed **+=** when I meant to type **+**. As a result, when concatUnsafe is called, it will modify the arguments out *and* s1, which may come as surprise to the user—who would expect a concatenation function to modify one of the source strings?

const to the rescue. Create a new function concatSafe, declare the variables const as in Example 15-3, and it won't compile:

```
void concatSafe(const std::string& s1,
                const std::string& s2,
                std::string& out) {
    out = s1 += s2; // Now you will get a compile error
}
```

concatSafe guarantees that the values in s1 and s2 will remain unchanged. It also does something else: it allows the user to pass const arguments. For example, code that needs to concatenate strings might look like this:

```
void myFunc(const std::string& s) { // Notice that s is const

    std::string dest;
    std::string tmp = "foo";

    concatUnsafe(s, tmp, dest);  // Error: s is const

    // Do something with dest...
}
```

In this case, myFunc won't compile because concatUnsafe does not maintain the constness guarantee of myFunc. myFunc has made a guarantee to the world that it won't modify the contents of s, which means that anything done to s within the body of myFunc must uphold this promise. Of course, you can get around this by using const_cast to cast away the const-ness, but that is just playing fast and loose with your variables, so you should avoid it. concatSafe compiles and runs fine in this situation.

Pointers add a wrinkle to this otherwise rosy portrait of const. When you declare a pointer variable as a parameter, there are two parts to it: the address itself and the thing that address refers to. C++ lets you use const to constrain what you can do to either one of these values. Consider yet another concatenation function that uses pointers:

```
void concatUnsafePtr(std::string* ps1,
                     std::string* ps2,
                     std::string* pout) {
    *pout = *ps1 + *ps2;
}
```

This has the same problems as concatUnsafe, described earlier. Add const to guarantee that the target strings aren't updated:

```
void concatSaferPtr(const std::string* ps1,
                    const std::string* ps2,
                    std::string* pout) {
    *pout = *ps1 + *ps2;
}
```

Great, now you can't change *ps1 or *ps2. But you can still change ps1 or ps2, or in other words, you can point them to some other string by changing the value of the *pointer*, not the value it points to. There's nothing to stop you, for instance, from doing this:

```
void concatSaferPtr(const std::string* ps1,
                    const std::string* ps2,
                    std::string* pout) {
    ps1 = pout;   // Uh-oh
    *pout = *ps1 + *ps2;
}
```

Prevent this sort of mistake by using const yet again:

```
void concatSafestPtr(const std::string* const ps1,
                     const std::string* const ps2,
                     std::string* pout) {
    *pout = *ps1 + *ps2;
}
```

By using const on either side of the asterisk, you have made your function as safe as it can be. This makes your intentions clear to consumers of your function, and it keeps you honest just in case you make a typo.

See Also

Recipe 15.4

15.4   Ensuring That a Member Function Doesn't Modify Its Object

Problem

You need to invoke member functions on a const object, but your compiler is complaining that it can't convert the type of object you are operating from const *type* to *type*.

Solution

Place the const keyword to the right of the member function declaration in both the class declaration and definition. Example 15-4 shows how to do this.

Example 15-4. Declaring a member function const

```cpp
#include <iostream>
#include <string>

class RecordSet {
public:
   bool getFieldVal(int i, std::string& s) const;
   // ...
};

bool RecordSet::getFieldVal(int i, std::string& s) const {
   // In here, you can't modify any nonmutable data
   // members (see discussion)
}

void displayRecords(const RecordSet& rs) {
   // Here, you can only invoke const member functions
   // on rs
}
```

Discussion

Adding a trailing const to a member declaration and its definition forces the compiler to look more carefully at what that member's body is doing to the object. const member functions are not allowed to invoke any nonconst operation on data members. If one does, compilation fails. For example, if, in RecordSet::getFieldVal, I updated a counter member, it wouldn't compile (assume that getFieldCount_ is a member variable of RecordSet):

```cpp
bool RecordSet::getFieldVal(int i, std::string& s) const {
   ++getFieldCount_;  // Error: const member function can't modify
                      // a member variable
   // ...
}
```

It can also help catch more subtle errors, similar to how const works in its variable-qualifier role (see Recipe 15.3). Consider this silly typo:

```cpp
bool RecordSet::getFieldVal(int i, std::string& s) const {

   fieldArray_[i] = s; // Oops, I meant the other way around
   // ...
}
```

Once again, the compiler will abort and give you an error because you are trying to change a member variable, and that's not allowed in const member functions. Well, with one exception.

In a RecordSet class, like the (bare-bones) one presented in Example 15-4, you would probably want member functions for moving forward and backward in the record set, assuming there is the notion of a "current" record. A simple way to do this is to keep an integer member variable that indicates the index of the current record; your member functions for moving the current record forward or backward increment or decrement this value:

```
void RecordSet::gotoNextRecord( ) const {
   if (curIndex_ >= 0 && curIndex_ < numRecords_-1)
      ++curIndex_;
}

void RecordSet::gotoPrevRecord( ) const {
   if (curIndex_ > 0)
      --curIndex_;
}
```

Clearly this won't work if these member functions are const. Both update a data member. But without this behavior, consumers of the RecordSet class won't be able to scroll through a const RecordSet object. This is a reasonable exception to the const member function rules, so C++ has a mechanism to support it: the mutable keyword.

To allow curIndex_ to be updated by a const member function, declare it as mutable in the class declaration like this:

```
mutable int curIndex_;
```

This gives you a free pass to modify curIndex_ from wherever you like. This should be used judiciously, however, since it has the same effect as leaving your member function nonconst to begin with.

Using const as in Example 15-4 is an effective technique for guaranteeing that a member function does not change its object's state. In general, this is good practice because it communicates the behavior of the member function to users of the class, and because it keeps you honest by forcing the compiler to validate your assertion that a member function won't do something it shouldn't.

15.5   Writing an Operator That Isn't a Member Function

Problem

You have to write a binary operator, and you can't or don't want to make it a class member function.

Solution

Use the operator keyword, a temporary variable, and a copy constructor to do most of the work, and return the temporary object. Example 15-5 presents a simple string concatenation operator for a custom String class.

Example 15-5. Concatenation with a nonmember operator

```
#include <iostream>
#include <cstring>

class String {  // Assume the String class declaration
                // has at least everything shown here
public:
   String();
   String(const char* p);
   String(const String& orig);
  ~String() {delete buf_;}

   String& append(const String& s);
   size_t length() const;
   const char* data() const;
   String& operator=(const String& orig);

   // ...
};

String operator+(const String& lhs, const String& rhs) {

   String tmp(lhs); // Copy construct a temp object
   tmp.append(rhs); // Use a member function to do the real work

   return(tmp);     // Return the temporary
}

int main() {

   String s1("banana ");
   String s2("rancher");
   String s3, s4, s5, s6;

   s3 = s1 + s2;          // Works fine, no surprises
   s4 = s1 + "rama";      // Constructs "rama" automatically using
                          // the constructor String(const char*)
   s5 = "ham " + s2;      // Hey cool, it even does it backward
   s6 = s1 + "rama " + s2;

   std::cout << "s3 = " << s3.data() << '\n';
   std::cout << "s4 = " << s4.data() << '\n';
   std::cout << "s5 = " << s5.data() << '\n';
   std::cout << "s6 = " << s6.data() << '\n';
}
```

Discussion

A standalone operator is declared and defined similarly to a member function operator. In Example 15-5, I could have implemented operator+ as a member function by declaring it like this:

```
String operator+(const String& rhs);
```

In most cases, this will work the same way regardless of whether you define operator+ as a member or nonmember function, but there are at least a couple of reasons why you would want to implement it as a nonmember function. The first is conceptual: does it make sense to have an operator that returns a new, distinct object? operator+ as a member function is not an inspector of the object's state, nor does it alter the object's state. It's a general utility function that happens to operate on Strings, and, therefore, should not be a member function.

The second reason is technical. You can't do the following with a member operator (from the example):

```
s5 = "ham " + s2;
```

This won't work because a character string doesn't have an operator+ that takes a String parameter. If, on the other hand, you have defined your standalone operator+ that takes two String parameters, your compiler will look to see if the String class has a constructor that takes a const char* argument (or whatever type you are using with a String) and construct a temporary object at runtime. The above code, therefore, is equivalent to this:

```
s5 = String("ham ") + s2;
```

The compiler saves you the extra keystrokes by just looking it up and invoking the constructor for you.

Overloading the left- and right-shift operators (<< and >>) for streams also requires that you use nonmember operators. For example, to put your new object to a stream using left-shift, you would have to declare operator<<, like this:

```
ostream& operator<<(ostream& str, const MyClass& obj);
```

Of course, you can subclass one of the standard library stream classes, and add all the left-shift operators you want, but is that really a good idea? If you do that, only code that uses your new stream class will be able to write your custom class's objects to it. If you use a standalone operator, any code in the same namespace can just write your object to an ostream (or read it from an istream) with no problem.

15.6   Initializing a Sequence with Comma-Separated Values

Problem

You want to initialize a sequence with a comma-delimited set of values, like you can with a built-in array.

Solution

You can use a comma-initialization syntax on standard sequences (such as vector and list) by defining a helper class and overloading the comma operator for it as demonstrated in Example 15-6.

Example 15-6. Utilities for comma initialization of standard sequences

```cpp
#include <vector>
#include <iostream>
#include <iterator>
#include <algorithm>

using namespace std;

template<class Seq_T>
struct comma_helper
{
  typedef typename Seq_T::value_type value_type;
  explicit comma_helper(Seq_T& x) : m(x) { }
  comma_helper& operator=(const value_type& x) {
    m.clear();
    return operator+=(x);
  }
  comma_helper& operator+=(const value_type& x) {
    m.push_back(x);
    return *this;
  }
  Seq_T& m;
};

template<typename Seq_T>
comma_helper<Seq_T>
initialize(Seq_T& x) {
  return comma_helper<Seq_T>(x);
}

template<class Seq_T, class Scalar_T>
comma_helper<Seq_T>&
operator,(comma_helper<Seq_T>& h, Scalar_T x) {
  h += x;
  return h;
}

int main() {
  vector v;
  int a = 2;
```

Example 15-6. Utilities for comma initialization of standard sequences (continued)

```
    int b = 5;
    initialize(v) = 0, 1, 1, a, 3, b, 8, 13;
    cout << v[3] << endl; // outputs 2
    system("pause");
    return EXIT_SUCCESS;
}
```

Discussion

Often time standard sequences are initialized by calling a push_back member function several times. Since this is somewhat repetitive, I wrote a function, initialize, which helps eliminate the tedium, by enabling comma initialization à la built-in arrays.

You may not have been aware that the comma is an operator, let alone an overrideable one. You are not alone; it is not common knowledge. The comma operator was allowed to be overloadable almost precisely for this purpose.

The solution uses a helper function initialize that returns a helper template, comma_helper. The helper template holds a reference to the sequence and overloads operator,, operator=, and operator+=.

This solution required that I define a separate helper function because of the way the compiler reads the statement v = 1, 1, 2, ...;. The compiler treats v = 1 as a subexpression that is not legal because the standard sequences do not support assignment from a single value. What initialize does is construct an appropriate comma_helper object that can hold the sequence while overloading the assignment and comma operator.

The comma operator, also known as the sequencing operator, has a default effect of grouping expressions from left to right and has the same type and value as the right-hand value. When overloaded, however, operator, takes on the new meaning and loses the original semantics. This has a subtle effect that the left-to-right evaluation of parameters is no longer guaranteed and code such as in Example 15-7 may not behave as expected.

Example 15-7. Overloaded comma arguments evaluation order undefined

```
int prompt_user( ) {
    cout << "give me an integer ... ";
    cin >> n;
    return n;
}

void f( ) {
    vector<int> v;
```

Example 15-7. Overloaded comma arguments evaluation order undefined (continued)

```
    // The following could result in v being initialized out of
    // sequence
    intialize(v) = prompt_user( ), prompt_user( );
}
```

The correct way to write f would be to place each call to prompt_user in a separate statement.

 The Boost Assign library by Thorsten Ottosen also supports a more complete form of comma list initialization of standard collections, among other forms of initializations. The library is available from *http://www.boost.org*.

Index

Numbers

2038 bug, 200

A

abstract base classes
    interfaces, creating with, 306–310
    rules, 309
Abstract Factory design patterns, 289
access
    containers, 253
    threads, serializing, 450–458
accumulate function, 406
adding
    classes, 294
    directories, 19
    margins, 185–187
    objects to vectors, 220
    rules, 71
    threads, 450
address-of operator, 543
-Ae option, 21
algorithms
    containers
        deleting objects, 256–258
        iterating through, 249–255
    ranges
        comparing, 260–263
        partitioning, 271
        printing to streams, 281–284
        sorting, 268–270
    sequences
        merging, 264–268
        randomly shuffling data, 259
        rearranging, 272–275
        transforming elements, 276–278
    String Algorithms library, 145
    strings, searching, 164
    writing, 278–281
aliases, namespaces, 116
aligning text, 352–356
alternating_many_reads mutex, 456
alternating_single_read mutex, 456
amortized constant time, 228
append function, 140
applications
    building
        Borland, 8
        C++Builder, 11
        CodeWarrior, 10
        Comeau, 8
        command-line tools, 33–37
        complex applications, 46–49
        complex applications with GNU make
            utility, 78–82
        complex applications with
            IDEs, 57–62
        Dev-C++, 11
        Digital Mars, 9
        dynamic libraries, 25–32, 45
        dynamic libraries with GNU make
            utility, 77
        dynamic libraries with IDEs, 53–56
        GCC, 5
        Hello World, 18–23, 40–43
        Hello World with GNU make
            utility, 64–71
        hellobeatles application, 11–15

We'd like to hear your suggestions for improving our indexes. Send email to *index@oreilly.com*.

instances
    classes, adding, 294
    variables, insuring one of, 108–110
    words, counting, 183–185
instantiation
    facets, 476
    templates, 313
integers
    hexidecimal, formatting as, 124
    large fixed-width, 439–443
Integrated Development Environments (see IDEs)
Intel C++ compilers, 6
interfaces, creating classes, 306–310
internal include guards, 108
internationalization
    currency, reading and writing, 477–481
    numbers, reading and writing, 468–472
    strings, sorting localized, 481–483
    Unicode strings, hardcoding, 467
intrusive serialization, 537
invoking rules, 41
istream_iterator class template, 401
iterators
    bidirectional, 254
    categories, 253, 255
    category abbreviations, 249
    containers
        interacting with, 217
        iterating through, 249–255
    declaring, 251
    forward, 254
    input, 254
    output, 254
    random-access, 254
    stride, implementing, 419–422
    valarray templates, 411

J

Jam build system, 4
JobQueue class, 460
join function, 449
joining strings, sequences of, 159–161
Julian calendar, 199
justifying text, 188–190, 352–356

K

keywords, extern, 108
kmatrix template, 428
kstride_iter.hpp, 421

kurtosis of sequences, computing, 403–406
kvector template, 412

L

large fixed-width integers, 439–443
leap years, 199, 208
least values, searching in
                containers, 396–399
left-justifying text, 188–190, 352–356
length
    of strings, getting, 151–153
    whitespace, formatting, 190
lexical_cast class, 122
lexical_cast function, 128
librarians, 2
libraries
    Boost Random, 408
    Boost serialization, 533
    Boost Threads, 446
    Boost.Filesystem, 373
    dynamic, 2, 45–46
    dynamically linked runtime, 33
    import, 28
    linkers, passing, 36
    static (see static libraries)
    String Algorithms, 145
    targets, 48
    XML, 484
libstdc++, 6
lines
    counting, 180–182
    text, wrapping, 178
linkers, 2
    libraries, passing to, 36
linking
    applications, 34
    hello.exe, 22
    source files, 99–101
Linux, ELF, 30
lists
    doubly linked, 229
    objects, storing in, 226–231
    strings, storing, 150
LoadFile( ) method, 485, 493
localeLessThan function, 483
locales
    behavior, 471
    class, 482
    global, 469, 483
    naming explicitly, 470
    sorting, 483

About the Authors

D. Ryan Stephens is a software engineer, writer, and student living in Tempe, Arizona. He enjoys programming in virtually any language, especially C++. His interests include information retrieval and data mining, and pretty much anything that has to do with algorithms and large data sets. When he's not working, writing, or programming, he plays with his kids, works on his house, or goes cycling.

Christopher Diggins is a freelance software developer and writer who has been programming computers since he was *haut comme trois pommes*. Christopher writes regularly for the *C++ Users Journal* and is the designer of the Heron programming lanugage.

Jonathan Turkanis is the author of the Boost Iostreams library and several other open source C++ libraries, covering areas such as smart pointers, runtime reflection, component architectures, and aspect-oriented programming. He is a PhD candidate in mathematical logic at the University of California at Berkeley.

Jeff Cogswell is a software engineer living near Cincinnati, Ohio. He has been programming in C++ since around the time the language was invented and has written extensively on the language, including two other C++ books. He also likes programming in other languages, especially Python. When not working (which is rare), he enjoys reading a good novel or playing the guitar.

Colophon

Our look is the result of reader comments, our own experimentation, and feedback from distribution channels. Distinctive covers complement our distinctive approach to technical topics, breathing personality and life into potentially dry subjects.

The animal on the cover of *C++ Cookbook* is a collie. The name refers to a type of sheepherding dog that originated in the highlands of Scotland and Britain in the 1600s. One variety of sheep in the Scottish Highlands had dark markings around its legs and face and was called the "Colley" sheep, a name derived from the Older Scots word for "coal." The modern version of the collie, lighter and more thick-boned than its Scottish ancestors, was bred in England in the late 19th century. Today, collies are primarily house pets, though they are still used as farm dogs in the United States.

There are two distinct breeds of collie: rough-coated collies were used to guard sheep, and the smooth-coated variety drove the livestock to market. Both are limber, streamlined dogs with a pronounced snout and pointed ears. They are 22–26 inches tall and weigh 50–75 pounds. Their fur is usually white with a second color that can vary from yellowish-white to brownish-red to coal-black.

Famous collies include Lassie, of course; Lyndon Johnson's pet Blanco; and Laddie from *The Simpsons*.

Matt Hutchinson was the production editor for *C++ Cookbook*. Octal Publishing, Inc. provided production services. Darren Kelly, Adam Witwer, and Claire Cloutier provided quality control.

Karen Montgomery designed the cover of this book, based on a series design by Edie Freedman. The cover image is a 19th-century engraving from *Cassell's Natural History*. Karen Montgomery produced the cover layout with Adobe InDesign CS using Adobe's ITC Garamond font.

David Futato designed the interior layout. This book was converted by Keith Fahlgren to FrameMaker 5.5.6 with a format conversion tool created by Erik Ray, Jason McIntosh, Neil Walls, and Mike Sierra that uses Perl and XML technologies. The text font is Linotype Birka; the heading font is Adobe Myriad Condensed; and the code font is LucasFont's TheSans Mono Condensed. The illustrations that appear in the book were produced by Robert Romano, Jessamyn Read, and Lesley Borash using Macromedia FreeHand MX and Adobe Photoshop CS. The tip and warning icons were drawn by Christopher Bing. This colophon was written by Matt Hutchinson.

Better than e-books

Buy *C++ Cookbook* and access the digital
edition FREE on Safari for 45 days.

Go to www.oreilly.com/go/safarienabled
and type in coupon code 7PL9-VR2M-AXYN-VLMP-TUXC

Search
thousands of
top tech books

Download
whole chapters

Cut and Paste
code examples

Find
answers fast

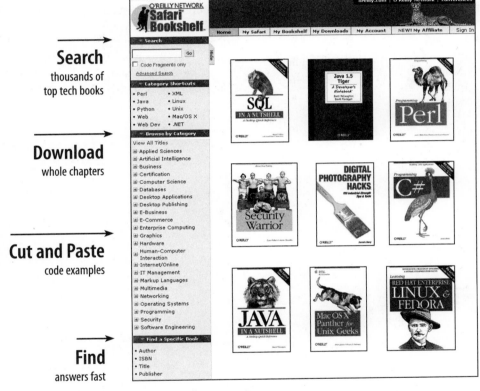

Search Safari! The premier electronic reference
library for programmers and IT professionals.

Related Titles from O'Reilly

C and C++ Programming

C Pocket Reference

C++ in a Nutshell

C++ Pocket Reference

C++: The Core Language

Mastering Algorithms with C

Objective-C Pocket Reference

Practical C Programming, *3rd Edition*

Practical C++ Programming, *2nd Edition*

Programming Embedded Systems in C and C++

Secure Programming Cookbook for C and C++

STL Pocket Reference

Keep in touch with O'Reilly

Download examples from our books

To find example files from a book, go to: *www.oreilly.com/catalog* select the book, and follow the "Examples" link.

Register your O'Reilly books

Register your book at *register.oreilly.com* Why register your books? Once you've registered your O'Reilly books you can:

- Win O'Reilly books, T-shirts or discount coupons in our monthly drawing.
- Get special offers available only to registered O'Reilly customers.
- Get catalogs announcing new books (US and UK only).
- Get email notification of new editions of the O'Reilly books you own.

Join our email lists

Sign up to get topic-specific email announcements of new books and conferences, special offers, and O'Reilly Network technology newsletters at:

elists.oreilly.com

It's easy to customize your free elists subscription so you'll get exactly the O'Reilly news you want.

Get the latest news, tips, and tools

www.oreilly.com

- "Top 100 Sites on the Web"—PC Magazine
- CIO Magazine's Web Business 50 Awards

Our web site contains a library of comprehensive product information (including book excerpts and tables of contents), downloadable software, background articles, interviews with technology leaders, links to relevant sites, book cover art, and more.

Work for O'Reilly

Check out our web site for current employment opportunities:

jobs.oreilly.com

Contact us

O'Reilly Media, Inc.
1005 Gravenstein Hwy North
Sebastopol, CA 95472 USA
Tel: 707-827-7000 or 800-998-9938
     (6am to 5pm PST)
Fax: 707-829-0104

Contact us by email

For answers to problems regarding your order or our products:
order@oreilly.com

To request a copy of our latest catalog:
catalog@oreilly.com

For book content technical questions or corrections: **booktech@oreilly.com**

For educational, library, government, and corporate sales: **corporate@oreilly.com**

To submit new book proposals to our editors and product managers:
proposals@oreilly.com

For information about our international distributors or translation queries:
international@oreilly.com

For information about academic use of O'Reilly books:
adoption@oreilly.com
or visit:
academic.oreilly.com

For a list of our distributors outside of North America check out:
international.oreilly.com/distributors.html

Order a book online

www.oreilly.com/order_new

Our books are available at most retail and online bookstores.
To order direct: 1-800-998-9938 • order@oreilly.com • www.oreilly.com
Online editions of most O'Reilly titles are available by subscription at *safari.oreilly.com*